Hine Brothers of Maryport

The Sailing Fleet

Based in Liverpool then Maryport

Vol. 1

Written and Compiled

by

Robert Peel

ISBN No. 978-0-9573870-0-3

Published by Cooil Publishing

I Cooilbane Cottages, Sulby, Isle of Man, IM7 2HR

Printed and bound in Great Britain

by

Titus Wilson & Son, Kendal

Contents

Acknowledgements

I should like to say thank you to the Maryport Maritime Museum for being so helpful and providing me with images. I should also like to thank Whitehaven Archive and Local Studies, the staff of the Maryport Library, the Carlisle Archive Centre and the Liverpool Maritime Museum (Archives and Library); all of whom did so much to assist me with my numerous enquiries with such kindness. A special thanks to Michael Freeman, Curator, Ceredigion Museum, Aberystwyth for his help and to allow me to use the material.

I am indebted to Karen Cook for the remarkable Aikshaw letter; Mrs. Law for the copy of the Glenfalloch painting; John Mounsey for the photograph of Abbey Holme, wreck; Ian Hine for his help and for providing images; David Kinrade for I.T. help; Des Clague for his artwork and John Wells, not only for images, but for much-appreciated encouragement.

I am extremely grateful to Titus Wilson and Son Printers in Kendal for going out of their way to accommodate me and to John Whitwell for his help and kindness.

My thanks also to Yvonne of the Curzon Grill Maryport for looking after me so well; to Juan Quirk for driving around Cumbria with me; to John and Vicky Peel for their support and encouragement and to Liz Forbes whose assistance was invaluable.

Introduction

Quite by chance, whilst visiting a friend, I saw a model of a stately sailing ship by the name of "Brier Holme" which captured my curiosity. After glancing at the internet, I thought I might prepare a small pamphlet on the vessel as a Christmas present for the model's owner. A second serendipitous occasion led me to the intriguing Maryport in Cumberland (now Cumbria) where the beautiful Maritime Museum again excited my interest.

My small pamphlet project then burgeoned to covering all the sailing vessels which formed part of the Hine Brothers (Wilfrid and Alfred) shipping line. In all there were, at least, twenty-six sailing vessels although some were connected with the Hine Brothers for only a short time. There could be more.

The more I researched these vessels and their voyages, the more intriguing tales I discovered. Indeed, my love of the salty sea would weave a fancy and run amuck. One such example is the uncovered tale of the honeymooners – the artist and his wife -- and the captain's wife (in Vol. 2). We shall leave the original writings to weave their own tapestry. Your own imagination will have to fill in the gaps during the calm passages, and the doldrums. The reports of voyages do show the terrible conditions; the stark fear during heavy seas; the thrill of the speed; the salt; the smell of the spray and wind; the fascination of the vastness of the ocean; and the solitude. For me, as for many others, there is the fascination engendered by the Mistress/Master, which is the Sea. One must love, yet respect and in no way, take it for granted. The most evocative writer of the sea in those times was Joseph Conrad and I have no compunction in using him for passages for describing gales and harbours.

On the whole, original newspaper cuttings are used to plot the courses and routes of these ships. Whilst such sources can be on occasions unreliable, it is the only way in which we can catch a glimpse of the history of these beautiful commercial ships coming towards the end of their era. We shall follow the vessels individually. The portraits of the barques and captains are only possible as the Australian and New Zealand governments have opened the newspapers on the web for free. Also I am grateful to the Californian and New York newspapers; and to those of the British Isles. I shall not attempt to comment on the narratives. Where possible, however, we try to verify the newspaper sources with Maritime Directories, crew lists and others sources such as personal letters and contemporary correspondence. The newspapers were on the whole good to report the outward journey; unfortunately the journeys back to Britain were not reported as often and so sometimes it is not easy to know whether the vessel went via the Horn or Cape of Good Hope. Sometimes sightings gave positions and of course, when the vessels went on to South America or indeed North Western America, they went back via the Horn.

The barques from the British Isles to eastern Asia and particularly to Australia and New Zealand used the route that ran west to east through the southern oceans to employ the high westerly trade winds. A typical route can be seen on the voyage of the Eden Holme in 1900:-- Bay of Biscay—Madeira—Island of Palma (Canaries)—Doldrums—Gough Island (S.E. of Tristan d'Acunha)—Cape of Good Hope—near Apostles' Islands—passed Kerguelen Island—Tasmania. This time no ice, but indications were that it was there near Apostles' Island. This time the "brave westerlies" were not met with till passing Cape of Good Hope in 43 deg. S.

Then, in the Roaring Forties, there was often a chance of meeting icebergs, however, the further south the vessels went, the more the winds increased enhancing the speed, and the curvature of the latitudes shortened the journey by hundreds of miles.

The return unfortunately is not so well documented (by Hine Bros.' vessels). There were normally three courses. One: via Cape of Good Hope. Two: direct from Australia, via south of New Zealand, into the 40th parallel South, under to 55th, to clear the Horn, which it passed on the port side. It had a particularly bad reputation with terrible conditions, high winds, shallow water, ice, and coasts without lighthouses.

The Hine Bros. never lost a vessel that way, that we know of. After the Horn, the vessel would have proceeded northward up the east coast of South America, then crossing the Equator, into the North Atlantic where she went east to Europe.

Three: leaving Australia, via Newcastle N.S.W. the vessel would go to South America with coal and then went round the Horn.

Another regular route was direct from the British Isles or Europe to the Pacific ports of the Americas and back via the Horn both ways. The trip from the Atlantic to the Pacific was considered the most feared, as the vessel had to beat through Drake's Passage into the prevailing winds.

1871 The Liverpool Mercury Mon. 16 Oct. p.3
The Robert Ritson [of Maryport, of 660 tons], *from Boston at Valparaiso Aug 23, was 64 days off the Cape Horn without making any progress, the wind blowing furiously all the time.*

Joseph Conrad from "Mirror of the Sea" Chapter 23

The one of the two great capes of the world, strangely enough, is seldom if ever called a cape (not like Cape of Good Hope). We say, "a voyage round the Horn"; "we rounded the Horn"; we got a frightful battering of the Horn," but rarely "Cape Horn" and, indeed, with some reason, for Cape Horn is as much an island as a cape.

And this is one of those gales whose memory in after-years returns, welcome in dignified austerity, as you would remember with pleasure the noble features of a stranger with whom you crossed swords once in knightly encounter and are never to see again. In this way gales have their physiognomy. You remember them by your own feelings, and no two gales stamp themselves in the same way upon your emotions. Some cling to you in woebegone misery; others come back fiercely and weirdly, like ghouls bent upon sucking your strength away; others, again, have a catastrophic splendour; some are unvenerated recollections, as of spiteful wild-cats clawing at your agonized vitals; others are severe, like a visitation; and one or two rise up draped and mysterious, with an aspect of ominous menace. In each of them there is a characteristic point at which the whole feeling seems contained in one single moment. Thus there is a certain four o'clock in the morning in the confused roar of a black and white world when coming on deck to take charge of my watch I received the instantaneous impression that the ship could not live for another hour in such a raging sea.

Another, strangely, recalls a silent man. And yet it was not din that was wanting; in fact, it was terrific. That one was a gale that came upon the ship swiftly, like a pampero, which last is a very sudden wind indeed. Before we knew very well what was coming all the sails we had set had burst; the furled ones were blowing loose, ropes flying, sea hissing -- it hissed tremendously -- wind howling, and the ship lying on her side, so that half of the crew were swimming and the other half clawing desperately at whatever came to hand, according to the side of the deck each man had been caught on by the catastrophe, either to leeward or to windward. The shouting I need not mention -- it was the merest drop in an ocean of noise -- and yet the character of the gale seems contained in the recollection of one small, not particularly impressive, sallow man without a cap and with a very still face. Captain Jones -- let us call him Jones -- had been caught unawares. Two orders he had given at the first sign of an utterly unforeseen onset; after that the magnitude of his mistake seemed to have overwhelmed him. We were doing what was needed and feasible. The ship behaved well. Of course, it was some time before we could pause in our fierce and laborious exertions; but all through the work, the excitement, the uproar, and some dismay, we were aware of this silent little man at the break of the poop, perfectly motionless, soundless, and often hidden from us by the drift of sprays.

When we officers clambered at last upon the poop, he seemed to come out of that numbed composure, and shouted to us down wind: "Try the pumps." Afterwards he disappeared. As to the ship, I need not say that, although she was presently swallowed up in one of the blackest nights I can remember, she did not disappear. In truth, I don't fancy that there had ever been much danger of that, but certainly the experience was noisy and particularly distracting -- and yet it is the memory of a very quiet silence that survives.

++++++++++

About 1862 Wilfrid Hine (23 years old) was in partnership (or at least a main employee) with Richard Nicholson & Son at the premises at 14 and 14½, South Castle-street Liverpool. By 1867 he was involved with at least four vessels, the Elizabeth (brig) 1862—lost 1862, the Hebe (brig) 1862--sold 1869; the Humberstone (barque) 1865--wrecked 1870; the Byron (brigantine) 1867--sold 1871.

During Wilfrid Hine's time in Liverpool from c 1860 up to the time he moved to Maryport in 1873, he had been intricately involved with Richard Nicholson and his son (William Henry). The following details of vessels illustrate this clearly.

Elizabeth
LR 1861-63 Elizabeth, W. Hine & c, Liverpool.
Liverpool Register: Elizabeth, William Henry Nicholson of Liverpool

Hebe
LR 1868: Hebe, Wilkinson: Wilkinson, Liverpool.
[**MLN** 1867: Wilfred (sic) Hine, 14, South Castle Steet, Liverpool.
[**MLN** 1868: Richard Nicholson, Liverpool.

Humberstone
LR 1870: Humberstone. W Robinson: W. Hine, Liverpool.
[**MLN** 1867: Wilfrid Hine, Liverpool.
[**MLN** 1868: Richard Nicholson, Liverpool.
[**MLN** 1870: W.H. Nicholson, 14, South Castle, Street, Liverpool.

Byron
LR 1870: Byron, E Ward: Nicholson &c., Liverpool.
[**MLN** 1868: Wilfrid Hine, 14, South Castle, Street, Liverpool.
[**MLN** 1870: Richard & W.H. Nicholson, 14, South Castle, Street, Liverpool.

Robert Hine
LR 1869-70: Robert Hine, J. Wilkinson: Nicholson &c., Liverpool.
[**MLN** 1870: Richd. Wm. Hy. Nicholson, 14, South Castle, Street, Lvrpl.
[**MLN** 1875 & 78: Wilfrid Hine, 14, South Castle, Street, Liverpool.
[**MLN** 1880: Wilfrid Hine, Maryport, Cumberland.

Abbey Holme
LR 1874: Abbey Holme, Robinson: Nicholson &c., Liverpool/ (amended) Hine Bros., Maryport.
[**MLN** 1870 & 75: Wilfrid Hine: 14, South Castle, Street, Liverpool.
[**MLN** 1878 & 80: Wilfrid Hine: Custom Ho. Bldgs., Maryport.
[**MLN** 1890: Wilfrid Hine: Custom Ho. Bldgs., Maryport. (Managing owner).

Note: (Elm Grove, barque, Official No. 47467, although a Nicholson vessel, not mentioned with Wilfrid Hine, was most probably connected with the latter. The captain was a Hine captain and Elm Grove was sold in 1872 in Australia by Captain Hurst.)

Also: John Abbott is mentioned in dispatches.

[Fl corr] *Liverpool 6 March 1873 referring you to mine of y'day please ....at once to barque "John Abbot"* [barque, Official No. 62,023] *now here care R. N & Sons, 28 stone of Flour same quality as for "Glenfalloch". Both these ships sail next week so it should be here by Tuesday or Wednesday. I have sent off 5 sacks today as per enclosed & paid 5d carriage. Yours truly Wilfred Hine.* [May have been a managing owner].

TSR 2/7 John Abbott: 1873: shares Wilfred Hine 2/64 & Alfred Hine 2/64.

In the next six years i.e. 1867-73 he had acquired one brigantine (Jane Harrison) in 1872 and 8 barques (one of which, the Queen of the Fleet, Wilfrid/Hine Bros., were managing owners).

The main types of sailing vessels this firm had were (s) ship – 3 masts yards with all square rigs: (bk) – barque (or bark) 3 masts with 2 square rigs with last or mizzen mast: (bg) -- brig with 2 masts with yards and square rig on both masts: (bn) -- brigantine with 2 masts with square rig on foremast only: (sr) – schooner with 2 masts with fore-and-aft sails.

In July 1873, Wilfrid Hine left Liverpool to join his younger brother Alfred in Maryport in Cumberland forming the Hine Brothers shipping company. Alfred had been mainly in marine insurance, but had been, at least once, a manager/owner of the Hope (brig) 1871-73.

Most of the Hine-vessels were mainly for deep-sea trade. However, in 1874 the new shipping company bought a small fleet from Sloane Richards of Birmingham consisting of two brigantines "Clara" and "Maggie Gross" one brig "Glastry" and one schooner "Tom Roberts", as well as their first steam vessel "Florence Richards". Apart from two small vessels, a flat "James" and a ketch "Clymene" bought later, that was the sum amount of sailing vessels for the coastal and Mediterranean trade, that we know of to date.

In 1875-6 Hine Brothers commissioned four brand new vessels between 800-1,000 tons, and was connected with another in 1875, of 570 tons, which they subsequently took over. Apart from one second-hand 1,000 ton barque in 1890, that was the last they acquired. From then the brothers began to concentrate on steamships which took precedence over the barques—indeed the Hine Brothers had had around 28 steamships forming the Holme Line for that purpose. The steamships mainly plied between the English and North American shores and the Mediterranean.

1881 Maryport Advertiser and Weekly News Fri. 17 June
A New Line of Steamers – Our readers will perceive by a reference to our advertising columns, that Messrs. Hine Brothers, of this town, have with their usual enterprise, determined to establish direct communication by sea between Maryport and America. A new line of splendid steamers, called the "Holme Line" has been formed, and these vessels will carry cargoes from New York to Maryport, via Plymouth. It is unnecessary, we hope, to solicit for this venture the support of the commercial men in the Western Division of the country. The new means of transit will be of great service to the public; it cannot fail, we think, to prove a commercial advantage; and we have no doubt, but that the well known readiness of Messrs. Hine to serve the trading community of the district, will be appreciated as it deserved.

1882 The Maryport Advertiser and Weekly News Fri. 15 Dec. p.8

Messrs. Hine Brothers: Steamers: Thorn Holme, 1,101 tons; West Cumberland, 897 tons; Alne Holme, 657 tons; Ardmore, 597 tons; Esk Holme, 595 tons; Glen Holme, 532 tons; Ovington, 444 tons; Horatio, 262 tons; Bavington, 47 tons. Sailing ships: Castle Holme, 1,042 tons; Myrtle Holme, 943 tons; Brier Holme, 920 tons; Eden Holme, 818 tons; Abbey Holme, 533 tons; Hazel Holme, 422 tons; Aikshaw, 596 tons; Glenfalloch, 459 tons; Robert Hine, 327 tons; Clara, 145 tons; Tom Roberts, 103 tons.

Often vessels were sold in 1/64 shares to others who become part owners. The Hines were either full owners or managing/owners or ships' husbands. [see Castle Holme 1889 Dec. 14 (Vol. 2)]

1885 The Liverpool Mercury Sat. 4 Apr. p.8
Ships of Sale: Valuable Steamship shares: To be Sold by Tender
Lot 1   Ten/ 64th shares steamship Morgan Richards of Liverpool
Lot 2   Ten/ 64th shares Capri of Liverpool
Lot 3   Three/ 64th shares Esk Holme of Maryport
Lot 4   Four/ 64th shares Ardmore of Maryport
Lot 5   Nine/ 64th shares Thorn Holme of Maryport
Lot 6   Eight/ 64th shares West Cumberland of Maryport
Lot 7   Nine/ 64th shares Alne Holme of Maryport
Lot 8   Six/ 64th shares Ovington of Maryport
Lot 9   Four/ 64th shares Fern Holme of Maryport
Lot 10   Six/ 64th shares Glen Holme (formerly called Margaret Banks) of Maryport

The managing owners of the ships are, as to lots 1 and 2, Messrs. Richard Nicholson and son, 14 and 14½, South Castle-street Liverpool, and to lots (3-10) Messrs. Hine Brothers, Custom House-buildings, Maryport.

1886 Maryport and Workington Advertiser Fri. 5 Feb. p.2
Messrs. Hine Brothers' Ships: Steamers: Fern Holme, 3,000 tons, cargo; Thorn Holme, 2,000 tons; West Cumberland, 1,600 tons; Alne Holme, 1,400 tons; Glen Holme, 1,300 tons; Esk Holme, 1,100 tons; Ardmore, 1,000 tons; Ovington, 800 tons; Horatio, 50 (sic) tons; Ivy Holme 280 tons; Elizabeth and Ann, 130 tons. Sailing ships: Castle Holme, 1,500 tons burthen; Myrtle Holme, 1,400 tons; Brier Holme, 1,300 tons; Eden Holme, 1,200 tons; Abbey Holme, 720 tons; Hazel Holme, 700 tons; Aikshaw, 870 tons.

This account of the sailing ships of the Wilfrid Hine/Hine Brothers tries to follow each vessel from the beginning, even before they were acquired by the Hines. The Queen of the Fleet (even though only a managed barque) was interesting as it had been involved in the North Atlantic trade (unusual for the Hine sailing vessels) in the very busy routes, contrasted to the lonely furrows made in the South Atlantic, Indian and Pacific Oceans.

During the 45 years Wilfrid Hine had sailing ships, we are following the end of the Tea Clippers (among which was the Cutty Sark), the real diminishing role of the barques (the working vessels), as the emergence of steamships which became faster and more reliable, and the opening of the Suez Canal in 1869, cutting out the tough passages via Cape of Good Hope and the Horn.

Most of the deep sea vessels had been clipper vessels: long, narrow and fast. Some had been ships like, Tea Clippers, but were soon converted to barques as they needed less crew, so were cheaper, and easier to deal with in often rapidly changing weather conditions, especially in the furious winds in the roaring forties and the furious fifties.

Castle Holme and Myrtle Holme were originally ships but were soon converted into barques, even the famous Cutty Sark had been converted and used, like the Hine Brothers' vessels, for the Australian trade.

+++++++++++++++++

Wilfrid Hine   John Wells of Kendal

Alfred Hine   John Wells of Kendal

{FS: Census 1861: Wilfred (sic) Hine. Male, 22, Boarder, born Maryport, Cumberland. 6 West Derby, St. Stephen, The Martyr – Liverpool}

1863 Adair's Maryport Advertiser Fri. 1 May p.8
Marriages: At the Baptist chapel, Maryport, on the 28th by the Rev. D. Kirkbride, Mr. Wilfred Hine shipbroker, Liverpool, to Jane, only daughter of Mr. Joseph Fletcher, Maryport.

{FS: Marriage—26 July 1865, Alfred Hine, 24—Isabella McLennan, 22—Maryport}

1871 Maryport Advertiser and Weekly News Fri. 5 May p.8
Mr. Alfred Hine, ship agent at this port, has been appointed agent for the Liverpool Underwriters' Association.

{bmd: Death, Mar. 1873, Isabella Hine, 30, Cockermouth 10b 390}
{bmd: Marriage—June 1875, Alfred Hine—Mary Eaglesfield: Cockermouth 10b 901}

[Dir: Post Office 1873 pp.861-4] Hine Alfred: Private Resident, 27 High st. Hine Alfred, Insurance Agents, Liverpool Underwriters Association, ship & insurance agent, commission merchant &c., Michley Coad Co. colliery proprietors (Alfred Hine, agent) [all at] Custom House buildings.
No Wilfrid Hine.

1880 The Liverpool Mercury Mon. 20 Sept. p.6
Birth: Hine—Sept. 6, at Camp Hill, Maryport, Cumberland, the wife of Wilfred Hine, of a daughter.

{FS: Census 1881}

Wilfred (sic) Hine	Head	M M	42	Maryport, Cumberland, Shipowner & Ship Broker
				Baptist Local Preacher
Jane Hine	Wife	M F	40	Maryport, Cumberland
Alfred Hine	Son	U M	12	Maryport, Cumberland, Scholar
Mary C. Hine	Dau	U F	10	Maryport, Cumberland, Scholar
Elfrida B.M. Hine	Dau	U F	6 m	Maryport, Cumberland.
Mary Elliot	Serv	U F	21	Ellenborough, Cumberland, Domestic, Cook.
Hannah M.C. Kenzie	Serv	U F	22	West Newton, Cumberland, Domestic, Housemaid.
Harriet Gorley	Serv	U F	18	West Newton, Cumberland, Domestic, Nurse.

(Camp Hill, Crosscanonby, Cumberland)

{FS: Census 1881}

Alfred Hine	Head	M M	39	Maryport, Cumberland, Shipowner & Ship Broker.
Mary Hine	Wife	M F	33	Maryport, Cumberland
Alfred Hine	Son	U M	12	Maryport, Cumberland, Scholar
John MC L. Hine	Son	U M	8	Maryport, Cumberland, Scholar
Mary Hine	Dau	U F	4	Maryport, Cumberland.
Ethel A. Hine	Dau	U F	3	Maryport, Cumberland.
Wilfred Hine	Son	U M	1 m	Maryport, Cumberland.
Betsy Pattinson	Serv	M F	52	Maryport, Cumberland, Sick Nurse.
Edith Roberts	Serv	U F	23	Nant Y Glo, Monmouth, Domestic, Cook.
Emily Roberts	Serv	U F	20	West Newton, Cumberland, Domestic, Cook.
Sarah Ann Bromley	Serv	U F	16	Maryport, Cumberland, Nursemaid.

(Park Hill, Crosscanonby, Cumberland)

1882 The Liverpool Mercury Fri. 3 Mar. p.6

Mr. David Ainsworth, M.B. for West Cumberland, Mr. Wilfrid Hine, of Maryport, and Mr. A. Mosses, of the firm of Mosses and Mitchell, had an interview on Wednesday with Admiral Sir Richard Collinson, K.C.B., deputy master of the Trinity House, with a view of the better lighting the Cumberland coast.

1882 The Liverpool Mercury Fri. 26 May p.6

Births: Hine--May 23, at Camp Hill, Maryport, Cumberland, the wife of Wilfrid Hine, of a son.

[Dir: Bulmer's 1883 p.557] Hine Alfred (Hine Bros.); h. Park hill.
Hine Wilfrid (Hine Bros.); h. Camp Hill.
Hine Bros., ship owners, ship brokers, insurance and commission agents, and coal importers, Custom House office, Glasson. (p.571) Coal Merchants; Hine bros., Fire and Life Insurance Offices, &c. Association of Underwriters (Liverpool) Hine Bros, Custom House buildings.
Workington: Hine Bros., steam and sailing ship brokers and owners, Commercial buildings, Falcon street.

1884 The Leicester Chronicle and Leicester Mercury Sat. 2 Aug. p.3

On Wednesday a meeting of non-electors of Cumberland was held on Ellenborough Moor, near Maryport, two thousand persons being present. Mr. Wilfrid Hine, shipowner, Maryport, presided. Addresses condemning the action of the House of Lords in throwing out the Franchise Bill were delivered by local Liberal leaders, and resolutions that the present constitution of the House of Lords is opposed to the true interest of the country, and ought to be reformed, and supporting the Government, were passed.

1886 The Times (London) 15 Feb. p.11

Mr. Harry H. Mitchell states that consequent upon the death of Mr. Alexander Mosses in October last, he has transferred the general shipping and insurance business hitherto carried on by Mosses and Mitchell to Messrs. Hine Brothers, of Maryport, and Mr. Edward P. Willis who will continue the same under the style and title of Hine Brothers and Willis.

1887 Maryport Advertiser Fri. 25 Feb. p.5
Death of Mrs. Hine—We regret to have to announce the death of Mrs. Hine, mother of Mr. Wilfrid and Mr. Alfred Hine of Camp Hill and Park Hill, Maryport, in her 80th year. She had been confined to her bedroom for some time, and her death was by no means unexpected. As soon as the sad event was announced on Friday night last, a large number of flags in the town and on the ships in the harbour were hoisted half-mast high.

1889 The Lancaster Gazette Wed. 7 Aug.
Formation of a Liberal Unionist Association for Maryport: The Liberal Unionists of Maryport and neighbourhood have just formed an association for the Maryport branch of the Cockermouth Division. Mr. Austin Hamill, of London, attended from the Central Association. Mr. Wilfrid Hine was elected president.

1890 The Lancaster Gazette Wed. 15 Jan.
A New Baptist Chapel for Maryport. The subscription towards the fund for the erection of the new Baptist chapel at Maryport are being promised most liberally. Messrs. Hine Brothers, shipowners, gave a donation of £500, and an offer of a further sum of £500 on condition that another £1,500 was raised before the church was opened. Seeing that upwards of £1,000 has been already secured, it is pretty certain that the balance will be forthcoming from Messrs. Hine's other £500. The new building, which is being erected at the corner of Station-road and Curzon-street, will have accommodation for 640 adults on the ground floor and 80 in the gallery. There will also be provided vestries for minister and deacons and a large lecture hall. The schoolroom will be erected in the rear of the chapel, and will have class rooms, and a separate room for the infants. The building will be of red sandstone, and erected in the early Gothic style, with a tower and spire 125 feet high.

[**Dir:** Kelly's 1894 p.198] Hine Alfred J.P., Parkhill, Maryport: Hine Wilfrid J.P., Camp Hill Maryport.
[**Dir:** Bulmer's 1901 p.755] Local Information: The Urban District Council of Maryport: Members: North Ward: Wilfrid Hine. Harbour Commissioners: W. Hine, Esq., Camp Hill; A Hine, Esq., Park Hill: Magistrates (Maryport Sub-Division)—Alfred Hine, Esq., Wilfrid Hine., Esq. [pp.765 & 768] Hine Bros, Shipbrokers, Ship Owners, Custom House buildings: Coal Merchants Hine Bros. (exporters). [p.99] Workington: Hine bros., shipowners, metal brokers, coal exporters, etc., 28 Falcon street:--Holme Line of Steamers, Hine Bros., owners, Maryport: branch Falcon street. [p.979 Appendix] The Fifth County Council Elected March 1901: County Councillors, Hine, Alfred—Park Hill, Maryport: Maryport South.

1902 The Maryport Advertiser Sat. 20 Sept.
Death of Mr. Alfred Hine, Maryport.
We regret to record the death of Mr. Alfred Hine, of Park Hill, the junior partner in the firm of Hine Brothers, shipowners, Maryport, which took place from nephritis at noon on Sunday. It is generally believed that Mr. Hine caught a chill in connection with the homecoming of his son, Captain Hine, from South Africa, but it was not till noon on Saturday the 6th inst., that he was taken seriously ill at his office. He was attended by Dr. Little, and on Thursday morning last such dangerous symptoms developed that it

was considered advisable to secure specialist advice, and on Friday afternoon, Professor Newman and Dr. Jowell, of Glasgow, attended and performed a minor operation, bleeding the patient in order to relieve the congestion of the kidneys, the seat of the disease. The deceased, who was 61 years of age, was a Justice of the Peace, and had sat for several years on the County Council as the representative of Maryport South. While deeply immersed in the world-wide mercantile pursuits of his firm, Mr. Hine found time to take an active part in most of the movements which had for their object the social, intelligence, and commercial welfare of the inhabitants of his native town. He was a lifelong abtainer (sic), a zealous temperance reformer, and while his brother, Mr. Wilfrid Hine, seceded over Mr. Gladstone's Home Rule Bill, and became a liberal Unionist, he remained true to the Liberal cause and took a leading part in connection with the Maryport branch of the Cockermouth Division Liberal Association. The deceased's most congenial work was, perhaps, associated with Trinity Baptist Church, a fine pile of buildings in Station Street, which would never have been erected but for the munificence of himself and Mr. Wilfrid Hine, and of which he was a deacon and zealous superintendent of the large and flourishing Sunday School. Mr. Hine was also widely known as a musician, and his gifts in that direction were reflected in a marked degree in both the musical portion of the service of Trinity Baptist Church and in the Sunday school. On the sad event becoming known in Maryport, on Sunday flags were displayed half-mast over all the public buildings and business houses in the town, and also by the vessels in the docks and harbour.

Mr. Alfred Hine was born at Maryport, April 30th, 1841, and was a younger son of the late Mr. Alfred Hine. He commenced business as shipbroker at Maryport in 1869 at the time the iron industry was established in the town. In 1873 he was joined by his brother Wilfrid, who brought with him from Liverpool his shipowning business, and the firm became Hine Brothers on the 1st July, 1873. From that time to the present the business of shipbrokers, shipowners, and merchants has been carried on by them. In addition to being a Justice of the Peace for the County of Cumberland, and a member of the County Council since its institution, and an alderman for six years, Mr. Hine filled various other public positions, including Maryport Harbour Commission, Secretary of Maryport British Schools for over 20 years, Superintendent of Grasslot and Trinity Baptist Sunday School for 30 years, Secretary of the Baptist Chapel for 25 years, and choirmaster for 15 years. He leaves a widow and grown-up family. The interment will take place at the Maryport Cemetery on Friday. A special service will be held in the Trinity Baptist Church at 2.30 p.m.

[Dir: Kelly's 1906 p.11] Cumberland County Council: Councillors: Maryport, South, Wilfrid Hine, Camp hill, Maryport. [p.204] Hine Brothers, ship owners, sailing & steamship brokers & coal exporters. Custom House buildings. [p.300] Workington: Hine Brothers, ship brokers, Falcon St.

1907 The Register, Adelaide Wed. 14 Aug. p.4

—A Meeting of Creditors—Messrs. Hine Brothers of Maryport, who also carry on business in London under the style of Messrs. Hine Brothers & Willis, the owners of the steamers Abbey Holme, Forest Holme, Greta Holme, Isel Holme and Nether Holme, and the well-known barques Castle Holme and Myrtle Holme, have called a meeting of their creditors. The circular from the firm's solicitors contains the following:— "After giving the matter the fullest consideration possible within the time at our disposed, we advised that Messrs. Lewis and Mounsey, chartered accountants, of Liverpool and London, who have special experience in shipping accounts, should be instructed to investigate the affairs of the firm with a view of preparing a statement for submission to the creditors. This course has been adopted. We hoped that the meeting of creditors might have been delayed until Messrs.

Lewis & Mounsey were able to make a complete investigation, but having regard to circumstances which have arisen since we were consulted we have thought it desirable, in the interests of the creditors, that the meeting should be called without delay, and the accountants will submit the result of their investigation so far as it has proceeded."

[**Dir:** Kelly's 1910 p.208] Hine Brothers, ship brokers & coal exporters, North Quay: p.323, under Private Residents, no Wilfrid Hine. [**Dir:** Kelly's 1914] no Hine Bros.
{**FS:** Census 1911: Wilfred (sic) Hine: Male, 72, Birthplace Maryport Cumberland: Household Paddington South, Paddington, London.}

1913: The Whitehaven News Thurs. 24 July.
Illness of Mr. Hine: Mr Hine of the Holme Line of Steam Shipping Company who left Maryport last week for London was taken ill on the journey, and collapsed on his arrival. He is now lying seriously ill in a nursing home. [Is this our Wilfrid Hine?]

1921 West Cumberland Times Sat. 26 Feb. p.5
We regret to record the death of Mr Wilfred (sic) Hine, which occurred in London on Wednesday.
Mr. Hine, who was 83 years of age, was one of the most prominent public men of Maryport during the last 50 or 60 years, and the memory of his innumerable activities for the welfare of the town will live for many generations. He had a deserved reputation as a keen-business man, a reliable counselor, a great public speaker, a generous philanthropist and one of the best benefactors of Maryport. Though he was at the head of a big commercial concern, Messrs Hine Brothers, shipbrokers and shipowners, and a very busy man, he found time to devote to public interests and associated himself with the chief local public bodies. It has often been said that the town of Maryport lost a good friend when he left the district. He worked unceasingly for the development of the town. The Holme Line fleet, which Messrs Hine owned, consisted of over a dozen steamers and about half-a-dozen sailing vessels, and they traded with all parts of the world, particularly South Australia. It was a big concern and a boon to Maryport. Not only did the line bring trade to the port and materially help local industries, but the ships were manned mostly by Maryport men. Mr Wilfred (sic) Hine was a great friend of the young men of Maryport, and dozens have him to thank for placing them on the road to promising careers. He was actively concerned in the management of the Maryport harbour. He was a member of the Board of Trustees for the District and Harbour of Maryport, and when, in 1894, the body was divided into the Urban District Council and the Harbour Commissioners he continued as a member of both bodies. He and his brother, the late Mr. Alfred Hine represented the ship-owners on the Harbour Commissioners for a long period of years. Always progressive and optimistic, he worked hard for the extension of the harbour, and it was due very much to his efforts that the Senhouse Dock was built, and after it met with disaster in course of erection, he endeavoured to get it on a sound financial footing again. He was also for some years chairman of the District Council, and afterwards he succeeded his brother as representative of the South Ward on the County Council. As a politician, he was a prominent figure on local platforms, being a fluent speaker and a man of great mental capacity. In his younger days he was a strong Liberal, but he differed from his party on the question of Home Rule, and joined the Unionist Party. He became president of the Maryport Unionist Association. He was a prominent Baptist and a deacon of Trinity Baptist Church, and it was mainly through the instrumentality of his brother Alfred and himself that the new Baptist Church, which is one of the most handsome buildings in the town, was built. He interested himself in most local charities, and was one of the most

liberal subscribers to the Victoria Cottage Hospital when it was built. The welfare of children also claimed his attention, and he was a manager of the British School. His services towards the school have been recognized by the hanging of his portrait, alongside his brother's, in the building. Though a man with a great strength of will, he had a genial and friendly disposition. He had a personality which was admired by all with whom he came in contact. Maryport owes much to his public spirit, to his great industry, both in his business and local affairs, and to his generosity. His wife pre-deceased him last year.   He lost his eldest son, John, at sea during the war, and his eldest daughter, Janie, died about a month ago. Maryport extends its sympathy to his family who are left to mourn his loss. Flags were flown at half-mast at the various public buildings in the town on Thursday and yesterday.
{**bmd:** Death, March 1921: Hine Wilfrid Death, 83, Paddington, 1a 107}

++

In terms of citation, the newspapers used are all named and individually dated. They ranged from Britain, Ireland, Australia, New Zealand, Singapore, North America, Honolulu, even the Netherlands etc., are shown. The Maritime Directories are cited using square brackets using the abbreviations set out below

[LR......]	The Lloyd's Register of Shipping.
[RAFS]	The Record of American and Foreign Shipping.
[ALRFS]	The American Lloyd's Register of American and Foreign Shipping.
[RA&ANZ]	The Register of Australian and New Zealand Shipping.
[MNL]	The Maritime Navy List.
[MNL&ANZ]	The Mercantile Navy List of Australian and New Zealand.

The registers must be used with caution especially dates, for ownership and captains, also small differences of tonnage and dimensions. However, dates for all surveys (with one exception) correspond with other sources and therefore are excellent references.

Liverpool Register of Shipping . At the Maritime Museum of Liverpool.

[TRS/ and TSR/]	Various crew lists and shares of vessels at the Records Office, Carlisle.
[DX/]	Correspondence at the Records Office, Carlisle.
[Dir]	Various Historical Directories
[Fl corr]	Robert Fletcher Correspondences at Whitehaven Archives. Letters and details of voyages of various Hine Bros' ships.
{.............}	From internet not verified.
{bmd:	Births, Marriages and Deaths: (freebmd.rootsweb.com)
{FS:	Census (FamilySearch.org-Search)

Dates

1861-65	American Civil War
1866	First really successful Atlantic cable laid by s.s. Great Eastern
1869	The Suez Canal opened
1870-71	France-Prussian War: German States—Second French Empire ends
1870	Cable: London to Bombay
1872	Cable: Australia linked to Bombay
1873	Cable: Lisbon to Portugal to Pernambuco (Brazil)
1872-76	Spanish Civil War
1876	Cable: British Empire—London to New Zealand
1876	Plimsoll-line introduced
1877	Cable: USA, Lima to Valparaiso
1879-84	The War of the Pacific: dispute between Bolivia and Chile: reason nitrate deposits. Chile also makes war against Peru.

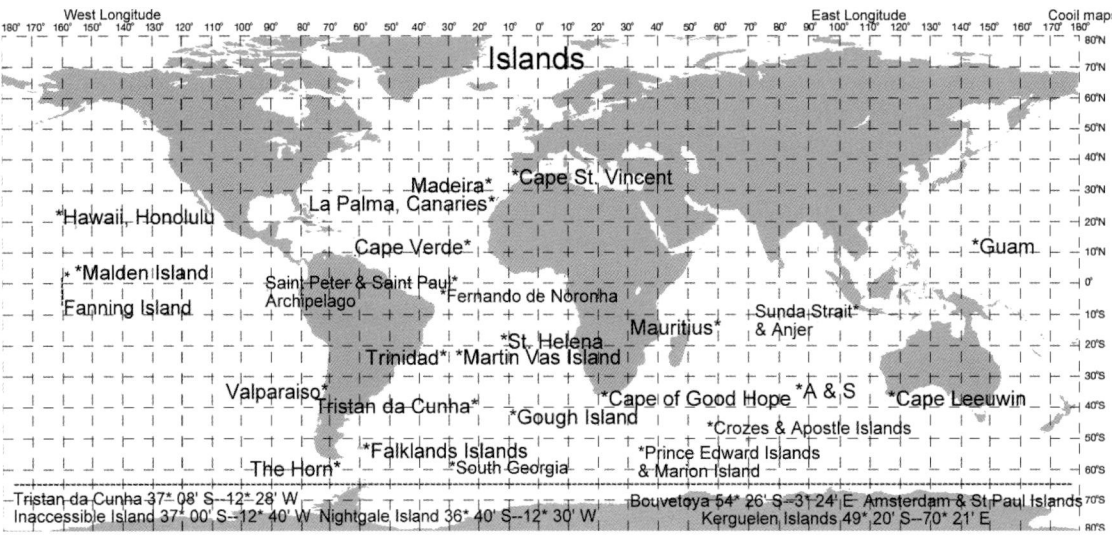

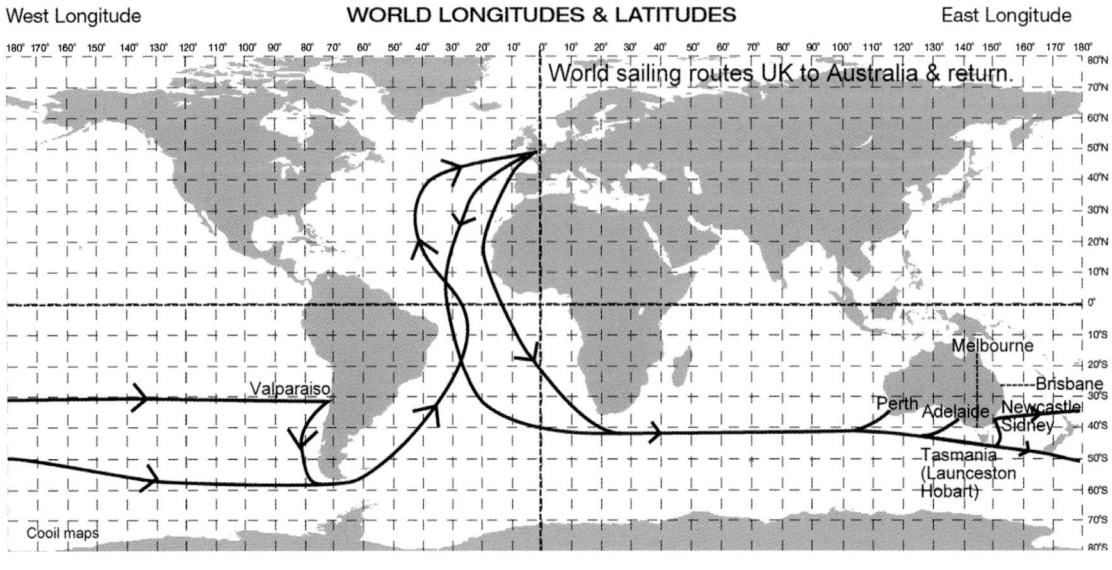

CHAPTER ONE

In the early days Wilfrid Hine was in partnership (or at least a main employee) with Richard Nicholson & Son at 14 & 14½, South Castle-street Liverpool. By 1867 he was involved with at least four vessels, the Elizabeth (brig) 1862—lost 1862, the Hebe (brig) 1863--sold 1869; the Humberstone (barque) 1865--wrecked 1870; the Byron (brigantine) 1867--sold 1871.

During Wilfrid Hine's time in Liverpool from c 1860 up to the time he moved to Maryport in 1873 he had been intricately involved with Richard Nicholson and his son (William Henry). The following details of vessels illustrate this clearly.

Elizabeth
LR 1861-63 Elizabeth, W. Hine & c, Liverpool.
Liverpool Register: Elizabeth, William Henry Nicholson of Liverpool

Humberstone
LR 1870: Humberstone. W Robinson: W. Hine, Liverpool.
[**MLN** 1867: Wilfrid Hine, Liverpool.
[**MLN** 1868: Richard Nicholson, Liverpool.
[**MLN** 1870: W.H. Nicholson, 14, South Castle, Street, Liverpool.

Byron
LR 1870: Byron, E Ward: Nicholson &c., Liverpool.
[**MLN** 1868: Wilfrid Hine, 14, South Castle, Street, Liverpool.
[**MLN** 1870: Richard & W.H. Nicholson, 14, South Castle, Street, Liverpool.

Hebe
LR 1868: Hebe, Wilkinson: Wilkinson, Liverpool.
[**MLN** 1867: Wilfred (sic) Hine, 14, South Castle Steet, Liverpool.
[**MLN** 1868: Richard Nicholson, Liverpool.

Apart from these, Wilfrid Hine had been involved with or part owner of the following:
Cereal, barque, 1871-72: Jane Harrison, brigantine, 1872-73 (Mr. Harrison had been also connected with the "Byron"): The Queen of the Fleet, barque, 1872-75 (Wilfrid/Hine Brothers managing owners):

Also included is "Hope", brig, c. 1871-72, Managing Owner: Alfred Hine, based in Maryport. This one was mainly for the coastal trade.

These vessels are the ones identified with the Hine Brothers with certainty. More will most probably be unearthed in time.

A schooner "North Branch" a venerable vessel has been linked with the Hines, however the only link is one mention in a newspaper and no other corroborative evidence.

1871 Maryport Advertiser and Weekly News Fri. 10 Mar. p.8
The North Branch, of Belfast, attempted to enter the harbour, amidst the teriflic (sic) gale which prevailed yesterday, at noon—but, no assistance being rendered by the tug, she was blown past [Maryport harbour].
May. 12 p.8
*Harbour Committee: Two letters were read from **Mr. Hine** (sic) [Mr. Hinde ???], owner of the "North Branch", claiming compensation from the Trustees for damage sustained by the said vessel, in consequence of alleged neglect on the part of the Steam Tug Co., in*

allowing her to go on shore, instead of taking her into the harbour.—The clerk read his letter in reply to Mr. Hine (sic) [Mr. Hinde ???]*, referring him to the Steam Tug Co.*

[MNL 1868: 37973 North Branch, Belfast, (Sr), 90, **William Hinde**, Belfast.] **[owner]**
[MNL 1870: 37973 North Branch, Belfast, (Sr), 82, William Hinde, Belfast.]

It had been a collier mainly running between Troon and Belfast. Who was the owner of the "North Branch"; Wilfrid Hine, Alfred Hine or William Hinde? We shall have to suspend judgement.

ELIZABETH

Official No.	**22859**	**Code JDHB**	
Built	**1848 May 8.**	Sunderland	
Deck	One	Build	Carvel
Masts	Two	Gallery	None
Rigging	**Snow/Brig**	Head	Woman Bust
Stern	Square	Framework	Wood.
Tonnage	**236.94**	Length 90.2 feet; Breadth 25.85 feet; Depth 15.65 feet.	

[**LR** 1848-60 Addendum: Sw [Snow], Moddrell, 254, Sunderland 1848. Hndmrsh of Shields A1]

1848 Newcastle Courant Fri. 22 Sept. part first p.2
Spoken: The Elizabeth, from Miramichi for Newcastle, Long Island bearing ESE, distant 30 miles, on the 13th instant, by the ship Madawska, of Liverpool, arrived at the Clyde.
Oct. 6 part first p.4
North Shields: Arrived: Oct. 2: Elizabeth, Modderel (sic), from Miramichi. Imports: 418 pieces of pine timber: 538 deals and deal ends: 8 cords lathwood: 2 pieces of maple: 8 spars: 12 oars—L. Hindmarsh.
Nov. 3 part first p.4
Newcastle: Exports: Oct. 26: Elizabeth, Moddrell, for Malta with 141 chs Buddle's West Hartley [coal]: Hall and Co.
Dec. 22 part first p.2
Malta: Arrived: Dec. 11: Elizabeth, Moddrel (sic) from Newcastle.
1849 May 25 Part First p.4
North Shields: Sailed: May 23: Elizabeth, for Petersburgh.

1849 The Dundee Courier Wed. 29 Aug.
Petersburg: Sailed: Aug. 11: Elizabeth, Moddrel (sic), for Dundee.

1849 Caledonian Mercury, Edinburgh Thurs. 6 Sept.
Sound intelligence: Aug 27: Elizabeth, Moddrell, Petersburgh, Dundee.

1849 The Dundee Courier Wed. 12 Sept.
Dundee: Arrivals: Sept. 6: Elizabeth, Moddrel (sic), Petersburgh, flax.
Sept. 19
Dundee: Departures: Sept 17: Elizabeth, Modrel (sic), Newcastle, ballast.

1850 The Liverpool Mercury Tues. 30 Apr. p.7
Liverpool: Loading: 254, Elizabeth, East Port, St. Andrew's N.B., and Quebec.
May 3 p.7
Liverpool: Sailed: Apr. 30: Elizabeth, Moddrell, St. Andrew's, N.B.
July 9 p.7
At St. Andrew: Elizabeth, Moddrell, hence.

1850 The Liverpool Mercury Fri. 13 Sept. p.7
Liverpool: Sailed: Sept. 10: Elizabeth, Moddrell, Alexandria, E.
Oct. 25 p.7
Elizabeth, Moddrell, hence at Malta, with loss of foremast &c. having been in contact with the Isabella, from Troon for Alexandria.
1851 Apr. 8 p.7
Liverpool: Sailed: Apr. 4: Elizabeth, Moddrell, Trieste.
June 6 p.7
At Trieste: Elizabeth, Maddrell (sic), hence.
June 27 p.7

Trieste: Sailed: June 16: Elizabeth, Modrell (sic), for this port.
Aug. 19 p.7
Liverpool: Arrived: Aug. 16: Elizabeth, Maddrell (sic), Trieste.
Sept. 19
Liverpool: Loading for Europe: Elizabeth, Moddrell, 254, Algiers &c.
Sept. 23 p.8
Liverpool: Sailed: Sept. 22: Elizabeth, Moddrell, Algiers.

1851 Newcastle Courant Fri. 14 Nov.
Algiers: Arrived: Oct. 30: Elizabeth, Capt. Moddrel (sic).

1853 New-York Daily Tribune Tues. 8 Mar. p.8
Antwerp: Sailed: Feb. 19: Elizabeth, Moddrell, Boston U.S.
May 16 p.8
Boston: Cleared: May 13: Elizabeth, Moddrell, Bactouche, N.E. to load for Liverpool.
June 4 p.8
Bactouche: Arrived: May 23: brig Elizabeth, Moddrel (sic), from Boston.

1853 The Liverpool Mercury Fri. 15 July p.7
Liverpool: Loading for Europe: Elizabeth Moddrel (sic), 254, Trieste.
Aug. 5 p.7
Liverpool: Sailed: Aug. 3: Elizabeth, Moddrell, Trieste.
Oct. 4 p.7
At Trieste: Elizabeth, Moddrel (sic), hence.

1854 The Liverpool Mercury Fri. 12 May p.11
Liverpool: Loading for Europe: Elizabeth, Maddrell (sic), 254, Alexandria E.
June 2 p.11
Liverpool: Sailed: May 31: Elizabeth, Moddrell, Alexandria.
Nov. 17 p.8
Liverpool: Arrived: Nov. 14: Elizabeth, Moddrell, Alexandria.

1855 The Liverpool Mercury and Supplement Fri. 5 Jan. p.3
Liverpool: Sailed: Jan. 4: Elizabeth, Moddrell, Alexandria, Egypt.
Mar. 6 p.7
At Alexandria: Elizabeth, Maddrell (sic), hence.

1855 Newcastle Courant Fri. 27 Apr. p.8
Malta: left: previous to the 15th: Elizabeth, Moddrell for Queenstown.

1855 The Liverpool Mercury Fri. 8 June p.3
At Queenstown: June 5: Elizabeth, Modrell (sic) from Alexandria.

1855 The Glasgow Daily Herald Fri. 29 June p.7
Glasgow: Arrived: June 25: Elizabeth of Shields, Moddrell, from Alexandria, with 1830 qrs. wheat.
July 23 p.8
[Advert] Now Loading at No. 16 South Side, will receive Goods all To-morrow, and clear for sea on the following day. At Glasgow--For Gibraltar and Venice. The A 1 coppered Brig Elizabeth, 254 tons register, Captain Moddrell. Apply to John & Robert Young. 107 Buchanan Street.
Aug. 1 p.7
Glasgow: Sailed: July 28: Elizabeth, Moddrell, Gibraltar and Venice.
Sept. 10 p.7
At Gibraltar: Aug. 26: Elizabeth, Maddrell (sic), from Clyde.

1855 Newcastle Courant Fri. 26 Oct. p.8
Leghorn: Arrived: Oct 8: Elizabeth, Moddrell, from the Clyde.

1855 The Glasgow Daily Herald Mon. 29 Oct. 11
At Santander: Oct. 15: Elizabeth, Moddrell, from Clyde.

1856 Newcastle Courant Fri. 13 June p.8
Dublin: Arrived: June 8: Elizabeth, Moddrell from Constantinople.

1857 Liverpool Mercury Wed. 28 Jan. p.3
Liverpool: Sailed: Jan. 26: Elizabeth, Moddrell, Constantinople.

1857 The Standard (London) Mon. 14 Sept. p.6
Gibraltar: Arrived: Aug. 30: Brig Elizabeth, J. Moddrell, 56 days from Taganrog, and 36 from Constantinople, with wheat for Cork, cleared.

1857 Royal Cornwall Gazette Fri. 18 Sept. p.8
Falmouth: Arrived: Sept. 14: Elizabeth, Moddrell, Taganrog.

1857 Newcastle Courant Fri. 9 Oct. p.8
Limerick: Arrived: Oct. 2: Elizabeth, Moddrell, from Taganrog.

1857 Royal Cornwall Gazette Fri. Dec. 25 p.8
Falmouth: Arrived: Dec. 21: Elizabeth, Modrill (sic), from Cardiff.
1858 Fri. Jan. 1 p.8
Falmouth: Sailed: Sat. [Dec. 26, 1857]: Elizabeth, Moddrill (sic), for Algiers.
Falmouth: Sailed: Mon. [Dec. 28, 1857]: Elizabeth, Moddrell, for Algiers.
Aug. 27 p.8
Falmouth: Arrived: Mon [Aug. 23]: Elizabeth, Moddrell, from Taganrog.
Falmouth: Sailed: Thurs. [Aug. 26]: Elizabeth, Moddrell for Rotterdam.

1859 The Glasgow Daily Herald Fri. 29 Apr. p.6
Greenock: Arrived: Apr. 27: Elizabeth, Moddrel (sic) from Alexandria, with wheat.
May 18 p.6 with Supplement.
Greenock: Sailed: May 16: Elizabeth, Moddrell, for Troon, to load for foreign.
May 19 p.4
Troon: Arrived: May 17: Elizabeth, Moddrell, from Glasgow for foreign.
May 27 p.7
Troon: Sailed: May 25: Elizabeth, Moddrell for Malta or Alexandria.

1859 Royal Cornwall Gazette Fri. 30 Dec. p.8
Falmouth: Arrived: Mon. [Dec. 26]: Elizabeth, Moddrell from Odessa.
1860 Fri. 13 Jan. p.8
Falmouth: Sailed: Tues. [Jan. 10]: Elizabeth, Moddrell, for Gloster.

1860 The Bristol Mercury, and Western Counties Advertiser Sat. 28 Jan. p.7
Gloucester: Foreign Imports: from Odessa, Elizabeth, 1822 qrs wheat.

1861 The Leeds Mercury Fri. 29 Nov. p.4
Deal: Nov. 26: The brig Elizabeth, of Sunderland, for Bordeaux, was in collision on the night, of 25th, with a brig, name unknown.
Nov. 28: The Elizabeth, from Sunderland, for Bordeaux. Captain reports that while riding in the Downs on the 25th instant, was run into by the Unity, of Whitby, and sustained damage.

1861 Royal Cornwall Gazette Fri. 13 Dec. p.5

Scilly: Arrived: Elizabeth, from Bordeaux.

1861 The Liverpool Mercury Wed. 18 Dec. p.3
Liverpool: Arrived: Dec. 16: Elizabeth, Maddrell (sic), Bordeaux.

++++++++++ **Wilfrid Hine**
[**LR** 1861-63: Sw, 254, Modrell (sic)/ J. Wilkinson, Hndmrsh of Shields/ W. Hine & C, Liverpool, A1]
Liverpool Register: Port No. 40/1862. William Henry Nicholson of Liverpool, Merchant. 64/64 shares. Dated 17 Feb. 1862. [No Masters given].

1862 [Survey: Liverpool in February & March]

1862 Adairs' Maryport Advertiser Fri. 14 Mar. p.8
The "Elizabeth" Capt. Wilkinson sailed from Liverpool for Trinidad on the 12th inst.
June 6 p.8
The brig "Elizabeth" Capt. Wilkinson, arrived at Trinidad from Liverpool on the 26th April., after a passage of 45 days. She commenced on the 7th of May, to load for the Clyde.

1862 The Glasgow Daily Herald Wed. 16 July p.6
Trinidad: Sailed: June 13: Elizabeth, Wilkinson, for Greenock.
July 22 p.4
Greenock: Arrived: July 20: Elizabeth, Wilkinson, from Trinidad, with molasses and sugar.

1862 Adairs' Maryport Advertiser Fri. 15 Aug. p.1
The brig "Elizabeth" Capt. Wilkinson, sailed from Ardrossan for Montreal on the 11th inst.—cargo of coals.
Oct. 31 p.8
The brig "Elizabeth" Capt. Wilkinson, from Adrossan at Quebec on the 7th inst. She had a long passage of 56 days, and experienced strong westerly winds nearly all the time. She would tow up to Montreal on the following day.

1862 The Glasgow Daily Herald Thurs. 30 Oct. p.4
Quebec: Arrived: Oct. 12: Elizabeth, Wilkinson from Ardrossan.

1862 Adairs' Maryport Advertiser Fri. 19 Dec. p.1
The brig Elizabeth, Wilkinson, bound for Montreal to load a cargo of grain, was abandoned off Cape Pine and the crew landed at St. John's N.F. on the 8th inst.

1862 The Harbor Grace Standard and Conception Bay Advertiser Wed. 17 Dec.
The brig "Elizabeth," Capt. Wilkinson, from Montreal, with a cargo of corn, bound for Queenstown, was abandoned on the 16th ult., about 8 miles off Cape Pine. The master and crew, when leaving the vessel, which was nearly half full of water and lying on her beams ends, made for Trepassy, where they safely arrived and remained there five days. On Wednesday morning procured a passage for St. John's, and were safely landed on Saturday afternoon. One of the seamen [was] badly frost-bitten.—The crew consisted of ten persons, all of whom were taken charge of and provided for by the proper authority.

[**LR** 1864: Elizabeth, Sw [Snow] 254, J. Wilkinson, W. Hine & C of Liverpool, A1 **LOST**]

HEBE

Official No.	42939	**Code TLVM**	
Built	1862 Aug.	Egmont Bay, Prince Edward Island McFadgn	
Deck	One	Build	Carvel
Masts	Two	Gallery	None
Rigging	**Brig**	Head	Female Bust Figure
Stern	Square	Framework	Wood (maple).
Tonnage	**199**	Length 105.5 feet; Breadth 24.0 feet; Depth 12.8 feet.	

[**LR** 1862 Supplement: Hebe, Bg, J Caffery/ Wilkinson, 200/199, P.E. Isl. (McFagn) 1862 8 mo, J. Duncan P.E. Isl./ Wilkinson &, Liverpool, A1]

[**LR** 1863-69: Hebe, Bg, Wilkinson, 199, Wilkinson &, Liverpool A1]

[**LR** 1870-73: Hebe, Bg, Wilkinson, 199, Wilkinson &, Liverpool --------]

1862 [Survey: P.E. Island in August]

1863 The Liverpool Mercury Tues. 3 Mar. p.3
Liverpool: Arrived: Mar. 2: Hebe, Cardiff &c. [Survey: Liverpool in April]

++++++++++ **Wilfrid Hine**
Liverpool Register: Registered in Liverpool 114/1863
Wilfrid Hine of Liverpool. Shipowner 64/64. Dated 2 April 1863.
Master Liverpool 4-4-63 Joseph Wilkinson, 10.151

1863 The Liverpool Mercury Tues. 5 May.
Liverpool: Sailed: Apr. 30: Hebe, Wilkinson, Trinidad. [Survey: Liverpool in April.]

1863 Adairs' Maryport Advertiser Fri. 15 May. p.1
The Hebe, Wilkinson, from Liverpool to Trinidad, off Scilly, on the 5th inst., all well.
July 17 p.1
The brig Hebe, Wilkinson, from Liverpool, at Trinidad on the 10th June, after a passage of 40 days, would load in cargo for London.
Aug. 28 p.1
The Hebe, Wilkinson, from Trinidad, at London on the 21st inst., after a quick passage of 33 days.
Oct. 30 p.8
The Hebe, Wilkinson, cleared out at London for Valparaiso and Callao on the 24th inst. General Cargo.

1863 The Morning Post (London) Oct. 28 p.7
Gravesend: Sailed: Oct. 27: Hebe to Valparaiso.

1863 Adairs' Maryport Advertiser Fri. 6 Nov. p.8
The brig Hebe, Wilkinson, from London for Valparaiso and Callao, when at anchor, in the Downs, off Deal during the heavy gale of the night on the 1st inst., came in contact with the schooner Queen of Beauty, and to prevent further damage slipped from Anchor and chain, has been supplied with another anchor and 90 fathoms of chain, from Deal.
1864 May 20 p.8
The Hebe, Wilkinson, from Valparaiso at Callao on the 5th inst
June 3 p.1
The Hebe, Wilkinson, sailed, from Callao for Mantua April 29th, to load general cargo for London.
Nov. 4 p.8
The Hebe, Wilkinson, sailed from Valparaiso for London, September 10th.

1865 Jan. 13 p.8
The Hebe, Wilkinson, from the West Coast of South America, at London on the 7th inst.
Mar. 3 p.8
The Hebe, Wilkinson, sailed from Swansea for St. Thomas, and Porto Rico, on the 23rd ult.
May 5 p.8
The Hebe, Wilkinson, from Swansea at St. Thomas, on the 4th ult.
June 23 p.8
The Hebe, Wilkinson, sailed from Porto Rico for Falmouth on the 22nd May for orders.
July 7 p.8
The Hebe, Wilkinson, from Porto Rico at Falmouth on the 30 ult., for orders, which were received on the following day and sailed for Dunkirk.
July 14 p.8
The Hebe, Wilkinson, from Porto Rico at Dunkirk on the 7th inst.
Sept. 8 p.8
The Hebe, Wilkinson, from Dunkirk at Cronstadt on the 28th ult.
Oct. 13 p.8
Hebe, Wilkinson, sailed from Cronstadt for Cork on the 4th inst.

1865 The Belfast News-Letter Thurs. Morning 2 Nov.
(By Magnetic Telegraph): Queenstown, Nov. 1: Arrived: Hebe, from Cronstadt, with hemp, for Cork: put in through stress of weather.

1865 The Liverpool Mercury Wed. 13 Dec. p.3
Liverpool: Sailed: Dec. 11: Hebe, Wilkinson, Guayaquil [Ecuador].
1866 Jan. 26 p.3
Liverpool: Sailed: Jan. 25: Hebe, Wilkinson, Guayaquil [Ecuador].
Mar 20 p.
((Two Vessels, supposed privateers, seen in Guayaquil Bay. Inquired about Spanish merchant vessels in that port.))
July 17 p.
At Guayaquil: Hebe, Wilkinson, hence [from Liverpool].
Dec. 13 p.3
Liverpool: Sailed: Dec. 11: Hebe, Wilkinson, Guayaquil.

[**MNL**1867: 42939: Hebe, Liverpool, 214, Owner, Wilfred Hine, 14 South Castle Street, Liverpool.]
[**MNL**1868: 42939: Hebe, Liverpool, 214, Owner, Richard Nicholson, Liverpool.]

1867 The Standard (London) Mon. 28 Jan. p.7
Deal: Arrived: Jan. 25: The Hebe, in the Downs from Guayaquil spoke the ship Orient, from Calcutta, 128 days out, in lat. 41 N. long. 37 W. short of provisions, and with twelve of the crew laid up with scurvy, supplied her with what she could spare.
Jan. 29. p.7
London: Custom House: Jan. 28: Vessels Entered Inward: Hebe from Guayaquil.
[Survey: London in February]

1867 The Dundee Courier and Argus Sat. 20 Apr. p.2
London: Left: Apr. 17: Hebe, Wilkinson for Launceston.

1867 Launceston Examiner (Tasmania) Thurs. 22 Aug p.4
Launceston: Arrivals: August 20: Brig Hebe, 273 (sic) tons, J. Wilkinson from London.
Captain J. Wilkinson, of the brig Hebe, reports-- Left London on the 21st April, and the Downs on the 25th. On 6th June crossed the Equator, having experienced tolerably fair weather; winds from the SW generally prevailing. When in the latitude of the Cape the weather was stormy, with tremendous sea, gales blowing from various quarters. It lasted about a week, when moderate winds blew from the NE. On the 19th July, when in latitude

46* 7' S and long. 55* E, saw a very large iceberg about four miles distant. It appeared to be fully one mile in length. In all directions within a radius of 10 miles there were large pieces afloat that appeared to have originally formed part of the great mass. From the above mentioned latitude experienced strong NE winds, by which the vessel was driven to the southward past Desolation Island. When off this island lost a man overboard named Andrea Neilson (a Norwegian.) He was engaged in loosening the foresail, and by some means lost his hold, and fell from the foreyard. In consequence of the strong gale blowing at the time and the darkness of the night it was impossible to save him. Were driven to latitude 50* 12' and long. 95* E, when the wind changed to NW on the 25th July, and continued to the 29th, at which date the vessel stood in latitude 47* S. and long. 91* 37' E. From thence experienced variable winds and calms until arriving at 42* 48' S and long. 121* 57' E. When in lat. 35* 45' S, long. 26* 35' W (sic), spoke a Schleswig Holstein vessel from Hamburg, 81 days out. She was bound for the Sandwich Islands. Could not make out her name. During the latter part of the passage had favorable winds and weather. Entered Tamar Heads at half-past eight a.m. on Tuesday, and brought up in the Tea Tree at about half-past six p.m. Came alongside the wharf yesterday.

Captain Smart, of the tug Tamar, informs us he took the Southern Cross, bound for Mauritius with breadstuffs, out to sea about three miles on Tuesday morning. Light west winds were blowing at the time. On returning he spoke the Hebe, but as there was a favorable wind blowing at the time she would not tow.
Sept. 28 p.4
The brig Hebe is fast filling up, already having on board over 100 bales wool, 5000 bushels wheat, and 50 tons bark. She will be getting away in a few days.
Oct. 10 p.4
Launceston: Departures: Oct. 8: Brig Hebe, 213 tons, Wilkinson for London.
Hebe left the wharf about half-past 7 a.m. yesterday in tow of the Tamar tug. When the Hebe was passing the bark Westbury the latter vessel hoisted her ensign, while the crews of both vessels gave several hearty cheers by way of "good bye." The Hebe was anchored in Lagoon Bay at 9 p.m. yesterday.
Oct. 12 p.4
The brig Hebe and the tug Tamar were both anchored in Bryant's last night, which is waiting to tow the Hebe to sea when the weather moderates.
1868 Apr. 18 p.4
The brig Hebe, Captain Wilkinson, from Launceston, arrived at Gravesend on February 19.

[LR 1868-69: Hebe, Bg, Wilkinson, P.E. Isl. McFagn: 1862 8 mo: Wlknson &, Liverp'l, A1]

Liverpool Register: Master, London 16.4.68, John Smith 13.207.

1868 The Dundee Courier and Argus Mon. 27 Apr. p.2
London: Left: Apr. 24: Hebe, Smith, for Lancaster (sic).
May 5 p.2
Dungeness: In the Roads: May 1: Hebe, Smith, from London for Launceston.

1868 Launceston Examiner (Tasmania) Tues. 18 Aug. p.2
Tamar Heads: Arrivals: Aug. 17—1 p.m. brig Hebe. Left London on 24th April.
Aug. 20 p.2
Launceston: Arrivals: August 19: Brig Hebe, Wilkinson (sic), from London. The Brig Hebe had not arrived at the wharf up to last night, so that we cannot yet give her manifest.
Aug. 22 p.4

The Brig Hebe, from London, arrived at the bar on Thursday afternoon, and at the wharf yesterday. Captain Smith reports leaving London Docks on the 27th (sic) April last. During heavy weather anchored off Dungeness on 29th of same month, and rode out a severe gale. Sailed again on 2nd May, and sighted Land's End on the 5th. From this to the line, which was crossed on the 3rd of June, experienced moderate weather, tolerably favorable winds, and strong NE trades. On the 19th of May, spoke the ship True Briton, 15 days out from Cardiff, bound to Callao. She sent a boat alongside, and got some nitre from the Hebe. On the 30th of the same month, the bark Colombo, 18 days from St. Helena, bound for London, was spoken, and asked to report the Hebe all well. Three or four days of baffling winds were experienced before falling in with the SE trades, which latter were strong. On the 27th June spoke the ship Corsica, of Thomastown, from Leith bound to Bombay. Sighted Gough Island in latitude 40* S, and longitude 10* W--the only land seen from leaving Land's End until sighting King's Island on the 18th instant. Had for the most part heavy weather from Gough's Island to Tamar Heads. Strong winds after leaving the Cape, veering from NW to SW, until within the influence of the Australian coast, when heavy northerly weather was experienced.
Sept. 17 p.2
Launceston: Departures: Sept. 16: Brig, Hebe, 214 tons, John Smith, for Sydney. In Ballast.
Sept. 19 p.4
The Brig, Hebe was to go over the bar with this morning's tide, and will sail to-day for Sydney, weather permitting.

{from the Internet: Source Authority of New South Wales Shipping Master's Office}
Sydney: Inward: Hebe of Liverpool, 213 tons, Launceston to Sydney, 3 Oct. 1868: John Smith, Master, 28, Gt. British; John Johns, Mate, 33, do; David Bailey, Carpt & Bsun, 27, do; Thomas Speed, Cook & Steward, 29. do; Jak Jak Sandiline, A.B., 30 Finland; Joseph Lidstone, A.B, 41 Gt. British; Val (?) H. Haile, apprentice, 18, Gt. British; Joseph Fletcher, apprentice, 14, do; Charles Hudson, apprentice 16 do.}

1868 The Sydney Morning Herald Fri. 2 Oct. p.4
Sydney: Arrivals: Hebe, brig, 216 tons, Captain Smith, from Launceston 16th ultimo, in ballast. Captain, agent.
Oct. 12 p.4
Sydney: Departures: Oct. 10: Hebe, for Newcastle.
Oct. 15 p.4
Newcastle: Arrivals: Oct. 13: Hebe, brig from Sydney.
Nov. 6 p.8
Newcastle: Departures: October 24: Hebe, Smith, for Manila, with 312 tons coal.

{from the Internet: Source Authority of New South Wales Shipping Master's Office}
Sydney: Inward: Hebe of Liverpool, 213 tons, Manila to Sydney, 15 Apr. 1869: John Smith, Master; John Johns, Mate, 33, Devon; David Bailey, Carpt & Boatswain, 27, Fritham; Thomas Speed, Cook & Steward, 29, London; Jak Jak Sundring, A.B., 30, Finland; Joseph Lidstone, A.B, 41 Dartmouth; Val (?) H. Halle, apprentice, 18; Joseph Fletcher, apprentice, 14; Charles Hudson, 16.

1869 The Sydney Morning Herald Fri. 16 Apr. p.4
Sydney: Arrivals: Hebe, Brig. 228 tons, Captain Smith from Manila 3rd February. She came through the straits of Gaspar and Sunda, and had favourable weather throughout. Hebe, brig, 214, Smith, in the Stream.
Imports: 61 cases cigars, 1000 packages hemp, 798 bags rice, 516 bags coffee.
May 1 p.1

Brig Hebe, from Manila. This vessel will be on Cuthbert's Patent Slip, Sussex-street, on Monday, the third of May, when intending purchasers are invited to inspect her. Joseph Ward and Co., Agents.
May 5 p.4

The brig Hebe; she has been stripped, caulked, and re-coppered, and is ready for launching again.
May 18 p.1

[Advert] *Brig Hebe, Captain J. Smith. All Accounts against this vessel must be rendered before noon, This Day, to the undersigned, otherwise they will not be recognised.*
May 19 p.10

*Vessels **Sold**: Hebe, brig. 214, to Captain Campbell for £2150.*

++++++++++

Liverpool Register: Cancelled 16th July 1869. Sold under Certificate of sale at Sydney and registered anew there No. 26/69 per Certificate of Registry received 19th July 1869.

[**RA&NZS** 1876-77] 42393: Hebe, Brig 214, Sydney, Date of Registry 1869. Master F. Fisher 104: Owner A. Campbell]

1893 The Sydney Morning Herald Fri. 10 Mar. p.5
The Weather. Sensational Reports from the Flooded Districts. The Southerly Gale on the Coast.
A Sydney-Owned Vessel Lost.
About 1 o'clock news came of the wreck of the brig Hebe on the north beach, about four miles from Stockton. Captain Thomas Wilson reports leaving Sydney for the port on Saturday in ballast, but was compelled to put back into Broken Bay owing to heavy seas and general bad weather. The Hebe took shelter there till Tuesday, when she put out to sea again. The brig was off Newcastle yesterday morning and hoisted signals for a tug boat. The Awhina put out, but was unable to reach the brig on account of the terrific squalls of driving rain almost blinding the crew. The captain of the brig appears not to have noticed the tug, and put out to sea again. After some time tacking about he made up his mind to get into Port Stephens, but could not make headway enough, and stood away to the south. A tremendous sea was running, and Captain Wilson was afraid the brig would never be able to stand against it. It was resolved to beach the brig in order to save the crew. He therefore called the crew aft and told them his intention, telling them that each would have to look out for himself when he beached her. Accordingly, at about 7 o'clock last night, he ran the brig on to the beach in 3ft. of water. All hands got ashore safely, but were compelled to remain on the beach all night, and at daylight started to walk to Stockton, about six miles away. All hands lost all they possessed, except what they stood upright in, and reached Stockton exhausted and wet through. As soon as possible they crossed from Stockton to Newcastle, where the captain reported himself and crew to the shipping-master, Mr. C. H. Hannell, who immediately saw to their comfort, and gave orders for clothing and admission to the Sailors' Home.
When the crew left the scene of the wreck the Hebe appeared to be fast breaking up. She was well known as running for years between Newcastle and Sydney. Captain Angus Campbell, of Sydney, is owner.
The Hebe came to Sydney many years ago from London, with a cargo, and was purchased by Captain Campbell for £2400 (sic). She has since been steadily employed in the Sydney-Newcastle trade, and during the quarter of a century she has run backwards and forwards has only once been in trouble. On that occasion she collided with a foreign vessel near Newcastle. She was in splendid order, only lately out of dock, at the time she went ashore on Wednesday night, and was in ballast.

HUMBERSTONE

Official No.	**46202**	**Code letters VHMC**	
Built	1863 June	In Quebec, Canada (Charles Jobin)	
Deck	One	Build	Carvel
Masts	Three	Gallery	None
Rigging	**Barque**	Head	Scroll
Stern	Round	Framework	Wood.
Tonnage	**322**	Length 120 feet; Breadth 26.5 feet; Depth 15.1 feet.	

[**LR** 1863 supplement: Humberstone, Bk, T Gibant/ Cook, 322, Quebec (Jobin) 1863, Berry & C, Quebec A1].
[**LR** 1864-67: Humberstone, Bk, Cook/ S. Johnst'ne, 322, Quebec, Berry & Co, Quebec A1].

1863 Liverpool Mercury Fri. 7 Aug. p.3
Queenstown: Arrived: Aug. 6: Humberstone, from New York.
Aug. 18 p.3
Queenstown: Sailed: Aug. 17: Humberston (sic), Liverpool.
Aug. 19 p.3
Liverpool: Arrived: Aug. 18: Humberstone, Quebec.
Nov. 25 p.3
At Holyhead: Humberstone, from Quebec for Dublin.

1863 The Glasgow Daily Herald Sat. 28 Nov. p.5
Dublin: Arrived: Nov. 27: Humberston (sic), Quebec.

1864 [Survey: Cardiff in January]

1864 The Liverpool Mercury Wed. 6 Apr. p.3
At Nassau: Humberstone, from Cardiff.

1864 The Cork Examiner Thurs. 11 June
Cork Harbour: Arrived: June 10: Humberstone, Cook, Cuba, sugar.

1864 The Liverpool Mercury Mon. 13 June p.3
Queenstown: Arrived: June 11: Humberston (sic), from Cuba.
June 16 p.3
Queenstown: Sailed: June 15: Humberstone, for Stockholm.

1864 Newcastle Courant Fri. 2 Sept. 2 p.6
Sundswald: Sailed: Aug. 21: Humberstone, Cook, for Sunderland.

1864 Hampshire Telegraph and Sussex Chronicle 22 Oct. p.5
Mercantile Shipping (From Mr. James Garrat, Lloyd's Agent): Tuesday, 18th October.—
Arrived—Humberstone, Johnston, Sunderland for Venice. [Survey: Sunderland in October]

1865 The Cork Examiner Mon. 1 May
Cork Harbour: Arrived: Apr. 29: Humberstone, Chittenden, Trieste, wheat.

1865 The Freeman's Journal Mon. 1 May
Queenstown: Arrived: Apr. 28: Humberstone, Enos [Knos?].
May 9
Queenstown: Sailed: May 8: Humberston (sic), Dublin.
May 15

Kingston: Foreign Arrival: May 14: Humberstone, Trieste, wheat, (one hundred and twenty days passage (sic ?)).

1865 The Liverpool Mercury Thurs. 13 July p.3
Liverpool: Arrived: July 12: Humberstone.

++++++++++ **Wilfrid Hine**
Liverpool Register: Registered in Liverpool 204/1865: Registry: formerly at Dublin. Wilfred Hine of Liverpool. Shipowner 64/64. signed 4th July 1865

Master: Liverpool 8.7.65: Wedgewood Robinson C. 16748

[**LR** 1868-69: Humberstone, Bk, S. Johnst'ne/ W. Robinson, 322, Berry & C/ W. Hine, Quebec/ Liverpool A1].
[**LR** 1870: Humberstone, Bk, W. Robinson, 322, W. Hine, Liverpool A1 *expired*].
[**LR** 1871-73: Humberstone, Bk, W. Robinson, 322, W. Hine, Liverpool ----------].

1865 The Liverpool Mercury Wed, 23 Aug. p.4
[Advert]: *Australia: Passengers for Adelaide, the A1 Clippers Barque: Humberstone: Has excellent Accommodation for a few Cabin Passengers,-- For terms of passage apply to Capt. Robinson, barque Humberstone.   Prince's Dock, Liverpool.   No Steerage Passengers taken by this vessel.*
Sept. 6 p.3
Liverpool: Sailed: Humberstone, Robinson, Adelaide.

1865 The South Australian Advertiser (Adelaide) Tues. 26 Dec. p.2
Arrived: Saturday, December 23: Humberstone, barque, 321 tons, Wedgwood Robinson, master, from Liverpool September 6. Acraman, Main, Lindsay, and Co., Town; R. and R. Main, Port, agents.   The Humberstone arrived from Liverpool on Saturday, and at tide time was towed to the North Arm, where she will discharge her powder. Vessels Spoken.—By the Humberstone, on October 23, in lat. 12* 49' S., long. 31* 5' W., the ship George Rayner, from Callao to Hamburg, 56 days out; on November 10, in 37* 43' S. 00* 25' E., the barque Restless, of Guernsey, from Liverpool bound to the Cape, 57 days out.
Dec. 29 p.3
Police Courts. Port Adelaide: Tuesday. December 26. [Before Mr. G. W. Hawkes, S.M.] Thomas Parks and Henry Lynch, seamen, were charged by Capt. Robinson, of the Humberstone, with disobedience of orders on the voyage from London. Mr. Dempster appeared for the informant.   The informant deposed to the facts of the case, but expressed a wish not to press for a heavy punishment in the case of Parks. His Worship committed Parks for 14 days, and Lynch for eight weeks with hard labour.
1866 Jan. 27 p.3
II: Anniversaries and Festivities. The Foundation of the Colony. Thursday, December 28. Thursday was observed with general rejoicing, as the 29th anniversary of the foundation of the colony. This year it was kept as a more general holiday, in consequence of the various trades in Adelaide having exchanged December 28 for another general holiday, which was previously on the calendar. Instead, therefore, of the shops opening during a part, if not for the whole of the day, they were closed altogether, and the opportunity was very generally embraced for pleasure-seeking and merry-making. Of course, the great attraction of the day were the sports at Glenelg, the first landing-place of the early immigrants. In addition to these, however, there were sports at the Semaphore, boating excursions at the Port, picnics in the hills and other such like holiday pastimes. These, however, are more particularly described below. We had forgotten to say that the

weather was enjoyable -- very much more so than the excessive heat of the previous day could have led to be anticipated.

Port Regatta. This entertainment was largely patronized. Great numbers of people from the town, suburbs, and country going by train in the hope of viewing the aquatic sports. Any one visiting the Adelaide Railway Station at 10 a.m. and 11 a.m. and seeing the crowds pushing and hurrying for tickets might have thought the Port was the only scene of interest on that day. More that 2,600 tickets were issued during Monday, and if we take into account those who joined at the various stations on the line, and others who gave cash instead of tickets at the terminus, we may calculate that more than 3,000 visitors to the regatta went by the train. Across the street at the station was a line suspended covered with flags, and the shipping appeared to be flying all the bunting they could muster. Many of the ships, all the balconies commanding a view, and the wharfs were crowded with spectators; even the railway vans were fully occupied. The boatmen plied a lively trade, and the stream was covered with boats of every size and description. At the commencement and finish of every race a gun was fired from the steamer, on board which were the Judges and Committee.

Fourth Race. Starting at 11 a.m.—Ships' Gigs, to be pulled by their own crews. Four-oar boats. From Buoy off Princes Wharf, round 2 boys off Red Buoy Spit, back to Government Steps. First prize, £10; Second prize, £2 10s. Entrance, 10s. Royal Shepherd, Samuel, Humberstone, Verulam. There was a severe contest between Royal Shepherd and Verulam, but one of the crew of the former broke an oar, and Verulam won easily.

1866 The Australian Register (Adelaide) Thurs. 1 Feb. p.2
Cleared Out: Wednesday, January 31: Humberstone, barque, 321 tons, Wedgewood, master, for Akyab [Burma]*: No Passenger. In ballast.*
Feb. 7 p.2
Sailed: Tuesday 6: Humberstone, barque, for Guam.

1866 The Glasgow Herald Sat. 6 Oct. p.7
Falmouth: Arrived: Oct. 4: Humberstone, Robinson, from Akyab .
Oct. 22 p.5
Gravesend: Arrived: Oct. 21: Hamberstone (sic), Akyab.

[**MNL** 1867: 46202 Humberstone of Liverpool, 322: Wilfred Hine, Liverpool.]
[**MNL** 1868: 46202 Humberstone of Liverpool, 322: Richard Nicholson, Liverpool.]
[**MNL** 1870: 46202 Humberstone of Liverpool, 322: W.H. Nicholson, 14, South Castle, Street, Liverpool.]

1867 The Mercury (Hobart) Thurs. 25 Apr. p.2
There have been no English arrivals at this port during the month, but the Humberstone is now expected, and will bring full stocks of winter goods, which, as the cold weather approaches, will doubtless meet with ready sale. Apropos of the weather, we are now enjoying a most glorious autumn, and the Easter holidays, just over, have been marked by a succession of fine days, which have contributed largely to the pleasure of the season.
May 1 p.2
The Humberstone, barque, Capt. Wedgewood Robinson, from London, with a very large general cargo, dropped anchor in the Cove at 6 o'clock on the morning of 29th ult. Capt. Robinson reports that he left London Docks on 10th January, and the Downs on 13th and had moderate northerly and easterly winds, with snow until 18th of that month, and had then until 25th a succession of S.W. and N.W. gales with a high cross sea. Sighted the Island of Madeira on 31st January, and got fresh N.E. trades. Crossed the Equator

on 18th February in 27.30 W. and had then light S.E. trades which carried the barque to 25.30, S, lat. and 25.20, W, long. Sighted the island of Tristan D'Acunha on the 12th March and had fresh winds from N.E. to N.W up to 17th of that month. On 21st March, the barque being then abreast of the Cape of Good Hope, experienced a strong N.W. gale accompanied with violent squalls which lasted for 48 hours. The gale was followed by a succession of strong winds from N.W. to S.W. which continued to 16th inst., when in lat. 45.10. S. and from 118 to 128 E. long, a violent gale from N.W., sprang up commencing shortly before midnight, with heavy rain. On the morning of the 17th the barometer fell to 29.50., the gale increasing in violence, the barque losing jib and foresail. At 4 a.m. on that day the barometer had fallen to 29.20. At 8 a.m. the gale blew with terrific violence and was still increasing, accompanied with heavy squalls, the barometer falling to 29.00. At noon the barometer had fallen to 28.70, the gale still blowing with great violence, with a terrific sea, the ship running under close-reefed topsails. At 4 p.m. the barometer had gone down to 28.50, steady, but at 6 p.m. the wind had shifted to W.S.W, blowing heavily, the barometer now commencing to rise. The ship, Captain Robinson reports, behaved admirably during the gales, but had her port bulwarks stove in during the last gale. At 2 a.m. on 18th the barometer was still rising the gale continuing with great fury, moderating only at 5 a.m. on 19th. The barque then made all sail and made the South West Cape at 3 p.m. on 25th ult. with northerly and N.N.E. winds and clear weather. Had then calms and light airs with dense fogs until 29th ult. when the weather cleared up with a light breeze from S.S.W. Got abreast of Adventure Bay at 8.30 p.m. on Monday, the night being very dark and cloudy and commenced sending up blue lights, with flare torches as a signal for a pilot and continued to show these lights at intervals until half an hour after midnight, but Captain Robinson was not successful in these attempts to obtain the assistance of a pilot. The Humberstone, which now makes her first trip to this port, is a Quebec built vessel, launched in 1864 (sic), and now owned by Mr. Wilfred (sic) Hine, Liverpool, and up to her present engagement from London to Hobart Town was in the Australian and Indian trade. She brought a very large cargo, and had also on board two heavy Armstrong guns for the Tasmanian Government, and was consigned to Messrs, McPherson and Co.
Passenger: Cabin: Mrs. Robinson.

1867 The Mercury (Hobart) Fri. 3 May p.2
Police Court. Thursday, May 2nd, 1867.
Before A.B. Jones Esq., Stipendiary Magistrate.
Insubordination on Board Ship.--Three seamen belonging to the Humberstone, British merchant ship, were charged by Captain Robinson with wilfully disobeying the lawful command of the chief mate that morning. Plea not guilty.
The captain deposed that the Humberstone arrived on Tuesday; this morning the defendants were told to work on board, which they refused to do. They asked for their discharge at first, but afterwards went. Complainant said he could not do it as their agreement was not fulfilled. Afterwards they again refused duty, and tried to create a disturbance in the ship. Witness then gave them in charge to the police.
By Sloane: It was a fit morning to go to sea.
Sloane: I can only say I have been ten years at sea, and have never been treated in the unmannly (sic) way as I have been with you. We scoured the ship all day yesterday.
By the Stipendiary Magistrate: The work was to wash the decks.
Edward Ward, the mate, gave corroborative testimony.
By Kellard: You have been laid up for three days.
Kellard complained of bad feed, and of having been worked like horses all the way.

By the Stipendiary Magistrate: There has been no ill treatment on board. Kellard has been under medical treatment.

The men wanted to make a statement of the treatment they had received on the voyage, but

The Stipendiary Magistrate said he could not let them say anything about any treatment on board. They must confine themselves to the charge that morning.

Kellard said a poor man went to the hospital yesterday with the same complaint as he had.

The Stipendiary Magistrate sentenced, the defendants to four weeks' hard labor, and to forfeit not exceeding two days' pay.

In consequence of the inclemency of the weather yesterday there is no shipping business done on the wharves. Owing to the rain.....could not open her hatches but is ready to commence discharging on the weather clearing up.

1867 The Mercury (Hobart) Fri. 10 May p.2
The Guns ex Humberstone.-- The chairman of the Board of Tenders calls for tenders for the immediate removal of two eight ton cases containing rifled guns which have arrived per barque Humberstone. We suggested the other day that the removal of the guns would have been appropriate exercise for our volunteer artillery, but this seems to be disapproved of. Tenders are therefore called for, and the person whose tender may be accepted will be required to enter into a bond to meet any claim made against the colonial Government for damage done in landing the guns. He will have no claim to the assistance of the crew of the vessel, nor to make use of her masts or rigging. The guns are to be deposited in the Ordnance Stores.

May 13 p.2.
Trinity Church Bells.-- The members of the Trinity Amateur Ringing Association on Saturday afternoon last rang a peal of one hundred and twenty changes, during their maiden practice with a set of new bell ropes received last week per Humberstone. The ropes, eight in number, arrived to the order of Mr. W. H. Gill. They are supplied with ornamental tufts of a description prevalent throughout Great Britain, and have been fixed by the sexton of Trinity Church, Mr. T. Swinnerton. The ropes were furnished by the eminent firm of Messrs. Mears and Stainbank, of Whitechapel, the successors of Mears and Co., by whom the Trinity bells were cast. With reference, to the durability of the former ropes it may be stated that previous to being replaced by the present ones, they were alone in use since the bells were hung in 1847. All that time, through the energy of a respected colonist and experienced ringer, still residing in Hobart Town, Mr. William Champion, not only was the public induced to contribute towards the expense of hanging the bells, but the first troupe of ringers was organized. During the past three years the ringing has been performed by gentlemen amateurs, who received tuition on what is termed the half-pull or grandsire system of change ringing, from the Lancashire Bell Ringers, when visiting Hobart Town some two years since. For those who do not indulge any prejudice against change ringing, it may be remarked that our amateur ringers have so far been successful in executing peals of one hundred and twenty changes on the grandsire method, a feat not yet accomplished by either the amateur or professional ringers in the adjoining colonies. It may further be mentioned that, in consequence of a very general desire, tune ringing on the Trinity Church bells will be recommenced in the course of a few weeks, by the amateurs who purpose, as in previous winter months, continuing the recreation on each Saturday afternoon.

May 17 p.2.
Police Court. Thursday May 16th 1867.

An Acting Mate Sent to Gaol.-- Thos. Wilson, of the Humberstone, was charged by Capt. Robinson with refusing to work.

Mr. Allport attended for the prosecution.

The Shipping Master was not present.

Defendant said he did refuse to work, he asked for his dinner, not having had any meals for 24 hours, when the captain said his dinner was in the pantry; and he told him the pantry was not the place for him take his dinner.

The captain said defendant had been with his wife all day, and he came to him and told him he had knocked off duty. He (the captain) had done nothing to provoke him. He had annoyed him two or three times on the wharf, requiring him to give him in charge, the captain said he should not do so until he attempted to leave the ship.

Defendant: I did not ask you to give me in charge. I asked you for my discharge.

The Stipendiary Magistrate: It's necessary that discipline should be kept up on board ship.

Defendant: It's not right to send me to the pantry to have my dinner.

The Stipendiary Magistrate (Mr. Jones) had often had his dinner in the pantry.

The captain expressed his regret at being obliged to bring him there on account of his friends at home; he had treated him like a brother, but his conduct towards him for the last twenty-four hours was scandalous.

Mr. Allport stated to his Worship that defendant was entered in the articles as boatswain, but he had been allowed to discharge the duties of second mate for the purpose of instruction, that was the reason he claimed to take his meals in the cabin, to which he was not entitled.

The Stipendiary Magistrate was afraid defendant had been taking bad advice, for unfortunately there were people here too ready to give it.

Defendant said he had not taken any advice.

The Stipendiary Magistrate said he was obliged to sentence him to be imprisoned and kept to hard labor for four weeks, unless the captain wished to take him on board.

Mr. Allport : Is it your wish to take him on board?

The Captain : No, sir.

The defendant was then committed.

May 21 p.3.

The London barque, Humberstone after sighting and having a few sheets of copper replaced was brought round to Ross's yard this morning to her former berth along the New wharf.

May 22 p.2

The rifled guns brought by the London barque Humberstone for the colonial Government will be landed this morning by the crew of the barque.

May 23 p.2

One of the guns brought by the Humberstone was landed from the vessel yesterday in the presence of a number of persons anxious to see the case containing this ponderous instrument upon the wharf. The other will be landed to-morrow.

May 24 p.2

The second of the rifled guns brought by the Humberstone was landed on the wharf yesterday morning.

May 25 p.3

The colonial Government have received two pieces of rifled cannon, a portion of the order forwarded to the ordnance department some time ago. These are rifled shunt guns, muzzle loaders, of the pattern approved by the ordnance select committee, and capable of throwing a projectile of l00 lbs. weight. The guns are complete with, sights, tompions, &c. Their calibre is 7 inches, and weight 7 tons each, while the charge necessary for the projectile is 12 lbs.

May 31 p.2

Police Court. Thursday May 30th 1867.

Insubordination. --James Sloane, a seaman belonging to the British merchant ship Humberstone was charged by Captain Robinson with having on the 29th refused to proceed to sea in the vessel without sufficient reason.

Defendant said he would go on board, and the captain agreeing after some discussion, the defendant was sent on board.

June 1 p.2

Cleared out: May 31: Humberstone, London barque, 322 tons, Wedgewood Robinson, for Guam. Passenger: Cabin: Mrs. Robinson.

June 4 p.2

Sailed: June 3: Humberstone, London barque, for Newcastle, New South Wales.

June 8 p.2

The New Guns and the Russian Trophy: The new rifled guns which arrived from England per Humberstone, were yesterday safely lodged in the Ordnance Stores by a fatigue party of the 14th Regt., detailed by Lieut.-Col. Dwyer, at the request of His Excellency the Governor. The Russian trophy gun was also removed by the same party and placed in Franklin Square. The gun has been placed in front of the statue of Sir John Franklin, and points towards the Commercial Bank. The party was in charge of Sergeant-Major Eccleston, R. A., and the work of fixing the gun was performed by the aid of the movable gyn [gin: a crane or windlass] *from the Queen's battery.*

1867 The Maitland Mercury & Hunter River General Advertiser Thurs. 13 June p.3.

Newcastle Shipping: Arrivals: June 11: Humberstone, barque, 322, Robinson, from Hobart Town.

1867 The Sydney Morning Herald Sat. 29 June p.4

Newcastle: Departures: June 27: Humberstone, barque, Robinson, for San Francisco with 403 tons coal.

1867 Daily Alta California Mon. 23 Sept. p.4

San Francisco: Arrived: Sept. 22: Per barque Humberstone, Robinson, 88 ds fm Newcastle N S W; coal, to Falkner, Bell & Co: First part of the passage had fine beezes from the W; crossed the equator Aug 16th, lon 121 W, since which have had moderate winds from NNE; Sept 21st, lat 34 50 N lon 125 W, spoke ship Enoch Train, hence Sept 18th for Liverpool.

Importations: 404 tons, coal.

Sept. 28 p.4

Vessel: Humberston (sic) Newcastle: tons 321: Amount Freight, $2,418. 00.

4 Oct. p.4

From San Francisco: To Liverpool: Per Br. Barque Humberstone Oct. 3. Wheat, 100lb. sks 9,339. Value $19,191. 25.

6 Oct. p.6

San Francisco: Sailed: Oct 5: barque, Humberstone, Robinson, Liverpool.

1868 The Brisbane Courier Wed. 29 Apr. p.2

The Bayswater spoken [to]: January 26: at lat. 5.30 N., and long. 25.17 W., the British, barque, Humberstone from San Francisco to Liverpool, 112 days out: sent a mail home by her.

1868 The Liverpool Mercury Thurs. 5 Mar. p.3

Liverpool: Arrived: Mar. 4: Humberstone, San Francisco.

Wed. 15 July p.3

Liverpool: Sailed: July 14: Humberstone, Robinson, Brisbane. [Survey: Liverpool in June]

1868 The Brisbane Courier Tues. 23 Nov. p.2

A vessel from Liverpool was signalled yesterday afternoon which turned out to be the Humberstone. This vessel was considerably overdue, having sailed, according to our advice, on July 24, and thus is 122 days out.

Nov. 25 p.2

Cape Moreton: November 24: The Humberstone, barque, got underweigh at 8 a.m. and went into the bay......at the anchorage afternoon....but [today] *up to the closing of the Telegraph-office we received no intelligence of her being admitted to pratique.*

Nov. 26 p.2

The Mary, s., has been engaged to tow the barque Humberstone from Brisbane Roads to the anchorage below Pinkenbar Flats. She will report at the Customs to-morrow.

Dec. 1 p.4

The Humberstone - This vessel sailed from Liverpool on July 14, and proceeded down St George's Channel with light weather, which lasted until she was off the Madeiras. These she passed on July 30, and then fell in with the north-east trades, which carried her as far as the 15th parallel of north latitude. After that she had strong southerly and south-westerly winds to the Equator, which she crossed on August 23, 47 days out. She crossed the meridian of the Cape of Good Hope, on the 81st day, having experienced moderate and variable winds from the Line. The easting was run down about the 45th parallel, and in the Southern Ocean had very rough weather, chiefly heavy gales from the westward ranging between north-west and south-west. The worst weather of the passage was experienced off the Leeuwin, between 116.0 and 128.0 east longitude, where she had gales of terrific violence from south-west to north-west. The south end of Tasmania was sighted on November 10, and thence she had strong southerly gales which continued to the 16th November, when she was off Smoky Cape. There she got northerly winds which afterwards shifted to the south-east and carried her into port. The barque rounded Cape Moreton on November 23, and the next day she anchored in Brisbane Roads. On the 26th she was towed up to the Flats by the "Mary", where she is now discharging cargo. On the passage the Humberstone spoke the following vessels -- On August 10, in lat. 15.10 N., long. 25.4 W., spoke the British ship Zephyr, from London to Swan River, 16 days from the Lizard. On August 19 exchanged signals with the ship Andromeda, of Liverpool, bound South.

Dec. 25 p.2

Clearances: Dec. 24: Humberstone, barque, 322 tons, Captain W. Robinson, for Guam, 42 casks, 9 casks earthenware – part of original cargo.

Passenger: Mrs. Robinson.

1869 Jan. 1 p.4

The Humberstone, barque, outward bound, was towed out of the river yesterday by the Francis Cadell, s [steamer]. *She was towed about three miles outside the shipping, and when cast off got canvas on her to beat across the bay; the wind being about easterly and a pleasant breeze. The Cadell then returned to Brisbane, having effected the towage from Harris' wharf to where she cast off the barque in four hours.*

{http://mariners.recorder.nsw.gov.au/}   Mariners and ships in Australian Waters.
Sydney: Inward: Ship Hamberstone (sic) of Liverpool, Wedgwood Robinson, Master, Burthen 321 Tons, from the Port of Brisbane to Sydney New South Wales 5th Jany. 1868 (sic) [1869?].
William Parkes, mate, 28: Adam Holliday, Bsn, 26: John Davis (?), S&C, 20: Andrew Gracie (?), AB 25: William Briscolm (?), AB 20: Harry George Turner, AB 20: Francis Burton Smith, AB 17, Joseph Todd, Cook 28, John Lewis (?), AB 26. (all from Gt. Britain). [No passenger registered]
Signed Sydney 5th Jany. 18: Wedgwood Robinson: Master.}

1869 The Sydney Morning Herald Wed. 6 Jan. p.4

Arrivals: January 5: The Humberstone, from Brisbane, in ballast, Captain agent, has come to this port seeking (charter).
Jan. 25 p.4
Clearances: January 23: Humberstone, barque, 322 tons, Captain Robinson, for Adelaide: Exports: 79 bales bags.
Passenger: Mrs. Robinson.
Jan. 26 p.4
Departures: January 25: Humberstone for Adelaide.

1869 The South Australian Register (Adelaide) Tues. 9 Feb. p.2
Arrived: Monday, February. 8: Humberstone, barque, 322 tons, W. Robinson, master, from Sydney, January 25: Imports: 72 bales sacks. Order.
Passenger: Mrs. Robinson, in the cabin.
Feb. 27 p.2
For Liverpool: Humberstone, barque, 2,797 bags wheat.
Mar. 4 p.2
Cleared: Humberstone, barque, 322 tons, W. Robinson, master for Liverpool: Exports: 2008 qrs. wheat.
No Passenger.
Mar. 5 p.2
Sailed: Mar. 4: Humberstone, barque, for Liverpool.

1869 The Dundee Courier and Argus Sat. 10 July
Spoken: Humberston (sic), Adelaide for Liverpool, May 10, lat. 35* S., long. 19* E. [suggests the voyage via Cape of Good Hope]

1869 The South Australian Advertiser (Adelaide) Wed. 31 Mar. p.7
Humberstone, with 2,008 quarters of wheat.

1869 The Liverpool Mercury Mon. 28 June p.3
Spoken: Humberstone (barque) from Adelaide for London, 78 days out, May 21, 24 S. 4 E.
July 15 p.3
Liverpool: Arrived: July 14: Humberstone, Robinson, Adelaide.
Sept. 18 p.8
Liverpool: Sailed: Sept.17: Humberstone, Clark, Bord'aux.

[LR 1870: Humberstone, Bk, W Robinson, 322, W. Hine, Liverpool, A1]
Liverpool Register: Master: Liverpool 15.9.69: William Clark C. 30750

1869 The Sydney Morning Herald Tues. 28 Dec. p.4
From Liverpool: Humberstone, 369, Clark. September 17. Sailed, via Bordeaux.

1870 The Argus (Melbourne) Tues. 15 Jan. p.4
The Humberstone, at Rochefort, loaded 45 hhds, 1,293 quarter-casks, 2,783 cases brandy for Melbourne and 6 hogsheads, 330 quarters, 1025 cases brandy for Sydney.
Apr. 11 p.4
The barque Humberstone, from Bordeaux, bound to this port, was spoken on the 3rd inst., to the westward of Cape Otway, by the schooner Cleopatra. [The Humberstone was telegraphed yesterday as having arrived at Port Phillip Heads.]
Apr. 12 p.4
The barque Humberstone is from Bordeaux and Rochefort, with a cargo consisting chiefly of bulk and case brandy for Melbourne and Sydney. Captain Smith reports leaving Rochefort on December 23, and experiencing strong N.N.W. and N.N.E. winds for the next five days. Fine weather then prevailed to the equator, which was crossed on

January 22, in long. 24deg. 28min. W., the meridian of the Cape of Good Hope being passed on February 28 in lat. 42deg. 28min. S. Moderate favourable winds were carried through the S.E. trades. The easting was run down in lat. 45deg., the winds being mostly from the northward. On March 17, a very heavy gale from W.N.W to N.W., and lasting for 24 hours, was encountered. The barque is consigned to Messrs. Curcier and Adet.

No passengers.

Apr. 21 p.1

[Advert] *For Sale, or Charter (after delivering balance of cargo in Sydney), the barque Humberstone, 322 tons register, built in Quebec in 1863, classed A1 seven years, which expires December 31,1870. Passed half time survey in 1868, when she was opened under the Inspection of Lloyd's, and at a cost of £800 was caulked from keel to combings, and had new pitch pine foremast; this voyage had new pitch pine main mast, and is now in excellent order; has delivered 500 tons of coal; stands and shifts without ballast; sails well, and delivers her cargoes in good order; is fitted with double topsail yards. Now discharging a general cargo from Bordeaux and Rochefort, at the Victorian Railways Pier, Williamstown, where she can be inspected.*

For further particulars, and list of inventory apply to: Captain Smith, on board.

May 4 p.4

The barque of Humberstone, from Bordeaux after discharging the Melbourne portion of her cargo, sailing from the bay yesterday, for Sydney, the balance of her cargo being for that port.

May 5 p.4

Port Phillip Heads: Sailed: May 4: Humberstone, barque, for Sydney.

Even in the "Sydney Morning Herald" the Humberstone was up for sale.

{http://mariners.recorder.nsw.gov.au/   Mariners and ships in Australian Waters.}
Sydney: Inward: Barque Humberstone of Liverpool, John Smith, Master, Burthen 322 Tons, from the Port of Melbourne to Sydney N.S.W.   11 May 1870
John Smith, Captain: Adam Holliday, Mate, 29, Maryport: Edward Heselton, 2nd Mate, 23, Scarborough: William Warwick, Carpenter, 54, Workington: John Davis, Cook & Std, 42, Plymouth: Charles Johnson, A.B., 31 Norway: Thomas Burton, A.B., 54, Whitby: John Brown, A.B., 24, Sunderland: Joseph Fletcher, Boy, 15, London: Ole Johansen, A.B., 22, Norway. Passengers: nil.}

1870 The Sydney Morning Herald Tues. 12 May p.4
Arrivals: May 11: Humberstone, barque, 450 tons (sic), from Melbourne 2ⁿᵈ instant.

June 29 p.4

Mails will close at the General Post Office as follows:-- For Hongkong: Humberstone this day, at noon.

July 5 p.4

Departure July 4: Humberstone, for Hongkong.

Oct. 31 p.4

Hongkong: Arrivals: August 30: Humberstone, from Sydney.

1870 The South Australian Advertiser (Adelaide) Tues. 22 Nov. p.3
A typhoon, the worst that has been experienced for three years, has swept over the Chinese coast, considerable damage was sustained chiefly amongst the native craft at Hongkong, and many lives are stated to have been lost. China: departures: Humberstone.

1870 Adairs Maryport Advertiser Fri. 23 Dec. p.8

*The Umberstone (sic) Smith, from Shangai, to Foochoo a total wreck in the China sea –
crew supposed to be saved.*

1871 The Argus (Melbourne) Tues. 25 Jan. p.4
*Foo-chow Markets. Mr. W. B. Kinnear, secretary of the Foo-chow General Chamber of
Commerce, reports under date Foo-chow, 5th December, 1870:*
The Humberstone which was expected to load at Foo-Chow has been lost on the coast of
Formosa.

1871 The Sydney Morning Herald Thurs. 26 Jan. p.4
Wreck of the British Barque Humberstone.
*We regret to record the total loss of the above vessel on the 21st ultimo. The
circumstances as related by Mr. Heselton, the second officer, are as follows: -*
The Humberstone left Hongkong on the 7th October on a voyage to Foochow, in ballast, and
had favourable weather until the 10th, when they were about 150 miles North East of
Hongkong, and experienced a heavy gale of wind which continued till the evening of the 12th,
when it moderated, and all possible sail was made. From that time they had fine weather
until the night of the 21st, when it was very thick and hazy with heavy rain and strong wind.
On that day at noon the south-east point of Formosa bore NE. by N. about 20 to 22 miles
distant. From noon till 6 p.m. the ship continued on an ESE. course, making about 45 miles,
and she then tacked to the northward and stood on that tack till 10 p.m., the course being
NW. west, distance about 22 miles. The master had been on deck from 8 p.m. About 10 p.m.
the man on the look-out sang out "broken water ahead." The helm was put to starboard, and
all the after canvas taken off, but notwithstanding this, she struck immediately afterwards,
and backed out from the reef into the deep water. They therefore proceeded to get out the
boat, into which they put provisions and other necessaries. All hands stepped into it, and the
second mate went on board again and reported to the captain that the vessel was fast settling
down. The captain shortly after got into the boat, but while it was being shoved off, the
vessel heeled over on to it, and capsized it. The boat, however, floated, and the mate and four
of the crew got to it, and the first mate was also got into it by Mr. Heselton, in a half drowned
condition. Neither the master nor any of the crew were found afterwards. The boat turned
over five times during the night before they were able to bale it out; and the first mate, being
unable to help himself, was lost. At last the survivors managed to get her baled out, and with
one sound oar and one broken, which were picked up attempted to reach the coast of Formosa.
Finding, however, that the wind was too strong off shore, and the sea too heavy, about noon
of the 23rd they were obliged to give up the attempt to reach the shore and put her before the
wind. They kept on that course till about 3 a.m. of the 27th, when they reached the Prata
Shoals, and were picked up there by a fishing junk. Though in a very weak and exhausted
state, having been without food and water for six days, through the kind treatment they
received, they partially recover their strength, and, after a thirty-one days' voyage they
reached Macao on the 27th ultimo, and came to Hongkong on the 28th -- China Daily Press,
December 13.

1871 Maryport Advertiser and Weekly News Fri. 13 Jan. p.8
Loss of the Humberstone.
*We have been favoured with the following copy of a letter from A.G. Hogg, & Co.,
Hongkong, to Wilfrid Hine, Esq., Liverpool:--*
"Hongkong, 28 Nov., 1870. "Humberstone."
"Dear Sir—We regret to be the transmitters of sad tidings concerning this vessel. As we last
advised you, she left this port (7 Oct.) for Foochow, under charter, to proceed from thence to
Melbourne—but, up to this day's steamer from the coast ports, we had heard nothing more of

her, and were becoming apprehensive for he (sic) safety. Yesterday, it appears that a junk arrived at Macao, bringing E. Heselton, second mate, John Dame (sic), cook, Burton Johnson, and a man who shipped here as a seaman. They reported that, on the night of the 21st Oct., the ship struck on a sunken rock, about 20 miles S.W. of the south end of Formosa, and went down in ten minutes. They had barely time to get one boat ready before she sunk, and the boat was then capsized. The drowned are Capt. Smith, Adam Holliday, chief officer, Thomas Warwick, carpenter, John Brown and Charles Johnson, seamen, and Joseph Fletcher, apprentice. The survivors tried to make for Formosa, but, after pulling for a day and a night, they found they could make no way against the sea. Their boat was upset three times; and they had neither food nor water for 6 days. They drifted down S.W., and were then picked up by a junk, on which they stayed 30 days, and were then landed at Macao. They came over, by steamer, to-day, and alll (sic) immediate requisite help has been given them—the men, having been placed in boarding house, or in the hospital (3 of them suffering from scurvy.) Mr. Heselton is one of the latter."

[Three of the unfortunate sufferers were well known in Maryport. Capt. Smith was remarkable for his unassuming manner and steadiness, and had distinguished himself for his great ability as a master mariner. He was only 33 years of age. We regret to add that Capt. Smith leaves a widow and four young children to mourn his loss.—Adam Holliday, mate, was also a native of Maryport, and was also favorably known here, though lately residing in Liverpool.—Joseph Fletcher was the eldest son of Mr. Joseph Fletcher, Crosby-st., in his 18th year. He was of a frank and generous disposition, and, being a young man of some promise, his premature death is felt as a severe blow to his aged parent.]

1871 The Liverpool Mercury Sat. 14 Jan. p.5   [some extra particulars]
[She] *was owned by Mr. F. Walker and Mr. Williamson of Maryport, and other gentlemen; Mr. Wilfrid Hine, of Liverpool being the managing owner.............Captain Smith......has left a widow and four children, two of whom are twins, and the oldest of the children is only about six years of age........Adam Holliday......was unmarried. Thomas Warwick....belonged to Workington, and was a married man, but had no children.*

BYRON

Official No.	**4621**	**Code JDHB**	
Built	1851	Annan (Scotland)	
Deck	One	Build	Carvel
Masts	Two	Gallery	None
Rigging	**Brig**	Head	Man's Bust
Stern	Square	Framework	Wood.
Tonnage	**174**	Length 92.5 feet; Breadth 22.8 feet; Depth 14.1 feet.	

[**LR** 1852-57: Byron, Bg, J. Crocket (sic), 196/ 190, Annan 1851, Nicholson, Annan A1]

1851 The Liverpool Mercury Tues. 2 Sept. p.7
Liverpool: Loading: Byron, Crocke (sic)t, 199. Rio Janeiro.
Oct. 14 p.7
Liverpool: Sailed: Oct. 12: Byron, Crocket (sic), Rio Janeiro.
1852 Feb. 17 p.7
At Rio Janeiro: Byron, Crocket (sic), hence.
May 11 p.7
Liverpool: Arrived: May 8: Byron, Crockett, from Paraiba, at this port, sailed 29th March. Left the Mary and Seraphina loading for Liverpool. Fever was very bad at Paraiba. On the 24th ult., southward of the Western Islands, experienced a severe hurricane, which lasted twelve hours.
The Seraphina, Gething, which has arrived here from Paraibo, reports that the fever continued very bad amongst the shipping in the river of the latter port; she lost first and second mates, carpenter, and two seamen, by it.
June 15 p.7
Liverpool: Loading: Byron, Crockett, 190, Monte Video &c.
July 9 p.7
Liverpool: Sailed: July 8: Byron, Roderick, Monte Video.
July 30 p.7
Byron, hence to Monte Video, 18th July in lat. 48 N., lon. 10 W.
[Survey: Annan in October]
Nov. 19 p.3
At Monte Video: Byron, Roderick, hence [from Liverpool].

1853 The Morning Chronicle Second Edition (London) Fri. 18 Feb. p.6
Port of Buenos Ayres: Sailed: Dec. 30: Brig Byron, for England.

1853 The Liverpool Mercury Tues. 22 Mar. p.7
Liverpool: Arrived: Mar. 19: Byron, Roderick, Buenos Ayres.
Mar. 25 p.7
Liverpool: Entered for Loading: For South America: Byron, Roderick, 199, Bahia.
May 6 p.7
Liverpool: Sailed: May 4: Byron, Roderick, Bahia.
July 16 p.7
At Bahia: Byron, from Liverpool.

[**LR** 1858: Byron, Bg, Bartlett, 196/ 190, H. Harrison, Liverpool A1]
[**LR** 1859-62: Byron, Bg, H. Jewson, 196/ 190, H. Harrison, Liverpool A1]
[**LR** 1863: Byron, Bg, H. Jewson, 196/ 190, H. Harrison, Liverpool A1] (scored out)]

1855 The Liverpool Mercury Tues. 27 Mar. p.7
Liverpool: entered for loading: Byron, 191, Vera Cruz.

1857 The Liverpool Mercury Fri. 12 June p.11
At Queenstown: June 9: Byron from Monte Video.

1857 The Morning Chronicle (London) Tues. 23 June p.8
Gravesend: Arrived: June 22: Byron from Monte Video.
Mon. July 27 p.7
Custom House, Coasters: Cleared Outwards: July 25: Byron for Liverpool.

1857 The Morning Chronicle (London) Thurs. 3 Sept. p.8
Liverpool: Sailed: Sept. 2: Byron for Buenos Ayres.

1857 The Daily News (London) Tues. 17 Nov. p.7
Spoken: Byron, Bartlett, from Liverpool for Buenos Ayres and Rosario 30 days, Oct. 3.

1858 The Liverpool Mercury Tues. 29 June
Liverpool: Arrived: June 26: Byron, Bartlett, Buenos Ayres.
Spoken: Byron, from Buenos Ayres for this port 20th May 18 N 38 W.
Sept. 29
Liverpool: Sailed: Sept. 27: Byron, Bartlett, Bahia.

1858 The Morning Post (London) Sat. 18 Dec. p.8
Spoken: Byron of and from Liverpool, for Bahia Nov. 5: 6N 24W.

1859 The Liverpool Mercury Mon. 4 Jan.
At Bahia: Byron, Bartlett, hence.

1859 The Glasgow Daily Herald 3 Mar. p.4
Falmouth: Arrived: Feb. 28: Byron, Bahia.
Mar. 12 p.4
Greenock: Arrived: Mar. 10: Byron. Bartlett, from Bahia, with sugar.

1859 The Morning Chronicle (London) Tues. 29 Mar. p.8
Greenock: Sailed: Mon. 26: Byron for Liverpool.

1859 The Liverpool Mercury Tues. 31 May.
Liverpool: Sailed: May 28: Byron, Jewson, Bahia.
Oct. 4 p.3
At Falmouth: Oct. 1: Byron, Jewson, from Bahia.

1859 The Glasgow Daily Herald Sat. 15 Oct. p.4
Falmouth: Sailed: Oct. 12: Byron, Jewson for Bremen.

1860 The Glasgow Daily Herald Mon. 25 June p.7
Falmouth: Arrived: June 22: Byron, Jewson, from Buenos Ayres.

1860 The Liverpool Mercury Wed. 27 June p.8
Falmouth: June 24.—The Byron, of Liverpool, from Buenos Ayres, for Bristol, in proceeding to sea last night in charge of a licensed pilot, drove on shore north side of the Black Rock, but was got off this morning on the flood, making a little water.

1860 The Bristol Mercury, and Western Counties Advertiser Sat. 30 June p.5
Bristol: Arrived: Byron, Jewson, from Buenos Ayres.
June 30 p.7
Bristol: Imports: Byron, from Buenos Ayres: 250 tons bone ash, 40 tons bones.
[Survey: Bristol in August]
Sept. 8 p.5

Bristol: Sailed: Byron, Jewson, for Pernambuco.

1860 The Daily News (London) Thurs. 6 Sept. p.7
Bristol: Sailed: Sept. 4: Byron to Pernambuco.

1861 The Liverpool Mercury Fri. 21 June p.7
At Bahia: Byron, Jewson, hence [from Liverpool].

1861 The Daily News (London) Wed. 4 Sept. p.7
Queenstown: Arrived: Sept. 2: Byron from Bahia.

1861 The Belfast News-Letter, Saturday Morning 7 Sept.
Queenstown: Sailed; Sept. 6: Byron for London.

1861 The Daily News (London) Wed. 11 Sept. p.7
Gravesend: Arrived: Sept. 10: Byron from Bahia.
Sept. 14 p.1
[Advert] *Reefing Topsails: Testimonial to Moore's Patent.*
We, the undersigned, having witnessed the principle of the fitting of the ship "Byron's" Topsailyard and Sail for Reefing, are of the opinion that it is a great improvement of all methods yet used or patent. We highly approve of the revolving power being independent of the hoisting and lowering power, and the retention of the ordinary single tye and haulyards. The principle of the parhackle, as adapted or applied in this case, adds additional strength and security to the slings of the yard, that doing away with that source of danger so very generally complained of with revolving yards—i.e., springing or breaking at the quarters. Its simplicity in fitting without any risk of getting out of order, besides economy in the outfit, is deserving of our recommendation. [21 signatures: 13 Master Mariners: 5 Captains: 1 R.N.: 1 Shipwright: and William G. Jewson, Commander of the "Byron."]

1863 The Liverpool Mercury Mon. Sept. 28 p.3
Liverpool: Arrived: Sept. 27: Byron (brig).
Liverpool Register: Registered in Liverpool 448/1863
John Langton & Thomas Longrigg of Liverpool, Merchants and Shipowners, 64/64 shares. Dated 9th Nov. 1863.
Master, Liverpool 13.11.63 R. Douthwaite 18.321.

Nov. 25 p.3
Liverpool: Sailed: Nov. 24: Byron, Brown (sic), Trinidad.
Dec. 12
Spoken: Byron of this port: Dec. 4, 49 N. 10 W.
1864 Feb. 15 p.3
At Trinidad: Byron, Daithwaite (sic), hence.
Liverpool Register: Master, British Consulate Hamburg 21.6.64 Peter Fea, 609.
July 21 p.3
Liverpool: Arrived: July 20: Byron, Hamburg.
[Survey: Liverpool in September]

[**LR** 1864 Supplement & 65: Byron, Bg, Fea, 196/ 190, Longton &, Liverpool A1]
[**LR** 1866: Byron, Bg, Fea, 174, Liverpool, Longton &/ T. Longrigg, Liverpool A1]

1865 The Liverpool Mercury Fri. 13 Jan. p.3
At Matamoras: Byron hence.
Feb. 23 p.3
Matamoras: Sailed: Jan. 9: Byron, Fea, for this port.

Feb. 23 p.3
Liverpool: Arrived: Feb. 22: Byron, Matamoras.
May 1 p.3
Liverpool: Sailed: Apr. 28: Byron, Fea, Vera Cruz.
July 21 p.6
At Vera Cruz: Byron, Fea, hence.
1866 Jan. 23 p.3
Liverpool: Arrived: Jan. 12: Byron, Fea, St. Nazaire. [Canada]
[Survey: Liverpool in February]
Mar. 22 p.3
Liverpool: Sailed: Mar. 21: Byron, Fea, Cienfuegos. [Cuba]
Mar. 27 p.3
Liverpool: Put back: Mar. 26: Byron, for Cuba. [Gale in the Irish Sea]
July 4 p.3
At Cienfuegos: Byron, hence.
Sept. 28 p.3
Spoken: Byron, of this port, from Santa Cruz for London, Sept. 8: 42 N. 55 W.
Oct. 2 p.3
Gravesend: Arrived: Oct. 1: Byron, Santa Cruz.
Nov. 12 p.3
Gravesend: Sailed: Nov. 11: Byron for Porto Rico.
Nov. 13 p.3
Deal: Passed: Nov. 12: Byron from London for Porto Rico.
1867 4 Feb. p.3
At Mayaguez [Porto Rico]: *Byron, Fea, from London.*

1867 The Glasgow Herald Tues. 2 Apr. p.4
Falmouth: Arrived: Mar. 29: Byron, Fea, from Arecibo. [Porto Rico]

++++++++++ **Wilfrid Hine**
Liverpool Register: Registered in Liverpool 151/1867
Wilfrid Hine of 14 South Castle Street, Liverpool. Shipowner Sixty Four/64. Dated 31 May 1867.

1867 Lloyd's List June 24 col. 12
London: Entered outwards: June 22: Byron, Fearon, B, 174, LD [London Dock], *Mosses.*

1867 The Liverpool Mercury Tues. 25 June p.3
Deal: Passed: June 24: Byron, from London for Callao.

1867 Lloyd's List June 28 col. 6
Falmouth: Arrived: June 27: Byron, Fearon, London for Callao: crew refusing duty.
July 1 col. 3
Falmouth: Sailed: June 29: Byron, Fearon, for Callao. [Peru near Lima]

1867 Lloyd's List Dec. 18 col. 20
Callao: Arrived: Nov. 11: Byron Jaeron (sic), from London.
1868 Jan. 15 col. 23
Callao: Sailed: Nov. 28: Byron, Fearon, for Valparaiso.

1868 The Liverpool Mercury Tues. 14 May p.6
At Iquique: Byron from Valparaiso. [Chile]

1868 Lloyd's List Sept. 3 col. 24
Spoken Byron, Fearon, Pisagua [Chile] *to Queenstown, 25th Aug. had lost foretopgallant mast and deck water casks in a gale off Cape Horn, by the Mississippi (s.s.) at New York.*
Sept. 11 col. 15

Spoken: Byron, Iquique to Queenstown, 27 Aug. 42 N. 31 W.
Sept. 17 col. 7
Crookhaven: Arrived: Sept 17 per E.T. at 12.39, Byron, Fearon, Iquique.
Sept. 28 col. 22
Penzance: Sept. 28: The brig reported yesterday at anchor in this bay is the Byron, of Liverpool, from Iquique to Newcastle: she is riding well.
Sept. 29 col. 22
Penzance: Arrived: Sept 28: Byron, Fearon for Newcastle, with sails split &c.
Oct. 12 col. 7
Shields: Arrived: Oct. 9: Byron, Fearon, from Iquique. [Survey: Newcastle in November]

[**MNL** 1867: 4621, Byron, Bg, Fea, Liverpool, 174, Owner, T. Longrigg/Nichlsn&S, Liverpool. A1]
[**MNL** 1868: 4621, Byron, Liverpool, 174, Owner, Wilfred (sic) Hine, 14, South Castle Street, Liverpool]
[**MNL** 1870: 4621: Byron, Liverpool, 174, Owner, Richard & W.H. Nicholson, 14, South Castle Street, Lvpl.]
[**LR** 1868-73: Byron, Bg, Fea/ E. Ward, 174, Nicholson, Liverpool A1]

1868 Lloyd's List Dec. 24 col. 3
Deal: Arrived: Dec. 23: Byron, Ward, for Bordeaux, from Shields.
1869 Jan. 23 col. 11
Bordeaux: Arrived: Jan. 20: Byron, Ward, from Newcastle.
Mar. 16 Col. 11
Bordeaux: Sailed: Mar. 12: Byron, Ward, for Yokohama.

1869 Strait Times Overland Journal Fri. 30 July p.6
Anjer [Java]*: Passed: July 17: Byron (British), Ward, from Bordeaux, to Yokohama.*

1869 Lloyd's List Nov. 23 col. 21
Yokohama: Sailed: Oct. 2: Byron, Wass (sic), for Nagasaki.
Dec. 28 col. 20
Nagasaki: Arrived: Oct. 16: Byron,------, from Yokohama.
col. 21
Nagasaki: Sailed: Oct. 22: Byron,------, for Chefoo.
Dec. 13 col. 29
Hong Kong: Arrived: Oct. 26: Byron, Ward, from Yokohama.
1870 Jan. 17 col. 24
Hong Kong: Sailed: Dec. 2: Byron, Ward, for Ningpo.

{Jardine Matheson Archive}
Charter party of the 'Byron' Reference: MS.JM/F7/95
The charter party of the British brig 'Byron' for a voyage from Taiwanfoo to Chefoo, dated Amoy, 5 February 1870.}

1870 Lloyd's List May 31 col. 41
Chefoo: Arrived: Mar. 18: Byron, Ward,---and sailed 26th for Amoy.
June 1 col. 23
Amoy: Arrived: Apr. 4: Byron,---------Chefoo.
July 26 col. 22
Shanghai: Arrived: May 31: Byron, Ward, from Takao.
Nov. 8 col. 30
Nagasaki: Arrived: Aug. 25: Byron, Ward, from Takao---and sailed 27th for Hiogo.
Kobe-Osaka [Capital of Hiogo prefecture]*: Arrived: Sept. 6: Byron, Ward, from Nagasaki.*
Nov. 29 col. 22
Kobe-Osaka: Sailed: Sept. 29: Byron Warde (sic), for Nagasaki.
Dec. 7 col. 24
Nagasaki: Arrived: Oct. 10: Byron, Ward, from Hiogo.

Dec. 21 col. 17

Shanghai: Arrived: Oct. 30: Byron, Ward, from Nagasaki.

1871 Jan. 5 col. 14

Shanghai: Sailed: Nov. 12 Byron, Ward, for Ningo & Taiwan.

Mar. 15 col. 14

Foo-Chow Foo: Arrived: Jan. 7: Byron, Ward ---and sailed 18th for Sydney.

{from the Internet: Source Authority of New South Wales Shipping Master's Office}
Byron of Liverpool, 174 tons, Port of Foo Chow to Sydney, 31 March. 1871: Edw. Ward: William Shilton, Mate, 33, English; William Allendale (alias Annandale), Boatswain, 22, Scotch; James Kerr, Cook & Steward, 26. English; Christian Bermister, A.B., 33, Hamburg; George Sliger (alias Myer), A.B, 22 Holland; John Alexander, A.B. 29, Scotch; James Kingham, A.B., 19, English; Johnson Mason, apprentice, 24, English; James Jenkins, A.B., 20, English..

1871 The Sydney Morning Herald Sat. 1 Apr. p.4

Sydney: Arrivals: March 31: Byron, Brig, 174 tons, Captain Ward, from Foo Chow [China] 19th January.

The brig Byron arrived in port yesterday, having been enabled to get clear of Jervis Bay when the southerly set in. She reports having sailed from Foo Chow on the 19th January, passed, Anjer Point [Island of Java] on the 6th February. She has had very unsettled weather throughout, the winds principally holding to the S.E. The Byron is to the consignment of Cowlishaw, Brothers.

p.10

Preliminary.

Congou Teas of the First Growth.

The entire cargo of the brig Byron, from Foo Chow, with a well-assorted shipment of Finest to Medium Congous, under instructions from Messrs, Cowlishaw, Brothers.

For Positive Sale, at the City Mart, on Tuesday, April 4th.

The Auctioneers are instructed to notify that this Cargo is placed upon the market for sale, it being the wish of the importers that every line should be closed out On The Fall of The Hammer.

Every facility will be afforded for liquoring the various chops; and the trade are respectfully invited to make themselves thoroughly acquainted with the fine flavour of those First Chop Teas prior to sale, as the vendors are determined to effect a clearance of the entire cargo. Muster packages now open.

R.F. Stubbs and Co. will sell by auction, at the City Mart, on Tuesday, April 4th, at 11 o'clock. The entire cargo of the Byron, comprising 4863 packages finest to medium kaisou congous. Full particulars in cards. Terms, liberal.

Apr. 4 p.4

Captain Ward of the brig Byron, from Foo Chow, reports that on the lst March, when in Latitude 35 2 S., longitude 97* 39 E., he sighted a large three-masted steamer steering a W.N.W. course, with the wind from the northward. She had her fore-and-aft canvas set, and was travelling very fast through the water. From the description of the vessel's rig, it must have been the Queen of the Thames (s.s.), from Melbourne bound to London.*

Apr. 13 p.1

For Sale, the A1 brig Byron, 178 tons register, 300 tons burthen, on a draught of 13 feet, built at Annan, Scotland, new wire rigged and coppered in 1868, shifts without ballast, and goes to sea with 45 tons. For inventory and information respecting vessel apply to Captain Ward, on board, at Campbell's Wharf ; or to Cowlishaw, Brothers, 50, Pitt-street.

Apr. 20 p.4

*The brig Byron, 174 tons register, recently arrived from Foo Chow, has been **sold** privately for £1400. The purchasers are Messrs. J. and S. Blue, Lewellyn, and W. S. Clarke. She will be employed in the coal trade between Sydney and Newcastle.*
May 4 p.6

Departures for England.: April 24: Brucklay Castle, Ship, 1014, Wallace for London: Passenger: Captain Ward.

[**RA&NZS** 1874: Byron Brig, 174, 4,621, Port 17, Sydney 1871: Built Scotland 1851: Captain W. Llewellin: Owners, John Blue and Others.]
++++++++++

1880 The South Australian Register Fri. 28 May p.5

The Brig Byron.—Our correspondent at Port Elliot writes thus—"Great anxiety has been felt at this port for the safety of the brig Byron, for although the place where she was anchored had good holding ground, yet the position was open and exposed, and in the event of a strong southerly wind setting in she would be exposed to great danger. From the time the vessel was anchored on Sunday up till Tuesday, morning she lay quietly, but the wind having changed about 10 a.m. on Tuesday, she then appeared to be rolling in a most unpleasant manner, and was by many persons considered in danger. She never dragged her anchors, however, or moved from the position she first took up. The lifeboat was all in readiness at Port Victor had it been required, but fortunately this was not the case. Pilot Brown and Police-trooper Bruce, with a number of the inhabitants, have been unceasingly on the watch, and have been prepared for any emergency. It was understood on Tuesday evening that the Cadell, steamer, had engaged to tow the Byron to Port Adelaide, but it was afterwards ascertained that the arrangement had not been completed, the captain considering the charge demanded too high. The captain has now engaged a steamer from Port Adelaide to take him through." The steamer Yatala, with the brig in tow, sailed at 8 o'clock yesterday morning and arrived off the Semaphore late last night.

1880 The South Australian Advertiser Sat. 10 July p.4

Auction Sale. Messrs. H. J. Wickstead and Co., of Port Adelaide, report:—"We offered the brig Byron this morning, but offers not being satisfactory she was passed in. We afterwards sold her privately at a fair figure."

1880 The South Australian Advertiser Summary for Europe (Gratis) Sat. 7 Aug. p.9S

The Fishing Company recently purchased the wrecked brig Byron, which after being repaired will be taken to Kangaroo Island and moored there. The brig will be chiefly used as a coal hulk, but the company have decided to fit up a portion of her for the reception of excursionists who visit the island for fishing during the summer months.

CEREAL

State Library of Victoria, Brodie Collection

CEREAL

Official No.	27518		Code letters PRNK
Built	1859 August. In Sunderland (Builder, Denniston)		
Deck	One	Build	---------
Masts	Three	Gallery	None
Rigging	**Barque**	Head	Woman Bust
Stern	Square	Framework	Wood (oak).
Tonnage	**299**	Length 114.3 feet; Breadth 25.25 feet; Depth 16.35 feet.	

Liverpool Register: Registered in Liverpool 111/1871: Sunderland 91/1859. Registered anew on transfer.

[LR 1860-61: Cereal, Bk, Alderson, 298, Sunderland 1859, R. Porrett, Sunderland A1]
[LR 1863: Cereal, Bk, M'Donald, 298, R. Porrett, Sunderland A1]
[LR 1863-67: Cereal, Bk, M'Donald/H. Sealy, 298, R. Porrett, Sunderland A1]
[LR 1868-70: Cereal, Bk, H. Sealy/ Legender 298, R. Porrett/ W. Legender, Sunderland A1]
[LR 1871: Cereal, Bk, Wilson 298, W. Legender/ W. Hine, Sunderland/ Liverpool A1]
[LR 1872: Cereal, Bk, Wilson 298, W. Hine, Liverpool A1 BURNT]

1859 The Liverpool Mercury Mon. 19 Sept. p.3
Deal: Passed: Sept. 17: Cereal, from the north for Venice.
1860 Feb. 27 p.3
Liverpool: Arrived: Feb. 25: Cereal, Klderson (sic), Venice.
Apr. 5 p.8
Liverpool: Sailed: Apr. 4: Cereal, Alderson, Malta.
May 15
At Malta: Cerlal (sic), Alderson, hence [from Liverpool].

1860 The Morning Post (London) Tues. 16 Oct. p.7
At Falmouth: Oct. 13: Cereal from Taganrog.

1860 The Caledonian Mercury, Edinburgh Tues. 6 Nov.
Leith: Arrived: Nov. 5: Cereal, Alderson, Taganrog, wheat.
Nov. 21
Leith: Cleared out: Nov. 20: Cereal, Alderson, Sunderland, ballast.

1861 The New York Evening Express 14 Mar.
Messina: Sailed: Feb. 20: Cereal, McDonald, NYk.

1861 Newcastle Courant Fri. 26 July p.6
Spoken: The barque Cereal, of Sunderland, from Constantinople for Queenstown or Falmouth, on the 12th July, nearly becalmed, off the North-west Coast of Sicily, by the steamer Stella, Farmer, arrived at Marseilles.

1861 The Standard (London) Wed. 25 Sept. p.6
Wreck on the Goodwin Sands.—Ramsgate, Sept. 23.—This morning, at daybreak, during a strong gale of wind from WSW and squally, a barque was observed on shore on the north part of the Goodwin Sands. The Northumberland life boat, in tow of a steamer, immediately put off from Ramsgate to the vessel's assistance. On proceeding to the wreck the tug took in tow the Broadstairs life boat. A deal lugger, which had been cruising about, was found, with the vessel. Through the joint exertions of the three boats' crews the vessel was fortunately got off. She proved to be the barque Cereal, of Sunderland, from Dunkirk to New York. The wreck having also been observed from

Walmer, the life boat on the station, belonging to the National Life-boat Institution, immediately put off to her assistance, and reached the vessel shortly after the boats, but her services were not required. The Walmer life boat is a new one. It was said that she behaved remarkably well on the occasion. Having to cross the Goodwin Sands through a heavy surf, she was frequently filled with water, which, however, she speedily freed herself of.

1861 Newcastle Courant Fri. 27 Sept. p.8
Ramsgate, Sept. 23:--The bark Cereal, Alderson, of Sunderland, from Dunkirk for New York (ballast), went on the Goodwin Sand at 3 o'clock this morning, and was assisted off this afternoon by the harbour tug Vulcan, also Ramsgate, Deal and Broadstairs lifeboats, and arrived at 3 p.m., making but little water, having lost sails.
[Survey: Sunderland in October]

1861 The Leeds Mercury Fri. 29 Nov. p.4
Deal: Put in and anchored: Nov. 27: Cereal from Sunderland, for Naples (sic).

1862 The Standard (London) Thurs. 3 Apr. p.7
Spoken: barque Cereal bound to Philadelphia, March 15, off Nova.

1862 The Daily News (London) Sat. 12 July p.7
Queenstown: Arrived: July 10: Cereal from Philadelphia.
July 22 p.7
At Cork: July 18: Cereal from Philadelphia.
Aug. 2 p.7
Queenstown: Sailed: July 30: Cereal to New York.

1862 New-York Daily Tribune Thurs. 11 Sept. p.3
New York: Arrived: Sept. 10: Bark Cereal (Br. of Sunderland) McDonald, Cork 58 days, in ballast to master. [Survey: New York in September.]

1862 The New York Evening Express 7 Oct.
New York: Cleared: Oct. 6: Br. bark Cereal, McDonald, Plymouth.

1862 The Daily News (London) Tues. 18 Nov. p.7
Plymouth: Arrived: Nov. 16: Cereal, from New York.

1862 The Morning Post (London) Mon. 22 Dec. p.6
Sunderland: Sailed: Dec. 18: Cereal to Messina.

1862 The Ipswich Journal and Suffolk, Norfolk, Essex and Cambridgeshire Advertiser Sat. 27 Dec. p.7
Lowestoft: From Thursday to Sunday morning we had a succession of gales from the North West, and on Sunday after the North and North East, with heavy squalls. On Sunday a number of vessels, with loss of anchors and chains and sundry damage, sought the harbour for refuge. Owing to the vessels that took the harbour without steam not having sufficient aft canvass to enable them to luff up to windward and take a clear berth, they fell to leeward upon the south pier; thereby damaging themselves and other vessels and the pier and blocking the entrance of the harbour, and a considerable amount of confusion was the consequence. ....The barque "Cereal," Mac'Donel (sic), of and from Sunderland, for Messina, towed in having been in collision with the brig "Kate," of Leamington. Hawse pipe broken and other damage. Agreement £40.

1863 New York Herald Tues. 9 Feb. Triple Sheet p.10
Boston: Sailed Feb. 6: bark Cereal.

1863 The Liverpool Mercury Wed. 1 July p.3
Queenstown: Arrived: June 30: Coreal (sic), from Baltimore.
July 9 p.3
Queenstown: Sailed: July 8: Cereal for Belfast.
July 13 p.3
At Belfast: July 11: Cereal from Baltimore.
July 25 p.8
Belfast: Sailed: Cereal, for New York via Cardiff.

1863 New York Herald Wed. 26 Aug. p.2
Cardiff: Sailed: Aug. 7: Cereal, McDonald N York.

1863 The New-York Times Sept. 25 p.8
New-York: Arrived: Sept 24: Bark Cereal (Br., of Sunderland), McDonald, Cardiff 44 ds., with coal. [Survey: New York in September.]
Oct. 23 p.8
New-York: Cleared: Oct. 22: Bark Cereal, (Br.,) McDonald, Cork.
Oct. 26 p.8
New-York: Sailed: Oct. 25: Bark Cereal (Br.,).
Dec. 12 p.8
Queenstown: Arrived: Nov. 29: Cereal from New-York.
Dec. 18 p.8
Dublin: Arrived: Dec. 7: Cereal from New-York.

[Survey: Swansea in January 1864]

1864 Jan. 29 p.3
Queenstown: Arrived: Jan. 28: Cereal from Swansea for Maranham, windbound.
Feb. 5 Feb. p.3
Queenstown: Sailed: Feb. 4: Cereas (sic), for Maranham [Brazil].

1864 The Times (London) July 15 p.12
Spoken: July 9: The Cereal bound east: 50N. 22W.
July 25 p.11
Gravesend: July 23: Arrived: The Cereal – from Trinidad.
[Survey: Sunderland in August.]
Sept 3 p.11
Deal: Anchored: Sept 2: Cereal from Sunderland for Naples.

1865 The Liverpool Mercury Thurs. 23 Feb. p.3
Gravesend: Arrived: Feb: Cereal, from Girgenti. [Sicily]
Mar. 2 p.3
Liverpool: off the port: Cereal.
Mar. 3 p.3
Liverpool: Arrived: Mar. 2: Cereal, Scaley (sic), Palermo.
Mar. 29 p.3
Liverpool: Sailed: Mar. 28: Cereal, Sulcy (sic) Bahia.
June 19 p.3
(per Telegraph): At Bahia: Cereal from Liverpool.

1865 The Times (London) Mon. 16 Oct. p.12
A Noble Lifeboat: During gales of wind by the Ramsgate lifeboat in conjunction with the harbour steamtug, during the past 11 years saved ......including the bark Cereal and crew saved [see 1861].

1865 The Glasgow Daily Herald Fri. 13 Oct. p.7
Falmouth: Arrived: Oct. 10: Cereal, Sealy, from Bahia.

Oct. 17 p.7
Falmouth: Sailed: Oct. 13: Cereal, Sealy, for the Clyde.
Oct. 23 p.7
Greenock: Arrived: Oct. 21: Cerial (sic), Siaby (sic) from Bahia with sugar.
1866 Jan. 27 p.7
At Messina: Jan. 14: Cereal, Sealy, from Ardrossan.

1866 The Belfast News-Letter Tues. 7 Aug.
[By telegraph] Queenstown: Arrived: Aug. 6: Cereal, from New York.

1866 The Daily News (London) Mon. 13 Aug. p.3
Gravesend: Arrived: Aug. 10: Cereal from Cronstadt.

1866 The Times (London) Mon. 13 Aug. p.12
Gravesend: Arrived: Aug. 11: The Cereal from Raumo. [Finland]

[**MNL** 1867 p. 66: Cereal of Sunderland: Owner: Robt. Burbank Porrett, Sunderland.]

1867 The New-York Times Mon. 22 July
New-York: Arrived: July 21: Cereal, (of Sunderland,) Bolt, Newcastle 53 ds., with mdse, to Barclay & Livingston. Had heavy weather, and lost sails, &c.

1867 New York Herald Fri. 9 Aug. p.7
New York: Cleared: Aug. 8: Bark Cereal, Bolt (Br.) Gibraltar via Philadelphia.
[Survey: New York in August.]
Oct. 24 p.10
Spoken: Bark Cereal, Boult (sic), from Philadelphia for Venice. Sept 22, lat 41, lon 28.
Nov. 30 p.8
Venice: Arrived: Nov. 13: Cereal, Bolt, N'York.

1868 The Glasgow Daily Herald Wed. 4 Mar. p.5
Court of Session.—Tuesday, March 3, Second Division: Advn.—Beun & Co. v. Porret and Sealy: This was an advocation from the Sheriff Court of Greenock of an action in which Beun & Co., merchants of Bahia, were pursuers, and Robert Burnbaut Porret, shipowner in Sunderland, owner of the barque Cereal, and Henry Charles Sealy, master of the vessel, were defenders. The summons concluded for payment of £258. 0s. 3d., being the amount of cash paid and advances made by the pursuers, Benn & Co., to or on the order and authority of the said Henry Charles Sealy, as master of the said vessel, for the purpose of paying the port charges and necessary disbursements of said vessel while she lay at Bahia in or about the months of July and August, 1865, and for which advances the defender Henry Charles Sealy was said to have granted to the pursuers Beun & Co., a certain document of debt. The document of debt libelled on was in the following terms:--"I, undersigned, master of the British barque Cereal, acknowledge that I have received from Messrs Beun & Co., of this place, the amount of £258 0s. 3d, necessary for port charges and disbursements of said vessel on present voyage to the Channel and port for orders, which I engage myself to reimburse on arrival to order of Messrs. Beun & Co. In witness whereof, &c:"
The defence was that the master of a vessel in a foreign port had no power to bind his owner by any such document as that founded on in the summons, and that the said document was illegally exacted from the master by the pursuers, who were bound by the terms of the charter, as agents for the charter of the vessel, to make the advances in question to the master, not as loans, but as payments to account of freight on behalf of the owner.

The Sheriff-Substitute (Tennent) sustained the defences, and assoilzied (sic) the defenders, holding (1) that it was established as matter of fact that the pursuers assumed the character of agents for the charterer, and took benefit from the character, and from the provisions of the charter party, in the shape of commission and otherwise; and (2) that that being so, they were bound by the provisions of the charter-party above referred to, which laid upon them, as agents, the obligation of making the advances sued for, not as loans, but to account of freight. On appeal, the Sheriff-Principal (Fraser) adhered substantially on the same grounds; and with reference to certain letters founded on by the pursuers as containing an intimation by them to the master that they would not make the advances except upon the footing of the obligation granted by him, he (the Sheriff) held that intimation to the captain was not intimation to the owner, and that in a question with the owner the pursuers were still bound by the provisions of the charter-party. The pursuers advocated, and to-day the case was advised, when the majority of the Court were for altering the interlocutors of the Sheriffs, and decerning in favour of the pursuer.

The Lord Justice-Clerk, Lord Benholme, and Lord Neaves held that the terms of the charter-party could not constitute a contract between the owner of the vessel and the pursuers, who were no parties of the charter-party. The charter-party was a contract solely between the owners and the charterers; and although the pursuers, as charters' agents, might have adopted the obligations of the charter-party, they did not do so in this instance, but made the advances in question on the express footing that they were not made in implement of the provision in the charter-party founded on, but in terms of the obligation granted by the captain, as above set forth.

Lord Cowan dissented, agreeing in substance with the view of the transaction taken by the Sheriffs.

1868 [Survey: Sunderland in June]

1868 New York Herald Wed. 26 Aug p.2
Cardiff: Sailed Aug. 7: Cereal, McDonald, N York.

1869 New York Herald Sun. 7 Feb. --triple sheet-- p.10
Boston: Cleared: Feb. 5: bark Cereal (Br), Legender, London. [Survey: Boston in January.]
Feb. 9 p.10
Boston: Sailed: Feb. 6: bark Cereal.
Mar. 15 --triple sheet-- p.10
Deal, In the Downs: Mar. 1: Cereal, Legender, from Boston for London.

1869 The Glasgow Daily Herald Tues. 7 Sept. p.7
Queenstown: Arrived: Sept. 6: Cereal, Salonica.
Sept. 10 p.6
Queenstown: Sailed: Sept. 9: Cereal, London.

1869 The Western Mail (Cardiff) Sat. 2 Oct. p.8
Pill and Kingroad: Passed to Bristol: Oct. 1: Cereal from Onega (sic).

1869 The Daily News (London) Mon. 4 Oct. p.7
Bristol: Oct. 1: The Cereal, from Salonika (sic) to London, has put in here to-day with damage, having been forced up.

1869 The Western Mail (Cardiff) Sat. 22 Oct. p.4
Pill and Kingroad: Sailed: Oct. 21: Cereal, (Legender) for Cardiff.
Oct. 27 p.4

Cardiff Entered Outwards, Oct. 26: Cereal, 299, Legender, Smyrna. [Turkey, Aegean Sea]
Nov. 9 p.4
Cardiff: Cleared: Nov. 8: Cereal, B, Smyrna, 450 coal.

1870 The Times (London) Fri. 8 Apr. p.10
Constantinople April 6 – The Cereal (bark) Captain Legender, from Odessa for England, with wheat, ran ashore at San Stefano, sea of Marmova on the 4th April, but was got off. Expenses £200. [Turkey, linking Black Sea to the Aegean Sea]
May 30 p.7
Queenstown: Arrivals: May 29: Cereal from Odessa. [Ukraine, Black Sea]

[**MNL** 1870 p. 65: Cereal of Sunderland: Owner: William Zegender (sic), Monkwearmouth.]

1870 The Dundee Courier & Argus Tues. 21 June
A Ship Captain Drowned at Sea.
On Saturday morning, the barque Cereal, of Sunderland, from Odessa, arrived in Leith, when the mate reported the loss of the captain, Walton (sic) [Wilton] Legender, who fell overboard, and was drowned on the 13th inst., off Cromar (sic) Light. The deceased man, who was fifty-two years of age, and a native of Sunderland, was suffering from the effects of drink when he met his unfortunate fate.

1870 The Glasgow Daily Herald Tues. 21 June p.7
Leith: Arrived: June 18: Cereal, Williams, from Odessa: wheat.
June 27 p.7
Leith: Sailed: June 24: Cereal, Williamson, for Sunderland: ballast.

1870 The Northern Echo Mon. 18 July
Deal: Passed: July 15: Cereal, Walton, for Malaga, from Sunderland.
[Survey: Sunderland in July.]

1870 The Standard (London) Tues. Aug. 16 p.7
Spoken: The Cereal, barque, Sunderland to Malta, July 30, lat. 36 N. long. 8 W.

1870 The Times (London) Wed. 24 Aug.
Monaco: Arrivals: Aug 14: The Cereal from Sunderland.

1870 The Glasgow Daily Herald Tues. 4 Oct. p.7
Queenstown: Arrived: Oct. 3: Cereal, Kustendjie. [Black Sea, Roumania]

1870 The Northern Echo Fri. 2 Dec. p.4
Stranding of a Sunderland Vessel. Constantinople, November 22: The Cereal barque, of Sunderland, Wilson, from Odessa for the United Kingdom (wheat), was stranded on the shoal of Dogani Aslan, near Gallipoli, on the 17th inst., but was assisted off next day at an expense of £300, and after losing about 15 fathoms of chain cable. A survey on the 19th declared her to be seaworthy. The cargo sustained no damage.

1871 The Standard (London) Sat. 4 Mar. p.7
Falmouth: Arrived: Mar. 3: The Cereal from Odessa, has lost bulwarks on port and starboard sides, and smashed skylight.

[**LR** 1871: Cereal, Bk, Wilson 298, W. Legender/ W. Hine, Sunderland/ Liverpool A1]

++++++++++ **Wilfrid Hine**

Liverpool Register: Wilfrid Hine, of 14 South Castle Street, Liverpool. Shipowner Sixty Four/64. dated 25th July 1871.
Master: Sunderland 1.8.71: James Ritchie C 93623

1871 The Liverpool Mercury Sat. 18 Nov. p.7
Spoken: Cereal of and from Sunderland for Rio Negro, Sept. 25, 2 N. 25 W.

1871 The Times (London) Mon. 4 Dec. p.11
Buenos Ayres: Arrivals: Nov 14: via Lisbon: the Cereal.

1872 Adair's Maryport Advertiser Fri. 28 June p.8
Maryport: Sailed: June 27: Cereal, Ritchie, for Swansea.

1872 The Times (London) Wed. 20 Nov. p.8
Wrecks & Casualties: Queenstown. Nov. 20. The "Cereal" from Swansea for Santos with coals, was burnt on the 28th of September, in lat. 4 S., long. 27 W., crew saved.

1872 Glasgow Herald Thurs. 21 Nov. p.6
Vessel Burned at Sea. By the arrival of the ship Portinscale, from Pisagua at Queenstown, we learn of the loss by fire of the fine Liverpool barque Cereal, bound from Savannah for Santos, with a cargo of coal, she having taken fire and been abandoned on the 27th September. The crew were taken off by the John Ritson, outward bound for Monte Video, but the captain and mate were transferred to the Portinscale, which landed them at Queenstown yesterday.

1872 Adair's Maryport Advertiser Fri. 22 Nov. p.8
The "Cereal" Burnt at Sea: This fine vessel, owned by Mr. W. Hine and others, when on her voyage from Swansea to the River Plate, took fire and was abandoned by the crew on the 27th September, in 4 S. All hands were saved by the barque "John Ritson", bound for Monte Video. The Captain, his wife, and the mate were transferred to the "Portinscale" at sea, and landed at Queenstown.

[**Fl corr**] Liverpool 20 Dec. 1872. I have lost one of my ships by fire but fully insured. Only had her about 16 months but in that time she cleared us over 40 per cent. I have just bought another for the same Captain as he is a first rate man & got her on very easy terms ---- Wilfrid Hine.

1873 Otago Daily Times (N.Z.) Mon. 10 Feb. p.2
News has been received of the total loss by fire of the barque Cereal, in lat. 4.30 S. She was from home to Montevideo hence to the Mauritius, then to Otago. All hands were saved by the British John Ritson. The Cereal was commanded by Capt. James Ritchie, formerly of the barque Eleanor, in the Newcastle trade connected with this port, and she was partly owned by Capt. Sewell, of Oamaru.
Feb. 14 p.2
We have been requested to state that Captain Sewell, of Oamaru, was not part owner of the barque Cereal, burned south of the line, as reported in our issue of the 10th. Captain Sewell regrets the mishap to Captain Ritchie, of the Cereal.

1873 Maryport Advertiser and Weekly News Fri. 16 May p.8
Capt. George Curwen, of the John Ritson, has been presented with a handsome gold watch by Capt. Ritchie, of the Cereal, for his gallant and Humane conduct towards Capt. Ritchie and his crew, whom he rescued from the ship when on fire at sea.

JANE HARRISON

Official No.	66308	The late **Rosslyn**	
Built	1872 August	Mount Stewart (Prince Edward Island, Canada)	
Deck	One	Build	Carvel
Masts	Two	Gallery	none
Rigging	**Brigantine**	Head	Woman bust
Stern	Square	Framework	Wood
Tonnage	**225**	Length 115.5 feet; Breadth 25.3 feet; Depth 12.5 feet.	

TSR 2/7 p.89: Registered Sale dated 7 Dec. 1872: Port No. 7/1872 Maryport, British. William Harrison 64 shares dated 10th Dec. 1872 sold to **Wilfrid Hine** of Liverpool, in Lancaster, Ship owner.

Jane Harrison had a very brief existence.
She started as the Rosslyn in Canada.
[**ALRAFS** 1873: Rosslyn, McRea, 225, P E Island 1872, P. E. Island Peake, Peake Bros & Co.]
[**LR** 1872 (supplement): Jane Harrison, ex Rosslyn, Bn, 238, J. Johnston, Hine & Co, Maryport, **FOUNDERED**]

1872 [Survey: P.E. Island in August] [Survey: Liverpool in November]

1872 Adair's Maryport Advertiser, Fri. 20 Dec. p.8
Jane Harrison, Johnston, sailed from Liverpool for Valparaiso on the 14th inst.

1873 The Standard (London) Tues. 21 Jan. p.7
Falmouth, Jan 19: The Jane Harrison of Maryport, from Liverpool to Valparaiso, was abandoned on the 6th of January, dismasted; crew saved by the Johannes, Norwegian, from Newport to Matanzas, and transferred to the Vesta, Austrian, arrived here yesterday.

1873 Adair's Maryport Advertiser, Fri. 31 Jan. p.8
Distressing Wreck of a Maryport Vessel.
The Jane Harrison, commanded by Capt. Johnstone, (a recent purchase by Mr. J. Harrison, of Maryport), sailed from Liverpool, on the 14th December, for Valparaiso. She encountered continuous gales till the 30th, when she was dismasted, and being much strained began to make water at a rate which baffled the pumps to keep her clear. Finding their vessel was sinking the crew with all speed launched the long boat; but had no time to save their clothes and only a little provisions. The sea running very high, beat heavily against the ship, and fears were entertained that the boat would be stove in under her quarters, when one of the crew, --John Scott, --fearlessly jumped on board the boat and kept her away from the ship till the rest got on board. The boat had not left many perches when the vessel went down. A Norwegian barque, the Johanna Rhodes observing that the vessel was in distress, bore down on them and picked up the crew, nine in number. They were afterwards transferred to an Austrian Schooner and safely landed at Falmouth, and sent to their respective homes by the agent of the Shipwrecked Mariners' Society.

Rolling Down to St. Helena: State Library of Victoria, Brodie Collection

Heavy weather, running the Easting Down. Both men are lashed at the wheel. Captain Bronlund of Excelsior in his Cape Horn suit: State Library of Victoria, Brodie Collection

QUEEN OF THE FLEET

Official No. 38058   **Code letters SHND**
Built   **1857**   In Yarmouth, Nova Scotia, Canada: Builder, Dennis Horton

Deck	One & Break	Build	Carvel
Masts	Three	Gallery	None
Rigging	**Barque**	Head	Female
Stern	Square	Framework	Wood (maple).
Tonnage	**593**	Length 147.3 feet; Breadth 31.4 feet; Depth 18.5 feet.	

[**ALRAFS** 1859: Queen of the Fleet, Mc Mullen, 595, Yarmouth N.S. 1857, of Yarmouth Abm. Gowdy & O]
[**ALRAFS** 1861-68: Queen of the Fleet, Hilton, 631, of Yarmouth Abm. Gowdy & O]
[**ALRAFS** 1869: Queen of the Fleet, Scott, 631, of Yarmouth Abm. Gowdy & O]
[**ALRAFS** 1870-73: Queen of the Fleet, McLeod, 595, of Yarmouth Abm. Gowdy & O]
[**ALRAFS** 1874-76: Queen of the Fleet, Holmes, 595, of Yarmouth Abm. Gowdy & O]
[**RAFS** 1875-85: Queen of the Fleet, Holmes, 593, of Liverpool, George Clark]

1857 The Liverpool Mercury Wed. 27 Dec. p.7
Liverpool: Arrived: Dec. 22: Queen of the Fleet, St. John, N.B.
1858 Jan. 12 p.4
On Thursday next, the 14th instant, at Twelve o'clock at noon, on the Quay Toxteth Dock: 13,878 Spruce Deals, 464 Spruce Scantling, 1,073 Boards, 1,351 Boards Deal Ends. Now landing ex Queen of the Fleet, from St. John, N.B. –On account of the Importers.
Feb. 19
Liverpool: Sailed: Feb. 18: Queen of the Fleet, M'Mullen for Halifax.
Apr. 9
At Halifax: Queen of the Fleet, M'Mullen.

1858 The Bristol Mercury Sat. 10 July p.5
Bristol: Arrived Queen of the Fleet, ------------, from St. John's, N.B.
July 17 p.7
Bristol: Imports: In the Queen of the Fleet, from Miramichi: Howell, Gibson and Leake, 13,087 pcs deals, 4546 pcs battens, 2292 pcs scantling, 1280 pcs deal ends.
July 31 p.5
Bristol: Sailed: Queen of the Fleet, McMullen for Miramichi.

1858 The Belfast News-Letter Thurs. 28 Oct. p.2
Belfast: Arrived: Oct. 27: Queen of the Fleet, M'Mullan, from Miramichi, with a cargo of deals.
Nov. 20
Belfast: Sailed: Nov. 19: Queen of the Fleet, M'Mullan, for Ardrossan.
Nov. 25
Ardrossan: Arrived: Nov. 20: Queen of the Fleet, M'Mullan, from Belfast.
Dec. 13
Ardrossan: Sailed: Dec. 9: Queen of the Fleet, M'Mullen for New York.

1859 New York Herald Wed. 2 Feb. p.8
New York: Arrived: Feb. 1: Bark Queen of the Fleet (Br.), McMullen, Ardrossan, Dec. 9 with pig iron to master. Had very bad weather during the month of December. Jan 22, lat 41 47, lon 61 24, fell in with a Br bark, of Liverpool, waterlogged and abandoned, could not ascertain her name, she had wooden stern davits, bright lower masts, mainmast iron hooped, zinc bottom to the bends, billet head, hull painted black,

maintopgallant mast, foremast head and all yards gone, mizzen topgallant mast housed. It being near night and blowing heavily did not board her. [Survey: New York in February]
1 Mar. p.8
New York: Cleared: Feb. 28: Bark Queen of the Fleet (Br.), McMullen, Newcastle.

1859 Newcastle Courant Fri. 27 May p.6
Newcastle: Imports: Queen of the Fleet, Muller (sic), Beaufort, 5,511 barrels, 50 barrels turpentine, 8,000 staves. – Order.
1 July p.6
Newcastle: Exports: June 29: Queen of the Fleet, Mullen (sic), New York, a general cargo.

1859 New York Herald Fri. 30 Sept. p.8
New York: Arrived: Sept. 29: Bark Queen of the Fleet (Br, of Yarmouth, N.S.), McMullen, Shields, July 4th, with Mdse to H & F W Myer. The first part of the passage experienced heavy gales from the westward, and calms, the latter part light winds and calms. Sept 14, lat 44 30, long 61 52, took a heavy gale from WNW; 15th, fell in with the schooner Princess, of and from Sydney, C B, for Boston, Sept. 9, in a sinking condition, coal loaded, having shipped a sea, carried away stanchions, tore up the covering board and swept deck in the gale of the 14th; took from her the captain, Charles Florian, and seven of her crew. Her owner, Mr. Francis Oliver, while getting on board the bark, fell into the sea; being a large heavy man, and thickly clothed, he was lost, although every exertion was made to save him. The mate of the schooner had previously been washed overboard, but was recovered. The bark, while lying to, came in contact with the schooner, losing her jibboom and damaging her cutwater. The Princess sunk soon after rescuing her crew. She was two years old, of 86 tons English measurement, and was insured in Halifax, N.S.
Nov. 15 p.8
New York: Cleared: Nov. 14: Bark Queen of the Fleet (Br), McMullen, Glasgow.

1859 The Glasgow Daily Herald Tues. 27 Dec. p.4
Glasgow: Arrived: Dec. 25: Queen of the Fleet, M'Millan (sic), from New York.
1860 Jan. 28 p.4
Glasgow: Sailed: Jan. 27: Queen of the Fleet, M'Millan (sic), for New York, with a general cargo.

1860 New-York Daily Tribune Mon. 19 Mar. p.8
New-York: Arrived: Mar. 18: Bark Queen of the Fleet (Br., of Yarmouth, N.S.), Mc Mullen Glasgow 50 days, pig iron, &c., to Thomas James. Had heavy weather.

1860 The New-York Times Fri. 6 Apr.
New-York: Cleared: Apr. 5: bark, Queen of the Fleet, McMullen, St. John.

1860 The Belfast News-Letter Thurs. Morning 31 May
St. John N.B: Cleared: 1 May: Queen of the Fleet, M'Mullen, for Belfast.
June 12
Belfast: Arrived: June 10: Queen of the Fleet, M'Mullen from St John N.B. with deals.
June 19
Auction: At Prince's Dock (North side), 20th June, the Cargo per "Queen of the Fleet" from St. John, N.B., consisting of Pieces.
12,166 Bright Spruce Deals 10 to 28 x 9 x 3
* 3,902   "   "   "   10 to 28 x 7 x 3*
*   707   "   "   "   10 to 26 x11 x 3   Ist, 2nd & 3rd quality.*
*   501   "   "   Ends 9, 7 & 11 x 3*

114 Birch Timber, 15 inch calliper
10,000 Paling Boards, 4½ ft.
2,000   do   4 ft.   11th June 1860 Belfast.

June 21 p.4
Belfast: Sailed: June 19: Queen of the Fleet, M'Mullen, for Ardrossan.
June 25 p.2
Ardrossan: Arrived: June 20: Queen of the Fleet, M'Mullen, from Belfast.

1860 The Glasgow Daily Herald Fri. 20 July p.7
Ardrossan: Sailed: July 18: Queen of the Fleet, M'Millan (sic), for Boston.
Sept. 19 p.7
Spoken: Queen of the Fleet, from Ardrossan for Boston, U.S., 23d ult., in lat. 56*N., long. 56* W.
Sept. 22 p.4
At Boston: Sept. 5: Queen of the Fleet, M'Millan (sic), from Androssan.
Oct. 31 p.6
New York: Cleared: Oct. 13: bark, Queen of the Fleet, Hilton, for Glasgow.
Dec. 14 p.7
Glasgow: Arrived: Dec. 13: Queen of the Fleet, Hutton (sic), from New York, with flour.

1861 The Morning Post (London) Wed. 16 Jan.
Great Flood of Ice on the Clyde: Queen of the Fleet, brig (sic), stern and rigging damaged.
Feb. 11
Clyde: Sailed: Feb. 8: Queen of the Fleet, to New York.

1861 The New-York Times Wed. 27 Mar.
New-York: Arrived: Mar. 26: Bark Queen of the Fleet (of Yarmouth N.S.) Hilton, Glasgow 44 ds. with iron to Edmiston Bros. 15 inst. Edward Martin seaman, fell from the main-rigging overboard, and was lost. [Survey: New York in March]
Apr. 24
New-York: Cleared: Apr. 23: Bark Queen of the Fleet (Br), Hilton, Cork.

1861 The Belfast News-Letter Morning Sat. 25 May
Queenstown: Arrived: May 24: Queen of the Fleet, New York.
June 13
Queenstown: Sailed: June 12: Queen of the Fleet, for Sydney, C.B.

1861 New-York Daily Tribune Sat. 27 July p.8
New York: Arrived: July 26: Bark Queen of the Fleet (Br. of Yarmouth, N.S.), Hilton, Cork 58 ds., in ballast to Edmiston Bros. July 1, lat. 15 50, lon. 48 52, passed a large iceberg. July 6, lat 44 20, lon. 51 02, spoke fishing schr Wm. Kinsrow, at Marblehead, anchored; reported fish scarce.   The Q of the F has experienced light W winds, with much fog, from the Banks.
Aug 22. p.5
New York: Sailed: Aug. 21: Bark Queen of the Fleet (Br), Cork.

1861 The Belfast News-Letter Morning Tues. 17 Sept.
Queenstown: Arrived: Sept. 16: Queen of the Fleet, from New York.
Sept. 24
Queenstown: Sailed: Sept. 23: Queen of the Fleet, Newry.

1861 The Glasgow Daily Herald Sat. 28 Sept. p.4
Queen of the Fleet, Hilton, from New York at Warrenpoint, 24th inst.

1861 The Daily News (London) Thurs. 26 Sept. p.7
At Newry: Sept. 25: Queen of the Fleet, from New York.

1861 The New-York Times Sat. 23 Nov.
New-York: Arrived: Nov. 22: Bark Queen of the Fleet (of Yarmouth N.S.) Hilton, Newry 34 ds in ballast to Edmiston Bros. 3rd inst. lat 44 48 lon. 43 24 spoke Br. bark Ann Carr from Falmouth for New-York.
Dec.8
New-York: Cleared: Dec. 7: Bark Queen of the Fleet (Br), Hilton, Cork.

1862 The Belfast News-Letter Mon. 13 Jan
Queenstown: Arrived: Jan. 11: Queen of the Fleet, from New York.
Feb. 6
Queenstown: Sailed: Feb. 5: Queen of the Fleet, New York.

1862 New York Herald Thurs. 20 Mar. p.8
New York: Arrived: Mar. 19: Bark Queen of the Fleet (Br. of Yarmouth, N.S.), Hilton, Cork, Feb 10, in ballast, to Edmiston Bros. Feb. 21 lat 41 33 lon 39 04, spoke Br ship Robert Treat, from Newry to New York; and took from her [i.e. Robert Treat] two mates and five men of the Br. bark Wolf, of Pictou, N.S, Capt. Munro, from Cardiff for Halifax, with a cargo of coal; she had sprung a leak during the gales of 18th and 21 of Feb, and when she was abandoned she had seven feet of water in her hold; had lost her rudder, and masts sprung. Capt. Munro and the remainder of the crew were on board [Robert Treat].

1862 New York Herald 9 May p.8
New York: Cleared: May 8: Bark Queen of the Fleet (Br) Hilton, Glasgow (sic).

1862 The Belfast News-Letter Thurs. 29 May
Londonderry: Arrived: May 23: Queen of the Fleet, Hilton, from New York.
June 17
Londonderry: Sailed: June 12: Queen of the Fleet, New York.

1862 New-York Daily Tribune Wed. 23 July p.2
New York: Arrived: July 22: Bark Queen of the Fleet (Br. of Yarmouth N.S.,) Hilton, Londonderry 37 days, in ballast.

1862 New-York Daily Tribune Fri. 7 Nov. p.7
New York: Arrived: Nov. 6: Bark Queen of the Fleet, Hilton, Glasgow 35 days, ballast.
Dec. 22 p.2
New York: Sailed: Dec. 21: Bark Queen of the Fleet (Br), Hilton, for Glasgow.

1863 The Daily News (London) 20 Jan. p.7
Arrived: Greenock: Jan. 17: Queen of the Fleet, from New York.

1863 The New-York Times Wed. 15 Apr.
New York: Arrived: Apr. 14: Bark Queen of the Fleet (Br. of Yarmouth N.S.,) Hilton, Glasgow 44ds. with pig iron to E. Bros. Had strong westerly gales to the Bank. March 27, a seaman named Laughlin McLunis, fell from the foreyard overboard and was drowned. March 29, lat. 43 50 long. 45 3(?) saw six large icebergs, 1st inst., John Jeffrey, a seaman, fell from the maintop to the deck, and broke his leg.
[Survey: New York in April]

1863 New York Herald Fri. 22 May p.8
New York: Cleared: May 21: Bark Queen of the Fleet (BR), Hilton, Glasgow.

1863 The Glasgow Daily Herald Wed. 24 June p.5
Greenock: Arrived: June 23: Queen of the Fleet, New York.
July 1 p.8
[Advert] Regular Trader: At Glasgow, for New York--The British Clipper Barque "Queen of the Fleet", 595 tons register, Captain Hilton, dead weight engaged, will have immediate despatch. For freight, apply to Inglis & Bow. 13 John Street.
July 13 p.7
Greenock: Sailed: July 11: Queen of the Fleet, Hilton, for New York.

1863 The New-York Times Sat. 22 Aug.
New-York: Below: Aug. 21: Bark Queen of the Fleet, Hilton, Clyde July 11.
23 Aug. 23
New-York: Arrived: Aug 22: Bark Queen of the Fleet (Br. of Yarmouth N.S.,) Hilton, Glasgow 35 ds. with pig iron to Edmiston Bros.

1863 New-York Daily Tribune Sept. 3
New-York: Cleared: Sept. 2: Bark Queen of the Fleet (Br.), Hilton, Quebec.

1864 The Glasgow Daily Herald Mon. 21 Mar. p.6
The barque Queen of the Fleet, Hilton, from Cardiff for New York, with railroad iron, put into Halifax, N.S., on the 5th March, leaking badly; she must discharge part of cargo.

1864 The New-York Times Fri. 25 Mar.
New-York: Arrived: Mar. 24: Bark Q of the F (Br. of Yarmouth N.S.,) Hilton, Cardiff Jan. 3, via Halifax 6 ds., (where she put in, in distress) with railroad iron to Edmiston Bros.
Apr. 30
New-York: Cleared: Apr. 29: Queen of the Fleet (Br.,) Hilton, for Quebec.
May 6
New-York: Sailed: May 4: Queen of the Fleet. [Survey: New York in April]

1864 The Glasgow Daily Herald Fri. 24 June p.7
Quebec: Loading: June: Queen of the Fleet for Warrenpoint.

1864 The Belfast News-Letter Thurs. Morning 4 Aug.
Auction: at our Wood Yards, Merchant's Quay, Newry, the Cargo now landing ex "Queen of the Fleet" from Quebec.
365 logs White Pine, 250 logs Red Pine, 5 logs Oak: 500 Pieces of Pine Deals, 12 feet, breadths 9 to 20x3 inches: 2500 Pieces Bright Spruce Deals 12x9x3 assorted 1st, 2nd, 3rds: 940 Pieces Deals assorted lengths and breadths x3 inch, principally 1sts: 5592 Pieces Staves, viz:--792 Large Pipes 2,400 Hogheads, 2,400 Barrel Staves, 9 Cords 4-feet Red Pine Lathwood. Newry, 1st August 1864.

1864 The New-York Times Sun. Nov. 6
Boston: Nov. 5: Arrived: Queen of the Fleet, Cardiff. [Survey: Boston in December]

1864 The Liverpool Mercury Mon. 14 Nov. p.3
Spoken: Queen of the Fleet, from Cardiff for Boston, Oct. 10, 47 N 40 W.

[**MNL** 1870: Queen of the Fleet of Yarmouth, N.S.: Owner: Aaron Goudey, Yarmouth, N.S.]

1865 The Glasgow Daily Herald Wed. 1 Feb. p.7
At Baltimore: Jan. 10; Queen of the Fleet, Hilton, from Bremen.

1865 The Belfast News-Letter Mon. 6 Feb.
Baltimore: Sailed: Jan. 31: Queen of the Fleet, Hilton, for Bremen.

1865 The Glasgow Daily Herald Sat. 4 Mar. 7.p
Bremen: Feb. 28: The Queen of the Fleet, Hilton, from Baltimore, which arrived here to-day, was aground, but came off with the assistance of a steamer.

1865 The New-York Times Wed. 6 July
Spoken: Queen of the Fleet: bark, Yarmouth, N.S., from Newcastle for Providence R.I. June 12, lat. 47 41, lon. 42 32.

1865 The Glasgow Daily Herald Sat. 19 Aug. p.6
Providence R.I: Cleared: Aug. 1: Queen of the Fleet, Hilton, for St. John, N.B.
Sept. 27 p.7
St. John, N.B: Cleared: Sept. 5: Queen of the Fleet, Hilton, Londonderry.
Oct. 11 p.7
Londonderry: Arrived: Oct. 7: Queen of the Fleet, Hilton, from St. John, N.B.
Nov. 1 p.7
[Advert] For Providence, R.I. The British Clipper Barque "Queen of the Fleet" 595 tons register, Captain Hilton, will sail end of this week. For Light Freight only, apply to Inglis & Bow. 13 John Street.

1865 New York Herald Sat. 2 Dec. --with supplement-- p.3
Ardrossan: Sailed: Nov. 11: bark Queen of the Fleet (Br), Hilton, Providence.

1865 The Glasgow Daily Herald Wed. 29 Nov. p.7
Lamlash, Nov. 27—The Queen of the Fleet, Hilton, from Ardrossan for Providence, U.S., put back here on the 26th inst. from the Tuskar, after being 9 days out, with sails split and cargo shifted, having experienced very heavy weather.
Dec. 13 p.7
Lamlash: Sailed: Dec. 10: Queen of the Fleet, Hilton, from Ardrossan for Providence, U.S.
1866 Jan. 27 p.7
Black Island, Jan. 2.—Off—A barque, supposed to be the Queen of the Fleet, Hilton, from Ardrossan for Providence, standing in for Newport.
Jan. 30 p.4
At Terceira: Jan. 16: Queen of the Fleet, Hilton, from the Clyde and left for Rhode Island.

1866 New York Herald Thurs. 1 Mar. with Supplement p.8
Providence: Below: Feb. 27: bark Queen of the Fleet (Br), Hilton, from Ardrossan via Terceira.
Mar. 3 with Supplement p.2
Providence: Arrived: Mar. 1: bark Queen of the Fleet (Br), Hilton, Ardrossan.

1866 Halifax Citizen Tues. 6 Mar.
Bark Queen of the Fleet, of Yarmouth, Hilton, from Ardrossan, below Providence, experienced very heavy gales of wind and severe weather during the passage, was struck by a heavy sea, which stove bulwarks, started stem; carried away head rails, shifted cargo and sprung a leak in the stem, was obliged to throw overboard about 50 tons of iron to lighten ship forward.

1866 The Liverpool Mercury Fri. 16 Mar. p.3
At Providence: Queen of the Fleet, from Ardrossan, in distress.

1866 The New-York Times Thurs. 22 Mar.
The Revenue Service: The Revenue Steamer Miami again at Work: The active revenue cutter "Miami", Capt, Daniel D Tompkins, has again rendered valuable service to private property as well as to the Government, having in one day rescued two vessels from a

very perilous position besides effecting a valuable and important seizure of a brig engaged in smuggling large quantities of cigars, tobacco, linen, &c., from Cuba to Boston. The facts are as follows: On Saturday last, while the Miami was proceeding to sea from Newport, a bark and brig were discovered by her, ashore on the rocks at "Castle Hill", and signals of distress flying. The "Miami" immediately proceeded to their assistance and found that on beating out of the harbour they came in contact with each other, and both drifted on the rocks. They proved to be the British bark "Queen of the Fleet", of Yarmouth, from Providence to St. John, N.B., in ballast, and the British brig "Crocus", of and for St. John, N.B., from Newport, in ballast. The brig had her foretopmast and all her head sails carried away, while the bark had lost her headstays and backropes. Hawsers were run out from the "Miami" to the "Queen of the Fleet", and after losing one she succeeded in getting her afloat, but found her so much disabled that she was compelled to tow her back to Newport at once. The "Miami" returned to Castle Hill as quickly as possible, and, after a great deal of difficulty, succeeded in getting the "Crocus" clear also, and, as she was not greatly damaged, she proceeded on her voyage.

Had the "Miami" not been near at the time, both vessels would have been "bilged" and probably gone to pieces, as before the rescue of the bark was effected a strong gale had sprung up from W.N.W. Any one familiar with the place on which the vessels drifted will be able to form an idea of the perilous in which they were placed.

After casting off from the brig the "Miami" steered S. and W., and when near Point Judith saw a brig standing N.E. She ran toward her and found her to be the brig "Redmond", from Cuba, Boyle, master, bound to Boston via Newport, with a cargo of molasses. From her suspicious movements Capt. Tompkins, of the "Miami", thought there was something in the wind, and determined to board her, but as it was blowing too hard to lower a boat he desired the captain of the "Redmond" to run into Newport, which was done. On examining the brig large quantities of cigars, tobacco, sugar and linen were found on board. No such articles being entered on the manifest, possession was at once taken of her and the case reported to the Collector of Customs at Newport. This contraband trade is extensively carried on by vessels sailing between the West Indies and the United States, but could easily be broken up by a few active revenue steamers like the "Miami", which has made several seizures during the past Winter and saved quite a number of vessels from destruction.

1866 The Glasgow Daily Herald Tues. 29 May p.7
In Mumbles Roads: May 25: Queen of the Fleet, Holdin (sic), from St. John, N.B.

1866 The Glasgow Daily Herald Thurs. 25 Oct.
Newcastle, Miramichi: Cleared: Sept. 24: Queen of the Fleet, Hilton, for Cork.

1866 The Liverpool Mercury Thurs. 1 Nov. p.3
Queenstown: Arrived: Oct. 31: Queen of the Fleet from Miramichi.
Nov. 3 p.8
Queenstown: Sailed: Nov. 2: Queen of the Fleet, for Dublin.

1866 The Freeman's Journal Fri. 23 Nov.
Charge Against a Sea Captain.
A court of inquiry, consisting of Mr. J. W. O'Donnell, Metropolitan Police Magistrate (who presided) and some members of the local Marine Board, sat on Wednesday and yesterday at the Custom-house, for the purpose of investing, under the Merchant Shipping Act, certain charges of misconduct made by the crew of the ship Queen of the Fleet against Captain Hilton, who is in command of her. Mr. Richardson Admiralty

Proctor, appeared for the complainants, and Mr. Hamerton, Queen's Proctor, appeared for Captain Hilton. On Wednesday last several of the crew were examined in support of the complainant. At the sitting of the Court yesterday the following evidence was given in corroboration:--

William Gorman examined by Mr. Richardson. He deposed as follows—I signed articles as an ordinary seaman of the Queen of the Fleet; remembered her being at Newcastle in September last; recollected the Monday on which she had all her cargo on board; all the men belonging to the vessel were there on that day, but the men were missing on the Tuesday morning; these were John Duggan, James Ryan, and James Craig; the carpenter sent me ashore to look for them; I went on shore in the ship's boat; I found the men together in a public-house in Newcastle; they were drinking.

The magistrate said he did not think this was evidence.

Mr. Hamerton, the Queen's Proctor, said he wanted to show that this was a most mutinous crew, and that the men who had left the vessel were taken up as deserters.

Examination resumed—The four of us then went down to the shore and returned to the ship with a strange man who came from her with the captain.

Mr. Richardson said he wished to examine the witness as to a threat made by the captain to shoot him.

Witness, in reply to Mr. Richardson, said that when the vessel was coming from Queenstown to Dublin on one occasion he went down to the cabin to see what time it was; the captain was not there, but in a quarter of an hour after, when the witness was on the look out, the captain that if he ever got witness down there again he would not bring his life out of it; the captain called witness a "bloody hound," and said that he went down there to rob something; it was necessary that he should go down to see the time, because they had no mate to keep time for them; he was often kept four hours at the wheel; witness was only about one minute in the cabin.

To the Queen's Proctor.—There was no strange man with the four of us on shore when we went on board. *After some further evidence the witness admitted that from the 25th of August to the 7th of October, when the ship was on the broad ocean, the captain never threatened him, not did he hear the captain threaten any other person on board.*

A man named Peter Donnelly deposed that on one occasion, when the wheel got foul, the captain shoved him from it and told him he would blow his (witness's) brains out if he did not go off the poop; the captain had a revolver in his hand at the time; on another occasion, when the captain was reading the log in the cabin, and when witness and some of the other men were present, witness asked to be allowed to make some remarks; the captain stood up and taking a revolver, which was on the table, said the first man who would say a word he should blow his brains out; the captain presented the revolver at witness; witness could not tell whether the revolver was loaded at the time.

John Duggan, one of the seamen, said that he recollected when the captain was reading the log in the cabin he had a revolver in his hand, and said that he would shoot Donnelly if he (Donnelly) would insult him in his cabin; Donnelly did not insult him, he said nothing but what was proper; their names were in the log-book.

This closed the evidence on the part of the complaints.

The Queen's Proctor said he would now produce his witnesses, and he would first produce the captain.

Mr. O'Donnell said that he could not hear the captain an oath, he could only hear his statement.

The Queen's Proctor said that unless this was a criminal prosecution against the captain, he thought the captain was entitled to give evidence on oath.

The Magistrate said that this was simply an investigation for the Board of Trade.

The Queen's Proctor said that he wished to make a statement previous to calling his witnesses. He appeared there for Mr. Hilton master of the ship Queen of the Fleet, a vessel the charge of which, from her nature and size, would only be entrusted to an experienced seaman. Amongst the witnesses whom he should produce would be the mate and the captain's wife.

The Magistrate said he could not take the evidence of the captain's wife no more than he could that of the captain.

Mr. Hamerton—You can take the evidence of the nurse?

Mr. O'Donnell—Yes.

Mr. Hamilton then said that he would call witnesses to prove the desertion of the first and second mate, and that the complainants had all arranged amongst themselves to desert the vessel. Gorman's story that he was sent after the other men was a pure fabrication, as he was one of the first to run. The evidence for the defence would show that the complainants were a most mutinous crew, and that some of them had threatened to take the captain's life. The captain never put any of them in irons, and never committed an act of tyranny towards them.

Mr. O'Donnell—Am I to understand that you mean to deny these acts about the pistol, or that you intend to justify them?

Mr. Hamerton—We deny them, and say that it is a gross fabrication. *Mr. Hamerton then said that he would give the log book in evidence which recorded the misconduct of the crew.*

Mr. Richardson objected to the book being received as evidence, on the grounds that it was not properly kept.

Mr. Abraham D. Craig, the mate of the vessel and brother-in-law to Captain Hilton was then examined, and his evidence went to contradict the charges brought by the crew against the captain. He never heard the captain threatening to shoot any of the crew, and the captain's manner towards them was always kind and friendly.

After the evidence of this witness had concluded this inquiry was adjourned to twelve o'clock this day.

Nov. 24

A man named Emsley, cook and steward on board the Queen of the Fleet, said he remembered the captain being in the galley when a man named Roche went aloft to furl the main royal after it was clewed up; the captain had no revolver in his hand then; he had a pipe and was smoking; did not hear the captain threaten violence; he told Roche to furl the sail as quick as he could and not let it blow away, and that if he could not furl it to come down and some one else would go up; never heard the captain threaten Roche with a pistol or bullets; if he had so threatened him witness must have heard him being three times nearer him than Roche; remember a flag of distress being hoisted by the captain; it was the ensign union down; did not know what it was for; remember the watches being called down to the cabin to read the log read, was in the cabin at the time; remembers Duggan and Donnelly remaining to hear a portion of the log after the men had left; was then in the pantry off the cabin, and the door was open; saw a pistol on the table; did not see the captain take the pistol off; if he had taken the pistol off the table and moved witness must have seen him do so; the captain told them be silent until he had done reading the log, and then say what they liked, and he would note it down; did not hear him use a threat while he was in the vessel; saw the captain laughing, and heard him say, "Go to your work like men and you will be treated as men" or something like that; did not hear the captain threaten to shoot a man while on board, and during the voyage across never saw the captain with a pistol in his hand on deck; heard a musket fired once or twice in the afternoon of one day; one of those discharges was in the Bay of Dublin; when the vessel first left Miramichi, witness slept in a room off the galley, and was afterwards removed aft to the captain's own cabin; so far as witness could observe, he saw no cruel treatment of the men; the men were supplied with corn bread in addition to the legal allowance, and when they began to complain of not getting more the corn bread was stopped; the flour was the same in quality as that used in the cabin.

Cross-examined by Mr. Richardson—Might have been below when the musket shots were fired; there was a great number of people knocking about at the landing-place at Newcastle.

Re-examined—On the morning of the day the men went ashore William Gorman got coffey (sic) shortly after five o'clock; he then left in a flat-bottomed boat that did not belong to the ship.

Eliza Anne Crooke, the stewardess, deposed that she knew a constable named Dalton, who lived at Newcastle Miramichi; from where the ship lay she could see the shore clearly and the houses on the day the men went ashore; knows Donnelly; saw him coming to the beach; the captain, Johnston, and Dalton were with him; the two latter were constables; saw Donnelly come off in the boat; was in the cabin when the captain read the log to the crew; saw a pistol lying on the table; the captain brought it there; never saw it there before, but saw it in the captain's drawer; when Donnelly and Duggan were in the cabin with the captain, after the last of the crew went up, they were interrupting the captain when he was reading the log; The captain told them to be silent until he was done reading and they had to say and he would write to down; when he had finished Donnelly said something which witness did not recollect and Duggan began to scold the mate, Craig, and to make a disturbance in the cabin; the captain told him to hold his tongue as he wanted to have order and discipline on board the ship; that he had not had it during the voyage and he would have it coming to land or he would make an example of some of them, and that the law would uphold him; the captain told them to go to work like men and he would treat them as such; the pistol was on the table all the time; did not see any person in the cabin take hold of the pistol, witness added "upon my solemn oath"; the captain did not take hold of the pistol on that occasion; he did not speak of shooting and never heard shooting mentioned then or at any other time.

Mr. Richardson—Are you going to be married to Craig?

The witness declined to answer the question.

Mr. Hamerton tendered the captain for examination, and the court declined to receive the evidence. He the proctor) then left the case without any comments to the court.

Mr. Richardson addressed the court for the complainants, and directed attention to the points of the captain's own case to show that his conduct, if truly related, was inconsistent with mutinous conduct in the crew. He conceded that the behaviour of the men was irreconsitable (sic) with the idea of desertion.

The court was cleared for consideration, and after the lapse of half an hour the court was opened.

Mr. O'Donnell expressed the opinion of the court. He said there was no evidence of there being danger to the ship on account of the desertion of the mates; yet it would have been more prudent for the captain to have procured mates before crossing the ocean. The board was unanimously of opinion that the captain was not guilty of threatening the crew with a pistol, or of cruelty with regard to the supply of provisions and water. Language may have occasionally been used by the captain in his unprotected state which, under other circumstances, would not have been justifiable; and the court hoped mates would be shipped, and that the crew would go on board and return amicably. As there might have been faults on both sides, the board would give no costs.

Mr. Hamerton said mates had been shipped.

Nov. 26

50

Police Court: (Before Mr. O'Donnell). Ship Desertion—
Patrick Roach was charged with having absconded from the ship Queen of the Fleet,
having signed the ship's articles, and with having been found on board a steamer about
to proceed to Liverpool on Friday night. The prisoner was discharged.

1867 The Glasgow Daily Herald Sat. 9 Mar. p.7
New York, Feb. 22.—The barque Queen of the Fleet, from Ardrossan, was ashore on
the Lower Middle, below Boston, yesterday, and would have to discharge part of her
cargo to get off. 23d.—The Queen of the Fleet, which was ashore below Boston, 21st
Feb. got off the same night at high water, and anchored in President Roads, without any
apparent damage.

1867 The Freeman's Journal (Dublin) Fri. 10 May p.4
Dublin: Arrivals: May 8: Queen of the Fleet, St. John's, deals.
May 13 p.6
Timber—Imported per Queen of the Fleet, from St. John's, N.B., 17,244 deals.

1867 The Belfast News-Letter Tues. 3 Dec.
Newry Extensive Sale of Wood Good: Per Barque "Queen of the Fleet" from St. John,
N.B: 22,492 Pieces Bright Spruce Deals as landed 9 to 26 feet 7, 9 and 11 x3: 1,339
Pieces Bright Spruce Ends: 7,000 Pieces Palings.

1867 The Glasgow Daily Herald Mon. 30 Dec. p.8
[Notice] For Boston, U.S.—The well-known Clipper Barque "Queen of the Fleet" 595 tons
register, having all her Deadweight engaged will have rapid despatch—For freight &c.
apply to M'Isaac & Murray. 11 Union Street.
1868 Feb. 21
Lamlash: Sailed: Feb. 19: Queen of the Fleet, Scott, Ardrossan for Boston.
Mar. 9 p.6
Lamlash: lying here: Mar. 6: Queen of the Fleet, from Glasgow for Boston.
Mar. 20 p.6
Lamlash: Sailed: Mar. 18: Queen of the Fleet, Scott, from Ardrossan for Boston.
Mar. 23 p.6
Lamlash: put in: Mar. 18: Queen of the Fleet, Scott, Ardrossan for Boston.
Mar. 24 p.2
Lamlash: Sailed: Mar. 22: Queen of the Fleet, Scott, Ardrossan for Boston.
June 13 p.7
Boston: off: May 29: Queen of the Fleet, Scott, from Ardrossan.
[Survey: Boston in August]

1868 The Freeman's Journal (Dublin) Wed. 9 Dec.
Belfast: Arrived: Dec. 9: Queen of the Fleet, from Miramichi.

1869 The Belfast News-Letter Wed. 20 Jan.
Belfast Police Court—Yesterday.
Summons for a Seaman's Wages.
    John Browning, a seaman, summoned Captain Whitmore for £10, wages alleged
to be due him.
    John Browning deposed he sailed as second mate on board a British North
American barque of which the defendant was captain. On the last voyage they
discharged at Belfast, and a sum of £14 was due to him for his services as seaman
since he shipped at St. John's. But of that he received £3, which with stoppages, left a
balance of £10 12s 6d.

Cross-examined by Mr. M'Lean—I signed my release at the Custom House before I was arrested in Newry.

After you were taken into custody did not the captain pay over to Mr. Guy, in Newry, £9, to indemnify him as one of your securities? I don't know.

Mr. Harper—What have we to do with that? The captain owes the money to the man, and he is responsible to him for it.

Mr. M'Lean said the money was handed over to Guy & Co., at the request of the prisoner.

Captain Whitmore deposed that he gave the complainant £4 in Belfast, which, with £9 he handed over to Mr. Guy for the benefit of Browning, and £1 expenses to Newry, amounted to £14—the full amount.

A receipt was handed in from Mr. Guy, acknowledging the £9. The defendant agreed to endorse this acknowledgement, with a request that the money would be paid back to the complainant; and with this understanding the summons was withdrawn.
Jan. 22

Charge of Manslaughter on the High Seas.

At the Newry Petty Session.--John Brownrigg, mate of the Queen of the Fleet, was brought up to custody of Constable Clingen, of the Belfast detective force, charged with manslaughter of a young man, named John Doyle on the passage home from St. John's to Newry. The prisoner, it will be remembered, ordered the deceased to do duty aloft, notwithstanding that he knew the deceased was not an experienced seaman. The boy fell from one of the yards, and was killed. The accused was arrested on his arrival in Newry, and bound over to take his trial at Down Assizes. The other day Captain Wetmore [J.K. Wetmore?] swore an information that he had reason to suspect the prisoner would not come forward for trial, the warrant was issued by the local magistrate for his immediate arrest. Constable Clingen accordingly arrested the man in Belfast, and brought him before the Court this morning. Mr. Browne, for the defendant, said the young man had not the slightest intention of leaving the country, and actually came home to stand trial. The man could not find bail, and he would have to go to jail till the holding of the Assizes. He was at present in bad health, and as he would likely get into hospital, it might just as well for him to go to jail. The man was then committed to Down Jail on the charge of manslaughter.—Newry Telegraph.
Feb. 11

Belfast: Sailed: Feb. 10: Queen of the Fleet, Whitmore, for Glasgow, in tow of the steam-tug Flying Mist.
Feb. 23

Auction: At Prince's Dock: the Cargo ex "Queen of the Fleet" from Miramichi: 5,880 Pine Deals and Battens: 12,240 Spruce all 7,9,11 x3. 10 to 24 feet long: 844 Pine Deals Ends.
Mar. 1

County of Down list of cases for Trial: John Brownrigg for feloniously causing the death of John Doyle on the high seas, on board of the barque Queen of the Fleet, on or about the 10th July, 1868.

1869 The Glasgow Daily Herald Fri. 12 Feb. p.6
Tail of the Bank: Arrived: Feb. 11: Queen of the Fleet, Whitmore, Belfast to Glasgow.
Mar. 10 p.6
Tail of the Bank: Sailed: Mar. 9: Queen of the Fleet, Wetmore, Glasgow, to Boston.
Apr. 29 p.6
Spoken: Queen of the Fleet (barque), from Glasgow to Boston, March 21: 45 N 42 W.

1869 The Glasgow Daily Herald Sat. 25 July p.7

Tail of the Bank: Arrived: July 23: Queen of the Fleet, M'Leod from St. John, N.B., for orders.

Aug. 12 p.7

Tail of the Bank: Sailed: Aug. 11: Queen of the Fleet, M'Leod, from Glasgow for St. Johns, N.B.

1869 New York Herald Thurs. 30 Sept. Triple Sheet p.10

Spoken: Bark Queen of the Fleet (Br), from Glasgow for Philadelphia Sept. 26 lat 40 31 lon 69 10 (by pilot boat Chas H Marshall, No 3).

[Survey: Philadelphia in October]

1869 Morning Chronicle (Halifax) Tues. 21 Dec. p.3

Dungeness: Off: Dec. 3: barque Queen of the Fleet, McLeod, from Philadelphia for Rotterdam.

1870 The New-York Times Fri. 11 Mar.

New-York: Arrived: Mar. 10: Bark Queen of the Fleet, (of Yarmouth, N.S.,) McLeod, Rotterdam 29 ds with old railway iron and petroleum bbls to Boyd & Hincken. Had easterly winds to the Banks, and was 11 ds from thence with N. gales.

Apr. 21

New-York: Sailed: Apr. 20: Queen of the Fleet, for Rotterdam. [Survey: New York in March]

1870 The British Colonist (Halifax) Tues. 14 June p.3

Off Dungeness: May 22: bark Queen of the Fleet, McLeod, N. York for Rotterdam.
Brouwershaven: Arrived: May 25: bark Queen of the Fleet, McLeod, N. York.

1870 New York Herald Sun. 18 Sept. Triple Sheet

Philadelphia: Arrived: Sept. 16: bark Queen of the Fleet (Br), McLeod, Rotterdam.
[Survey: Philadelphia in September]

1871 The New-York Times Sun. Apr. 30

Arrived: New-York: Apr. 29: Bark Queen of the Fleet, (of Yarmouth, N.S.,) McLeod, Hamburg 39 ds., with mdse. To Funch, Edge & Co. Came the northern passage, and had fine weather; April 16, lat 45 10, lon 49, passed a number of icebergs, and had to stand S. to clear them. [Survey: New York in May]

1871 The London Register June 17 col. 21

New York: Cleared: June 3: Queen of the Fleet: McLeod: Rotterdam.

1871 New York Herald Tues. 3 Oct. Quadruple Sheet p.12

New York: below: Oct. 2: Bark Queen of the Fleet (Br), McLeod, from Rotterdam Aug 9.

Oct. 6

New York: Arrived: Oct. 5: Bark Queen of the Fleet, (Br), McLeod, Rotterdam 56 days, with old iron and empty barrels to Boyd & Hincken. Had strong westerly gales up to Cape Race; thence 20 days, with light moderate weather. [Survey: New York in October]

1871 New-York Daily Tribune Sat. 7 Oct. p.3

Freights: British bark Queen of the Fleet, 4,000 bbls. Refined Petroleum, same voyage and rate.

1871 The World: New York Tues. 24 Oct. p.8

New York: Cleared: Oct. 19: bark Queen of the fleet (Br.), McLeod, Amsterdam.

1871 The British Colonist (Halifax) Thurs. 28 Dec. p.3
Off the Lizzard (sic): Dec. 4: Queen of the Fleet, McLeod, from New York for Amsterdam.

1872 The Freeman's Journal Fri. 16 Feb.
Dublin: Arrived: Feb. 14: Queen of the Fleet, Amsterdam.

1872 The Glasgow Daily Herald Fri. 15 Mar. p.8
[notice] *At Ardrossan, for St. John, N.B. To Sail Early in March—The favourably known Barque "Queen of the Fleet" 595 tons register, classed A 2 America's Lloyd's, Coppered in 1870. This Vessel is open to a limited quantity of Cargo for St. John N.B. Apply to Francis Carvill & Son. 3 Water Street, Liverpool.*
Mar. 16 p.6
Ardrossan: Arrived: Mar. 14: Queen of the Fleet from Dublin.
Apr. 10 p.7
Ardrossan: Sailed: April 9: Queen of the Fleet, St. John, N.B.

1872 Lloyd's List June 11 col. 13
St. John, N.B: Arrived: May 24: Queen of the Fleet, Holmes, Ardrossan.
[Survey: St. John in July]

1872 The North Wales Chronicle (Bangor) Sat. 17 Aug. p.5
Carnarvon: On Wednesday, the 14th August, at five p.m., the tide at the time being high water, the weather hazy and the wind from the N.E., light, the barque Queen of the Fleet, of Yarmouth, Nova Scotia, from St John's, N.B., to Carnarvon, with timber, grounded on Carnarvon Bar whilst being towed in; part of the deck load was discharged, and the vessel towed off at 5.30 this morning and is expected to arrive at Carnarvon evening in safety.
Oct. 5 p.4
On Thursday last: barque Queen of the Fleet, (Dublin), after having completed her discharge of timber at Carnarvon, was taken in tow from the latter port by the steam-tug Warrior, of Liverpool at 3.30 p.m. Whilst attempting to get through the Penmon Sound, where a very high sea was running at the time, the tow rope snapped and the vessel was driven on Puffin Sound at 4.30 p.m. Three of the crew swam to the island, and the remainder were taken on board the tug by means of a boat. The barque remained on the rocks until the tide flooded, when the Penmon pilots, arrived by some fishermen, got her off, and she towed back to Beaumaris yesterday (Friday) by the Warrior, and left under Beaumaris Bank, where she will have to remain for the present. We were unable to ascertain the extent of the damage, which is, however, very considerable.

1872 The Times (London) Mon. 7 Oct. p.12
Mr. W. Preston reports under date Penmon, Anglesey, October 4, that during a fresh wind on Thursday afternoon the bark, Queen of the Fleet, bound from Caernarvon for Liverpool, in ballast, drove on Puffin Island, and exhibited a signal of distress. The Christopher Brown lifeboat, belonging to the National Institution, went out to the vessel and took from the island the master, two women, and three of the nine men forming the crew, who, at their request, were put on board the steamer Warrior.

1872 The Leeds Mercury Tues. 15 Oct. p.4
Liverpool: Arrived: Oct. 13: Queen of the Fleet, Holmes, Caernarvon.

1872 The Morning Post (London) Thurs. 24 Oct. p.3
A Brave Life-Boat Man.

A correspondent of the North British Daily Mail *furnishes the following barque Queen of the Fleet, which was driven upon a ledge of rocks a few days ago, near Beaumaris, during a heavy gale, while being towed from Carnarvon to Liverpool:--* "The crew consisted of Captain Holmes, his son, and eight men, the captain's wife and daughter being also on board. Signals of distress were made as soon as possible, and were seen from the Penman (sic) life-boat station. At the critical juncture – the vessel seeming to open with every blow, and the sea, which was making a clean breach over her, threatening to sweep every soul out of her – one of the crew, named James Moore, a Liverpool boatman, and also one of the crew of the tubular life-boat, gallantly came forward and volunteered to swim to the island with a rope, to effect a means by which the rest could be landed. At least 100 yards lay between the vessel and where Moore could effect a landing, the sea breaking all along the island most terrifically, but, nothing daunted, Moore, having divested himself of part of his clothing, and the deep sea leadline fastened round his body, heroically plunged into the angry sea. For a time he was entirely obscured, and when first seen was half way to the island, struggling forward most bravely at one moment, and the next moment almost carried back to the vessel. Still he struggled on to accomplish his praiseworthy aim, and at length he successfully reached the shore, having been dashed against some of the points of the rocks and sustained severe injuries to several parts of his body. After recovering himself a little, three others of the crew were in turn hauled through the surf by Moore, and an attempt was made to haul a fourth one, but the line got entangled with the rocks, and it was with much difficulty the poor fellow was hauled back to vessel in an exhausted state. It was now resolved, as those already landed had been more or less injured by the rocks, not to attempt the same means again, but as the tug steamer Warrior lay at the lee side of the island, and Captain Green, with some of his crew, had landed, with the assistance of the four men already saved the steamer's punt was carried round the island, and by means of the rope attached to the vessel the boat was launched through the surf, and, after being hauled backwards and forwards several times, the rest of the crew, with the two females, were safely landed on the island. The courage of Moore cannot be too highly commended. He has on four occasions rescued lives on the Mersey at the risk of his own, and his also been instrumental in saving lives by means of his boat, in each case having appeared before the Liverpool Shipwreck and Humane Society and received rewards in recognition of his gallant services."

[Survey: Liverpool in November]

++++++++++ **Hine Brothers managing owners**
Liverpool Register: Registered in Liverpool 201/1872:
George Clarke, of 72 Queen's Street of the city of Dublin, Merchant 64/64. date 16th Dec. 1872

Master: Liverpool 17.12.72: Wilson Holmes C. 42494

[**Fl Corr**. In Hine Brothers' accounts sent to The Owners of Barque "Queen of the Fleet". 1st & 2nd Voyages [unknown destinations]. 3rd Voyage was from Liverpool to Quebec & back to Grangemouth [Scotland]. 4th Voyage, Grangemouth to Genoa [Italy] thence to Miramichi [N.B. Canada] & back to Maryport. Damages in North Sea in Winter of 1874 when she was put back first the Tyne & afterwards to Grimsby. [The] last incompleted Voyage .... Damages in consequence of which vessel put back to Barrow.
Maryport 18th April 1876 [signed] Hine Brothers.]

[Voyage 1]

1872 The Glasgow Herald Tues. Dec. 24 p.6

Liverpool: Sailed: Dec. 23: Queen of the Fleet, New York.

1873 The New-York Times Fri. 28 Mar.
New-York: Arrived: Mar. 27: Bark Queen of the Fleet (of Liverpool,) Holmes, Liverpool, 63 days, with mdse, to Russell, Howes & Co.
May 2
New-York: Cleared: May 1: Queen of the West (sic), (Br.,) Holmes, Liverpool, Russell, Howes & Co.

1873 Adair's Maryport Advertiser Fri. 13 June p.8
Liverpool: Arrived: June 10: Queen of the Fleet, Holmes, from New York.
[Voyage 2]
July 11 p.8
Liverpool: Sailed: July 7: Queen of the Fleet, Holmes, for Quebec.
Aug. 15 p.8
Spoken: July 31: Queen of the Fleet, Holmes, Lat. 46N Long. 40W.
Sept. 12 p.8
Quebec: Arrived: Aug. 23: Queen of the Fleet, Holmes, from Liverpool.
Oct. 3 p.8
Quebec: Sailed: Sept. 19: Queen of the Fleet, Holmes, for Liverpool.
Oct. 17 p.8
Queen of the Fleet, Holmes, off S.W. coast off Pentacosti on Sept. 27.

1873 The Liverpool Mercury Thurs. 30 Oct. p.3
Liverpool: Arrived: Oct 29: Queen of the Fleet, Quebec. [Survey: Liverpool in November]
[Voyage 3]
Nov. 27 p.3
Liverpool: Sailed: Nov. 25: Queen of the Fleet, Doboy. [Darien: Georgia U.S.A]

1873 Adair's Maryport Advertiser Fri. Dec. 5 p.8
Liverpool: Left: Dec. 2: Queen of the Fleet, Holmes, for Doboy. [Why the two sailings?]
1874 Feb. 6 p.8
Doboy: Arrived: Queen of the Fleet, Holmes, from Liverpool. – By telegram.
Mar. 27 p.8
Doboy: Left: Feb. 27: Queen of the Fleet, Holmes, for Liverpool.

1874 The Liverpool Mercury Mon. Apr. 13 p.3
Liverpool: Arrived: Apr. 10: Queen of the Forest (sic) [Fleet ?], *Darien.*

1874 New York Herald Tues. 14 Apr. --quadruple sheet-- p.12
Telegram to New York Herald: London April 13, 1874: Bark Queen of the Fleet (Br), Holmes, from Darien, arrived at Liverpool to-day with loss of spanker and boats washed away, having experienced a heavy gale on March 10. She has a list to port and has been making water. Arrived at Liverpool 13th (sic).

1874 The Western Mail (Cardiff) Wed. 15 Apr. p.7
Liverpool: The Queen of the Fleet, from Doboy, encountered a gale March 10, when she shipped a heavy sea, which carried away cabin skylight, and lost mainsail, maintopsail, and maintopsailyard. The vessel has a slight list, and makes water through bow port.
[Survey: Liverpool in May]

1874 Adair's Maryport Advertiser Fri. 31 July. p.8
Queen of the Fleet, Holmes, bound up St. Lawrence, off Camanraska on the 20th.
Aug. 1 p.8
Grangemouth: Sailed: July 22: Queen of the Fleet, Holmes.
Sept. 4 p.8

Off Wick: Aug. 31: Queen of the Fleet, Holmes.

1874 The Glasgow Herald Sat. 12 Sept. p.6
Grangemouth: Arrived: Sept. 11: Queen of the Fleet, Quebec.
Sept. 24 p.6
Grangemouth: Arrived: Sept 23: Queen of the Fleet, Quebec.
[Voyage 4]
Oct. 28 p.6
Grangemouth: Sailed: Oct. 27: Queen of the Fleet, Genoa.

1874 The Liverpool Mercury Tues. 10 Nov. p.3
Shields: Put in: Queen of the Fleet, from Grangemouth for Genoa, leaky.

1874 Adair's Maryport Advertiser Fri. 18 Dec. supplement
Grimsby: Put into: Dec. 14: Queen of the Fleet, Holmes.

LR 1874: 38058, Queen of the Fleet, Bk, -----------, 593/569, G. Clarke, Liverpool ---------]
MNL 1875: 38058: Queen of the Fleet, Liverpool, 593, Owner, George Clark, 72 Queen Street, Dublin.

Liverpool Register: Master: Grimsby 21.1.75: James Tarney C. 94517

1875 Adair's Maryport Advertiser Fri. 5 Feb. p.8
Grimsby: Sailed: Feb. 1: Queen of the Fleet, Farney (sic), sailed for Genoa.
Feb. 12 p.8
Dover: Passed: Feb. 4 at 1 p.m.: Queen of the Fleet, Tarney, and passed Prawl Point on Feb. 6 at 4 p.m.
Mar. 12 p.8
Genoa: Arrived: Mar. 6: Queen of the Fleet, Tarney, from Grimsby.
May 28 p.8
Queen of the Fleet, Tarney, steering N.W. lat. 47 N long. 53 W.
July 16 p.8
Miramichi: Left: June 24: Queen of the Fleet, Tarney, for this port. [Maryport].
[New Brunswick, Gulf of St. Lawrence, Canada]
Aug. 6 p.8
Maryport: Arrived: Aug. 3: Queen of the Fleet, Tarney, from Miramichi.
[Voyage 5 uncompleted]
Sept. 3 p.8
Maryport: Sailed: Aug. 28: Queen of the Fleet, Tarney, sailed for Miramichi.
Sept. 17 p.8
Put into Belfast Lough: Sept. 8: Queen of the Fleet, Tarney.
Sept. 24 p.8
Barrow: Left: Sept. 22: Queen of the Fleet, Tarney, for Miramichi.
Oct. 8 p.8
Spoken: Sept. 26: Queen of the Fleet, Tarney, in lat. 55-16 N. long. 12-50 W.

1875 The Liverpool Mercury Thurs. 16 Dec. p.3
The barque Queen of the Fleet from Barrow for Miramichi, was the vessel reported on the 7th instant abandoned at sea, and not the Queen of the West.

1875 The Belfast News Thurs. 16 Dec.
Abandonment of a Barque,--Captain Smith of the ship Norma, which has arrived at Sharpness Point from Chatham, N.B., reports that on the 11th ult. he spoke the barque Enchantress, of and for St. John's, N.B., from Belfast, latitude 45, longitude 51* 40. He took from on board her the captain and five seamen of the barque Queen of the Fleet,*

which was abandoned at sea. Before parting with the Enchantress he supplied her with all the provisions he could spare.

1875 Adair's Maryport Advertiser Fri. 31 Dec. p.8
The "Queen of the Fleet." Important Board Trade Inquiry:

     Yesterday at 11 o'clock, an enquiry touching the loss of the "Queen of the Fleet" took place. The assessors sent from the Board of Trade were Messrs. Parfit and Holt. The solicitors Mr Atter, Whitehaven, appeared for the owners, and Mr. P. de E. Collin for the Board of Trade. The captain was not represented. The Justices present were Messrs. R. Ritson and H.P. Senhouse.

     Mr. P. de E. Collin said the "Queen of the Fleet" was built in 1857 at Yarmouth, Nova Scotia. She left Maryport on the 28th of August for Miramichi, and the crew had to pump her, and after nine days they insisted on putting into Belfast Lough, and she was ordered to Barrow for repairs. After undergoing repairs at Barrow she sailed on the 22nd Sept. and encountered a squall, and on the 14th Oct. there was a heavy gale, and she commenced to make water worse than ever. The crew then went to the master and persisted in putting back, as they considered her unseaworthy. They then came up to the "Enchantress," and all were taken on board. The enquiry was instituted in the interests of the public without any imputation implicating anyone.

     Mr Atter asked whether the owners stood acquitted and the charge was to be confined to the captain. The Court ruled that the whole case should be gone into.

     Joseph Kendall, carpenter on board the "Queen of the Fleet," said she was 592 tons register, and was barque rigged. She had 14 hands of a crew all told, and sailed in ballast from Maryport on the 28th August, bound for Miramichi: it was fine weather, and she was well found in everything; was in good sailing trim, had two pumps and three boats provided with the necessary equipments, and she had two anchors. The pumps were manned every watch after leaving Maryport: it took about 10 or 15 minutes to suck her. As they proceeded on the voyage the leak increased with ordinary weather. Remembered the crew going to the captain after being ten days at sea to ask him to bear up as the ship was not fit to go to the westward. The ship was then put about and they proceeded to Belfast Lough, where she was surveyed, and the surveyors recommended them to go to Barrow. They then proceeded to Barrow, where the ship was caulked in a dry dock to the top side of the beams, and several bolts were put into her, and some repairs on the deck. In witness's opinion these repairs were satisfactory, and the crew were willing then to go to sea with her. They sailed from Barrow on the 22nd Sept., the weather being fine for three or four days; a gale then came on and they lost their fore topmast head, and main top gallant mast, spanker boom and gaff; the sails were also blown away. After clearing away the wreck, the pumps were tried night and morning, and she still kept tight. The weather was still getting worse. Three weeks afterwards she broke out and made a great deal of water; the pumps were manned watch and watch, until she got very bad, and then all hands were at her. The captain, second mate, cook and steward, and witness went into the hold. She seemed all working together forward and straining very much. The plank ends forward were loose and working from an inch to an inch and a half. The listing was off the sheathing. They got oakum and the cabin carpet to try to stop the leaks, and nailed a piece of plank against them; but this did no good. They then looked over the bows, and they found the listing was gone. They put a sail over the open seams, but it was soon washed away. All this time the pumps were kept going night and day. They then tried to sail her before the wind, the canvas was taken off. It was agreed to keep at the pumps till some ship came in sight, or to go down with her. They pumped about three days and nights before a ship hove in sight. They signalled a barque, the "Enchantres (sic)," of St. John's, and eight were put on board the long boat, and afterwards the rest of the crew were put on board the "Enchantress," and the "Norma," also of St. John's, the latter vessel landed them at Gloster, and were forwarded by the Ship-wrecked Mariners' Society.

Cross-examined by Mr Atter: The pumps were new when we sailed; she was well found and well manned. Captain Melmore and Captain Palmer, surveyors of the two local Mutual Insurance Associations, were at Barrow at the time the vessel was undergoing repairs, and Mr A. Hine was at Barrow, the harbour master and the master carpenter of the Ship Building Company of Barrow were instructed to make an independent survey. Also the Board of Trade surveyor, Mr Hannah, was occasionally there. All the crew joined without any hesitation. We had stone as ballast. The captain worked his turn at the pumps, and each watch had four hours at the pumps and two hours off. The chronometer and sexton and carpenter's tools, besides all other things were lost. There was seven feet of water in the hold at the time we abandoned the ship.

Henry Hodgson, seaman, cook and steward on board the "Queen of the Fleet," was then called and said: As soon as we got out we went to the pumps. The vessel was pumped dry in about ten minutes. This continued eight or nine days, during which time the leak increased. The weather was good. The crew, finding the leak increasing, refused to proceed further to the westwards. We went to Barrow, and were repaired to the satisfaction of the crew. We sailed from Barrow about the 22nd Sept., and two or three days after we sailed we had a squall, which carried away the fore topmast head, spanker boom, jack, and sails. We then put on fresh sails. 17 days after this we found she had broken out, making water very fast. The crew then went aft to the captain, refusing to proceed further to the westward. The captain then said they must try to get the vessel home again. She was put on the course home, but she would not fetch us home. We then shortened sail and manned the pumps – the leak increasing. We took off the sail and hove to, agreeing to keep at the pumps till we met with some vessel to take us off. Three days after we saw a vessel, and we hove down on her and signalled. The barque hove to, and we put the long boat off with eight of the crew. We put out the other boat and she swamped with as alongside, and we were all saved with life buoys. The property on board was all lost.—*The rest of the evidence of this witness was merely a confirmation of the carpenter.*

William Colman, was called and stated that he agreed in the main with the other witness. Jomes (sic) Musgrave, another of the crew, agreed with the evidence given by the other witnesses.—William Lenaghan also agreed with the others.

James Tierney (sic), master of the "Queen of the Fleet," was called, whose evidence was a repetition of the carpenter's. (He was cautioned by the Bench not to give any evidence that might criminate himself, or in fact answer any question.) We were as far a-head when we were out 18 hours as when we were out 19 days. I know that she was insured.—*Cross-examined:* The Board of Trade surveyor visited the vessel very often, and expressed himself quite satisfied with the state of the vessel after being repaired. When the crew first wished to return I tried to persuade them to proceed on the voyage, till at length I saw we had no chance, as the vessel was so leaky, and the men becoming exhausted. I deemed it better to abandon her when the "Enchantress" came in sight. I don't think there was any possibility of getting the vessel home, and besides the crew told me point blank they would not attempt more than to keep her afloat till some vessel should come in sight. The surveyor thoroughly examined her and pronounced her perfectly sea-worthy at Barrow.

After some consultation as to the evidence to be called by Mr Atter for the defence, who intended to call Messrs, Melmore and Palmer, marine surveyors for the local insurance societies, it was agreed to adjourn the court till to-day at 10 o'clock.

Jan. 7 p.8

The Board of Trade Enquiry.

Which was opened on Thursday, the 30th, and adjourned, was resumed on Friday, the 31st, when Mr. Atter addressed the Court in defence of the owners, and captain of the "Queen of the Fleet," and called Mr T. Melmore, who said he had been a master mariner for many years, and had gone to Barrow at the request of Messrs. Hine, managing owners of the "Queen of the Fleet." He attended to the vessel when undergoing repairs there, and having been instructed by Messrs. Hine to have everything done to the vessel that was required to make her strong and fit for sea. The foreman carpenter of the Barrow Shipbuilding Co. was also frequently in attendance on the ship as well as the Board of Trade surveyor, Mr Hannah. Mr. Melmore in reply to questions by the assessors: described the nature of the repairs, and estimated the worth of the barque when she went to sea, at nearly double the sum she was insured for. Mr. Henry Palmer, also master mariner, acting as surveyor for the Maryport Insurance Club, bore testimony to the completeness of the repairs at Barrow, as did also Mr. Welsh, the foreman carpenter, who added that it was not a contract job, and therefore nothing was left undone which might be deemed requisite to make the ship sea-worthy.—The assessors retired for about half-an-hour to consider their decision, and on returning to the court read the following—

Judgment.

"The court having duly weighed and considered the evidence before us, are of opinion that the "Queen of the Fleet," when she sailed from Barrow, was in a sufficient state of repair, and that afterwards when she sprang a leak and made a great deal of water, everything was done to keep her afloat, but the crew having resolved on leaving her so soon as any vessel bore in sight, left no option but to abandon her. If, however, the captain had been willingly supported by his crew, it is possible the vessel might have been kept afloat longer and got into a port of safety. The court accordingly returns the master's certificate." *Mr Ritson added that the captain left the court without the slightest stain on his character.*

Liverpool Register:
Register closed 17 December 1875 Vessel abandoned at Sea on her voyage from Barrow to Miramichi 21st Oct. 1875 per Certificate of Registry received 18th Dec. 1875.

HOPE

Official No. **8093**
Built 1810   Chester
Deck   One   Build   Carvel
Masts   Two   Gallery   None
Rigging **Brig**   Head   None
Stern   Square   Framework   Planking Wood.
Tonnage   **153**   Length 74.2 feet; Breadth 23.1.5 feet; Depth 14 feet.

[**LR** 1818-21: Hope, Bg, E. Vernon 161, Chestr (8 old), Thmpsn &, A1]
[**LR** 1822-25: Hope, Bg, E. Vernon 161, Chestr (12 old), Thmpsn &, E1]
[**LR** 1826-28: Hope, Bg, E. Vernon 161, Chestr (16 old), Rchdsn &, E1]
[**LR** 1829: Hope, Bg, Middleton, 161, Chestr (19 old), Capt. & Co., E]
[**LR** 1830-33: Hope, Bg, J. Middleton, 157, Chestr (20 old), Capt. & Co., E]
[**LR** 1839-41: Hope, Bg, Middlet'n, 157, Chestr 1810, Middlet'n, Maryport, AE1]
[**LR** 1842-43: Hope, Bg, Middlet'n, 157, Middlet'n, Maryport, --------]
[**LR** 1845-46: Hope, Bg, Middlet'n, 157, Middlet'n, Maryport, AE1]
[**LR** 1847: Hope, Bg, Middlet'n, 157, Middlet'n, ----------------------]
[**LR** 1852: Hope, Bg, Morrison, 148, Russell & c., Belfast, AE1]
[**LR** 1853: Hope, Bg, Morrison, 148, Russell & c., Carikfrg, AE1]
[**LR** 1854: Hope, Bg, Morrison, 148, Russell & c.------------------]
[**LR** 1855: Hope, Bg, W. Price, 148, H. Brown, Belfast, AE1]
[**LR** 1856-57: Hope, Bg, J. Burton, 148, J. Bradfrd, Belfast, AE1]
[**LR** 1858-63: Hope, Bg, J. Burton, 148, J. Bradfrd, Belfast, ------------]
[**MNL** 1858: 8093, Hope, Belfast]
[**MNL** 1859-61: 8093, Hope, Maryport]
[**MNL** 1867 & 70: 8093, Hope, Maryport, LCQF, 154, B.D. Dawson, Maryport]

1815 The Liverpool Mercury Fri. 7 Apr. p.8
Liverpool: Arrived, from West Indies: The Hope, E. Vernon from Barbadoes, with 106 hhds, 190 tces 2 brls sugar 63 bales cotton 8 doz cocoa nuts 1 box-sweetmeats 6 jars tamarinds.

1815 The Lancaster Gazette Sat. 22 July. p.3
At Barbadoes: The Hope, Vernon, from hence [Liverpool].

1816 The Liverpool Mercury Fri. 29 Mar. p.7
At Barbadoes: Hope, Vernon, from St. Andrew's N.B.

1816 The Liverpool Mercury Fri. 2 May p.8
Liverpool: Arrived from West Indies: Hope, E Vernon, from Barbadoes, with 140 hhds 103 tcs 4 brls sugar 78 bags cotton 204 casks 93 bags coffee 46 pchs rum, order.

1817 The Lancaster Gazette Sat. 8 Mar. p.3
At Barbadoes: The Hope, Vernon, from hence [Liverpool].

1817 The Liverpool Mercury Fri. 2 May p.8
Liverpool: Arrived: Hope, E. Vernon, from Barbadoes, with 140 hhds 103 tcs 4 brls sugar 4 pchs rum 18 bags 3 pockets cotton 75 bags ginger 48 brls 30 bags cocoa 2 casks 1 box old copper for Gibbs, Thompson and co---8 tcs 1 brl sugar E Vernon---20 hhds sugar 4 pchs rum, order.

1817 The Lancaster Gazette Sat. 16 Aug. p.3

At Barbadoes: Hope, Vernon, from hence [Liverpool].

1817 The Liverpool Mercury Fri. 12 Sept. p.7
Liverpool: Arrived: from West Indies: Hope, E. Vernon, from Barbadoes, with 70 hhds 46 tces sugar 31 bales 2 pockets cotton 2 boxes sweetmeats 90 pieces furniture wood for Gibbs, Thompson and co---100 tces rice Duff, Findlay---1 hhd 9 brls sugar 3 bags cotton 5 bags ginger 200 cocoa nuts, order.

1817 The Lancaster Gazette Sat. 3 Mar. p.3
At Barbadoes: Hope, Vernon, from hence [Liverpool].

1818 The Lancaster Gazette Sat. 28 Feb. p.3
At Barbadoes: Hope, Vernon, from hence [Liverpool].

1818 The Liverpool Mercury Fri. 7 Aug. p.7
Hope, Vernon, hence, at Madeira on the 26th June, and sailed for Bahia the same day.

1819 The Liverpool Mercury Fri. 14 May. P.7
At St. Lucia: Hope, Vernon, hence.

1819 The Lancaster Gazette Sat. 16 Oct. p.3
The Hope, Vernon, hence [Liverpool] *at Barbadoes, and sailed for St. Lucia.*

1820 The Morning Post (London) Fri. 4 Feb. p.4
Deal, Feb. 2—Came down the River last evening, and sailed with the whole outward bound, the Hope, Vernon, for Barbadoes.

1820 The Liverpool Mercury Fri. 29 Dec. p.7
Liverpool: Imports: Brazil: Hope, E. Vernon, from Bahia with 128 bg cotton for Rathbone Hodgson and co---21 do Cropper, Benson and co--- 57 do B. Hollingshead and Stewart---30 t pig iron W. and J. Thompson---692 bg cotton 8 brl ipecacuanha 1 case vanelloes 267 planks jacaranda 1 paper pcl returned good order.

1821 The Liverpool Mercury Fri. 25 May p.7
Barbadoes: Sailed: Apr. 4: Hope, Vernon, for this port.

1822 The Morning post (London) Mon. 11 Mar. p.4
Margate, March—Arrived the Hope, Vernon, from Aux Cayes for London, with loss of anchor and cable, and windlass disabled.

1822 The Lancaster Gazette Sat. 26 Oct. p.3
At Jamaica: Hope, Vernon, hence [Liverpool].

1822 The Liverpool Mercury Fri. 29 Nov. p.7
Liverpool: Imports: Hope, E. Vernon, from Jamaica with 43 bl cotton, J. Simpson--- 23 do, T.C. Wakefield---157 do, Tavinie and Hill---40 do, T. and W. Earle and co---50 do, 28 serons indigo, 2 tc old copper, Campbell and Mackie---130 bl cotton, 7 serons indigo, 13t logwood, 18ft fustic, Moravia and co---11t logwood, Gibbs, Thompson---17 do, 17t Nicaragua-wood, T. Hatton---20t Braziletto-wood, R. Hutchison---3t Nicaragua-wood J. Tenant and co---5 tc coffee, said master---1h 1904 lb old copper, 3 bl cotton, order.— King's Dock.
page 4

Liverpool: Auction: This day (Friday) the 29ʰ inst at Twelve o'clock, South and King's Dock. 17 tons solid Nicaragua Wood: 28 Tons Jamaica Logwood. Now loading ex Hope, Vernon from Jamaica.

1823 The Liverpool Mercury Fri. 25 May p.7
Barbadoes: Sailed: Apr. 4: Hope, Vernon, for this port.
Oct. 10 p.3
At Domingo: Hope, Vernon, hence.
Dec. 12 p.7
At Kinsale: Hope, Vernon from St. Domingo.

1824 The Liverpool Mercury Fri. 7 May p.7
At Barbadoes: Hope, Vernon from London.
July 9 p.7
Liverpool: Imports: Hope, E. Vernon from Barbadoes with 168 h 28 tc sugar, Gibbs, Bright and co---13hd do, Barton Iram and Higginson---10 do, J. Heyes and co---15, do, Hall M'Garrel and co---2400 coker nuts, J.A. Harwell---45 bl cotton, 3 tc sugar, 1 pcl goods returned, 1 brl yams, 1 Kg 1 jar tamarinds, order.
1825 Jan. 28 p.7
Liverpool: Sailed: Jan. 22: Hope, Vernon, Barbadoes.
Feb. 4 p.7
At Studwall Roads: Hope, Vernon, for Barbadoes.
May 6 p.7
At Barbadoes: Hope, Vernon, hence.
Dec. 30 p.7
Hope, Vernon, from Pernambuco at Ceara, 14ᵗʰ ult. and sailed for Maranham.

1827 The Liverpool Mercury Fri. 19 Jan. p.7
Liverpool: Arrived Jan. 18: Hope, Vernon was to proceed to Paraibo, to load for this port.
Apr. 6 p.7
Liverpool: Sailed: Mar. 27: Hope, Vernon, Barbadoes.

1827 The Morning Chronicle Tues. 7 Aug. p.4
Deal: Arrived: Aug. 4: Hope, Vernon, from La Guayra.

1828 The Liverpool Mercury Fri. 5 Sept. p.7
At Dublin: Hope, Middleton, from Barbadoes.

1829 {theshipslist.com   Canadian newspapers---
Quebec: Arrived: July 17: brig Hope, Middleton, Dublin (sailed 7 weeks), 184 settlers, in ballast.}

1829 The Liverpool Mercury Fri. 18 Sept. p.3
At Dublin: Hope, Middleton, from Quebec.

1830 {theshipslist.com   Canadian newspapers---
Quebec: Arrived: Oct. 2: brig, Hope, Middleton, Dublin (sailed Aug. 7), 10 settlers, in ballast.
Quebec: Cleared: Oct. 19: brig Hope, Middleton, (for) Dublin.

1830 The Morning Post (London) Thurs. 30 Dec. p.4
Newry: Arrived: Dec. 26: Hope, Middleton, Quebec.

1833 The Morning Chronicle (London) Tues. 15 Oct. p.3
Cork: Arrived: Oct. 12: Hope, Middleton from Quebec.

1834 The Morning Chronicle (London) Fri. 21 Feb. p.4

Deal: Arrived: Feb. 19: Hope, Middleton, Waterford.

1835 The Morning Chronicle (London) Tues. 26 Jan. p.4
Gravesend: Sailed: Jan. 24: Hope, Middleton, for Calais.

1835 {theshipslist.com   Canadian newspapers---
Quebec: Arrived: June 23: brig Hope, Middleton, Maryport (sailed 28 April), 1 settler, in ballast.}

1837 The Morning Post (London) Tues. 31 Oct. p.4
Maryport: Arrived: Oct. 28: Hope, Middleton, from Quebec.

1838 The Morning Post (London) Tues. 31 Aug. p.4
Dublin: Arrived: Aug. 28: Hope, Middleton, from Bathurst.
Sept. 5 p.4
Maryport of port: Arrived: Sept. 2: Hope, Middleton, from Quebec.

1839 The Standard (London) Fri. 26 Apr. p.3
Maryport: Sailed: Apr. 24: Hope, Middleton for Quebec.
Sat. Aug. 10 p.3
Maryport: Arrived: Aug. 8: Hope, Middleton, from Quebec.
Sept. 2 p.3
Maryport: Arrived: Aug. 30: Hope, Middleton, fm Miramichi.

1840 The Standard (London) Mon. 29 June p.3
Maryport: Sailed: June 27: Hope, Middleton, for Quebec.

1841 The Freeman's Journal (Dublin) Tues. 30 Mar. p.4
Dublin, Pier head: Arrived: Mar. 28: Hope, Middleton, Chepstow, timber.

1844 Caledonian Mercury, Edinburgh Mon. 14 Oct. p.4
Dreadful Gale and Shipwreck in the Bay of Luce.
For eight days bypast the weather has been unusually boisterous, accompanied by high winds and heavy showers of rain and hail, but on Tuesday night the weather waxed into quite a tempest, and we fear we shall ere long hear, many and bad accounts of the gale. Wednesday night was no better, it blowing a hurricane, as on the previous night, from ESE. On Tuesday, the following disasters occurred in the Bay of Luce, near Drumore and Ardwall:--The Hope, Middleton, of and bound to Maryport, with timber from Quebec, brought up in Drumore Roads during the late gales. Last night it blew a hurricane from the ESE, when one of her chains burst, the other held on till eight o'clock this morning (Wednesday), when it snapt, and the brig was driven on shore in Chapelrossan Bay, where she now lies stranded. She will be got off (as the tides are making) by discharging her deck timber. The damage she has sustained cannot yet be ascertained, as she is into the bilges in sand; it is thought not to be very extensive.

1846 The Liverpool Mercury Fri. 13 Nov. p.3
At Kingston: Hope, Morrison, hence for Dordt.

1852 The Belfast News-Letter Fri. 17 Sept. p.4
Arrived at Greenock, on the 11th instant, the Hope, Morrison, from Cronstadt.

1856 The Belfast News-Letter Tues. 13 May p.4
Entered at Liverpool, on the 9th instant: the Hope, Burton, for Riga.

1856 The Liverpool Mercury Mon. 2 June p.3
Liverpool: Sailed: May 30: Hope, Burton, Riga.

1856 Caledonian Mercury, Edinburgh Wed. 3 Sept. p.4
Stornoway: Sailed: Hope, Burton for Belfast.

1858 The Belfast News-Letter Wed. 13 Jan p.1
List of Shipping Registered at the Port of Belfast, Year Ending 31st December 1857: Registed de Novo, or Sold in 1857: Foreign Trade: Hope, Tons 148, Owner: P. Quin, at Maryport.

1858 The Belfast News-Letter Tues. 9 Sept. p.4
Belfast: Arrived: Sept. 6: the brig Hope, Burton, from Riga, with a cargo of timber.

++++++++++ ? **Alfred Hine**
1870 The Glasgow Daily Herald Tues. 24 May p.7
Troon: Arrived: May 22: Hope, Fearon, Dublin.
June 4 p.7
Troon: Sailed: June 3: Hope, Fearon, Dublin.
June 28 p.7
Troon: Arrived: June 26: Hope, Fearon from Dublin.
July 4 p.7
Troon: Sailed: July 2: Hope, Fearon, Dublin.

TRS 1/64
Hope 8093 Port of Registry Maryport 5/1858 Tonnage 153
Managing Owner: John Fearon, Ellenbro place, Maryport. Master: John Fearon (51) Maryport (no certificate), continues as Master.
1870-71: Voyage: Dublin 3.10.70: Newport to Queenstown to return to a portion of the Bristol Channel. Joined at Newport 30.12.70 and also 6.1.71
Received at Maryport 5.5.71. (signed) **Alfred Hine** part owner.

TSR 8/142
Shares: John Patterson 58/64 & Alfred Hine 4/64 dated 11th July 1871.

TRS 1/64
1871: 1 Jan.—30 June.
Managing Owner: Alfred Hine, High St. Maryport. Master: John Patterson, 49 King St. (33) Cumberland (from "Eleanor More, Maryport) Oct 27/70 at Liverpool, joined Maryport 11.4.71 as Master. 7 crew.
Voyage: From Maryport to Bristol Channell (sic) from there to a Port no (sic) East Coast of Ireland & Back to Maryport.

1871: 1 July—31 Dec.
Managing Owner: Alfred Hine. Master: John Patterson. 12 crew.
1. Newport: Sailed: July 18. to Dublin: Arrived: Aug. 8 & back to Maryport.
2. Maryport: Sailed Sept. 13. Newport: Arrived Sept. 18: Sailed Oct. 6. to Halbohrig (??): Arrived Oct. 12. & back to Maryport.
3. Maryport: Sailed: Nov. 11 for Dublin: Arrived Nov. 13 & back to Maryport.
4. Maryport: Sailed to Dublin: Sailed: Dec. 16 put into Whitehaven Dec. 18 and remains.

1872: 1 Jan.—30 June.
Managing Owner: Alfred Hine. Master: John Patterson, address Whitehaven.

1. Whitehaven (joined Jan. 7) Belfast Jan 12 Iron ore
1a. Jan, 25 Belfast to Maryport, ballast.
2. Feb. 3 Maryport to Belfast Feb 9, coal.
3. Mar. 8 Belfast to Maryport, ballast.
4. Apr. 3 Maryport to Belfast, coal.
5. Apr. 25 Dublin to Maryport, ballast.
6. June 5 Maryport to Dundalk, coal.
7. June 18 Dundalk to Maryport, in ballast.
8. June 26 Maryport to Newport, pig iron.
1872: 13 July—31 Dec.
 Managing Owner: Alfred Hine. Master: John Patterson. 9 crew.
1. Newport: Sailed: July 17.
2. Dublin: Arrived: July 21. Sailed: July 30.
3. Maryport: Arrived: Aug. 2. Sailed: Aug. 18.
4. Swansea: Arrived: Aug. 22. Sailed: Sept. 17.
5. Dublin: Arrived: Sept. 30. Sailed: Oct. 14.
6. Maryport: Arrived: Oct. 15. Sailed: Nov. 12.
7. Dublin: Arrived: Nov. 13. Sailed: Dec. 23.
8. Maryport: Arrived: Dec. 24 and remains.

1873:
Managing Owner: Alfred Hine. Master: John Patterson (34) Maryport.
Sailed from Maryport for Swansea January 29 1873. Has not since been heard of. The papers having been lost with the vessel there are all the particulars that can be obtained.
(signed) Alfred Hine managing owner.
Thomas Patterson nephew of the Master Boy 13, Maryport, drowned on or about 31 Jan 1873.

1871 The North Wales Chronicle Sat. 22 Apr. p.5
Holyhead: Arrived: Hope, Patterson, Maryport.

1872 The Belfast News-Letter Morning Sat. 13 Jan.
Belfast: Arrival of Coal-laden vessels: Jan 12: Hope from Maryport.

1872 The Belfast News-Letter Morning Sat. 10 Feb.
Belfast: Arrival of Coal-laden vessels: Feb. 9: Hope from Maryport.

1872 The Belfast News-Letter Morning Tues. 7 May
Belfast: Sailed: May 6: Hope for Ardrossan.

Hazel Holme at Mauritius, 1874: State Library of South Australia, Brodie Collection

Abbey Holme, wreck at Sunderland April, 1890: John Mounsey

Valparaiso etched by Albert Charles Cooke & Walter Hart: State Library of Victoria

Bombardment of Valparaiso, by the Spanish, 1866: State Library of Victoria

Rounding Cape Horn in Illawarra: State Library of Victoria, Brodie Collection

Off the pitch of Cape Horn in Castleton barque: State Library of Victoria, Brodie Collection

Fearful earthquake & tidal wave at Arica, South America, 1868, engraver C.T. Winter: State Library of Victoria

Arica, Peru (now Chile), after earthquake & Tsunami 1868: Library of Congress, Washington, D.C., USA

Later view of Arica: Library of Congress, Washington, D.C., USA

CHAPTER TWO

In July 1873, Wilfrid Hine left Liverpool to join his younger brother, Alfred, in Maryport in Cumberland, forming the Hine Brothers' shipping company. Alfred had been mainly in marine insurance, but had been, at least once a manager/owner, that of the "Hope" 1871-73.

Most of the Hine-vessels were mainly for deep-sea trade. However, in 1874 the new shipping company bought a small fleet from Sloane Richards of Birmingham consisting of two brigantines "Clara" and "Maggie Gross", a brig "Glastry" and a schooner "Tom Roberts", as well as their first steam vessel "Florence Richards". These carried various cargoes. However, they were often used as colliers. This makes sense as the Hine Brothers were also coal importers amongst other things.

By 1883 this venture into coastal sailing vessels was terminated, all four being sold at various times.

Apart from two small vessels a flat, "James" and a ketch, "Clymene" (bought later for leisure), the above constituted the total number of sailing vessels for the coastal and Mediterranean trade, that we know of.

GLASTRY

Glastry brigantine wrecked 1880, Sunderland during the storms: North Yorkshire County Council Collection

GLASTRY

Official No.	**60319**	The late **Pallas**	
Built	1861	In Barth, Germany	
Deck	One	Build	Clincher
Masts	Two	Gallery	none
Rigging	**Brig**	Head	none
Stern	Elliptical	Framework	Wood (oak)
Tonnage	**169**	Length 87.7 feet; Breadth 24 feet; Depth 12.6 feet.	

[**ALRAFS** 1862: Pallas, Bn, G. Tessin, 170, oak, C.I., Barth, Stralsund 1861, C.L. Weyer]
[**ALRAFS** 1863-71: Pallas, Bn, T.H or J. Tessen, 230, oak, I, Barth, Stralsund 1861, C.L. Weyer]
1861 [Survey: Stralsund (Germany in the Baltic Sea) in May]

1862 The Glasgow Daily Herald Sat. 3 May p.7
Queenstown: Arrived: Apr. 30: Pallas, Tesin (sic), from Trieste with wheat.

1862 The Daily News (London) Fri. 16 May p.8
At Fleetwood: May 14: Pallas from Trieste.
Aug. 20 p.7
Sunderland: Sailed: Aug 17: Pallas to New York.

1862 The New-York Times Fri. 17 Oct. p.8
New-York: Arrived: Oct. 16: Bark Pallas, (Pruss.,) Tessin, Sunderland 56 days, with coal to Wm Salem & Co. [Survey: New York in November]

1863 The Aberdeen Journal Wed. 16 Sept. p.8
Aberdeen: Arrived: Sept. 11: Pallas, Tessin, Riga.
Sept. 30 p.8
Aberdeen: Sailed: Sept. 23: Pallas, Jessin (sic), Stralsund.

1863 The Caledonian Mercury, Edinburgh 27 Oct.
Riga: Arrived: Oct 17: Pallas, Tessin, from Aberdeen.

1865 [Survey: Stralsund (Germany in the Baltic Sea) in September]
1867 [Survey: Stralsund (Germany in the Baltic Sea) in April]

1867 The Dundee Courier and Argus Wed. 10 July
Memel: Left: July 3: Pallas, Tessin, for Aberdeen.

1867 The Aberdeen Journal Wed. Oct. 9 p.8
Aberdeen: Sailed: Oct. 8: Pallas, Tessen (sic), Lossiemouth.
Nov. 13 p.8
At Stettin: Nov. 4: Pallas, Tessin, from Lossiemouth.

1869 The Belfast News-Letter Fri. Jan 15
Belfast: Arrived: Jan 14: Pallas, Brumshagen from Stralsund, with wheat.
Feb. 8 p.
Belfast: Sailed: Feb. 6: Pallas, for Runcorn.

1869 The Liverpool Mercury Tues. 9 Feb. p.3
The Prussian Schooner Pallas from Belfast for this port with oats and meal, went ashore off the Long Rock, Ballywalter, on the 6th instant. Cargo saved without any damage, and

is being brought to Belfast in small craft. The ship has been dismasted and scuttled until the weather moderates.

1869 The Belfast News-Letter Tues. 9 Feb.
The Prussian brig Pallas, which got on the Long Rock, Ballywalter, during Saturday [Feb. 6] *night, is reported to have gone to pieces; crew saved.*
Feb. 11 p.
Yesterday, as the smack Mary, of Belfast, was coming up the lough, laden with stores; &c., belonging to the Pallas (which was wrecked at Ballywalter on Saturday last), a man named M'Ilroy, a native of Belfast, was washed overboard, and drowned.
Feb. 12 p.
[Advert] Sale:-- This Day: Seed Oats For Sale. To be sold by Public Auction, at the Stores of the undersigned, Corporation Square, on Friday the 12th, at Twelve o'clock: About Ten Tons Seed Oats, Very slightly damaged by salt water on board the Prussian Brig "Pallas," wrecked at Ballywalter, on her voyage from Belfast to Liverpool. For further particulars, to apply to – Sinclair & Boyd; or to Hugh Hamilton, Auctioneer.
Shipwreck: Sale:-- To be sold by Public Auction (on account of whom it may concern), on Monday , the 15th instant, at Ballywalter , County Down, at Eleven a.m. The Hull of the Prussian Brig "Pallas" of Stralsund, 169 Tons Register (wrecked on her voyage from Belfast to Liverpool), as it may lie on the Long Rock off Ballywalter. –Also, the sails, Boats, Spars, Ropes, Running Rigging, Anchors, Chains, Compasses, &.c., and all her stores, consisting of Bread, Beef, Paints, Oils, &c., &c. – Terms –Cash, and 5 cent. Auction Fees: Gustavus Heyn, Royal Prussian Vice-Consul, Agent of Captain and Owners of the "Pallas." -- H. C. Clarke & Sons, Auctioneers. – N.B. –Cars will be in attendance at Newtownards station on arrival of 7.40 a.m. Train from Belfast.

++++++++++   [A special examination in Belfast in May 1869.]

1869 The Liverpool Mercury Thurs. 2 Sept. p.3
Liverpool: Sailed: Sept. 1: Glastry, M'Cune, Riga [Latvia].

1869 The Belfast News-Letter Wed. 15 Sept. p.
Pentland Frith (sic) [Firth]: *Passed: Sept. 10: the brig Glastry (of Belfast), M'Cune, from Liverpool for Riga.*

1869 The Liverpool Mercury Fri. 1 Oct. p.3
Riga: Arrived: Sept. 30: Glastry from Liverpool.

1869 The Belfast News-Letter Thurs. 23 Dec.
Bruntisland: Arrived: Dec. 18: at anchor in the roads, the brig Glastry, of and for Belfast.
1870 Sat. 8 Jan.
Belfast: Put into: Jan 7: Bruntisland Roads, the brig Glastry (of Belfast), from Riga for Dublin.
Jan. 28
Dublin: Arrived: Jan. 24: the Glastry (of Belfast), M'Cune, from Riga. [Latvia]

[**ALRAFS** 1870 & 72: Pallas, Bn, ---------, 230, oak, I, Barth, Stralsund 1861, H. McKelvey, Belfast]
[**MNL** 1870: Glastry of Belfast (tons 169): Owner: Hugh Mc Kelvey, Kirkcubbin, co., Down.]

1870 The Western Mail (Cardiff) Wed. 2 Mar. p.4
Cardiff: Arrival: Bute West Dock: Mar. 1: Glastry, 168, Hamilton, Dublin, ballast.

1870 The Glasgow Herald Wed. 11 May p.6
Troon: Arrived: May 10: Glastry, Hamilton, from Dublin.

1870 The Glasgow Herald Wed. 8 June p.6
Troon: Arrived: June 5: Glastry, Hamilton, from Dublin.
June 14. p.7
Troon: Sailed: June 12: Glastry, Hamilton, for Dublin.
July 4 p.7
Broomielaw: Sailed: July 2: Glastry , 168, Smith, last from Dublin to Glasgow, timber.
Aug. 6 p.7
Troon: Arrived: Aug. 5: Glastry (Smith) from Dublin.
Sept. 29 p.7
Troon: Sailed: Sept. 27: Glastry (Smith) for Dublin.
1871 Mar. 21 p.6
Troon: Arrived: Mar. 20: Glastry (Black), from Dublin.
Mar. 25 p.7
Troon: March 24: The Brig Glastry, of and for Dublin, ran ashore on Lady Isle this morning, but is likely to be got off next tide.
Mar. 27 p.6
Troon: March 24: The Glastry, ashore on the Lady Isle, was towed off at high water, and proceeded.
Apr. 15 p.6
Troon: Arrived: Apr. 14: Glastry (Smith) from Dublin.
May 8 p.6
Troon: Sailed: May 6: Glastry (Smith) for Dublin.
May 24 p.6
Troon: Arrived: May 23: Glastry (Smith) from Dublin.
June 23 p.6
Troon: Sailed: June 22: Glastry (Smith) for Dublin.
Oct 6 p.6
Troon: Arrived: Oct. 5: Glastry (Smith) from Dublin.
Oct. 13 p.6
Troon: Sailed: Oct. 12: Glastry (Smith) for Dublin.

1873 The Liverpool Mercury Mon. 13 Jan. p.3
Liverpool: Sailed: Jan. 11 Glastry
Jan. 12: The Glastry, outward bound, was left at three p.m. on the 11th inst. off the Bell Bouy by the tug Marseilles. Wind S.S.W., moderate breeze.

1873 The Freeman's Journal (Dublin) Thurs. 13 Feb. p.8
Kingstown: The harbour is not crowded, not withstanding the prevailing east and North winds. The Glastry, with general cargo, bound for Bilboa, entered to-day.

1873 The Western Mail (Cardiff) Mon. 28 Apr. p.4
Newport: Imports: Glastry, B, Bilboa, iron ore.
May 12 p.4
Swansea: Entered Outwards: May 10: Glastry, B, 148, Collick, Corunna.
June 16 p.4
Swansea: Cleared: June 14: Glastry, B, Corunna, 250 coal.
Aug. 5 p.4
Newport: Imports: Glastry, B, Bilboa, iron ore, order.
Aug. 23 p.4
Cardiff: Arrival: Aug. 22: Bute West Dock: Glastry, 148, Vellacott, Newport, light.
Sept. 2 p.4
Cardiff: Cleared: Sept. 1: Glastry, B, Lisbon, 270 coals.
Nov. 26 p.4
Cardiff: Arrivals: Nov. 25, Bute West Dock: Glastry, 148, Vellacott, Milford, ballast.
Cardiff: Entered Outwards: Nov. 25: Glastry, B, 181 (sic), Vellacott, Corunna.

Dec. 4 p.4
Cardiff: Cleared: Dec. 3: Glastry, B, Corunna, 251 coal.
Dec. 6 p.4
Cardiff, Bute West Dock: Sailed: Dec. 5: Glastry, Vellacott, Corunna.

++++++++++++++++++ **Hine Brothers**
1874 Apr. 18 p.7
Swansea: Entered Outwards: Apr. 17: Glastry, B, 148, Shepherd, Lisbon.
Apr. 24 p.7
Swansea: Cleared: Apr. 23: Glastry, B, Lisbon, 268 coal.
May 14 p.7
Lisbon: Arrived: Glastry from Swansea.
June 25 p.
Lisbon: Sailed: Glastry for Swansea.
July 4 p.7
Swansea: Imports: July 3: Glastry, 148, Lisbon, 100 boxes onions, Burgess, Shaddick, and Co.; 255 tons iron ore, Hannan and Co., Glasgow.
July 24 p.7
Swansea: Entered Outwards: July 23: Glastry, B, 148, Shepherd, Santander.
July 29 p.8
Swansea: Cleared: July 28: Glastry, B, Bilbao, 261 coal.
Oct. 24 p.7
Cardiff: Arrivals: East Bute Dock Oct. 23: Glastry, 148, Shepherd, Boulogne, ballast.
Nov. 14 p.6
Cardiff: Sailings: East Bute Dock: Nov. 13: Glasbury (sic), Shepherd, Dublin.

[**LR** 1874: (60319) Glastry, Bg, R. Shephrd: 148/ 167, Prussia, 1861, G. Shaddick, Dublin, --------]
[**LR** 1876: Captain R. Shephrd: Owners, Hine Bros., Dublin.
[**LR** 1877: Captain R. Shephrd: Owners, Hine Bros. amended to J. Davidson, Maryport.
[**MNL** 1875: 60319 Glastry, Dublin,148, Owner: Sloane Richards, Birmingham]
[**MNL** 1876: 60319 Glastry, Dublin,148, Owner: Evan Matthew Richards, Swansea]
[**MNL** 1878: 60319 Glastry, Maryport,148, Owner: Joseph Davidson, 1, Sussex St., Birkenhead]

1875 The Western Mail (Cardiff) Sat. 24 Apr. p.7
Milford: Arrivals: Apr. 23: Glastory (sic), 148, Saul, Maryport, iron ore.
Apr. 27 p.7
Swansea: Arrivals: Apr. 25: South Dock: Glastry, 148, Saul, Maryport, iron.
May 17 p.7
Swansea: Sailings: May 15: North Dock: Glastry, Saul, Cork.

1875 Adair's Maryport Advertiser Fri. 21 May p.8
Cork: Arrived: May 17: Glastry, Saul.

1875 The Western Mail (Cardiff) Fri. June 11 p.7
Yarmouth, June 5.
John Saul, master of the brig Glastry, of Dublin, 148 tons, from Cork, May 27th, for Newcastle, with limestone, reports:-- Proceeded on her voyage, and nothing of importance occurred till about midnight of the 3rd inst., when the weather became foggy, which afterwards increased in density, the wind being W.S.W., moderate, St. Catherine's being supposed to be N.N.E., 28 miles. We were under all plain sail, steering E. by S., and going about four knots. On Friday, the 4th, at 2.15 a.m., tide being ebb, dense fog, wind W.S.W., a moderate breeze, the brig continuing her course, when I observed a green light one point on our port bow. I immediately ordered out helm hard a-starboard, and before she had time to answer her helm a large sailing ship, apparently in ballast, struck us about the port forerigging with his port bow, carrying away both the masts by the board, and staving in our port side, abaft the forerigging, down to the water's edge. The stranger then threw lines over the side,

which my men appeared to get hold of, and jumped overboard. I remained by my wife. The stranger having got out of sight, I hailed her, and kept our bell ringing, but got no further communication with her. I and my wife succeeded in getting out our boat, and kept her alongside. I then endeavoured to ascertain how much water she was making, but could not get at the pumps on account of the wreck on deck. On going to the lazarette I heard the water coming in, but could not find what quantity she made. I and my wife remained on board till six a.m., when a French brigantine hove in sight, named the Hippolyte et Marie, of Bayonne. I hailed him, and asked him to tow us, or spare me some of his men, which he could not do; and they came alongside with their boat, and suggested we should go on board their vessel, which we did, and were treated with the utmost kindness by the master, who landed us at Yarmouth last night, about 7.30 o'clock. Our lights were burning brightly before and at the time of collision, and I kept the fog-horn going every few minutes. No lives were lost that I am aware of, and believe they (the crew) were saved by the other ship; but nothing further concerning the strange ship or my crew has come to my knowledge. I have just received a telegram, saying my vessel has been taken into Portsmouth by the Maggie, of Llanelly, where I am now bound.

Portsmouth, June 5.

John Richards, master of the brig Maggie, of Llanelly, 199 tons, from Caen, June 3, for Llanelly (in ballast), reports:- On Friday, the 4th, on 10 a.m., tide being ebb, weather fine, wind W. by S., a fine breeze, with a smooth sea, the brig was on a port tack under whole sail, St. Catherine bearing N.N.W., distant about 25 miles, when I observed the hull of a vessel bearing N. by E., distant about two miles, and discovering she was dismasted and her sails hanging about her hull, I bore down for the wreck and launched a boat. After sending three hands on board, I found she was abandoned, and that she was the Glastry, of Dublin. Took her in tow for a port of safety, and brought her into Portsmouth Harbour, and placed in safety about 2 p.m. to day.

1875 Adair's Maryport Advertiser Fri. 18 June p.8

Collision at Sea.—The brig Glastry, Capt. Saul, of this port, was run into off the Isle of Wight, on the morning of the 8th inst. (sic), during a dense fog, by a full rigged ship, apparently an American. The Glastry's two masts were carried away by the board with all attached and the port side of the vessel stove in. The crew of the large ship threw ropes to those on board the brig, and they were all saved. She bore away, leaving Capt. Saul and his wife on board. Mrs. Saul's escape was almost miraculous. She was standing by the companion when the mainmast fell, and would have been killed on the spot were it not that the wheel house caught the mast and spars and so broke their fall. The captain was almost dragged overboard by one of the ropes from the large vessel getting entangled with his limbs as he lay on the deck half conscious from the effects of the collision. They launched the boat, but a French vessel appearing in sight took them off the wreck, landing them at Yarmouth, Isle of Wight, on the following day.

1875 The Manchester Times Sat. 12 June p.3

Shipping Disasters.

The barque Enos Soule, of Freeport, State of Maine, arrived at Cardiff on Thursday, and the captain, Mr. John Baldwine Drinkwater, reported to the Collector of Customs that a collision had occurred between his vessel and the Glastiny (sic) on the 3rd June. The Enos Soule left Hamburg for Cardiff on the 31st May. All went well up to the night of the 2nd June, when a dense fog arose, the vessel being then about 12 miles from St. Catherine's Light. He had a north sea pilot on board, who kept to the helm, and the watch was set for the night. Lights were hoisted, and the fog horn blown very frequently. About half-past two on the morning of the 3rd the lookout man shouted "Red light ahead."

The helm was put hard aport, but before she answered to the helm she struck a vessel under sail, which afterwards proved to be the Glastiny (sic), of Dublin. The blow only deadened the way of the Enos Soule, but cut the other down. The ships drifted alongside each other, and the mate threw ropes overboard, as the other vessel was believed to be sinking. Five of the crew caught the ropes, and came on board the Enos Soule, leaving the captain and his wife on board the Glastiny (sic). The vessels soon parted, and the captain heard a man's voice cry out for help. He shouted back that help would be sent, and the voice replied "All right." A boat was got out, and part of the crew of the Glastiny (sic) and chief mate of Enos Soule got into it, and rowed in the direction that it was believed the ship had drifted. For half an hour they rowed about, but neither saw nor heard anything of the vessel, and at one time they lost sight of the Enos Soule, and almost gave themselves up for lost. The captain took the boat in tow, and tacked his vessel about in every direction in which it was thought the other vessel might be, but when the fog cleared away at seven o'clock nothing could be seen, and it was believed that the Glastiny (sic) must have sunk soon after the collision. The Enos Soule then came on to Cardiff.

1875 The Hampshire Advertiser Sat. 6 Nov. p.8
The brig Glastry is at the Albion shipbuilding and repairing yard, Landport, which vessel it may be remembered, was brought into the port some mouths (sic) since a derelict, having been dismasted and received considerable damaged through having been in collision in the Channel.

1876 Adair's Maryport Advertiser Fri. 14 Jan. p.8
Portsmouth: Sailed: Jan. 8: Glaslry (sic), Saul, for Cardiff.
Feb. 4 p.8
Dublin: Arrived: 28th ult: Glastry, Saul.
Mar. 31 p.8
Glastry at Maryport.
Apr. 14 p.8
Glastry at Port Maryport.
Apr. 21 p.8
Glastry at Port Maryport.

++++++++++

TSR 2/7 p.125: Wilfrid Hine shares Sixty Four/64: 16 Mar. 1876.
TSR 2/7 p.123:   Transferred from Dublin to Maryport 3/1877.
Shares: Joseph L. Davidson of 207 Sussex Street, Birkenhead, appointed Managing owner by letter dated 18th May 1876 owning 64 shares.
Joseph L. Davidson of No 1 Sussex Street Birkenhead, Managing owner, dated 18.5.1876.

1876 The Freeman's Journal (Dublin) Sat. 6 May
Dublin: Sailing: May 4: Glastry, Maryport, manure.
June 15 p.8
Maryport: Arrived: June 14 from Dublin.
July 21 p.8
Maryport: Arrived: July 30: Glastry from Dublin.
Aug. 18 p.8
Maryport: Sailed: Aug. 17: Glastry, for Dublin.
Sept. 28 p.8
Maryport: Arrived: Sept. 27: Glastry, from Dublin.

1876 Adair's Maryport Advertiser Fri. Oct. 20 p.8
Maryport: Sailed: Oct. 17: Glastry, Sheffield, Dublin.

Oct. 27 p.8
Dublin: Arrived: Oct. 24: Glastry from Maryport

1876 The Freeman's Journal (Dublin) Fri. 10 Nov. p.8
Maryport: Sailed: Nov. 9: Glastry for Dublin.

1876 Adair's Maryport Advertiser Fri. 24 Nov. p.8
Maryport: Sailings: Nov. 18: Glastry, Sheffield, Dublin.

1876 The Freeman's Journal (Dublin) Mon. 27 Nov. p.3
Dublin: Arrivals: Nov. 26: Glastry, from Glasgow (sic) [Maryport ?]*, with coal.*

1876 Adair's Maryport Advertiser Fri. 8 Dec. p.8
Dublin: Arrived: Tues. 5 [??]*: Glastry from Maryport.*

1876 The Freeman's Journal (Dublin) Sat. 9 Dec.
Dublin: Departures: Dec. 8: Glastury (sic), for Maryport, in ballast.

1877 The Freeman's Journal (Dublin) Tues. 16 Jan. p.5
Shipping Casualties: On Saturday night last the brigantine Glastry, belonging to Dublin, with a cargo of coals from Scotland (sic) [??] *to Dublin, put into Carlingford Lough, and struck on a rock at Greencastle, County Down. However, notwithstanding that the rudder was broken, the crew, by great effort, managed to keep the vessel from going ashore. The Glastry was towed into Warrenpoint dock on yesterday (Monday) by the steam tug Wave of Life. It is believed she has received some injury, as she is making a good deal of water.*

1877 Adair's Maryport Advertiser Fri. 6 Apr. p.8
Maryport: Arrivals: Apr. 5: Glastry, Sheffield, Londonderry.
May 25
Port Maryport: Arrivals: May 18: Glastry, Sheffield, Londonderry.

1877 The Freeman's Journal (Dublin) Wed. 13 June p.3
Maryport: Sailed: June 12: Glastry for Dublin.
Aug. 6 p.5
Dublin: Arrivals: Aug. 4: Glastry, from Maryport, with coals.

1877 Adair's Maryport Advertiser Fri. 24 Aug. p.8
At Maryport: Glastry.
Sept. 21 p.8
Maryport: Sailings: Sept. 17: Glastry, Sheffield, Dublin.

1877 The Freeman's Journal (Dublin) Fri. 21 Sept. p.3
Dublin: Arrivals: Sept. 20: Gastria (sic) from Maryport, coals.
Oct. 6 p.7
Maryport: Arrived: Oct 5: Glastry from Dublin.
Nov. 28 p.3
Maryport: Sailed: Nov. 27: Glastry, for Dublin.

TRS 1/ p.575
1878: Glastry (60319) Maryport Registered 3/1877 Tonnage 148.36/100: Managing Owner. Joseph Davison, Liversedge Road, Higher Tranmere, Birkenhead. Master, Benjm. Sheffield (aged 38), 85, King Street, Maryport. 12 Crew.

Jan. 78—Dec. 78

Maryport sailed Jan. 2: Londonderry arrived Jan. 5, sailed Jan. 24: Maryport arrived Jan. 25, sailed Feb. 2: Londonderry arrived Feb. 8 sailed Mar. 26: Maryport arrived Mar. 27, sailed Apr.

4: Londonderry arrived Apr. 8 sailed May 14: Maryport arrived May 17, sailed June 4: Londonderry arrived June 7, sailed July 4: Maryport arrived July 6 sailed July 17: Londonderry arrived July 25, sailed Aug. 17: Maryport arrived Aug. 19, sailed Aug. 26 : Londonderry arrived Aug. 29, sailed Oct. 11: Maryport arrived Oct. 12, (Vessel being repairing from Oct. to Dec. 13th) 1878. sailed Dec. 13: Llanelly arrived Dec. 18.

1878 The Liverpool Mercury Tues. 29 Oct. p.3
Maryport, Oct. 28: The schooner (sic) Glantry (sic), Sheffield, hence for Dublin, in putting back took the ground a little to the south of the south pier. She is lying on a good soft and level bottom. There in every probability that she will be got off next tide without any material damage.

1879 The Western Mail (Cardiff) Sat. 4 Jan. p.4
Llanelly: Cleared: Jan. 3: Glastry, B, Dublin, 230, coal.

TRS 1/ p.575
     Jan. 79—June79
Lanelly sailed Jan. 3: Foynes arrived Jan. 8, sailed Jan. 21: Clare arrived Jan. 26, sailed Feb. 7: Garston arrived Mar. 2, sailed Mar. 24: Newcastle arrived Apr. 8, sailed May 4: Ramsgate arrived May 7, sailed May 21: South Shields arrived May 26, sailed June 2: Waterford arrived June 14, sailed June 30.
     July 79—Dec.79
Maryport arrived July 4, sailed July 15: Swansea arrived July 21, sailed Aug. 9: Gravesend arrived Aug. 21: Silvertown sailed Sept. 10: Swansea arrived Sept. 21, sailed Oct. 6: The Western Mail Wed. 1 Oct. p.4 *Swansea: Entered Outwards: Sept. 30: Glastry, B, 148, Fecamp.* Oct. 4 p.4 *Swansea: Cleared: Oct. 3: Glastry, B, Fecamp, 270 coal.* Fecamp arrived Oct 17, sailed Oct 29: Llanelly arrived Nov. 6, sailed Nov. 19: Newcastle arrived Dec. 21, sailed Dec.30.
     Jan. 80—June 80
Fecamp arrived Jan. 11, sailed Jan. 20: Llanelly arrived Jan. 27, sailed Feb. 24: Fecamp arrived Feb. 29, sailed Mar. 11: Maryport arrived Mar. 28, sailed Apr. 4: Swansea arrived Apr. 19. The (Western Mail Mon. Apr. 26 p. *Swansea: Cleared: Apr. 24: Fecamp, Glastry, b, 280 coal.)* sailed Apr. 26: Fecamp arrived May 6, sailed May 19: Sunderland arrived May 25, sailed June 10: Portsmouth arrived June 18.

TRS 1/ p.575
     July 80—Dec. 80
Portsmouth sailed July 2: Llanelly arrived July 24, sailed Aug. 2: Fecamp arrived Aug. 9, sailed Aug. 18: Llanelly arrived Aug. 30, sailed Sept. 24: Fecamp arrived Oct. 13, sailed Oct. 25: Scarborough arrived Oct. 28.

[MNL 1878: 60319 Glastry, Maryport, 148, Owner: Joseph Davidson, 1, Sussex St., Birkenhead]

1880 The York Herald Fri. 29 Oct. p.5
Shipwrecks and Loss of Life at Scarbro'. : During the whole of Wednesday night, and up to yesterday, morning, a strong gale of E.N.E. prevailed at Scarbro', bringing up a very heavy sea, and, we regret to say, causing the wreck of three ships and the loss of one life.
Two other vessels were seen making for the harbour, and these were more fortunate than those which had preceded them, but they sustained some damage. The first of the pair, a brigantine name Maria, of Yarmouth, rounded the pier, and a rope being got to her she was being hauled into the harbour, when the rope parted, and before she could

be got out of the way the Glastry brigantine, of Maryport, ran into her port quarter, and both vessels sustained considerable damage.
Oct. 30 p.6
The Glastry, which we reported as successfully making the harbour on the previous afternoon, was blown out of the harbour during the night, and came ashore opposite Mr. Woodall's boat house.

1880 The Leeds Mercury Mon. 1 Nov. p.6
The Storm and Floods: The Gale at Scarborough.
During the whole of Thursday night the gale at Scarborough continued to rage with unabated force, and the disastrous results will long be remembered in the annals of the port, for it is now many years since such sights have been witnessed as have taken place this week. The sea literally ran mountains high. About eight o'clock the schooner (sic) Glantry (sic), of Maryport, Isle of Wight (sic), captain Sheffield, laden with plaster of Paris, from Fecamp for Newcastle, which had entered the harbour during the early part of the evening, was observed to be in extreme danger of being carried out to sea by the extraordinary force of the current. She was moored above the narrow bridge connecting the St. Vincent and Lighthouse piers. As soon as the danger was seen, under the directions of the Mr. Appleyard (harbour master), extra warps and tow lines were run out to her from the pier and made fast to one of the pillars, and all possible efforts made to keep her to her moorings. But the strain proved too much for the lines, which snapped asunder like thread, at the same time almost wrenching the pillar from its socket in the pier, loosening the stonework down to the very foundations. A massive chain cable was quickly got out and made fast to the pillar at the Lighthouse Pier head with hopes of checking the Glantry (sic) in her course, the crew meanwhile, seeing the imminent danger they were in, scrambling on to the pier. As soon as the strain got into the chain it also broke in two, and by about two o'clock yesterday morning the vessel was stranded on the beach opposite the Aquarium. The pillar to which the chain cable had been attached was also severely wrenched, and the stonework of the pier, down to its base, was opened to the extent of nearly a foot.

1880 The York Herald Thurs. Nov. 4
Scarbro'.- We hear that, owing to the strong remonstrances of several individuals Harbour Commissioners a meeting of the committee has been held to investigate the conduct of the Harbour Master with reference to the course pursued by the steam tug Alexandra during the recent storm. It has already been stated in these columns that a generally expressed opinion was prevalent to the effect that most of the ships wrecked could have been saved had the Alexandra been employed as she ought to have been. The committee have made diligent inquiry into this point and we understand will report to the Commissioners as the next quarterly meeting, some three weeks hence. Yesterday a good deal of interest was excited by preparation being made with a view to getting one of the skips which came ashore a week ago to-day off the sands. Workmen were seen busily clearing the Glastry of ballast, and others were engaged in caulking her seams. This work was not quite completed when the tide reached her, and the further advance of the tide was keenly watched to see whether she was likely to float. The tide was at its height about four o'clock, and shortly before that hour men on board the vessel started hauling on the anchor cable with the windlass, and presently it was seen that though the ship made a large quantity of water she began to show signs of floating, and then the steam tug Alexandra came up and took her in tow, and succeeded in getting her once more into the harbour. It will be remembered that the Glastry was one of the ships which succeeded in getting into the harbour during the storm last Thursday, and subsequently

broke away and drifted on to the sands. She is a good deal strained and beaten about, and will require a considerable outlay to refit her.

Nov. 11 p.7

Claim for Salvage Services Rendered During the Late Storm.

At the Town-hall yesterday, before Ald. Champley and other magistrates, Benj. Sheffield, [see Benjamin Sheffield "Clara" 1883] master of the brig Glastry of Maryport, Cumberland, was summoned by Wm. Leonard on the 28th October. Mr. Watts appeared for the salvors, and in opening the case said they had agreed to the value of the vessel being between £400 and £500, exclusive of her cargo. The claim was made by Leonard and fourteen others for having rendered salvage services to the brig Glastry on Thursday, the 28 October, on which day there was a terrible gale and storm, and about 4 p.m. on the day the Glastry on her way to Newcastle, with about 150 tons of stone, was seen endeavouring to get into the harbour. When coming round the pier head her head sails were blown away, and she ran into another vessel, which stopped her, and she then began to drift away. The claimants boarded her and secured her. When the tide began to flow it was necessary to get the vessel further up, and by the instructions of the harbour master they had her made fast by the pier, using the vessel's own ropes and borrowed ones as well, and made her perfectly fast. They continued on board from six in the evening to two o'clock the next morning. She broke loose and drifted unto the sands, but had since been recovered and put into the harbour. The salvors, claimed £20 which he submitted could not be considered a gross claim. It might be submitted in defence that their services were of no avail, but under ordinary circumstances the vessel would have been safe when moored in the harbour.-- Wm. Leonard said on the 28th October he, along with a number of others, noticed the Glastry making for the harbour, about half-past four, at which time there was a very heavy gale. They were in boats watching for vessels to sea if they could render them any assistance. They saw the Glastry come round the salt pier head, and they saw her there lose her headsails, which were blown away. When she got past the pier head she ran into another vessel, which stopped her, and she began to drift south. Two or three of them then boarded her, and endeavoured to make her fast. The tide ebbed about five o'clock, and the sea was very rough. They succeeded in getting her along the Lighthouse pier, and they made her as fast as they could. She remained on the ground about an hour. They went on board again to see the captain and asked him to make some arrangements, but he would not. The Harbour Master said when the tide began to flow they must have plenty of force, and they went on board when it began to flow. It would be about half-past six, and they continued on board till nearly two o'clock. They finally made use of all the vessel's ropes and others as well, and made her tight. Under ordinary circumstances it would have been, and in fact they did more than they should under ordinary circumstances. About two the storm increased in violence, and in spite of anything they could do she broke loose and drifted unto the beach, but had since been got off and put into the harbour. They risked their lives, and if they had not assisted the ship would not have got in.-- The captain, in reply to Mr. Woodall, the magistrates' clerk, said the men gave him every assistance.-- Mr. Appleyard, harbour master, said the last witness's account was very straightforward. They rendered every assistance, and would have been safe under ordinary circumstances. The Glastry when she broke loose damaged warps and the pier to the extent of £150.-- Mr. Watts said he was told the Glastry was insured for £700.-- The captain said he was willing to pay what was fair and just, and was instructed by the owner to offer the sum of £5.-- Mr. Watts said he could not entertain it.-- Chas. Harwood said on the night in question he had some conversation with the captain, who asked him if he could get him 12 or 14 men for a tide's work; that was between five and six o'clock.

-- Cross-examined: He asked £40, but the captain told he thought about 5s each.-- The captain said he had been told that the chain was maliciously let go, and after staying there for nine hours it looked very suspicious, and he had also a rope on board at the present time which had been cut through in the middle.-- The magistrates retired, and on their return into court, Ald. Champley said they unanimously allowed £12 and the costs.

TSR 2/7 p125
Vessel stranded and afterwards sold to be converted into a hulk at Scarborough. Certificate cancelled and register closed 4th December 1880.

1881 The York Herald Sat. 19 Mar. p.6
Scarbro' : Sailed: March 18: Glastry, Husband, Hartlepool, ballast.

1881 The Daily Gazette (Middlesbrough) Sat. 19 Mar. p.4
Hartlepool: Arrivals: Mar. 18: Glastry, Husband, from Scarborough, ballast.
Mar. 22 p.4
Hartlepool. Exports. Mar. 21: Glastry, Husband, Scarborough, 260 tons of coals, from East Helton Colliery. W.H. Porter, shipper.

1881 The Northern Echo (Darlington) Mon. 2 May p.4
H'pool: Sailed: Apr. 30: Glastry, Warwick, for Scarboro'.

……………..
1885 The Northern Echo (Darlington) Mon. 2 May p.4
Scarborough, May 1: The hulk Glastry, Short, of and for Scarborough, from Hartlepool in tow of tug, came ashore about two miles north of Scarborough this morning. Assistance gone from here.

1885 The North-Eastern Daily Gazette (Middlesbrough) Tues. 29 Apr.
Glastry (in tow of St. Dauntless), Cowell, Scarborough, 250 tons of large coals. W.H. Scaffe shipper.

1895 [2] The Northern Echo Wed. 4 Sept.
W H'pool: Arrived: Aug. 2: Glastry (hulk), Short, Scarborough, light.

1895 The North-Eastern Daily Gazette (Middlesbrough) 7 Sept. Fourth Edition.
Hartlepool: Sailing, September 6: Glastry, Short, Scarborough.

1895 The Yorkshire Herald Wed. 13 Nov. p.7
Hartlepool: Sailed, November 9: Glastry, Scarborough.

[**MNL** 1888-96: 60319 Glastry, Scarborough, 169, Owner: George T. Williamson, Scarborough]
[**MNL** 1898-1900: 60319 Glastry, Scarborough, (no rig specified) 169, Owner: Mrs. Jane Fenwick, Scarborough: Manager, M. Fenwick, St. Martin's Place, Scarborough]

This is the last news up to date. She was a tough one.

MAGGIE GROSS

Official No.	59256	Code letters	JGPM
Built	1869 July	Moncton, New Brunswick, Canada	
Deck	One	Build	
Masts	Two	Gallery	None
Rigging	**Brigantine**	Head	Female
Stern		Framework	Wood (maple).
Tonnage	**185**	Length 101.8 feet; Breadth 25.9 feet; Depth 11.4 feet.	

As most of the small sailing vessels, she was not in the fleet for long.
She was owned and worked by Captain J. S. Gross, out of Canada from 1869 until she was sold in Swansea 1873 to G. Shaddick & J. H. Burgess.

[**MNL** 1870: Maggie Gross of St. John, N.B.: Owner: William Haines, Moncton, N.B.]

1869 The Belfast News-Letter Thurs. Morning 16 Sept.
In Belfast Lough, the Maggie Gross, from St. John, N.S.—for orders.

1869 The Glasgow Herald Sat. 18 Sept. p.7
Tail of the Bank: Arrived: Sept. 16: Maggie Gross, Gross, Moncton, N.B., to Greenock.
Oct. 5 p.7
Greenock: The shipments of coal during the past week: 310 tons coal, per Maggie Gross, for Cienfuegos. [Cuba]
Oct. 7 p.7
Tail of the Bank: Sailed: Oct. 6: Maggie Gross, Gross, from Greenock to Cienfuegos.
Oct. 11 p.6
Lamlash: Put in: Oct. 8: Maggie Gross, Gross, from Greenock to Cuba.
Oct. 15 p.6
Lamlash: Sailed: Oct. 13: Maggie Gross, Gross, from Greenock to Cuba.

1870 New York Herald Fri. 4 Feb. --triple sheet-- p.10
Holme's Hole: Arrived: Feb. 2: brig Maggie Gross (Br.), Gross, Cienfuegos for Portland.
May 5 --triple sheet-- p.10
New York: Arrivals: May 4: Brig Maggie Gross (Br), Gross, Matanzas 18 days, with sugar and molasses, to order.—vessel to master. Had light winds and calm the entire passage. Has been 6 days N of Hatteras. The M G is anchored in the lower bay.

1870 The New-York Times Wed. Aug. 13
New-York: Arrived: Friday Aug 12: Brig Maggie Gross (of St. John N.B) Gross. Miik (sic) River in Ja., 22 ds., with logwood to A.H. Salomon & Co. – vessel to Honey & Parker; crossed the equator July 5 in lon. 33 30, and since had light variable winds and calms, and been 4 ds. N. of Hatteras. [Maggie Gross had gone to Milk River in Jamaica.]
Aug. 27
New-York: Cleared: Friday, Aug. 26: Brig: Maggie Gross, (Br.,) Gross, St. John, N.B.

1870 New York Herald Sun. 28 Aug. --triple sheet-- p. 10
Passed Through Hell Gate: Aug. 27: Bound East: Brig Maggie Gross, Gross, New York for St. John, N.B.
1871 Mar. 12 p.12
New York: Cleared: Mar. 11: Brig Maggie Gross (Br), Gross, Matanzas, Snow & Burgess
Apr. 22
Matanzas: Arrived: Apr. 7: brig Maggie Gross (Br), Gross, New York.
May 28 p.12
St. John, N.B: Arrival: May 25: brig Maggie Gross (Br), Woodhouse, New York.

1871 The New-York Times Fri. May 19
Port of New-York. Cleared: May 18: Brig Maggie Gross (Br.), Outhouse (sic), St. John N.B.
June 22
Port of New-York: Arrived: June 21: Brig. Maggie Gross, (Br.,) Gross, St. John, N.B. 12 ds. with lumber.
June 29
Port of New-York: Cleared: June 28: Brig Maggie Gross (Br), Gross, Lingan. C.B. [coal mine Nova Scotia]
[Survey: Boston in August.]

1871 The Glasgow Herald Fri. 6 Oct. p.6
Wilmington [North Carolina]: *Cleared: Sept. 20: Maggie Cross (sic), for London.*

1871 The Standard (London) Mon. 30 Oct. p.7
Gravesend: Arrived: Oct 28: Maggie Gross, from Wilmington.
Nov. 4 p.7
London: Custom House: Entered Out: Nov. 3: Maggie Gross, for Porto Rico.
Dec. 4 p.7
Gravesend: Sailed: Dec. 1: Maggie Cross (sic) for Porto Rico.

1871 The Morning Chronicle (Halifax) Thurs. 21 Dec. p.3
Reports, Disasters, &c.: Portland, Dec 4, The Maggie Gross brigantine of St. John N B, Gross, from London for Porto Rico, has put into the roads and landed Mr. Denton, channel pilot, having lost anchor and chain in Prince's Channel.

[Survey: Baltimore in April 1872.]

1872 New York Herald Sun. 19 May Quadruple Sheet p.12
St. John, N.B: Arrived: May 16: brig Maggie Gross (Br), Gross, Baltimore.
Sept. 5 Triple Sheet
Satilla River: Arrived: Aug. 7: brig Maggie Gross (Br), Gross, Cardenas (and cleared 24th for St. John, N.B).
Sept. 15 p.12
St John, N.B, Arrived: Sept. 12: brig Maggie Gross (Br), Gross, Satilla.

{http://daryl.chin.gc.ca:8000/} (The voyages in small type are furnished by "Canada Heritage, Memorial University 1869-1883)

Saint John	01-10-1872
Parsboro (Nova Scotia)	18-10-1872 to 30-10-1872
Liverpool	21-11-1872 to 06-12-1872
Cienfuegos	22-01-1873 to 10-02-1873
Saint John	02-03-1873

1872 The Glasgow Herald Wed. 23 Nov. p.6
Liverpool: Arrived: Nov. 22: Maggie Gross from Parrsbro'. [Canada]

Saint John	11-03-1873
Workington (Cumbria)	02-04-1873 to 13-04-1873
Swansea (Wales)	19-04-1873

{http://daryl.chin.gc.ca:8000/}
[Under Owners of Maggie Gross;   Remarks: Sold to G. Shaddock (sic) and J.H. Burgess of Swansea on February 24, 1873.]

1873 The Western Mail (Cardiff) Thurs. 8 May p.4
Swansea: Entered Outwards: May 7: Maggie Gross, B, 18?, Kelso, Brest.
May 20 p.4
Swansea: Cleared: May 19: Maggie Gross, B, Brest, 311 patent fuel.

1873 The Liverpool Mercury Thurs. 4 Sept. p.3
Liverpool: Sailed: Sept. 2: Maggie Gross, Brest.

1873 The Western Mail (Cardiff) Fri. 10 Oct. p.4
Cardiff: Entered Outwards: Oct. 9: Maggie Gross, B, 170, Kelso, Corunna, Burgess, Shaddick, and Co.
Oct. 20 p.4
Cardiff: Cleared: Oct. 20: Maggie Gross, B, Corunna 341 coal, Burgess & Co.
Dec. 31 p.4
Newport: Imports: Dec. 30: Maggie Gross, B, Santander, iron ore.

++++++++++ **Hine Brothers**
[Survey: Swansea April 1874.]

1874 The Standard (London) Mon. 24 Aug. p.7
Off the Lizard: Arrivals: Aug. 22: Maggie Cross (sic), Swansea.

1874 Adair's Maryport Advertiser Fri. 28 Aug. p.8
Falmouth: Arrived: Aug. 22: Maggie Gross, Kelso.
Sept. 11 p.8
Plymouth: put into: Sept. 10: Maggie Gross.
Nov. 13 p.8
Troon: Sailed: Nov. 10: Maggie Gross, Kelso, for Bilbao.
Dec. 4 p.8
Bilbao: Arrived: Nov. 22: Maggie Gross, Kelso.

1875 The Glasgow Herald Mon. 8 Mar p.6
Troon: Arrived: Mar. 6: Maggie Gross, Bilbao.
Mar. 25 p.6
Troon: Sailed: Mar. 24: Maggie Gross, Maryport.

[**LR** 1875: Captain: blank. Owner: J.H. Burgess, Swansea.]
[**MNL** 1875 & 1876: Maggie Gross, Swansea: Owner: Sloane Richards, Birmingham]
[**LR** 1876-77: Captain: blank. Owners: Hine Bros., Swansea.]
[**LR** 1878: Captain: blank. Owners: Hine Bros. amended to S. Morrison, Swansea.]

1875 Adair's Maryport Advertiser Fri. 2 Apr. p.8
Maryport: Arrived: Mar. 28: Maggie Gross, Kelso, from Troon.
May 21 p.8
Maryport: Sailed: May 15: Maggie Gross, Holmes, for Llanelly.
Llanelly: Arrived: May 19: Maggie Gross.
June 11 p.8
Dublin: Arrived: June 7: Maggie Gross, Holmes, arrived at Dublin from Llanelly.
July 2 p.8
Maryport: Arrived: June 25: Maggie Gross, Holmes, arrived here on the 25th and sailed
Maryport: Sailed: June 29: Maggie Gross, Holmes, for Llanelly.
July 9 p.8
Llanelly: Arrived: July 3: Maggie Gross, Holmes.
July 30 p.8
Dublin: Arrived: July 25: Maggie Gross, Holmes.

Sept. 10 p.8
Cardiff: Sailed: Sept. 4: Maggie Gross, Holmes, for Lisbon.
Oct. 29 p.8
Ardrossan: Arrived: Oct. 26: Maggie Gross, Holmes, from Lisbon.
Nov. 12 p.8
Ardrossan: Sailed: Nov. 9: Maggie Gross, Holmes, for Waterford.
Nov. 19 p.8
Waterford: Arrived: Nov. 12: Maggie Gross.
Dec. 17 p.8
Garston: Arrived: Dec. 13: Maggie Gross, Holmes.
1876 Jan. 21 p.8
Garston: Sailed: Jan. 12: Maggie Gross, Holmes, for Dublin.
Dublin: Arrived: Jan. 13: Maggie Gross, Holmes.
Feb. 4 p.8
Dublin: Sailed: Jan. 31: Maggie Gross, Holmes, for Maryport.
Maryport: Arrived: Feb. 1: Maggie Gross, Holmes.
Feb. 11 p.8
Maryport: Sailed: Feb. 6: Maggie Gross, Holmes, for Dundalk.
Dundalk: Arrived: Feb. 10: Maggie Gross, Holmes.
Mar. 17 p.8
Maryport: Sailed: Mar. 12: Maggie Gross, Wedgwood, for Dundalk.
Dundalk: Arrived: Mar. 15: Maggie Gross, Wedgwood.
Apr. 28 p.8
Swansea: Sailed: Apr. 22: Maggie Gross, Wedgwood, for Dublin.
Dublin: Arrived: Apr. 25: Maggie Gross, Wedgwood.

1876 The Western Mail (Cardiff) Fri. 7 July p.7
Cardiff, West Dock: Sailings: July 5 and 6: Maggie Gross, Wedgwood, Southampton.

1876 The Hampshire Advertiser County Newspaper Sat. 22 July p.8
Southampton: Discharging: At the Dock: Maggie Gross, from Cardiff, coals.

1876 The Western Mail (Cardiff) Wed. 16 Aug. p.7
Cardiff, Penarth Roads: Arrivals: Aug. 14 and 15: Maggie Gross, Wedgewood (sic).
Aug. 18 p.7
Cardiff, West Bute Dock: Arrivals: Aug. 16 and 17: Maggie Grosy (sic), 179, Wedgwood, Southampton, ballast.

1876 The Belfast News-Letter Tues. 29 Aug. p.
Belfast: Arrival of Coal-laden Vessel: Aug. 27 and 28: Maggie Cross (sic), from Cardiff.

1876 Adair's Maryport Advertiser Fri. 29 Sept. p.8
Port of Maryport: Sailing: Sept. 22: Maggie Gross, Wedgwood, Newport.

1876 The Western Mail (Cardiff) Fri. Sept. 29 p.7
Newport, Dock: Arrivals: Sept. 27 and 28: Maggie Gross, 196, Wedgwood, Maryport, pig iron.
Oct. 12 p.7
Newport, Dock: Sailings: Oct. 10: Maggie Gross, Wandsworth, Dunkirk.

1876 The Freeman's Journal (Dublin) Fri. 24 Nov. p.3
Kingstown: Arrivals: Nov. 23: Maggie Cross (sic), from Workington, with pig iron, for Newport, windbound.
Nov. 29 p.3
Kingstown: Arrivals: Nov. 28: Maggie Cross (sic) M'Clean (sic), from Workington, with pig iron, for Newport, windbound.

1876 The Western Mail (Cardiff) Sat. 2 Dec. p.7
Newport, River: Arrivals: Dec. 1: Maggie Gross, 179, Wedgwood, Workington, pig iron.
Dec. 4 p.7
Newport, Dock: Arrivals: Dec. 1: Maggie Gross, Wedgwood, River, light.

1877 The Belfast News-Letter Wed. Morning 9 May
Belfast: Arrival of Coal-Laden Vessels: May 8: Maggie Gross from Swansea.
May 23
Belfast: Sailed: May 22: Maggie Gross for Maryport.

1877 Adair's Maryport Advertiser Fri. 1 June p.8
Maryport: Arrivals: May 24: Maggie Gross, Saul, Belfast.

1877 The North Wales Chronicle Sat. 30 June p.5
Holyhead: Arrived: Maggie Cross (sic), Wedgwood, Newport: Sailed: for Dundalk.
+++++++++++ ?

[**MNL** 1878: Maggie Gross of Swansea: Owner: Samuel Morrison, Ann St., Ironworks, Belfast.]

1878 The Western Mail (Cardiff) Sat. 9 Jan. p.4
Neath: Cleared: Jan.8: Maggie Gross, Dublin, coal.

1878 The Freeman's Journal (Dublin) Wed. 16 Jan. p.7
Dublin: Arrivals: Jan. 15: Maggie Gross, from Swansea, with coals.
Feb. 26
Workington: Sailed: Feb. 25: Maggie Gross, for Dublin.
Mar. 1 p.3
Dublin: Arrivals: Feb. 28: Maggie Gros (sic), from Workington, with railway iron.

1878 The Liverpool Mercury Tues. 10 Sept. p.3
Spoken: Maggie Cross (sic) (brig) bound E. Sept. 6, 51 N. 22 W.

1878 The Isle of Man Times and General Advertiser Sat. 21 Sept. p.4
Suit for Seamen's Wages.—On Wednesday last John McIvoie (sic), the master of the brigantine Maggie Gross, was summoned before the High Bailiff and Col. Price, by Samuel Stevenson, the mate, and four of the seamen of the Maggie Gross, for wages due to them. The crew had been discharged on the previous day, and were offered, as the owner alleged, the full amount of wages due to them. They refused to take what was offered, claiming a day's pay more, and as the owner declined to pay the extra day, the crew brought this suit to recover. Mr. Kellett appeared for the crew, and Mr. Cannell for the master. The latter took a preliminary objection that the court had no jurisdiction, and that in the absence of the ship's articles no claim beyond the certificate handed in to the Collector of Customs by the defendant in terms of the Merchant Shipping Act could be claimed. He offered, however, to admit to the extent of the tender made, less his costs, and on the advice of the Court the plaintiff's accepted the compromise rather than incur the loss of further delay.

1878 The Freeman's Journal (Dublin) Tues. 22 Oct. p.3
Belfast: Arrived: Oct 21: Maggie Gross, from Troon, with coals.

1879 The Western Mail (Cardiff) Tues. 4 Mar. p.4
The brigantine Maggie Gross of Swansea, collided with the schooner Candace, of Aberyst., Jones master, in Milford Haven, on Sunday morning. The Candace carried away her bulwarks and stanchions on the starboard side.

1879 The Freeman's Journal (Dublin) Sat. 8 Mar. p.3

Newry: Arrived: Mar. 7: Maggie Gross, of Swansea, Marston (sic), master, from Swansea, coal.

Mar. 25

Newry: Sailings: Mar. 24: Maggie Cross (sic) of Swansea, Morrisson (sic) master, for Liverpool, stones.

1879 The Liverpool Mercury Wed. 2 Apr. p.3

Liverpool: Arrived: Apr. 1: Maggie Cross (sic).

1879 The Belfast News-Letter Mon. 21 Apr. p.6

Belfast: Arrivals of Coal-laden Vessels: Apr. 19: Maggie Gross, from Liverpool.

May 26 p.3

Belfast: loading at this port May 24: the brigantine Maggie Gross, Morrison, for Denmark, with salt rock.

1879 The Daily (London) Wed. June 4 p.3

Belfast: Sailed: June 2: Maggie Gross for Copenhagen.

1879 The Freeman's Journal (Dublin) Thurs. 10 July p.3

Frederica [Denmark]*: Arrived: June 27: Brigantine Maggie Gross, Morrison, from Belfast.*

Sept. 2

At Stornoway, on the 26 ult, the brigantine Maggie Gloss (sic), of Belfast, Morrison, from Gondswall (sic) for Douglas.

1879 The Belfast News-Letter Thurs. 11 Sept. p.1

Deaths: Morrison--September 7, at sea, on passage from Sundswall to Douglas, Captain William Morrison, 20 Dunluce Terrace, Belfast.

Sept. 22 p.6

At Douglas, September 15, the brigantine Maggie Gross, Stevenson, of Belfast, from Sandswall (sic).

Nov. 8 p.1

[Advert] Vessel for sale. To be Sold by Public Auction, at the Queen's Quay, Belfast (unless previously disposed of by private treaty), on Friday, 14 November, 1879, at One o'clock p.m.

The Well Known Brigantine Maggie Gross, of Swansea, built at Moncton, N.B., 1869: Length 101 ft, 8-tenths, Breadth 25 ft 9 tenths, Depth 11 ft. 4 tenths. 179 tons Register; has just discharged 325 tons coal. This vessel is extra heavily iron-kneed, and strongly fastened for the Iron and Copper Ore Trades; was docked in 1878, when she was thoroughly overhauled. Is well found in Anchors, Chains, Ropes, Sails &c.; would cross Channel without ballast; will be found a most desirable vessel for the general Coasting Trades, carrying a large cargo on light draught of water. Is ready for immediate employment, provisions only required to send her to sea. For further particulars, apply to: Morrison & Gough, 32 Garmoyle Street: Henry Gowan, Ship Valuer and Auctioneer.

[**MNL** 1880: Maggie Gross of Swansea: Owner: Samuel Morrison, Ann St., Ironworks, Belfast.]

1880 The Glasgow Herald Wed. 7 Jan. p.6

Troon: Sailed: Jan. 6: Maggie Gross, Dundalk.

1880 The Belfast News-Letter Sat. 7 Feb. p.6

Belfast: Arrived: Feb. 6: Coal Laden Vessels: the Maggie Gross, from Garston.

Feb. 18 p.3

Belfast: Sailed: Feb. 17: Maggie Gross, for Troon.

Mar. 12 p.6
Belfast: Arrived: Mar. 11: Coal Laden Vessels: the Maggie Gross, from Garston.
Mar. 23 p.6
Belfast: Sailed: Mar. 21 & 22: Maggie Gross, for Newport.

1880 The Bristol Mercury Sat. 16 Oct. p.7
Pill [Port Pill, near Bristol]: *Arrived: Oct. 15: Maggie Gross, Cardiff.*

1880 The Glasgow Herald Mon. 6 Dec. p.3
Lamlash: Put in, Dec. 3: Maggie Gross, for Tralee.

1880 The Daily News (London) Fri. 17 Dec. p.7
A telegram from Bowmore, Scotland, Dec. 16, states that the Maggie Gross is reported on the rocks at Lochindaal, and is a total wreck; saving what can of top gear. The Maggie Gross, brigantine, of Swansea, laden with coals, was bound from Greenock for Tralee.

1880 The Western Mail (Cardiff) Fri. 17 Dec. p.7
The brigantine Maggie Gross of Swansea, from Greenock to Tralee, has been totally wrecked at Port Charlotte Islay.

1880 The Glasgow Herald Tues. 21 Dec. p.2
Last Week's Wreck: Maggie Gross (11): S (sail): Swansea: 185: Coals: Crew and Pass: Lost none: Saved all.

{http://canmore.rcahms.gov.uk/}
Royal Commission of the Ancient and Historical Monuments of Scotland.

[Contemporary] source: Lightkeeper, Loch Indaal Lighthouse.
Maggie Gross, 179 ton, brigantine, master Martin, of Swansea bound from Greenock to Tralee, cargo coals. Crew 6, all saved. Lost 14 Dec 1880, 11 p.m. Near Port Charlotte. 1 mile from Loch indaal Lighthouse. 'Missed stays, anchor failed to bring her round, she became helpless and drove ashore'.

Source: PP Abstracts Returns of Wrecks and Casualties on Coasts of the UK 1880-81}
14 December 1880, Maggie Gross, 11 yrs old, of Swansea, wooden brigantine, 179 tons, 6 crew, Master N. Martin, Owner S. Morrison, Belfast, departed Greenock for Tralee, carrying coal, wind WSW 9, stranded, total loss, near Port Carlotte, Arygyleshire.

CLARA

Official No.	**50799**		
Built	1865 July	In Truro, Nova Scotia, Canada	
Deck	One	Build	--------
Masts	--------	Gallery	None
Rigging	**Brigantine**	Head	Woman
Stern	---------	Framework	Wood (maple).
Tonnage	**145**	Length 90.0 feet; Breadth 23.2 feet; Depth 11.2 feet.	

There are too many Claras. The Newspapers did not distinguish the different Claras. So mistakes may arise, great care has been made to avoid them.
{Ship Building in Nova Scotia, Canada, 1859-1891
Clara, Brgt, N/A (tons), 1865, J. Crowe (Owner), J. Crowe et al (Builders) Old Barns (where) P.A.N.S. (source)}

[**ALRAFS** 1866-71: Clara, White, N168, 1 Deck, 1865 Truro N.S., Truro Jas Crow, (86, 22, 11)]
[**ALRAFS** 1875: Clara, Burns, 144, 1865 Truro N.S., St. John, Wm. Donelly (sic)]
[**ALRAFS** 1876: Clara, --------, 144, 1865 Truro N.S., Swansea, Shaddick & Burgess]
[**ALRAFS** 1876-77: Clara, G. McLeod, 144, 1865 Truro N.S., Swansea, Hine Bros.]
[**ALRAFS** 1878-83: Clara, G. McLeod, 145, 1865 Truro N.S, Swansea, Hine Bros. (90, 23.2, 11.2)]
[**RAFS** 1871-76: Clara, White John, 12B, Br, Truro, 144, 1865 Truro N.S., James Crow]
[**MNL** 1870: 50799 Clara, St. John's, Newfoundland, 145 tons. Owner: William Henry Mare, St. John's, Newfoundland.]

.

1865 New York Herald Thurs. 6 Oct. p.8
New York: Cleared: Oct. 5: Clara (Br.,) White, Maitland, N.S.--J. F. Whitney & Co.
[Survey: New York in October]

1865 Halifax Citizen Tues. 14 Nov.
Ship News—Disasters: Portland, Nov. 9: brig Clara, from Truro, N.S. for New York, put into this port this A.M. and reported that Morton Buckworth, a seaman, fell from the maintop and was killed.

1865 The New-York Times Tues. 21 Nov.
New-York: Arrived: Nov. 20: Brig Clara, White, Windsor, N.S., 18 ds., with plaster to J. F. Whitney & Co.

1866 New York Herald Tues. 30 Jan. --with supplement-- p.5
Demerara: Arrived: Jan. 6: brig Clara, White, N. York.
Feb. 1 p.6
St. Thomas Jan. 22: In port brig Clara (Br), White from New York via Demerara for charter.

1866 Evening Express New York Fri. 1 Feb.
New York: Arrived: 31 Jan: Brig, Clara, White, from San Juan, Nic.

1866 New York Herald Tues. 13 Mar. --with supplement-- p.5
New York: Arrived: Mar. 12: brig Clara, White, Trinidad (Cuba), 25 days, with sugar and molasses to J.F. Whitney & Co.
May 1 p.8
St. John, N.S. Arrived: Apr. 9: brig, Clara, White, N. York.
June 8 p.8
New York: Cleared: June 7: Brig Clara (Br.), White, Halifax--J. F. Whitney & Co.
July 24 p.3

New York: Arrived: July 23: Brig. Clara, (Br.,) White, Lingan [coal mine in Nova Scotia]*, with coal to J. F. Whitney & Co.*
Sept. 14 p.8
St Johns, N.F. Arrived: Aug. 23: brig Clara, White, N. York 9 and cld [cleared] *for Lingan.*

[Surveys: New York in November 1866: in December 1867: in October 1868: and at Boston in October 1870]

{Her port of registry in November 1873 was Swansea.}

1873 The Western Mail (Cardiff) Sat. 18 Jan. p.4
Newport: Entered Outwards, Jan. 17: Clara, B, 144, Richards, Bilbao.
Jan. 25 p.4
Newport: Cleared, Jan. 24: Clara, B, Bilbao &c, 250 coal.
Feb. 26 p.
Bilbao: Arrived: Feb. 15: Clara, from Newport.
Apr. 1 p.4
Newport: Imports, Mar. 31: Clara, B, Bilbao, iron ore.
May 17 p.4
Swansea: Entered Outwards, May 16: Clara, B, 144, Pyman, Corunna, Burgess, Shaddick and Co.
May 27 p.4
Swansea: Cleared: May 26: Clara, B, Corunna, 273 coal.
June 12 p.4
Corunna: Arrived: June 4: Clare (sic), Pyman, from Swansea.

1873 Adair's Maryport Advertiser Fri. 12 Sept. p.8
Maryport: Arrived: Sept. 10: Clara, Pyman, from Bilbao.

1873 The Western Mail (Cardiff) Mon. Dec. 8 p. 4
Swansea: Entered Outwards: Dec. 6: Clara, B, 144, Pyman, Abiento.
Dec. 11 p.4
Swansea: Cleared: Dec. 10: Clara, B, Alicante, 230 coal.

1874 The Western Mail (Cardiff) Fri. 27 Mar. p.8
Swansea: Entered Outwards: Mar. 26: Clara, B, 144, Pyman, Carthagena.

++++++++++ **Hine Brothers**
{Captain George McLeod (Master Cert. No. 33008), signed on 10.04.1874. (His previous ship had been the s.s. Laorna).}
Apr. 15 p.8
Swansea: Cleared: Apr. 14: Clara, B, Carthagena, 230 patent fuel.
June 4 p.6
Carthagena: Homeward Bound: Clara for Swansea.
July 1 p.7
Swansea: Imports, June 30: Clara, 144, Porman [Port of Porman near Cartagena, Spain]*, 330 iron ore.*

[LR 1874: 50799 Clara, Bn, G. M'Leod: 144/135, N.Scot. 1865, G. Shaddick & J.H. Burgess, Swansea. -------]
[LR 1875: Captain: G. M'Leod. Owners: G. Shaddick & J.H. Burgess, Swansea.]
[LR 1876: Captain: G. M'Leod. Owners: Hine Bros. Swansea.]

1874 The Western Mail (Cardiff) Thurs. 27 Aug. p.7
Newport: Imports: Aug. 26: Clara, B, Santander, iron ore.

1874 Adair's Maryport Advertiser Fri. 28 Aug. p.8
Newport: Arrived: Aug. 25: Clara, McLeod, from Santander.
[Survey: Swansea in October.]
Nov. 20 p.8
Falmouth: Arrived: Nov. 17: Clara, McLeod.

1875 The North Wales Chronicle Sat. 19 June p.
Holyhead: Arrived: Clara, McLeod, Maryport.
Holyhead: Sailed: Clara, McLeod, Port Talbot.

1875 Adair's Maryport Advertiser Fri. 25 June p.8
Port Talbot: Arrived: June 19: Clara, McLeod, from Maryport.

[MNL 1875 & 1878: 50799 Clara of Swansea, Owner: Sloane Richards, Birmingham.]

1875 The Western Mail (Cardiff) Tues. 29 June p.7
Swansea: Arrivals: South Dock, June 28: Clara, 144, M'Leod, Port Talbot, ballast.
June 30 p.7
Swansea: Entered Outwards, June 29: Clara, B, 144, McLeod, Lisbon.

1875 Adair's Maryport Advertiser Fri July 30 p.8
Clara, McLeod, spoken July 12 for Lisbon.

1875 The Glasgow Herald Wed. 15 Sept. p.6
Ardrossan: Arrived: Sept. 14: Clara from Lisbon.
Oct. 1 p.6
Ardrossan: Sailed: Sept. 30: Clara, Santander.

1875 Adair's Maryport Advertiser Fri Nov. 5 p.8
Santander: Arrived: Oct. 26: Clara, McLeod.
Dec. 17 p.8
Port William: Arrived: Dec. 14: Clara, McLeod.
1876 Jan. 7 p.8
Portwilliam: Left: Jan. 3: Clara, McLeod, for Maryport.
Maryport: Arrived: Jan 4: Clara.
Jan. 14 p.8
Swansea: Arrived: Jan. 13: Clara, McLeod.
Feb. 11 p.8
Swansea: Sailed: Feb. 6: Clara, McLeod, for Dublin.
Feb. 18 p.8
Dublin: Arrived: Feb. 16: Clara, McLeod, from Swansea.
Mar. 17 p.8
Swansea: Sailed: Mar. 12: Clara, McLeod, for Maryport.

1876 The Freeman's Journal (Dublin) Mon. 24 Apr. p.8
Dublin: Sailings: Apr. 21: Clara, Maryport, manure.

1876 Adair's Maryport Advertiser Fri 28 Apr. p.8
Maryport: Arrived: Apr. 24: Clara, McLeod.

1876 The Western Mail (Cardiff) Tues. 29 June p.7
Swansea, South Dock: Arrivals: June 28: Clara, 144, M'Leod, Port Talbot, ballast.

1876 The Western Mail (Cardiff) Thurs. 14 Sept. p.7
Swansea, North Dock: Arrivals: Sept. 13: Clara, 144, M'Leod, Maryport, pig iron.
Sept. 29 p.7
Swansea, North Dock: Sailings: Sept. 28: Clara, M'Leod, Belfast.

1876 The Belfast News-Letter, Wed. Morning, 18 Oct. p.
Belfast: Sailed Oct. 17: Clara, for Maryport.
Oct. 25 p.8
Maryport: Arrived: Oct. 24: Clara, from Dublin.

1876 The Western Mail (Cardiff) Mon. 20 Nov. p.7
Swansea, North Dock: Arrivals: Nov. 18: Clara, 144, Cloud (sic), Maryport, pig iron.

1876 The Belfast News-Letter, Wed. Morning, 13 Dec. p.
Belfast: Arrival: Dec. 12: Coal-laden Vessel: Clara, from Swansea.

1880 The Glasgow Herald Tues. 28 Sept. p.6
Glasgow: Arrived: Sept. 27: Clara 144, Hoddson (sic) [Hodgson ?], from Port-Talbot--coal.

[**MNL** 1880 & 1882: 50799 Clara of Swansea, 145, Owner: Sloane Richards, Birmingham.]

1882 The Maryport Advertiser and Weekly News Fri. 21 July
Maryport: Arrived: July 20: Clara, M'Cullough.

1882 The Maryport Advertiser and Weekly News Fri. 15 Dec. p.8
Messrs. Hine Brothers: Sailing ships: (barques) Castle Holme, Myrtle Holme, Brier Holme, Eden Holme, Abbey Holme, Hazel Holme, Aikshaw, Glenfalloch, Robert Hine; (Brigantine) Clara; (Schooner) Tom Roberts.
++++++++++?

[**MNL** 1880-3: 50799 Clara, Swansea, Bn, 145. Owner: Sloane Richards, Birmingham]
[**LR** 1883: 50799 Clara Bn, G. M'Leod/ W. Shilton, 145/135, W. Hine/ W. Shilton, Swansea. -----]

1884 The Belfast Newsletter Tues. 15 Nov. p.7
Lisbon: Sailed: Nov. 3: Clara, Wood, for Belfast.

1884 The Freeman's Journal 30 Dec. p.3
Belfast: Arrived: Dec. 29: Brigantine Clara, Wood, from Lisbon, with phosphate of lime.
1885 Jan. 9 p.3
Belfast: Sailed: Jan. 8: Brigantine Clara, Wood, for Swansea.
++++++++++?

1885 Maryport and Workington Advertiser Fri. 21 Aug. p.3
Messrs. Hine Brother's Ships: Sailing ships (only) Castle Holme, Myrtle Holme, Brier Holme, Eden Holme, Abbey Holme, Hazel Holme, Aikshaw. [No Clara]

[**LR** 1889: Clara, Bn, Sheffield, 136/135, B. Sheffield, Swansea, --------------]
[**MNL** 1888-91: 50799 Clara, Swansea, Bn, 136. Owner: Benjamin Sheffield, 49, Nelson St., Maryport.] [A Benjamin Sheffield had been the captain of the Glastry when it had been pummelled at Scarbrough in 1880]
[**MNL** 1892 & 93: 50799 Clara, Swansea, 136. Owner: x James Willcock, Manchester]

TOM ROBERTS

TOM ROBERTS

Official No.	**18904**	**Code letters MPSF**	
Built	1838	Milford	
Deck	One	Build	----------
Masts	Two	Gallery	none
Rigging	**Schooner**	Head	none
Stern		Framework	Wood
Tonnage	**117**	Length 74.5 feet; Breadth 21.0 feet; Depth 12.0 feet.	

[**LR** 1838-44: Tom Roberts, Sr, J. Samuel, 117, Milford, 1838 (3 mths): Capt. & Co. Milford. A1]

1838 The Morning Post (London) Sat. 28 July p.7
Off Dover: Arrived: July 26: Tom Roberts, Martin, from Galway.

1840 The Liverpool Mercury Fri. 11 Dec. p.411
On the 24th ult. saw the Tom Roberts putting into Gibraltar for supplies.

1840 The Morning Post (London) Sat. 12 Dec.
London: Entered Inwards: Tom Roberts, Samuel, from Cephalonia.

1841 The Morning Chronicle (London) Mon. 1 Mar.
Liverpool: Cleared Outwards: Feb. 27: Tom Roberts for Smyrna.
Mar. 11 p.8
Liverpool: Sailed: Mar. 10: Tom Roberts, Samuel, for Genoa.
Mar. 31 p.7
Cork: Sailed: Mar. 27: Tom Roberts for Algiers.

1841 The Liverpool Mercury Fri. 25 June p.211
Marseilles: Sailed: June 13: Tom Roberts, Samuel, for this port.

1841 The Morning Chronicle Fri. 23 July
Spoken: Argo from Hamburg, for the Pacific 17th lat 47 by the Tom Roberts, arrived at Milford.

1841 The Standard (London) Fri. 6 Aug.
Liverpool: Arrived: Aug. 5: Tom Roberts, from Marseilles.

1841 The Liverpool Mercury Fri. 27 Aug. p.287
Liverpool: Entered for Loading, for Europe: 117, Tom Roberts, Samuel, Leghorn.
Sept. 10 p.307
Liverpool: Sailed: Sept. 5: Tom Roberts, for Leghorn.
Oct. 22 p.7
At Leghorn: Tom Roberts, Samuel, hence.

1842 The Morning Post (London) Mon. 17 Jan.
London: Entered Inwards: Jan. 16: Tom Roberts, Samuel, from Leghorn.
Apr. 16 p.7
Liverpool: Entered for Loading: Apr. 15: Tom Roberts, Samuels, for Riga.

1842 The Liverpool Mercury Fri. 29 Apr. p.139
Liverpool: Sailed: Apr. 25: Tom Roberts, Samuels, Riga.
June 10 p.7
At Riga: Tom Roberts, hence.

1842 Caledonian Mercury, Edinburgh Mon. July 11
Riga: Sailed: June 30: Tom Roberts, Samuel, Dublin.

1842 The Morning Post (London) Fri. Sept. 2
Liverpool: Entered for Loading: Sept. 1: Tom Roberts, Samuel, for Leghorn.

1842 The Liverpool Mercury Fri. 30 Sept. p.319
Liverpool: Sailed: Sept. Tom Roberts, Samuel, Leghorn.

1843 The Liverpool Mercury Fri. 1 Sept. p.291
Aug. 27: Tom Roberts, Samuel, from Petersburgh for this port, at Milford, with loss of foreyard, having been in contact with the Edward of Aberdeen.

1843 The Morning Post (London) Tues. 5 Sept.
Liverpool: Arrived: Sept. 4: Tom Roberts, from St. Petersburgh.
Oct. 7 p.8
Liverpool: Cleared Outwards: Oct. 6: Tom Roberts, Samuel, for Syra and Salonica.
Oct. 19
Liverpool: Sailed: Oct. 18: Tom Roberts, Samuel, for Syra.
1844 June 7
Gravesend: Arrived: June 5: Tom Roberts from Smyrna.
Aug. 8 p.7
The Late Hurricane.—During the height of the gale of Saturday last, the Tom Roberts, a fine schooner, commanded by Captain Samuels, whilst making for Messina, having left Swansea some time previous, was struck by a sea from the eastward, and having sustained some damage, the captain thought the most prudent step to take would be to get the vessel to the first place, and have her repaired. Accordingly he bore up to Milford. In entering the harbour, just as they were going to tack the ship, a tremendous squall set in, which carried away the cleat at the bowsprit end of the jib-stay; thereby rendering the jib useless, and prevented the vessel from either wearing or staying. The ship was expected every minute to the carried upon the rocks, when Captain Samuels, with great presence of mind, had every one of the sails cut away, and both anchors dropped, which stopped the ship from striking the rocks. Had it not been for cutting away the sails, the ship must have been lost, and probably every soul on board, for when she was brought up, she was only a cable's length for this dangerous shoal.

1844 The Liverpool Mercury Fri. 20 Dec. p.429
At Milford: Tom Roberts, Samuel, from Sicily.

1845 Cornwall, Royal Gazette Fri. 3 Jan.
Falmouth: Arrived: Friday [1884 Dec. 26]: *Tom Roberts, from Catania.*
Jan. 10
Falmouth: Sailed: Friday [Jan. 3]: *Tom Roberts, Samuel, for Stockton.*

1845 Newcastle Courant Fri. 31 Jan. p.1
Sanders, Weatherall, & Co., Importers and General Wholesale Merchants. Have on Sale.
Ex. "Tom Roberts," Captain Samuel, from Messina. Stockton on Tees, 1st Mo. (Jan.) 29th 1845.

[**LR** 1845: Tom Roberts, Sr, J. Samuel/ W. James, 117, Capt. & Co/ Samuel & Co. Milford. A1]
[**LR** 1846-54: Tom Roberts, Sr, W. James, 117, Samuel & Co. Milford. A1]
[**LR** 1855-56: Tom Roberts, Sr, W. James, 117, Samuel & Co. Milford. AE1]

[LR 1857: Tom Roberts, Sr, W. James, 117, Samuel & Co. --------------------]
[LR 1858-59: Tom Roberts, Sr, -------------, 117, Samuel & Co. Milford. AE1]
[LR 1860-63: Tom Roberts, Sr, H, Jenkins, 117, Richards & Co. Milford. AE1]
[LR 1864-65: Tom Roberts, Sr, H, Jenkins/ D. Lewis, 117, Richards & Co. Milford. A1]
[LR 1867-72: Tom Roberts, Sr, D. Lewis/D. Wiilliams, 117, Richards & Co. Milford. A1]
[LR 1873: Tom Roberts, Sr, D. Williams, 117, Richards & Co. Milford. ---]

1845 The Hampshire Advertiser Sat. 1 Feb. p.8
Cowes, Isle of Wight: Arrived: Jan. 30: Tom Roberts, James, from Stockton, with coals for the market.

1845 The Morning Post (London) Sat. 16 Aug. p.7
Liverpool: Arrived: Aug. 15: Tom Roberts, from Cronstadt.

1845 The Liverpool Mercury Fri. 10 Oct. p.5
At Helyoet (?): Tom Roberts, James, hence.

1847 The Morning Chronicle (London) Fri. 12 Mar. p.8
Liverpool: Sailed: Mar. 11: Tom Roberts, for Beirout, Alexandria, and Galatz.
[Survey: Liverpool in March]

1847 Lloyd's Weekly London Newspaper Sun. 4 Apr. p.12
Tom Roberts from Liverpool for Alexandretta, put into Belfast, March 18th, with loss of foremast.

1847 The Liverpool Mercury Fri. 26 Mar. p.11
Tom Roberts, hence for Beirout at Belfast, with loss o (sic) foremast, sails, jibboom, &c. and one man overboard.

1847 The Standard (London) Tues. 9 Nov.
Spoken: Tom Roberts, 20th ult. off Cape de Gatt [Spain].

1848 The Liverpool Mercury Fri. 18 Feb. p.8
Liverpool: Sailed: Feb. 17: Tom Roberts, James, Galatz.

1848 Caledonian Mercury, Edinburgh Thurs. 6 Apr.
Malta, March 26.—The Tom Roberts, James, from Liverpool to Galatz, arrived here 22d inst. with loss of part of her starboard bulwarks, and skylight stove, having been struck by a sea which filled the cabin with water; vessel tight; but cleared 21st for Galatz.

1848 The Liverpool Mercury Fri. 16 June p.7
At Galatz: Tom Roberts, James, hence [from Liverpool].
1849 Mar. 27 p.7
Liverpool: Sailed: Mar. 16 (sic) [Mar. 23]*: Tom Roberts, James, Galatz.*
May 15 p.7
At Constantinople: Tom Roberts, James, cleared for the Danube.
1850 July 19 p.7
At Ibrail: Tom Roberts, Jones (sic), hence [from Liverpool].
July 30 p.7
Galatz: Sailed: July 11: Tom Roberts, James, for Queenstown or Falmouth.

1850 The Freeman's Journal (Dublin) Mon. 7 Oct.
Dublin: Arrived: Oct. 5: Tom Roberts, Galatz, Indian corn.
Oct. 8

Spoken: By the Tom Roberts, arrived on the 5th instant, the schooner Sphynx, of Liverpool for Cork or Falmouth, on the 3d ultimo off Lisbon, from Ibrail; all well.

1850 Caledonian Mercury, Edinburgh Thurs. 12 Dec.
At Paimboeuf: Dec. 5: Tom Robert (sic), Jones, from Clyde.

1851 The Morning Post Wed. 8 Jan. p.8
Liverpool: Arrived: Jan. 7: Tom Roberts, from Nantes.

1851 The Liverpool Mercury Fri. 17 Jan. p.7
Liverpool: Entered for Loading, Europe: Tom Roberts, James, 117, Galatz, &c.
Mar. 8 p.8
Liverpool: Sailed: Mar. 7: Tom Roberts, Galatz.
Mar. 18 p.7
At Milford: Mon. 16: Tom Roberts, James, hence [from Liverpool], *for Galatz.*

1851 The Standard (London) Wed. 2 Apr.
Milford: Sailed: Mar. 31: Tom Roberts, for Galatz.

1851 The Liverpool Mercury Fri. 30 May p.7
At Constantinople: Tom Roberts, Jones, hence.
Aug. 29 p.683
At Milford: Tom Roberts, Jones, from Galatz.

1853 The Morning Post (London) Thurs. 15 Sept. p.8
Deal: Arrived and Passed: Sept. 14: Tom Roberts, from Galatz to London.
Sept. 17 p.7
Gravesend: Arrived: Sept. 14: Tom Roberts, from Galatz.
Nov. 4 p.8
London: Cleared out: Nov. 3: Tom Roberts, for Corfu.

1855 The Glasgow Herald Friday Morning 2 Feb. p.7
At Havre: Jan. 23: Tom Roberts, James, from Clyde.

1855 Royal Cornwall Gazette Fri. 16 Feb. p.8
Penzance: Arrived: Tom Roberts, James, from Havre.
Mar. 16 p.8
Penzance: Sailed: Tom Roberts, James.

1855 The Bristol Mercury, and Western Counties Advertiser Sat. 15 Dec. p.7
Bristol: Imports: Tom Roberts, from Palermo, 77 tons brimstone, 1273 bags shumac, 6 cases Kernels of nuts, 247 cases lemons, 18 bags hempseed, 10 boxes 10 cases manus (??).

1856 The Liverpool Mercury Sat. 14 June p.7
Messina: Sailed: May 25: Tom Roberts, for Licata and Liverpool.

1856 The Standard (London) Tues. 15 July
Milford: Arrived: July 12: Tom Roberts, from Alicata.

1856 The Morning Chronicle (London) Wed. 30 July
Gravesend: Arrived: July 29: Tom Roberts, from Licata.
Sept. 3 p.8
London: Cleared outwards: Sept. 2: Tom Roberts, for Naples, Galatz, and Ibrail.
Sept. 6 p.8
Gravesend: Sailed: Sept. 4: Tom Roberts, for Naples.

1857 The Morning Post Wed. 6 May p.7
Sailed for Liverpool.—Tom Roberts from Tunis for Queenstown, has put into Malta, having struck on a rock near Cape Bon.

1857 The Standard (London) Wed. 1 July p.8
Milford: Arrived: June 29: Tom Roberts from Ibrail.

1858 The Glasgow Herald Monday Morning 1 Nov. p.7
Falmouth: Arrived: Oct. 28: Tom Roberts, Jenking (sic) from Gallipoli.

1858 Royal Cornwall Gazette Fri. 5 Nov. p.8
Falmouth: Sailed: Friday [Oct. 30]: Tom Roberts, Jenkins, for Liverpool.

1858 The Morning Post Wed. 24 Nov. p.8
Liverpool: Arrived: Nov. 23: Tom Roberts from Gallipoli.

1860 The Glasgow Daily Herald Fri. 3 Feb. p.6
At Kingston: Jan. 30: Tom Roberts, from Ardrossan for Dieppe.
Feb. 11 p.4
At Dieppe: Feb. 6: Tom Roberts, Jenkins, from Ardrossan.

1860 The Belfast News-Letter Sat. 8 Sept.
Belfast: Arrived: Sept. 6: Tom Roberts, Jenkins, from Villa Nova, with brimstones.

1860 The Freeman's Journal (Dublin) Fri. 21 Sept.
Belfast: Sailed (by Magnetic Telegraph): Tom Roberts, Ardrossan.

1860 The Glasgow Daily Herald 4 Oct.
Ardrossan: Sailed: Sept 27: Tom Roberts, Jenkins, for Genoa.
Nov. 27 p.4
At Genoa: Nov. 19: Tom Roberts, Jenkins, from Ardrossan.

1861 The Liverpool Mercury Tues. 19 Feb. p.3
Liverpool: Arrived: Feb. 17: Tom Roberts, Jenkins, Genoa.

1861 The Birmingham Daily Post Wed. 27 Feb. p.1
To be Sold by Auction: on the Quay, South-east corner of the Canada Dock, Liverpool. 207 Planks Italian Walnut. Now landing ex Tom Roberts from Genoa.

1861 The Liverpool Mercury Tues. 26 Mar.
Liverpool: Sailed: Mar. 22: Tom Roberts, Jenkins, Dordt.
Sat. 20 Apr.
Sale at Canada Dock, Liverpool: Ex Tom Roberts from Genoa: 116 Planks Italian Walnut: On account of the Importers, Farnworth & Jardine.

1861 The Liverpool Mercury Fri. 20 Sept. p.3
Gravesend: Arrived: Sept. 19: Tom Roberts from Palermo.

1861 The Morning Post (London) Thurs. 3 Oct. p.3
Gravesend: Sailed: Oct. 2: Tom Roberts to Caen.

1862 [Survey: Milford in April]

1863 The Liverpool Mercury Mon. 2 Mar. p.3

Hull: Arrived: Feb. 26: Tom Roberts, from Palermo.

1863 The Leeds Mercury Fri. Mar. 6 p.4
Goole: Arrived: Mar. 4: Tom Roberts, shellac, Palermo.

1863 The Hull Packet and East Riding Times Fri. 10 Apr. p.2
Goole: Sailed: weekly list: Tom Roberts, Naples.
May 22 p.2
Naples: Arrived: May 11: Tom Roberts, Jenkins, from Hull.
May 25 p.2
Rutter v. Hammond.—The plaintiff claimed £5 18s. 7d. as half commission in respect of the chartering of two vessels, the Lydia and Mary, and the Tom Roberts. It appeared that the plaintiff had chartered the vessel on behalf of the parties he represented, and he claimed the half commission from the defendant, who had been the broker.—The defendant alleged that he had not received the commission from the captain, and also that the plaintiff had agreed to give up his share of the commission in consideration of another transaction.—The plaintiff was non-suited.
July 17 p.2
Smyrna: Sailed: June 20: Tom Roberts, Jenkins, for Hull.
July 31 p.2
Cagliari: Arrived: July 18: Tom Roberts, Jenkins, from Smyrna for Hull.
Sept. 11 p.2
Hull: Arrived: Sept. 5: Tom Roberts, Jenkins, Smyrna. Imports: Four Roberts (sic), Smyrna, 150 tons valonia.
Oct. 9 p.2
Hull: Sailed: Oct. 3: Tom Roberts, Jenkins, Oporto.
Dec. 25 p.2
Oporto: Arrived: Dec. 10: Tom Roberts, Henry (sic ?), from Hull.
1864 Jan. 29 p.2
Cadiz: Sailed: Jan. 16: Tom Roberts, Jenkins, for Hull.
Feb. p.2
Hull: Arrived: Jan. 30: Tom Roberts, Jenkins, Cadiz.—Imports: from Oporto and Cadiz: 51 pipes 9¼ pipes Oporto wine, 111 butts 59 hdds 24¼ casks 6 vats Cadiz wine.
Mar. 25 p.2
Off Deal: Mar. 19: Tom Roberts, Jenkins, from Middlesbrough for Naples.
June 10 p.2
Palermo: Sailed: May 25: Tom Roberts, Jenkins, for Goole.
Aug. 26 p.2
Goole: Sailed: Goole Weekly list: Tom Roberts, for Messina.

1864 The Glasgow Daily Herald Tues. 29 Nov. p.3
Deal: Passed: Nov. 26: Tom Roberts (of Milford), Palermo.
Dec. 1
Gravesend: Arrived Nov. 30: Tom Roberts, Smyrna.

1865 [Survey: Milford in February]

1865 The Standard (London) Wed. 8 Mar. p.7
Cardiff: Mar. 6: The Richard Roper, schooner, of Ulverstone, ran into the Tom Roberts, schooner, of Milford, at anchor in Penarth Roads this afternoon, doing her so much damage that it is feared she will have to return into dock and discharge part of cargo.

1865 The Glasgow Daily Herald Thurs. 17 Aug. p.4
Glasgow: Arrived: Aug. 16: Tom Roberts, Lewis, from Gioja [Italy], with olive oil.
Nov. 10 p.7
At Palermo: Oct. 26: Tom Roberts, Williams, from the Clyde.

Dec. 29 p.7
Spoken: Tom Roberts, bound north-east, 20 Dec., in lat. 45 N, long. 23 W.

1866 The Leeds Mercury Wed. 3 Jan. p.4
Goole: Arrived: Jan. 1: Tom Roberts, sulphur, Palermo.

1867 The Liverpool Mercury Tues. 5 Mar. p.6
Liverpool: Arrived: Mar. 4: Tom Roberts, Williams, Catania [Sicily].
Apr. 16
Liverpool: Sailed: Apr. 13: Tom Roberts.

1867 The Bristol Mercury, and Western Counties Advertiser Sat. 2 Nov. p.7
Bristol Imports: Thursday's "Presentment": Tom Roberts, from London, 870 qrs. wheat.

1868 [Survey: Milford in July]

1869 The Western Mail (Cardiff) Thurs. 27 May p.3
Swansea: Arrivals: May 26: Tom Roberts, Williams, Harfleur.
July 5 p.3
Swansea: Entered Outwards: July 2: Tom Roberts: 121, Williams, Gibraltar.
July 10 p.
Swansea: Cleared: July 9: Tom Roberts, Gibraltar, 195 coal.

1869 The Liverpool Mercury Wed. 15 Sept. p.3
Gravesend: Arrived: Sept. 14: Tom Roberts, from Sines (Portugal).

1869 The Standard (London) Thurs. 16 Sept. p.7
London: Custom House: Entered Inwards: Sept. 15: Tom Roberts from Pomaron.

1869 The Western Mail (Cardiff) Tues. 26 Oct. p.4
Swansea: Entered Outwards: Oct. 25: Tom Roberts, Havre, Walter & Davies.
Dec. 21 p.4
Cardiff, Bute West Dock: Arrivals: Dec. 20: Tom Roberts, 117, Williams, Honfleur [near Le Havre]*, ballast.*

[**MNL**1870: 18904 Tom Roberts, Milford, 117: Owner: Jno. Richards, Haverfordwest]

1870 The Belfast News-Letter Thurs Morning. 3 Mar. p.
Belfast: Arrived: Mar. 2: Tom Roberts, Williams, from Kilrush, with flag-stones.
Mar. 10 Morning
Belfast: Sailed: Mar. 9: Tom Roberts, for Glasgow.

1870 The Glasgow Herald Wed. 16 Mar. p.7
Troon: Arrived: Mar. 14: Tom Roberts, Williams, from Belfast.

1870 The Western Mail Tues. 14 June p.4
Cardiff, Bute West Dock: Arrivals: June 11: Tom Roberts, 117, Williams, Limerick, pitwood.

1870: [Survey: Milford in August & September]

1870 The Western Mail Mon. Nov. 21 p.4
Newport: Entered Outwards: Nov. 18: Tom Roberts, 117, Williams, Genoa.
Dec. 3 p.4
Newport: Cleared: Dec. 2: Tom Roberts, Genoa, 200 iron.

1871 The Daily News Tues. 17 Jan. p.7
Genoa: Arrivals: Jan. 11: Tom Roberts, from Newport.

1871 The Standard (London) Mon. 3 Apr. p.7
Queenstown: Arrived: Apr. 1: Tom Roberts, from Marseilles.

1871 The Daily News Fri. 15 Sept. p.7
Off Scilly: Sept. 12 and 13: Tom Roberts, from Scilly.

1871 The Freeman's Journal Tues. 19 Sept.
Falmouth: Arrived: Sept. 18: Tom Roberts, San Stefano [near Genoa in Italy].

1872 The Glasgow Herald Tues. 6 Feb. p.6
Queenstown: Arrived: Feb. 5: Tom Roberts, Mazagan [Morocco, Atlantic].

1872 The Daily News Mon. 24 June p.6
Gravesend: Arrived: June 21 and 22: Tom Roberts, from Gibraltar.

1872 The Glasgow Herald Tues. 15 Oct. P.6
Gravesend: Arrived: Oct. 13: Tom Roberts, from St. Ubes. [Setubal, Portugal]

1873 The Western Mail (Cardiff) Wed. 1 Jan. 1. p.4
Newport: Cleared, Dec. 31: Tom Roberts, B, Bilbao and Marseilles, 200 coal.
Apr. 22 p.4
Bilbao: Sailed: Apr. 11: Tom Roberts, for Swansea.

[**MNL**1875 & 1878: 18904 Tom Roberts, Milford, 103: Owner: Sloane Richards, Birmingham]

[**LR** 1874: Tom Roberts, Sr, D. Williams/ E. Hall, 117, Richards & Co./ Hine Bros, Milford. ---]

1873 The Hampshire Advertiser County Newspaper Wed. 24 Dec. p.4
Portsmouth: Arrived: Dec. 22: Tom Roberts, Hall, Newcastle, coals.

1874 The Western Mail (Cardiff) Wed. 1 Apr. p.8
Newport: Imports: Mar. 30: Tom Roberts, B, Santander, iron ore.
Apr. 15 p.7
Cardiff: Arrivals: Bute East Dock: Apr. 14: Tom Roberts, 177, Moore, Newport, light.

++++++++++ **Hine Brothers**
Cardiff: Entered Outwards: Apr. 14: Tom Roberts, 177, Hall, Santander. [New Captain]
Apr. 29 p.7
Cardiff: Cleared: Apr. 28: Tom Roberts, B, Santander, 200 coal, Aberdare.
Apr. 30 p.7
Cardiff, Bute East Dock: Sailings: Apr. 29: Tom Roberts. Mull (sic), Santander.
June 5 p.7
Newport: Imports: June 4: Tom Roberts, B, Santander, iron ore, order.
June 13 p.6
Newport: Entered Outwards: June 12: Tom Roberts, B, 117, Hall, Lisbon.
July 10 p.7
Lisbon: Arrived: Tom Roberts, from Newport.

1874 The Liverpool Mercury Thurs. 10 Sept. p.3
Liverpool: Arrived: Sept. 8: Tom Roberts, Pomaron. [Portugal]
Nov. 7 p.7
Liverpool: Sailed: Nov. 5: Tom Roberts. Dordt. [Survey: October, in Liverpool]

1874 Adair's Maryport Advertiser Fri. 20 Nov. p.8

Falmouth: Put in: Nov. 12: Tom Roberts, Hall.
Dec. 4 p.8
Dordt: Arrived: Nov. 24: Tom Roberts, Hall.

1875 The Belfast News-Letter Mon. 18 Jan.
Belfast: Arrival: Jan. 10: (coal-laden vessel) Tom Roberts, from Swansea.

1875 Adair's Maryport Advertiser Fri. 2 Apr. p.8
Maryport: Arrived: Mar. 28: Tom Roberts, Hall.
June 4 p.8
Lisbon: Arrived: May 17: Tom Roberts, Hall.
June 25 p.8
Ardrossan: Arrived: June 18: Tom Roberts, Hall, from Lisbon.
July 9 p.8
Ardrossan: Sailed: July 3: Tom Roberts, Hall, for Lisbon.
Sept. 10 p.8
London: Arrived: Sept. 7: Tom Roberts, from Lisbon.
Oct. 15 p.8
The Downs: Put into: Tom Roberts, Hall.
Oct. 29 p.8
Douglas: Arrived: Oct. 22: Tom Roberts, Hall, from London.
Nov. 12 p.8
Port of Maryport: Arrived: Nov. 5: Tom Roberts, Hall, Douglas.

1875 The Dundee Courier and Argus Wed. 29 Dec.
Charente: Sailed: Dec. 20: Tom Roberts, Hall, left for Auquillon. [both France]

1876 Adair's Maryport Advertiser Fri. 7 Jan. p.8
Arguillon: Arrived: Dec. 28: Tom Roberts, Hall, from Tonnay-Charente.
Jan. 28 p.8
Newport: Arrived: Jan. 20: Tom Roberts, Hall, from Arguillon (France).
Feb. 11 p.8
Dublin: Sailed: Jan. 31: Tom Roberts, Hall, for Maryport.
Maryport: Arrived: Feb. 1.
Mar. 3 p.8
Lisbon: Arrived: Feb. 22: Tom Roberts, Hall, Newport (Mon).
Apr. 7 p.8
Cork: Arrived: Apr. 4: Tom Roberts, Hall, from St. Ubes.
May 12 p.8
Maryport: Sailed: May 8: Tom Roberts, Hall, for Tonnay Charente.
June 9 p.8
Charente: Sailed: June 6: Tom Roberts, Hall, for Cardiff.
June 30 p.8
Cardiff: Arrived: June 27: Tom Roberts, Hall, from Tonnay Charente.
July 14 p.8
Cardiff: Sailed: July 6: Tom Roberts, Clark, sailed for Dundalk.
Dundalk: Arrived: July 9.

1876 The Western Mail (Cardiff) Fri. 7 July p.7
Cardiff, West Dock: Sailings: July 5 and 6: Tom Roberts, Hall (sic), Dundalk.
July 25 p.7
Cardiff, Penarth Roads: Arrivals: July 22, 23, 24: Tom Roberts, 103, Clark.
Cardiff, West Bute Dock: Arrivals: July 22, 23, 24: Tom Roberts, 103, Clark, Dundalk, ballast.
Aug. 1 p.7
Cardiff: Inquests: An Inquest was held on Monday morning (before Mr. Grover, deputy coroner), on the body of David Thomas, who was drowned early on Monday morning by

falling from the vessel Tom Roberts, which had just arrived from Milford Haven. The jury returned a verdict of "Accidental death."

Aug. 5 p.7
Cardiff, West Bute Dock: Sailings: Aug. 3 and 4: Tom Roberts, Clark, Dundalk.

Aug. 24 p.7
Cardiff, West Bute Dock: Arrivals: Aug. 22 and 23: Tom Roberts, 103, Clark, Dundalk, ballast.

Sept. 27 p.7
Swansea, South Dock: Arrivals, Sept. 25: Tom Roberts, 106, Clarke, Waterford, pitwood.

Oct. 19 p.7
Swansea, South Dock: Sailings: Oct. 18: Tom Roberts, Clarke, Dublin.

1876 The Freeman's Journal (Dublin) Fri. 20 Oct. p.8
Swansea: Sailed: Oct. 19: Tom Roberts for Dublin.

1876 Adair's Maryport Advertiser Fri. 22 Dec. p.8
Maryport: Sailings: Dec. 18: Tom Roberts, Clark, Portalbert (sic).

1877 The Belfast News-Letter Thurs. Morning 18 Jan.
Belfast: Arrival of Coal-laden Vessel: Jan. 17: Tom Roberts, from Port Talbot.

1877 The Western Mail (Cardiff) Tues. 20 Mar. p.4
Llanelly: Cleared: Mar. 19: Tom Roberts, B, Belfast, 185 coal.

1877 The Freeman's Journal (Dublin) Thurs. 17 May p.3
Swansea: Sailed: May 16: Tom Roberts, for Dublin.

1877 [Survey: Maryport in July]
Nov. 28 p.3
Maryport: Sailed: Nov. 27: T. Roberts, for Dublin.

1878 The Belfast News-Letter Tues. 15 Jan.
Belfast: Arrival: Jan.13 and 14: Tom Roberts, from Swansea.

1879 Mar. 5 p.8
Belfast: Arrival of Coal-Laden Vessels: Tom Roberts, from Burryport.

Mar. 18 p.8
Belfast: Sailed from this port on the 16th and 17th inst: the Tom Roberts, for Workington.

1879 The Western Mail (Cardiff) Thurs. 29 May p.4
Signalled off the Mumbles Head: May 28: Schooner, Tom Roberts, of Milford.

June 6 p.4
Cardiff: Entered Outwards: June 5: Tom Roberts, B, 103, Dieppe.

June 7 p.4
Cardiff: Cleared: June 6: Tom Roberts, B, Dieppe, 191 coal.

1879 The Liverpool Mercury Mon. 21 July p.3
Liverpool: Arrived: July 20: Tom Roberts, Dieppe.

1880 The Belfast News-Letter Tues. 23 Mar. p.6
Belfast: Sailed: Mar. 21 & 22: Tom Roberts, for Maryport.

1880 The Western Mail (Cardiff) 13 Sept. p.4
Penarth Roads: Arrivals: Sept 12: Tom Roberts, 103, blocks.

Sept. 15
Cardiff, West Bute Dock: Arrivals: Sept. 14: Tom Roberts, 103, Maryport, 192 tons sandstone blocks.

Oct. 28 p.4

The schooner Tom Roberts from Maryport to Lydney with pig iron, put into Milford Haven on the 27th inst. with topsail split and other damage.

[**MNL** 1880 & 1882: Tom Roberts: Owner: Sloane Richards, Birmingham.]
[**MNL** 1883: 18904 Tom Roberts, Milford, 103: Owner: Sloane Richards, Birmingham.]

{Census 1881 3rd April}

John Fearon	Other	M M 41 Maryport	Master
Edward Jones	Other	U M 27 Beachley Gloucester	Mate
William Forsyth	Other	U M 23 Maryport	A B
Joseph James	Other	U M 19 Sunderland	Apprentice

(Vessel "Tom Roberts": Milford Haven, Pembroke, Wales)

1882 The Western Mail (Cardiff) Wed. 5 Apr. p.4

Collision at Milford Haven: On Monday night as the Tom Roberts, of Milford, and the Maria M'Millan, of Glasgow, were both coming up Milford Haven they fouled each other off Gellyswick. Both vessels received damage, but not to any very serious extent. Each attributes the blame to the other. The Tom Roberts was bound from Swansea to Workington with coals.

1882 The Maryport Advertiser and Weekly News Fri. 2 June p.8

Port of Maryport: Sailed: May 26: Tom Roberts, Tully, Londonderry.

1882 The Northern Echo (Darlington) Tues. 4 July p.4

Stockton July 3: Tom Roberts, Tully, from Derry, bog ore.
July 8 p.4
Stockton: Sailed: July 7: Tom Roberts, Tully, for Middlesbro': light.

1882 The York Herald Sat. 8 July p.7

Middlesbro': Arrived: July 7: Tom Roberts, Tully, Stockton.
July 11 p.7
Middlesbro': Sailed: July 10: Tom Roberts, Tully, Newport.

1882 The Western Mail (Cardiff) Wed. 2 Aug. p.4

The Mumbles Head: Signalled off, Passed East: Aug. 1: schooner, Tom Roberts of Milford.

1882 The Belfast News-Letter Mon. 14 Aug. p.8

Belfast: Coal-Laden Vessels: Aug. 11& 12: the Tom Roberts, from Swansea.

1882 The Maryport Advertiser and Weekly News Fri. 27 Oct. p.4

At Maryport, port: Tom Roberts has loaded iron from the Maryport Company for Llanelly.
Dec. 15 p.8
Messrs. Hine Brothers: Sailing ships: [barques] *Castle Holme, Myrtle Holme, Brier Holme, Eden Holme, Abbey Holme, Hazel Holme, Aikshaw, Glenfalloch, Robert Hine;* [brigantine] *Clara;* [schooner] *Tom Roberts.*

[**LR** 1883: Tom Roberts, Sr, R. Carswell, 103/118, Hine Bros, Milford. ---]

1883: The Times (London) Tues. 30 Jan. p.10

The Tom Roberts of Milford, Captain Kendal, from Londonderry for Ardrossan, in ballast, while leaving Lough Foyle, was caught in a squall and thrown on her beam ends, which shifted the ballast. She lost her foresail, topgallant sail and topgallant yard, and ran for Portrush and struck on the North Pier. Damage to hull not yet ascertained.

1883 The Freeman's Journal (Dublin) Tues. 30 Jan.
The schooner Tom Roberts, of Milford, Londonderry to Ardrossan, has returned to Portrush damaged and with her cargo shifted. She struck twice whilst entering the harbour but makes no water.
++++++++++ ??

1884 The Glasgow Herald Wed. 27 Feb. p.8
Ayre: Sailed: Feb. 26: Tom Roberts, Cardiff, pig iron.

1884 The Western Mail (Cardiff) Fri. Mar. 7 p.4
Cardiff, West Bute Dock: Arrivals: Mar. 6: Tom Roberts, 103, Ayr. Imports: 190 tons, pig iron, Taff Vale Railway.
Mar. 17 p.4
Cardiff: Entered Outwards: Mar. 15: Tom Roberts, B, 103, Fecamp. [France]
Mar. 19 p.4
Cardiff: Cleared: Mar. 18: Tom Roberts, B, 190 coal, Fecamp.

1884 The Freeman's Journal (Dublin) Wed. 15 Oct. p.10
Dublin: Arrived: Oct. 14: Sailing carriers: Tom Roberts, Newport, coals.

1885 The Western Mail (Cardiff) Fri. 20 Feb. p.4
Cardiff, West Bute Dock: Arrivals: Feb. 19: Tom Roberts, 103, Londonderry. Imports: 90 tons, pitwood, order.
Mar. 11 p.4
Cardiff, West Bute Dock: Sailings: Mar. 8: Tom Roberts, M'Clure, Gravesend.

1885 Maryport and Workington Advertiser Fri. 12 June p.3
Maryport: Sailings: June 22: Tom Roberts, M'Clure, Portrush.

1885 Maryport and Workington Advertiser Fri. 21 Aug. p.3
Messrs. Hine Brother's Ships: Sailing ships (only) Castle Holme, Myrtle Holme, Brier Holme, Eden Holme, Abbey Holme, Hazel Holme, Aikshaw. [No Tom Roberts]

1885 The Dundee Courier and Argus Wed. 29 Dec.
Charente: Left: Dec. 20: Tom Roberts, Hall (sic), for Arguillon.

[**MNL** 1888: 18904 Tom Roberts, Sr, 103. Owner: William Walker, Maryport]

1887 The Isle of Man Times and General Advertiser Sat. Nov. 19 p.4
Schooner Ashore: About o'clock on Wednesday night the schooner Tom Robert (sic), of Liverpool, (Smith, master) went ashore at Ballaugh, about eight miles south of the Point of Ayre. She was bound from Belfast to Workington, and had about 90 tons of iron ore on board. The cause of the disaster had not transpired, but as the spot where she went ashore is several miles out of her course, the compass may have got out of order. The men, not knowing the nature of the shore, thought their lives were in jeopardy, and prepared to leave in their punt, but it was carried away, and they remained on board until the tide receded and left the vessel high and dry. It is doubtful if she can be got off without discharging the cargo.
Dec. 3 p.1
[Advert] *On Wednesday, next, December 7, 1887: To Farmers, Mine Agents, Builders, and others.*

Wreck! Wreck! Wreck!

For the Benefit of whom it may concern – W.J. Craige will Sell by Auction on Wednesday next, Dec. 7, 1887 the whole of the Wrecked Schooner "Tom Roberts", of Milford Haven, as the Hull and Wreckage may then lie on Ballaugh Beach. The vessel is of 190 tons burthen, copper fastened throughout, and will be sold in lots, which will comprise the whole of her Spars, Sails, Ropes, Running Gear, Tow Rope and Warps, Cargo Winch, Anchors and Chains, Small Boat, &c., &c. – Terms, cash. – By order of Richard Smith. Auction alongside the vessel at 12 o'clock, noon. Auctioneer's Office – 52, Athol-st., Douglas.

Dec. 31 p.4

High Court of Justice, Common Law Division: Douglas, Monday, December 12. 1887 (Before Sir W. L. Drinkwater)

The Wrecked Vessel at Ballaugh J. W. Kaneen v. Robert Greig, Belfast.-- This suit was brought for £18 3s 9d. Mr. C. Cannell appeared for plaintiff, and Mr. G. A. Ring represented defendant.-- Mr. Cannell said that the suit was brought in respect of the cartage of certain steel borings from the schooner Tom Roberts of Milford Haven, which was wrecked on Ballaugh Beach on the 16th November.-- John Smith, master, of the schooner, said the vessel had on board a quantity of scrap iron, and she went ashore on the Ballaugh coast on the 16th of November. He was the owner of the vessel, and Mr. Greig owned the cargo. She loaded at Belfast. Witness agreed with Kaneen for him to take the cargo out of the vessel on to the beach for 2s. a ton, and Kaneen was also to have is (sic) a ton from the beach to the railway station. The cargo was not carted from the beach, because the weather turned out better, and as witness thought they could get the vessel off again.-- The witness, in cross-examination by Mr. Ring, said that he had signed several papers denying that he had authorised plaintiff to cart the cargo from the beach to the station but he was not sober at the time.-- In reply to Mr. Cannell, the witness said that since the vessel was wrecked he had been more or less on the spree. (Laughter) – At this stage the further hearing of the case was adjoined.

1888 Jan. 7 p.4

John William Karran v. Robert Greig. Mr. Cannell appeared for plaintiff, Mr. Ring defending.-- The case had been continued from the last court, when it was partly heard.-- Plaintiff, sworn, said: I live at Ballaugh, and remember a vessel coming ashore on the 17th November last. Her name was the "Tom Roberts". The captain's name was Smith. I went down to see the vessel next day: and I made a contract with the captain to bring the cargo from the vessel to the beach for 2s. a ton. I removed the cargo during the next two days, taking away altogether from twenty to thirty tons. On the Sunday following, the captain of the vessel and Mr. Greig came down to me, and in answer to the latter I told him what I had got for carrying out my contract. He said he had been requested by his uncle to look after the cargo, and he wanted to know what I could cart it to the railway station for. The job was to be done as soon as possible, a number of carts and men to be employed. I said I could do it for 6s. a ton, and he agreed to give that. We discharged all from the vessel, with the exception of a few tons, which had to be left in as ballast. We carted six loads to the station on the Wednesday following, and then Mr. Cameron told us we were to stop working until the trucks would come, which was on the 3rd December. On Tuesday, the 29th Nov., I spoke to Mr. Greig, and he said the price agreed upon was too much, and that he was going to do the cartage himself, as it would be cheaper. He came down next morning with three carts, and I gave him notice, in the presence of a number of people, that I was carrying out the contract agreed upon between us. We brought up 25 loads, being from 30 to 35 tons.-- Cross-examined: Mr. Greig made the contract with me on the Sunday: he did not say that he would give me a final answer the next day. I never said that I would cart the stuff to the station for 2s. a load. -- *John Collister gave corroborative evidence, and a number of witnesses were present prepared to give evidence with respect to the cartage.-- Defendant, sworn, said:* I agreed with plaintiff that he should do the cartage from the vessel to the top of the beach, and for this he was to be paid at the rate of 2s. per ton.-- *At this stage the suit was adjourned to the next sitting of the court.*

Feb. 11 p.2

John W.C. Karren v. Robert Greig. This suit which was part heard at a Court held in December, was for £18 3s 9d for carting a quality of steel filings &c. from the schooner Ann (sic) Roberts, which was wrecked on Ballaugh beach in November. After the defendant and other witnesses had been examined, his Honour said that the plaintiff had not employed the defendant to cart the cargo, and gave judgment for £6 2s., loss plaintiff's costs.

JAMES

Official No.	**70856**		
Built	1873	Bootle (Lancs.) James Crook	
Deck	One	Build	Carvel
Masts	Two	Gallery	none
Rigging	**Flat**	Head	none
Stern	Elliptic	Framework	Wood
Tonnage	**35**	Length 66.9 feet; Breadth 14.7 feet; Depth 5.05 feet.	

Liverpool Register: Registered in Liverpool 125/1874: First Registry: William Heaps of Liverpool. Flat Owner sixty four/64 Dated 6th August 1874
Registered in Liverpool 125/1874
Master: Henry Barrow.

[MNL 1880 & 1882: James of Liverpool: Owner: Wm. Heaps, 134, Gt. Mersey St., Liverpool.]

1882 The Liverpool Mercury Wed. 21 Apr. p.8
[Advert] *By order of the Executors of the late William Heaps deceased – To close a trust. To-morrow (Thursday), the 27th instant, at Twelve o'clock, at the Broker's Saleroom. Walmer-buildings, Water-street, Liverpool (if not previously disposed of by private treaty).*
The Coasting Flat James 35 tons register. Built at Bootle in 1873. In good repair and gear in good order. Flat has a small boat.
C.W. Kellock & Co., Brokers, Walmer-buildings, Water-street, Liverpool and at 72, Cornhill, London E.C.

+++++++++++ **Hine Brothers**
1882 The Freeman's Journal (Dublin) Mon. 22 May p.3
Shipping Casualties (Lloyd's Telegram). London, Sunday Night.
The Flat James of Liverpool, from Douglas, Isle of Man, to Duddon, in ballast, was stranded eastward of Clayhead, near Douglas, this morning, and is a total wreck. Crew saved.

1882 Mona's Herald & Fargher's Isle of Man Advertiser Wed. 24 May p.4
The flat James, of Liverpool, which left Douglas on Thursday without ballast, James Coleman, master, and a crew of two hands, for Duddon, got becalmed, and an inshore wind swept her on to Garwick about four o'clock on Saturday morning. Being daylight, the crew scrambled up the rocks. The vessel has since become a total wreck.

Liverpool Register: Transferred to Maryport 3 in 82.
Master Liverpool, 5.5.82: Jas. Coleman.

TSR 8/155
James (70856) (Maryport) 35 tons, Hine Bros, Custom House Blgs., Maryport. Master James Colman (Queen St. Maryport).
Left Garston 11 May / 82. Arrived at Douglas 14 May. Sailed from Douglas 18th May. Vessel struck and went to pieces 20 May at Clay Head. Crew saved.
James Colman (born 1838) Maryport (60006) (former Ann Fallon Maryport) 1882 joined 5-5-82 Liverpool). Master.
Robert Hinde (born 1838) Maryport (70406) (former Hippolyte, Maryport) Mate.
William Henry Carswell (born 1862) Maryport (former Industria, Maryport).

CLYMENE

Official No.	**89483**	Code letters MWPJ	
Built	1873	Port St. Mary, Isle of Man	
Deck	One	Build	Carvel
Masts	Two	Gallery	None
Rigging	**Ketch**	Head	None
Stern	Elliptic	Framework	Wood.
Tonnage	**26**		

TSR 2/7 p.189: Registry Maryport 1/1893: Wilfrid Hine & Alfred Hine both of Maryport with Sixty four/64 Shares. Joint Owners.

Alfred Hine died 14th Sept. 1902 Probate granted is the District Registry Carlisle on the 15th May 1903.

Wilfrid Hine Sixty four/64 March 6th 1908, Bill of Sale to Alfred Catt of Kinston-by-Sea.

Sold March 6th 1908 to Alfred Jarman Catt, of Kingston-by-Sea in the County of Sussex. Harbour Master.

[MNL 1893 (Too Late-Insertion) & 1907: 89483, Clymene, Maryport K.: Port St. Mary, 1873, MWPJ, 26 tons: Managing owner, Wilfred (sic) Hine, Camp Hill, Maryport.]

The address suggesting the vessel was a private one.

[MNL 1911: 89483, Clymene, Maryport K.: Port St. Mary, 1873, MWPJ, 26 tons: Managing owner, Ernest A.F. Chipperfield, 8 Marine Avenue, Hove, Sussex]

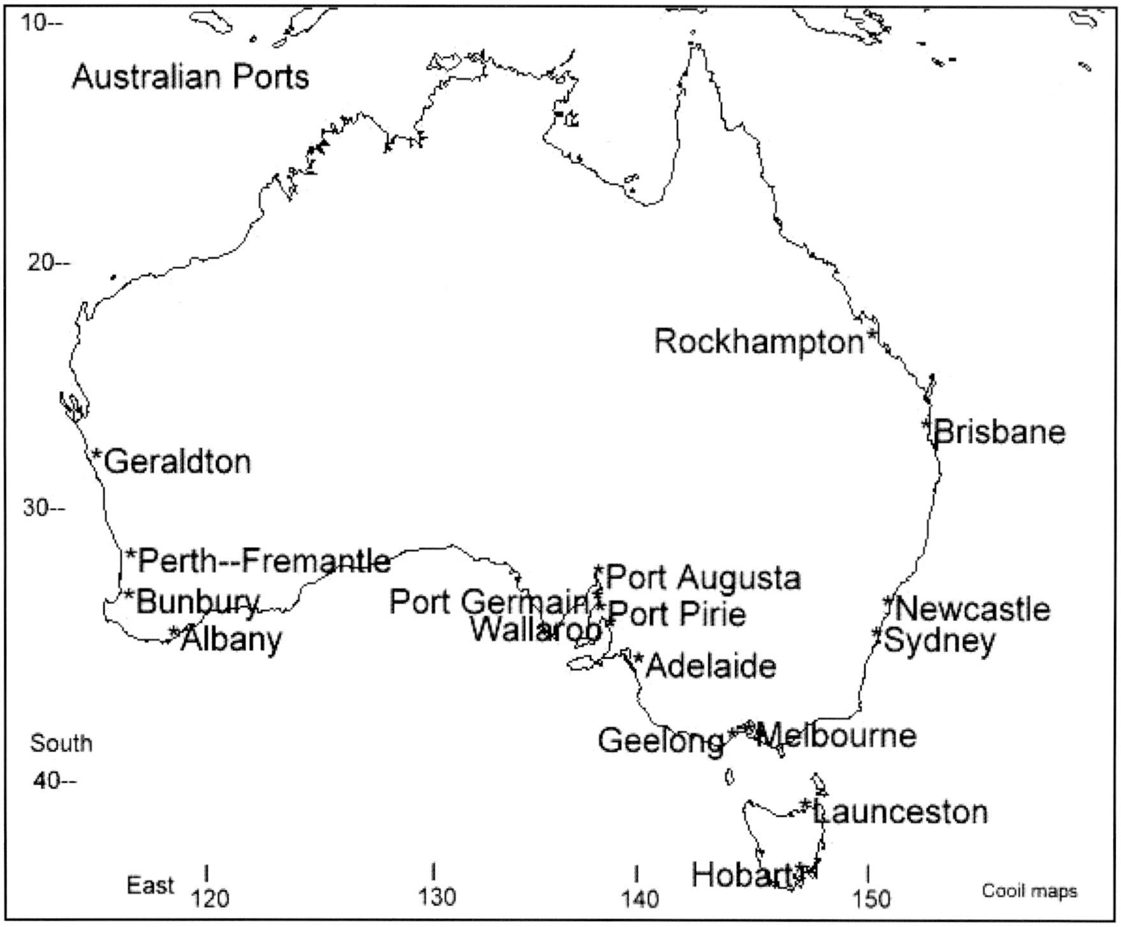

Australian Ports

10--

Australian Ports

20--

Rockhampton*

*Brisbane

*Geraldton

30--

*Perth--Fremantle
*Bunbury
*Albany
Port Germain* *Port Augusta
Wallaroo* *Port Pirie
*Adelaide
*Newcastle
*Sydney

South
40--

Geelong* *Melbourne

*Launceston

Hobart*

East 120   130   140   150   Cooil maps

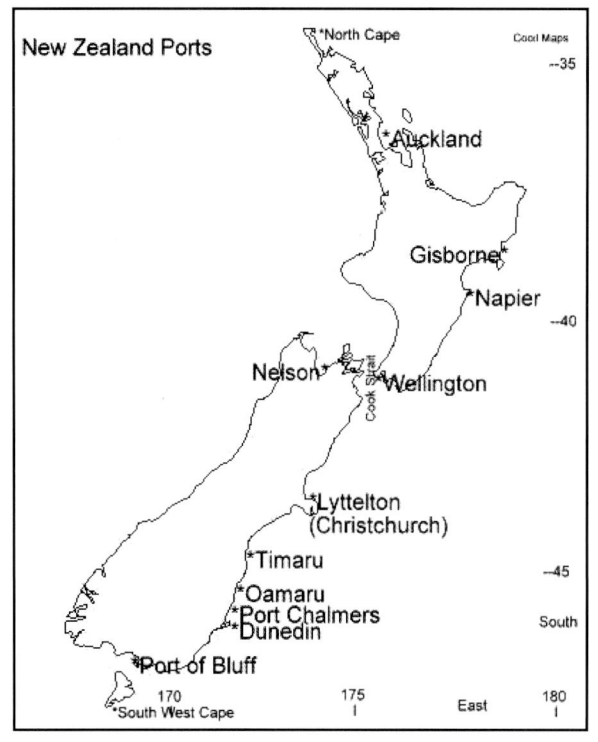

New Zealand Ports

*North Cape Cool Maps
--35

*Auckland

Gisborne*

*Napier
--40

Nelson* *Wellington Cook Strait

*Lyttelton
(Christchurch)

*Timaru
--45

*Oamaru
*Port Chalmers
*Dunedin
South

*Port of Bluff

170   175   East   180
*South West Cape

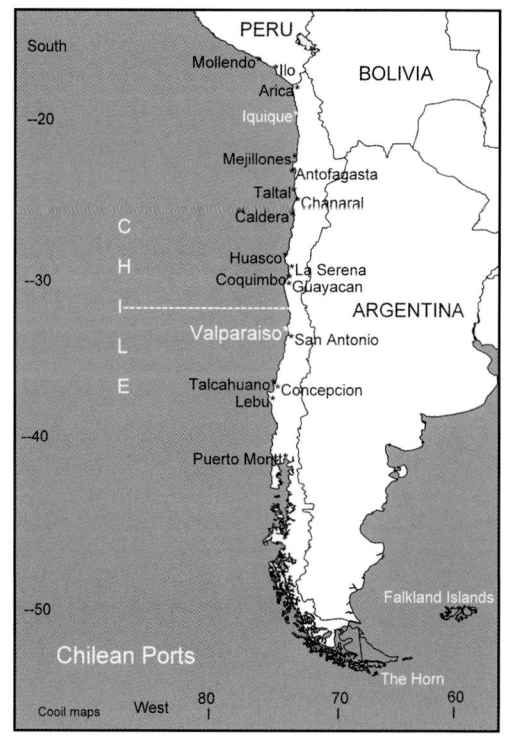

Chilean Ports

South
PERU
Mollendo* *Ilo
*Arica
BOLIVIA

--20
Iquique*

Mejillones* *Antofagasta
Taltal* *Chanaral
Caldera*

C
H
Huasco*
--30
Coquimbo* *La Serena
*Guayacan
ARGENTINA
I
Valparaiso* *San Antonio
L
Talcahuano* *Concepcion
E
Lebu*

--40

Puerto Montt*

--50
Falkland Islands

The Horn

Cooil maps   West   80   70   60

112

Glenfalloch in full sail: Courtesy of Mrs. Law. Artist E.L. Greaves

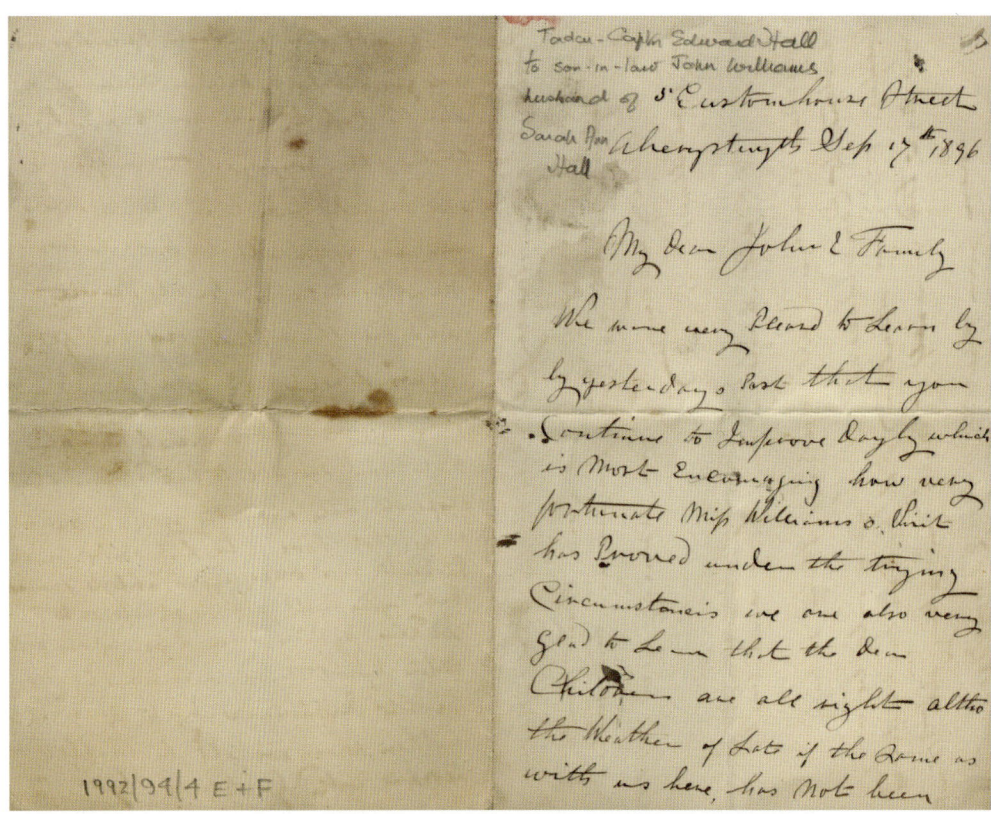

Robert Hine barque, Captain Hall, Letter (part one): Ceredigion Museum Aberystwyth

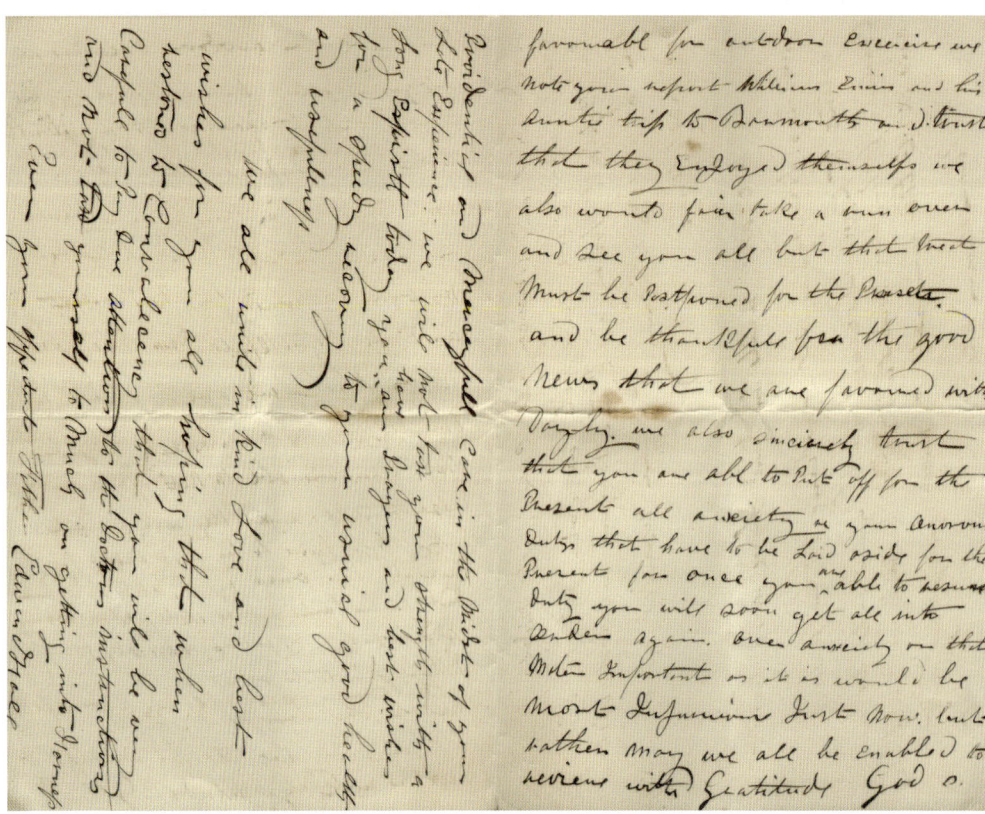

Robert Hine barque, Captain Hall, Letter (part two): Ceredigion Museum Aberystwyth

Robert Hine barque: Ceredigion Museum Aberystwyth

Robert Hine barque at Fanning Island: Ceredigion Museum Aberystwyth

Captain Hall & family: Ceredigion Museum Aberystwyth

Clipper 'Barque' Aikshaw, drawn by W.T. Baldwin: Maryport Maritime Museum (Allerdale Borough Council)

Old Cape Horn. He has watched the Fleets of the World go Past: State Library of Victoria, Brodie Collection

Tristan de Cunha, Nightingale & Inaccessible Island bearing S.E. Artist Ludwig Becker:
State Library of Victoria,

Launceston, Tasmania, engraver Fredrick Grosse: State Library of Victoria

Hobart Town from the new wharf. H. Grant Lloyd, Del. W.L. Walton, Litho:
Tasmanian Archive & Heritage Office

Liverpool Dock quayside 1861, artist Gavin Herdman: Liverpool Record Office

CHAPTER THREE

Wilfrid Hine, still in Liverpool, acquired six barques between 1868-1872, between 327 and 533 in tonnage. These vessels were all for deep-sea trading.

By July 1873 they were incorporated into the Hine Brothers' Fleet. In 1868 the "Robert Hine" was commissioned new, as the "Abbey Holme" was in 1869. They most probably were Nicholson-Hine ventures.

Robert Hine

LR 1869-70: Robert Hine, J. Wilkinson: Nicholson &c., Liverpool.
[**MLN** 1870: Richd. Wm. Hy. Nicholson, 14, South Castle, Street, Lvrpl.
[**MLN** 1875 & 78: Wilfrid Hine, 14, South Castle, Street, Liverpool.
[**MLN** 1880: Wilfrid Hine, Maryport, Cumberland.

Abbey Holme

LR 1874: Abbey Holme, Robinson: Nicholson &c., Liverpool/ (amended) Hine Bros., Maryport.
[**MLN** 1870 & 75: Wilfrid Hine: 14, South Castle, Street, Liverpool.
[**MLN** 1878 & 80: Wilfrid Hine: Custom Ho. Bldgs., Maryport.
[**MLN** 1890: Wilfrid Hine: Custom Ho. Bldgs., Maryport. (Managing owner).

The Aline, Hazel Holme, John Norman and Glenfalloch (all barques) were all bought in 1872.

By 1890, all the barques had been either sold or wrecked. Abbey Holme, wrecked in 1890, had been replaced by an old big barque (tons 998) called Star of Denmark. The Hine Brothers had changed its name to Denton Holme. It, too, was wrecked the same year. Both were captained by John Hoare Rich.

In 1875-76 five new vessels, all iron ships, were commissioned in Sunderland. The Aikshaw (573 tons) will be dealt with in this volume, but the magnificent four: the Eden Holme, Brier Holme, Castle Holme and Myrtle Holme will be dealt with in Volume 2.

ROBERT HINE

Robert Hine barque: Ceredigion Museum Aberystwyth

ROBERT HINE

Official No.	**60079**	**Code letters**	**HDSN**
Built	1868 May	In Sunderland (Davison)	
Deck	One & Break	Build	Carvel
Masts	Three	Gallery	None
Rigging	**Barque**	Head	¾ man
Stern	Elliptic	Framework	Wood (oak & teak).
Tonnage	**327**	Length 119.8 feet; Breadth 27.3 feet; Depth 16.4 feet.	

Liverpool Register: Registered in Liverpool 128/1868: **New ship**
Wilfred (sic) Hine, of Liverpool, Shipowner Sixty Four/64. date 8th July 1868.

Master: Liverpool 8.7.68: Joseph Wilkinson C. 10151

[**LR** 1868 Supplement-70: Robert Hine, Bk, J Wilknsn, 327, Sunderland 1868, Nich'lsn & S, Liverpool, A1]
[**LR** 1871-72: Robert Hine, Bk, J Wilknsn/ E. Ward, 327, Nich'lsn & S, Liverpool, A1]
[**RAFS** 1870-1: Captain J. Wilkinson: W. Hine, Port Liverpool.]

1868 [Survey: Sunderland in June]

1868 The Argus (Melbourne) Sat. 18 Apr. p.4
We observe from our South Australian files, to hand by the Aldinga, that a screw-pile lighthouse, for Cape Jaffa, is to be despatched from England on the 1st of July. A lighthouse at the point named -- the western entrance of Backstairs Passage -- is much needed.
Nov. 5 p.4
The materials for the erection of a lighthouse on Cape Jaffa have arrived at Adelaide. The artificers who are to erect it have also reached that city. The work, we believe, will be commenced at once. It would be well, however, if the South Australian Government changed the locality of this light, and built the house on Cape Jervis, at the western entrance of Backstairs Passage, where it is more wanted.

1868 The Liverpool Mercury Mon. 27 July p.3
Spoken: Robert Hime (sic), from Shields for Adelaide July 20, 48N 7W.

1868 The South Australian Register Tues. 27 Oct. p.2
Adelaide: Arrived: Oct. 26: South Australian, ship, 1,040 tons, David Bruce, master from London July 28, via Plymouth, August 1: By South Australian.... arrived a party of men who have been sent out to put up the Cape Jaffa screw-pile lighthouse. The party is under the charge of Mr. Wm. Fairbairn King, and includes an assistant and three men. The lighthouse has not yet arrived, but it is on board the Robert Hine which is now daily expected, she having left Newcastle-on-Tyne on July 8.
Oct. 31 p.2
Adelaide: Arrived. Friday, October 30. Robert Hine, barque, 327 tons, J. Wilkinson, master, from Newcastle-on-Tyne July 10. Watts and Wells, Town; J. Stilling and Co., Port, agents. At the Lightship.
Imports: Robert Hine, from Newcastle-on-Tyne-194 tons Tanfield Moor coals; materials for Cape Jaffa Lighthouse, viz.:—1 steamboat, 82 pieces ironwork, 10 boxes rivets, 2 coils rope, 1 boiler, 1 cask cement, 10 pieces machinery, 53 piles, 180 tie-rods, 54 pieces, 27 girders, 16 bells iron, 7 do. steel, 3 ladders, 2 boats davits, 39 cross pins, 21 pieces iron, 1 hoddy, 32 bars and plate, 1 anvil, 21 brackets, 2 capstan-heads, 2 tube-doors, 21 principals, 7 piles, 4 plates, 119 caps, 27 couplings, 1 spur wheel, 41 cases

galvanized iron, 5 casks paint, 6 tubes, 16 castings, 2 casks, 92 boxes glass, 13 cases woodwork, 5 casks tar, 5 coils rope, 4 tanks, 6 spears, 91 pieces oak, 194 pieces timber, 1 bdl. rods, 21 capstan bars, 3 boathooks, 2 lifebouys, Watts and Wells.

The Robert Hine arrived early yesterday morning, after a lengthy voyage of 112 days, but this may in a measure be accounted for by her being quite a new vessel with a cargo principally of dead weight. The master reports no very bad weather, but a succession of contrary winds throughout, which delayed every stage of the voyage, and especially since rounding the Cape of Good Hope.

The Cape Jaffa Lighthouse is now in a very fair way to become an accomplished fact. There are many persons curious about the length of time its erection will occupy, as the necessity for a light on the Cape has long been sufficiently obvious. The Robert Hine, which arrived yesterday from Newcastle brought about 500 tons material for the work. A glance at the shipping column will show that the contractors have furnished a good plant: for in addition to capstans and tools a steamboat is on board, which must be put together before the work commences. The principal artificer arrived a day or two back in the South Australian, and it is probable no time will elapse before operations are commenced.

Nov. 3 p.1

Tenders for Lightering: Tenders are invited on or before the 3rd day of November now next ensuing for Lightering the Materials for the Cape Jaffa Lighthouse at Port Caroline, now on board the Robert Hine.

1868 The South Australian Advertiser (Adelaide) Mon. 2 Nov. p.5
Vessels in Harbor: Robert Hine, barque. In the Stream.
Nov. 4 p.3
At Levi's Wharf.
Nov. 6 p.2
Cape Jaffa Lighthouse. -- By the Flinders, on Wednesday evening, the President of the Marine Board and one of the members sailed for the reef with a view to fixing the site for the new lighthouse. Mr. King also accompanied the schooner.

1868 The Argus (Melbourne) Thurs. 19 Nov. p.4
Port of Adelaide: Sailed: Nov. 17: Robert Hine for Kingston.

1868 The South Australian Register (Adelaide) Thurs. 26 Nov. p.2
Port Caroline: Arrived: November 21: Robert Hine, barque, J. Wilkinson, master, from Port Adelaide. Cargo: Lighthouse for Cape Jaffa Lighthouse.

1868 The South Australian Advertiser (Adelaide) Mon. 30 Nov. p.3
Port Caroline, November 24. [From a Correspondent (sic)] The barque Robert Hine arrived in the Bay, with the Cape Jaffa Lighthouse, on the 21st, and anchored at the Cape on the evening of the same day. She is chartered to take wool and bark from this Bay to England as soon as she has discharged her cargo; the schooner Crest of the Wave is engaged to discharge her. Nothing can show the need of dispatch in opening the seaboard country of this district more than the fact, however ridiculous it may appear, that wire and station stores are now being carted overland from Geelong, a distance of above 300 miles, and wool taken back the same road from a station only 30 miles inland from Port Caroline. The want of a proper road through our frontage is doing this. This want is a disgrace to South Australia.

1868 The South Australian Register (Adelaide) Sat. 5 Dec. p.3
Lacepede Bay. Our smooth waters at Port Caroline had quite a lively appearance last week, and looked something like the beginning of what we hope soon to see—a busy

shipping port here. There were no less than four vessels in the port at the same time, viz., the Swallow, the Resolute, the Crest of the Wave, and the brigantine Camilla, and towards the end of the week the barque Robert Hine, with the Cape Jaffa Lighthouse on board, came in to the bay. Mr. King and his men are now at the reef making preparations for the erection of the lighthouse.

Dec. 15 p.3

Guichen Bay, December 5. Vague rumours are abroad that the Robert Hines (sic) cleaned her bottom a bit by lying on the ground for a night off Port Caroline; but as that is said to be the finest harbour on the coast, it can hardly be considered correct.

1869 South Australian Advertiser Thurs. 4 Feb. p.4

Arrived: Wednesday, February 3: Robert Hine, 327 tons, J. Wilkinson, master, from Lacepede Bay January 29. Watts and Wells, agents. Cargo -- 307 tons bark, Bean Brothers; 139 bales wool, Saunders; 55 tons copper ore, Paramatta Mining Company.

The Robert Hine has landed the Cape Jaffa Lighthouse at Lacepede Bay, and, having loaded up with bark and sundries, returned to the anchorage Wednesday to procure sea stock and a few seamen prior to sailing for England.

Feb. 8 p.2

Sailed: Feb. 6: Robert Hine, barque, for London.

Feb. 15 p.3

Lacepede Bay. February 11: The barque Robert Hine has taken away about 300 tons [bark] and a quantity of wool, for London, via Port Adelaide.

1869 The South Australian Register Sat. 27 Feb. p.3

A letter from the Collector of Customs stated that, owing to the Robert Hine having sailed without paying the light dues, he had issued instructions to the boarding officers not to grant clearances in future without production of the receipt for the dues.

Mar. 4. p.3

Port Adelaide, Monday, March 1. [Before Mr. G.W. Hawkes S.M.]

Robert Kent, seaman, a deserter from the Robert Hine, was fined £5 for being found in the province after the departure of the vessel without a proper discharge.

Mar, 13 p.3

Port Adelaide, Friday, March 12. [Before Mr. G.W. Hawkes S.M.]

Peter Manson, a deserter from the Robert Hine, was fined £5 on a charge for being found without a discharge.

Nov. 3 p.3

The Parliament: Legislative Council: Tuesday, November 2.

The Jaffa Lighthouse. The Commissioner of Public Works in reply to Mr. J. Fisher said— "Amount paid by the Government to the contractor for the Cape Jaffa Light-House to the present date is £14,250. Estimated value of work done to the present date £14,600. Total amount of the contract £20,870 11s. Probable date of completion of the erection about July 1870."

{The Cape Jaffa Lighthouse was established in 1872. It took three years to construct, due to terrible weather and rough seas hampering progress. The Lighthouse was finally replaced in 1973. Luckily, the National Trust of South Australia (Kingston Branch) operates it as a museum having been able to reconstruct it and place it in a park in Kingston.}

1869 The Liverpool Mercury Tues. 15 June p.3

Robert Hind (sic), from Port Adelaide for London, 115 days out, June 4, 45 N. 17 W.

1869 The Dundee Courier & Argus Wed. 16 June

Ships spoken: Robert Hine, from Adelaide for London, 118 days, June 5 lat 47 N. long. 13 W.

125

1869 The Daily News (London) Thurs. 17 June p.7
Deal: Arrived: June 15: Robert Hine, from Adelaide.
June 18 p.7
Gravesend: Arrived: June 17: Robert Hine, from Port Caroline.
June 19 p.7
London: Custom-House: Vessel entered inwards: June 18: Robert Hine, from Adelaide.
July 2 p.7
London: Custom House: Entered out: July 1. Robert Hine, for Valparaiso.
Aug. 18 p.1
[Advert] Australia - Orient Line of Ships - West Coast of America, West Indies &c.
Valparaiso - Robert Hine - J. Wilkinson – London - Fitting up.
Aug. 24 p.7
Gravesend: Sailed: Aug. 23: Robert Hine, Valparaiso. [Chile]

1870 The Dundee Courier & Argus Thurs. 3 Feb.
Valparaiso: Arrived: Dec. 2: Robert Hine, from London.
Mar. 22
Valparaiso: Left: Feb. 1: Robert Hine, Caldera. [North of Santiago, Chile]
Mar. 30
At Caldera: Feb. 11: Robt. Hine, from Valparaiso.

1870 The New-York Times Sun. 12 June
New-York: Arrived: Saturday June 11: Bark Robert Hine, (of Liverpool,) Wilkinson, Iquique 84 ds., with nitrate of soda to Hazard Powder Company, vessel to Geo. F. Bulley. Passed Cape Horn April 12, and crossed the equator May 12, in lon. 36. Has had light winds the entire passage, and been 10 ds. W. of Bermuda, with N.E. winds and fogs. [Survey: New York in June 1870.]
July 9
New-York: Friday: Sailed: July 8: Bark: Robt. Hine, for Havre.
July 18
Bark Sabine: [on] July 12, to the S.E. of George's Banks, saw bark, Robert Hine, (Br.,) hence for Antwerp.

1870 New York Herald Fri. 8 July p.8
New York: Cleared: July 7: Bark Robert Hine, (Br.), Wilkinson, Antwerp.

[**MNL** 1870: Robert Hine of Liverpool: Owner: Richd. & Wm. Hy. Nicholson, 14, South Castle St. Liverpool]
[**MNL** 1875: Robert Hine of Liverpool: Owner: Wilfred (sic) Hine, 14, South Castle St. Liverpool]

1870 The Standard (London) Wed. 2 Nov. p.7
Gravesend: Sailed: Nov. 1: Robert Hine, for Callao.

1871 Lloyd's List Wed. 15 Mar. col. 15
Callao: Arrived: Feb. 4: Robert Hine, Wilkinson, Lndn.
Nov. 11 col. 36
The Van Diemen, from Liverpool to San Francisco put into Stanley, Falkland Islands, previous to 29th Aug, with rudder damaged. The Robert Hine has also put into Stanley for provisions.
Nov. 17 col. 7
Falmouth: Arrived: Nov. 16: Robt. Hine, Williamson (sic), (coffee), Guatemala.

1871 The Standard (London) Fri. 17 Nov. p.7
Falmouth: Arrived: Nov. 16: Robert Hine, from Guatemala: reports that the Flower of the Forest was at the Falkland Islands leaky.

Nov. 23 p.7
London: Custom House: Nov. 22. Vessels Entered Inwards: the Robert Hine, from San Jose de Guatemala.

1871 The Daily News (London) Tues. 26 Dec. p.1
[Advert] *Australia - Orient Line of Ships - West Coast of America, West Indies &c. Guayaquil and Buenaventura - Robert Hine - J. Wilkinson – S.W.I. – Jan 10*
[Survey: London in January 1872.]

1872 **Liverpool Register**: Master: London 23.2.72: Edward Ward C. 27720

1872 The Glasgow Herald Thurs. 7 Mar. p.6
Gravesend: Sailed: Mar. 6: Robert Hine, Guayaquil [Ecuador on Pacific Ocean].
Mar. 12 p.6
Deal: Sailed: March 10: Robert Hine, Guayaquil.

1872 Lloyd's List Tues. 13 Aug. col. 26
Guayaquil: Arrived: July 11: Robert Hine, Ward, London.

1872 Adair's Maryport Advertiser Fri. 13 Sept.
Death of Capt. Ward. –Yesterday morning brought the melancholy tidings of the death of Edward Ward, of the ship "Robert Hine." It appears the deceased had experienced indifferent health on the outward voyage, and when at Guayaguil (sic) his illness culminated in the breaking of a blood vessel on the 9th of August, and he was interred on the following day. Capt. Ward was in the prime of life, a young man who was greatly esteemed, and held a high character, and good prospects in his profession in the merchant service. –Shortly before sailing from this country, he married the eldest daughter of Mr. Sherwood, the photographer, and the tidings of this sudden calamity to his young widow and family is a severe shock.
Sept. 27 p.8
Birth: On the 24th, the wife of late Capt. Ward, of a daughter.

1872 Lloyd's List Tues. 1 Oct. col. 27
Guayaquil: Sailed: Aug. 23: Robert Hine, Brown, Buenaventura [Colombia, Pacific Ocean]

[**LR** 1873: Robert Hine, Bk, E. Ward/ G. Brown, 327, Nich'lsn & S/ W. Hine, Liverpool/ Maryport A1] Projected voyage: London to Guayaquil amended to Liverpool to Arica.
[**LR**. 1874: Robert Hine, Bk, G. Brown, 327, Hine Bros, Maryport A1]

1873 The Times (London) Mon. 31 Mar. p.8
Plymouth: March 29: The bark "Berean" 526 tons register, Captain John Wyrill, to discharge in W.I. Docks, spoken the British bark, Robert Hine, 88 days from Magdalena, for London. March 4, in lat 3 14 N., long., 36.58 W.

We shall encounter Captain Wyrill later in Vol, 2, on the Eden Holme.

Liverpool Register: Master: London 24.4.73: George Brown C. 31031

1873 Adair's Maryport Advertiser Fri. 11 Apr. p.8
London: Arrived: Apr. 8: Robert Hine, Brown, from Magdalena Bay. [Mexico]
Death of Daniel Bowes, June. – This promising boy, so well known and beloved in Maryport, eldest son of Mr. D. Bowes, when at sea on board the Robert Hines (sic) fell from aloft and was killed, on the 6th of Jan. last. He was in his 16th year – this being his first voyage as an apprentice.

June 7 p.8
London: Sailed: May 30: Robert Hine, Brown, to Valparaiso.
Nov. 21 p.8
Valparaiso: Arrived: Sept. 27: Robert Hine, Brown.

1873 New York Herald Wed. 19 Nov. --triple sheet-- p.10
Valparaiso: in port: Oct. 16: bark, Robert Hine (Br.) for Pisagua, to load nitrate for New York.
Dec. 19 p.10
Valparaiso: Sailed: Oct. 3 (sic): bark Robert Hine (Br), for Pisagua (to load for New York).

1874 Lloyd's List 29 Jan. col. 15
Iquique: Cleared: Robert Hine, [for] *New York.*

1874 The New-York Times Wed. 22 Feb. p.8
New-York: Arrived: Saturday, Feb. 21: Bark Robert Hyne (sic), (of Liverpool,) Brown. Pisaqua 96 ds. With nitrate of soda to Brown Bros. & Co. – vessel to Russell, Howes & Co.

1874 Adair's Maryport Advertiser Fri. 27 Mar. p.8
New York: Left: Mar. 12: Robert Hine, Brown, for Liverpool.
Apr. 10 p.8.
Liverpool: Arrived: Apr. 3: Robert Hine, Brown, from New York. [Survey: Liverpool in May.]

1874 Lloyd's List 4 June col. 7
Liverpool: Sailed: Robert Hine: Arica, off June 3, 12.40 p.m.
June 11 col. 22
Robert Hine (barque), 7 June, off the Saltees [off the southern coast of County Wexford in Ireland].

Book: Capt. Brown's Experiences on board the barque "Robert Hine".

It was in fine, clear weather that we left Liverpool in the year 1873 (sic) [1874?], bound for Arica and Mollendo with a general cargo. All went well until we got within 100 miles of the Straits of Le Maire, when we encountered a heavy gale of wind from the south-east. The sea was running very high and we shipped heavy water on deck. We were on the port-tack with two lower topsails and foretop-mast staysail set. At the commencement of the gale we should be about 70 miles from the land.

We headed for the land, and when it was about ten miles distant were obliged to wear ship and put her on the starboard tack, for fear of being driven on shore. No sooner had we gone on the starboard tack than a heavy sea struck the vessel, carrying away nearly all our bulwarks, rails, and stanchions on the starboard side, also starting decks and waterways, damaging the crew's houses, and flooding the cabin. This would be about midnight. At daybreak we found that our fore rigging had been carried away and the vessel leaking. I decided to run for Stanley Harbour, in the Falkland Islands, to get my vessel repaired, as she was not in a fit state to proceed on her voyage round Cape Horn. In due time we arrived in Stanley Harbour -- one of the best I have ever visited. We found the inhabitants to be mostly Scotch carpenters; there would be from 100 to 150 men in the place, but very few ladies, I should say not more than six. Several of the men asked me, should I visit their island again, if I would kindly bring them some wives.

1874 Lloyd's List Sept. 29 col. 20
Falkland Islands (Lisbon 28th Sept., 8.45 p.m.) Robert Hine, from Liverpool to Arica, has put into Stanley with damage to bulwarks and part of stanchions.

Oct. 6 col. 30
Stanley F.I.: arrived: Aug. 13: Robert Hine, Brown, Liverpool for Arica. (see Falkland islands paragraph in list of 29th Sept.).
Nov. 16 col. 14
Stanley F.I. sailed: Aug. 29: Robt. Hine, Brown, Arica.

1874 The Times (London) Thurs. 19 Feb.
[The results of the Imperial Census, so far as they refer: The Falkland Islands, with 803 inhabitants, close the list of our American possessions.]

We were six weeks in repairing the ship, and then we sailed again, enjoying fine weather and favourable wind until we reached Cape Horn, where we encountered another south-east gale. I decided to run under the land for shelter and go through Nassau Straits, which we entered about 6 p.m., in daylight. Having heard and read so much about the Patagonian Savages, I did not anchor but kept under weigh until the gale moderated.

Before entering Nassau Straits I gave orders for all guns, cannon, and revolvers to be got ready for action, as a precaution, in case the natives attempted to board our ship. We had also a plentiful supply of hot water ready, and the carpenter sharpened all his axes, adzes, and other cutting instruments. When all this had been done, I told Mrs. Brown she had better retire to rest. Sleep was out of the question for myself, as I was bound to be on deck until the weather moderated and we were safely through the Straits. But Mrs. Brown answered "No; I am afraid of the savages; but if you will make further preparation for keeping them from boarding the ship I will go to my room." Then she told me that in the storeroom there were a large number of pickle and preserve bottles, which she suggested should be broken and spread upon the deck, in case the natives attacked us. This I thought was an excellent plan and was not long in getting the bottles broken, as suggested.

We were two nights and days in this place before the gale moderated sufficiently to allow us to go through into open water. Several times when we were passing the small islands we heard the natives shouting and screeching, but no boats came off to us, for which we were very thankful. An American vessel four years before this was not so fortunate, as she lost half her crew fighting these men, who had boarded her. In the fight twenty natives were killed and the remainder jumped overboard and were drowned.

We had a nice passage from False Cape Horn to Arica and Mollendo. [Both were in Southern Peru]. After discharging the cargo and loading nitre for Hamburg ....

1874 Adair's Maryport Advertiser Fri. 4 Dec. p.8
Arica: Arrived: Oct. 23: Robert Hine, Brown. [Now Chile: in 1874 Peru]
1875 Jan. 1 p.8
Mollendo: Arrived: Robert Hine, Brown.
Jan. 22 p.8
Pisagua: Arrived: Dec. 7: Robert Hine, Brown, from Mollendo.
Apr. 30 p.8
Spoken: Feb. 6: Robert Hine, Brown, from Pisagua for Hamburgh lat. 37 south long. 91 west [off Chile].
May 14 p.8
Hamburgh: Arrived: May 11: Robert Hine, Brown, from Pisagua.
July 16 p.8
Hamburgh: Sailed: July 8: Robert Hine, Brown, for Valparaiso.
July 23 p.8
Beachy Head: Passed: July 17: Robert Hine, Brown.
Oct 1 p.8
Spoken: Aug. 14: Robert Hine, Brown, Lat. 6* 54' North, Long. 25* 23' West.

On another voyage namely from Hamburg to South America, (Valparaiso, Iquique) and back to Hamburg. Where was Mrs. Brown? --

...........we set out for Valparaiso. We had a pleasant and quick passage to within fifty miles of Cape Horn. Then the barometer commenced to fall very rapidly, and the weather to southward looked bad. I decided to run for Good Success Bay. This would be about two o'clock in the afternoon, and at six in the evening we anchored.

Just before anchoring we noticed a small fore and aft schooner lying at anchor, flying the English ensign. Thinking this craft might possibly be a pirate schooner, I gave orders for all guns to be loaded and made ready for action; at the same time I did not forget to muster all the broken bottles ready for spreading on the deck. When we had been to anchor about two hours, a small boat with four men came alongside from the schooner. The men looked rather like foreigners, and seeing this I shouted for them to keep away; they answered back that they were Missionaries. Seeing that they only four in number, I asked them to come on board, which they did. It turned out in conversation that they were from Stanley Harbour, Falkland Islands, and bound for Beagle Channel Missionary Station, and that their schooner's name was "Allan Gardner No. 3" so called after the first Missionary to the Patagonians. The schooner was loaded with beef, potatoes, geese, and rabbits. We were kindly asked if we would like some fresh meat and potatoes. I answered "Yes," but asked them not to bring too much, as I had very little money on board. They at once very generously replied that the provisions should be a free gift.

Before dark our visitors left the ship and returned to their own schooner, promising to come again the next morning. This they did, bringing with them three quarters of fresh meat, six bags of potatoes, altogether sufficient to last us a month. As they had been so kind I offered to let them have whatever clothing they require for themselves, their wives and families, at cost price. I had invested in this clothing as a speculation when in Hamburg. They were very pleased to accept my offer, and bought of my stock to the extent of £65. Like myself, they had no money, but they gave me a letter addressed to a gentleman in Liverpool, of whom I was to receive payment.

I was then asked to accompany them on shore, as they were anxious to learn for themselves what the natives were like. The information that had reached them was to the effect that the people were very wild and treacherous -- indeed, perfect savages, I, however, declined the invitation, as the manner in which I had seen the people dancing and jumping like madmen around their fires all night convinced me that it was wiser to remain aboard my ship. I also suggested that the best plan for us would be to heave up anchor and clear out. But they were very anxious to land, as they desired to learn whether they knew the language of the natives or not. If they were ignorant of it, they agreed not to land. With this I promised to accompany them, providing they did not object to me taking two "bulldogs" with me. They looked round, and asked where I kept the bulldogs? I produced two revolvers, which they said I could take on condition they were only used in self-defence. We then went within a hundred yards of the shore in the schooner's boat; from that distance the Missionaries hailed the natives in the language they knew, and received from one of the tribe a response in the same tongue. The knowledge that at least one man could understand them was very pleasing to the Missionaries

After a lot of talk the native was asked if it was safe to land? Certainly the prospect was not very inviting, as the people all appeared to be painted ready for war. Not one of them had any clothing on whatever. Men, women, and children were all quite naked, although it was freezing hard and exceedingly cold. The man answered back, that under the circumstances it was perfectly safe to land, but that it would not have been so had he had not been able to act as interpreter.

We then landed, and immediately the natives came crowding around us; they commenced taking hold of our clothes, shaking them vigorously -- first our coats, and then every article we had on. I asked the Missionary the meaning of this, and he said it was the way they had of expressing their desire to become possessed of our clothing. As we were shivering with cold, of course this was out of the question. After this they sat around their fires, first one and then another going close up to the burning sticks to get warm.

I may say these people have no places of shelter whatever, neither houses nor huts; their only comfort is a wood fire, and, what appeared very strange to me, they always sat on that side of the fire where the wind was blowing towards them. I asked the reason of this, and was told, if they were sheltered by the land it would be draughty and they would be more liable to take cold.

During the whole of our visit I hardly took my eyes off the natives, as I feared they might treacherously attack us. Once I struck a match to light my pipe, and in an instant they were all round me, amazed at the sight; they had never seen a match before, and when I gave them one or two their delight was very great. I thought what a good plan it would be to bring all the matches we could spare on shore and barter them for the bows and spears, they had, for whilst they carried these I was very uneasy. This was done. For a box of matches they gave me a bow and arrow, and in a short time I had their weapons, which we placed on board so as to be out of their reach.

The Missionaries gave to the natives some meat and a quantity of geese and rabbits; at the same time I also gave them salt meat and bread. These people possessed a large oval pan which they had found on an old wreck lying on the beach. Up to the time of our visit they had been unable to find a use for it. One of the Missionaries now told them to fill it with water, and promised to show them how to cook the meat, &c. First he placed all the geese and rabbits, and salt meat and the bread, upon the beach, and then told the natives to arrange themselves in families around the provisions. He then proceeded to divide the meat and other things, according to the number in each family, cutting the meat up into portions and giving to each a share. I asked him why he did this, and he replied that if it was left with the natives to distribute they would arrange themselves for war, and the strongest side would take the whole lot. After he had apportioned the meat out, he put some in the pan to cook, but it had not been there long before the people were pulling it out and eating it. So delighted were they with the meat that more was placed in the pan, together with a goose, two rabbits, and a quantity of shell fish; these latter were put in just as they had been killed – skins, feathers, and all – and in the same state they were eaten, of all that was thrown away after the meal were a few shells.

After this we took three of the natives on board the "Robert Hine," for the purpose of showing them over the ship. I went down into the cabin first, our visitors following. The first, who was some distance from the other two, on reaching the room, almost the first thing he was saw a picture of himself in the mirror upon the stern-post casing. The shock to him was tremendous; he made a terrific leap, through the skylight, and dropping down upon the floor fainted right away. His friends would not venture any further, the reason of their brother's fright being quite incomprehensible to them, and they stood bewildered. After we had brought the fellow round, they become somewhat reassured, and then the fun commenced. First one and then another would peep at the mirror, and then give a big jump backwards. This was for at least a dozen times. At length the Missionary succeeded in explaining the mystery to the man who acted as interpreter, and was at least able to satisfy them that the person who they saw were themselves and none others. Then the sailors let them see through their quarters, and when they came again on deck, they were dressed in some of the old clothes belonging to the crew. They were all highly delighted with their costumes, and their exhibitions of joy were amusing to watch. But the greatest fun was after they had returned ashore, indeed, it was a real "Jubilee" occasion amongst them. The next day three of the ladies were dressed in the sailors' clothes, and day by day they were passed on to three fresh persons until all had enjoyed the new sensation.

One day, about noon, we set off to climb the mountains, so that we might see the view on the other side. We had great difficulty in persuading one of the natives to accompany us, as the people suspected that we intended to kill our guide. The ascent of the mountains was accomplished after a deal of hard work, as the sides were very steep and covered with small trees and shrubs. It was rather late and getting quite dark when we came down, and aboard the ship they were beginning to get uneasy on our account; to warn us of the oncoming night they had commenced to pull the flags up and down. We were a ragged-looking lot, our clothes being almost torn off our backs; but although I took particular notice of our native guide, I could not see that he had a single scratch about him, notwithstanding he had gone through the bushes like a rabbit.

The next day we had moderate weather, and both vessels sailed together, keeping in company for about eight hours, after which we parted, the Missionary schooner making for Beagle Channel and the "Robert Hine" for Nassau Straits once again.

When we got as far as False Cape Horn it commenced to blow, and we had to run back and anchor in Orange Bay, where we laid three days and nights. During our first day there we saw several natives walking about, but none afterwards. We landed on the second day and cut about twenty fine spars, of which there were a large quantity; it was well sheltered from all winds. When the gale abated we started again and passed safely through the Straits. We made a splendid voyage from thence to Valparaiso, the time being only fourteen days, whereas I have been as much as six weeks doing the same passage.

1875 Adair's Maryport Advertiser Fri. 17 Dec. p.8
Valparaiso: Arrived: Oct. 22: Robert Hine, Brown.

After our ship had been reported to the Customs, almost all the Captains and officers of the vessels in Port came on board, to enquire what kind of places Good Success and Orange Bays were; they were also anxious to know what we thought of the natives – whether in case of a wreck near their shores they would kill and eat the unfortunate sailors? I replied, that although I should not care to be cast amongst them, yet at the same time I would prefer landing before keeping to sea in an open boat. One man especially, who, as Mate of the "Peckforton Castle," came to me many times to enquire my opinion of the natives, my reply to him being the same as above.

This poor fellow (Capt. McAdams) got command of the "San Rafael," of Liverpool, on his return home with the "Peckforton". He sailed in October, 1874 (sic), carrying a cargo of coal for Valparaiso, and with a crew of twenty-two hands. His wife also accompanied him. On New Year's Day, 1875 (sic), after rounding Cape Horn, they found the vessel on fire. They were compelled to take to the three boats; the Captain, his wife, and part of the crew were in the largest boat, the officers and the remainder of the crew being in the other two. During a fog the officers lost sight of the Captain's boat and never saw it again.

It transpired subsequently, however, that the Captain and his companions landed on a small island a few miles from the mainland, hoping there to attract the notice of some passing ship. But no ship came, and after enduring dreadful hardships all perished of starvation. During the time their little stock of food lasted, cooking operations were conducted at night for fear of drawing the attention of the natives on the mainland. It appears the natives did see the blaze of their fire, but were too afraid to venture a visit whilst the fires lasted. When these had ceased they went to the island and found the dead bodies of the Captain and Mrs. McAdams and crew of the boat. They returned and told the sad story to the Missionaries, walking for that purpose a distance of about 100 miles. The Missionaries at once proceeded to the island in the "Allen Gardner" and reverently buried the dead bodies.

The diary of Captain McAdams, which he had kept until he could see to write any longer, was also found, and from its pages the dreadful fate of himself and his companions was learned.

The officers kept to sea in their boats, and after tossing about for twenty-seven days were picked up by a passenger ship from Melbourne, bound for London.

1876 Liverpool Mercury Mon. 6
The Crew of the San Rafael: Further Details: A paper was issued on Saturday from the Colonial Office. Containing the correspondence with reference to the discovery of a portion of the crew of the Liverpool ship San Rafael on Hoste Island, as briefly reported in our last issue. We make the following extracts:-- "Enclosure 1.
" From the Rev. T. Bridges to his Excellency Governor Callaghan "Received June 16. 1876" ...."On board the Allen Gardiner, Button Island, Fireland, Tierra de Fuego."
"Sir,--I feel it a duty to apprise you of the probable loss of a Liverpool vessel called San Rafael belonging to Balfour, Williamson and Co. I say probable loss, because we are only sure of the death of part of her crew and officers, and have no proof whatever of the loss of the vessel, though we are strongly of opinion that she is lost. On April 22 a large party of Indians reached Ooshooia from New Year's Sound and neighbourhood, and brought news of the death of nine men by starvation and exposure on an exposed part of the coast, which we judged to be somewhere between Waterman and Henderson Island. They brought proof of their statements in their clothing they wore and an English sovereign they offered for sale. [etc. etc.]

With reference to the Missionary schooner frequently referred to in the above narrative, it should be stated that she was called "Allen Gardner (sic)" after two previous Missionary ships of the same name, the former of which was so-called in memory of the first Missionary to the Patagonians When this devoted man, in company with several others, left England for South America, only sufficient water and stores were taken out to last one or two months, beyond the time time (sic) occupied in the passage out. It was arranged before sailing that a large brig-rigged vessel should carry out to them an adequate stock of provisions, but, unfortunately, this ship became disabled and was compelled to return to England to repairs. When at length she did arrive in South America, they found all the Missionaries were dead, having been starved.

A short time after this another ship – the "2nd Allen Gardner," went out with another band of Christian Pioneers, but she too met with disaster. When passing through the Beagle Channel she ran around, and all her passengers and crew, with the exception of one man, were cruelly killed by the savage natives. The one man who escaped was picked up a passing vessel and landed on the Falkland Islands. The natives also tried to set fire to the ship, but failed to do so because of the copper that was in the bottom. Some time afterwards a gunboat towed her off and took her to the Falkland Islands, where I saw her.

The "3rd Allen Gardner" [see note below] was the one I met in Good Success Bay, loaded with provisions and bound for Beagle Channel Missionary Station, as mentioned earlier.

Unfortunately, although the book is most interesting, some of the facts are misleading. The 1st missionary vessel used by the missionary Allen Gardiner was not named the Allen Gardiner. The first "Allen Gardiner" was the schooner bought in 1854 and used up to 1875 which Captain Brown called "2nd Allen Gardner". The Allen Gardiner II (called "3rd Allen Gardner" by Capt. Brown) was a ketch or yawl.

[**MNL** 1876: 40499 Allen Gardiner, Bristol: Sr. Dartmouth 1854 SVPT 89 tonnage: Isaac Braithwaite, 4, Glo'ster Sq., Hyde Park, London.]
68338 Allen Gardiner, Bristol: Yl. Turnchapel 1874 NQPM 39: [same address].

Allen Gardiner III was a schooner with a steam engine, but this is later than our narrative.

1874 The Times (London) Thurs. 29 Oct.
The South American Missionary Society. – A new mission yawl, constructed for the South American Missionary Society, has just been launched at Turnchapel (Plymouth, Devon). It is to take the place of the Allen Gardiner, [belonging to the] *mission school, which has sailed for 20 years between the Falkland and Tierra del Fuego, carrying supplies and taking missionaries and natives to and from the Falklands. Previous to the launch a meeting was held in the National School-room, the Rev. J.J. Tapson, Vicar of Hove, in the chair: and there were present the Bishop of the Falklands, Vice-Admiral Sir B.J. Sulivan, K.C.B., ………………………Admiral Sir H. Keppel, G.C.B. was present in the Admiralty yacht Vivid.*

{www.cms-uk.org/DocumentManager/tabid/81/…../410/….}
Sams Magazine – Illustrations: (Photos have been scanned and saved on computer (in Archives): 1875 Inside Front Cover: New Mission Yawl 'The Allen Gardiner' (sailed from Plymouth February 6 1875)

1875 Lloyd's List Dec. 28 col. 30
Valparaiso: Sailed: Nov. 9: Robert Hine, Brown, Iquique.
1876 Jan.21 col. 17
Iquique: Loading for Nov. 30: Peckforton Castle for the Channel. Robert Hine for the Channel.
Feb. 24 col. 14
Iquique: Cleared: Prev. Jan. 1: Robert Hine for the Channel.
Apr. 19 col. 7
Falmouth arrived Apr. 18: Robert Hine, Brown, Iquique (nitrate) for Hamburg.

1876 Adair's Maryport Advertiser Fri. 11 Feb. p.8
Iquique: Sailed: Dec. 21: Robert Hine.
Apr. 28 p.8
Falmouth : Arrived: Apr. 18: Robert Hine, Brown, from Iquique: sailed for Hamburg on the 19th and reported to have passed Cuxhaven on the 26th.
June 30 p.8
Hamburg: Sailed: Robert Hine, Brown, for Valparaiso.

1876 Lloyd's List July 1. col. 12
Hamburg: sailed: June 27: Robert Hine, Brown, (for) Valparaiso.
July 6 col. 14
Cuxhaven: Sailed: July 2: Robert Hine, Brown, (for) Valparaiso.
July 15 col. 2
Portsmouth: Arrived: July 13: Robert Hine, Brown, Hamburg for Valparaiso.

Liverpool Register: Master: Portsmouth 13.7.76: Edward Hall C. 30864.

1876 Adair's Maryport Advertiser Fri. July 21 p.8
Lizard: Passed: July 16, at 3.20 p.m: Robert Hine, Hall.
July 28 p.8
Spoken: July 18, westward: Robert Hine, lat. 47-15 N., long. 9-5 W.

1876 The London Register Aug. 3 col. 24
Lisbon: Arrived: July 27: Robert Hine, Brown (sic), Hamburg.

A Voyage in the "Sunbeam" Author Annie Allnut Brassey: Release Date January 31, 2005 [eBook #14836] www.gutenberg.net.
A Voyage in the "Sunbeam": Our Home on the Ocean for Eleven Months, by Mrs. Brassey. Chicago: Belford, Clarke & Co. 1881
p.115-116
Some account of the disaster [of the fire on board the Monkshaven, barque, rescued by the Sunbeam] as gathered from the lips of various members of the crew at different times, may perhaps be interesting. It seems that early on Monday morning [Sept. 25 1876], the day following that on which the fire was discovered, another barque, the "Robert Hinds (sic)," of Liverpool, was spoken. The captain of the vessel offered to stand by them or do anything in his power to help them; but at that time they had a fair wind to Monte Video, only 120 miles distant, and they therefore determined to run for that port. .... In the course of the night, however, a terrible gale sprang up.

Shipwrecked Crew coming on Board.

1876 The London Register Dec. 26 col.12
Valparaiso: Arrived: Nov. 4: Robert Hine, Hall, Hamburg.

{http://pilgrim.ceredigion.gov.uk/} According to the museum in Aberystwyth: "The collection of curiosities belonged to Captain Edward Hall (1827-1901) of Aberystwyth. His sea voyages around the world led to his collecting shells, coral, beads and other exotic and unusual mementoes. The pots, covered in stamps, were made by his three children. The Captain sent letters to them from all over the world and so they used the stamps to decorate these items. Captain Hall, from Aberystwyth, is known to have travelled around the world three times in a barque named "Robert Hine."

1877 The Liverpool Mercury Tues. 24 Apr. p.3
Falmouth: Arrived: Apr. 23: Robert Hine from Iquique [northern Chile].
Apr. 26 p.3
Falmouth: Sailed: Apr. 24: Robert Hine for Plymouth: Arrived: April 25: Robert Hine, from Iquique.

1877 The Western Mail Wed. 4 July p.4
Swansea: Entered Outwards: July 3: Robert Hine, B, 327, Valparaiso.
July 14 p.4
Swansea: Cleared: July 13: Robt. Hine, B, Valparaiso, 307 coal and 130 bricks.
[Survey: Swansea in July]

1878 The Liverpool Mercury Wed. 13 Feb. p.3
Valparaiso: Arrived: Dec. 31 [1877]*: Robert Hine, from Swansea.*

[A personal letter]
From Thomas Francis Guayacan, Chile, to Capt. Edward Hall as he sailed in the Robert Hine. Dated: January 28th 1878.

1878 The Liverpool Mercury Wed. Dec. 18 p.3
Spoken: Robert Hine, from Iquique for Falmouth, Sept. 28, 51 S, 52 W. [near the Falklands].

1878 The Times (London) Fri. 20 Dec. p.11
Lizard: Arrivals: Dec. 19: Robert Hine from Iquique.
Dec. 28 p.8
Swansea: Arrivals: Dec. 27: Robert Hine from Iquique.

1878 The Western Mail Sat. 28 Dec p.4
Swansea: Imports: Dec. 27: Robert Hine, Iquique, 500 tons nitrate soda.

1879 The Times (London) Fri. 21 Feb. p.2
[Advert] *Devitt & Moore's Australian Line of Clipper Ships:*
Launceston - Robert Hine - Hall – S.W.I. - Feb. 22.

1879 Launceston Examiner Thurs. 10 July p.2
Launceston: Inwards: July 9: Bark Robert Hine, 327 tons, Jas. (sic) Hall, commander, from London.
The Bark Robert Hine, from London, entered Tamar Heads last evening, after a protracted passage of 131 days. The bark left the London Docks on the 1st March, and passed the Lizard on the 25th (sic), arriving as above, and anchoring in Lagoon Bay for the night. The vessel may be expected to reach the Wharf about midday to-day, as the steamer Amy will no doubt be sent down to meet the vessel, and tow her up to town.
July 11 p.2

The steamer Amy proceeded down the river yesterday morning for the purpose of towing up the bark Robert Hine from Lagoon Bay. The bark left the bay at 1.30 p.m., but had not reached the Wharf at 9 last evening.
July 12 p.2

The bark Robert Hine, which arrived yesterday from London, is a smart looking vessel of 327 tons register, owned by Messrs Hine Bros., of Marypool (sic), Cumberland, and built by Messrs. Davison, of Sunderland, and classed A1 for 11 years at Lloyd's. Since she has been built she has been employed on the colonial and West Coast trade, during which she has made some very quick passages. The vessel is commanded by Captain James (sic) Hall, and comes consigned to Messrs Dalgety, Moore, and Co. The voyage, although it has been a lengthy one, has been almost devoid of incident, but we regret to say that one of the apprentices, named Thomas Dimelow, aged 16, expired at 1 a.m. yesterday from pleurisy, supervening on bronchitis, he having been confined to his bunk from an attack of the latter disease for three weeks previous. On the 19th June another apprentice, named Robert Lorraine, fell from the upper fore topsail yard while reefing in a gale, and fractured his thigh, but is now doing well. Of the passage Captain Hall reports leaving London on March 1, and passed the Lizard on the 15th (sic). From that time no land was sighted until King Island was made on Sunday last, and Tamar Heads were entered on Wednesday afternoon. A pleasant run was experienced to the Equator, which was crossed in long. 32° E., when the S.E. trades were encountered, which were not favourable, the vessel having to beat and tack right through. Northerly winds were then experienced to long. 142°, thence easterly and variable winds to port. A strong westerly gale was experienced off Kangaroo Island, during which part of the bulwarks were washed away. The vessel berthed alongside the Wharf last evening, having been detained at Town Point to discharge a quantity of gunpowder.
July 14 p.2

The agents of the bark Robert Hine announce that that vessel will commence discharging cargo tomorrow morning, provided sufficient entries have been passed to enable her to do so without unnecessary trouble and inconvenience. It is to be hoped that merchants and others having consignments on board will at once pass their entries, and thus facilitate the unloading of the vessel after her long and protracted voyage.

A Sailor's Funeral.--The remains of Thomas Dimelow, an apprentice on board the bark Robert Hine, who died at one o'clock on Friday morning from a combined attack of pleurisy and bronchitis, were conveyed to their last resting place in the Church of England Cemetery on Saturday afternoon. The coffin, covered with the Union Jack, was borne to the hearse and thence to the grave by shipmates of the deceased, Captain Hall and the officers following as chief mourners. Two or three sympathizing residents of the town also joined the procession. The funeral service was read by the Rev. W. Hogg, the Ven. Archdeacon Hales was also present. The poor lad was an only son, and the captain and all the ship's company speak very kindly of him. A few hours before his death, during a brief period of delirium, he called several times for his mother, but consciousness returned again and remained until the last. When his illness assumed a serious character Capt. Hall had a berth provided for him in his own cabin, and everything was done for his comfort that circumstances would permit. As soon as the ship came to an anchor in the river the medical officer was telegraphed for, but on arrival said that nothing further could be done. It was a sudden and sorrowful termination to a nautical career commenced some five months ago amidst all the hilarity and enthusiasm of youth. But though he came to Tasmania only to find a grave, the melancholy satisfaction remains to his friends that he received a decent Christian burial; and that though in a land of strangers there are many hearts touched with pity at his untimely

death, and probably some loving hands that will now and again scatter memorial flowers over the sleeping place of the lone sailor boy.
Aug.1 p.2
The bark Robert Hine finished the discharge of her inward cargo on yesterday. We are informed that the vessel will take in ballast and proceed to Malden Island and there load for guano and proceed to Hamburgh.
Aug. 11 p.2
Launceston: Cleared out: Aug. 9: Robert Hine, 327 tons, Edward Hall, master for Malden Island.

Robert Hine Accident.--We are glad to learn that Robert Lorraine, the apprentice on board the Robert Hine who had the misfortune to break his leg on the passage out, is so far recovered that yesterday he was able to get about on crutches. It is expected that he will be in a fit state to join the ship as soon as the latter is ready for sea, though of course he will not be in a condition to undertake his usual work for a considerable time.

1879 The Mercury (Hobart) Thurs. 13 Aug. p.2
Four sailors were engaged and proceeded by train yesterday, to join Robert Hine which has been delayed at Launceston owing to some of her crew having deserted.

1879 Examiner Launceston Fri. 14 Aug. p.2
The bark Robert Hine was towed down the river yesterday morning by the Tamar tug, but was delayed at the Heads waiting for seamen, which arrived from Hobart Town yesterday morning.
Aug. 15 p.2
Tamar Heads: Sailed: August 14, bark Robert Hine, Malden Island. [Northern South Pacific, Kiribati]

1880 The Times (London) Wed. 17 Mar. p.14
The Robert Hine of Liverpool from the South Pacific for orders 125 days out was spoken on February 24 in lat. 31.46 N. long. 41.43 W. with no foretopgallantmast, and topmast head gone, by the Bremen, ship, arrived at Liverpool from San Francisco.

1880 The Liverpool Mercury Sat. 22 May p.6
Liverpool: May 21: The master of the tug Lord Lyons, reports having towed into the Mersey this day the Robert Hine, from Hamburg.
[Surveys: Liverpool in May, June, July and August] a lengthy stay.
Aug. 3 p.3
Liverpool: Sailed: Aug. 1: Robert Hine, Monte Video.

[**MNL** 1880 & 1882: Robert Hine of Liverpool: Owner: Wilfrid Hine, Maryport, Cumberland.]

1880 The Times (London) Tues. 19 Oct. p.12
Speakings: Robert Hine from Liverpool for Montevideo: She was spoken on Sept 10, 10.13 N. 27 W.

1880 The Liverpool Mercury Wed. 8 Dec. p.7
Pernambuco: Arrived: Robert Hine, from Liverpool.

1881 The Maryport Advertiser and Weekly News Fri. 12 Aug. p.8
Plymouth: Arrived: Aug. 8: Robert Hine, Hall, from the West Coast, South America.
Aug. 19 p.8
Plymouth: Sailed: Aug. 10: Robert Hine, Hall, for Dunkirk.
Dunkirk: Arrived: Aug. 13: Robert Hine, Hall.

1881 Het Nieuws van den Dag (Amsterdam) van Dinsdag 16 Augustus p.6

Plymouth, Vertr [sailed]: *Aug. 11: Robert Hine, Hall, Rotterdam.*

1881 The Times (London) Mon. 3 Oct. p.2
[Notice] *Fiji (direct) the Regular Line: Levuka and River Rewa: Robert Hine: 327: A1 12yrs: E.I.D (East India Dock): Sailed.*

1881 The Maryport Advertiser and Weekly News Fri. 7 Oct. p.8
London: Sailed: Oct. 1: Robert Hine, Hall, for the Fiji Islands.

1881 The Liverpool Mercury Mon. 3 Oct. p.7
Deal: Passed: Oct. 2: Robert Hine for Fiji, from London.

1881 The Glasgow Herald Fri. 2 Dec. p.10
Spoken: Robert Hine (of Liverpool), steering south, Nov. 2 in lat 4 N., long. 28 W.

[**MNL** 1882: 60079 Robert Hine, Liverpool, 327. Owner: Wilfred
Hine, Maryport]

1882 The Sydney Morning Herald Tues. 17 Jan. p.4.
The ship "Darling Downs" spoken ships that desired to be reported "all well". The British barque Robert Hine from London to Fiji, November 27, lat. 34* 27 S., long. 39* 3 W.
Apr. 13 p.7.
Fiji: Levuka April 1: The barque Robert Hine from England, has arrived after a most protracted voyage. So long had the consignees of her cargo been looking for her that at length some of them began to write up to the insurance officers concerning their claims; but "all's well that ends well."

1882 The Evening Post (N.Z.) Tues. 19 Apr. p.2
Fiji News: Auckland 18th April: The Barque Robert Hine reached Fiji 180 days out from London. Some of the shippers had given up, and forwarded claims for insurance.

1882 The Maryport Advertiser and Weekly News Fri. 26 May p.8
Robert Hine, Hall, at Levuka [Fiji] from London, on the 22nd March

1882 The Liverpool Mercury Tues. 6 June p.6
Wrecks and Casualties: Robert Hine, from London at Levako (sic). The report of the 30th May that this vessel had sprung a leak was erroneous.

1882 The Maryport Advertiser and Weekly News Fri. 29 Sept. p.7
Letter from a Maryport Man in Figi.
We have been favoured with a copy of a letter dated Suva Figi, 5th June, 1882, written by Captain Hall, of the barque Robert Hine, to a gentleman resident in Maryport:--
Suva Figi, June 5th, 1882
Dear Sir,--It is not to be expected that in our short letter, I can state half the blessings that have come to the natives of these once and until lately cruel and barbarous isles; for they certainly were full of cruelty and oppression. It is something to be marveled at, to think that only a few years ago—say twelve years—human life was not safe, and that to satisfy a barbarous appetite; and to go about among the people now and see them civil, kind, and well behaved: very much so. They are remarkably civil. I have not once seen them quarrel or fall out either among themselves or with foreigners, and I understand from good authority that family worship prevails through out of the length and breadth of the land. Every night before retiring to rest, when employed on shipboard and in out-of-the-way places far from their homes, their well sung songs of praise and earnest prayers are to be heard. I have found their

places of worship well attended, and the people to all appearance seem both devout and earnest worshippers. Their morals are good, especially under present circumstances; for I am sorry to say that there are many things that work against their advancement. One sad drawback is that the native chiefs don't seem to take any real interest in their peoples' spiritual or temporal welfare; indeed, they don't seem inclined in any way, as far as I can learn, to improve their condition. Unfortunately the immorality and infidelity of many of the white people tend to anything but the improvement and advancement of natives; for you must understand that as yet they are but big children, and in many things faulty. But, after all, they are but children's faults. When the Gospel of Jesus Christ proves to be the power of God to a child, he must still grow to be a man. It is then that his renewed nature will properly appear in his Christian manhood, but he is a Christian when a child with his childish faults. For instance, a Figian teacher may even not be perfect, but the same teacher will go with his life in his hand, as it were, to New Britain and the Solomon groups to carry the glad tidings that have done so much for him and his fellow-countrymen. I am sorry to inform you that in the above-named groups cannibalism, with its horrible and debasing consequences, is still commonly practiced. But the same agency is at work there, in spite of its pestilential and deadly climate, which has been so wonderfully blest in this group, I mean our Wesleyan friends. No pen nor tongue can do them justice so far as to make known the amount of good that under God they have been instrumental in doing here since the day that they first put foot in this group with their lives in their hands, and with no one but God to protect them, and their strong faith and spirit of love to cheer them on in the face of indescribable difficulty. But their teaching was wonderfully blessed, and that most abundantly and quickly. For what, after all, are 30 or 40 years to bring about such a change in the face of such obstacles and prejudices, and cruel practices for ages of this benighted people? There is one thing that speaks well for the present Government, whatever may be its faults or failings—that is, that no one dare sell or give any native any sort of intoxicating drink under a penalty of £20, and the enactment is well carried out. I understand that no one dare sell or give the natives drink; and the law here has the power to prohibit it being given to white people also if complaints are laid against them. Instances of this have occurred during my short sojourn here. I know of more than one instance in that time, and anyone who supplies them with drink when once prohibited by a magistrate is also liable to a fine of £20. It would be well for Sir Wilfrid Lawson to know that, and that both the browns and whites submit quietly to the law. I really believe that as they have been so long in approving of Sir Wilfrid's bill he might add another clause to it, that is, that the magistrate should be empowered in like manner to deal with inebriates if a complaint was lodged against them that they were injuring their families and their employers. Perhaps the old country is not ripe for such a radical change as this, our legislators believe; but it answers here. Sir Wilfrid might just as well agitate for the whole thing. It must come to that. Men cannot always be permitted to ruin their families with no law to protect their wives and children, let alone a law to protect employers and the public.

Just a word about native education. I am informed on good authority, that every native village has its day-school, which is well attended. The consequence is that I find most of the natives able to read and write. Of course there are seminaries and colleges for those of the natives who are being trained for the ministry, which speaks well for the Wesleyan brethren, for I know of no school except those that are connected with their cause—I mean among Protestants. There are a few Roman Catholic schools.—Yours obediently, Edward Hall.

1882 The Maryport Advertiser and Weekly News Fri. 1 Dec. p.8
Robert Hine, at Iquique for Mediterranean ports on the 30th September.

[**LR** 1883: Robert Hine, Bk, E. Hall, 327, Hine Bros, Maryport A 1]

1883 The Maryport Advertiser and Weekly News Fri. 16 Mar. p.5
Gibraltar: Arrived (her orders): Mar. 9: Robert Hine, Hall, from Iquique.
Gibraltar: Sailed: Mar. 13, for Marseilles.
Mar. 30 p.7
Marseilles: Arrived: Mar. 23: Robert Hine, Hall, from Iquique. [Survey: Marseilles in April.]
June 15 p.8
Marseilles: Sailed: June 12: Robert Hine, Hall, for Valparaiso.
Dec. 21 p.8
Valparaiso: Arrived: Dec. 15: Robert Hine, Hall, from Marseilles.
1884 Aug 22 p.8
Plymouth (port of call): Aug. 16: Robert Hine, Hall, at Plymouth from Lobos-de-Afusia.
Plymouth: Sailed: Aug. 21: Robert Hine, Hall, for Antwerp.
Sept. 5 p.8
Antwerp: Arrived: Aug. 29: Robert Hine, Hall, from Lobos-de-Afusia via Plymouth.

++++++++++

Liverpool Register: Master: Antwerp 18.11.84: H. J. Phillips C. 95144.

1884 The Western Mail (Cardiff) Sat. 20 Dec.
Swansea: Entered outwards: Dec. 19: Ensenada, Robert Hine, Phillips, 318.

1885 The Morning Post (London) Thurs. 1 Jan. p.7
Swansea: Sailings: Dec. 30: Robert Hine, Ensenada.

1885 Maryport and Workington Advertiser Fri. 21 Aug. p.3
Messrs. Hine Brother's Ships: Sailing ships: Castle Holme, Myrtle Holme, Brier Holme, Eden Holme, Abbey Holme, Hazel Holme, Aikshaw. [No Robert Hine]

1885 The Liverpool Mercury Tues. Oct. 27 p.3
Queenstown: Arrived: Oct. 26: Robert Hine, from Jamaica.
Oct. 28 p.3
Queenstown: Sailed: Oct. 27: Robert Hine for Goole.

1885 The Glasgow Herald Sat. 7 Nov.
Casualties: The Princess (s), Webb, master, from London for Hull, with a general cargo, fouled the Robert Hine, Phillips, master, from Black River for Goole, with logwood, in Hull Roads last night. The former lost bowsprit cutwater. The latter is apparently undamaged.

1885 The York Herald Tues. 10 Nov. p.8
Goole: Arrived: Nov. 8: Robert Hind (sic), Phillips, Black River, logwood.
Dec. 8 p.8
Goole: Sailed: Dec. 6: Robert Hind (sic), Phillips, Plymouth, coals.

1885 The Liverpool Mercury Thurs. 10 Dec. p.3
St. Catherine's Point: Signalled Off: Dec. 9: Robert Hine (barque) of Liverpool.

Liverpool Register: Master: Swansea 29.1.86: David Williams C. 31226.

1886 The Standard (London) Fri. 5 Feb. p.6
Swansea: Sailings: Feb. 3: Robert Hine, Algoa Bay. [Survey: Swansea in February.]

1886 The Bristol Mercury Thurs. 10 June p.7
At Algoa Bay: Robert Hine ss (sic), Swansea.

1886 The York Herald Thurs. Dec. 16
Goole: Arrived: Dec. 15: Robert Hine, Williams, Belize, logwood.
1887 Jan. 26 p.8
Goole: Sailed: Jan. 25: Robert Hine, Williams, Para (via Hull), coals.
Feb. 11
Hull: Sailed: Feb. 9: Robert Hine, Para.

Liverpool Register: Master: Goole 5.2.87: H.J. Phillips C. 95144.

1887 Maryport Advertiser Fri. 13 May p.5
Para: Arrived: May 2: Robert Hine from Hull.

1887 The Freeman's Journal (Dublin) Thurs. 25 Aug. p.3
Queenstown: Arrived: Aug. 24: Robert Hine, British, 319, Phillips, Belize, logwood.
Aug. 26
Queenstown: Sailed: Aug. 25: Robert Hone (sic), Goole.

1887 Western Mail (Cardiff) Wed. 31 Aug. p.4
Signalled Off the Lizard: Aug. 30: Passed East, Robert Hine of Liverpool, from Queenstown for Goole.

1887 The York Herald Sat. 3 Sept. p.8
Goole: Arrived: Sept. 2: Robert Hind (sic), Phillips, Belize, logwood.
Sept. 22 p.6
Goole: Sailed: Sept. 21: Rob... Hind (sic), Philips, Plymouth, coals.

In 1887 the Robert Hine had a voyage from February to November. From Goole (Hull) to Para (Brazil) to Belize and back to the U.K.

[Survey: Appledore (Bideford, Devon) in December 1887.]

Liverpool Register: Master: Newport 20.1.88: Jas. Rees C. 21542

[**MNL** 1888: 60079 Robert Hine, 319. Owner: William Barrett, Sailor's Home, Swansea]
[**RAFS** 1889: Captain Rees: Owner W. Barrett: Port Liverpool]
[**LR** 1889: Robert Hine, Bk, Rees --87-87--, 319/ 311, S. Cann, Liverpool A 1]
[**MNL** 1889: 60079 Robert Hine, 319. Owner (managing owner) Samuel Cann, Chudleigh, Devon]

1888 The Times Mon. 9 July p.7
Probate, Divorce, and Admiralty Division (Before Mr. Justice Butt.)
In this case, on Friday, the plaintiff, who was master of the barque Robert Hine, from February to November, 1887, claimed a sum of £77 3s. 3d., which he alleged to be due to him in respect of wages and disbursements. The owners of the ship having become bankrupt, the action was defended by the mortgagee in possession, who had intervened. It appeared that the voyage in respect of which the wages were claimed had been from Goole to Para, thence to Belize, and back to the United Kingdom. At Para the master had received the outward freight, and at Belize certain advances in respect of the homeward freight, and the sums so received be claimed to be entitled to keep in payment of a debt due to him from the owners of the vessel. On the arrival of the vessel in this country the mortgagee took possession, and, on the accounts being delivered, disputed the master's right to retain the sums received in respect of freight.
Mr. Robson appeared for the plaintiff; Sir W. Phillimore and Mr. Holman for the mortgagee. Mr. Justice Butt was of opinion that until the mortgagee had taken

possession of the ship the master was entitled to appropriate any money of the owners in his hands in payment of a debt due from them to him. He, therefore, gave judgment for the plaintiff for the balance claimed, subject, if the intervener desired it, to a reference.

1888 The Western Mail (Cardiff) Wed. 18 Jan.
Newport: Entered Outwards: Jan. 17, Paysandu, Robert Hind (sic), B, Phillips, 318.
Jan. 24
Newport: Cleared: Jan. 23: Paysandu, Robert Hine, B, 235 rails, 15½ [sic?] fish plates, 2 bolts and nuts, and 240 creosoted sleepers.

1888 The Standard (London) Mon. 31 Jan. p.6
Sailings: Newport, Jan. 28: Robert Hine, Paysandu. [Uruguay near Buenos Ayres]

1888 The Aberdeen Weekly Journal Wed. 11 Apr. p.3
Casualties (From Lloyd's – Tuesday). The Robert Hine, British barque, Newport for Paysandu, arrived at Monte Video with deck swept. Lost bulwarks.

[Survey: Appledore in May]

1888 The Liverpool Mercury Wed. 5 Dec. p.8
Falmouth: Arrived: Dec. 4: Robert Hine, from Paysandu
Dec. 8 p.7
Falmouth: Sailed: Dec. 7: Robert Hine, for Antwerp.
Dec. 12 p.7
Flushing: Arrived: Dec. 11: Robert Hine, from Paysandu.

Liverpool Register: Master: 27.2.89 Samuel Ca[nn] C. 89357

1889 The Western Mail (Cardiff) Sat. Jan. 26 p.4
Swansea: Imports: Jan. 25: Antwerp, Robert Hine, 252 tons clay, order.
Jan. 28 p.4
Swansea, Prince of Wales Dock: Arrivals: Jan. 25: Robt. Hine, 318, Antwerp, clay.
Feb. 22 p.4
Swansea: Entered Outwards: Feb. 21: Port Natal, Robert Hine, B, Evans, 319.
Mar. 4 p.4
Swansea, South Dock: Sailings: Mar. 1: Robert Hine, (Cann), Port Natal. [Brazil]

1889 The Glasgow Herald Tues. 18 June p.11
Spoken: Robert Hine (English barque), Swansea to Port Natal, April 15, 19 S. 32 W.
June 27 p.11
Port Natal: Arrivals: Robert Hine, from Swansea.

1890 The Yorkshire Herald and The York Herald Thurs. 9 Jan. p.8
Hull: Arrived: Jan 7: Robert Hine, Belize.
Feb. 7 p.8
Hull: Sailed: Feb. 5: Robert Hine, Grimsby.
Grimsby: Arrived: Feb. 5: Robert Hine, Hull.

1890 The Western Mail (Cardiff) Fri. 28 Mar. p.4
Cardiff: Entered Outwards: Mar. 27: Buenos Ayres, Robert Hine, B, Cann, 306.
Apr. 18 p.4
Cardiff: Cleared: Apr. 17: Buenos Ayres, Robert Hinde (sic), B, 623 coal.
Apr. 21 p.4
Cardiff: Sailings: Apr. 19: Robert Huine (sic), s, (Laren) (sic) [Cann?], Buenos Ayres.

1891 New York Herald Tues. 13 Jan. Triple Sheet --with supplement-- p.10
Spoken: Bark Robert Hine (Br), Cann, from Rio Janeiro for Macao, Nov. 28, lat 21 S, long 28 W.

1891The Rio News Tues. 3 Feb. p.6
Imbituba: Arrivals: Jan. 27: Br bk Robert Hine: 303 tons: Cann: 21 ds: salt to Max. Nothmann & Co, from Macao.
Mar. 17 p.6
Imbituba: Departures: Mar. 14: Br bk Robert Hine: 310 tons: Cann, do [ballast].
May 19 p.6
Imbituba: Arrivals: May 17: Br bk Robert Hine: 306 tons: Cann: 11 ds timber to Queiroz.
June 9 p.8
Freights & Charters: The only charter is Br bk Robert Hine, Imbituba and Rio, timber p. t
June 30 p.,6
Imbetuba: Cleared and Ready for Sea: Br bk Robert Hine: do [sundries].
July 7 p.6
Imbetuba: Departures: July 1: Br bk Robert Hine: 307: Cann: Sundries.

1891 New York Herald 22 Aug. --twelve pages-- p.10
Disasters: Bark Robert Hine (Br.), Cann, from Rio Janeiro July 1 for Imbetuba, has been wrecked at Imbetuba. No lives were lost.

1891 The Liverpool Mercury Fri. 21 Aug. p.7
Robert Hine—"St.." (?), Aug. 19, British barque Robert Hine ashore Imbituba [Brazil]. *No further particulars.*
Aug. 22 p.7
Robert Hine—Santa Catharina, Aug. 20: Robert Hine totally wrecked. Crew saved. Broken in two.
Liverpool Register: 128/1868: Robert Hine wrecked at Imbituba 18th August 1891; registry lost with vessel.

1891 The Times (London) Fri. 28 Aug. p.5
Maritime Losses and Casualties: at Lloyd's on Lost-book between midnight, Wednesday August 19 and midnight Wednesday August 26 1891. Robert Hine: Sail: 307 tons: British Built 1858: Ashore no survivors (??).

ALINE

ALINE

Official No.	**58064**	**Code letters**	**HPLB**
Built	1867 May	In Sunderland (James Hardie)	
Deck	One & Break	Build	Clinker
Masts	Three	Gallery	None
Rigging	**Barque**	Head	Billet
Stern	Elliptic	Framework	Wood (oak & teak).
Tonnage	**474**	Length 141.3 feet; Breadth 29.7 feet; Depth 18.2 feet.	

[**LR** 1867 supplement-71: Aline, Bk, G. James'n, 474, Sundrl'd 1867, Ord & Co, Sundrlnd, A1]
[**MNL** 1868 p.16 & 1870 p. 15: Aline, Sunderland: Owner: Robert Ord, Sunderland.]

[Survey: Sunderland in May, 1867]

1867 The Liverpool Mercury Wed. 5 June p.3
Deal: Passed: June 4: Aline, Jameson, from Sunderland for Valparaiso.

1868 New York Herald Thurs. 6 Aug p.8
Disasters in the Bahamas: July 12: Br bark Aline, Jameson, from St. Jago de Cuba for Swansea, with copper ore, touched on Bird Rock Reef, took assistance, threw part cargo overboard, got off, settled for £100 to wreckers and proceeded.

1868 The Standard (London) Wed. 21 Oct. p.7
Swansea: Sailed: Oct. 18: Aline for Cuba.   [Survey: Swansea in October]

1869 The Daily News (London) Fri. 2 Apr. p.7
Nassau, March 6.—The copper ore, which was recovered after being thrown overboard by the Aline, from St. Jago de Cuba to Swansea, when stranded on the Bird Rock 12th Jan. (sic), has been brought here and arrangements have been made to ship it in the Prospero, which is to sail in a few days for London.

1870 The Western Mail (Cardiff) Wed. 26 Jan. p.4
Swansea: Entered Outwards: Jan. 24: Aline, 474, Jameson, Valparaiso. [Chile]
Jan. 31. p.4
Swansea: Cleared: Jan. 29: Aline, 680 coal, Valparaiso.

1870 Lloyd's List 15 Aug. col. 17
Caldera: Arrived: July 2: Aline, Jameson, from Valparaiso.

1870 The Mercury (Hobart, Tasmania) Fri. Morning, 4 Nov. p.2
The Aline, Captain Jameson, which arrived at Valparaiso on the 19th of June from Swansea, passed the River Plate on the 11th of April, and thence to Staten Island, which was passed on the 30th April, experienced strong south-west gales. She sighted Cape Horn on the 10th of May, after which she encountered continuous gales from W.N.W. to S.S.W. until the 15th of June, in lat. 41 S., long. 79 W.

1870 The Western Mail (Cardiff) Wed. 7 Dec. p.4
Swansea: Entered Outwards: Dec. 6: Aline, 474, Jameson, Valparaiso.
Dec. 12
Swansea: Cleared: Dec. 10: Aline, Valparaiso, 680 coal.
1871 May 15 p.4
Valparaiso: Arrivals: Mar. 17 to 28: Aline from Swansea.

1871 The Daily News Sat. 9 Sept. p. 7
Spoken: Aline, from the West Coast [of America] *for Swansea, Aug. 3, 15 N. 32 W.*
Sept. 9 p.5
Mumbles [near Swansea]: *Arrivals: Sept. 7: Aline, from Caldera.* [Northern Chile]
Sept 14 p.7
Swansea: Arrivals: Sept. 12: Aline, from Chili.

1871 The Western Mail Sat. 30 Sept. p.4
Swansea: Entered Outwards: Sept. 29: Aline, B, 474, Jameson, Valparaiso.
Oct. 12 p.4
Swansea: Cleared: Oct. 11: Aline, B, Valparaiso, 675 coal. [Survey: Swansea in October]

1872 The Times (London) Fri. 15 Mar. p.10
Valparaiso: Arrivals: Jan 17 to 30: the Aline from Swansea.

1872 Lloyd's List July 20 col. 6
Swansea: Arrived: July 18: Aline, Jameson, Carrizal.

++++++++++ Wilfrid Hine

[**LR** 1872: Aline, Bk, G. James'n, 474, Ord & Co/ W Hine, Sundrlnd/Liverpool A1]
[**LR** 1873: Aline, Bk, G. James'n/ Turney, 474, W Hine, Liverpool A1]
[**LR** 1874: Aline, Bk, J. Turney, 474/450, W Hine, Liverpool A1]
[**MNL** 1875 & 1876: Aline, Liverpool: Owner: Wilfred (sic) Hine, Liverpool.]
[**MNL** 1878 & 1880: Aline, Liverpool: Owner: Wilfred (sic) Hine, Custom Ho. Blgs. Maryport.]

Liverpool Register: Registered in Liverpool 153/1872
Wilfrid Hine, of Liverpool Sixty Four/64 Dated 3 Oct. 1872.
Master: John Graham Turney, cert. 19279.
Changes of Masters none.

1872 Adair's Maryport Advertiser Fri. 15 Nov. p.8
Swansea: Sailed: Nov. 12: Aline, Turney, for Valparaiso. [Survey: Swansea in October]

[**Fl corr** Liverpool 20 Dec. 1872. I now enclose you cheque for £10-0-6 in payment of flour & oatmeal sacks for the "Aline" & my own a/c............Wilfrid Hine.]

1873 Lloyd's List Tues. 1 Apr. col. 20
Valparaiso: Arrived: Feb. 11: Aline, Turney, Swansea.
Apr. 16 col. 28
Valparaiso: Sailed: Feb. 18: Aline, Chanaral. [North of Valparaiso Chile]
July 24 col. 25
Valparaiso: Arrived: June 3: Aline, Turney, Tome. [North of Talcahuano, Chile]
July 30 Col. 17
Valparaiso: 13th June: The Aline, Turney, from Tome, with wheat, which put in here, 3rd June, was leaky; she is discharging for repair.
Aug. 29 col. 19
Valparaiso: Cleared: July 15: Aline, Liverpool.
Oct. 21 col.10
Liverpool: Arrived: Oct 20: Aline, Valparaiso. [Survey: Liverpool in November]
1874 Lloyd's List Fri. 16 Jan. col. 7
Liverpool: Sailed: Jan. 15: Aline, Buenaventura. [S. America Colombia. Pacific Ocean]
July 23 col. 23
Speakings: Aline: Apr. 15: Liverpool to Guatemala, 56 S. 63 W. [near the Horn]
Sept. 30 col. 29
Leon, Nic.: Arrived: July 19, Aline, Turney, Liverpool. [Nicaragua, Central America; Pacific]

1874 Adair's Maryport Advertiser Fri. 18 Sept. p.8
Real-e-jo: Arrived: Aline, Turney, from Punta Kana. [Punta Cana, Dominican Republic Haiti]

1874 Lloyd's List 2 Oct. col. 19
Nicaragua: arrived: Aline.
1875 Feb. 15 col. 13
Realejo [Nicaragua; Pacific Ocean]*: Sailed: Nov. 10: Aline, Turner (sic), England.*

1875 The Glasgow Herald Fri. 26 Mar. p.6
Falmouth: Arrived: Mar. 25: Aline, Realejo.

1875 The Western Mail (Cardiff) Sat. 27 Mar. p.8
Late shipping: Vessels signalled off the Lizard: (Special telegram from the Lizard Signal Company): Mar. 25: passed East, afternoon, barque Aline of Liverpool, for Falmouth.

1875 Lloyd's List Mar. 27 col. 5
Falmouth: Arrived: Mar. 25: Aline, Turney.
Mar. 30 col. 8
Falmouth: Sailed: Mar. 28, Aline, London. [Survey: London in May.]

1875 The Standard (London) Mon. 5 Apr. p.7
Deal: Arrivals: Apr. 3: Aline, Realejo.
Gravesend: Arrivals: Apr. 4: Aline, Realejo.
June 10 p.7
Gravesend: Sailings: June 9: Aline, Valparaiso.

1875 The Glasgow Herald Wed. 16 June p.6
Gravesend: Put Back: June 15: Aline for Valparaiso.
Deal, June 15: The Aline (barque), of Liverpool, Captain Turney, from London for Valparaiso, and the Trosita (Spanish barque), Captain de Renleria, from London to Havana, were in collision early this morning in the Downs. The former vessel, after slipping anchor and chain, proceeded to the river in tow of the City of London (tug); damages received not ascertained. The latter had bowsprit carried away, besides other damage, and also slipped from an anchor and chain. The vessel remains at anchor in the Downs.

1875 The Times (London) Sat. 26 June p.2
[Advert] *Anderson & Co's, Orient Line for Australia: West Coast & America West Indies & Co: Valparaiso: Aline: 474: J.G. Turney: S.W.I.: She was expected to voyage from Liverpool to Guatemala.*

1875 Adair's Maryport Advertiser Fri. 16 July p.8
Gravesend: Left: July 13: Aline, Turney, for Valparaiso [Northern Chile].
July 23 p.8
Hastings: Passed: July 15: Aline, Turney, and landed pilot.
Sept. 17 p.8
Spoken: Sept. 10: Aline, Turney, 10 N and 25 W.

1876 Lloyd's List Jan. 3 col. 14
Valparaiso: Arrived: Nov. 16 [1875]*: Aline from London.*
Feb. 9 col. 19
Valparaiso: Sailed: Dec. 10 [1875]*: Aline, Furney (sic), for Liverpool.*
Feb. 24 col. 15
Iquique: Loading: Dec. 31 [1875]*: Aline, for the Channel*

1876 Adair's Maryport Advertiser Fri. 10 Mar. p.8

Iquique: Sailed: Jan. 24: Aline, Turney, for London.

1876 The Glasgow Herald Mon. 24 Apr.
Spoken: Aline (barque), of Liverpool, steering southward (sic), March 17, in lat. 25 S., long. 20 W.

1876 Adair's Maryport Advertiser Fri. 19 May p.8
Off the Lizard: May 12: Aline, from Iquique for London.
May 26 p.8
London: Arrived: May 22: Aline, Turney, from Iquique.
June 2 p.8
London: Entered Out: May 27: Aline, Turney, for Callao. [near Lima in Peru]

1876 Lloyd's List Sept. 16 col. 31
London: Cleared Outwards: Sept. 15: Aline, Turney, B, 474, VD [Victoria Dock], *Mosses, for Callao.*
Sept. 18 col. 1
Gravesend: Sailed: Sept. 16: Aline for Callao.
Sept. 19 col. 2
Deal: anchored from the River for Sept. 18, Aline, Turney, Callao.
Sept. 20 col. 2
Deal: sailed: Sept. 19: Aline for Callao.

1876 The Liverpool Mercury Mon. 9 Oct p.3
Spoken: Sept. 26: Aline of this port, 49 N. 7 W.
Dec. 1 p.3
Spoken: Oct. 25: Aline (barque), of this port, 13 N. 27 W. [Survey: Callao in February 1877.]

1877 The Liverpool Mercury Wed. 18 July p.3
Liverpool: Arrived: July 17: Aline, Callao. [Survey: Liverpool in September]
Aug. 13
[Advert] *Australia: "Liverpool" Line of Packets to Brisbane with Quick Despatch. The beautiful Clipper Barque: Aline: 474 tons: Captain Turney. This splendid vessel was built under special survey, and classed A1 at Lloyd's for 14 years. She has always delivered her cargo in excellent order, and offers to shippers an unrivalled conveyance. Loading in Prince's Dock. For freight apply to: Thomas Marwood & Co., 15, Water-street, Liverpool.*

{www.archives.qld.gov.au/downloads/Indexes/immigration/*U-V.pdf*}
Index to Registers of Immigrant Ship' Arrivals 1848-1912. Series ID 13086.
Aline: 27 Jan 1878: IMM/115 1478 Z1959 M1698
Turney J.G. (Master): Parker William Geo 38: Parker - (Mrs) 24: Russell Richard 55: Russell Maria 54: Russell Richard 14: Russell Alice 9: Russell Louisa 6: McGrath Martin 24

1877 The Brisbane Courier Tues. 20 Nov. p.2
Departures from Liverpool: Sept. 19: Aline, barque, (Marwood's line), Captain Turney for Brisbane. Passengers: Mr. and Mrs. Parker; Mr. and Mrs. Russell and family. Consigned Bright Brothers & Co.
1878 Jan. 28 p.2
Brisbane: The Aline, barque, of Marwood's line, arrived off Cape Moreton from Liverpool on Saturday afternoon. The vessel, which has occupied 128 days on the passage, is consigned to Bright Brothers and Co. The barque anchored in the Brisbane Roads yesterday afternoon, and passed the Heath Officer.
Jan. 30 p.2
Entered Inwards.

January 29.-Aline, barque, 474 tons, Captain John S. Turney, ... reported at the Customs yesterday.

Imports. (A Special charge is made on consignee's announcements inserted in this column.)

Aline, Barque, from Liverpool : 37 packages earthenware, 750 cases bottled beer, 500 sacks crushed rock salt, 8 octaves 10 quarter-casks 26 cases wine, 10 quarter-casks 3011 cases whisky, 650 cases stout, 2300 sacks salt, 300 hogsheads beer, 111 drums soda, 400 boxes tinplates, 25 cases bath bricks, 70 cases table salt, 68 packages bottled ale, 20 tons rock salt, 5-casks palm oil, and 12 packages sundries.

Ex. Aline, barque, from Liverpool : 600 cases Tennent's quart ales, 100 boxes I.C. coke 100 boxes I.C. 100 boxes Ix 100 boxes Ixx charcoal tinplates. Parbury, Lamb, and Co.
page 3

The case of a stowaway on board the barque Aline, from Liverpool, was heard before the Assistant Police Magistrate yesterday. The man, Martin McGrath, was found stowed away on board after the vessel had left, and, as is customary, was obliged to work his passage. He proved to be a refractory character, and was in hot water during the whole voyage; in consequence, the master of the vessel proceeded against him for illegally obtaining a passage. McGrath pleaded "Guilty" and was fined £10 or a month's imprisonment. Had McGrath behaved himself in even a decent manner it is very doubtful if he would have been prosecuted.
Feb. 1 p.2

Aline will be towed up the river by the Boko, this morning.
Feb. 4 p.2

Captain Turney reports that the Aline, barque, left Liverpool on September 21, 1877. Experienced fine, light easterly weather down Channel; then strong north-easterly, winds to 35° north, succeeded by calm, and light variables to 31° north, when the north-east trade wind was felt, which we found very light, and lost them in 7° north; thence to Equator had light baffling wind, with much rain. The Line was crossed on November 2, in longitude 29° 80' west; [The Liverpool Mercury Mon. 26 Nov: *Spoken: Aline hence for Brisbane, Nov. 4, 2S. 31W.*] fell in with the south-east trade wind in latitude 4° 40' south, they hanging well to southward. Crossed the meridian of the Cape on December 5, and St. Paul's on December 20, with thick, cloudy, dirty weather. Rounded Tasmania on January 6, 1878, and from thence up the coast to Cape Byron had light, variable, thick weather. Was off Cape Moreton on January 24, but the weather being thick and dirty, stood off shore. Anchored at Yellow Patch, under Cape Moreton, on January 26. October 1, 1877, spoke a ship showing German colors, from Cardiff to Singapore. October 20, 1877, British barque, Mary Wiggin, from Madras to London, 90 days out, 11° 21' north, and 26° 12' west. October 21, 1877, ship Northbrook, 68 days out, from Java to London ; barque Rover of the Seas, from Cochin to London.
Feb. 20 p.2

Departures: Feb. 19.- Aline, barque, 474 tons, Captain John S. Turney, for Callao, in ballast. Bright Brothers and Co., agents. The Aline, barque, for Callao, was towed down the river yesterday morning by the Boko.
Feb. 23.

The Aline, barque, for Callao, was crossing Moreton Bay yesterday afternoon, wind light from the northward.
Feb. 25.

The Aline, barque, for Newcastle, was on Saturday at anchor off the Pilot Station.

1878 The Queenslander (Brisbane) Sat. 2 Mar p.32
Departures: Aline, barque, for Callao, in ballast, on Feb 25.
Mar. 1 p.3

Southern and Western Railway: Extension.

The commission appointed to enquire into the best means of connecting the railway with deep water. ....Witness would have bought 700 tons for the Lady Douglas a few days ago, but Mr. Thomas could not bind himself to time owing to the wet season coming on ; a similar reason had prevented the barque Aline from taking a cargo of coal for Callao; she subsequently left in ballast; in some instances ships bringing cargoes here were sent to Newcastle for orders ; the cost of ballast was 4s, per ton ; did not know anything of the market in Adelaide, but had always been advised not to send coals there; they had a prejudice against Queensland coal there, because it was doubtless inferior to that from Newcastle.

[Survey: Callao in May]

[**MNL** 1878: Aline, Liverpool: Owner: Wilfred (sic) Hine, Custom Ho. Bldgs. Maryport]

1878 The Liverpool Mercury Sat. 12 Oct. p.7
Liverpool: Arrived: Oct 11: Aline, Callao. [Survey: Liverpool in November]
Dec. 14 p.6
Liverpool: Sailed: Dec. 13: Aline, Adelaide.
1879 Jan. 21 p.3
Spoken: Aline, of this port, Jan. 4, 4N., 26W.

1879 The South Australian Advertiser (Adelaide) Tues. 8 Apr. p.4
What has become of the barque Aline? She sailed from Liverpool for Port Adelaide on November 22.
Apr. 9 p.5
Respecting a paragraph in Tuesday's Advertiser touching the barque Aline, from Liverpool, Mr. Gordon, on behalf of the firm of Messrs. D. & W. Murray, who are the agents of the vessel, informs us that she did not sail from Liverpool on the 22nd November, as stated, but on December 13, and therefore there is not the slightest cause for uneasiness respecting her safety.
Apr. 28 p.4
Adelaide: Arrived: Saturday, April 26: Aline, barque, 474 tons, Jno, G. Turney, from Liverpool December 11. No passengers.
The Aline from Liverpool is a barque of 474 tons, which has been 133 days on the passage on account of contrary winds and light airs. After leaving Liverpool there were a few days of coarse weather, but subsequently nothing but calms and light airs marked her progress down the trade region. After passing the prime meridian the weather became boisterous, and the passage of the Southern Ocean was a long one throughout. She left Liverpool on December 11, and at first had strong south and and (sic) south-west winds until reaching the Isle of Madeira on January 7. There were no north-east trades worth speaking of, and the light airs which followed were against her making good progress. On January 31 she crossed the line in 26 18' west; on February 3 sighted Fernando de Norhone (sic), and on the 4th the Pyramid, which bore N.E. by N., distant 14 miles. Very moderate and light breezes continued down the south-east trade region, and on March 14 she was on the prime meridian in 38* 13' south. She headed away down to 40* 56' south, longitude 20* 27' east, and on March 11 there began a series of heavy gales veering from north-west to south-west. During the excessive violence of the weather the sea broke on board in immense volumes. On March 28, while hove-to under low canvas, the sails were blown from the belt-ropes and the vessel for a time lay gunwale under. After sighting Cape Borda she was 10 days before reaching the anchorage, and then having made signal for a tug she was at tide-time towed into harbor*
May 10 p.6
Marine Board: Friday, May 9.
The Harbor-Master at Noarlunga forwarded a piece of paper with the following sentence written on it: "April 16, 1879: Barque Aline, of Liverpool, foundered 120 miles south-west of

Kangaroo Island. Captain, mate, and crew got away in boats. Please send to the rescue. God have mercy. A. Smidt, A.B." *This document was enclosed in a glass bottle which was picked up at Port Noarlunga. As the Aline arrived at the Port safely on April 26 the probability was that the bottle was thrown overboard as she was coming up the Gulf. The President considered the affair a disgraceful hoax. He stated that enquiries had been made with the view of finding the writer, but they had been unsuccessful, as there was no one on board the Aline named Smidt, and the writing on the document did not appear to correspond with that of any of the crew.*
May 13 p.4
It now appears, however, from information imparted by Captain Turney, of the Aline to the Secretary of the Marine Board, that on April 16 she was in latitude 38* 32' S. and longitude 130* 8' E., and it was not till April 19 that she made Neptune Island, which is over 100 miles from Port Willunga, where the bottle was picked up. By this statement the affair is still more shrouded in mystery.

1879 Supplement of The South Australian Register (Adelaide) Sat. 17 May p.7S
General Merchandise
Ale and Porter.—Bulk ales in the early part of the month were in demand, stocks having run out. The Aline, from Liverpool, after a long passage, arrived a few days ago, and brought the first shipment of Marrian's new Brew. This has for the present stocked the market. A parcel of Ashby's is now afloat, and the importer is asking £7 10s. per hhd. for it to arrive. Bottled ale is in better supply, owing to previously purchased parcels having come to hand during the month. Traders are not buying so eagerly to arrive as formerly. The last sales noted are Bass's, bottled by Byass, at 11s , and Jeffrey's at 8s. 9d. per dozen for quarts. Bulk stout has been dull of sale, and we have heard of no transactions. In bottle there has been some enquiry for Guinness's, bottled by Foster, and for Byass's in quarts, both of which are out of the market. Sales of the former brand to arrive have been made at 9s. 3d. to 9s. 6d., and of the latter at 8s. 9d. per dozen. Of other brands the market is fairly supplied, large quantities having come to hand per Campana and other late arrivals.
May 21 p.4
The windbound vessels is the roadstead on Tuesday were the Aline, Bengal, Albert Victor, Lotus, and Craig Alvah, all bound to the westward, but from the sudden fall in the glass and the appearance of the weather they preferred awaiting the conclusion of a gale to making a start to meet one.
May 24 p.4
Sailed: May 23: Aline barque, for Callao. [near Lima in Peru].
There was a complete exodus from the roadstead on Friday morning, when the whole of the wind-bound vessels weighed anchor, and were joined by the Hermoine, which had been towed out. The first wind was very light from the northward, but there was no prospect of settled weather, and at sunset much lightning was seen.

1879 Lloyd's List Mon. 15 Sept. col. 23
Callao: Arrived: Aug. 1: Aline, Turney, Adelaide. [Survey: Callao in August]
Sept. 17 col. 27
Callao: Sailed: Aug. 12: Aline, Furney (sic), Payta.
Sept. 30 col. 32
Payta: Arrived: Aug. 17: Aline, Purney (sic) from Callao.
Oct. 21 col.27
Payta: Sailed: Sept. 9: Aline, Turney for Callao.
Nov. 14 col. 23
Callao: Arrived: Oct. 11: Aline, Turney from Payta.
Dec. col. 25

Callao: Cleared: Nov. 24: Aline, Turney, Liverpool.
1880 Apr. 20 col. 9
Liverpool: Arrived: Apr. 17: Aline, Turney, Chimbote [Peru, North of Callao]
June 22 col.10
Liverpool: Sailed: June 21: Aline, Turney, Montevideo. [Uruguay]

1880 The Manchester Weekly Times Sat. 25 Sept. p.3
Wreck of a Liverpool Ship: Information was received in Liverpool on Saturday of the total loss, of the iron barque Aline, a vessel of 474 tons, which left the Mersey on the 21st June bound for Montevideo. The announcement of her wreck states that the disaster occurred at a place called Juacio. The master of the Aline (Captain Turner (sic)), as well as the crew, was saved. The Aline was built at Sunderland in 1867, and registered at Liverpool. She was classed A 1 at Lloyd's, and was owned by Mr. W. Hine, of Maryport.

1880 Lloyd's List Oct. 16 col. 34
Montevideo: Sept. 16. Aline, British barque, from Liverpool for this port (general cargo) has been totally lost (as telegraphed) at San Ignacio. Some of the crew are saved.

Liverpool Register:
Wrecked at Ignacio on the 13th Sept. 1880 as per letter dated 8th November 1880 from Wilfred (sic) Hine the Managing owner. Certificate of Registry lost with the vessel.

1880 The Maryport Advertiser and Weekly News Fri. 5 Nov. p.3
Wreck of a Maryport Barque: Sufferings of the Crew. –An Apprentice Drowned.
This week we are able to give some particulars respecting the loss of the Alina (sic), of this port, which occurred on the 13th of September last, at Josignacio, a place 75 miles distant from Monte Video. The Aline, a wooden barque of 474 tons, John Turney, master, and owned by Messrs. Hine Bros. of this town, left Liverpool on the 21st of June last, for Monte Video, with a general cargo and a crew of 14 persons, consisting of J. Lewthwaite, A.B., Joseph Story (?), carpenter, T. Nutter, and H. Golightly, apprentices and the captain – all from Maryport, excepting the apprentice Golightly, who belonged to Whitehaven. [Sept. 24 p.8: Henry Golightly, son of Mr. Thomas Golightly, late of Maryport, now of Cleator.] *The remaining portion of the crew were taken on board at Liverpool. Nothing unusual occurred during the voyage out until the morning of the 13th September – the 84th day out. A heavy sea was running, and a slight fog prevailed, when a light was observed at some distance off. This, it was discovered, was a light on land and duly recorded on the chart, but immediately or passing it another light came in view, and there being no record of anything of the kind on the chart, the light was immediately set down as that of some steamship, and the mistake was not discovered until the vessel ran ashore. From about three o'clock in the morning, till daylight, the crew remained on board the barque, which was in the meantime swept by a heavy sea, jeopardising the lives of the crew at every moment. In this terrible position the unfortunate men remained until a number of the natives began to assemble, and then a line was attached to a life-buoy which drifted ashore. This the natives seized, and, holding the line tight, the crew began by its assistance to struggle through the surf to the beach. The task, however, as may easily be imagined, was no easy one; nor by this time every man had become drenched to the skin and benumbed with cold, and it was just at this juncture that the most melancholy incident in connection with the affair occurred. Henry Golightly, a lad sixteen years of age, and belonging to Whitehaven, as we have stated, but formerly of Maryport, and on his first voyage as an apprentice, was attempting to make his escape when he lost his hold of the line. He disappeared beneath the waves and was no more seen by his companions, although they remained on the outlook during the whole of the day. The natives – a mixture of Spaniards and Portuguese – were exceedingly kind to*

the rescued men, for they roasted a whole sheep and asked them to partake of it, which of course they did willingly. For the next three days the party took up their quarters in a "ranch" or mud hut, about three miles from the wreck. During that time they saw the vessel go to pieces. While on one of their visits to the shore they were fortunate enough to pick up a quantity of provisions. No clothing, however, or personal property was saved, beyond what the men were wearing at the time of the wreck. At the end of three days the party set out on their journey to Maldonado, 3? miles distant, in company with a team of bullock wagons, and reached that place at the end of two days' journey. From Maldonado they proceeded in a small schooner to Monte Video, and from thence to Liverpool, in the Corderlara (sic) [Cordillera?], a vessel belonging to the Pacific Steam Navigation Company. They landed at Liverpool on the 26th ult., and from thence came to Maryport, which was reached about eight o'clock in the evening of the same day. Captain Turney, who is expected home by the next mail steamer, has written to the owners of the Alina (sic) to say that he has been tried by a Naval Court at Monte Video, and acquitted of all blame; but the event, he adds has given him a very severe shaking.

Cereal barque: State Library of South Australia, A.D. Edwardes Collection

Glastry brigantine wrecked 1880, Sunderland during the storms: North Yorkshire County Council Collection

155

Port Louis, Mauritius, engraver Fredrick Grosse: State Library of Victoria

Port Chalmers, New Zealand, photographer Mr. A.C. Green: State Library of Victoria

Newcastle N.S.W., Harbour, dock with unidentified barque: State Library of Victoria

Sydney, Darling Harbour, 1871: State Library of Victoria

The West Melbourne Dock: State Library of Victoria

London, South-West India Dock, 1874: State Library of Victoria

JOHN NORMAN

Official No.	**6044**	**Code letters**	**JMDV**
Built	1855 July	Barnstaple (J. Westacott)	
Deck	One & break	Build	Carvel
Masts	Three	Gallery	None
Rigging	**Barque**	Head	Man Bust
Stern	Round	Framework	Wood (oak).
Tonnage	**511**	Length 150.0 feet; Breadth 27.3 feet; Depth 17.5 feet.	

Liverpool Register: Registered in Liverpool 207/1860: 351/1855 registered anew.
Registered de novo 121 in 72 per transcript – received 21 August 1872.
John Norman, of Liverpool. Ship owner 64/64. signed 12th Oct. 1860

[**LR** 1856-58: John Norman, S, C. Gilbart, 511, Bnstpl 1855, N. Devon Sh. Co., Liverpool, A1]
[**LR** 1859-60: John Norman, S, Bond, 511, N. Devon Sh. Co., Liverpool, A1]
[**LR** 1861: John Norman, S, D. Bond, 511, N. Devon Sh. Co., (scored out) Liverpool, A1]
[**LR** 1862-63: John Norman, S, D. Bond, 511, B. Patchett, Liverpool, A1]
[**LR** 1864-65: John Norman, S, D. Bond/ J. Edwards, 511, B. Patchett, Liverpool, A1]
[**LR** 1866: John Norman, S, J. Edwards, 511, B. Patchett, Liverpool, A1 (expired)]
[**LR** 1867-69: John Norman, S, J. Edwards, 511, B. Patchett, Liverpool, ------------]
[**LR** 1870: supplement -71: John Norman, Bk, ----------, 511, Redway & C, Exeter, A1]
[**LR** 1872: John Norman, Bk, ---------------, 511, Redway & Co/W. Hine, Exeter/Liverpool, A1]
[**LR** 1873: John Norman, Bk, Hurst/J.N. Hurst, 511, W. Hine, Liverpool, A1]
[**LR** 1874: John Norman, Bk, J.N. Hurst/W. Bryce, 513/461, W. Hine, Liverpool, A1]
[**ALRAFS** 1866-69: John Norman, J. Edwards, 513, Liverpool, B. Patchitt & Co.]
[**ALRAFS** 1870: John Norman, Gardner, 513, Liverpool, B. Patchitt & Co.]
[**RAFS** 1870-71: John Norman, R. Chandler, S, Br, Liverpool, 513, B. Patchett]
[**ALRAFS** 1871: John Norman, ----------, 513, Liverpool, B. Patchitt & Co.]
[**RAFS** 1872: John Norman, R. Burke, S, Br, Liverpool, 513, B. Patchett]
[**ALRAFS** 1872-73: John Norman, ----------, 513, Liverpool, Exeter, Redway & Co. (x ship)]
[**RAFS** 1874-75: John Norman, G.N. Hurst, S, Br, Liverpool, 513, B. Patchett]
[**ALRAFS** 1874-75: John Norman, J.N. Hurst, 511, Liverpool, Exeter, Redway & Co.]
[**RAFS** 1876-77: John Norman, G.N. Hurst, S, Br, Liverpool, 513, W. Hine]
[**ALRAFS** 1876-77: John Norman, W. Bryce, 513, Liverpool, Hine Bros.]
[**RAFS** 1878-79: John Norman, J. Tarney, S, Br, Liverpool, 513, Hine Bros.]
[**ALRAFS** 1878-80: John Norman, J. Tarney, 513, Liverpool, Hine Bros.]
[**ALRAFS** 1881-82: John Norman, Nicholson, 513, Liverpool, Hine Bros.]

Before John Norman came into the Hine Bros. fleet, her history was most interesting.

1855 Trewman's Exeter Flying Post Thurs. 1 Nov. p.8
Barnstaple: The "John Norman."—This splendid ship, 800 tons burthen, and the largest built at Barnstaple, was towed down the river on Thursday last, by the steam tug Tartar, to Appledore Pool, thence she will cross the channel for the Welsh coast to be coppered. The John Norman is a beautiful specimen of modern ship-architecture, and reflects the highest credit on the superior ability of the builder, Mr. J. Westacott.

1855 The Morning Chronicle (London) Mon. 3 Dec. p.7
Newport: Sailed: Nov. 30: John Norman for New Orleans.

1856 The Liverpool Mercury Wed, 23 April p.3
Off Kinsale: Apr. 18: John Norman from Quebec for hence [for Liverpool].
Apr. 25 p.7

Liverpool: Arrived: Apr. 24: John Norman from New Orleans.
July 25 p.3
Liverpool: Sailed: July 25: John Norman, Gilbart, for Valparaiso.
1857 June 8 p.7
Liverpool: Arrived: June 5: John Norman, Gilbert (sic), San Felipe.
Spoken: John Norman, for this port, 2nd June, in lat. 50 N. lon. 11 W.
Aug. 10 p.7
Liverpool: Sailed: Aug. 8: John Norman, Gilbart for Valparaiso.
1858 June 22 p.3
Liverpool: Arrived: June 21: John Norman, Bond, from Cobija.
Oct. 11 p.3
Liverpool: Sailed: Oct. 9: John Norman. Bond, Valparaiso.

1859 The Morning Chronicle (London) Thurs. 14 July p.8
Spoken: John Norman, from Iquique for Hamburg, June 23, in lat. 38 N., 36 W., out 75 days.
July 16 p.8
Deal: July 15: Put in and anchored in the Gull Stream the John Norman, from Iquique for Hamburg.
1860 July 17 p.8
Liverpool: Arrived: July 16: John Norman from Iquique. [Survey: Liverpool in September]

1860 The Liverpool Mercury Mon. 15 Oct. p.3
Liverpool: Sailed: Oct. 13: John Norman, Bond, Shangae.

1861 The Daily News (London) Tues. 14 May p.7
Spoken: John Norman, from Liverpool for Shanghai, 115 days, March 11.
Sept. 28 p.7
Shangae: Departures: July 18: John Norman, Norman, Foochow.

1861 The Standard (London) Thurs. 17 Oct. p.6
China Shipping: Fuchan: Departures: Aug. 15: The John Norman, Norman, for London.
Nov. 29 p.7
Manilla: Oct 5. The John Norman, British ship, Foo-chow-foo to London was fallen in with, Sept. 9, in lat. 8 N. long. 131 E., with her master dead, by the Acis, schooner, arrived here from the Pelew Islands. [W. Pacific Ocean]. *The mate of the John Norman, the only mariner on board, requested an officer from the Acis, but the latter could not render any assistance in that respect.*

{"Rocks and Storms I'll Fear No More":
Anglo-American Maritime Memorialization, 1700 - 1940
A Dissertation by David James Steward
Submitted to the Office of Graduate Studies of Texas A&M University in partial fulfillment of the requirements for the degree of Doctor of Philosophy May 2004}
By far the most amazing of the memorials that describes a body being brought home for burial is that of Captain John Norman of Liverpool (MR #126). Norman's story is one of the nine recorded on the family gravestone in St. James's Cemetery, Liverpool. After detailing the names of four other family members, including his mother, the gravestone states: **Also Captn John Norman, son of the above Mary Norman who died on board the Ship "John Norman" in the China Sea on his homeward voyage from Foochow to London, August 31st 1861, Aged 52 Years. His remains were brought to England by his Wife and interred here February 9th 1862**
Captain Norman's wife Frances, the last person to be added to the stone following her death in 1886, must have been an extremely determined woman to bring his body halfway around the world in the face of prevailing maritime superstitions against such a practice. The fact

that she was able to do so was most likely due to her husband's position as captain of the vessel.}

1862 The Morning Post (London) Tues. 30 Jan. p.3
Falmouth: Arrived: Jan. 27: John Norman from Foo-chow-foo.
Feb. 7 p.7
Gravesend: Arrived: Feb. 6: John Norman from Foo-chow-foo.

1862 The Daily News (London) Thurs, 30 Jan. p.3
The John Norman, Finzel, and Primula have arrived from China with 1,600,000 lbs. of tea. [Survey: London in March]
May 12 p.7
Gravesend: Sailed: May 10: John Norman to Adelaide.

Liverpool Register: Master: London 6.5.62: John Miles C. 44027.

1862 The South Australian Advertiser Mon. Aug. 18 p.2
Adelaide: Arrived: Aug. 16. John Norman ship, 513, J. Miles, master from London May 12. Passengers: Mr. Mainwaring, and Misses Clarke, Steadman, and West, in the cabin: and Robert Price, and Michael Condon, in the steerage.
The John Norman, from London, arrived on Saturday, after a favourable passage, which has not been marked by any extraordinary occurrence. She left the Downs on the 14th of May, and in about five days after was clear of the Channel, and up to the period of crossing the line, on June 12, she encountered a continuation of remarkably fine weather; but subsequent to rounding the Cape strong-gales have been felt, though no serious damage to the vessel has resulted beyond springing the mainroyalmast. Captain Miles reports the following vessels: On July 1 in lat. 30* 50' S., long. 31* 30' W., the steamer, Rattler, 79 days out from Glasgow, bound to Calcutta; on June 5, in lat 7* 58' N., long. 20* 4' W., the barque Penelope, 25 days out from the west coast, bound to Bristol.

1862 The South Australian Police Gazette: Adelaide Friday, September 12, 1862 No. 75.
Deserted Seamen: Warrants have been issued (5th September) at Port Adelaide, for the apprehension of the undermentioned deserted seamen:--From the ship "John Norman": James Brown, a Scotchman, 30 years of age, dark complexion, dark hair, large whiskers, middle height.
John Hunt, a Canadian, 23 years of age, light complexion, light hair, no whiskers, short and stout; has friends in Adelaide and Port Adelaide.

1863 The South Australian Goverment Gazette: Adelaide Feb. 26, 1863 p.171
Felony Cases: No. 50: Dec. 27: Stolen from on board the ship John Norman, some plates and a plated spoon at Port Adelaide (property recoved) Francis Jones (prisoner): P. C. Burchell (apprehended by): Sum. convict.

1862 The South Australian Register Tues. 23 Dec. p.2
The John Norman was towed to the Lightship on Monday morning.
1863 Mon. 26 Jan. 26 p.8
Adelaide: Departures: Dec. 27: John Norman, ship, 513 tons, J. Miles for London: Cargo—wool, copper &c: 1 passenger. {www.slsa.sa.gov.au/webdata: Mr. J. Holden. Passenger for London U.K. Dep. 19/12/1862}
Apr. 31 p.4
The Hotspur, Captain H. Toynbee, which arrived in Table Bay on the 11th February, reported having spoken the John Nornam, in lat. 34 49' S., long. 26 43 E., out from Adelaide to London 42 days. [suggests going via Cape of Good Hope]

1863 The Times (London) Thurs. 16 Apr. p.13

Gravesend: Arrived: April 15: John Norman from Adelaide (110 days).
May 15 p.2

[Advert] Adelaide direct. The fast and favourite clipper John Norman: A1 now at the jetty London Docks. Passage to Adelaide last year 87 days. Has a superb saloon, with every comfort and convenience for passengers.

1863 The South Australian Register Thurs. 8 Oct. p.2

Adelaide: Arrived: Oct. 7: John Norman ship, 515, J. Miles, master from London July 6. Passengers: Mrs. Miles, Mrs. West, Messrs. Henderson, Brooks, and Armstrong, in the cabin.

The John Norman: It was quite a picture to see this smart little ship heading for the anchorage after a 94 days' passage from London; for she had every stitch of canvas set when first made out, and the skysails aloft indicated what vessel it was long before she was boarded. During the passage nothing remarkable occurred worthy of note beyond some very heavy weather in lat. 37* 26', long. 50* 38' which continued for several days without intermission, but no serious damage resulted beyond the detention caused by the contrary winds. On nearing the land strong easterly weather is noted in the log book, which prevented the run in from Cape Leuwin, which would have materially improved the passage. Although there are pilots on the look-out down the Gulf, yet the John Norman came to an anchor without being boarded; all the officials at the Port being engaged.
Oct. 30 p.3

Port Adelaide: Thursday. October 29. [Before Mr. G. W. Hawkes. S.M.]

John Mallis, seaman of the John Norman, was charged with being absent without leave. Constable Mooney deposed to having arrested him on the wharf with a bundle of wearing apparel under his arm. Captain Miles stated the prisoner had had (sic) received no permission to leave the vessel. His Worship ordered him to be sent to gaol for two months

1863 The South Australian Advertiser Thurs. 12 Nov. p.3

Local Court—Port Adelaide. Tuesday, November 10. [Before Messrs. G.W. Hawkes, S.M., B. Douglas, and R. Tapley.] Full Jurisdiction.

Disobeying Orders.--John Henry Howard, and Charles Ollershisser, seamen of the John Norman, were charged with disobeying orders on Sunday last. The prisoners had refused to pump out the ship on Sunday night, which was usual, and were insolent at the same time. They were committed to gaol for four weeks.
Nov. 24 p.2

Adelaide: Sailed: Nov. 23: John Norman, ship, for Port Augusta.
Dec. 3 p.2

Port Augusta: Vessels in Harbour: At Hacket's Jetty, the ship John Norman, Miles, Master, Discharging coasting cargo preparatory to taking in wool for England.
1864 Jan. 25 p.2

Port Augusta: Sailed: Jan. 18: The John Norman. 513 tons, John Miles, master, for London. Passenger, Mrs. Miles.

1864 The Times (London) Mon. 13 June p.6

Gravesend: Arrived: June 11: John Norman from Port Augusta. [Survey: London in July]
Liverpool Register: Master: London 12.8.64: John Gilbert Edwards C. 9255
Aug. 15 p.11

Deal: Passed: Aug. 14: John Norman from London for Shanghai.

162

1865 New York Herald Fri. 1 Sept. p.8
New York: Arrived: Aug. 31: Ship John Norman (Br), Edwards, Shanghai April 7, with teas to master. Passed Anjer May 25, Cape of Good Hope July 9, St. Helena 21st, crossed the equator 31st, in lon. 27; since then had very light winds and calms.
[Survey: New York in September]

1865 The Glasgow Daily Herald Tues. 21 Nov. p.5
Queenstown: Arrived: Nov. 20: John Norman, New York.

1866 The Times (London) Mon. 26 Mar. p.10
Spoken: John Norman 30 days from Cardiff for Yokohama, Feb. 27, 5.16 N long. 24.30 W.

1867 The New-York Times Sun. 30 June
New-York: Arrived: June 29: Ship John Norman, (of Liverpool), Edwards, Singapore March 28, with mdse, to master. Passed Angier (sic) March 28, Cape of Good Hope April 26, St. Helena May 20, and crossed the equator May 30, in lon. 24; from the gulf had light winds and thick fogs.

1867 {Immigrant Ships Transcribers Guild: Ship John Norman, Singapore to New York, 1 July.
John G. Edwards, Master of the Ship John Norman: List of Manifest of all the Passengers taken on board the Ship John Norman, from Singapore, burthern 513 Br. tons. 1. Mr. Hore 31, Male, Co????, U.S., U.S., Cabin. 2. Mrs. Hore, 28, Female, Wife, U.S., U.S., Cabin. 3. Mr. Pancratz (?), 23, Male, Clerk, Olinberg (?), Olinberg (?) [(suggest) Oldenburg, Germany], Cabin.}

1867 The New-York Times Sun. 27 Oct.
New-York: Cleared: Oct. 26: Ship, John Norman, (Br.,) Gardner, Hong Kong and Shanghai. [Survey: New York in October]

1868 New York Herald Tues. 15 Dec. --triple sheet-- p.10
Shanghae, Oct. 14: in port ship John Norman (Br.) Gardner, for NYork.

1869 The New-York Times Fri. Jan. 22 p.8
China and Japan: San Francisco, Thursday, Jan 21: The steamer Japan arrived yesterday with advices from Hong Kong to Dec. 16 and Yokohama Dec. 28: Left the following vessels at Yokohama: ship John Norman, loading for New-York.

1869 New York Herald Tues. 23 Mar. --triple sheet-- p.10
Yokohama: In Port: Jan. 9: John Norman (Br), Gardner for New York, ldg [loading ?].

1869 Sacramento Daily Union (California) Sat. 24 July p.1
Letter from Japan
Yokohama. June 29, 1869. Yokohama. This settlement is situate on the south side of the bay of Yedo, eighteen miles by water and twenty-two by land from that city, and twenty-nine miles from the entrance to the bay. The bay is a fine one, and the natural scenery is lovely, but the site chosen for this settlement is not very good for harbor convenience, being more like a roadstead. Ships are obliged to lie at anchor, moored in the channel which makes up between this and Kanagawa, and much delay and inconvenience are caused when it blows from the north, as it often does, in consequence of the roughness of the sea. There are no wharves or docks here for ships to discharge or load at, and this is all done by native lighters which work very cheap — too cheap to be efficient; but we shall soon have a company of Europeans started here who will have lighters and tugs ready for public patronage, and perhaps, in conjunction therewith, a ferriage or Whitehall boat business. The present means

for public conveyance between vessels and shore are most contemptible; the boats used for this purpose are the commonest kind of native fish boats, without seats or covering, and resemble very much in design and neatness the top of an old-fashioned skate with the iron pulled out. They are propelled on the screw principle with huge heavy oars settled midway on a wooden peg attached to an outrigger; the upper end is then slipped through a rope noose made fast to the boat, and the boatman, whose costume seldom consists of more than a strip of cotton around the groin and loins, guides this, standing, in a skillful manner, by pushing to and fro. These boats make fair time through the water, but are by no means safe, particularly to "Jack" when he has just "taken some benzene," and not a few accidents have happened in this harbor from that cause. These boats are owned by the native Custom-house authorities, and may be engaged at either of the two "hatobas" or landing places. These "hatobas," like nearly everything Japanese, are very primitive, and as all cargoes are landed and shipped from these places, they are by no means pleasant quarters for ladies to pass through. Custom-house inspection officers are established at each, and all goods have to be examined here for landing or shipment. There are very fine bonded warehouses adjacent to one of these "hatobas," which, from the time of their establishment, over three years ago, have been under the superintendence of Thomas Hogg, an American gentleman, and one of the pioneers of this settlement. He goes home by next steamer on leave of absence. Should he not return, this community will lose one of its most useful members. Yokohama lies on a piece of flat or swamp land that makes in like a horse-shoe, and is set in a surrounding ridge of high or bluff land that lends a charm to the appearance of the place, and looks green the year round, back of which Mount Fusigama is plainly visible, rearing its symmetrical and snow-capped peak up into the clouds a distance of 14,000 feet, and fifty-six miles from this place, although it does not seem more than five. This place is surrounded by a canal, the continuation of the channel in which the vessels in harbor anchor. This piece of land measures about three square miles; one-half of which is devoted to the use of foreigners, and the other to Japanese. In the Japanese portion the houses are of the tent order, similar to Chinese, but cleaner, and seldom over one story high, without paint, built of wood or mud-stone with tiled roofs and windows of paper, or none at all. They open their doors by lifting out a convenient side of the house, close them by putting the side back again, and fasten them with an anchor latch. They are generally large enough to hold all hands, and at night there is about as much spare room as in a Fulton Ferry car on a rainy evening. A six-foot darkey, boatswain from the tea clipper John Norman, for New York, was arrested a short time ago for making confusion in one of these dwellings and brought before the Consul. It appears that he wrathfully pulled out an opposite side to the one open, thereby causing things to come together in a confused manner. He was fined twenty-five "boos" (about eight dollars) and went on his way sailorizing, soliloquizing or swearing, whichever you like to call it. The native population of this quarter is estimated at 20,000 — largely increased during business hours by people from Kanagawa, or villages on the other side of the canal, and the scene is very animated in fine weather, the people flocking through the streets — which are, with two exceptions, very narrow — like so many ants.

1869 New York Herald Sat. 21 Aug p.8
New York: Arrived: Aug. 20: Ship John Norman (Br), Gardiner (sic), Yokohama, March 2, with teas &c. to Francis Hathaway. March 4, took a heavy gale, which carried away foretopsail yard and split the topsail; had light baffling winds down the China Sea; was 5 days working through the Straits of Sunda; left Anjier (sic) April 25; had very light winds throughout the trades; was 10 days from lat. 23 to 27. 30; Aug 12, lat 20 12 N, lon 70 10, encountered a heavy gale from S W, and, from appearances, judged a hurricane was travelling to the N. E., on the 13th weather moderated, since which time had light variable winds. Passed Cape of Good Hope June 5; St. Helena 27th, crossed the Equator July 9 in lon 22 W, and arrived off Sandy Hook, 3 a.m. 20th inst after a passage of 170 days.

Aug 8 no lat, &c, boarded brig Clytic, of Spearsport, from NYork for Cienfuegos, who kindly supplied a barrel of beef and some other stores, which were much needed.
1869 The New-York Times Sat. 21 Aug.
Had light variable lights and calms almost the entire passage; experienced a heavy N.E. gale in the Gulf of Yoddo [c. 10 miles below Yokohama], *during which lost fore topsail yard, and split fore topsail; had also heavy N.E. gales between Madagascar and the Cape. Passed Anjer April 24; .... and crossed the equator July 9, in lon. 20 W. Aug 8. lat. 20 44, lon. 68 46, spoke brig Clytic, (of Spearsport). Hence for Cienfuegos, who kindly supplied us with a barrel of beef and some small stores, of which we were short.*
Sept. 16
New-York: Cleared: Sept. 15: Ship John Norman (Br.,) Chandler (sic), London.
[Survey: New York in September]

Liverpool Register: Master: New York 31.8.69: Richard Gardiner – vice S.S. Gardiner

1869 The Glasgow Herald Tues. 5 Oct. p.7
A cable telegram from New York states that the John Norman, Gardner (sic), master, from New York to Liverpool was at Halifax, leaky.

1869 The British Colonist, Halifax, Nova Scotia Thurs. 11 Nov.
Sales at Auction: 11 o'clock: Underwriter's Sale: By Edward Lawson, At O'Conner's Wharf, To-morrow, Friday, at Eleven o'clock: Two Tons Old Metal: From off the ship John Norman, and sold for the benefit of the Underwriters and all concerned. Nov 11.

1869 The Glasgow Herald Sat. 9 Dec. p.7
New York, Nov. 27: The John Norman (ship), from New York for London, which put into Halifax in distress, repaired and cleared for her destination on the 22d inst.

1869 The Liverpool Mercury Tues. 7 Dec. p.3
The John Norman, from New York for London, which put into Halifax leaky on the 30th Sept. broke adrift there 19th Nov., and damaged her stern considerably, but was afterwards securely moored.

[**MNL** 1870: 6044 John Norman, Liverpool, 513. Owner: Benjamin Patchett, Liverpool.]

Liverpool Register: Master: Newcastle 30.3.70: George Avon

1870 The Times (London) Tues. 19 Apr. p.5
Exmouth: April 17: The John Norman (ship), from Shields, arrived here in charge of a pilot and steamer took the ground on the ridge at high water, and remained, lying very badly. She got off the following tide, after discharging part of her cargo. She is greatly strained and hove up in midships, and to all appearance seriously damaged.

[Survey: Dartmouth in December]
Liverpool Register: Master: Dartmouth 16.12.70: Charles Ascon C 12409

1870 The Western Mail (Cardiff) Wed. 28 Dec. p.4
Cardiff: Arrivals: Bute East Dock: Dec. 27: John Norman, 513, Axon, Dartmouth, ballast.
Dec. 31 p.4
Cardiff: Entered Outwards: Dec. 30: John Norman, 513, Axon, Bahia. [Brazil]
1871 Jan. 24 p.4
Cardiff: Cleared Out: Jan 23: John Hennan (sic), B, Bahia, 750, coal.
Liverpool Register: Master: Cardiff 30.1.71: John Burke 2986

1871 The Glasgow Daily Herald Sat. 4 Feb. p.6

Queenstown: Arrived: Feb. 3: John Norma (sic), Cardiff for Bahia; reported leaky.
Feb. 24 p.6
The John Norman, Cardiff to Bahia, fouled the Nordens Dronning, at Queenstown, on the 17th, and was obliged to slip. The Nordens Dronning first broke her windlass, and had to slip her anchor.

1871 The Times (London) Wed. 17 May p.12
Bahia: Arrivals: Apr.- 9 and 25: The John Norman from Queenstown. [Cobh, Ireland]

1871 The Liverpool Mercury Fri. 25 Aug. p.3
Liverpool: Arrived: Aug. 24: John Norman, Bahia. [Northeast Brazil]
Nov.14 p.3
Liverpool: Sailed: Nov. 12: John Norman, Pernambuco. [Northeast Brazil]
Nov. 15 p.3
The John Norman, hence for Pernambuco, was left at eight p.m. on the 13th instant off Point Lynas by Mr. J.B. Sumner, pilot wind S.S.W., strong breeze.
Dec. 20 p.8
Dispute of Freight: Greenup and Another v. Sweet and Another-----Messrs. Greenup and Co. are Merchants at Manchester and having also a house in Liverpool------the defendants are Messrs. Sweet and Redway, who are owners of the barque John Norman.-----A voyage from Bahia to Liverpool.-----The ship arrived at Liverpool at the end of August. His Lordship ruled that there was no defence, and the verdict was entered for the plaintiffs.

1871 The Sun & Central Press, London Fri. 17 Nov. p.5
Collision at Sea: The barque, John Norman, Captain Burke (sic), from Liverpool, with a general cargo for Pernambuco, three days out, has put in at Queenstown for repairs, having experienced a fearful gale on Tuesday. She also collided with a barque whose name is unknown. The John Norman lost her bowsprit, jibboom, cut water and foreyard, and has her sails split. [Survey: Queenstown in November.]

1871 The Standard (London) Sat. 18 Nov. p.6
Queenstown: The John Norman, Liverpool to Pernambuco, has put in with loss bowsprit and foreyard, having been in collision with a vessel off Tuskar. [County Wexford, Ireland]
Dec. 7 p.7
Queenstown: Sailed, Dec. 6: John Norman for Pernambuco.

1872 The Glasgow Herald Fri. 26 Jan. p.6
Pernambuco: Arrivals: previous to Jan. 11: John Norman, from the United Kingdom.
June 4 p.6
Liverpool: Arrived: June 3: John Norman, Pernambuco.

++++++++++ **Wilfrid Hine**
[LR 1872: John Norman, Bk, ----------, 511, Redway & C/ W. Hine, Exeter/ Liverpool, A1]
[LR 1873: John Norman, Bk, J.N. Hurst, 511, W. Hine, Liverpool, A1]
[LR 1874: John Norman, Bk, J.N. Hurst/ W. Bryce, 511/461, W. Hine, Liverpool, A1]

Liverpool Register: Registered de novo 121 in 72 per transcript – received 21 August 1872.

1872 The Glasgow Herald Thurs. 5. Sept. p.6
Liverpool: Sailed: Sept. 4: John Norman, Callao. [Lima, Peru]
Dec. 6 p.6
Spoken: John Norman, from Liverpool for Callao, Oct 23, in lat. 18 S., long. 29 W.

1873 The Liverpool Mercury Sat. 3 May p.6

Wreck of a Liverpool Trader and Loss of Life.
We learn by telegraph from Lisbon of the total loss of the well-known Liverpool and River Plate trader John Norman, bound from Liverpool for Buenos Ayres with a general cargo, she having gone ashore at Garzon. A telegram states that the master and seven men were lost. The John Norman was a barque of 511 tons, built in Barnstaple in 1855, and owned by Mr. Wilfred (sic) Hine, of Liverpool.
May 5 p.3
To the Editors of the Liverpool Mercury.

Gentlemen,--Observing in the Mercury of to-day the reported loss of the John Norman, of this port, I shall feel obliged by your correcting the same, as the John Norman is at present loading for Liverpool on the coast of Peru. You have no doubt confounded this vessel's name with that of the Norman, of Maryport, whose loss is reported on a voyage hence for Monte Video.

Wilfrid Hine.

Managing owner of the barque John Norman, of Liverpool, 14, 14½, and 16, South Castle-street, Liverpool, May 3, 1873.
Aug. 21, p.3
Liverpool: Arrived: Aug. 20: John Norman, Chereppe.

1873 Adair's Maryport Advertiser Fri. 22 Aug.p.8
Liverpool: Arrived: Aug. 20: John Norman, Hurst, from Valparaiso.
[Survey: Liverpool in September.]
Oct. 24 p.8
Liverpool: Sailed: Oct. 17: John Norman, Hurst, for Valparaiso.

1873 The Liverpool Mercury Tues. 28 Oct. p.3
Oct. 27: John Norman, hence for Valparaiso, put into Queenstown with rudder damaged.
Oct. 31 p.3
The John Norman, hence for Valparaiso, which put into Queenstown, had jettisoned part of cargo, was much strained, and making a good deal of water.

[Survey: Cork in December.] [New captain]

1874 The Standard (London) Fri. 10 Apr. p.7
Spoken: John Norman, Liverpool to Valparaiso, February 16, lat. 20 S. long. 36 W.

1874 Adair's Maryport Advertiser Fri. 19 June p.8
Valparaiso: Arrived: Apr. 23: John Norman, Bryce.
Valparaiso: Sailed: Apr. 29: John Norman, Bryce for Iquique.
Oct. 30 p.8
Queenstown: Arrived: Oct. 24: John Norman, Bryce, for orders, and has since sailed for Glasgow.

1874 The Liverpool Mercury Thurs. 29 Oct. p.3
Queenstown: Sailed: Oct. 28: John Norman, for Glasgow.

1874 The Glasgow Herald Thurs. 5 Nov. p.6
The Broomielaw: Arrived: Nov. 4: John Norman, 513, Bryce, from Iquique, nitrate of soda.
1875 Jan. 1 p.6
The Broomielaw: Sailed: Jan. 7: John Norman, for Napier, N.Z.
Jan. 14 p.6
Lamlash: Put in: Jan 11: John Norman, from Glasgow for Napier, N.Z.
Jan. 25 p.6
Lamlash: Sailed: Jan. 21: John Norman, from Glasgow for Napier, N.Z.

[**MNL** 1875 & 1876: 6044 John Norman, Liverpool, 513. Owner: Wilfrid Hine, Liverpool.]

1875 Adair's Maryport Advertiser Fri. 23 Apr. p.8
Spoken: Feb. 23: John Norman, Bryce, lat. 18.40 north, long. 21.50 west.

1875 The Evening Post (N.Z.) Mon. 12 June p.2
Napier: Arrived: June 11: John Norman from Glasgow, with plant for the gasworks.

((Evening Star (Auckland) (N.Z.) Sat. 12 Jan. p.2 1878
Auckland: Arrivals: Jan. 11: Abbey Holme arrived from London. Captain Bryce, who is in command, has not been in Auckland, but visited Napier the year before last as commander of the barque John Norman.))

"White Wings" NZETC p.215
1875: John Norman, sailed from London (sic) January 5th and Lamlash January 21st arrived June 11th. A long voyage of 153 days owing to heavy weather experienced throughout.

1875 The Daily Southern Cross (N.Z.) Wed. 14 July p.3
The long-expected gas plant has at last arrived by the "John Norman". The works are progressing rapidly. The premises are close to the railway, on the White Road but I do not think the town can be lighted sooner than six or seven months, seeing that none of the pipes are yet laid down anywhere.

1875 Adair's Maryport Advertiser Fri. 1 Oct. p.8
Valparaiso: Arrived: John Norman, Bryce, from Napier, New Zealand, about Sept.
Nov. 19 p.8
Valparaiso: Arrived: Sept. 19: John Norman, Bryce.
Dec. 10 p.8
Valparaiso: Sailed: Sept. 24: John Norman, Bryce, for Iquique, and arrived Oct. 4.
Dec. 17 p.8
Iquique; Arrived: Oct. 4: John Norman, Bryce, and sailed again on Oct. 7.
1876 Feb. 18 p.8
Queenstown: Arrived: Feb. 12: John Norman, Bryce, from Iquique.
Feb. 25 p.8
Queenstown: Sailed: Feb. 19: John Norman, Bryce, for Hamburgh.
Mar. 3 p.8
Hamburgh; Arrived: Mar. 1: John Norman, Bryce, from Queenstown.
[Survey: Hamburg in April]
May 5 p.8
North Shields: Arrived: May 1: John Norman, Bryce, from Hamburgh.
[**LR** Captain W. Brice (sic) amended to J. Tarney]
May 26 p.8
The Tyne: Sailed: May 20: John Norman, Tarney, for Valparaiso.
June 2 p.8
Off the Bill of Portland: May 28: John Norman, Tarney, for Valparaiso.

1876 The Liverpool Mercury Wed. 16 Aug. 16
Spoken: John Norman, from Newcastle for Valparaiso, June 27, 5 N. 26 W.

1877 The Liverpool Mercury Mon. 2 Apr. p.3
Queenstown: Arrived: Apr. 1: John Norman, from Pacamayo [Peru].

1877 The Western Mail (Cardiff) Tues. 10 Apr. p.4

Signalled off the Lizard: April 9, afternoon, passed east: barque John Norman, of Liverpool.
[Survey: London in June.]

1877 The Liverpool Mercury Mon. 23 July
Deal: Passed: July 22: John Norman for Callao [Peru], *from London.*
1878 May 11 p.7
Liverpool: Off the Port: May 10: John Norman, Callao.
May 13 p.7
Liverpool: Arrived: May 11: John Norman, Malabrigo. [Chicama: Peru]
June 12 p.
Liverpool: Sailings: June 11: John Norman for Callao. [Survey: Callao in September.]

[**MNL** 1878: John Norman, Liverpool: Owner: Wilfrid Hine, Custom Ho., Bldgs., Maryport.]
[**LR** 1879 Captain J. Tarney/ J. Turney/ Nicholson. Owners Hine Bros., Liverpool]

1879 New York Herald Tues. 19 Aug. With Supplement p.10
Arica: Sailed: June 19: ship John Norman (Br), Queenstown or Falmouth (with cargo ex bark Jennie S Barker).

1879 The Daily News (London) Tues. 30 Sept. p.2
Queenstown: Arrivals: Sept. 27: John Norman, from Arica, nitrate.

1879 The Freeman's Journal (Dublin) Tues. 30 Sept. p.3
Cork Harbour: Arrived: Sept.29: John Norman, 513, Turnay(sic), Arica, wheat (sic).
Oct. 3 p.3
Cork Harbour: Sailed: Oct. 2: John Norman, Hamburg.

1879 The New-York Times Sun. 30 Nov. p.2.
The British ship John Norman, Capt. Turney, which sailed from Hamburg on Nov. 26 for Philadelphia, has put into Harwich very leaky, having been ashore.

1879 The Ipswich Journal, and Suffolk, Norfolk, Essex, and Cambridgeshire Advertiser Tues. 2 Dec. p.3
On Nov. 29: the John Norman, English barque, 513 tons, from Hamburg for Philadelphia, with scrap iron, sprung a leak at sea. She was making about 10 inches an hour of water and got on shore on the Halladay Flats, but took assistance and was towed in by the tug Harwich.

1880 New York Herald Tues. 27 Jan. --triple sheet-- p.10
Gravesend: Sailed: Jan.25: bark John Norman (Br), Turner (sic) (from Hamburg), Philadelphia, having repaired.

1880 New Liverpool Mercury Mon. 26 Jan. p.3
Deal: Passed: Jan. 25: John Norman, for New York, from London.
Jan. 27 p.3
Deal: Passed: Jan 26: John Norman, for Philadelphia.

1880 New York Herald Tues. 3 Feb. --triple sheet-- p.10
London Feb. 2: Bark John Norman (Br), Turney, from Hamburg for Philadelphia, which put into Gravesend Dec 3 in distress, and sailed again Jan 25 for her destination, put into Queenstown to day leaky.

[**MNL** 1880 & 1882: John Norman of Liverpool: Owner: Wilfrid Hine, Custom Ho., Bldgs., Maryport.]

1880 The Liverpool Mercury Mar. 24 p.3
Queenstown: Sailed: Mar. 23: John Norman, for the United States.
Apr. 1 p.3
Liverpool: Arrived: Mar. 31: John Norman, Queenstown. [Survey: Liverpool in May.]
June 24 p.6
Liverpool: Sailed, June 23: John Norman, Sourabaya.
July 8 p.6
Spoken: July 2: John Norman of this port, 48 N 7 W.
Sept. 8 p.7
Spoken: July 31: John Norman hence for Batavia 15 N. 28 W.

1880 De Locomotief—Nieuws—Handels—en Advertentieblad—Vrijdag (Friday) 31 Dec. No 308.
Vertrokken [Departure]: *Batavia 28 Dec. Eng. Bark John Norman, Nicholson, n. Samarang. Invoer* [Import] *te Samarang. Aaangebracht van Engeland, per z.s. John Norman, gez. Nicholson, zeep* [soap] *4902 c., ijzer* [steel] *30 c.,--Order.*
1881 Jan. 6 no 4
Scheepsberichter [Shipping News]: *Samarang: Aangekommenn* [arrived]: *6 Januari, Eng. Bark John Norman, gezagvoerder* [commander], *G. Nicholsen (sic), van Batavia, agt, Gezagvoerder.*
Jan. 15 p.1
Vertrokken: Samarang 15 Jan. Eng. Bark John Norman, Gez. Nicholson, van Soerabaja.

1881 The Maryport Advertiser and Weekly News Fri. 4 Mar. p.6
Samarang: Sailed: Jan. 14: John Norman, Nicholson, for Sourabaya. [both Indonesia]
Apr. 14 p.8
Sourabaya: Sailed: Mar. 4: John Norman, Nicholson, for Padang.
{www.plimsoll.org/ Southampton: Wreck Report for Fanny (47,667) 1881. Finding of a Court of Inquiry held .....at Sourabaya...3rd. day March 1881: Present; Isaac Nicholson, Master of the English ship "John Norman".]
June 10 p.8
Padang: Arrived: Apr. 16: John Norman, Nicholson, from Sourabaya.
July 29 p.7
Padang: Sailed: May 18: John Norman, Nicholson, for Rouen.

1881 The Liverpool Mercury Thurs. 15 Sept. p.7
St. Helena (via Madeira, Sept. 14): Arrived, John Norman.

1881 The Maryport Advertiser and Weekly News Fri. Sept. 23 p.8
At St. Helena: Sept. 19: John Norman, Nicholson, at St. Helena from Padang, and sailed for Rouen, on the 21st.

1881 New York Herald Fri. 4 Nov. --triple sheet-- p.10
Steamer Denmark (Br): Oct. 22, lat 50.06, lon 13.24, passed bark John Norman (Br), from Padang for Rouen.

1881 The Liverpool Mercury Sat. 5 Nov. p.6
Spoken: John Norman, Oct. 31, off Wolf Rock Lighthouse.

1881 The Maryport Advertiser and Weekly News Fri. Nov. 11 p.5
Rouen: Arrived: Nov. 7: John Norman, Nicholson, from Padang.
Dec. 2 p.5
Rouen: Sailed: Dec. 1: John Norman, Nicholson, for Swansea.

1881 The Liverpool Mercury Thurs. 8 Dec. p.3
Falmouth: Arrived: Dec. 7: John Norman, from Rouen for Swansea.

1881 The Maryport Advertiser and Weekly News Fri. Dec. 16
Falmouth: Sailed: Dec. 11: John Norman, Nicholson, for Swansea.

Swansea: Arrived: Dec. 14: John Norman from Rouen.

1881 The Western Mail (Cardiff) Thurs. 15 Dec. p.4
Signalled off the Mumbles Head: Dec. 14: Passed East, barque John Norman of Liverpool.
Dec. 26 p.4
Saturday's Police: Swansea: (Before Mr. J.G. Hall, Mr. J.T. Jenkin, and Mr. T.A. Marten): Cornelius Bowen was charged with stealing a quantity of rope from the barque John Norman. Joshua Jones, who had been working on board the vessel, deposed to a piece of rope produced being part of the stern mooring of the ship. Witness further stated that he saw prisoner on Thursday with a bag of rope, and followed him to a marine stores, where the stolen property was subsequently found. Prisoner was committed for trial at the next quarter sessions.
Dec. 28 p.4
Swansea: Cleared: Dec. 27: John Norman, B, 700 coals, Valparaiso.

1882 The Maryport Advertiser and Weekly News Fri. 6 Jan. p.8
Swansea: Sailed: Jan. 3: John Norman, Nicholson, for Valparaiso.
Jan. 13 p.5
Swansea: Put back: Jan. 5: John Norman, Nicholson, from Swansea, for Valparaiso.
Jan. 20 p.5
Swansea: Sailed: Jan. 18: John Norman, Nicholson, for Valparaiso.

1882 The Freeman's Journal (Dublin) Tues. 28 Feb. p.3
Lloyds' Telegram: London, Monday: The John Norman, British barque, from Swansea for Valparaiso, was at St. Vincent, Cape Verds, leaky upper works, and probably will be able to repair without discharging.

1882 The Liverpool Mercury Tues. 14 Mar. p.7
Swansea: Sailed: Mar. 13: John Norman for Cadiz. (sic) [??].
Thurs. 16 Mar. p.7
John Norman, from Swansea for Valparaiso, at St. Vincent., C.V., leaky. The surveyors declare that the cargo total ex this vessel is not fit to be carried on in the vessel, and advise that it should be sold if possible.

1882 The Maryport Advertiser and Weekly News Fri. 5 May p.8
St. Vincent: Sailed: Apr. 29: John Norman, Nicholson, for Valparaiso.

1882 The Daily News (London) Wed. 28 June p.2
John Norman, British barque, from St. Vincent to Valparaiso, is reported by telegram from Pernambuco, to have struck on the bar north of Bahia; crew taken off by the Mondego steamer.

1882 The Times (London) Fri. 30 June p.12
Posted as missing between midnight Wednesday, June 21, and midnight. Wednesday June 28 1882: John Norman – Sail – 513 – British – 1855 – Struck -- # (Crew saved).
July 1 p.12
St. Vincent (Cape Verd) June 30. The Royal Mail Steam Packet Company's steamer "Mondego", from Brazil, has arrived here, having been detained out beyond the usual time. She proceeds for Lisbon and Southampton.
July 11 p.10
Disaster at Sea:- The Mondego, which arrived at Southampton last night, brought home the crew of the barque John Norman, of Liverpool, official number 6,044, who were picked up at sea off Bahia on the 21st ult. The master reported having abandoned his vessel on the previous night.

1882 The Freeman's Journal (Dublin) Wed. 12 July p.3
Southampton, Monday: The Royal Mail Company's steamer Mondy (sic), with mails from Brazil and River Plate, which arrived here to-day, bring the usual complement of passengers, and specie to the value of £2,100 and full general cargo among the passengers are the crew of the barque John Norman, of Liverpool, picked up at sea off Bahia on 23rd ult by Mondego; master of John Norman reports having abandoned his vessel on the previous evening.

HAZEL HOLME

Hazel Holme: State Library of Victoria, Brodie Collection

HAZEL HOLME

Official No.	**58782**	**Code letters JNFM**	
Built	1870 May	In Whitby (T. Turnbull & Son)	
Deck	One	Build	Carvel
Masts	Three	Gallery	None
Beams	Iron		
Rigging	**Barque**	Head	Male figure
Stern	Elliptic	Framework	Wood (oak).
Tonnage	**399**	Length 138.9 feet; Breadth 28.5 feet; Depth 17.5 feet.	

Liverpool Register: Registered in Liverpool 20/1873: Hazel Holme (formerly called King Arthur) name allowed to be changed in 1873.
Wilfred (sic) Hine, of Liverpool. Owner Sixty Four/64. signed 17th February 1873

For eighteen months, Hazel Holme was the King Arthur. Owner/Captain: J. Pearson.

[**LR** 1870 Supplement-71: King Arthur, Bk, J. Pearson, 399, Whitby 1870, T. Turnbull, Whitby, A1]
[**LR** 1872-73: King Arthur, Bk, J. Pearson, 399, T. Turnbull, Whitby, A1 *see supplement.*
        Hazel Holme, Bk, J. Pearson, 399, W. Hine, Liverpool A1 *late King Arthur*]
[**LR** 1874: Hazel Holme, Bk, J. Pearson/ W. Clark, 399/415, W. Hine, Liverpool/ Maryport A1]
[**ALRAFS** 1874: Hazel Holme, J. Pearson, 399, Liverpool, W. Hine *x King Arthur*]
[**ALRAFS** 1875-77: Hazel Holme, W. Clark, 399, Maryport, W. Hine]
[**ALRAFS** 1878-79: Hazel Holme, W. Holme, 399, Maryport, W. Hine]
[**ALRAFS** 1880-81 & 83: Hazel Holme, Mellican, 405, Liverpool, Hine Bros.]

1870 The York Herald Sat. 21 May p.10
Whitby: Launch of the "King Arthur". On Tuesday afternoon this fine barque, intended for the Indian trade, was launched from Messrs. Turnbull and Son's shipbuilding yard, in the presence of a large concourse of spectators. The vessel glided into the water very smoothly, with colours flying, and amid the loud huzzas of the assemblage. Miss Turnbull broke a bottle of gin over the ship's stem (according to custom), and named her the "King Arthur." She is a fine-looking vessel, beautifully modelled, and finished throughout in a most superior style. She is classed A1 for about fourteen years, is about 420 tons register, and is 188 feet 7 inches in length. She is fitted with all the latest improvements, and will be commanded by Capt. John Pearson.
[First survey: Whitby in May]

1870 The Northern Echo (Darlington) Fri. 3 June p.3
The Last Wooden Ship at Whitby.
Yesterday morning, between five and six o'clock, the barque "King Arthur" recently launched from the stocks of Messrs. Turnbull and Son, left the harbour of Whitby. As she is, in all probability, the last new wooden vessel that will sail from Whitby, the fact is worth recording. Early as the hour was, many persons turned out to witness the spectacle, and to a few, who remembered "when George the Third was King," it would perhaps, be the cause of some melancholy reflections. Whitby was always famous for its wooden ships, Captain Cook preferring the vessels built at that port before all others. But it cannot be denied that wooden vessels have gone almost entirely out of fashion, and we cannot be surprised at the conclusion arrived at by the shipbuilders at Whitby, namely, to build no more wooden vessels, unless expressly ordered. Iron shipbuilding will shortly be commenced at the port. And we, knowing how Whitby abounds in mineral wealth, have no doubt that, when once begun and carried on to a fair extent, the business will be followed as enthusiastically as at Hartlepool and at Middlesbrough.

Whitby people are naturally slow in seizing new ideas or projects but we are certain that when they do, and prove them to be sound, they will prosecute them with ardour, and who knows what Whitby may not one day be famous for its iron shipbuilding?

Mon. 20 June p.4

Great Yarmouth: Passed south: June 17: King Arthur of Whitby.

June 25 p.4

Prawle Point: Passed: June 23: King Arthur, of Whitby.

1870 The Standard (London) Sat. 15 Oct. p.7

Falmouth: Arrived: Oct. 13: King Arthur, from Constantinople.

Nov. 1 p.7

Falmouth: Sailed: Oct. 31: King Arthur, for Waterford.

1870 The Western Mail Wed. 16 Nov. p.3

Cardiff, West Bute Dock: Arrivals: Nov. 15: King Arthur, 399, Pearson, Waterford, ballast.

Entered Outwards: for Constantinople.

Nov. 30 p.4

Cardiff: Cleared: Nov. 29: King Arthur, B, Constantinople, 700 coal.

1871 The Daily News (London) Thurs. 12 Jan. p.7

Dardanelles : Arrivals: (previous to Dec. 27): King Arthur from Cardiff.
Constantinople: Arrivals: Dec. 26, 27, and 30: King Arthur from Cardiff.

1871 The Standard (London) Mon. 3 Apr. p.7

Falmouth: Arrived: Apr. 1: King Arthur, from Varna. [Bulgaria, Black Sea]

{rootsweb: Cornwall Online Census 1871

Merchant Shipping: Civil Parish of Falmouth Folio 52.

King Arthur, Whitby, Vessel No. 57782 (sic) 399t. foreign: Record x-ed-out.

Master: John Pearson, 27, Whitby Yorkshire. -- Number of crew 15.}

1871 The Bristol Mercury and Western Counties Advertiser Sat. 8 Apr. p.8

Pill: In Kingroad: Friday: King Arthur, Black Sea.

Apr. 15 p.7

Bristol: Arrived: Apr. 10: King Arthur, Pearson, Varna. Imports: 12,500 cwt. barley.

1871 The Liverpool Mercury Fri. 6 Oct. p.3

Falmouth: Arrived: Oct. 5: King Arthur, from Nicolaieff [Ukraine]*, with loss of bulwarks, backstays carried away, and sails split.*

++++++++++ **Wilfrid Hine**

[**Fl corr**. Liverpool 20 Dec. 1872. I have lost one of my ships by fire ["Cereal" under J. Ritchie] but fully insured. Only had her about 16 months but in that she cleared us over 40 per cent. I have just bought another for the same Captain as he is a first rate man & got her on very easy terms. Wilfrid Hine.]

1873 The London Gazette, 17 Jan. p.227

Official Notice:- Proposal to Change a Ship's Name. I, Wilfrid Hine, of Liverpool, hereby give notice, that in consequence of my ships being called after various "Holmes" in Cumberland, it is my intention to apply to the Board of Trade, under Section 6 of the Merchant Shipping Act, 1871, in respect of my ship "King Arthur", of Whitby, official number 58,782, of gross tonnage 422 tons, of register tonnage 399 tons, heretofore owned by

Thomas Turnbull and son, of Whitby, for permission to change her name to "Hazel Holme," to be registered under the said new name at the port of Liverpool as owned by myself.

Any objections to the proposed change of name must be sent to the Assistant-Secretary, Marine Department, Board of Trade, within fifteen days from the appearance of this advertisement.

Dated at Liverpool, this 14th day of January, 1873.   Wilfrid Hine.

[**MNL** 1875: Hazel Holme, 405. Owner: Wilfred (sic) Hine, Liverpool. (formerly King Alfred)]

1873 The Western Mail (Cardiff) Thurs. 30 Jan. p.4
Cardiff: tered (sic) Outwards: Jan. 29: Hazel Holme, B, 422, Ritchie, Mauritius.
Feb. 7 p.4
Cardiff: Entered Outwards, Feb. 6: Hazel Holme, B, 399, Ritchie, Mauritius.
Feb. 24 p.4
Cardiff: Cleared: Feb. 23: Hazel Holme, B, Mauritius, 673, coal.

1873 Lloyd's List Mon. 26 May col. 24
Speakings: Hazel Holme: Cardiff to Mauritius 14th Apr. 4 S 26 W.

1873 Adair's Maryport Advertiser Fri. 25 July p.8
Mauritius: Arrived: July 10: Haze (sic) Holme, Ritchie, from Cardiff.

1873 The Otago Daily Times (N.Z.) Fri. 26 Sept. p.2
Port Chalmers: At the Heads: Hazel Holme, barque, Ritchie, from Port Louis (Mauritius), 16th August. Hazel Holme, is command of Captain James Ritchie, a gentleman well-known in the Newcastle trade while in command of the barque Eleanor. She remains at anchor outside last night, but will be towed up early this morning.
Sept. 27 p.2
Port Chalmers: Arrival: Sept. 26: Hazel Holme, a pretty and powerful-looking barque, reported in our yesterday's issue at the Heads from the Mauritius—was towed up yesterday, and berthed at the Railway Pier. She left Port Louis on the 16th ult., and had favourable Trades to reaching 29 S.; from thence a continuance of heavy gales was encountered , from S.W., veering round westerly to N.E., either of which did not last for more than 24 hours, carrying away portion of bulwarks, and flooding the cabin with water. Sighted the Snares on the 23rd inst, and anchored at the Heads at 11 a.m, on Thursday. She brings a full cargo of sugar, part being consigned to her agents, Cargills and M'Lean, and the remainder for Auckland. We thank Captain Ritchie, her master, for Mauritius papers.
Passenger: Mrs. Ritchie.

1873 The Wellington Independent (N.Z.) Thurs. 2 Oct.
The barque Hazel Holm (sic), which arrived at Port Chalmers on the 26th ultimo from the Mauritius, with a cargo of sugar, experienced exceedingly rough weather during the voyage. On the 29th August she had a gale of wind from the north-west, with an extremely low barometer, during which the ship was straining very much, the decks being continually under water, and the cabin full from the 1st September till the 17th. Had nothing but gales continually veering from S.W. to N.E. back and forth every twenty-four hours. At 6 a.m. on the 6th the barometer was down to 29; and a perfect hurricane came on at 7.30 a.m. At 1.30 p.m. a sea struck her, lifting the skylight top, and filled the cabin with water. At 2 p.m. the barometer was 29.8; another sea struck her, carrying away starboard boat and everything moveable on deck. For three days the bulwark was running level with the water. On Sunday (14th) shipped another very heavy sea, which, breaking on deck, carried away the bottom of the main hatch, bursting it open, and a

quantity of water got into the hold before it could be secured; it also broke the main winch.

1873 The Daily Southern Cross (N.Z.) Mon. 6 Oct. p.2.
Sugars are still dull; 'Hazel Holm (sic)' has reached Otago from Mauritius, ...brings 13,155 bags and 510 pockets for Dunedin and 12,118 bags and 605 pockets for Auckland.

1873 The Otago Daily Times (N.Z.) Fri. 17 Oct. p.2
Port Chalmers: Departures October 16: Hazel Holme, barque, 397 tons, Ritchie, for Auckland.
Oct. 20 p.12
At the railway sheds an auction was held of the damaged portion of the Hazel Holme's cargo, consisting of 1168 pockets, in bond. The prices realised were as follows:—Good browns, slightly sweated, at from L27 to L28 10s; fine yellow counters, at from L28 15s to L29 15s; yellow crystals and finest yellow crystals, at from L30 15s to L31 15s; white crystals, L32; fine white crystals, L32 to L 33; finest white crystals, L33 10s to L36. We consider that these prices ruled rather under those last realised for similarly damaged parcels.

1873 The New Zealand Herald Mon. 27 Oct. p.2
Port of Auckland: Arrivals: Oct. 25: Hazel Holme, barque, Nicholl, from Mauritius via Dunedin: Imports, 328 tons sugar, Owen and Graham (agents).

1873 The Daily Southern Cross (N.Z.) Mon. 27 Oct. p.2
Port of Auckland: Arrivals, October 26: Hazel Home (sic) 399 tons, Ritchie, from Mauritius, via Dunedin, arrived in harbour last evening, after a fine weather passage of ten days. Captain Ritchie reports having sailed from Dunedin on the 16th instant, and had southward winds to the East Cape, which was rounded on the 23rd, thence light airs and calms.
Oct. 31 p.2.
At Messrs. Tonks and Co.'s sale of sugar ex "Hazel Holme", all the principal merchants and tradesmen of the city were present. So far as prices are concerned they equalled the importers' expectations. Fully two-thirds of the cargo were realized at prices corresponding with Canterbury and Otago rates. It is to be regretted that for small lines of 100 bags, should have been placed upon the market prejudicial to larger transactions which might have been carried out at the upset prices. However, the sale was a success, and we congratulate Messrs. B. Tonks and Co. on the result of their usual efforts which always prove so successful.

1873 The New Zealand Herald Tues. 11 Nov. p.2
Port of Auckland: Depatures: [for] Newcastle, Hazel Holme, barque, this morning.
Nov. 12 p.2
Port of Auckland: Depatures: Nov. 11: Hazel Holme, barque, for Newcastle.

1873 The Sydney Morning Herald Thurs. 27 Nov. p.4
Newcastle: Arrivals: November 25: Hazel Holme, barque, Ritchie, from Auckland.
Dec. 20 p.6
Newcastle Shipping: Departures: December 19: Hazel Holm (sic); barque, Ritchie, for Mauritius, with 656 tons coal, 3 bales leather, 100 bags flour.

1874 Otago Daily Times (N.Z.) Wed. 21 Jan. p.4
Shipping: Port Chalmers: Departures Otago, ship, 992 tons, Stewart, for London: Passengers: Saloon, Mrs. Ritchie and two children. [see Addenda of Captains and Family]

1874 Otago Witness (N.Z.) Sat. 25 Apr. p.9
Mauritius: (From a correspondent) February 25th, 1874.: Arrivals: 11th Feb: Barque, Hazel Holme, from Newcastle, N.S.W.

Liverpool Register: Master: Port Louis (Mauritius) 29.4.74: Samuel Wilson C. 91122 vice James Ritchie C.93623 --- 1.5.74: James Mitchell C. 27088.

1874 The Standard (London) Tues. 28 July p.6
Gravesend: Arrivals: July 27: Hazel Home (sic), Mauritius. [Survey: London in August.]

Liverpool Register: Master: London 18.9.74: William Clark C. 30750.

1874 The Glasgow Herald Thurs. 1 Oct. p.6
Deal: Sailed: Sept. 30: Hazel Home (sic), Mauritius.

1874 Adair's Maryport Advertiser Fri. 9 Oct. p.8
The Downs: Left: Oct. 4: Hazel Holme, Robinson (sic), for Mauritius.

1874 The Liverpool Mercury Thurs. 15 Oct. p.3
Hurst Castle: Passed: Oct. 14: Hazel Holme.

1875 The Glasgow Herald Sat. 20 Feb. p.6
At Mauritius: Feb. 5: Hazel Home (sic).

1875 Adair's Maryport Advertiser Fri. 16 Apr. p.8
Mauritius: Sailed: Mar. 5: Hazel Holme, Clark, for Sydney.

{http://mariners.recorder.nsw.gov.au/   Mariners and ships in Australian Waters.}
Hazel Home (sic) of Liverpool, William Clark, Master, Burthen 399 Tons, from the Port Louis to Sydney New South Wales.   14 April 1875
William Mclean, Chief Mate, 35, Dumfries: John Barr, Boatswain, 20, St. Johns: x Attaque, Steward, 35, Canton: G.F. Bergnes, Carpenter, 47, Finland: William Cuthbertson, A.B., 30 Scotland: John Austin, A.B., 24, Liverpool: Martin Masten, A.B., 20, Norway: John Bird, A.B., 22, North Shields: George Smith, A.B., 42, Hamburgh: Alexander Adamson, O.S., 21, Liverpool: William Lee, O.S., 17, Melbourne: L. Kumina (?), O.S., 23, Germany.   Stowaways: Geo. Leslie & J. King: Sydney 15 April 1875 signed Wm. Clark, Master.}

1875 The Sydney Morning Herald Thurs. 15 Apr. p.4
Sydney: Arrivals: April 14: Hazelholm (sic), barque, 399 tons, Captain Clarke (sic) left Mauritius on the 6th March, and reached as far as latitude 40 S. before she commenced making her easting, which was ultimately run down on a parallel of latitude 39* 30 S. – Cape Otway being passed on the 11th instant. On the 20th March, in latitude 36* 30 S., longitude 75 E., spoke the barque Formosa, from Mauritius to Freemantle (sic), 16 days out. Imports: 340 tons sugar.*
May 11 p.4
Clearances: May 8: Exports. Hazel Holme, for Hongkong: 620 tons coal.
May 13 p.4
Sydney: Departures: May 12: Hazel Holme, for Hongkong.

1875 Adair's Maryport Advertiser Fri. 16 July p.8
Hong Kong: Arrived: July 1: Hazel Holme, Clark, from Sydney.
Oct. 1 p.8
Ilo Ilo [Iloilo City, Philippines]*: Arrived: Aug. 7: Hazel Holme, Clark.*
Oct. 29 p.8

Ilo Ilo: Sailed: Sept. 8: Hazel Holme, Clark, for United Kingdom.
1876 Jan 7 p.8
St. Helena: touched at: Nov. 26: Hazel Holme, Clark.
Jan. 21 p.8
Queenstown: Arrived: Jan. 16: Hazel Holme, Clark, from Ilo Ilo. And received orders for London.

1876 The Liverpool Mercury Mon. 24 Jan. p.3
Queenstown: Sailed: Jan. 23: Hazel Holme for London.
Jan 27 p.3
Gravesend: Arrived: Jan. 26: Hazel Holme, from Iloilo.

Liverpool Register: Master: London 3.3.76: Wilson Holmes C. 42494.

1876 The Glasgow Herald Wed. 8 Mar. p.6
Deal: Anchored: Mar. 7: Hazel Holme, for Hobart Town.

1876 The Liverpool Mercury Thurs. 9 Mar. p.3
Deal: Passed: Mar. 8: Hazel Holme, for Hobart Town.

1876 Adair's Maryport Advertiser Fri. 16 June p.8
Spoken: Hazel Holme, Holmes, from London to Hobart Town, spoken April 29 lat. 14.17 S. long., 28.50 W.

1876 The Mercury (Hobart) Thurs. 29 June p.2
Hobart: Arrived: June 28: Hazel Holme, barque, 399 tons, Wilson Holmes, from London. The barque Hazel Holme arrived in port yesterday morning, about 10 o'clock, and anchored off Macquarie Point to discharge gunpowder. Captain Holmes reports that he left London on the 4th March, but inconsequence of heavy N.W. and W. weather, he did not get clear of the channel until the 19th. The vessel was anchored off Deal during part of the time. The departure was taken from the Eddystone on the 21st of March, and very heavy breezes, varying from N.W, to W., were experienced until the 27th. From that date to the 1st of April variable winds from W., S.W., N.W., and N.E., were experienced. The Equator was crossed on the 19th of April, on the 29th day from the Eddystone. On the same day, when in 0deg. 3min. S. lat., and 25deg. 8min. W. lon, the ship going about four knots per hour, with light variable winds, four distinct shocks of a submarine earthquake were felt. The second and third shocks were the most severe, causing the crockery in the pantry to knock about, and the railway iron and other cargo to work together. The deep sea lead was hove, but no bottom was got. The S.E. trades were fallen in with shortly after crossing the Equator, and the meridian of the Cape of Good Hope was crossed in lat. 39*31 S., on the 21st of May, 61 days from the Eddystone. Good weather was experienced until the 24th of May, and on that day a very heavy gale came on which lasted till the 29th, and varied from W. to N.N.E. The vessel was hove to for 72 hours under storm canvas. From the 29th May fresh breezes varying from S.W. to N.W. were experienced to Tasmania. The S. W. Cape of Tasmania was made on the 27th June, distant 30 miles,and bearing N. by E., the voyage from land to land, thus having been made in 98 days. Was becalmed off South Bruni for two hours on the same night, and the wind then sprang up from the S.W. Was boarded by Pilot Bleach off the Iron Pot at half-past 7 yesterday morning, and the anchorage was reached as above. The Hazel Holme is a smart looking clipper vessel of 399 tons register, and was built in Whitby, near Sunderland in 1870. She is a wooden vessel with iron beams and binding, and is owned by Messrs. Hines Bros, of Maryport. She is

consigned to Messrs. W. Crosby and Co., and on discharging her gunpowder will be berthed at the New Wharf to land cargo.

The Captain of the Hazel Holme reports that he spoke the ship Cairnbulg, from Sydney to London, on the 27th of April, in lat. 14*29 S. and long. 28*26 W.

July 7 p.3

Rails.

The inspecting Engineers assured me that no fault could be found with any of the rails except the "I.S.R." brand, which were, as often before stated, purchased and sent out when we were greatly in need of rails here, and the manufacturers were so extremely busy that it was totally impossible to procure any others at the time. A surplus was sent to replace any that might prove defective, and those in the track are most carefully watched, and renewed whenever necessary. Independently of former extra supplies, the Hazel Holme now in port here has 100 tons of first class rails on board, for maintenance purposes, and a much larger quantity has been ordered, and is probably now on the way out. I can only say that I am fully aware of the doubtful wearing quality of some of these rails, and that each one found imperfect will be renewed. The large majority of these questioned rails will doubtless have a longer life than, any other kind, on account of the hard, strong character of the iron.

Aug. 2 p.2

The barque Hazel Holme has completed discharging cargo, and was yesterday taking in ballast.

Aug. 4 p.2

Entered Out: Aug. 3: The Hazel Holme, barque, 399 tons, W. Holmes, for Sydney (sic).

Aug. 7 p.2

Hazel Holme cleared out for Port Pirie S.A., on Saturday in ballast. She afterwards left the wharf and anchored in the stream.

Aug. 8 p.2

Hazel Holme was ready for sea yesterday but was detained by bad weather. Should the weather be favourable she will sail to-day.

Aug. 9 p.2

Hobart Town: Sailed: August 8: Hazel Holme, for Port Pirie: Mount Nelson: Outward: August 8th: 8.30 a.m.: off Sandy Bay Point: Noon: off Trumpeter Bay: 3.30 p.m.: passed to east.

1876 The South Australian Register (Adelaide) Sat. 26 Aug. p.4

Port Pirie: Arrived, Aug. 24: Hazel Holme, barque, from Hobart Town.

Supplement of The South Australian Register (Adelaide) Sept. 13 p.2S

The barque Hazel Holme, 400 tons, the largest vessel which has hitherto reached our jetties, after taking part of the cargo on board was towed down to the anchorage by the steamer Derwent to complete her loading. She went out without hitch or hindrance on a draught of 11 feet of water.

Sept. 25 p.4

Port Pirie: Sailed: September 23: Hazel Holme, brig (sic), United Kingdom.

1876 The South Australian Police Gazette 13 Sept. p.147

From the Barque "Hazel Holme" at Port Pirie on the 3rd instant. -- Charles Peterson, aged 22 years, 5 ft. 6 in. high, fair complexion, little hair on chin, small moustache; a Dane. -- Robert McKay, aged 25 years, 5 ft. 5 in. high. sandy hair, small whiskers and moustache; Scotchman. -- £1 reward for each.

1876 The Argus (Melbourne) Tues. 21 Nov. p.4

The barque Hazel Holme, from Adelaide for Cork, has spoken by the Lady Turner on October 29, in lat. 24deg. S., and lon. 96deg. E. [It suggests a return via Cape Good Hope]

1877 The Liverpool Mercury Tues. 23 Jan. p.3
St Helena: Arrived: Jan. 21: Hazel Home (sic).
Feb. 16
Queenstown: Arrived: Feb. 15: Hazel Holme, from Port Pirie.
Feb. 19 p.3
Queenstown: Sailed: Feb. 19: Hazelholme (sic), for Dublin.

1877 The Freeman's Journal (Dublin) Tues. 20 Feb. p.3
Dublin: Arrival: Feb. 19: The Hazelholm (sic), from Peri (sic), with wheat.
Mar. 23 p.3
Swansea: Arrived: Mar. 22: Hazel Home (sic), Holmes, from Dublin, in ballast.

1877 The Western Mail (Cardiff) Thurs. 22 Mar. p.4
Swansea: Entered Outwards: Mar. 21: Hazel Holme, B, 399, Rockhampton.
May 9 p.4
Swansea: Cleared: May 8: Hazel Holme, B, Rockhampton, 593 steel rail: 24 axles and wheels. [Survey: Swansea in April]

Liverpool Register: Master: Swansea 8.5.77: Thomas Sawle C. 84419

1877 The Bulletin, Rockhampton (Queensland) Wed. 19 Sept. p.2
The Hazel Holme, barque, 399 tons, from Swansea on May 11, was in sight to the south of Keppel Bay yesterday. She is principally loaded with railway iron.
Sept. 22 p.2
The Hazel Holme, barque, from Swansea, now in Keppel Bay, brings the following cargo for the railway works:--53 wheels and axles, 6 loose wheels and 4131 rails. Messrs. W. and M.C. Thompson are the agents of the vessel.
The arrival of two English vessels in this port is an occurrence which does not often happen, but during the week The Hazel Holm (sic) and Scottish Bard both entered Keppel Bay, the former on Tuesday and the latter on Thursday, as reported in our shipping colums (sic). The Hazel Holm (sic) is a neat trim barque of 405 tons, and is under the charge of Captain T. Sawle. She left Swansea on the eleventh of May last, and experienced fine weather during the voyage. She is laden with railway iron only, and brings no passengers. The Health Officer, Dr. Salmond, having visited the vessel on Thursday and granted practique, she will be brought up to the Central Island anchorage, where some of the cargo will probably be taken out, after which she will come up to the wharf.
Sept. 28 p.2
The Hazel Home, barque, was towed up to Central Island anchorage by the Mary steam-tug on Wednesday.
Oct. 6 p.2
The Hazel Holme, barque, was to be towed up from Central island to the deep water wharf last night.
Oct. 13 p.2
The Hazel Holme will have discharged her inward cargo shortly, and loads for London, some 400 bales wool waiting shipment already.
On Thursday night a man named Musgrave, employed on the steamer Nowra, met with an accident which fortunately was not attended with any serious result. It appears that Musgrave, having occasion to go on board the Hazel Holme, lying at the Railway Wharf, stopped on the staging leading from the wharf to the vessel. By some means not yet ascertained, he was precipitated into the water, from which he was rescued by three men who happened to be near at hand, none the worse for his immersion. It is said there was only one hand rail on the staging, and no light near the gangway, but for the truth of this report we cannot vouch.

Rockhampton Police Court: Tuesday, October 16. Before the Police Magistrate.

Breach of Harbour Regulations.--Police v. T. Sawle. Mr. D'Arcy appeared for the prosecution and Mr. Milford for the defence. Senior-Sergeant Brannelly deposed that the Hazel Holme, ship, was lying at the Railway Wharf; she was secured by the usual ropes; he went on board the vessel on Thursday night last to make inquiries concerning a man who had fallen off the staging into the water; he examined the staging, on the right side of which was a handrail stretched from the wharf to the ship; there was a light on the gangway at that time; he laid the information next day. By the Bench: He believed the gangway was 2 feet 6 inches wide.--Robert Henry Musgrave, seaman, deposed that on Thursday night last, about 8 o'clock, he had occasion to go on board the Hazel Holme; he fell off the staging into the water, a height of about 10 or 11 feet at ebb tide; the planking of the stage seemed substantial enough; he believed there was only one rope across the staging; he did not catch hold of it; he fell over the side; there may have been a light at the gangway, but he did not notice it; the police came to him and he made a statement the same night. By Mr. Milford: He was not tight that night, having only had about three glasses that day; he saw the rope, but did not catch hold of it; he was a seaman on board the Nowra, but was left behind when she went to the Bay. --John Connor, labourer, deposed that he was near the Hazel Holme on Thursday night, and hearing a noise he went to see what had happened; a man with him said some one was in the water; he saw the mate of the vessel, and helped to pull the man out; Musgrave showed him where he slipped off the staging; a portion of it was broken; there was no light at the gangway. By Mr. Milford: Musgrave appeared, to have had a drink or two. By the Bench: It was a dark night, there was neither a light on the ship nor on the wharf. This closed the case for complainant.--Robert Miller Hunter, merchant, deposed that he had been for many years a master of a vessel; he saw the staging of the Hazel Holme made; he had been in the habit of using and making gangways for many years; he considered the gangway a perfectly safe one for transit to and from the vessel; had usually seen the gangways with one man rope and one rail.--J. W. Milligan (sic), Chief Officer, Hazel Holme, deposed that he recollected the man falling from the staging; the staging consisted of two stunsail booms from the wharf to the ship, and cross pieces and planks between; there were three stanchions about three feet in height and 4 feet 6 inches apart; there was a man rope; the staging was about three feet wide; he had been nine years at sea and in his opinion the gangway was sufficient to insure safe transit; had seen two ropes used sometimes. By Mr. D'Arcy: The pilot in Keppel Bay furnished a copy of the regulations to the ship. By the Bench: The staging was in the same condition with the exception that the rope was slackened.--George Davis, ships carpenter, stated that he had been accustomed to erect stages ; the one in question was in his opinion sufficient for the purpose of transit; it was 3 feet wide; the stanchions were of wood.--Joseph William Bray, apprentice, deposed that he belonged to the Hazel Holme; he saw Musgrave the night he fell over; he was tipsy; there was a light on the gangway at the time. By Mr. D'Arcy: Musgrave might have been staggered by the fall. Mr. Milford addressed the Court. The Police Magistrate, in giving his decision, read the following clause in the Harbour Regulations.--"Every vessel, while berthed alongside any wharf, shall have a sufficient gangway placed between such vessel and the wharf, to ensure safe transit to and from such vessel, and every such gangway shall not be less than 2 feet 6 inches in width, and shall be fitted on either side with stanchions of sufficient strength on either side of such gangway, and every such vessel shall also, between sunset and sunrise, exhibit a bright light from such a position as to throw its full light upon such gangway." *He stated that the case rested upon the construction placed upon the word "either" in the clause, which he ruled referred to both sides. Several authorities were quoted in support*

of this ruling, and the defendant was fined 10s., 21s. professional costs, 7s. 2d. costs of Court, and 10s. witnesses expenses. The lowest penalty under the Act was inflicted, as it was evident the defendant had such staging erected as complied with his reading of the clause.
Oct. 27 p.2

The Rev. J. F. Orr will preach on board the barque Hazel Holme to-morrow afternoon, and in Kent street Church in the evening.
Nov. 3 p.2

The Rev. J. F. Orr will preach in the Kent-street Wesleyan Church to-morrow morning and evening. Mr. Layman will conduct service on board the Hazel Holme in the afternoon at four.
Nov. 20 p.2

Hazel Holme, barque.--Has completed the Stowage of over 1000 bales of wool and a quantity of bones and horns. She appears to be rapidly filling up, as she only commenced loading about a fortnight since, and the agents, Messrs. R. M. Hunter and Co., expect to be able to despatch her within a fortnight for London.
Nov. 28 p.2

At the Police Court yesterday, before the Police Magistrate and Captain R. M. Hunter, J. P., James Price, on remand, was charged with unlawfully absenting himself from the barque Hazel Holme. Thomas Sawle deposed that he was master of the barque Hazel Holme; the prisoner, whose signature was attached to the articles produced, was shipped at Swansea, South Wales; the prisoner had no authority to leave the ship; the information was laid and a warrant obtained in consequence of his doing so. Joseph William Milligan (sic), chief officer, stated that the prisoner deserted from the ship, and took his clothes with him; witness corroborated the evidence of Captain Sawle. The Bench, after hearing a statement from the prisoner, committed him to gaol for six weeks, and ordered the amount paid for a substitute on board the vessel to be deducted from his wages. Prisoner to be returned to the ship, if required by Captain Sawle, before the expiration of the sentence.
Dec. 15 p.2

Rev. J. F. Orr will preach morning and evening at the Kent-street Wesleyan Church, and for the last time on board the Hazel Holme at four in the afternoon.
Dec. 21 p.2

Hazel Holme, barque.—Left yesterday morning in tow of the steam-tug Mary for Keppel Bay.
Dec. 22 p.2

Hazel Holme for London with 1065 bales washed wool, 385 bales greasy, 26 bales scoured, 1797 horns, 16½ tons bones and hoofs and sundries.
Dec. 29 p.2

In shipping intelligence we note the departure of the Hazel Holme with a general cargo.

1877 The Queenslander (Brisbane) Sat. 20 Oct. p.22

Central Queensland Wool.—It its worthy of note that over 1100 bales of wool arrived in Rockhampton by train and steamer, from Broadsound, during the week, the latter bringing 286 bales. This may be in a great measure accounted for by the spurt put on by teamsters, who calculated upon having a full supply of grass and water after discharging their loading, and procuring more, so that they could travel with speed and at a moderate expense. On one day during the week there were twenty bullock and ten horse teams laden with wool. Two ships are on the berth, the Hazel Holme and the Scottish Bard. The former has the whole of her cargo engaged, and is expected to be away at the end of November, although she has not yet discharged her cargo; and the latter, which has nearly completed discharging, has every prospect of being loaded rapidly, a large portion of her cargo being on hand.

1878 The Argus (Melbourne) Wed. 24 Apr. p.5
London: Arrived: April 18: From Rockhampton: Hazel Holme ship, sailed December 25. [Survey: London in May]

1878 Royal Cornwall Gazette Fri. 10 May p.5
Deaths: Sawle: At sea (while on a voyage from Australia to London). March 1, Capt. Thomas Sawle, of the barque Hazel Home (sic) (late of Portscatha), aged 36.

There are several snippets about him and his family through the internet (not verified) but interesting. [See Addenda of Captains and Family].

1878 The Morning Bulletin, Rockhampton (Queensland) Tues. 16 July p.2
The numerous acquaintances and friends of Captain Thomas Sawle, of the barque Hazel Holme, will be sorry to hear of his death on the passage home from this port. It may be remembered that the vessel left Keppel Bay last Christmas. About 22nd February, the Captain took ill of rheumatic fever, which was followed by an epileptic fit, and on the 1st March, shortly after rounding Cape Horn, the Captain died. Mr. J. W. Millican assumed command of the ship, the second officer, Mr. Caulthard, was promoted, and Mr. Price, who absconded on the vessel arriving here, and was recaptured, behaved so well on the homeward run, that the new captain appointed him second officer. The vessel arrived in London after a passage of 118 days, and Mr. Millican was thanked by the owners, Messrs. Hyne (sic) Brothers, for the manner in which he brought the vessel to port. Captain Sawle was only here four months, but during that time he made many friends.
July 20 p.2
Rev. J. F. Orr will preach in Kent street Church to-morrow evening, making special reference to the death of the late Captain T. Sawle.

1878 The London and China Telegraph 1 June p.16
[Advert] With despatch: For Yokohama and Hiogo, the favourite composite clipper Hazel Holme, A1 14 years, 422 tons register, South West India Dock, --------------, Commander. Freight or Passage apply to Robertson and Co., 25, Booth-street, Manchester; and 5, Newman Cornhill, London, E.C.

Liverpool Register: Master: London 8.6.78: Joseph Wm. Millican C. 21977

1878 The Liverpool Mercury Mon. 3 June p.3
Return of Masters who were reported to have passed their examinations before the Local Marine Board under the provisions of the Merchant Shipping Act, for the week ending June 1: Joseph W. Millican: O.C. (Master Ordinary).
June 14 p.7
Deal: Passed: June 13: Hazelholme (sic), for Yokohama.
Sept. 18 p.3
Spoken: July 31: Hazel Home (sic), from London for Japan, 21 S. 30 W.

1878 The Inquirer and Commercial News (Perth) Wed. 25 Sept p.3
Local Telegrams: Geraldton. Sept. 22: Arrived, barque Hazel Holme, 399 tons, Captain Millican, 101 days from London, bound for Yokohama (Japan), laden with general merchandise. She has put in here for water.
Oct. 2 p.3
Geraldton. September 25.

We were rather surprized on Monday on observing a strange barque coming into port, wearing a somewhat crippled appearance, part of her starboard bulwarks having been carried away. This was all we could make out with the glass, her name, destination, etc., remaining unknown until the water police came ashore with the intelligence that it was the British barque Hazel Holme, 405 tons register, Capt. J. W. Millican, from London, bound to Yokohama, with a cargo of sundries, chiefly iron. She had been 102 days out, and had experienced very heavy weather after rounding the Cape. Her tanks having become leaky she ran short of water and bore up for this port for a supply. She sailed again this morning.

— The shipmasters speak in high terms of the Point Moore Lighthouse. As a proof of its excellence I may mention that Capt. Millican, of the Hazel Home (sic), saw the light distinctly a distance of upwards of twenty miles the night before his arrival.

1879 Lloyd's List Feb. 13 col. 3
Yokohama: Arrived: Dec. 17 [1878]: *Hazel Holme from London.*
Mar. 11 p.28
Yokohama: Sailed: Jan. 16: Hazel Holme, Millican for Kobe
Mar. 25 col. 29
Kobe: Arrived: Jan. 23: Hazel Holme, Millican, from Yokohama.
Apr. 10 col. 23
Kobe: Sailed: Feb. 15: Hazel Holme, Mellican (sic), for Melbourne.

1879 The Argus (Melbourne) Apr. 8 p.5
The Rotoruna which arrived from New Zealand, reports that on Sunday she spoke the barque Hazel Holme, Yokohama to Melbourne, 60 days out.
Apr. 14 p.4.
Hazel Holme, barque, 405 tons, J.W. Millican, with 640 tons of rice.
Reports having left Kobe, Japan, on February 15, with a fresh north west wind. Had a continuance of the same until February 22, when the wind hauled to the S.S.E., and blew a hurricane. There was also a tremendous sea. This was in lat. 32deg. 14min. N., and lon. 144deg. 14min. E. The vessel was thrown on her beam ends for 12 hours by the sheer force of the gale, and there was not a possibility of showing a stitch of canvas. The sea was also unusually high and very confused, and caused the vessel to roll very heavily. A portion of the lee bulwarks had to be knocked away to keep the decks clear, as the vessel lay with the water up to her main hatch combings by reason of the force of wind. The position of the barque at this time was critical, and the master had everything in readiness to cut away the masts if necessary. The wind, however, shifted into the west, and the weather cleared up. The whole of the cargo of rice sagged bodily over to port, and thus gave the vessel an additional list, but it was afterwards righted. Since then the barque has had fine weather and moderate winds. The island of Oulan, in the Caroline group, was sighted on the 9th ult. and the barque passed over a shoal not marked on the charts. The soundings were from 18 to 20 fathoms, and coral and shells at the bottom were plainly visible from deck. This was in about lat. 12deg. 44min. S. lon. 174deg. E. {www.ngdc.noaa.gov/mgg/global/relief/: this is now designated "Hazel Holme Bank"; a seamount (submarine rise) 12.49 S. 174.03E} *Lord Howe's group of islands was sighted on the 5th. inst., and fine weather and N.E. winds with continual deluges of rain were afterwards experienced till off Cape Howe. The wind then shifted to the south, and remained so till arrival to port. Deal Island was sighted on the 10th inst, and Wilson's Promontory was passed on the 11th, the Heads being entered yesterday morning. The passage has occupied 57 days from port to port.*
May 3 p.4
Discharging [the rice] *at the Sandridge town pier during the week ending Friday, May 2:* [she] *entered out for Newcastle.*

The Argus Summary for Europe May 14 p.2S
Cleared out: May 5: Hazel Holme, 405 tons, J.W. Millican in ballast.
For Hong Kong, the Hazel Holme was taken up to load breadstuffs at Port Pirie £600.
May 8 p.4
The barque Hazelholme (sic) left Hobson's Bay yesterday for Port Pirie.

1879 The South Australian Advertiser (Adelaide) Fri. 16 May p.4
Port Pirie: Arrived: May14: Hazel Holme, barque, Adelaide.
[Port Pirie: Sailed: June 6: Hazel Holme for Hongkong.]
Fri. 16 Sept. p.5
Hongkong: Arrived: Aug. 7: Hazel Holme, barque, from Port Pirie June 6.
[Survey: Hongkong in September].

1879 Lloyd's List Oct. 3 col. 28
Hong Kong: Sailed: Aug. 24: Hazel Holme, --------, for Quinhon [Vietnam].
Dec. 1 col.28
Hong Kong: Arrived: Oct. 30: Hazel Holme, Millican, from Quinhon.
1880 Feb. 26 col. 23
Hong Kong: Sailed: Jan. 17: Hazel Holme, Millican, for Taiwan.
Mar. 5 col. 32
Hong Kong, Jan. 27: Hazel Holme, barque, Millican, hence for Taiwanfoo put back Jan. 22 in consequence of having stranded on the Pratas Shoal. She has been docked and found to have lost false keel and a few sheets of copper. The vessel will have to be recoppered [reported by telegraph].

1880 The Liverpool Mercury Wed. 4 Aug. p.3
Queenstown: Arrived: Aug. 2: Hazel Holme, from Formosa [sugar]*, took the ground inside Camden Point whilst beating into Queenstown harbour on the 1st instant, and remained for a short time, but floated off with the rising tide apparently uninjured.*
Aug. p.3
Queenstown: Sailed: Aug. 4: Hazel Holme, for London.
Aug. 9 p.7
Deal: Passed: Aug. 8: Hazel Holme, from Formosa [now Taiwan]*, for London.*

1880 The Daily News (London) Mon. 9 Aug. p.3
Gravesend: Arrived: Aug. 8: Hazelholme (sic), from Formosa.

[**MNL** 1880: Hazel Holme, 405. Owner: Wilfred (sic) Hine, Maryport.]

1880 The Times (London) Fri. 15 Oct. p.2
[Advert] *Taylor, Bethell & Robert's London Line: Swan River: Hazel Holme: 405: A.1: L.D.* [London Dock] *(to sail) Nov 5.*
Nov. 15 p.12
Gravesend: Sailing: Nov. 12: Hazel Holme, Swan River.

1880 The West Australian (Perth) 14 Dec. p.2.
Anglo-Colonial Shipping: When the last mail left England (Nov 6) the only vessels remaining on the berth at London for Fremantle were the Daylight and the Hazel Holme.
1881 Jan. 25 p.2
According to Cosen's circular, the Hazel Holme, daily expected at Fremantle from London, brings 318 gallons of red, and 700 gallons white; 1610 gallons of brandy; 800 gallons rum and 440 do gin.
Mar. 1 p.2
[Classified Advertising] *Consignments by the "Hazel Holme": On Arrival of the above vessel, we purpose having sold by Public Auction the following consignments :*

62 Barrels Soda Crystals: 200 Casks Portland Cement: 30 Tons best Coals: 20 Half boxes Gun Powder: 70 Quarter Barrels Blasting do.
As these goods will be sold to cover cost and freight, an opportunity will be afforded to Merchants and others of buying on better terms than usual.
W. D. Moore & Co. Fremantle, 11th Jan., 1881.
Mar. 11 p.2
Fremantle: Arrivals: March 8: Hazel Holme, barque, 405 tons. J. Millican; discharging; W.D. Moore & Co., agents.

There is important news. Captain Joseph William Millican, had been in correspondence with Miss Lydia Caroline Jones of Rockhampton since his visit three years before. On this trip they managed to arrange her to get to Fremantle and there they were married.

1881 The Capricornian, Rockhampton, Queensland Sat. 12 Mar. p.11
A pleasing recognition of a teacher's services was made at the William-street Public School on Monday afternoon, when Miss L. C. Jones, assistant in the Girls' School, was made the recipient of a handsome testimonial on the occasion of her resigning her position, which she had held for nine years. The presentation, which took the form of a piece of plate, was made by Miss Morrison, the head teacher, on behalf of the teachers and scholars. Miss Morrison expressed her regret at losing the assistance of Miss Jones, whom she said was greatly respected by both the teachers. Miss Jones had won the good will of all by her excellent qualifications and kindly manner. Miss Jones acknowledged the gift in suitable terms.
Apr. 2 p.16
Departures: (From Keppel Bay: Mar. 30: Alexandra, s.s., 600 tons, Capatin W. Hill for Sydney via Brisbane. Passengers: Mrs. (sic) Jones, and six in the steerage.

1881 The Queenslander (Brisbane) Sat. p.480
Brisbane Arrivals: Apr. 1: Alexandra ASN Company's 546 tons Captain W. Hill from Cooktown, via intermediate ports: Passengers: Miss Jones.
Departures: Apr. 2: Alexandra for Sydney. Passengers: Miss Jones.

1881 The Sydney Morning Herald Tues. 5 Apr. p.4
Sydney: Arrivals: Apr. 4: Alexandra (s) 600 tons, Captain W. Hill from Cooktown: Passengers: Miss Jones.
Apr. 7 p.4
Sydney: Clearances: R.M.S. Cathay 2983 tons, Captain W. M. Robbie for Bombay and Galle, via Melbourne and Adelaide: Passengers: For King George's Sound Miss L. C. Jones.

1881 The South Australian Register (Adelaide) Fri. 15 Apr. p.4
Adelaide Sailed: Thurs. April 14: R.M.S. Cathay ......Passengers: for King George Sound, from Sydney—Miss L.C. Jones.

1881 The Inquirer and Commercial News (Perth) Wed. 20 Apr. p.2
The R.M.S. Cathay arrived at Albany [King George Sound] *at 8.30 p.m. on Sunday* [17th] *evening. The Cathay brought the following passengers for the colony: Miss Jones.*

1881 The Capricornian, Rockhampton, Queensland Sat. 30 Apr. p.1
Marriage.
Millican--Jones. On the 23 instant, at the Johnston Memorial Church, Freemantle (sic), West Australia by the Rev. Joseph Johnston, Joseph William Millican, captain of the barque Hazel Holme, and eldest son of the late Captain John Millican of Maryport, Cumberland, England, to Lydia Caroline (Lily) eldest daughter of Edward Jones, of

Rockhampton and Townsville, and formerly of Knockvicar House, County Roscommon, Ireland.

Certificate of Marriage : Form no. 282 :
April 23rd. 1881 Fremantle Wn. Australia : Joseph William Millican Above 21 years : Master Mariner : Fremantle Residence of the time of Marriage : John Millican Father's Name and Surname : Master Mariner Rank or Profession of Father : Lydia Caroline Jones : Spinster : Edward Jones : Contractor : Married in the Johnston Memorial Congregation Church. Signed in the presence of N. D. Moore and [unclear].

There is no certain news that she accompanied him, i.e. a long honeymoon, but it is probable.

1881 The West Australian (Perth) Tues. 10 May p.3
[In a long court case]
The case as stated by the Magistrate (Mr. Slade) was as follows :
"At a petty sessions held at Fremantle, before the undersigned, one of Her Majesty's Justices of the Peace and Resident Magistrate at Fremantle aforesaid, on the 29th day of March last, one Ephraim Hines, the above-named defendant, was charged in and by a certain information, for that be, being master of the licensed steamer City of Perth, did, on the 24th March, land on the North or River Jetty, twenty-nine hogsheads of ale from the barque Hazel Holme, from London, contrary to the Jetty Regulations of the 23rd December, 1873. ....
The regulation itself provides that goods may be so landed if proper permission be obtained. The warrant was in accordance with the form prescribed by the schedule to the Customs Ordinance, and was as follows : "Suffer to be landed from the Hazel Holme, William (sic) Millican, master, from London, the undermentioned goods, duty paid."
May.17 p.2
Cleared at Customs: Hazel Holme, barque, 405 tons, Jno. Millican, for Shanghai. Cargo: 406½ tons sandalwood.

1881 The Inquirer and Commercial News (Perth) Wed. 18 May p.2
Perth: Sailed: May 17: Hazel Holme, barque, 405 tons, J. Millican, for Shanghai.

1881 The Maryport Advertiser and Weekly News Fri. 8 July p.8
Shanghai: Arrived, on or before July 6: Hazel Holme, Millican, from Fremantle.

1881 The Liverpool Mercury Mon. 19 Dec. p.3
Deal: Passed: Dec. 17: Hazel Holme, from Shanghai, for London.
Dec. 21 p.3
Gravesend: Arrived: Dec. 20: Hazel Holme, from Shanghai.

1882 The Western Mail (Cardiff) Wed. 4 Jan. p.2
The Crimping System.
We pointed out some time since the many evils arising from "crimps" and "touts" being allowed to board vessels upon their arrival in port. The fifth section of the enactment passed in 1880, and known as "The Payment of Wages and Rating Act," states that a person unauthorised by law cannot legally go on board a vessel without the master's permission. And that a person boarding a ship in defiance of these regulations becomes subject to a penalty. It also provides that before a person has a right to board a ship the vessel must give permission; the seamen must have been officially discharged; and lastly, the intruder must not have been warned to leave the ship by an official. The

greatest difficulty, however, is experienced in preventing masters and sailors being beset by a swarm of human mosquitoes the moment a vessel arrives in port. Upon the arrival of a ship at her destination the entire attention of the master and officers is engrossed in getting their craft safely moored. It is at once a painful and disastrous thing for the commander of a ship to have overcome the dangers of a voyage and then to get his vessel stranded, sunk, or damaged just as he reaches his destination. It is not too much to expect that the crew should be equally solicitous in getting the vessel safely moored. To be interrupted in their work, teased and cheated by a lot of rowdy and so-called "business" men is, therefore, most obnoxious at such a time. A captain has such a inborn objection to legal proceedings that he endures, with a patience truly Jobian, being teased and tormented by a host of touters for outfitters, chandlers, grocers, and other tradesmen, rather than go to the trouble and cost of prosecuting these marine pests for illegally boarding his ship before the crew has been discharged. The evils arising out of this state of things were so great that it was found necessary last year to empower the Board of Trade to give "crimps" and "touts" into custody instead of merely summoning them. An important case under this new Act was heard before Mr. Slade at the Southwark police-court on Monday. A young man named Chapman Barnett.......

1882 The Standard (London) Tues. 3 Jan. p.6
Police Intelligence: Southwark.
Cheepma (sic) Barnett, 20, who described himself as an outfitter's agent, appeared before Mr. Slade, on remand, charged with being unlawfully on board the ship Hazel Holme at Hayes's Wharf, Tooley-street, and refusing to leave when requested by the Chief Officer and an Officer of the Board of Trade. – Mr. Strong prosecuted on behalf of the Board of Trade, and Mr. Keith Frith appeared for the Defendant. – Charles Leathwaite, an Officer of the Board of Trade, stated that on the arrival of the Hazel Holme at Hayes's Wharf, Tooley-street, on the 19th, from China, he went on board and found the Prisoner on deck. Knowing him to be a crimp he ordered him to leave. He refused, stating that he was invited on board by the carpenter, and yet the mate had allowed him to remain. Witness spoke to the mate, when the latter said, "Had I known him to be a crimp, I would not have allowed him on board," and ordered him to leave. As he refused to do so, Witness gave him into custody. In answer to Mr. Slade, he said he knew the Prisoner to be a "crimp." – Thomas O'Brien, the mate of the vessel, said that, in the absence of the captain, the carpenter brought the Prisoner on board the vessel as his friend. Not knowing him to be a "crimp," he allowed him to remain until he was pointed out by last Witness, when he ordered him to leave the vessel. He refused to do so, when last Witness gave him into custody. – Mr. Frith, on the part of the Prisoner, contended that he was not a "crimp," but a respectable young man, the son of an outfitter, at Ratcliffe; and, knowing the carpenter of the vessel, he was asked on board by him. He had frequent dealings with his father when he came from a voyage. He (Mr. Frith) denied that the Prisoner was a crimp, and the Board of Trade officer had no right to interfere with him. – He called Robert Marshall, the carpenter of the vessel, who said he had known the Prisoner about eighteen months, and seeing him near the ship on the arrival he invited him on board, and the mate allowed him to remain. – Mr. Strong here observed that this case was the first under the new Act that gave the Board of Trade power to give the crimps into custody instead of summoning as hitherto, he, therefore, should not press for the full penalty. – Mr. Slade ordered the Prisoner to pay a fine of £10., and £2, 2s. costs, allowing him to find bail, and pay the amount in a fortnight.
Jan. 12 p.1
[Advert] *Devitt and Moore's Australian Line: Clipper Ships: Launceston: Hazel Holme: J.W. Millican: E.I: To follow.* [Survey: London in February.]

1882 The Morning Bulletin, Rockhampton (Queensland) Mon. 17 Apr. p.1
Birth: Millican:--On the 18th February, at her residence, 32 High-street, Maryport, Cumberland, England, the wife of Captain J. W. Millican, of a daughter (Elsie Hazel).

1882 Launceston Examiner (Tasmania) Mon. July 3 p.2
Launceston: The Hazel Holme, a smart looking bark of 415 tons, arrived in the port yesterday after-noon, after a rather lengthy passage of 106 days from London. Captain Millican reports having left London in tow of a tug on March 16. On March 21st experienced a fresh gale from W. and N.W. During its course one of the seamen fell from aloft to the deck, cutting his head severely, and otherwise injuring himself. On March 27th, during a heavy gale from the N.W., a terrific sea broke on board, sweeping away the forecastle hatch, flooding the weather side of the galley and stove, and washing the whole to leeward. The temporary loss of the cooking apparatus by this accident caused a great amount of inconvenience and unpleasantness. On March 29th got clear of the land at last, with wind from the N.W. Sighted Porto Santo on April 5th, with pleasant northerly breeze, which continued until the 10th, when the north-east trade wind was fallen in with, the position at the time being 27 N. and 21 W. The north-east trade wind carried the vessel to the Equator, which was crossed on April 22nd, in longitude 25 deg. W., the wind veering to S.E. Thence to the prime meridian which was crossed on May 10th, in latitude 39 deg. S., experienced ordinary winds and weather. On May 13th fell in with a fresh gale from the eastward, which lasted three days, during which time the sea was constantly breaking on board, washing away a large quantity of bulwark planks, and smashing the main rail. Passed the meridian of the Cape of Good Hope on May 19th, being then 55 days out. On May 27th, in latitude 39 deg. S., longitude 49 leg. E., fell in with easterly winds, which continued until June 9th, the position of the vessel being then 42 deg. S. and 70 deg. E. Experienced on June 10th, in latitude 42 deg. S. and longitude 73 deg. E., a fresh gale from the south, which continued until the 12th, the sea breaking on board with great force, and starting the ring bolts on deck. A fresh gale from the north, accompanied with a high sea, commenced on June 16th. At 4 p.m. on the same date a big sea struck the ship, breaking the main rail and a number of bulwark planks. Passed the longitude of Cape Llewn (sic) on June 23rd. On June 28th met with a strong N.W. wind which continued until the next day, when Cape Otway was passed. At 4 p.m. the wind hauled W., and at 9 p.m. to S., throwing the vessel to leeward. Sighted Ninth Island at daylight on Friday, and was off Tamar Heads at 9 p.m. the same day. Lay too (sic) outside until daylight, and entered at 8.30 a.m. on Saturday. Took the pilot on board, and dropped anchor at Town Point at 1 p.m. The Hazel Home (sic) was built at Whitby, England, in 1870, and the present is her first trip to Tasmania. Besides a large cargo of general merchandise, the Hazel Home (sic) brings a quantity of gun powder which will be landed to-day. She will be entered at the Customs to-day, and consignees are requested by Messrs. Dalgety, Moore, and Co., the agents, to pass their entries without delay. Captain Millican, of the Hazel Holme, reports having, on May 20, in 40 deg. S. and 25 deg. E., spoken a French bark showing the letters H. N. P. B. The vessel was bound from Monte Video to Mauritius, 33 days out, and reported all well. Captain Millican also reports that, on May 6, in latitude 35 deg S. and longitude 17 deg W., at 6 p.m., the Hazel Holme sustained a severe shock as if she had struck something. As nothing could be seen in the locality to account for the circumstance, he concluded it was caused by the bark striking a floating spar or other wreckage.

Passengers: Cabin: Mrs. J. W. Millican and daughter [only 4½ months old] *and Mr. W. Strugnell.*
July 5 p.2

The bark Hazel Holme, which arrived at Town Point on Saturday night last from London, discharged the gunpowder she had on board yesterday morning, and hauled alongside the wharf at 3 o'clock in the afternoon. She will probably break bulk to-day.
Aug. 1 p.3

Launceston Police Court, Monday, July 31. Ship Deserters.---Thos. Steele and John Fry were charged with being deserters from the English bark Hazel Holme now in port, and pleaded guilty. Captain Milligan (sic) wished to press the charge, and stated that the men had refused to work. Fry stated that his reason for refusing to work was that £9 were due to him for wages, and he could not get the money. The captain acknowledged the truth of this statement, and defendants were each sentenced to a fortnight's imprisonment.
Aug. 8 p.2

The bark Hazel Holme left the wharf at 7.15 a.m. yesterday, in ballast, for Guam; she was towed down the river by the tug Tamar, and cleared Tamar Heads at 11.35 a.m.
page 4

Y.M.C.A. To the Editor of the Examiner.

Sir,-- During our stay in port we have had the pleasure of reading your valuable paper (for which we tender you our thanks), and as we find your columns always open to those who wish to make their views known, it occurred to us that you would allow a small place to express our thanks for the many kindnesses we have received at the hands of the people of Launceston, and more especially of the Young Men's Christian Association. As soon as we were alongside the wharf some members of the Y.M.C.A. came on board and gave all hands a cordial invite to make use of their rooms whenever we wished. They did not ask are you Christians? or infidels ? drunkards ? or teetotalers ? No, they said by their actions you are fellow-creatures, and as strangers far away from all home influences we will endeavour to make your stay here pleasant and profitable to you. This quite surprised us for we had never before seen or heard of such considerations for sailors, and, of course, we were anxious to see this Association's rooms. We went and met with such a kind hearty welcome that we felt at home in a moment. We were agreeably surprised to find such nice cosy rooms and thought a young man here need not go to the bar parlour of a gin palace to seek comfort or amusement. There were no Glenfield starch countenances there that would think it a sin to smile. No, they all seemed to be at home with one another, enjoying themselves as members of one family and as rational beings. When we had been in port a few days they gave us all a welcome in the shape of a nice tea and some amusement afterwards; had we not felt at home before, we certainly should have then. We have visited at the rooms almost every day since, and have always found the same warm, earnest, Christian welcome, making us feel less embittered against the world, for in most seaports sailors are courted only for what can be got out of them. One or two have been silently convinced of the beauty of total abstinence, and have signed the pledge there. The prayers of one praying mother will go up for the Y.M.C.A. when she hears that a prayer she has been sending to Heaven for some years has been answered. None of us will leave here without much regret, but we carry with us the consciousness that we have been benefited both temporally and spiritually; and our prayers will ever be God bless and prosper the Y.M.C.A. of Launceston.

J. Wm. Millican,

Bark Hazel Holme.

Launceston, August 7.
Aug. 8 p.2

Launceston: The bark Hazel Holme, left the wharf at 7.15 a.m., yesterday, in ballast for Guam; she was towed down the river by the tug Tamar, and cleared Tamar Heads at 11.35 a.m.

1882 The Sydney Morning Herald Thurs. 10 Aug. p.5

Mutiny on Board the Barque, Hazel Holme. (From our own correspondent) *Melbourne. Wednesday.*

The barque Hazel Holme, which left Launceston on Monday for Tal Cuano, Conception Bay, on the West Coast of South America, put in here to-day in consequence of the mutiny of the crew. Prior to the vessel leaving Launceston, two of the crew -- Steele, the cook and steward, and Fry, an able seaman -- who had been lodged in gaol for refusing duty while in port, because the captain would not advance all the money they required, were released and placed on board the vessel. A coloured man, named Green, the carpenter of the vessel, also refused duty, on the plea of illness; but certificates were obtained to show that he was fit for duty. The vessel left at noon on Monday, and, after the tug left her, shaped a course for Kent's Group. Two seamen, Thompson and Jorquensen, joined the refractory hands, and all efforts to induce the men to perform their duty were unavailing. The working of the barque, therefore, devolved on the captain, mate, second mate, and four apprentices. Two of the crew who were sent from Melbourne had received a month's pay in advance. The captain, finding the men obdurate, came on here, and the offenders have been arrested on warrant.

1882 The Argus (Melbourne) Fri. 11 Aug. p.10

Five mutinous seamen named Green, Stich, Thompson, Fry, and Jorgensen, whose conduct while at sea necessitated the captain or the barque Hazel Holm (sic), bound for South America, putting into this port, was charged at the Williamstown Court yesterday with wilful disobedience of orders. Upon the men pleading guilty, Mr. Plummer, who appeared for Captain Millican, of the barque, asked the Bench to inflict the severest penalty allowed by the act, Captain M'Callum, presiding magistrate, remarking that he considered the punishment allowed altogether inadequate in such serious cases, sentenced the prisoners to four weeks' imprisonment, Green to pay £5 12s. costs; the others, £2 9s. costs,, and each of them forfeit two days' pay.

Aug. 12 p.8

Melbourne: Cleared Out: Aug. 11: Hazel Holme, 405 tons, Joseph W. Millican, for Guam, in ballast.

Aug. 16 p.4

Port Phillip Head: Sailed: Aug. 15: Hazel Holme for Guam.

Aug. 26 p.10.

The sentences passed on the refractory crew of the barque Hazel Holme, bound from Launceston to Guam, and which put into Port Phillip, have struck us as being very light. In connexion with this little mutiny there is one incident associated with it worth recording. When the Hazel Holme arrived at Launceston from home, the Young Men's Christian Association in that town showed the visitors every kindness. The secretary went down to the ship and gave the crew a cordial welcome. He invited them to the institute, and told them to make the place their home while in port. The crew took full advantage of this generous offer, and the day before leaving wrote a letter to the local paper expressing their obligations to the members of the Young Men's Christian Association. It was a somewhat gushing effusion, but it breathed such a Christian spirit throughout, and spoke of the welcome extended to the crew, that the news of their mutiny rather took us by surprise. The writer of the letter asserted that "one or two of the crew had been silently convinced of the beauty of total abstinence, and had signed the pledge." He further remarked that "they had been benefited both temporally and spiritually;" but this benefit does not include the proper performance of duty on board ship. It is to be regretted that the benefits derived at the Y.M.C.A. did not send to suppress a mutinous spirit on board, as it would have saved the captain of the barque much expense, and the crew two months' incarceration.

1882 The Morning Bulletin (Rockhampton, Queensland) Wed, 13 Dec. p.2
Rockhampton: Departures: Dec. 12: Queensland s., 309 tons, Captain J.H. Meaburn for Brisbane via ports: Passengers: Mrs. Millican and child.

1882 The Brisbane Courier Sat. 16 Dec. p.4
Brisbane: Arrivals: Dec. 15. Queensland, A.S.N. Company's 309 Captain J.E. Meaburn from Rockhampton, via Bundaberg and Maryborough. Passengers: Mrs. J.W. Millican.

[see Mrs Millican: Addenda of Captains and Family]

1883 The Maryport Advertiser and Weekly News Fri. 9 Mar. p.5
Hamburg: Arrived: on the 20th ult. Hazel Holme, Millican, from Iquique.
May 4 p.7
Hamburg: Sailed: Apr. 29: Hazel Holme, Austin, for Callao.

[**LR** 1883: Hazel Holme, Bk, Mellecan, 399/415, Hine Bros, Liverpool A1]

Liverpool Register: Master: Hamburg 25.4.83: John Austin C. 22542.

1884 Maryport and Workington Advertiser Fri. 14 Mar. p.8
Liverpool: Arrived: Mar. 9: Hazel Holme, Austin, from Cheripee.
Apr. 25 p.4
A Visit to Peru.
Captain James Austin, of the British barque Hazel Holme, sends the following account of a recent visit he paid to Cayalti, Peru, the Hacienda of Messrs. Aspillago Hermanos. He says:--

At nine a.m., horses and guide being in attendance, we started from Cheripee for Cayalti, across the sandy desert of zana, which is situated in about 70.10 S. (sic) latitude. There being very little wind and the sun now nearly overhead, the heat was so overpowering that we wished ourselves safe back at Cheripee. But after three hours good riding we entered the monte, or bush, which in this part being moderately thick and a good road made it a little more pleasant. There was likewise something to draw our minds from the fearful thirst which we suffered, having forgotten to bring water with us. Parrots and other birds of almost every coloured plumage hopped from branch to branch and flew from tree to tree. Lizards ran from bush to bush, some of them as much as eighteen inches long, attracting our attention in every direction. The ride through the bush was really delightful. About two p.m. we arrived at Ucabe Hacienda, about two leagues from the village of Zana, and within a half mile of the ruins of an old church, which my guide told me was formerly the church of Laguna. The inhabitants having removed to a place called Laguna at present, some twelve or fourteen miles distant, the ancient village and church had been left to go to ruins, and very little remains. At Ucabe a good lunch was prepared for us with plenty of first-class milk, which after the long ride through the sun we enjoyed as never lunch before. The Administrator at Ucabe is a young gentleman named Alejandro de la Torre Ugarte, who on my return from Cayalti showed me over most of the estate, which is large. They send their sugar from here to England in blocks (concrete). It has to go through other processes when it gets to its destination.

At five p.m. we arrived at Cayalti and the spectacle even at a distance was something seldom seen in this country. The well kept road, the good and regular built walls on each side, extending upwards of a mile from the establishment with the bridges over the cuttings well filled with water for irrigating the different parts of the Hacienda, were all in first-class order. As we draw nearer the establishment we see dozens of bullock wagons coming from one part of the Hacienda loaded with sugar cane, which is stacked near the feeder of the crushing machine, a number of Chinamen standing on each side keeping this feeder full. The Chinamen stand aback of the rollers to heave back any pieces not sufficiently crushed, which are but few. The extent of this Hacienda is about 9,600 acres plentifully supplied with water. About 2,400 are planted with sugar cane, 320 with pasture, and the remainder with Indian corn, rice and other things. They have likewise a magnificent garden of about 70 acres well kept and watered, and producing all kinds of vegetables, fruits, and flowers. There might be seen the vegetables of Europe and all kinds of fruits that abound in the tropics. By means of the sluices in different parts of the river which runs half around the estate, the water can be sent into any part of the Hacienda. There are about 600 people working on this establishment, and Mr. Aspillago informed me they have plenty of employment for 400 more if they could get them. Labour appears to be very scarce. There is a rice mill in course of erection, which the engineer told me would be on rather a large scale. Next day I had the pleasure of visiting Zana, a small village, on the outskirts or (sic) which stand the ruins of seven very large churches. The inhabitants say that this place and the churches were formerly very rich, but were robbed and partly destroyed by some English pirates, who landed at Cheripee and marched here some two hundred years. After spending a very pleasant day among the ruins of the churches and under the shelter of the wide-spreading tamarind trees, we finished our outing by another visit to the Church of St. Mercedes and to St. Isabel. I was introduced to the proprietors and dinner not being ready for an hour or so they took me through the engine department which is said to be the finest in Peru. It was fitted by Messrs. Fawcett, Preston, and Company, of Liverpool, and S. S. Hepworth, of New York and is kept in beautiful order. It is under the control of Mr. Colstow, a Scotch gentleman, and the proprietors have great faith in him. This machinery is very powerful, and will turn out 40,000 lbs, of sugar a day. The distillery is likewise very large and in keeping with the rest of the establishment. The buildings are very massive, without stone foundations and plenty of ventilation, but the engineer told me it was never very warm inside the engine-house, although so warm outside. The flooring is of cement on a foundation of brick, which they burn on the establishment. There is in course a construction, but nearly finished, a magnificent house with central court and garden, officers, and rooms for the large staff of assistants. They expected to move into it in the course of a month. It remained for the next day to visit the Hacienda. It is situated in the valley of Zana, in the providence of Chiclayo. This valley was well and very favourably known to the Spaniards for its good soil, which is suited for the growth of sugar cane and all other tropical productions, besides many of those of Europe. We finished a very pleasant day at Cayalti at seven next morning, when we bade adieu to Cayalti and Don Antero and Ramon Aspillagos, and were soon on our road to Cheripee, stopping to lunch at Ucabe. We arrived at Cheripee at four p.m. after the most pleasant outing ever I had in this country.

1884 The Liverpool Mercury Sat. 5 Apr. p.7
Liverpool: Sailed: Apr. 4: Hazel Holme, Valparaiso.

1884 The Liverpool Mercury Wed. 25 June p.3
Spoken: May 10: Hazel Holme, hence for Valparaiso, 4 S, 28 W.

1884 Maryport and Workington Advertiser Fri. 1 Aug. p.5
Valparaiso: Arrived: on or before the 29th ult., Hazel Holme, Austin, from Liverpool.

1885 Maryport and Workington Advertiser Fri. 9 Jan. p.5
Scilly: Passed: Jan. 3: Hazel Holme, Austin, on passage from Iquique to Hamburg.
Jan. 16 p.5
Hamburg: Arrived: Jan. 12: Hazel Holme, Austin, from Iquique.
Jan. 23 p.7

Hazel Holme, Austin, which arrived at Hamburg from Iquique on the 12th inst. reports that off the Falkland Islands, she passed the bottom of a vessel. It was coppered, and Captain Austin thinks the vessel must have been in contact with an iceberg or in collision.

Feb. 13 p.8
Cuxhaven: Sailed: Feb. 11: Hazel Holme, Austin, for London.

Feb. 20 p.8
London: Arrived: Feb. 19: Hazel Holme, Austin, from Hamburg.

2 Apr. p.8
London: Sailed: Mar. 30: Hazel Holme, Austin, for Valparaiso.

1885 [Survey: Valparaiso in July]

1886 The Morning Post (London) Fri. 19 Feb. p.6
Wrecks and Casualties: The Hazelholme (sic), barque, from Coronel [just south of Talcahuano, Chile], laden with coal, has been driven ashore on the rocks at Sas Vilas (sic), and is reported full of water.

1886 The Times (London) Tues. 24 Feb. p.12
Wrecks and Casualties:- Intelligence from Valparaiso, dated January 8, reports that the Hazel Holme, with coals, struck a rock in entering Los Vilas, but got off and the leak stopped by a diver. Extent of damage not known.

1886 New York Herald Sat. 27 Feb. –with supplement-- p.10
Valparaiso. Jan. 16.—Bark Hazel Holme (Br), from Lota for Los Vilas, on anchoring at latter port struck a rock and was badly damaged.

1886 The Maryport Advertiser & Weekly News Fri. May 28
Valparaiso: Sailed: Apr. 14: Hazel Holme for Pisagua. [Northern Chili, nitrate port]

1886 The Times (London) Mon. 12 July p.7
A telegram from Valparaiso reports that the Hazel Holme, with nitrate, has put into Valparaiso leaking. [Survey: Valparaiso in August.]

1887 **Liverpool Register**: (20/1873).
Addition: Condemned at Valparaiso & afterwards sold by auction. The Certificate of Registry handed to ? M. Consul there for advice received from Hine Bros. agents to the owners dated 24 Jan. 1887.

++++++++++

[**RAFS** 1886-87: Hazel Holme, J. Austin, Bk, Br, of Liverpool, 399, Hine Bros.]
[**RAFS** 1888: Hazel Holme, Marsh, Bk, Chl [Chile], of Valparaiso, 399, H. Battle]

1887 Daily Alta California Wed. July 27 p.8
Pisagua: Sailed: May 29. Br bark Hazel Home (sic) for San Francisco.

page 4
[Advert] *Walnuts. Walnuts: 1,000 Sacks of New Crop Chile delivery Walnuts now fully due, ex "Hazel Home" (sic) from Valparaiso which we offer to the Trade. Send in your orders in time to secure immediate delivery on arrival. J. Ivancovich & Co. 500 Washington Street.*

Aug. 2 p.8
Arrived: Monday August 1: Chil (sic) bark Hazel Home (sic), Marsh, 63 days from Pisagua; 580 tons saltpeter, 100 tons Walnut, to J W Grace & Co.

Aug. 3 p.7

The Chilian (sic) bark Hazel Holme loads lumber from Puget Sound to Valparaiso ......will dock to-day at the bulkhead between Spear and Steuart-street wharf.

1887 The Daily Colonist (Victoria B.C. Canada) Sun. 7 Aug. p.4
Marine: Chilian (sic) Hazel Holme, 405 tons, is chartered by J.W. Grace to load lumber at one of Puget Sound ports for Valparaiso. [Survey: San Francisco in August.]

1887 Daily Alta California Tues. 20 Aug. p.7
The Chilean bark Hazel Holme cleared yesterday for Puget Sound to load Lumber for Valparaiso. She took a small quantity of merchandise, valued at $ 1700.
Aug. 21 p.8
Sailed: August 20: Bark Hazel Home (sic) Marsh, Burrard Inlet.

1887 The Daily Colonist (Victoria B.C. Canada) Oct. 16 p.4
Chilean bark Hazel Holme, has hauled out of the Hastings wharf. Her cargo consists of 159,255 feet of T&G [Tongue & Groove] flooring and 63,619 feet of rough lumber for Iquique (Chile). She was to have sailed yesterday.

1888   Book: p. 605-6: Algunos: Naufrajios: Ocurridos: En las Costas Chilenas: Desde Su Descubrimiento Hasta Nuestros Dias: por Francisco Vidal Cormaz: Santiago—Imprenta Elzeviriana, 1901. [Some shipwrecks and Calamities, occurred on the Chilean coasts from the beginning up to date]
"Hazel Holme" Barca chilena del porte de 399.09, toneladas de rejistro, construida con material de madera en Whitsy (sic), en 1870, que ingreso a la Matricula de la Marina Mercante nacional en 1886, propiedad de H. Batle (sic), de Valparaiso. En viaje del puerto de Ancud para de Carrizal Bajo, con un cargamento de durmientes para el ferrocarril. Al entrar al puerto de su destino, choco en una roca submarina que destaca el islote de Carrizal, abriendole una via de agua, por lo que fue, necesario, vararla en la paya del N., el 4 de junio de 1888, donde se declaro inutil para navegar. El placer o rodal roqueno que destaca el islote de Carrizal es mui insidioso i ha dado orijen a numerosos naufrajios, que se recuerdan en esta estadistica.

"Hazel Holme" Chilean barque, burthen 399.09 tons register, built in wood in Whitby [sic] in 1870, was registered in the National Merchant Navy in 1886, owner H. Battle [sic], of Valparaiso. On a voyage from the Port of Ancud to Carrizal Bajo, with a cargo of railway sleepers, when entering the destination of the harbour, hit an underwater rock by the islet of Carrizal, and cracked the bottom of the vessel letting water in, so it was necessary to beach it on the northern beach, on 4 June 1888, where it was declared useless for sailing. The sandbank or the rocky areas around the islet of Carrizal is very treacherous and has caused many shipwrecks that are mentioned in this survey.

GLENFALLOCH

Glenfalloch barque at Brisbane River at anchor: John Oxley Library, State Library of Queensland

GLENFALLOCH

Official No.	**29821**	Code letters	QHGB
Built	1861 July	In Troon Scotland (Duke of Portland's yard)	
Deck	One & Break	Build	----------
Masts	Three	Gallery	----------
Beams	Two tiers	Bulkhead	One (cemented)
Rigging	**Barque**	Head	Female
Stern	---------	Framework	Wood (oak).
Tonnage	**449**	Length 140 feet; Breadth 28.1 feet; Depth 17.5 feet.	

[**LR** 1861 supplement-67: Glenfalloch, Bk, J Buch'an, 449, Troon 1861 W. Grieve, Greenock, A1]

1861 The Glasgow Daily Herald Mon. 5 Aug.

[Advert] *From Glasgow for Rangoon and Moulmein* [near Rangoon].—*The beautiful new Clyde built Ship Glenfalloch, 450 tons register, just launched, and classed 13 years A1 at Lloyd's, John Buchanan, Commander, has the greater part of the cargo engaged, and will meet with quick despatch. For freight or passage.* [Survey: Clyde in August]

Aug. 13 p.4

Troon: Sailed: Aug. 10: Glenfalloch, Buchanan, Glasgow.

Sept. 20

Greenock: Sailed: Sept. 16: Glenfalloch, Buchanan, for Rangoon and Moulmein, with a general cargo.

Oct. 17 p.4

Spoken: A barque, No. 7124, 3d d.p. (Glenfalloch); from Clyde for Rangoon, 4ᵗʰ inst.

1862 Apr. 1 p.4

At Rangoon: Feb. 10: Glenfalloch, Buchanan, from Glasgow.

Apr. 30 p.6

At Moulmein: Glenfalloch, Buchanan from Glasgow.

July 19 p.7

At Helena: June 5: Glenfalloch, Buchanan, from Moulmein, sailed for Queenstown or Falmouth.

Aug. 6 p.7

Falmouth: Arrived: Aug. 4: Glenfalloch, Buchanan, from Moulmein.

1862 Royal Cornwall Gazette Fri. 8 Aug. p.5

The Glenfallock (sic) arrived here reports:--July 17 lat. 36 N 35.10 W. wind light, weather fair, passed close to the wreck of a vessel full of water; took her to be American built of 150 tons or 200 tons had been rigged as a brigantine, maintopmast gone by the cap; foremast gone about 10 feet above the deck; bowsprit standing, rudder gone; rudder case and stern stove; saw no appearance of cargo in her; had a house aft with rose deck at sides and a house at foremast; no figure-head.   On one side of stern in large white letters had "Queen" no other letters legible. Appeared likely to keep afloat and hold together for a long time. Had been stripped of everything remarkable.

1862 The Glasgow Daily Herald Wed. 24 Dec. p.7

Pernambuco [Brazil]*: Sailed: Nov. 22: Glenfalloch, Buchanan, for Clyde.*

1862 The Freeman's Journal (Dublin) Tues. 30 Dec.

Queenstown: Arrived: Dec. 29: Glenfallock (sic), Pernambuco.

Dec. 31 p.

Queenstown: Sailed: Glenfallock (sic), Greenock.

1863 The Glasgow Daily Herald Sat. 3 Jan. p.7

Greenock: Arrived: Jan. 2: Glenfalloch, Buchanan, from Pernambuco, with sugar.

Jan, 16 p.8
[Advert] *From Greenock for Kurrachee: The very beautiful new Clyde-built Clipper Barque "Glenfalloch", 449 tons register, 13 years A1, J. Buchanan, Commander.*
Feb. 9 p.6
Lamlash: Put In: Feb. 3: Glenfalloch, Buchanan, from Glasgow for Kurrachee. [Karachi]

1863 The Brisbane Courier Wed. 30 May p.5
The ship Merrie England, from London, 34 days out, bound to Sydney, was spoken on the 2nd April the barque Glen Fallock (sic), 41 days out from Greenock, bound to Kurrachee.

1863 The Glasgow Daily Herald Wed. 8 July p.7
Off Kurrachee: June 3: Glenfalloch, Buchanan, from the Clyde.
Sept. 8 p.4
Kurrachee: Sailed: July 27: Glenfalloch for London.

1863 The Standard (London) Wed. 18 Nov. p.7
London, Custom House: Entered Inwards: Nov. 17: Glenfalloch from Kurrachee.

1864 The Glasgow Daily Herald Wed. 17 Aug. p.7
Madras: Sailed: July 4: Glenfalloch, Edwards, for Liverpool.

1864 The Liverpool Mercury Tues. 18 Oct. p.9
Liverpool: Arrived: Oct.14: Glenfallach (sic), Madras.
 Dec. 7 p.3
Liverpool: Sailed: Dec. 6: Glenfallock (sic), Edwards, Madras.
Dec. 8 p.3
Dec. 7: The barque Glenfallock (sic), Edwards, hence for Madras, was left at 2.40 p.m., this day, off the Great Ormshead, by steam tug Relief. Wind S.W., fresh breeze.

1865 The Glasgow Daily Herald Fri. 24 Mar. p.6
Spoken: Jan. 21: Glenfallock (sic), Liverpool to Madras, 42 days out.
May 17 p.7
At Madras: Apr. 10: Glenfalloch, Buchanan, from Liverpool.
Aug. 18 p.6
At Penang: June 2: Glenfalloch, Buchanan from Madras.
Sept. 25 p.6
Penang: Sailed: Aug. 2: Glenfalloch, Buchanan, for Calcutta.
Oct. 12 p.4
Calcutta: Arrived: Aug. 17: Glenfalloch, Buchanan, from Penang.
Nov. 8 p.7
Calcutta: Sailed: Sept. 29: Glenfalloch, Buchanan, for Mauritius.
Dec. 8 p.7
Mauritius: Arrived: Oct. 27: Glenfalloch, Buchanan, from Calcutta.
1866 Jan. 24 .4
Queenstown: Arrived: Jan. 24: Glenfalloch, Buchanan, from Mauritius.
Feb. 1 p.7
Greenock: Arrived: Jan. 31: Glenfalloch, Buchanan, from Mauritius, sugar.
Mar. 10 p.6
Man Missing:--On Saturday last, a man named Alexander Donaldson, employed as a watchman on board the ship Glenfalloch, went missing, and has not since been heard of. The harbours have been trawled, but no clue to his whereabouts has yet been ascertained. The missing man is aged about 60 years, and is a widower.
Mar. 16 p.8
[Advert] *At Greenock for Madras. The beautiful 13 years A1 Clipper Barque "Glenfalloch" 449 tons register, J. Buchanan, Commander will have immediate despatch.*

Mar. 21 p.7

Glasgow: Sailed: Mar. 20: Glenfalloch, Buchanan for Madras, a general cargo.
Mar. 26 p.4

Serious Collision at Sea: At an early hour yesterday morning the fine new barque Glenfalloch, 449 tons, Captain Buchanan, bound from the Clyde to Madras, put back to Greenock in a dreadfully crippled state, having been in collision off Holyhead on Thursday night with a large ship, supposed to be the Anna Frame, of Liverpool outward bound. The Glenfalloch left the Tail of the Bank on Tuesday last, and proceeded down the channel with a fair wind from the eastward. The barque passed Wicklow Lightship on Thursday, the wind still being light and favourable. On Thursday, however, toward the afternoon, the wind veered to the southward, and increased to a fearful gale towards evening. The ship's sail was shortened and made snug, and ultimately her sails were close reefed. About 3 o'clock the master ordered the foretop sail to be taken in and the ship "laid to." The weather at this time was very thick, with small rain falling. About 6 o'clock same evening, the Glenfalloch then being on the starboard tack, and beating down channel, a large ship was suddenly seen ahead, close to her, coming along on the port tack, and under close reef sails. A collision was seen to be all but inevitable. However, the foretopmast staysail was ordered to be set, in the hope that the Glenfalloch would wear round. When that sail was set, however, it was blown into ribbons by the force of the gale. The strange vessel then drifted down upon the Glenfalloch, when a scene of confusion and destruction took place which baffles description. The sea was running Mountains high, and the two ships, being fastened together, tore and plunged, the crews of the various vessels expecting every moment that both would founder. The Glenfalloch lost all her lower yards, rigging on the starboard side, boats stove, topgallant bulwarks torn away, anchor and chain lost, jibboom and head gear broken and torn away, besides the copper being torn from her side, and other damage of a very serious character. The stranger ship also lost all her topmasts, yards, and sustained severe injury to rigging and other gear. The crews of the two vessels made several narrow escapes from injuries from the falling rigging. In the course of an hour a cry arose that the Glenfalloch was going down, when seven of her crew jumped on board the stranger. At that moment the vessels, which had been closely knit together for an hour, separated, and soon there after lost sight of each other. The Glenfalloch was headed towards the Clyde, and the gale being favourable she reached Corsewall Light on Saturday, and was taking in tow of the tug steamer Terrible and brought to Greenock early yesterday morning.—The Glenfalloch is making very little water. No accounts of the strange ship have yet reached Greenock, and much anxiety is expressed as to her fate, as she appeared to be badly disabled. She is believed to be the Anne Frame, of Liverpool, bound to the East Indies. The Glenfalloch which is a comparatively new ship, will, it is believed, require to go into dock for repairs. The crew were much exhausted upon their arrival here.
Mar. 27 p.2

Greenock: The Late Serious Collision at Sea,--We learn that the ship which was in collision with the barque Glenfalloch was the Alicia Bland, from Liverpool to Bombay. The collision took place on the 23d inst., 15 miles W.S.W. of the Calf of Man. The Alicia Bland was abandoned, and seven of the crew of the Glenfalloch have been landed at Holyhead. The Alicia Bland is a Quebec-built ship, classed 7 years A1, and owned in Liverpool by Messrs. Farnworth. We understand that only a portion of the cargo of the Glenfalloch will require to be discharged. The latter ship belongs to Mr. Walter Grieve of this port, and was built in Troon about three years ago. One of the crew states that the storm which raged when the collision took place was of a more violent character than the

one during which the ill-fated s.s. London foundered, our informant having been on board a vessel in the immediate vicinity of the disaster, and experienced the gale.
Shipments of Coal and Iron—469 tons coal, by Glenfalloch, for Madras.
Mar. 31 p.5
Captain John W. Brown, late master of the ship Alicia Bland, which, it will be remembered, came into collision with the Glenfalloch, on the 23d inst., reports as follows:--Left Liverpool 22d March in tow of the streamtug Retriever, out of the River Mersey. On 23d, at 10 A.M., wind S., a strong gale, the hawser parted, and tug being unable to tow vessel, made sail, gale increasing, Holyhead bearing E.S.E., distant about 9 miles. At noon took a cast of the lead in 60 fathoms sandy bottom. At 3 P.M., weather squally, with rain, wind S. by E., a heavy gale, proceeding under two close-reefed topsails, squall continuing with heavy rain, and being very thick during squalls, Holyhead bearing about S.S.E., distant about 15 miles, vessel close hove to on port tack, observed a ship about three points on the starboard bow about two and a half miles off. Attempted to wear ship by putting the helm hard aport and squaring afteryards. The foretopsail blew away from the bolt ropes, and ship again broached to, and the other vessel the helm starboard, trying to wear, both vessels came into collision falling alongside each other, carrying away our mainmast at the masthead, breaking in covering boards, stanchions, and channels, three beams, and tearing up stern frame and quarter. Sounded pumps at 5 P.M. and found 18 inches in the well; sounded again in 10 minutes, and found 24 inches. The other vessel, the Glenfalloch, of Greenock, got clear and bore away, leaving seven of her men on board of us, they having jumped on board during the collision; both pumps were manned. At 6 P.M. again sounded and found 30 inches, and gaining fast at the rate of 18 inches per hour, with both pumps going, the masts and rigging thumping alongside, still blowing a gale, and sea making a complete breach over the vessel, put her on starboard tack. Cut away the stump of mainmast to clear the wreck; all hands kept at the pumps all night. At 5 A.M. on the 24th, water gaining, and sea washing the men from the pumps, there was 11 feet water in the ship, and fast increasing, and the men being exhausted, it was impossible to keep her afloat, she being unmanageable, and seeing two vessels to leeward hoisted a signal of distress, and prepared to abandon vessel. Receiving no answer, got into the boat and pulled to schooner, the Star of West, Searle, of Bridgewater. Having put some of the crew on board the schooner, returned to ship for the remainder, four in number, when I found they had left in another boat, and pulled towards a ship to leeward. Sounded, and found 16 feet water in her, and that she was evidently settling down. I then returned to the schooner, which proceeded to Holyhead, and arrived at 8 P.M. The remaining four of the crew are supposed to have got on board the ship Charles Challoner (sic), of Liverpool."

1866 The Liverpool Mercury Tues. 3 Apr. p.8
The Wreck of the Alicia Brand (sic):--On Saturday morning two trawling boats belonging to Douglas, Isle of Man, and named the Governor Ready and Paroquet, were fishing off the Calf of Man, when they discovered an immense quantity of small boxes of soap and other articles floating about. They succeeded in picked up about 200 of the boxes, which were marked "crown soap." They were brought to Douglas and have been taken possession of by the receiver of wrecks. The crew of the above trawlers report that several Irish fishing vessels were also engaged in picking up the floating cargo. There is no doubt that these goods formed a portion of the cargo of the fine ship Alicia Brand (sic)............A ship's longboat, with the name Alicia Brand (sic) painted on her stern, has been washed ashore on the southern coast of the Isle of Man.

1866 The Glasgow Daily Herald Thurs. 5 Apr. p.4

Port St. Mary I.M., March 31.—Several small pieces of wreck, apparently from a vessel of about 800 to 1000 tons, have come on shore in this neighbourhood, viz., pieces of deck plank, poop and hold ladders, pieces of topgallant and mainrail. A wheel grating or stand, with the name in brass letters, "Alicia Bland", has been also been picked up.
Apr. 14 p.7
Greenock: Sailed: Apr. 12: Glenfalloch, Buchanan, for Madras, a gen. cargo.
Sept. 6 p.4
Spoken: Glenfalloch (barque) from Greenock for Madras, 60 days out, 16th June, in lat. 37 30 S., long. 17 30 E, by the ship Berar, at Madras.
Sept. 18 p.4
Madras: Arrived: July 27: Glenfalloch, Buchanan, from Greenock.
Oct. 24 p.7
Madras: Sailed: Sept. 17: Glenfalloch, Buchanan for the Northern Ports.
Nov. 14 p.7
Coringa: Arrived: Sept. 9 Glenfalloch, Buchanan, from Madras.
Nov. 24 p.7
Madras: Arrived: Oct. 16: Glenfalloch, Buchanan, from Cocanada. [North of Madras and south of Vishakhapatnam]
Nov. 30 p.7
Madras: Sailed: Oct. 25: Glenfalloch, Buchanan for Cocanada.
1867 Apr. 15 p.6
Calcutta: Sailed: Mar. 12: Glenfalloch, Buchanan, for Melbourne.

1867 The Argus (Melbourne) Mon. 20 May p.4
Melbourne: Arrived: May 18: Glenfalloch, barque, 449 tons, J. Buchanan, from Calcutta. Passenger: cabin: Mr. J. S. Hamilton. Imports: 10,000 bags rice, 400 cases castor-oil, 200 cases gunny bags, 80 [?] bales tobacco leaf, 127 bundles linen, 7 cases.
The clipper barque Glenfalloch, of Greenock, 449 tons register, from Calcutta, anchored in Hobson's Bay on Saturday night, with a cargo of rice, oil, gunny bales, tobacco, &c. She sailed from Calcutta on the 10th March, and from Sand Heads on the 13th, and experienced very light winds coming down the Bay of Bengal, being twenty days to the equator, and thirty-one days from Sand Heads before getting the south-east trade winds, in lat. 11deg. south. Had very stormy weather in about 17deg. south, splitting sails, and had the bulwarks in port gangway washed away; also had bad weather for several days about the end of April, in about 35deg. S. and 100deg. E. During the latter portion of the passage experienced a succession of light easterly winds, and in consequence made very slow progress since 3rd of May. In the last eight days she made only about 260 miles. The Glenfalloch is a very fine vessel of her size. She is classed for Al thirteen years, and was built, we believe, in the Duke of Portland's yard, at Troon, in Ayrshire, and is in the very best of order.
page 7
Rice: The Glenfalloch, reported among the arrivals to day, brings nearly 500 tons. For Indromago rice £25 is wanted, but we have no sales to record.
Jun. 3 p.7
Rice: A rumour is current that the Glenfalloch's cargo has also changed hands, and though we have not had any actual confirmation of the same, we have no reason to doubt its correctness.
Jun. 6 p.4
The handsome clipper barque Glenfalloch, which arrived here a few weeks ago, has been chartered to take wheat to England. She is loading at the Sandridge Town Pier.

{www.prov.vic.gov.au/} Vessel Glenfalloch Captain John Buchanan, May 1867: Passenger: Mr. Jno. Scott Hamilton 36 age.

[**MNL** 1867: 29821, Glenfalloch, Liverpool: Q.H.G.B.: 499: Walter Grieve, Greenock.

1867 The Argus (Melbourne) Sat. 15 June p.4

Hobson's Bay: Cleared out: June 14: Glenfalloch, 449, tons, J. Buchanan, for Liverpool: A portion of the Glenfalloch's Patna rice was offered for auction sale, when about bags found buyers at £25: Exports (for Liverpool): June 14: Glenfalloch: 5,799 bags wheat, 93 bales wool.

1867 The Liverpool Mercury Fri. 8 Nov.

Liverpool: Arrived: Nov. 6: Glenfalloch, Buchanan, Melbourne.

Unusually, a report was sent back for the return voyage, Australia to Liverpool. A very interesting voyage it was.

1868 The Argus (Melbourne) Sat. 18 Jan. p.4

The following particulars relative to the protracted passage of the clipper barque, Glenfalloch from this port to Liverpool, are from a letter sent out by Captain Buchanan, master of the vessel. The Glenfalloch arrived here in May last, with a cargo of rice, from Calcutta, after a very rapid passage, and was chartered to take home wheat. From her clipper build, and having already proved herself a good sailer, it was anticipated that she would make a quick passage to Liverpool. Captain Buchanan states that he made a very bad start from Port Phillip Heads: the wind was foul (about E.S.E.) and the same night it came on to blow a determined gale about E., with a heavy confused sea in the Straits. It was Captain's Buchanan's intention to proceed by the Cape Horn route, and he kept the barque to the eastward, in hopes that the gale would not last, but it did, and he could not fetch the Heads, to get inside again. With the great pitching and violent lurching caused by the heavy cross-sea, the cargo settled down to starboard, giving the barque a heavy list, and she lay down in the squalls with the lee rail under water, and made fearful weather, during which one of the boats was stoven, and the bulwarks, ports &c., were washed away. After knocking about the Straits for several days, it was decided to try and get under King's Island, to trim the cargo, and then pass round to the westward of Tasmania. The gale continued, however, and the weather kept thick; so the barque was kept on to the westward, and reached the parallel of Kangaroo Island before the gale abated and the hands could get below to trim her upright. The barque then had moderate winds to King George's Sound, where bad weather again set in, and very little progress was made for fifteen or sixteen days. The gales kept backing from W. and W.S.W to N.W., with a mountainous sea all the time; and although the barque shipped several heavy seas, she lost nothing of consequence, except two topsails and all the headrails. After getting round Cape Leuwin, the barque fell in with more propitious weather and made an average passage from thence, via the Cape of Good Hope, to Liverpool. Captain Buchanan states that the passage of the Glenfalloch between the different points stands thus - From Port Phillip Heads, round Cape Leuwin, thirty eight days; thence to abreast Mauritius, twenty one days, thence round Cape of Good Hope twenty days, from the Cape to St. Helena, fourteen days, and from thence to the Equator, eleven days. From the line to the Azores (Flore's Island (sic)), eighteen days; and from Flore's Island (sic) to Liverpool, sixteen days; not withstanding the very tempestuous weather encountered at the outset of the voyage, and the injuries the barque sustained, her cargo was turned out in much better order than was expected.

[**LR** 1869-71: Glenfalloch, Bk, J Buch'an/ Skinner, 449, W. Grieve, Greenock, A1]

1867 The Liverpool Mercury Mon. Dec. 9 p.3

Liverpool: Sailed: Dec. 8: Glenfalloch, Skinner, Bombay.
1868 Feb. 27 p.6
Spoken: Glenfallock (sic), hence for Bombay, Jan. 19, 11 S. 28 W.

1868 The Glasgow Herald Wed. 13 May p.6
Bombay: Arrived: Apr. 11: Glenfalloch, Skinner, from Liverpool.

1868 The Dundee Courier and Argus Wed. 22 July
Futocorin (sic): Left: June 4: Glenfalloch for London.

1868 The Liverpool Mercury Tues. 22 Sept. p.3
Off Penzance: Glenfalloch, from Colombo.

1868 The Standard (London) Thurs. 24 Sept. p.7
Gravesend and Custom House: Arrived: Sept. 23: Glenfallock (sic), from Tuticorin. [now
Thoothukudi, Tamil Nadu, India]

1868 The Dundee Courier and Argus Mon. 2 Nov. p.
Cardiff: Left: Oct. 28: Glenfalloch, Skinner, for Bahia [Brazil].
Nov. 4
Cardiff: Left: Oct. 30: Glenfalloch, Skinner, for Bahia.
1869 Jan. 8
At Bahia: Dec. 9 [1868] *Glenfalloch, Skinner, from Cardiff.*
Apr. 20
Queenstown: Sailed: Apr. 15: Glenfalloch, Skinner, for Greenock.

1869 The Glasgow Daily Herald Wed. 21 Apr. p.6
Tail of the Bank: Arrived: Apr. 20: Glenfalloch, Skinner, from Bahia to Greenock.
June 7 p.8
[Advert] *Rangoon and Maulmain: The Barque "Glenfalloch" 449 register, A1 at Lloyd's for
13 years, will receive Goods up till Friday, 11th. For freight or passage.*
[Survey: Clyde in May]
June 15 p.7
Tail of the Bank: Sailed: June 14: Glenfalloch, Skinner, from Glasgow to Rangoon.

1869 The Scotsman Wed. 3 Nov. p.8
Rangoon: Arrived: Sept. 22: the Glenfalloch, Skinner, from the Clyde.

1869 The Glasgow Herald Thurs. Nov. 25 p.7
Glenfalloch, Skinner, sailed from Rangoon for Bombay Oct. 15.

[**MNL** 1870: 29821 Glenfalloch, of Greenock: Owner: Walter Grieve, Greenock.]

1869 The Dundee Courier and Argus Wed. 22 Dec.
At Bombay: Nov. 20: Glenfalloch from Rangoon.
1870 Jan. 18
Bombay: Sailed: Dec. 22: Glenfalloch, for Calcutta.
Mar. 2
At Calcutta: Jan. 24: Glenfalloch from Bombay.
Mar. 30
Calcutta: Left: Feb. 24: Glenfalloch for Bombay.
May 11
Bombay: Arrived: May 9: Glenfalloch, Skinner, from Calcutta.
June 4
Bombay: Left: May 28 (telegraph): Glenfalloch for Havre.

1870 The Glasgow Herald Fri. 30 Sept. p.6
Havre: Arrived: Sept. 28: Glenfalloch, Skinner, from Bombay.

1870 The Western Mail (Cardiff) Wed. 19 Oct. p.4
Cardiff, Bute East Dock: Arrivals: Oct. 18: Glenfalloch, 449, Skimmiers (sic), Havre, ballast.
Oct. 20 p.4
Cardiff: Entered Outwards: Oct. 19: Glenfalloch, 449, Skinner, Bahia.
Nov. 4 p.4
Cardiff: Cleared: Glenfalloch, B, Bahia, 627 coal.

1870 The Dundee Courier and Argus Wed. 9 Nov.
Cardiff: Left: Nov. 5: Glenfalloch for Bahia.

1871 The Glasgow Herald Wed. 22 Feb. p.6
Bahia: Sailed: Jan. 13: Glenfalloch, Skinner, for the Clyde.
Mar. 1 p.7
Queenstown: Arrived: Feb. 28: Glenfalloch, Bahia.
Mar. 10 p.6
The Tail of the Bank: Arrived: Mar. 9: Glenfalloch, 449, Skinner, from Bahia to Greenock: sugar. [Northeastern Brazil]
Mar. 13 p.4
Sudden Death at Sea: An able seaman on board the barque Glenfalloch, of Greenock, just arrived at the port, named John Montgomery, while that vessel was lying at Queenstown, on the 2d, took a violent fit of coughing, burst a blood vessel, and expired in a few minutes.
[Survey: Clyde in March]
Apr. 3 p.6
The Tail of the Bank: Sailed: Apr. 1: Glenfalloch, 449, Skinner, from Greenock to Matanzas; coal. [Cuba]
June 15 p.6
Matanzas: Arrived: May 25: Glenfalloch, from Greenock.
Aug. 21 p.6
The Tail of the Bank: Arrived: Aug. 19: Glenfalloch, 449, Skinner, from Matanzas; sugar.
[Survey: the Clyde in September.]
Oct. 5 p.6
Tail of the Bank: Sailed: Oct. 4: Glenfalloch, 449, Skinner, from Greenock to St. John's N. F.: general cargo.
1872 Jan. 12 p.6
Pernambuco [Brazil]: *Arrived: Glenfalloch, Skinner, from St. John's N.F., in 25 days.*
Feb. 17 p.6
Point Lynas [Anglesey]: *Off: Feb. 16: Glenfalloch, Skinner, from Pernambuco, in 30 days.*
Apr. 13 p.6
St. John's N.F.: Arrived: Apr. 11: Glenfalloch, Skinner, from Liverpool.
May. 6 p.6
St. John's N.F.: Sailed: May 1: Glenfalloch, Skinner, for Barbadoes.
May 29 p.6
Barbadoes: Arrived: May 24: Glenfalloch, Skinner, from St. John's N. F.
June 17 p.6
Barbadoes: Sailed: June 11: Glenfalloch, Skinner, for Queenstown.

{1872 Star and Conception Bay Semi-weekly Advertiser Tues. 3 Sept.}
Ship News: Port of St. John's: Cleared: 26 Aug: Glenfalloch, Skinner, Pernambuco. W. Grieve & Co.

Queenstown: Arrived, Dec. 18: Glenfalloch from Pernambuco.
Dec. 25 p.6
Liverpool: Arrived, Dec. 24: Glenfalloch from Pernambuco.

++++++++++ **Wilfrid Hine**
[**LR** 1872: Glenfalloch, Bk, Skinner, 449, W. Grieve, Greenock/ W. Hine, Liverpool, A1]
[**LR** 1873: Glenfalloch, Bk, Skinner/ Johnston, 449, W. Hine, Liverpool, A1]

1873 The Liverpool Mercury Tues. 7 Jan. p.8
[Advert] *Commercial Sales: On Thursday next, the 9*[th] *instant at Half-past One o'clock at the Public Saleroom, B 10, Exchange-buildings West, Liverpool, if not previously disposed of by private treaty.*
The very handsome Clipper Barque Glenfalloch 449 19-100 tons register. Built by the Portland Shipbuilding Company, Troon, in 1861, and classed A1 13 years; is copper-fastened, and was sheathed with yellow metal in September 1872; passed half-time survey 1869. Carries 675 tons dead weight, shifts with about 50 tons ballast, is a noted fast sailer, and is well found in stores. Dimensions, length, 142 7-15 feet; breadth, 28 2-10 feet; depth 17 5-10 feet. Lying in the Queen's Dock.

[**Fl corr**. Liverpool 6 March 1873 referring you to mine of y'day please ....at once to barque "John Abbot" now here care R. N. & Sons, 28 stone of Flour same quality as for "Glenfalloch". Both these ships sail next week so it should be here by Tuesday or Wednesday. I have sent off 5 sacks today as per enclosed & paid 5d carriage. Yours truly Wilfrid Hine.]

1873 The Liverpool Mercury Mon. 17 Mar. p.3
Liverpool: Sailed: Mar. 15: Glenfalloch, St. John's.

1873 Lloyd's List 2 May col. 20
St. John's N.B: Arrived: Apr. 7: Glenfalloch, Johnston, L'pool.

1873 Adair's Maryport Advertiser Fri. 13 June p.8
By Cable. Glenfallock (sic), Johnston, hence from Picton at Quebec, on the 8th *inst.*

1873 Lloyd's List 10 July col. 28
Montreal: Sailed: June 23: Glenfalloch, Johnston.

1873 Adair's Maryport Advertiser Fri. 18 July p.8
Glasgow: Arrived: July 16: Glenfalloch, Johnston, from Montreal, after a smart passage of nineteen days.

1873 The Glasgow Herald Fri. 18 July p.7
The Broomielaw: Arrived: July 17: Glenfalloch, from Montreal: gen. cargo.
[Survey: Cly (Glasgow) in August]
Tues. 12 Aug. p.6
The Broomielaw: Sailed: Aug. 11: Glenfalloch, for Montreal.
Aug. 16 p.6
The Tail of the Bank: Sailed: Aug. 15: Glenfalloch, 449, Johnstone (sic), from Glasgow to Montreal: general cargo.

1873 Adair's Maryport Advertiser Fri. 19 Sept. p.8
Montreal: Arrived: Sept. 15: Glenfalloch, Johnston, after a passage of 29 days.
[Survey: Montreal in September.]

Oct. 3 p.8
Spoken: Glenfalloch, Johnston, the Horatio, of Maryport, for Montreal off the S.W. Point of Anticosta of the 11th last.
Oct. 17 p.8
Montreal: Sailed: Sept. 30: Glenfalloch, Johnston, for Glasgow.

1873 The Glasgow Herald Mon. 3 Nov. p.7
The Broomielaw: Arrived: Nov. 1: Glenfalloch, 449, Johnston, from Montreal, gen. cargo.
Dec. 8 p.6
The Tail of the Bank: Sailed: Dec. 6: Glenfalloch, 449, Johnston, from Glasgow to Genoa: pig iron.
Dec. 13 p.6
Belfast: Put In: Dec. 11: Glenfalloch, from Glasgow for Genoa (windbound).

1874 Adair's Maryport Advertiser Fri. 30 Jan. p.8
Genoa: Arrived: Jan. 22: Glenfalloch, Anderson, from Glasgow.
Feb. 13 p.8
Genoa: Sailed: Feb. 3: Glenfalloch, Anderson, for Porman. [near Carthagena, Spain]
Feb. 20 p.8
Porman: Arrived: Feb. 12: Glenfalloch, Anderson, from Genoa.
Mar. 20 p.8
Carthagena: Sailed: Mar. 8: Glenfalloch, Anderson, sailed for Maryport.
Apr. 3 Supplement
Maryport: Arrived: Mar. 31: Glenfalloch, Anderson, from Carthagena. [Spain]
Apr. 24 p.8
Maryport: Sailed: Apr. 20: Glenfalloch, Johnston, for Pictou. [Nova Scotia]
May 22 p.8
Pictou: Arrived: May. 15: Glenfalloch, Johnson, from Maryport.
June 26 p.8
Montreal: Arrived: June 10: Glenfalloch, Johnson.
July 10 p.8
Montreal: Sailed: June 22: Glenfalloch, Johnston, for Glasgow.

1874 The Scotsman Sat. 25 July p.7
Greenock: Arrived: July 24: Glenfalloch, 449, Johnstone (sic), from Montreal, for Glasgow, grain and flour.

1874 The Glasgow Herald Tues. 25 Aug. p.6
Tail of the Bank: Sailed: Aug. 24: Glenfalloch, 449, Johnston, from Glasgow to Montreal—general cargo.

1874 Adair's Maryport Advertiser Fri. 2 Oct. p.8
Spoken: Glenfalloch, Johnston, bound Westward Sept 15th 49.36 N long 46 W.
Oct. 9 p.8
Montreal: Arrived: Oct. 6: Glenfalloch, Johnston.
Nov. 13 p.8
Montreal: Sailed: Oct. 25: Glenfalloch, Johnston, for Liverpool.
Nov. 27 p.8
Liverpool: Arrived: Nov. 23: Glenfalloch, Johnston.
[Surveys: Liverpool in January and February.]

[**MNL** 1875: 29821 Glenfalloch, Greenock, 449, Owner: Wilfred (sic) Hine, Liverpool.]

1875 The Liverpool Mercury Wed. 10 Feb. p.4
[Advert] *Australia: Liverpool Line of Packets for Brisbane: Glenfalloch: 449 tons Register. Captain Johnston: This splendid A1. 13 years Clipper, built at Troon under special survey has just come out of graving dock, re-classed and newly coppered, and offers to*

shippers a superior conveyance for goods to Brisbane direct. For freight or passage apply to: Thomas Marwood & Co., 15, Water-street, Liverpool. [Survey: Liverpool in February]
Mar. 12 p.8
Liverpool: Sailed, Mar. 11: The Glenfalloch, hence for Brisbane, was left at 3.45 p.m., this day off the Bar Lightship by the tug Relief. Wind S.E. strong breeze.

1875 Adair's Maryport Advertiser Fri. 24 Sept. p.8
Interesting Ocean Race to the Antipodes between two Maryport Ships.
The Eden Holme, Capt. Robinson, a new iron ship of 818 tons register, and the Glenfalloch, Capt. Johnston, a wood vessel of 450 tons, sailed in March last for Brisbane, Australia, the former from London on the 12th, the smaller vessel thus getting the start by twelve days. The Eden Holme crossed the line on the 24th, and the Glenfalloch on the 25th day out. The Glenfalloch was the first to arrive at Brisbane which was on the 29th June, and the next morning the Eden Holme put in an appearance, thus beating her rival by eleven days. The race was a well-contested one, and when difference of size and power is taken into account speaks well for both ships and the skill with which were navigated. Their passages were the two fastest that have been made to Brisbane this year.

1875 The Brisbane Courier Wed. 30 June p.2.
Brisbane: Arrivals: June 29: Glenfalloch, barque, 449 tons, Captain J. Johnson. The Glenfalloch, Barque, from Liverpool arrived off Cape Moreton yesterday morning, at half-past 7 o'clock and would probably anchor off the Bar last evening. The vessel, which has made a passage of 110 days, comes to the agency of Messrs. Bright Brothers and Co., and brings a general cargo of the value of £6600; the principal shipments being 160 tons white salt, 95 tons rock salt, 20 tons pig iron, 20 tons galvanised iron, and 40 tons of fencing wire.
July 3 p.4
The Glenfalloch, barque, from Liverpool, reported at the Customs yesterday, at noon. The vessel requiring to be lightered, the Francis Cadell yesterday afternoon towed the Samson, lighter, to the Bay for that purpose, the steamer, probably, returning with one of the recent arrivals from Adelaide in tow.
July 8 p.2.
Captain John Johnston reports that the Glenfalloch barque, sailed from Liverpool on March 11, and parted with pilot off Point Lynas on the 12th, at 1 a.m. wind E.N.E.; had variable winds and fine weather to the 22nd, when Maderia (sic) is sighted, bearing S.S.W 25 miles; met with the N.E. trades in latitude 31° 36' N., longitude, 19° 5' W.; on the 30th sighted St. Antonia, Cape Verde Islands, distant about 25 miles; on April 2 spoke the barque Evelyn Wood, from Sunderland, bound to Auger, 21 days out, in latitude 8° 12' N., longitude 23° 42' W., lost N.E. trades in latitude 3° 17' N., longitude 21° 3' W.; had light N.W. and westerly winds until 4° S., when we got S.E. trade winds. Spoke the German ship Jedo, from Bale for Rotterdam, ninety-one days out, latitude 1° 13 S., longitude 20° 1' W. 18th April, spoke the barque Aurora Australis, from Liverpool for Java thirty-nine days out, latitude 22° 23' S., longitude 27° 8' W., where we lost the trade winds; had fine weather with variable westerly winds to the Cape of Good Hope, which we passed on the 5th May, latitude 39° 50' S. 6th May, spoke the ship Royal George, from London to Melbourne, fifty-six days out, latitude 39° 50' S., longitude 19° 10' E. 9th May, had a very heavy gale from S. W.; shipped a heavy sea, washing long boat out of chocks, smashing after hatch, and washing tarpaulins off, and bulwarks on starboard side were stove in; from thence had a succession of gales, veering from N.N.E. to S. From June 5 until the 24th had light N. and E.N.E. winds, when we sighted Smoky Cape; from then until 26th had strong N.N.W. winds, when we got a brisk gale from the south; made Cape Moreton

light 10 p.m. of the 28th. On the 29th came into Moreton Bay, received pilot, and anchored off station same day.

July 9 p.2

The owner of Eden Holme (now alongside Raff's wharf) Mr. Winefred (sic) Hine, Maryport, whose line of vessels (the Holme line) includes amongst the Abbey Holme and the Glenfalloch.

July 15 p.1

*Advert: For **Sale** the splendid Barque Glenfalloch 449 Tons Register, built at Troon, 1861 under special survey, of best material: length 141 7-10 ft., breadth 28 2-10 ft, depth 17 ½ ft; is coppered-fastened throughout: originally classed A1 for 13 years, and was re-classed in March last for 4 year from July 1st instant; is now discharging her Liverpool cargo at Messrs. Bright Brothers and Co's. wharf, where she may be viewed, and all particulars obtained of the captain, on board.   John Johnston, Master.*

Aug. 2 p.3

At the City Police Court on Saturday Frederick Beach, charged with being absent without leave from the ship Glenfalloch, was discharged.

Sept. 4 p.4

At the City Police Court yesterday. A.D. Graham, for desertion from the ship Glenfalloch, was sent to gaol for one month, to be returned to the ship in the meantime if required.

Sept. 10 p.2

The Glenfalloch which cleared at the Customs yesterday afternoon, for Valparaiso, in ballast, will be towed down the river to-day by the Francis Cadell.

Sept. 15 p.2

Departures: Sailed: Sept. 14: Glenfalloch, barque, 449 tons, Captain J. Johnston, for Valparaiso....cleared Cape Moreton yesterday morning.

1875 Adair's Maryport Advertiser Fri. 17 Dec. p.8

Valparaiso: Arrived: Nov. 2: Glenfalloch, Johnston.

1875 Lloyd's List 28 Dec. col. 30

Valparaiso: Sailed: Nov. 7: Glenfalloch, Johnson, Pisagua.

1876 Adair's Maryport Advertiser Fri. Jan. 21 p.8

Pisagua: Sailed: Nov. 29: Glenfalloch, Johnston.

Mar. 17 p.8

Falmouth: Arrived: Mar. 15: Glenfalloch, Johnston, from Pisagua.

Mar 31 p.8

Falmouth: Sailed: Mar. 23: Glenfalloch, Johnston, for Rotterdam.
Rotterdam: Arriving: Mar. 29.

May 5 p.8

Rotterdam: Sailed: Apr. 30: Glenfalloch, Johnston, for Montreal.

May 12 p.8

Off the Lizard: Glenfalloch, Johnston, bound for Montreal.

June 9 p.8

Montreal: Arrived: June 7: Glenfalloch, Johnston.

June 30 p.8

Montreal : Sailed: June 21: Glenfalloch, Johnston, for Dublin.

July 28 p.8

Milford Haven: Arrived: July 26: Glenfalloch, Johnston, from Montreal and has received orders to proceed to Dublin.

1876 The Liverpool Mercury Tues. 1 Aug.

Milford: Sailed: July 31: Glenfalloch, for Dublin.

1876 The Freeman's Journal (Dublin) Tues. 1 Aug. p.8

Dublin, Pier Head: Arrivals: July 30: Glenfallock (sic), Montreal, wheat.

Aug. 28 p.8
Portmadoc: Glenfalloch, from Dublin.

The Mercury (Hobart) Sat. 30 Sept. p.2 (1882)
Captain John Saul: has been in command of the vessel [Glenfalloch] *since Sept. 1876.*

1876 Lloyd's List Nov. 15 col. 32
Speakings, Glenfalloch (barq.), of Greenock, Swansea to Valparaiso 24 Oct., off Paraibo.
1877 Feb. 13 col. 18
Valparaiso: Arrived: Dec. 30: Glenfalloch, Swansea.
Mar. 3 col. 18
Valparaiso: Sailed: Jan. 3: Glenfalloch, Saul for Chanaral.
May 2 col. 23
Pebellon de Pica: Loading: Mar. 19: Glenfalloch.
May 15 col. 24
Pebellon de Pica: Loading: Mar. 31: Glenfalloch.
July 19 col. 26
Speakings: Glenfalloch, Pabellon de Pica to Jamaica 29th May 2 S. 29 W. [near North Brazil]

1877 The Liverpool Mercury Mon. 14 May
Telegrams received in Liverpool and London report that the town of Iquique was destroyed by an earthquake on Thursday, the 10th inst.
May 22 p.8
The tidal wave which lately caused so much destruction at Iquique extended its ravages to other portions of the western coast of South America, and a telegram from Valparaiso announces the total destruction of no fewer than 17 on the Peruvian coast, while 40 others have been more or less seriously damaged. Of those lost, 15 are known to have been with guano [from Pabellon de Pica].
June 2 p.
Intelligence received at New York from the Sandwich Islands announced that simultaneously with the earthquake at Iquique, Peru, a tidal wave struck the group of islands. On May 10, between four and five a.m. the sea suddenly receded, and returned with great violence in a wave 16 feet high.
June 13 p.7
The destructive tidal wave experienced at Callao and the ports north of that place extended as far south as the northern boundary of Chili. The almost complete destruction was reported of Antofogasta, Iquique, Arica, Tambo de Mozo, Pabellon de Pica, and Ilo. The destruction was caused by the upheaval and ingress of the sea. Iquique is a complete ruin. At Arica the sea washed over the town to the hill at the back of the church and destroyed much valuable property. ..... The sea in some places rose over 60 feet.
July 26 p.3
Queenstown: Arrived: July 25: Glenfalloch from Pabellon. [Chile south of Iquique]
July 28 p.6
Queenstown: Sailed: July 27: Glenfalloch, for Glasgow.
Spoken: Glenfalloch, of Greenock, from Iquique for Cork.
Aug. 1 p.3
Greenock: Arrived: July 31: Glenfalloch from Pabellon de Pica.

1877 The Aberdeen Journal Mon. 30 July
Spoken: Glenfalloch, from Iquique for Cork, lat. 39 N., long. 39 W., July 17.
Aug. 3
Glasgow: Arrived: July 30: Glenfalloch, Sangster (sic), from Pabellon de Pica.

1877 The Scotsman Wed. 11 Sept. p.7
Glasgow Harbour: Sailed: Glenfalloch, 449, Saul, for Lisbon (sic), coal.
Sept. 12 p.7
Glasgow Harbour: Sailed: Glenfalloch, 449, Saul, for Callao, coals.

1877 The Liverpool Mercury Wed. 12 Dec. p.3
Spoken: Glenfalloch, from Glasgow for Callao, Oct. 20, 5 N. 21 W.

1878 The Liverpool Mercury Sat. 10 Aug. p.6
Spoken: Glenfalloch, from Callao for this port, August 5. 51 N 12 W.
Liverpool: Arrived: Aug. 9: Glenfalloch, Altonia. [Survey: Liverpool in September]
Sept. 26 p.3
Liverpool: Sailed: Sept. 25: Glenfalloch, Eten, Peru. [near Cartagena]

1879 The Glasgow Herald Tues. 7 Jan. p.6
Glenfalloch (of Greenock), from Liverpool, steering south, Oct. 31, in lat. 6 8 N. 27 14 W.
Feb. 18 p.6
Glenfalloch, steering west, Dec. 19, in lat. 56 S., long. 74 W. [Near the Horn.]

1879 The Liverpool Mercury Mon. 23 June
Liverpool: Arrived: June 21: Glenfalloch, Eten.
Fri. 22 Aug. p.3
Liverpool: Sailed: Aug 21: Glenfalloch, Bett's Cove, N.F. [Newfoundland, copper mine]

1879 New York Herald Sun. 2 Nov. Quintuple Sheet p.14
Liverpool: Arrived: Oct. 20: Glenfalloch, Saul, Bett's Cove.

1879 The Liverpool Mercury Thurs. Nov. 13 p.3
Liverpool: Sailed: Nov. 11: Glenfalloch, Boston.
Severe Gales: The Gale, which commenced to blow off this port on Tuesday evening, continued to rage with great violence all through the night and during yesterday.
Nov. 12 p.3
Glenfalloch hence for Boston, put back.
Nov. 17 p.3
Liverpool: Sailed: Nov. 15: Glenfalloch, Boston.

1879 New York Herald 18 Dec. Triple Sheet p.10
Madeira, Dec. 17—Bark Glenfalloch (Br), Nicholson, from Liverpool Nov. 17 for Boston, put into Teneriffe on the 14th inst. leaking badly. It will be necessary to discharge her cargo.

1880 The Glasgow Herald Mon. 19 Jan. p.6
Teneriffe, in port: Jan. 9: Glenfalloch.

[**MNL** 1880: Glenfalloch, of Greenock. Owner: Wilfrid Hine, Maryport.]

1880 The Liverpool Mercury Mon. 16 Feb. p.
Liverpool: Arrived: Feb. 14: Glenfalloch, Boston.
Sunday, Feb. 15. Glenfalloch (barque), which left this port for Boston, Nov. 15 has put back leaky, making about two inches of water per hour. She docked in Birkenhead yesterday.

1880 The New-York Times Tues. 17 Feb. p.2

The British bark Glenfallock (sic) Capt. Nicholsen (sic), before reported at Teneriffe, leaky, (having put in there on her voyage from Liverpool for New-York,) has returned, and been docked at Birkenhead.
Apr. 28 p.8
By cable: London April 27: Sailed: 24th inst. Glenfalloch, having repaired.
[Survey: Liverpool in April.]

1880 The Glasgow Herald Mon. 28 June p.6
Boston: Arrivals: June 26: Glenfalloch from Liverpool.

1880 New York Herald Sun. 25 July ---quadruple sheet--p.12
Boston: Cleared: July 24: Glenfalloch, (Br), Saud (sic), Maryport.

1880 The Liverpool Mercury Sat. 28 Aug. p.6
Spoken: Glenfalloch, from Boston for Maryport, Aug. 25, off Kinsale. [near Cork]

1880 New York Herald Sat. 25 Sept. Triple Sheet p.10
Maryport: Sailed: Sept. 23: bark Glenfalloch (Br), Saul, Boston.
Oct. 20 p.10
Spoken: Bark Glanfallock (sic) (Br), Saul, from Maryport for Boston; Oct. 18, 150 miles E of Boston Light.

1880 Adair's Maryport Advertiser Fri. Oct. 29 p.8
Boston: Arrived: Oct. 23: Glenfalloch, Saul, from Maryport, after a quick run of 28 days.

1880 The Maryport Advertiser and Weekly News Fri. 19 Nov. p.2
Boston: Sailed: Nov. 12: Glenfalloch, Saul, for Maryport. [Survey: October in Boston.]

1880 New York Herald Wed. 8 Dec. --Triple Sheet-- p.10
Maryport: Arrived: Dec. 6: bark Glenfalloch (Br), Saul, Boston.

1880 The Liverpool Mercury Wed. 8 Dec. p.7
Glenfalloch (barque) which arrived at Maryport yesterday from Boston with grain, whilst in tow of the Iron King (s.s) from Holyhead, took the ground off Duddon yesterday morning, and remained for about ten minutes. Part of her false keel is gone, and she is making a little water.

1881 The Liverpool Mercury Mon. 24 Jan. p.7
Liverpool: Arrived: Jan 22: Glenfalloch, Maryport. [Surveys: Liverpool in February & March]
Mar. 31 p.7
Liverpool: Sailed: Mar. 30: Glenfalloch, Batavia.
Apr. 1 p.6
Liverpool: Thurs. Mar. 31. The Glenfalloch, hence for Batavia, was left at 6.30 p.m. on the 30th instant off Point Lynas by the tug Sunshine.

1881 The Glasgow Herald Apr. 26 p.6
Spoken: Glenfalloch, from Liverpool for Batavia: signalled "Report me: Burt dead": April 14, in lat 27 N., long. 22 W.

1881 The Maryport Advertiser and Weekly News Fri. 27 May p.8
St. Vincent [Algarve, Portugal]*: Sailed: Apr. 27: Glenfalloch, Saul, for Java.* [Indonesia]
July 15 p.7
Spoken: Glenfalloch, from Liverpool to Batavia, 13th May 19 S. 32 W.
July 22 p.7
Batavia: Arrived: July 15: Glenfalloch, Saul, from Liverpool.
Nov. 4 p.8

Samarang: Sailed: Sept. 8: Glenfalloch, Saul, for Sourabaya. [both Indonesia]
[Survey: Sourabaya in September.]
Nov. 18 p.3
Sourabaya: Sailed: Oct. 3: Glenfallock (sic), Saul, for Australia.

1881 The Argus (Melbourne) Sat. 22 Nov. p.6
Port Phillip Heads: Arrived: Nov. 21: Glenfalloch, bq, from Java.

The Glenfalloch is from Java, and in consequence of the presence of cholera there she had to go into quarantine on arrival at the Heads. After due inspection, however, the barque was released yesterday afternoon and got to the bay toward evening. She sailed from Sourabaya, her port of loading, on the 5th ult. And had the winds very light and shy in the S.E. trade down to lat. 26deg. S. and long. 98deg. E., which crossed on the 23rd ult. Light variables followed to the meridian of 105deg, E., which was crossed in 34deg. S. on the 4th inst; and thence strong southerly and S.S.W. winds prevailed to Cape Otway.
Hobson's Bay: Arrived: Nov. 21: Glenfalloch, 499 tons, John Saul, from Sourabaya 5th ult. Victoria Sugar co., agents. 2,125 bskts (580 tons) sugar.
Nov. 29. p.1
[Advert] *For Boston, U.S.A., direct: The A1 barque despatch having the bulk of her cargo ready. For freight apply to: Newell and Co. 114 Collins street west.*
Dec 27. p.4
Exports. Dec 24. Glenfalloch for Boston: 1,952 bls wool, 36 pkgs. wine, 2 cs belting; 11 cs flannels; 1 cs specimens, 18 pkgs sewing-machines, 2 cs platedware.
1882 Jan. 2 p.4
Port Phillip Heads: Sailed: Jan. 1: The barque, Glenfalloch, for Boston, took her departure on Saturday night [Dec. 31], *in tow of the tug Hercules and cleared Port Phillip Heads at 5 a.m. yesterday.*

1882 The Maryport Advertiser and Weekly News Fri. 21 Apr. p.8
Boston: Arrived: Apr. 14: Glenfalloch, Lambe (sic), from Melbourne.
[Survey: Boston in April.]
June 9 p.8
Boston: Sailed: June 5: Glenfalloch, Saul, for Launceston and Brisbane.

1882 The Argus (Melbourne) Thurs. 3 Aug. p.6
Commercial Intelligence: At Boston, Glenfalloch cleared on 7th June, with 2,000 cases oil and 100 barrels plaster, &c., for Launceston, besides 5,020 cases oil &c., for Brisbane.

1882 The Glasgow Herald Thurs. 31 Aug p.7
Spoken: Glenfalloch (of Greenock) from Boston Bay for Launceston July 18, in lat. 4 N. long. 24 W.

1882 Examiner Launceston (Tasmania) Wed. 27 Sept. p.2
Launceston: Inwards: Sept. 26: Bark, Glenfalloch (sic), 499 tons, Lane (sic), master; from Boston; agents Wm. Hurst and son, and Lindsay Tulloch and Co.

The bark Glenfallock (sic), which left Boston on June 7th, entered Tamar Heads at 7.15 a.m. yesterday, and had reached Rosevear's at noon, when the state of the tide compelled her to drop anchor. She will probably reach Town Point to-day, having made the passage in 111 days.
Sept. 28 p.2
The bark Glenfallock (sic) arrived at Town Point yesterday, and dropped anchor in the stream after a passage of 111 days from Boston to Tamar Heads. The Glenfallock is not as was generally supposed an American vessel, but British, having been built in Troon, Ayrshire, Scotland, in 1862, by the Portland Shipbuilding Company, and is at present

owned by Messrs. Hine Bros. of Maryport, England, being a sister ship of the bark Hazel Home (sic) which visited this port some little time ago. The bark has been a general cruiser since her launch, trading chiefly between America and the colonies and England. She is commanded by Captain John Saul, who brings with him as passengers his wife and child, and who has been in command of the vessel since Sept. 1876. The Glenfallock (sic) is a smart little bark, and has the reputation of being a fast sailer, but has been unfortunate this trip, having met with adverse and unfavourable winds during the passage, the first fortnight of which the vessel might as well have remained in port. No casualties occurred on the trip to either crew or ship except the latter carrying away her foretop gallant yard. The following are the ship's dimensions :--Length, 150ft, : beam, 28ft. : depth, 17ft. 6in. registering 449 tons with a carrying capacity of about 700 tons dead weight, Captain Saul gives the following account of his voyage :-- Left Boston on June 7th with a fresh S.S.W. wind, passing Cape Cod the same day, thence till lat. 39deg. N. long. 50deg. W. experienced mod. S.S.W. and S. breezes, and thence till lat. 36deg. W. light southerly airs. From here till picking up the N.E. trades light and variable winds were had, they being found in lat. 32deg. N. and long. 30deg. W., clearing them in lat. 10deg. N. and long. 26deg. W. Thence to the Equator light and baffling winds were had, the line being crossed on July 20, 43 days out in long. 28deg. W. Took the S.E. trades in lat. 2deg. N. and 25deg. W., dropping them in lat. 19deg. S. and long. 35deg. W., they having been strong and squally throughout and the wind far south. Thence till passing the meridian of the Cape of Good Hope had the general run of usual winds, passing the meridian on August 21 in lat. 40deg. S. From the meridian of the Cape on the parallel of 41deg. to 50deg. E. fresh to moderate gales were had from N.E. to N.W. Thence on same parallel to 74deg. E. fresh W. to S.W. moderate gales were encountered, and to the meridian of Cape Leuwin fresh W. moderate W. and N.W. winds were had on Sept. 16 carrying away the foretopgallant yard. On Sept. 24, a 4 p.m., King's Island was sighted, it blowing a heavy gale from the W. and N.W., that and the following day, at times blowing with hurricane force accompanied by hail stones and heavy lightning. At 10 p.m. on the 26, sighted Low Head light, and at 8 next morning entered Tamar Heads, taking the pilot on board and proceeded up the river to Freshwater Point anchoring for the night, leaving at 1 p.m. yesterday, and arrived at Town Point at 2.20 p.m. *The Glenfallock (sic) will haul alongside the wharf to-day, and commence discharging cargo immediately. She comes consigned to Messrs. Wm. Hart and Son and Lindsay Tulloch and Son, and after discharging the Tasmanian portion of her cargo will proceed to Brisbane, probably loading there for the United States.*
Oct. 9 p.2

The bark Glenfallock (sic) will clear out this morning for Brisbane, and sail to-morrow, weather permitting. She takes about 40 tons of cargo from here for Brisbane, principally bark, together with a portion of her original freight.
Oct. 13 p.2

Launceston Police Court. Thursday October 12. Before H. T. A. Murray, Esq., P.M., and T. Corbett, Esq., J.P. Refractory Seamen.-- Stephen Lindsay, Alfred Nelson, Andrew Jerrel, Peter Rasmussen, and Peter Heckloom, were charged by Captain J. Saul, of the bark Glenfallock (sic), with having refused to do duty on board the vessel, on which they were articled seamen. Defendants pleaded guilty, and refused to go back to the ship. Mr. Coulter explained that on the previous day when the Glenfallock (sic) was prepared to go to sea defendants left the vessel and refused to return. They were each sentenced to ten weeks' imprisonment, and ordered to forfeit two days' pay.
Oct. 16 p.2

The departure of the bark Glenfallock (sic) has again been postponed, Capt. Saul having been disappointed by the non-arrival of the seamen expected to join the bark in the s.s.

Manguna which arrived on Saturday from Melbourne. Efforts were made to obtain seamen from Hobart, and probably the vessel will sail this evening or to-morrow.
Oct. 17 p.2
The bark Glenfallock (sic) left Town Point at 2 p.m. yesterday for Brisbane, and was towed down the river by the tug Tamar.
Oct. 18 p.2
The bark Glenfallock (sic), which left Town Point on Monday for Brisbane, remained in Lagoon Bay yesterday.

1882 The Brisbane Courier Thurs. 19 Oct. p.4
Glenfalloch, barque, Messrs. Alfred, Shaw & Co. were advised by wire yesterday that the barque, Glenfalloch from Boston for Brisbane left Launceston yesterday.
Nov. 4 p4
Brisbane: Arrivals: November 3: Glenfalloch, barque, 449 tons, Captain Saul, from Boston, via Launceston, with cargo, arrived off Cape Moreton at 7.45 a.m. yesterday, crossed the Bay, and was towed up the river by the Boko in the evening.
Nov. 6 p.2
The Glenfalloch which arrived on Friday [3rd], is expected to have all her cargo out by Thursday; she landed about 400 tons of her original cargo at Launceston, leaving 480 tons for Brisbane.
Nov. 28 p.4
Glenfalloch, barque, for Newcastle, in ballast, passed out of the river in tow of the Boko at 12.55 p.m. yesterday, and anchored in the roadstead at 1.30 p.m.
Dec. 1 p.4
Glenfalloch anchored off the Pilot Station on Wednesday evening and left at 1.30 p.m. yesterday.
Dec. 2 p.4
Moreton Bay: Departures: Dec. 1: Glenfalloch, barque, 449 tons, Captain John Lane (sic), for Newcastle, in ballast.

1882 The Mercury (Hobart) Tues. 19 Dec. p.3.
Launceston: The annual festival given by Mrs. Henry Reed to the sailors in port, took place this evening at the mission chapel, Wellington-street. There was a large attendance of sailors and their wives and friends. After tea practical addresses were given by Pastor Hiddlestone and Missionary Marshall. The latter alluded to the desertions after last year's meeting from the Glenfalloch, and hoped the men would be faithful to their captains and the service.

1883 The Maryport Advertiser and Weekly News Fri. 26 Jan. p.8
Newcastle (N.S.W.): Arrived: Dec. 8: Glenfalloch, Saul, from Brisbane.
Feb. 16 p.5
Newcastle (N.S.W.): Sailed: Dec. 22: Glenfalloch, Saul, for Valparaiso.
May 4 p.7
Valparaiso: Arrived: Mar. 6: Glenfalloch, from Newcastle (N.S.W.).

1883 The Newcastle Courant (Newcastle-upon-Tyne) Fri. 13 July p.8
The Glenfalloch, British barque, with nitrate, has put into Valparaiso leaky; she will discharge for repairs.

1883 The Liverpool Mercury Mon. 27 Aug. p.3
Glenfalloch, from Caleta Buena [nitrate shipping port, north of Iquique, Chile] *for the Channel, which put into Valparaiso leaky, has been condemned.*

[**MLN** 1883: 29821 Glenfalloch, Greenock. 449. Owner: Wilfrid Hine, Maryport]

[**LR** 1883: Glenfalloch, Bk, Saul, 449/422, Hine Bros. Greenock. A1 **CONDEMNED**]
++++++++++

1888 Book: p. 662: Algunos: Naufrajios: Ocurridos: En las Costas Chilenas: Desde Su Descubrimiento Hasta Nuestros Dias: por Francisco Vidal Cormaz: Santiago—Imprenta Elzeviriana, 1901. [Some shipwrecks and Calamities, occurred on the Chilean coasts from the beginning up to date]
"Natalia" Barca chilena, del porte de 463 toneladas de rejistro, construida en Proon (sic) (Escocia) con material de madera, en 1862 (sic), e ingresada a lat Matricula de la Marina Mercante nacional en 1883, destinandola a la navegacion jeneral su dueno don Esteban Escanriaga (sic), armador de Valparaiso.

Suta la "Natalia" on (en?) la rada de San Antonia de las Bodegas, con un cargamento de cebada in frutos del pais, un fuerle (fuerte?) viento del NO la bizo faltar las amarras i dio al traves sobre la costa, perdiendose totalmenta el dia 24 de mayo de 1891. La tripulacion salvo en los botes de la nave.

"Natalia" Chilean barque, burthen 493 tons register, built in Troon [sic] (Scotland) [sic], built from wood, in 1861 [sic] and registered in the National Merchant Navy in 1883, intended for general sailing, its owner is Mr. Esteban Escauriaga [sic], of Valparaiso.

The "Natalia" was in the area of "San Antonio de las Bodegas" [a seaport of Santiago province, Chile, about 25 miles S. of Valparaiso], with a cargo of barley and agricultural produce, when a strong NW wind made her miss the moorings, she capsized along the coast, and was totally lost on 24 May 1891. The crew was saved by using the vessel's lifeboats.

ABBEY HOLME

State Library of Victoria, Brodie Collection

ABBEY HOLME

Official No.	63204	Code letters	JHPP
Built	1869 Sept.	In Sunderland (John Blumer and Co.)	
Deck	One	Build	Clincher
Masts	Three	Gallery	None
Beams	Two tiers	Bulkhead	One (cemented)
Rigging	**Barque**	Head	Billet
Stern	Elliptic	Framework	Iron.
Tonnage	**533**	Length 157.7 feet; Breadth 28.2 feet; Depth 17 feet.	

Liverpool Register: Registered in Liverpool 217/1869. **New Ship**.
Wilfrid Hine of 14 South Castle Street, Liverpool Shipowner 64/64. Dated 6th Oct. 1869

Master: Sunderland, 8-10-69, Wedgewood Robinson, 49237

[**LR** 1869 supplement-73: Abbey Holme. Bk, Robinson, 516, Nicholson & Co. Liverpool, AA1]
[**MNL**: 1870 p.1: Abbey Holme of Liverpool: Owner: Wilfrid Hine, 14, South Castle Street, Liverpool.]
[**LR** 1874: Abbey Holme. Bk, Robinson, 516/492, Nicholson & Co. Liverpool/ Hine Brs, Maryport, AA1]

[**Fl corr**.
14 & 14½, South Castle, Street, Liverpool, 10 September 1869.

Mr. Isaac Fletcher, High House, Frizington, near Whitehaven.
Dear Sir,
I was glad to learn thro' Capt. Robinson you were going to join us in our new iron ship & have now much pleasure in informing you he & I proceeded to Sunderland yesterday to examine her & were so well satisfied with her that we made the contract for her at once. We get her quite £150 less than I was prepared to give & she has every indication of being a profitable ship & if she get fair freights have no doubt she will do well barring accidents. She is 522 tons register is the highest class at Lloyds & will we expect carry 750 tons. I would have liked you to take 1/16 as the payments are very easy, ½ cash now, 1/3 6 mos. & 1/3 9 mos. 1/16 costs £450 but as Capt. R. informed me you would prefer taking 1/32 I put you down for the share which of course only costs £225.
I have called her the "Abbey Holme" after a well known district in Cumberland, & I hope she will be a good investment for us.
Trusting to have soon the pleasure of your personal acquaintance & assuring you I will do all in my power to make her a paying concern.
I remain, Dear Sir, Yours truly Wilfrid Hine.
I may add all the owners are Cumberland people with one single exception. W.H. (signed).
The vessel was launched yesterday afternoon & Capt. R & self were present.]

1869 The Liverpool Mercury Tues. 14 Sept. p 7
Ship Launch.-- An iron barque, named the Abbey Holme, of 587 builders' measurement, and 522 N.N. register, was launched from the building yard of Messrs. John Blumer and Co., of Sunderland, on the 9th instant. The following are the dimensions:-- Length, 157 feet; beam, 28.2 feet; and depth of hold, 17 feet. She is of the highest class at Lloyd's, and 20 years in the Liverpool book. She is intended for the West Coast and Australian trade, and is under the management of Mr. Wilfrid Hine of this town.

1869-70 [1st voyage]   [Survey: Sunderland in October]

1869 Lloyd's List Wed. 13 Oct. col. 10
Sunderland: Sailed: Oct. 12: Abbey Home (sic), for Valparaiso.
1870 Mar. 18 col. 10
Coquimbo: Arrived: Jan. 28: Abbey Holme, Robinson, Valparaiso.
May 13 col.19
Coquimbo: Sailed: Mar. 30: Abbey Holme, Robinson, Valparaiso.
June 1 col. 25
Valparaiso: Arrived: Apr. 12: Abbey Holme, Robinson, Coquimbo.
July 13 col. 17
Valparaiso: Sailed: May 30: Abbey Holme, Robinson, Havre.
Sept. 1 col. 29
Speakings: Abbey Holme (barque), Valparaiso to Havre, July 13, 25 N [?] 31 W.
Sept. 13 col. 37
Havre: Arrived: Sept. 12: Abbey Holme,------,Valparaiso.
Dec. 17 col. 5
Plymouth: Arrived: Dec. 15: Abbey Holme, Robinson, Havre.

1871 The Standard (London) Tues. Mar. 7 p.7
Gravesend: Arrived: March 6: Abbey Holme, from Havre.
Custom House: March 6: Entered Out: Abbey Holme, for Brisbane.
Mar. 4 p.1
[Advert] *Queensland, - Brisbane Direct – The fine ship Abbey Holme, classed double A 1 at Lloyd's. First-rate accommodation; taking 1st and 2^d classes only,- Brokers, George Quick and Co., 35, Leadenhall-street, London.*
Mar. 11 p.1
[Advert] *Brisbane Direct (Forty-Acre Land Grants),- The magnificent double A 1 Clipper Abbey Holme taking first and second classes.* [Survey: London in April.]

1871-2 [2nd voyage]

1871 The Standard (London) Tues. 31 May p.6
Gravesend: Sailed: May 30: Abbey Holme, for Brisbane.

1871 The Scotsman Thurs. 9 Nov. p.8
Spoken: The Abbey Holme, from London to Brisbane, on the 4th July in lat. 7 S., long. 27 W. by the City of Adelaide, of Adelaide.

{www.archives.qld.gov.au/downloads/Indexes/immigration/*U-V.pdf*}
Index to Registers of Immigrant Ships' Arrivals 1848-1912. Series ID 13086.
Abbey Holme: 13 Sep 1871: IMM/114 142 Z1958 M1697
Robinson - (Master): Farmer Margaret, 32: Farmer Annie H, 6: Morley William P, 50: Morley Sophia 40: Morley Arthur 20: Morley Sophia 18: Morley William 16: Morley Florence 11: Morley John 10: Morley Harvey 8: Morley Frederick 5: Morley George 3: Morley Henry C, 1: Foley Catherine 30: Simmons Henry 23: Hethorn John H, 33.

1871 The Brisbane Courier Wed. 13 Sept. p.2
Brisbane: Arrivals: Sept. 11: The Abbey Holme, barque, 516 tons, Captain W. Robinson, from London. Passengers: Mrs. Farmer & Miss Farmer, Mr. W.P. Morley and Mrs. W.P. Morley and family (8) Mrs. Catherine Foley, Messrs. W.P. Morley, Henry Simmonds and John Hethorn.
Captain Robinson reports that the barque Abbey Holme left the Downs on the 31st May; passed the Lizard, June 2 ; Madeira, on the 11th, 12 days out; spoke ship Kurrachee same day, also 12 days out, from Greenock, bound to Batavia; June 22nd, spoke ship W. J. Wright, 104

days from Akyab to Falmouth; on the 25th, spoke barque Mountain Ash, 25 days from London to Vancouver's Island; experienced moderate north-east trades to latitude 7 degrees north, from thence to the equator variable winds from south to west, the equator was crossed on the 30th June, the vessel being 30 days out from the Downs; had moderate light south-easterly trades till 17 degrees south latitude, and from thence to about 2 degrees east longitude had light south and south-south easterly winds; passed the meridian of the Cape of Good Hope on July 30, 61 days out, on the 4th July spoke the ship City of Adelaide, 33 days from the Downs, bound to Adelaide, passengers and crew all well. From the meridian of the Cape of Good Hope to Tasmania encountered very unsettled stormy weather, on the 2nd instant rounded Tasmania, and had strong southerly winds to abreast Sydney, where strong northerly winds were met with for three days, and from thence to Cape Moreton had moderate southerly winds and fine weather, passed Cape Moreton on the 11th, at noon, and took pilot on board; anchored the same night at the Bar, after in passage of 103 days, passengers and crew all well.

The vessel, after being lightered, will come up to the Flats, probably about Thursday.

The Emma, ss, brought up the captain and the passengers from the Abbey Holme yesterday.

Sept. 30 p.1

[Advert] Harris: London and Queensland Lines: of Clipper Passenger Ships. The Splendid Clipper: Abbey Holme: A A1 20 Years: Wedgewood Robinson, Esq. Commander, whose inward cargo is landing in unexceptionable order and condition, will follow the Indus on the London Berth, with utmost dispatch, a large quantity of wool being already engaged. For freight or passage apply to J. & G. Harris. Brisbane and Ipswich: Mr. G.H. Wilson & Co., Ipswich: Agents.

Oct. 16 p.2

At the Police Court on Saturday, before Mr. J. Petris J.P., John Benson, a seaman belonging to the ship Abbey Holme was charged with deserting from the vessel last September. The prisoner being found guilty was sentenced by the Water Police Magistrate to two months' imprisonment.

Nov. 25 p.4

The Abbey Holme, being the second of the Harris' line of wool ships, is quite full, and will sail for London on Monday or Tuesday next, with nearly 2000 bales wool, besides 500 bags bone dust, 800 cases preserved meats, 30 tons tallow, 700 hides, &c.

Nov. 30 p.2

The fine barque, Abbey Holme, ... was towed down the river during the course of the morning.

Passenger: Mrs. Robinson:

By Electric Telegraph: Lytton: Nov. 29: The barque, Abbey Holme went aground in Francis' Channel.

Dec. 2 p.4

Cape Moreton: Dec. 1: A barque supposed to be the Abbey Holme in sight to E.S.E. at daylight, beating off.

1872 The Scotsman Fri. 12 Apr. p.7

Gravesend: Arrived: April 11: Abbey Holm (sic), from Brisbane.

For once we have a report of the return voyage even if it is brief.

1872 The Mercury (Hobart, Tasmania) Wed. 12 June p.2

The Abbey Holme, at London, left Brisbane, November 30th, 1871, and had light, moderate weather for 21 days; passed North Cape of New Zealand December 13th; off Cape Horn January 17th, 1872; had fine weather off the Cape, with S. and S.W. winds, and several vessels passed, bound west ; had fresh westerly winds from Hatten Island to lat. 44 S.; from thence had a succession of heavy gales from N.E. to W. to 34 S. From thence had fine light weather through the S.E. trades, wind northerly, E. to E.N.E. Crossed the Equator March 1st in long. 28 W. Had N.E. trades and fine weather to 37 N., 34 W., where we met with heavy gales from S.W. to N.N.W. Had very strong, unsettled weather from Western Islands to 46 N., 19 W. From thence for London fine, moderate weather, wind from W.S.W. to N.W -- European Mail.

She had had a lengthy stay in London. [Survey: London in May]

1872 The Daily News (London) Fri. 3 May p.1
[Advert] *Devitt and Moore's Australian Line of Clipper Packets. The following high-classed Vessels and favourite Passenger Ships will be despatched as under: (Port) Brisbane; (Ship) Abbey Holme; (Captain) W. Robinson; (Dock) S.W.I; (to sail) June 10. For terms of freight or passage apply to Devitt and Moore, 109 Leadenhall-street, E.C.*

1872-3 [3ʳᵈ voyage]

1872 The Glasgow Herald Mon. 1 July p.6
Deal: Passed: June 29: Abbey Holmes (sic), from London for Brisbane.

1872 Hampshire Telegraph and Sussex Chronicle (Portsmouth) Wed. 3 July
The Camel, steam tug, master, William Main, was sent yesterday (Tuesday) morning to the assistance of a merchant barque in distress off the east end of the Isle of Wight. The barque was towed into harbour in the afternoon.
July 6 p.10
The Collision off the Isle of Wight: Later particulars respecting the fatal collision between the barque Abbey Holme and the Lapwing, screw steamer, off St. Catherine's Point on Tuesday morning last, which we reported in our impression of Wednesday, have come to hand, and show that at least one more person beyond the three who escaped by jumping on board the Abbey Holme from the steamer had been saved. The person in question was picked up during Tuesday by a fishing smack, the man on board which found him floating on a bale of cotton. He was conveyed to Brixham, near Torbay. The Vega, Mathews master, which arrived at Cowes from Cherbourg on Tuesday, reported that she passed a number of bales of cotton and logs of mahogany about ten or twelve miles off the Needles. The master of the Alliance, screw steamer, from Cherbourg, which arrived at Southampton on Tuesday, states that about half-past nine o'clock that morning when about ten miles off the Needles, he passed four bales of cotton and a small cask, apparently a boat's water breaker. On the following day the Traveller and the Stornoway (Deal lugger), arrived here, the former with 23 bales and the latter with 34 bales of cotton, which they picked up off St. Catherines. There can be no doubt that these goods formed a portion of the cargo of the Lapwing. The Lapwing, of which Mr. Cullen was the master, belonged to the Cork Steamship Company, and traded between Liverpool and Rotterdam. She was a vessel of 800 tons gross register, and was built on the Tyne in 1858. At the time of the collision, she had on board four passengers, and the crew numbered 24. The Abbey Holme, which is the property of Mr. Hine, of Liverpool, is an iron vessel rigged as a barque, and is of 530 tons register. She was built in 1869. She belongs to the highest class on Lloyd's books, and is certified for 20 years on the Liverpool register. She is a handsome vessel, built in compartments, and to this latter circumstance must her salvation be attributed. She is manned by a crew of 17 hands, including the master (Mr. Robinson), the first mate (Mr. Randall), and the second mate (Mr. Sharer). The version given of the terrible catastrophe by those on board the Abbey Holme, is that the vessel, which was laden to the hatches with a general cargo,

and bound from London to Brisbane, in Australia, left the first-named port on Thursday evening, and arrived in the Downs on Friday night. Shortly before twelve o'clock on Tuesday morning she was off St. Catherine's Point, Isle of Wight, bearing east by north, and distant about 18 miles. The night was moderately dark, and there was a fresh breeze blowing from the westward. The two mates, Messrs. Randall and Sharer, were conversing on the upper deck, the first-named being about to relieve the latter, and at about a quarter-past twelve they, on looking over the port bow, noticed a bright light burning at the mast-head of what afterwards turned out to be the ill-fated Lapwing. The vessel in question was bearing west by south, and appeared, when first seen, to be about two miles distant and coming on towards the bow of the Abbey Holme. The captain and men of the Abbey Holme hailed those on board the steamer when they saw her approaching too closely, and told them to "Look out where they were coming to," and to keep off, in reply to which those on board the Lapwing shouted "All right." At this time the three lights of the steamer could be plainly seen, and she appeared to be coming straight towards the barque. Capt. Robinson feeling confident that the steamer intended passing across the stern of his vessel, in which case no danger was to be apprehended, turned to issue some directions to his men, and on looking at the steamer again saw that she had ported her helm for the purpose of crossing the barque's bows. Captain Robinson now being persuaded that a collision was inevitable put her helm hard down to port, in order to ease the shock. About two minutes after the helm was put down to port the Abbey Holme struck the steamer abaft the beam as she was crossing the bows. The crash was terrible, the force of the collision almost "halving" the steamer. The vessels remained in contact about five minutes, during which time the steamer, which was going at full speed, about ten knots per hour, at the time of the collision, consequently having great weigh, dragged the barque with her, and opened still wider the frightful gap which had been made. After much difficulty the vessels were separated, and almost immediately afterwards the steamer disappeared from view. No one on board the Abbey Holme saw the steamer go down. Captain Robinson at once ordered the pumps to be sounded, and the result of this sounding was that only two inches of water was discovered in the well. It was now found that three of the steamer's crew were on board, namely Mr. Stewart, the chief engineer, Alice Frazer, the stewardess, and William Stalk, the quartermaster, and at the request of the first-named gentleman, Captain Robinson allowed him to have a boat to search for any of the steamer's crew who might be floating about. The boat in question (the pinnace) was manned by Mr. Stewart, Stalk, the Quartermaster, and some men belonging to the barque. Other boats were then lowed, and all exertions made to rescue the unfortunate crew of the Lapwing, but they returned an hour afterwards withou (sic) having picked up a soul. It was discovered that the starboard bow of the barque had been forced open, and that the orifice measured no less than 6 feet by 3 feet 8 inches. A second hole was also discovered on the port bow under water at the eight feet mark, the dimensions of which have not up to the present time been ascertained. The fore compartment was filled with water, but fortunately the heavy pressure of the cargo against the bulkhead had the effect of strengthening it and resisting the immense quantity of water. The hole was stuffed with sails and roughly planked over. At daylight a large ship, which had been lying by the barque during the night, bore down and offered to render any assistance, but the offer was declined. The captain of the ship in question reported that he had picked up three of the Lapwing's crew, and proceeded on his course up channel. About five o'clock a steamboat passed the barque, bound down channel for Santander, and reported that she had picked up one of the stokers of the Lapwing, and offered to render assistance which offer was also declined. The barque managed to get before the wind having previously "tommed" over the hole with a large topsail, weighted at the bottom, to prevent the sea forcing in the planking and canvas, and passed St. Catherine's light at a quarter to nine o'clock, and at half-past eleven o'clock was taken in tow by the Camel, which had been telegraphed for, and brought into Portsmouth harbour, where she now remains.

1872 The Standard (London) Mon. 15 July p.6
Arrived: Cardiff: July 10. The Elaine, screw steamer, from St. Nazaire, has landed one of the crew of the Lapwing, steamer, which was sunk in the English Channel on the 1st inst.

1872 The Daily News (London) Wed. 17 July p.4
A short time ago a Cork steamship called the Lapwing was run down in the Channel by a barque named the Abbey Holme. Nearly all on board the Lapwing were lost, and some curious details of the catastrophe have been furnished by a Portuguese fireman named Mordel, who escaped from the wreck. The steamer was struck on the port side, where the port lifeboat was hanging, and the funnel was driven over upon the starboard lifeboat, so that both were rendered useless. It is then stated that the captain of the disabled vessel called on the Abbey Holme for rescue, but his appeal was disregarded. There was a small punt still remaining to the Lapwing, in which the captain, a pilot, and his daughter, the carpenter, and two of the crew sought refuge, but Mordel, who saw the little craft was much overcrowded, held back, and in less than a minute the dingy went down suddenly, Mordel looking on. Mordel by this time had fastened a life-belt round his waist, and thought he was alone on board the steamer. The second engineer, however, appeared, and asked Mordel to give him his life-belt. Thereupon ensued a furious struggle between the two men. "Before the encounter could be decided the steamer gave a heavy lurch, precipitating the combatants for the life-belt, locked in each other's arms, into the sea. It would seem that this lurch was occasioned by the settling down of the Lapwing, and the suction attendant on the foundering of the steamer carried the men a considerable depth under water. When Mordel came to the surface both steamer and barque had disappeared." He had then lost his life-belt, but, being an able swimmer, he paddled about for an hour, and finally struck on a bale of cotton, from which he was taken off by a collier, finally arrived in Cork on Thursday night last. This is Mordel's own narrative, and besides being a story of singular dramatic interest, it definitely implies a grave charge of neglect and inhumanity against the Abbey Holme barque, which no doubt will be duly investigated. Mordel expressly states that the Lapwing did not sink for twenty minutes after she was struck, during which there would have been ample time for the barque to have lowered boats to her assistance.

July 20 p.7

The Lapwing and the Abbey Holme.

To the Editor of the Daily News.

Sir,- We have read with much pain the article in your issue of yesterday on the collision which recently took place in the English Channel between the screw steamer Lapwing and the sailing vessel Abbey Holme. Without going fully into the details of the case, which we have no desire to do just now, as it may form a subject of legal proceedings, this much we can say: that there is ample evidence from the crew of the Abbey Holme as well as from the survivors of the Lapwing to show that the steamer was entirely to blame. In regard to the charge of inhumanity and neglect, we beg to state that the chief engineer, quartermaster, and stewardess of the Lapwing were rescued by the Abbey Holme, and that immediately after the collision Captain Robinson had a boat launched which was manned by two of his own crew and the said engineer and quarter-master, and despatched in search of survivors, but after an hour's absence returned without any success, the vessel all the time burning blue lights as signals. She was also hove to for five hours after the collision. We feel sorry to trespass so

much on your space, but must respectfully ask you to give this letter that prominence which your article of yesterday entitles it to.- We are your truly, Richard Nicholson and Sons, Per Wilfred (sic)Hine, Agents for the Owners of the barque Abbey Holme.
14, South Castle-street, Liverpool, July 18.

1872 The Brisbane Courier Fri. 30 Aug. p.2
According to later particulars the loss of life will not be so great as had been anticipated. J. R. Jordan, master of the ship Rhine, arrived in the Thames from New York, reports having taken off from a bale of cotton two men belonging to the steamer Lapwing. Hendrich Wardenburg, of Rotterdam, another of the crew of the steamer Lapwing, was picked up on a bale of cotton off the Isle of Wight on July 2 by a fishing smack, and landed at Brixham next day. The Abbey Holme had discharged part of her cargo on July 9, and had been hauled into the dry dock to have the necessary repairs effected.
Oct. 1 p.2
The Abbey Holme has been repaired, and she left the dockyard on August 1. She is now being reloaded. The Cargo was not damaged, though the damage done to the ship by the collision was such as must have sunk her had it not been for the seamanlike promptness and fortitude of Captain Robinson – European Mail.
[Survey: Portsmouth in August.]

1872 The Sydney Morning Herald Tues. 22 Oct. p.4
The Abbey Holme, having completed her repairs and reloaded her cargo, was towed out of Portsmouth harbour, and proceeded for Australia on August 19.

1872 The Times (London) Thurs. 28 Nov. p.12
Portsmouth: Wednesday: Forty casks of palm oil were washed up on the beach at Ventnor; they are supposed to be part of the cargo of the Lapwing, of Liverpool, which foundered some time since off Ventnor, and is supposed to be now breaking up.

1872 The Glasgow Herald Tues. 26 Nov. p.6
Abbey Holme, from London for Brisbane, Sept. 30, in lat. 16 S., long. 28 W.

1872 The Brisbane Courier Sat. 21 Dec. p.4
There are three vessels now considerably overdue from London – viz., the Abbey Holme, Harmodious, and the Naval Bridge, which have been respectively 123, 113 and 110 days on passage. They each bring full cargoes of assorted goods, and Christmas supplies, which must now arrive too late for the holiday season.

That's what happened. Just too late!

1872 The Brisbane Courier Fri. 27 Dec. p.4
Cape Moreton: Dec. 26: Abbey Holme got underweigh at 10 a.m. and went into the bay.
Dec. 28 p.4
The barque Abbey Holme was towed up to Brisbane by the Francis Cadell yesterday morning. No passengers.
Captain Robinson reports that the barque Abbey Holme having completed her repairs, rendered necessary by the collision with the Lapwing, took her departure from Portsmouth on the 19th August with a fair easterly wind. The Island of Madeira was passed on the 30th August, and the Equator was crossed on the 21st September, in longitude 22 degrees west, 33 days out. The Martin Vas Rocks were passed on the 2nd October, when moderate S.E. trades were fallen in with, succeeded by moderate southerly winds to the meridian of the Cape, which was passed on the 64th day out. From the Cape to Tasmania fine light easterly weather was experienced, and after

rounding Tasmania encountered a succession of north-easterly and northerly gales, with a strong current setting to the southward, running from 27 to 30 miles per day. When about 40 miles to the eastward of Sydney a very remarkable phenomenon was experienced. The sea suddenly rose in immense waves for some considerable distance round the vessel without any discernible cause, it being almost calm at the time. This extraordinary occurrence lasted for some five or six hours, the sea running very high all the time, and heavy seas breaking against and over the vessel, with hurricane fury, causing her to labor heavily as in a severe gale. On the 21st instant, off Newcastle, a fresh southerly gale was encountered, which lasted for two days. The weather then moderated, and light south and south-easterly winds with calms were met with until arrival at Cape Moreton, after a tedious passage of 128 days. The Abbey Holme brings a large general cargo, consigned to Messrs. Bright Brothers and Co.
1873 Jan. 14 p.2

Central Police Court. Monday, January 13. "Jack" and his Brother. James Nutkins, 31, seaman, and James Barter, 26, seaman, both belonging to the Abbey Holme, were charged with being drunk and disorderly on Sunday afternoon, at the Diggers' Arms, Boundary-street. George Staeheli, the landlord, and James Watt, a boarder, gave evidence, from which it appeared that the prisoners, went to the house and called for drinks, but were refused, the landlord, whom they found enjoying his pipe, telling them that they had imbibed too much already. This irritated the seamen, and Barter, the shorter and stouter of the two, struck the landlord in the face, while his companion dealt him a blow on the back of the neck. Blood streamed from his nose, and he went down on one knee, seeing which, and hearing, probably, that a policeman had been sent for, the irate tars beat a hasty retreat, and in their flight encountered James Watt, the boarder, who tried to stop them, and whose coat they "tore to ribbons". On getting out, "they pelted the house with stones," and it was stated that the bombardment had done some damage to the front. The defence was of an indefinite character. Nutkins had a dreamy recollection of seeing a woman slap his mate in the face -- an incident which he said was "the first origination of the affray". Barter, in cross-examining the landlord, asked -- Didn't you and the other man (the boarder) knock me down and kick me?" *Nutkins (replying for the landlord):* "No, it was the other man only, not the landlord". *Both the landlord and Watt denied assaulting the prisoners, or seeing any one else do so. A fine of 20s each was imposed.*
Feb. 11 p.2

Cape Moreton: Departure: February 10, Abbey Holme, barque, for Adelaide.

1873 The South Australian Register (Adelaide) Wed. 26 Feb p.2
Arrived: Tuesday, February 25: Abbey Holme, 515 tons, W. Robinson master, from Brisbane February 10: In ballast.
The Abbey Holme, from Brisbane, a handsome iron barque, has arrived to join the wheat fleet, and the master reports another vessel to follow. On leaving, the Abbey had a strong southerly wind, which continued till as far south as Solitary Island; then it veered to the north, and continued so to Cape Howe. She passed through Bass's Straits with the wind fresh from south-east, and had a favorable slant at the finish. Immediately on reaching the roadstead the tug took her to the harbour.
Mar. 25 p.3

Police Court. Port Adelaide: [Before the Mayor and Captain Bickers J.P.] Four seamen of the Abbey Holme, charged with being absent without leave, were ordered on board.
page 4

Exports: Abbey for London, 6,145 bags wheat. No passengers. The Abbey Holme was towed out on Sunday [23rd] evening.
Mar. 27 p.4 Thursday

Sailed: March 26: Abbey Holme, barque, for London, weighed anchor on Wednesday morning, and proceeded down the Gulf with a fine breeze, which enabled [it] *to get out of sight before sundown.*

1873 The South Australian Advertiser (Adelaide) Wed. 23 Apr. p.3
Exports : Abbey Holme: Sailed 24 March: 3,253 (Qrs.) £6,506.

1873 The Times (London) Wed. 5 Mar. p.10
The Quail, a vessel of 600 tons burden, with a general cargo on board, from Liverpool bound for Rotterdam; went ashore yesterday morning during a thick fog at Atherfield Ledge, west of Black Gang Chine, on the south-west coast of the Isle of Wight. All hands; have been landed safely, and an attempt will be made to-day to get the vessel off. Success is considered to be very doubtful. The Quail is a sister-vessel to the Lapwing, which foundered off the Isle of Wight in May last.

1873 The Queenslander (Brisbane) Sat. 5 July p.2
Wharfage Accommodation.
SIR,—Constant complaints are made by importers and others, both privately and in the columns of the Press, as to the inefficiency of the present, and necessity for increased, wharfage accommodation ; and looking a little in advance, there can be do doubt of the deficiency being more severely felt, as it is to be hoped and expected our shipping trade will increase.

But great as the delay and inconvenience is to ship owners, a much heavier loss is entailed upon importers and consignees; caused by the extreme delay with which ships are discharged. Ship captains and their agents loudly proclaim the rapid passages made of their vessels, and justly hope to secure future freight from the good sailing qualities or skilful navigation of their ships; but as far as any benefit to the importers of the goods is concerned, it seems to be the last thing thought of. When the vessel reaches the bay or a wharf a lethargy seems to fall upon the ship's company, and the cargo is doled out at a miserably slow rate, usually requiring as many weeks as it should take days, to discharge. One instance will illustrate many. A vessel arrived in this port in May, in which I had over a dozen packages of merchandise. On the 22nd of that month one parcel was received, the next was not delivered until the 18th June, more than three weeks intervening, and up to the present time some of the parcels still remain on board the ship; it is very provoking for merchants to have enquiries for saleable goods, which they are compelled to decline, although in the port for weeks.

In this case there was no possible excuse, as the freight was paid in London, and the duty and shipping charges before a single package was discharged. I knew that ships are much impeded by delay in the entries being passed at the Customs, but that is no reason why those who are prompt in doing what is right, should suffer from others' carelessness. The remedy is in the hands of the ship-captain, if he will only use it.

It may be said that no convenience exists for rapid discharge; but it is not so. On Raff's wharf stands a steam crane; but as the using would entail a little expense on the ship, it is left alone. At the present day no wharf is complete without a steam crane; but it is no use to get them, as they will not be employed.

The ship Abbey Holme was loading in London about the month of May last year. She met with misfortune, and had to put back and discharge her cargo, entailing delay and expense on the shippers and consignees. She arrived here about the end of the year, after a very long voyage. It would naturally be thought that some effort would have been made to discharge the cargo quickly after such great delay, but no; it was doled out in the usual miserable manner, until the consignees were tired out of all patience.

The ships of the A.S.N. Co. are constantly discharged and reloaded in twenty-four hours, showing what can be done. It will be said, they have steam winches. Then let the ships hire or get steam winches, if they wish to retain their freights. Neither in Sydney nor Melbourne would the system prevailing here be permitted to exist.

One other instance will suffice. A large importing firm here directed certain goods to be sent out directly; some were shipped in a vessel which started quickly, others were sent via Sydney, as no other ship was about sailing for Brisbane. Now mark the result. The goods which came by Sydney, in the ship sailing latest, were discharged, re-shipped to Brisbane, and actually disposed of, before the other vessel had discharged her cargo. This requires no comment; it speaks for itself. If the ship-owners and agents of vessels trading to this port wish to retain their trade, they must alter their ways. I for one, and also others, are trying the experiment as to whether it is not cheaper and quicker to get goods by Sydney, as we can count within a month at the farthest as to the time they will be delivered to us here. Apologising for the length to which I have extended this letter, and pleading the importance of the subject as my excuse,—

Yours, &c.,

Importer.

1873 The Standard (London) Fri. 1 Aug. p.7
Off the Lands End: July 31: The Abbey Holm (sic), from Adelaide.
Aug. 2 p.7
Deal: Arrived: July 31: Abbie (sic) Holme, from Adelaide.
Aug. 4 p.7
Gravesend: Arrivals: Aug. 1: Abbey Holme, from Adelaide. Aug. 2, entered the Custom House.
Aug. 11 p.1
[Advert] Devitt and Moore's Australian Line: Clipper Packets: Brisbane: Abbey Holme: Robinson: S.W.I: sailing due Aug. 20.

Liverpool Register: Master, London 1-9-73 John Henry Randall 28286

1873-4 [4th voyage]

{www.archives.qld.gov.au/downloads/Indexes/immigration/*U-V.pdf*}
Index to Registers of Immigrant Ships' Arrivals 1848-1912. Series ID 13086.
Abbey Holme: 12 Jan 1874: IMM/114 567 Z1958 M1697
Randall - (Captain): Drake James George 24: Battestbey [Battersby?] William 23: Marsh Edwin 33: Stevens George.

1874 The Brisbane Courier Thurs. 15 Jan. p.2
Brisbane: Arrivals: January 13: Abbey Holme, barque, 515 tons, Captain J.H. Randall, from London. Passengers: Messrs. J.G. Drake, William Battersly [Battersby?], *Edwin Marsh, and G. Stevens: Abbey Holme was towed up to Brisbane by the Francis Cadell on Tuesday evening* [and] *is berthed alongside Bright Brothers' wharf.*
Jan. 16 p.2.
Captain Randall reports that the barque Abbey Holme left Gravesend at 3 a.m. on the 8th September and discharged pilot off Deal, at 1 o'clock the same afternoon. In the evening the wind veered to SW, with drizzling rain, increasing to a gale, the weather being changeable to the 20th September, when a strong breeze set in from SE, and lasted for a couple of days, succeeded by heavy gales from S and SW; on the 4th October passed the island of Madeira with light winds and fine weather, which continued to the Equator; crossed in 28.30 W on the 24th of the same month. Light variable winds then continued to the 2nd November, when the

wind freshened and veered from ESE to ENE, the weather proving very squally and variable to the Cape of Good Hope, which was passed on the 22nd November; light winds and fine weather prevailed until the 29th, when a strong easterly wind was met with, which lasted to the 6th December, when it veered to WSW, with strong gales and heavy sea, the weather being very thick and squally. On the 17th December a heavy gale was encountered from SSW, during the continuance of which the ship was hove-to on the port tack. The weather moderated somewhat on the 18th, but again became very boisterous on the 22nd, necessitating the vessel being again hove-to. The weather continued very changeable until the 25th, on which date the Island of Tasmania was passed, a strong gale from WSW blowing at the time. From January 1 to the 11th instant had strong north-easterly weather; anchored in Moreton Bay the following day.

At the Central Police Court, yesterday, George Stephens, a new arrival by the Abbey Holme, was fined 40s for resisting the police, one of whom got a kick on the neck; defendant said he was drunk at the time.
Apr. 10 p.2

Marriage: Holmes A'Court- Anderson - On the 8th April, at St. John's Church, Brisbane, the Hon. Charles George Holmes a'Court, to Mary, eldest daughter of late J. H. Anderson, Esq.
Apr. 24 p.2

Cleared: April 23. Abbey Holme, 515 tons, Captain Randall, for London. Passengers: Mr. & Mrs. Holmes A'Court.
Apr. 29 p.2

By Electric Telegraph: Lytton: April 28: Abbey Holme, barque, anchored at Bar, outward bound.
Apr. 30 p.2

By Electric Telegraph: Cape Moreton: Departures April 29, Abbey Holme barque at 9.50 a.m. for London.

1874 The Queenslander (Brisbane) Sat. 30 May p.8
Australian Tin in England.
The last shipment of tin direct to the English market, by the barque Abbey Holme, justifies the anticipations expressed in a former letter as to the probable falling-off in the export of ore and the increase in the export of metal, and evidences, moreover, the rapid development of smelting operations in the colony. The vessel named carried 3296 ingots metal, and only 147 casks of ore; but as the weights are not given in the manifest it would be difficult to arrive at a correct estimate of the gross amount in tons. I am informed that, in consequence of advices received from England, the Queensland Smelting Company have altered the size and weight of their ingots, and are now running the metal into 84-lb. moulds, instead of 1cwt, as before. At least two-thirds of the ingots exported per Abbey Holme were of the old shape, running twenty to the ton, the remainder being of the new pattern, counting about twenty-five to the ton. The works at Bulimba—the Q.S. Co.'s—have been turning out fifty tons of metal per week for some time past, with four furnaces going ; a fifth has just been completed, and then operations will be correspondingly enlarged.
Nov. 23 p.2

Arrived at London: September 4: Abbey Holme, barque, 516 tons, Captain J.H. Randall, from Cape Moreton, April 29. Passage 128 days.

1874-5 [5th voyage]

1874 The Scotsman Fri. 23 Oct. p.7
Gravesend: Sailed: October 22: Abbey Holme for Brisbane.
Deal: Sailed: October 22: Abbey Holme for Brisbane.

{www.archives.qld.gov.au/downloads/Indexes/immigration/*U-V.pdf*}
Index to Registers of Immigrant Ships' Arrivals 1848-1912. Series ID 13086.
Abbey Holme: 9 Feb 1875: IMM/115 859 Z1958 M1698
Randall - (Captain): Wells Seymour 20: Patterson Imogene 23: Patterson Samuel 25: Roberts Sarah 30: Roberts Richard 2: Johnson John Fredk 20: Dodds Henry 30: Haynes Thomas 21: Bryan George 21: Johns William 26: Taubman James 19.

1875 The Brisbane Courier Wed. 10 Feb. p.2

Brisbane: Arrival: February 9: Abbey Holme, barque, (Devitt and Moore's line), 516 tons, Captain J.H. Randall from London, arrived off Cape Moreton from London, yesterday afternoon after a passage of 109 days from Deal.
Feb. 13 p.4

The Abbey Holme, barque, from London, will probably be reported at H.M. Customs this morning. The vessel brings the following passengers: Saloon: Mr. S. Wells. Second Cabin; Mr. and Mrs. Patterson, Mrs. Roberts & child, Messrs. J.F. Johnson, H. Dobbs, T. Haynes, G. Bryan, W. Johns and M. Taubmann [Taubman?]

In the import markets business during the week has continued quiet in all branches, and some weeks must elapse before we shall be able to report a more active state of things. The demand for goods from the northern ports continues extremely languid, and little improvement can be looked for during the prevalence of the rainy season. There is no great activity noticeable in the inland trade, and the more immediate local enquiry for merchandise becomes daily more limited, as the number of houses importing direct from the home markets increased. Since our last report we have to record the arrival of the Abbey Holme, barque, from London, with a general cargo, valued at £25,900, some lines of which will be very acceptable to stocks which have been bare of late, such is pickles, bottled fruit, tinned fish, and other like articles in daily consumption.
Feb. 15 p.3

At the City Police Court on Saturday, before John Petrie, Esq., J.P., James Tolman and George Macklay, who pleaded guilty to the larceny of cargo on board the ship the Abbey Holme on December 24 last, were each fined £1, or one month's imprisonment.
Feb. 17. p.1

Public Notice: Mr. Henry Dodds, late passenger in the Abbey Holme from London, begs to thank publicly his Christian friends who, under cover of anonymous communications have succeeded in their malicious intentions. Sullivan's Temperance Hotel. George-street Brisbane.
Feb.23. p.3

Detention of Cargo.

To the editor of the Brisbane Courier.

Sir,-- I desire to draw your attention, and, through your columns, that of the proper officers to look after such matters, to the great and unnecessary delay which now takes place in discharging cargo from ships arriving in this port.

This is really becoming a serious matter to the mercantile interest, and if the power does exist to prevent a continuance it appears strange it is not exercised. Take a frequent case: A ship arrives with goods in demand, the consignee sells, with promise to ship or deliver within a certain time, but is forced to break his promise, and possibly lose the sale of his goods, for the simple reason that they are still in the ship.

A present instance illustrates the neglect on the part of agents to hasten discharge of cargo. The ship Abbey Holme was reported at the Customs on the 13th instant, and all consignees notified to pass then entries, the limit of time for doing so being four days. Hundreds of pounds have been paid to the Customs as duty, but to the present time, the 22nd, not one package has been discharged, and the ship still swings at anchor in the river, and from all I can learn she is not likely to open her hatches for some days to come.

It is stated that the ship Fontenaye occupies the wharf at which the Abbey Holme is to be discharged, and that one must leave before the other can unload. It may be so, but if the Fontenaye had been discharged with reasonable celerity, the Abbey Holme might now have had half her cargo out.

Several consignees were lately fined at the Police Court for not passing entries within the time specified by the Act: and in common justice the same measure should be dealt out to the ship agents who fail to comply with the terms of the Act, which provides that the ship must discharge within seven days.

Yours, &c.   Importer

Feb. 26. p.2

Complaints on the part of consignees of goods on board the English ships Blenheim and Abbey Holme have reached us, on the subject of the delay in their discharge. Making all allowances for the wants of importers, they are hardly reasonable in expecting agents to run the risk of bringing these vessels alongside the wharf during the present flooded state of the river. A secure anchorage in mid-stream seems at present the most desirable berth attainable.

Apr. 1 p.2

The Abbey Holme, barque, on her present visit to this port does not take the berth for London, but clears in a few days for Newcastle, future destination not yet fixed.

Apr. 5 p.2

The Abbey Holme, barque, for Newcastle, in ballast, was towed to the Bay by the Frances Cadell on Saturday [3rd] and yesterday morning left the Bar.

Apr. 19 p.2

The following arrivals: Movements at Newcastle from Brisbane are reported: April 12. Abbey Holme, barque.

Jun. 5 p.4

The Abbey Holme, barque, Captain Randall, sailed from Newcastle for San Francisco, on Saturday last, with 750 tons coal.

1875 Daily Alta California Tues. 24 Aug. p.4

Spoken: Aug 22d. lat 37.30N. long 137 50W: Br bark Abbey Holme from Newcastle (N.W.S.) for San Francisco.

Aug. 27

San Francisco: Arrived: Aug. 26: Br. Bark Abbey Holme, Randall, 89 days from Newcastle (N.S.W.) 750 tons coal to Order. Memoranda: Per Abbey Holme. Left May 29th., crossed equator July 14th. lon. 14S. 37W. : had light winds throughout, except on Aug 23rd when 70 miles SW of Farralones, had a strong N NW gale during which carried away main top-gallant mast.

Sept. 20 p.1

At Harrison street: The Abbey Holme discharging coal and to load for Liverpool.

Sept. 23

The engagements since last Wednesday have been as follows: Abbey Holme, 534 tons, wheat for Liverpool £2.11s.

Here she had a survey in September. (This is one time the Registers of Shipping surveys have failed. They both placed surveys at New York in May of 1875. Otherwise the survey dates are very dependable, not like the dates for captains and owners which can be quite misleading. One has to be very circumspect with those latter details.)

1875 Adair's Maryport Advertiser Fri. 1 Oct. p.8

San Francisco: Sailed: Sept. 27: Abbey Holme, Randall, for Liverpool.

1876 Feb. 25 p.8

Abbey Holme, Randells (sic), spoken from San Francisco for Liverpool, lat 18* S., long. 30* 30' W., January 16th, all well, 110 days.

1876 The Liverpool Mercury Sat. 26 Feb.p.6
Spoken: Abbey Holme from San Francisco for this port Feb. 8: 21 N., 43 W.

1876 Adair's Maryport Advertiser Fri. Mar. 3 p.8
Liverpool: Arrived: Mar. 1: Abbey Holme, Randall, from San Francisco.

1876 The Liverpool Mercury Wed. 17 May p.4
[Notice] For Brisbane: Taking Cargo to the Wharf, with Immediate Despatch, The Iron Clipper; Abbey Holme: 515 tons register: Captain J.R. Randall. This fine iron clipper is of the highest class at Lloyd's.

Liverpool Register: Master, Liverpool, 29-5-76 William Bryce 32636

J. H. Randall, promoted, joined the newer and bigger Eden Holme in London (Vol. 2).

1876-7 [6th voyage]

1876 The Brisbane Courier Fri. 13 Oct. p.2
Brisbane: Arrived: Oct. 12: Abbey Holme, barque, 516 tons, Captain Bryce, from Liverpool June 2. No passengers [? where was Mrs. Bryce—see captains' addendum].
The Abbey Holme, barque, from Liverpool, a previous visitor to this port, arrived off Cape Moreton yesterday morning, and anchored off the Bar in the afternoon, at 4 o'clock. The vessel which has occupied some 130 days in the passage, brings a general cargo, valued at £9400, principally salt and bulk beer.
Oct. 17. p.2
The Abbey Holme, barque from Liverpool, now lying alongside the agents' wharf, Messrs. Bright Brothers and Co, was reported at the Customs yesterday. Of his passage, Captain Bryce reports that he left Liverpool, June 2. Encountered a strong gale on the 4th, with heavy confused sea; from thence had fine weather to the Equator, which was crossed on July 8, in 30°20' W.; had very bad S.E. trade winds mostly from S. and S.S.W. and squalls. Sighted Tristan d'Acunha August 10; passed meridian of the Cape of Good Hope on the 18th; on the 21st, encountered a very heavy gale; lost the long boat, poop ladder, &c., and had a continuance of bad weather until passing Tasmania, which was passed on the 23rd of September, from thence had fine weather, with the exception of one or two heavy thunderstorms. Sighted Cape Moreton on the 12th of October, and arrived at Brisbane on the 13th.
Oct. 19 p.3
The stone-breaking machine ordered by the Brisbane Municipal Council has arrived from England by the ship Abbey Holme, and will be landed in a few days. At the last municipal meeting the Council accepted Alderman Sinclair's offer to inspect the machine on its being landed, and if found in good order and condition, to take delivery for the Council. The cost of the machine is about £500, and authority has been given, contingent upon Alderman Sinclair's certificate, to hand over a cheque for the amount. Arrangements have also been made by the Council for a supply of road metal, the Government having granted the Corporation permission to take stone from the quarry reserve at Bundamba, and the railway authorities are to charge the Corporation 1s. 6d. per ton for its conveyance thence by rail and delivery in Brisbane. The stone is extensively used for ballasting the railway line, and if its quality for the purposes of road metal be as good as appearances or a hasty examination would indicate, the citizens of Brisbane will have just cause to complain on that score, we understand that its cost

delivered in Brisbane and broken ready for spreading on the streets, will be about five shillings a cubic yard, which is less than one-half of the exorbitant cost of laying down in Brisbane the metal from Lytton, under the contract that terminated some time since. Brisbane aldermen seem at last convinced of the false economy of using inferior metal at any price for the top covering of the streets.

1876 The Queenslander (Brisbane) Sat. 11 Nov. p.29
Enoggera Water [Reservoir].
It is understood that the Mayor of Brisbane has undertaken, at the request of the Municipal Council, to have samples of the Enoggera water submitted to microscopical examination and chemical analysis; but no plan seems to have been considered for getting the work done in a manner that will afford reliable data as to its actual quality, and for adopting the best means of preventing the contamination and impurities which now unquestionably make it unwholesome, if not positively injurious to health. It will be of little use taking samples at haphazard, without regard to locality or conditions that may affect the quality of the water. In Sydney, the city water supply has been tested by Professor Liversidge in a most thorough and painstaking fashion. Numerous samples were taken under his own personal supervision from the several reservoirs, at different depths and different times; and also from the mains, at certain hours and at various points, throughout the city, noting particularly those places where contamination appeared more than ordinarily probable. There is reason to believe that the Enoggera water, judging from tests applied some years' since, is naturally above the average purity, and contains a very small quantity of mineral or other deleterious substances. But no one who uses it, as drawn from the mains in Brisbane, will give it that character; and complaints of its bad color, smell, and taste are heard daily. We are informed that the barques Harmodius and Abbey Holme, now lying at Bright's wharf, filled their tanks on arrival in port with Enoggera water from the main at the junction of Eagle and Queen-streets, but it made the men ill, and its smell and taste were so offensive that it had to be got rid of. We mention this as a specimen of the complaints made respecting the water with which the inhabitants of this city are supplied at a great expense; and it must be acknowledged on all hands that the evil has been too long quietly submitted to without proper measures being tried to effect an improvement. We think that the Corporation, although not entrusted with the charge of the waterworks, have done right in deciding upon an examination being instituted; but it is evident that little good can come of their efforts, unless the work be done in the most unexceptionable manner. It would perhaps be advisable to communicate with Professor Liversidge, or some other analytical chemist of the highest standing available, and ascertain what steps had better be taken to have the water properly tested.

Abbey Holme and Eden Holme were at the port together that month until the latter departed on December 28.

1877 The Brisbane Courier Thurs. 18 Jan. p.2
The commission appointed to enquire into the navigation of the Northern entrance of Moreton Bay, met on Tuesday morning, and continued their sitting until a late hour in the afternoon, there being present -- Commander Heath (chairman), the Hon. W, G. Simpson, M.L.C., Lieutenant Connor, R.N., Mr. F. Beattie, M.L.A., and Captains Knight, Almond, and Brown. The witnesses examined were, Captain Bryce, of the Abbey Holme, and Captain Woods, of the Pilot Service. The commission meet again this morning at half-past ten o'clock.
Feb. 24 p.4

Abbey Holme, barque, for London, is at anchor off the Pilot Station.
Feb. 27 p.2
The Abbey Holme, barque, for London, after being windbound off the Pilot Station for some days, cleared Cape Moreton yesterday afternoon, at half-past 3 o'clock.
Feb. 28 p.2
The Abbey Holme, barque, for London, was in sight from Cape Moreton yesterday afternoon, beating off to the eastward.

1877 The Queenslander (Brisbane) Feb. 24 p.36
February 20: Abbey Holme, barque, 516 tons (Devitt and Moore's line), Captain T. (sic) Bryce, for London. No passengers. Exports: 1856 bales wool and skins, 500 cases meat, and 6 cases tortoiseshell.

1877 Lloyd's List Sat. 28 July col. 28
Abbey Holme, of Liverpool, Brisbane for London 11th July 37 N. 42 W.

1877 The Aberdeen Journal Mon. July 30 p.2
Spoken: Abbey Holme, from Brisbane for London, 134 days, all well, lat. 39 N., long. 41 W., July 14.

1877 Lloyd's List Tues. 31 July col. 4
Dover passed East: July 30: Abbeyholme (sic) (barq., of L'pool) for London—in tow of the Darling (tug).

1877 The Standard (London) Wed. 1 Aug. p.7
Deal and Gravesend: Arrivals: July 31: Abbey Holme, Brisbane. [Survey: London August.]

1877 The Brisbane Courier Thurs. 18 Jan. p.2
Arrivals at London: July 31: Abbey Holme, barque, 516 tons, Captain Bryce, from Brisbane February 26. Passage, 154 days. [That had been a long voyage.]

1877 The Times (London) Fri. 31 Aug. p.2
[Advert] *The New Zealand Shipping Company: Clipper Ships for N.Z.: Auckland – Abbey Holme Bryce.*

1877-8 [7th voyage]

1877 The Standard (London) Wed. 12 Sept. p.7
Sailings: Gravesend, Sept 11: Abbey Holme for Auckland.

1878 Evening Star (Auckland) (N.Z.) Sat. 12 Jan. p.2
Auckland: Arrivals: Jan. 11: Abbey Holme, barque, 51? tons, Captain Bryce, from London.
The barque Abbey Holme arrived from London this afternoon after a lengthy passage of 119 days. Captain Bryce, who is in command, has not been in Auckland, but visited Napier the year before last as commander of the barque John Norman. The following is the report of the passage which it will be seen has been of an uneventful description with the exception that one death occurred:-- Left the Downs on the 15th September. Passed the Lizard on the 17th, and sighted Madeira on the 25th. Had fine weather and fair winds for the first part of the voyage. Lost the N.E. trades in 12 N., and did not catch the S.E. trades until reaching 1? N., being baffled for 10 degrees by variables. Crossed the Equator on the 21st Oct. Carried the S.E. trades to 20 S. Sighted Trinidad on the 30th Oct., and Tristam (sic) D'Acunha on the 11th Nov. Crossed the Meridian of the Cape in 44. 38 S. on the 21st Nov. ran down the eastings on the parallels of 43. 44. to 46. S. Had the usual strong N.W. and S.W.

233

breezes. Sighted the Eddystone Rock off Tasmania on the 24th December. Thence to Three Kings had easterly winds and dirty weather. Sighted them on the 8th inst. Down the coast Southerly and S.W. winds. Arrived off the North Head this afternoon at 2 o'clock, and anchored at half-past three. *The Abbey Holme is a fine iron barque about 8 years old, built by Blumer and Sunderland. She comes to the agency of the New Zealand Shipping Company, and brings a valuable cargo, but no passengers. Walter Chancellor Bryant, the youngest apprentice, a lad between 17 and 18, died of consumption on 26th November.*
Jan. 16 p.2

The barque Abbey Holme was brought alongside the Queen-street Wharf yesterday afternoon. She will start to discharge her cargo immediately.
Jan. 30 p.3

The Regatta.

Merchant Ships' Gigs: Iron Queen, Smith 1. Loch Fleet, Robertson 2. May Queen, Tatchell 3. Lorraine, Gronsund; and Taupo, Carey; also started. There was considerable unpleasantness over this race. The foreign-going ships' captains declined to pull against the crews of the local steamers, alleging that neither they nor their boats came within the conditions ef (sic) the race. The Argyle and Rotomahana boats were consequently the only ones left in it, and the starter, in accordance with the rules of the regatta, declared it no race. Some time afterwards the Rowena's boat was sent out; but the starter having once pronounced the race void, declined to alter his decision. A special collection was made on the flagship for a race among the foreign-going ships' boats, and the race came off with the above result. The Abbey Holme boat really came in first, but she was disqualified because not entered on Saturday. The Loch Fleet boat led for the first half of the distance, but the Iron Queen was quickest at the turn, and came in a length behind the Abbey Holme boat, and 2 lengths ahead of the Loch Fleet. The May Queen crew, who finished third, rowed in a much shorter boat than their opponents, and would have shown up well had they not laboured under this disadvantage.
Feb. 5 p.2

The barque Abbey Holme cleared out to-day for Valparaiso in ballast. She is to sail early to-morrow morning.
Aug 1 p.2

The barque Abbey Holme has arrived at Valparaiso from this port after a passage of six weeks' duration.

1878 Lloyd's List Mon. 29 Apr. col. 21

Valparaiso: Arrived: Mar. 13: Abbey Holme, Bryce, Auckland N.Z.
May 27 col. 20

Valparaiso: Sailed: Apr. 1: Abbey Holme, Bryce, Iquique.
June 21 col.18

Iquique: Loading: May 1: Abbey Holme for the Channel.
July 18 col. 19

Iquique: Cleared: prev. to June 1: Abbey Holme, Channel.
Sept. 18 col. 7

Queenstown: Arrived: Sept. 17: Abbey Holme, Brice (sic), Mexillones (nitrate).
Sept. 24 col. 8

Queenstown: Sailed: prev. to Sept. 24 [Sept. 23]*: Abbey Holme, King's Lynn.*
Oct. 3 col. 10

Lynn: arrived: --------: Abbey Holme, Robinson, Iquique.
Dec. 7 col. 22

London Customs: Entered Outwards: Dec. 6: Bluff Harbour N.Z. Abbey Holme, Bryce, B, 516 EID [East India Dock] *Shaw, Saville.*

1878-80 [8th voyage]

Abbey Holme from London 09-12-1878: Bluff 10-04-1879: 122 days: Bryce: No passengers.

1879 The Southland Times (N.Z.) Fri. 11 Apr. p.2

Bluff Harbor: Arrived, April 10: Abbey Holme, Barque 515 tons, Bryce, from London.
The barque Abbey Holme, Captain Bryce, left London on the 7th December, dropped down to Gravesend, and took a quantity of powder and dynamite; and on the 9th was towed to the Foreland, where she landed the pilot and anchored. On the 10th, weighed and sailed with a light northerly wind. Passed Start Point on the 13th; and then was headed by strong winds and high seas for several days, when the wind veered, and held fair to Madeira, which was sighted on the 30th December. Then baffling winds set in for ten days, when she got the N.E. trade in latitude 10, and held it till the 18th January, then losing it in 4 north. Regular doldrum weather then set in— wind light and variable, and very heavy rains— until she crossed the equator on the 24th, and met the S.E. trade at the same time. The trade held till February 3, and died away in lat. 23 south, long. 33 west, after that light winds, chiefly from north, prevailed for 5 days; fresh westerly winds with heavy rains succeeded, then variable weather until the 22nd when a heavy S.W. gale set in during which the ship labored heavily, the gale blowing terrifically. This brought in the westerlies. The barque passed the Meridian off Greenwich 19th February; sighted Prince Edward's Island on March 2nd during a heavy fog, and Tasmania on April 9th. Experienced strong variable winds across the middle ground, and sighted the Solanders on the 8th, and had light weather in the Straits till arrival yesterday. She brings a full general cargo.

Apr. 21 p.2

The dynamite brought on Saturday by the Abbey Holme and transhipped into the cutter Rapid, was taken on board the Pioneer schooner, which left immediately for Dunedin. The Abbey Holme still remains at anchor in the north channel.

Apr. 22 p.2

It seems somewhat extraordinary that the Abbey Holme should be still lying in the North Channel without any steps having been taken to remove her powder and allow her to come alongside the wharf. This vessel arrived in port on the 10th inst., so that after making all due allowances for weather, &c., this delay must be considered excessive.

Apr. 24 p.2

Bluff Harbour: The last of the powder was discharged from the Abbey Holme yesterday morning and during the afternoon she hauled up alongside the wharf, and will begin discharging the rest of the cargo to-day.

May 16 p.2

The barque Abbey Holme has almost finished discharging her cargo, and only retains enough iron to ballast her until sufficient grain is taken in. She has been chartered to load grain for Sydney, and began taking in cargo yesterday.

May 29 p.2

The Abbey Holme was engaged yesterday forenoon in taking in cargo, the afternoon being spent in levelling ballast and preparing the after hold for the reception of cargo.

June 7 p.2

The Abbey Holme was busy yesterday bending sails and making preparations for her voyage.

June 10 p.2

The barque Abbey Holme left her berth at the wharf yesterday morning, and came to on anchor off the Point, the wind not being favourable.

June 11 p.2

The barque Abbey Holme cleared at the customs yesterday and will sail at day-light this morning.

June 27 p.2

The wharf clerk at Bluff ....records: Abbey Holme: 7644 sacks oat.

1879 The South Australian Advertiser (Adelaide) Thurs. 10 July p.4
Adelaide: Arrived: July 9: Abbey Holme, barque, 516 tons, W. Bryce, master, from Bluff Harbour, New Zealand, June 11. John Hart and Co., agents. No passengers.
Imports: Abbey Holme, from New Zealand: 7,700 bags oats.
The Abbey Holme, which was towed into harbour on Wednesday, has a cargo of oats from New Zealand. She made a fair passage, though some heavy weather was experienced. Bluff Harbour was left on June 11, and on the fifteenth day out the vessel passed through Bank's Straits, and had a continuation of bad weather as she headed to the westward. On Sunday night she reached in for the land, and almost weathered Cape Borda, but the wind headed the barque off, and she was in consequence obliged to enter the Gulf by way of Backstairs Passage. The vessel was pretty well weather-worn on arrival, and but for her name would hardly have been recognised as the trim barque which was here a few years back.

July 26 p.4
Sale of Oats. Messrs. E. E. Priestly & Co. offered at auction yesterday the entire cargo of New Zealand oats, ex Abbey Holme, and cleared nearly every line at from 2s. 8d. to 3s. 2½d. per bushel. There was a very large attendance of buyers, and spirited competition for each line offered. We cleared all but five lines at auction and privately, and the balance we are in treaty for. The following is a copy of the catalogue submitted, and the prices realized :— B1 and 2, 178 bags, 2s. 10d.; MD. 178 do., 3s. 0½ d.; H, 130 do., 2s. 11½ d. ; K over dash, 138 do, 2s. 8½ d.; 26, 259 do. 2s. 11¼d.; CT, 391 do, 2s. 10¼d.; Napdale, 1,708 do., 2s. 11¼d.; K, 190 do., 2s. 9d.; W, 298 do., 2s. 9¼d.; P, 80 do, 3s.; T, 56 do., 3s. 2d.; Two Spots, 1,096 do., 2s. 10¼d.; WY, 110 do., 2s. 8d.; MD, 30 do., 2s, 9d.; MCM, 198 do., 2s. 8¼d.; M, 85 do., 2s. 8d.; E, 68 do., 2s. 9d.; One Spot, 78 do., 2s. 8d.; S, 228 do, 2s. 8d. ; S, 222 do., 2s. 8d. : A. 299 do. 2s. 8d.

Aug. 6 p.4
Exodus: There was a general clear-out of vessels on Tuesday afternoon, as the steamtugs towed out the Niagara, Abbey Holme, Southern Belle, and Natal Queen, while the Louisa, under all plain sail, chased the towing fleet through the Narrows.

Aug. 8 p.4
Sailed: Aug. 7: Abbey Holme, barque, for Newcastle.

Aug 21 p.4
Newcastle: Arrived: Aug. 19: Abbey Holme, Port Adelaide.

1879 The Sydney Morning Herald Tues. 30 Nov. p.6
Newcastle: Departures: Sept 3: Abbey Holme for Callao (Peru) with 697 tons of coal.

1879 Lloyd's List Fri. 14 Nov. col. 23
Callao: Arrived: Nov. 6: Abbey Holme, Bryce, Australia.

1880 The Freeman's Journal Thurs. 24 June p.3
Queenstown: Arrived: June 23: Abby (sic) Holme, British, Bryce, Talcahuano, wheat.
July 1 p.7
Queenstown: Sailed: June 30: Abbey Holme, for Dunkirk.
Aug. 14 p.3
Queenstown: Arrived: Aug. 13: Abbey Holme, British, Bryce, Dunkirk, in ballast, for Workington, short of provisions.

[**MNL** 1880: Abbey Holme of Liverpool: Owner: Wilfrid Hine, Custom Ho. Bldgs., Maryport.]

1880-1 [9th voyage]

1880 The Liverpool Mercury Thurs. 4 Nov. p.7
Spoken: Abbey Holme: Oct. 29: 18 miles N.E. of Porto Santo. [Northern island of Madeiras]

1881 The South Australian Advertiser (Adelaide) Fri. 21 Jan. p.4
Adelaide: Arrived: Thursday, January 20: Abbey Holme, barque, 516 tons, Wm. Bryce: imports, 3,786 steel rails. No passengers.

The Abbey Holme, from Workington, has a full cargo of steel rails, and left there on October 6. She had a fresh easterly wind at starting, and passed the Tuskar on the 7th. She then had light winds, chiefly from S.W. and W.S.W., until nearing the region of the north-east trades, and on October 27 sighted and passed Porto Santo. The north-east trades were very light at first, but gradually increased in force, though they were entirely lost on November 11, when variables met in till the 14th. The south-east trades were tolerably brisk, and the line was crossed in 27* west, on November 16. On December 5 she sighted and passed Tristan d'Acunha, and on the 9th crossed the prime meridian. On the 14th of December she reached the meridian of the Cape of Good Hope, in 42* south, and on January 8 passed the meridian of the Leuwin, and concluded the passage against adverse wind.

Feb. 23 p.4
Cleared: Tuesday February 22: Abbey Holme, for United Kingdom: 6,273 bags wheat.
Feb. 24 p.4
At the Anchorage for United Kingdom.

1881 The Maryport Advertiser and Weekly News Fri. 1 July p.8
Abbey Holme, from Adelaide for Cork, 90 days, all well. May 27th: 19 S 1 W, by the Arundel Castle at St. Helena.

1881 The Standard (London) Wed. 27 July p.6
Queenstown: Arrivals: July 25: Abbey Holme, Adelaide.
[From Lloyd's List.] Abbey Holme, which has arrived at Queenstown, reports that on April 30 experienced a strong gale from N.W. A large sea broke aboard the after part of the ship, washing away the binnacle and ventilator, smashing the glass of the skylight and flooding the cabin to the depth of a foot, starting the top plate of the ship's side in the wake of the mizen chains and nearly washing the man at the wheel overboard.

1881 The Maryport Advertiser and Weekly News Fri. 5 Aug. p.7
Queenstown: Sailed: July 31: Abbey Holme, Bryce, for Honfleur.
Aug. 12 p.8
Honfleur: Arrived: Aug. 6: Abbey Holme, Bryce, from Queenstown.

1881 The Liverpool Mercury Mon. 29 Aug. p.7
Gravesend; Arrived: Aug. 28: Abby (sic) Holme, from Honfleur.

[Surveys: London in August and September.]

1881-2 [10th voyage]

1882 The South Australian Advertiser (Adelaide) Tues. 31 Jan. p.4
Arrived: Monday, January 30: Abbey Holme, barque, 516 tons, Wm. Bryce, from London October 22. D. and J. Flower, agents. No passenger.

The Abbey Holme was anchored in a very safe position in the outer roadstead during Sunday night, and after dawn on Monday the Triton, station cutter, headed out to her, put a pilot on board, and as soon as practicable the tug was on hand and the vessel towed into harbor. The master reports leaving London on October 22, Gravesend 23,

and Dungeness the same day at midnight. Easterly winds marked the commencement of the passage, and lasted down to 43* N., when there was a change to south and south-west until the north-east trades were met with on November 14 in 27* N. There were three days variables, and the southerly trades commenced in 60* 42' N. The line was crossed on November 25 in 25* W. and brisk trades terminated in 18* S. Trinidad was sighted on December 4, and on December 19 Tristan d' Acunha was sighted. The vessel passed the prime meridian on the 23rd, and the longitude of the Cape on the 28th. The Southern Ocean was crossed in 43* with occasional strong winds, and the meridian of Cape Leuwin was reached on January 22. On Saturday she made Cape Borda, and came to anchor on Monday morning early.
Mar. 13 p.4
Exports: Abbey Holme, for United Kingdom: 6,164 bags wheat. J Darling and Son.
Mar. 16. p.4
Sailed: March 15: Abbey Holme, barque for London.

1882 The Maryport Advertiser and Weekly News Fri. 18 Aug. p.4
Queenstown: Arrived: Aug. 14: Abbey Holme, Bryce, for orders, from Adelaide.
Aug. 25 p.4
Queenstown: Sailed: Aug. 21: Abbey Holme, for Rouen.
Sept. 1 p.8
Rouen: Arrived: Aug. 29: Abbey Holme, from Queenstown.
Sept. 29 p.8
Prawle Point: Passed: Sept. 22: Abbey Holme, for Liverpool.

1882 The Liverpool Mercury Fri. 29 Sept. p.6
Abbey Holme, from Havre, has not arrived at this port as before reported.

1882-3 [11ᵗʰ voyage]

[LR 1883: Abbey Holme. Bk, W. Bryce/ J.H. Rich, 516/492, Hine Bros, Liverpool AA1]

Liverpool Register: Master, Workington, 12-10-82 John Hoare Rich 22773

1882 The Maryport Advertiser and Weekly News Fri. 20 Oct. p.8
Abbey Holme, Rich, sailed from Workington for Port Augusta, on the 13ᵗʰ inst.
Dec. 15 p.8
Gallant Rescue by a Maryport Captain.
For some time considerable anxiety has been felt in Maryport with respect to the safety of the barque Abbey Holme, of this port. The vessel, which is owned by Messrs. Hine Brothers, of this town, sailed from Workington on the 13ᵗʰ of October, with a cargo of steel rails for Port Adelaide, South Australia. On the 8ᵗʰ of November a paragraph appeared in Lloyd's List headed "Abbey Holme," and stated that the head-board of a ship, with the name "Abbey Holme" on it, had washed ashore on Borth beach, four miles to the south of Aberdovey; also, that a quantity of small boards, forming part of a round-house, had been washed a shore at the same place, and that they appeared not to have been long in the water. In consequence of this paragraph the underwriters, and a great many persons who had friends on board the Abbey Holme, became very anxious, thinking probably that the vessel had collided with some other vessel, or that some other accident had happened to her. The owners, however, were very confident that the Abbey Holme was all right, and their confidence has been fully justified; for a Lloyd's telegram, dated Cape Town, 12ᵗʰ Dec., states "that the splendid iron four-masted ship, Shakespeare, 1,814 tons register, owned in Liverpool bound from Cardiff to Calcutta, with a valuable cargo, had run ashore on an inaccessible island [Inaccessible Island]—a reef of rocks in the South Atlantic Ocean—during a thick fog, and became a total wreck. The whole of the crew and passengers, 60 in number, were saved, and after spending several weeks on the island,

were taken off by the Abbey Holme, and landed at Simon's Bay on Tuesday." *As the master, Captain J.H. Rich, the mate, four seamen, and two apprentices on board the Abbey Holme, belong to Maryport, the news of her safety will be hailed with pleasure.*

1883 Sheffield and Rotherham Independent Sat. 13 Jan p.3
Shipwrecked Sailors left on an Island.
Information received from London states that the Shakespeare, of Liverpool: floundered, but the whole of the crew and several passengers who were on board got away safely in the boats and reached the neighbouring island of Tristan d'Acunha, where they remained for eight days, when their signals of distress were seen by the emigrant ship Abbey Holme, bound for New Zealand, which sent off and took the master and nine men on board, and landed them at the Cape of Good Hope. Twenty persons were left on the island, but assistance will be sent as soon as possible.

1883 The Glasgow Herald Wed. 17 Jan. p.8
The Shakespeare ran on a reef off Inaccessible Island, an uninhabited wooded rock, the most westerly of the group of Tristan d'Acunha. The vessel floated off, but was so damaged that she sank in deep water. All hands were saved in the ship's boats, and reached Tristan d'Acunha. Capt. Carrey considered the accident must have arisen from an error in his chronometers. The court of inquiry at the Cape considered he erred in proceeding in the fog when he was near land, and suspended his certificate for three months. The shipwrecked crew were conveyed to Simon's Bay by the Abeona (sic) of Liverpool, bound for Port Augusta.

1883 The Morning Post (London) Wed. 17 Jan. p.5
The remained of the crew of the Shakespeare (20 in number) wrecked recently on Inaccessible Island, were landed at Port Elizabeth on Christmas Day, having been brought from Tristan D'Acunha by the Norwegian schooner Spica.

1883 The South Australian Register (Adelaide) Mon. 22 Jan. p.4
Cape Borda: January 20, 9.30 a.m: Barque, Abbey Holme, passing inwards for Port Augusta, foretopgallantmast and jibboom gone.
Jan. 23 p.4
Port Augusta: January 20: barque in sight, supposed Abbey Holme.
Jan. 25 p.7
Port Augusta, January 24: The barque Abbey Holme from England, arrived this morning, having been detained twenty hours through running ashore. This is another case of non-compulsory pilotage. The captain, owing to the unsatisfactory state of pilot affairs, could not get a pilot.
Jan. 26 p.6
Marine Board: Accidents.--Grounding of the Abbey Holme near Port Pirie was reported. Captain Legge thought that accidents were increasing under the voluntary pilotage system. Other Wardens differed.
Supplement to the South Australian Register (Adelaide) Feb. 5 p.1S
The Pilotage Question: The Marine Board having visited Port Augusta [discussed] *the deleterious effect of the non-compulsory system of pilotage which obtains in the outports. ………………*
It was only last week that the Abbey Holme ran aground, but fortunately an unexpectedly high tide enabled her to get off. Had this fortunate circumstance not happened the cost of a steamtug, lightering, &c, would have been £250, and all caused through there not being a pilot, as the men had left because their certainty of finding an occupation was gone.
Feb. 9 p.4

Abbey Holme: Cargo: Railway material.
Feb. 15 p.7

Augusta. February 13. At the Police Court to-day, before Mr. Donaldson S.M., three foreign seamen named Rohdolf, Hysendorn, and Sergergier were charged with deserting from the barque Abbey Holme. Captain Rich applied to have the men imprisoned for safe keeping, but the Court had no power to do so, and made an order that they should forfeit two weeks' wages and pay 5s. costs.
Mar. 7 p.4 and 6.

Port Augusta: Sailed March 5: Abbey Holme, in ballast for New Zealand.

1883 Otago Daily Times Sat. 31 Mar. p.2

Port Chalmers: Arrivals: Abbey Holme, barque, 376 (sic) tons, Rich, from Port Augusta. Master, agent.

The barque Abbey Holme was towed into Port Chalmers and anchored in Mansford's Bay at 5 p.m. yesterday. The Abbey Holme comes in ballast from Port Augusta for orders. She is a handsome iron vessel of 516 tons register, and was built under special survey by Messrs J. Blumer and Co., of Sunderland, in 1869, for Messrs. Hine Brothers, of Liverpool, her class at Lloyd's being +AAI. She left Port Augusta on March 6th with southerly winds, which carried her down to Cape Borda on the 13th; thence she had S.E. winds for 24 hours, followed by westerly winds and fine weather until the 23rd inst., when a fierce S.W. gale and heavy sea was encountered. The gale continued for 48 hours, and she passed the Suares on the 25th inst.; thence she had westerly winds along the cost (sic), and arrived off Godley Head, Lytte ton (sic), on the 28th inst.; received orders to proceed to Otago; had S.E. winds, and passed Akaroa at 6 p.m. on the 29th, and thence had strong S.E. winds to arrival off Otago Heads at 2 p.m. yesterday.
Apr. 5 p.2

Will be berthed at the wharf to-day.
Apr. 6 p.2

Was shifted from the stream and berthed at the George street Pier yesterday.
Apr. 28 p.2

Has nearly completed her loading, and should be a full ship to-day.
May 1 p.2

Port Chalmers: Outwards: Abbey Holme, 376 (sic) tons, Rich, for Cork, with cargo. Neill Bros. agents. Has finished loading with 6500 bags wheat.
May 5 p.2

Port Chalmers: Departures: Abbey Holme, barque, 376 tons (sic), Rich, for Cork, was towed to sea yesterday forenoon by the s.s. Plucky, and sailed.

1883 The Maryport Advertiser and Weekly News Fri. 6 July p.6

Dunedin (N.Z.): Sailed: Apr. 30 (sic): Abbey Holme, Rich, for Cork.
Aug. 17 p.8

Falmouth: Arrived: Aug. 15: Abbey Holme, Rich, (for orders) from Lyttelton New Zealand.
Aug. 24 p.8

Falmouth: Sailed: Aug. 20: Abbey Holme, Rich, for London.

1883 The Argus (Melbourne) Wed. 3 Oct. p.8

In cargoes arrived at ports of call there has been a good continental demand for New Zealand during last week, but this is now apparently satisfied, and many of the later arrivals are in such doubtful condition that they will probably have to be ordered round unsold to London or Hull. Abbey Holme [has] been ordered round unsold to London.

1883 The Liverpool Mercury Mon. 27 Aug. p.3

Gravesend: Arrived: Aug 25: Abbey Holme, from Port Chalmers.

1883 The Standard (London) Thurs. 30 Aug. p.1
[Advert] *Devitt & Moore's Australian Line of Clipper Ships: Launceston: Abbey Holme: J.H. Rich: Sept. 28.*

1883-4 [12th voyage]

1884 The Mercury (Hobart, Tasmania) Sat. 5 Jan. p.2
Launceston: Tamar Heads: Inward: January 4: 7.15 a.m. Abbey Holme, barque.
Captain J. H. Rich, of the barque Abbey Home, reports having left London on October 1; passed Dover next day, and Point Lizard on the 7th; had strong N.W. winds down the Channel, and fresh winds from N.N.E. to S.W. across the Bay of Biscay; passed Madeira on October 15; got trades in 34deg. N., and carried fresh trades to 7deg. 53min. N., and from this to 2deg, 15min. had light variable winds and calms; crossed the equator on November 9, and got S.E. trades in 2deg. 15min, N., and carried fresh trades to 28deg. S., and afterwards fresh west winds. Passed Inaccessible Island on November 28, with strong westerly wind blowing. When in lat. 51deg. S., and long 5deg. 47min. W., met with a very heavy gale, blowing with hurricane force from N.E. to N.W. Barometer down to 28'45. This lasted about eight hours, and there then blew a steady gale from W. for the next 24 hours. Ran easting down in lat. 42deg, and 43deg. S., and carried strong westerly winds. Met with southern gales, with very heavy sea, and carried the same to long. 136deg. E. From this to King's Island, which was passed on the 2nd of January, had moderate winds and fine weather, and had strong W.S.W. winds and squally weather to port. Arrived off Port Dalrymple at 5 a.m. on 4th ; received Pilot on board at 7 a.m., anchored in West Bank at 8 a.m., and left again at 10 a.m., arriving at bar at 4 p.m. Spoke to barque Ellen Douglas in lat. 4'49deg. S., and 27deg. 18min. W., from New York to Balpwargen, 45 days out. *The Abbey Home is an iron vessel of 516 tons, and is owned by Hine Bros, of Maryport, England. She is 14 years old, and was built at Sunderland in England, by John Blumer and Co. She is a splendid sea boat, and has formerly been trading to the Australian Colonies. The vessel is consigned to Mr. Samuel Tulloch, and will haul alongside the wharf to-morrow.*
Jan. 19 p.3
Launceston from our own correspondent -- Friday
An incident occurred this morning upon the wharf. Whilst some cases of ale were being unloaded out of the barque Abbey Holme, six of them slipped out of the sling and fell into the water. A number of thirsty souls at once assembled on the wharf and bank, no doubt contemplating something light, but, unluckily for them, the cases were, with the aid of a few willing hands and a boathook, recovered undamaged.
Jan. 30 p.2
The barque Abbey Holme will leave in ballast for Port Pirie about Saturday next, where she will take in a general cargo for London.
Feb. 11 p.2
The barque Abbey Holme bound for Port Pirie, passed through Tamar Heads at 4.47 p.m. on the 9th inst.

1884 The South Australian Register (Adelaide) Fri. 15 Feb. p.4
Cape Borda. Feb. 14, 10.15 a. m.--Barque Abbey Holme, of Liverpool, from Launceston, bound for Spencer's Gulf—reports fine voyage. Wind, S.E., fresh, sea moderate.
Feb. 19 p.4
Port Pirie: Arrived: Feb. 16: Abbey Holme, Tasmania
Mar. 10 p.6
Port Pirie: March 9: The barque Abbey Holme has taken in a full cargo at Cave's Wharf, and is the first vessel of any size that has done so.
Mar. 19 p.4

Port Pirie: Sailed: March 17: Abbey Holme, United Kingdom.
Mar. 24 p.5
Wheat Shipments: Abbey Holme, 6402 bags. Cave & Co.
Supplement to the South Australian Register Sept. 13 p.1S
The grain trade: wheat: The Abbey Holme at 39s. 3d. (less ½ per cent), for Lowestoft.

1884 Adair's Maryport Advertiser Fri. 11 July p.8
Falmouth: Arrived: July 9: Abbey Holme, Rich, (for orders) from Port Pirie.

1884 The Liverpool Mercury Tues. 29 July p.7
Falmouth: Sailed: July 28: Abbey Holme for Lowestoft.

1884 Adair's Maryport Advertiser Fri. 1 Aug. p.5
Lowestoft: Arrived: July 31: Abbey Holme, Rich, from Port Pirie, via Falmouth.
Aug. 15 p.8
Lowestoft: Sailed: Aug. 14: Abbey Holme, Rich, for London.
Aug. 22 p.8
London: Arrived: Aug. 15: Abbey Holme, Rich, from Lowestoft..

1884 The Standard (London) Wed. 20 Aug. p.7
London Dock: Arrived: Abbey Holme, from dry dock.

1884-5 [13th voyage]

1884 The Morning Post (London) Fri. 26 Sept. p.8
Deal, Sept. 25: Passed: Abbey Holme, Fremantle and Champion Bay.

1884 The West Australian (Perth) Sat. 4 Oct. p.2
Weekly Commercial Report: Perth: Oct 4th: Prices: Cement is still scare, but in the Abbey Holme, which cleared from London on 23d September and is due here about Christmas there are 200 casks. On board there are also about 20 tons galvanized iron, which ought to come to a good market, as stocks by that time will probably be much lower.
Dec. 27 p.3
Perth: Arrivals: Dec. 23: Abbey Holme, barque, Rich, from London. Passengers: Mr. and Mrs. Carter, T. Anderson, Elizabeth Bates, Wm. Bates, C. Mortimer, Elizabeth Mortimer, Mary Markham and Alice Markham.
Dec. 30 p.2
The Abbey Holme, with a good supply of general merchandise is now discharging.
1885 Jan. 1 p.2
Gage's Road: Abbey Holme discharging.
Jan. 17 p.4
For Freight or Charter. The Al Iron Clipper Barque Abbey Holme, 516 tons, Capt. J. H. Rich, is open for employment. Apply to Geo. Shenton, Agent. Fremantle, Jany. 10th, 1885.
Jan. 24 p.5
The barque Abbey Holme is about to proceed to Champion Bay to complete discharging.
Jan. 27 p.3
Departures: Jan. 24: Abbey Holme, barque, Rick (sic), for Champion Bay.

1885 South Australian Register (Adelaide) Fri. 13 Mar. p.4
Port Germein: Arrived: March 11: Abbey Holme, Western Australia.
Mar 26 p.6
Port Germein, March 25: The barque Abbey Holme, which arrived at this port last week, has completed taking in a full cargo at the jetty end, consisting of 6,550 bags or wheat. Captain Rich is satisfied with the dispatch, and would not hesitate to load here again.
Apr. 11 p.3S

Port Germein: Sailed: March 29: Abbey Holme, for the United Kingdom.

1885 The Freeman's Journal (Dublin) Tues. 18 Aug. p.3
Queenstown: Arrived: Aug. 17: Abbey Holme, 518, British, Roche (sic), Port Germein, wheat.
Aug. 31 p.3
Queenstown: Sailed: Aug. 30: Abbey Holme, for Newry.

1885 South Australian Register (Adelaide) Sat. Oct. 10 p.4
Newry: Arrivals: Sept.2: Abbey Holme, from Port Pirie.
In Australian wheat cargoes: Brier Holme has been sold at 34s. per 480lb. for Dublin, the Eden Holme at 33s. 4 ¼d for Fleetwood, Abbey Holme at 34s 1¼d for Newry.

1885 The Freeman's Journal (Dublin) Mon. 21 Sept. p.3
Newry: Sailed: Sept. 19: Abbey Holme, of Liverpool, Rich, master, to London, with ballast.

1885 The Liverpool Mercury Thurs. 24 Sept. p.3
Dungeness, passed: Sept. 23: Abbey Holme, from Adelaide.
Sept. 25 p.7
Deal: passed: Sept. 24: Abbey Holme, from Adelaide.

1885 The Standard (London) Wed. 30 Sept. p.6
East India Dock: Arrived: Abbey Holme, from dry dock to load for Hobart
Oct. 12 p.1
[Advert] Devitt and Moore's Australian Line: Hobart: Abbey Holme: J.H. Rich: E.I., Oct 31.

1885-6 [14th voyage] [Survey; London in November.]

1885 The Times (London) Fri. 6 Nov. p.12
The London Docks: Departures: East India Dock: Abbey Holme: Hobart.

At Hobart "The Mercury" (1886) featured several pieces about the Abbey Holme.
1886 Feb. 5 p.2
The defences. A quantity of ammunition is on the way by the barque Abbey Holme from England, for defence purposes. It includes 1,000 lb. gunpowder for the B.G.L. service guns, 50 lbs. for the R.F.G. service do. And 25 lbs. P. shell. These are expected to arrive in a very short time in the colony and will no doubt add to the effectiveness of our defence.
Feb. 9. p.2
Hobart: Arrived: Feb. 8: Abbey Holme, barque, 516 tons, J. H. Rich from London.
Passengers – Saloon: Mrs. Rich and son.
The barque Abbey Holme, from London, dropped anchor in the stream at 5 p.m. yesterday, after a passage of 94 days from Gravesend. The Abbey Holme is a smart beamy looking iron barque, of 516 tons register, and was built in 1869. She is owned by Messrs. Hine Bros., of Maryport, but her port of registry is Liverpool. This is the barque's first appearance in these waters, but about three years since she was at Launceston, to which place she brought a large cargo. The voyage has been rather a lengthy one for such a first-class vessel, but this is attributable to adverse weather and several heavy gales met with during the voyage. On November 17, when off Madeira, a sad accident, which threw a gloom over the whole of the ship's company, happened. On this date William Swift, a fine strapping young fellow, of l8 years of age, an apprentice on board of the vessel, was engaged on the top gallant forecastle doing some necessary work. At this time it was blowing a heavy gale from the W.S.W., with a very high sea running, and

the vessel at the time giving a heavy lurch to windward, Swift lost his hold, tumbled across the guard chain, and fell overboard. The helm was at once put hard down, the main yard laid aback, and as Swift was passing the weather quarter a life-buoy was thrown him, but he did not succeed in grasping it. He, however, buffeted bravely with the seas, and got hold of the patent log line which was trailing out over the weather quarter. The vessel by this time had stopped going through the water, and some of the crew commenced, to haul on the log-line until Swift was well under the stern of the vessel. At this juncture the second officer, Mr. Mathewson, and an A.B. named George Lestrup thought they would be able to get a rope round the lad if lowered over the stern. This they succeeded in doing, but owing to the vessel plunging heavily, the rope got entangled and slipped off the boy's body. Ineffectual efforts were made to get it round him again but the poor fellow owing to having heavy oilskins and sea boots on, soon lost his strength and let go the log line and drifted astern, but still grimly trying to keep himself afloat by swimming. One of the hands was at once sent aloft to watch him, and the second officer and the other man were then got on board in a very exhausted state. One of the ship's boats was then got out as speedily as possible, and pulled away in the direction the buoy was last seen. After an absence of about an hour and a half they returned, and stated that they had seen nothing of Swift or the life buoy. When the boat was sufficiently near the vessel a line was thrown to the men, which they caught, but on getting alongside the barque gave a tremendous heavy roll to leeward, which completely filled the boat, and with the heavy surge the painter carried away, and as the boat drifted astern lines were thrown the crew, and it was with great difficulty they were hauled on board. The boat in the meantime got under the lee quarter, capsized, drifted rapidly astern, and was lost with the whole of her gear. Feeling confident that everything had been done to save the poor lad's life, and seeing that it was useless to make any further efforts in the face of the heavy weather, the vessel was once more put on her voyage. The young fellow was a general favourite, and considered as one of the smartest seamen on board. Only recently he lost his father, who was drowned at sea off the coast of England, and he leaves a widowed mother to mourn his loss. The following is the log account of the voyage:- Hauled out of the East India Docks on November 5, 1885, and at 3.30 p.m. same day arrived at Gravesend, where 17 tons of gunpowder was taken on board. Left again at 7 a.m. on November 6, and at 9 p.m. discharged steam-tug off Dungeness. At 2 p.m. on November 7 arrived off Beachy Head, when the wind came in from the eastward, and a fair run was made down the English Channel, but as the weather was hazy saw no land. Had fair winds and fine weather across the Bay of Biscay and to lat. 37 N., and long, 18 W., when the wind came from the W.S.W. and S.W., and increased to a gale with a high sea. Carried this to lat. 33 N., and 10 W., where the accident William Swift occurred. The wind keeping westerly passed to the eastward of Madeira, and carried westerly winds and fine weather to Palma, Canary Islands, which were passed on November 20. The same winds held to 25½ N. long. 20 W., when the N.E. trades were picked up. Had fresh north-easterly winds and fine weather to San Antonio Cape, De Verde Islands, which were breasted on November 26. Fresh N.E. trades were carried to 6deg. N. lat, when the wind shifted to the S.E. Crossed the Equator in long. 28 W. 29 days out. To lat. 30 S. long 33 W., had moderate S.E. trades. Sighted Tristan's Island on Christmas Day. From thence had westerly winds and high seas till passing Cape Leeuwin. From thence till sighting the S.W. Cape had heavy westerly gales and mountainous sea. Passed the S.W. Cape at 10 a.m. on 7th inst., and at 9 a.m. yesterday received the pilot on board and arrived in the cove as above."
The barque has under the poop deck a very spacious cabin nicely fitted up, some of the state rooms being very spacious. The barque is fitted with a full number of boats, and is a first class ship in all respects. The Abbey Holme has 17 tons of gunpowder on board

for the Government and about 1,300 tons of general merchandise. She is commanded by Captain John H. Rich, who has with him as first and second officers respectively, Mr. Swinbourne and Mr. G. Mathewson. The barque is consigned to Messrs. W, Crosby and Co.

Feb. 10 p.2

The cove yesterday presented a lively appearance owing to the numerous vessels anchored in it, viz., the Shaw Savill and Co's fine steamer Arawa, H.M. ships Nelson, Miranda, Raven, and Swinger, whilst farther out lay the fine iron clipper barques Countess of Rothes and Abbey Holme. It is many years since the cove had such a fine number of vessels lying in it, a fact which was pretty freely commented on during the day.

The barque Abbey Holme discharged her gunpowder yesterday in splendid condition, and afterwards was towed to a berth at the New Wharf. She will break bulk, to-day.

Feb. 11 p.2

Captain Rich, of the barque Abbey Holme, which arrived here on Monday last from London, reports that on running the easting down between 45 deg. and 46 deg. S. lat., he saw no ice, which is rather an unusual thing in these latitudes. On the 16th January the ship Windsor Castle passed the Abbey Holme bound to the eastward.

Mar. 9 p.2

A Horse Drowned.--About 11 o'clock yesterday morning a horse and dray, belonging to Mr. James Elliot, carter, was loading fruit from the establishment of Messrs. Johnson Bros., New Wharf. After about 20 cases had been packed on the dray the horse was startled by some object, and at once bolted at a mad pace across the New Wharf. On reaching the corner where the barque Abbey Holme is berthed the frightened animal leaped sheer over the wharf, its head striking the bow of the barque, and before assistance could be procured it was drowned. The whole of the fruit, with the exception of one case, was recovered. The owner, who is a steady, industrious man, was offered £40 for the animal only a few days since, and much sympathy is expressed with him on his loss.

Mar. 16 p.2

City Police Court. Charles Hogherson, seaman, pleaded guilty to having behaved in a disorderly manner on board the Abbey Holme on Saturday [13th], and was fined 10s. 6d., with the option of 14 days in prison.

Mar. 19 p.2

Sailed: March 18: Abbey Holme, barque, 516 tons, J. Rich, for South America, in ballast.

Mar. 20 p.2

City Police Court. George Lestrup and Carl Jensen, accused of having deserted from the barque, Abbey Holme, was discharged, as the vessel had sailed and there was no one to prosecute.

1886 Maryport and Workington Advertiser Fri. 7 May p.8

Talcahuano: Arrived: May 3: The Abbey Holme, Rich, from Hobart Town.

1886 The Freeman's Journal (Dublin) Wed. 6 Oct. p.6

Queenstown: Arrived: Oct 5: Abbey Holme, British, 516, Ritch (sic), San Antonio, wheat.

14 Oct. p.3

Queenstown: Sailed: Oct. 13: Abbey Holme, Stockton-on-Tees.

1886 The North-Eastern Daily Gazette (Middlesbrough) Second Edition Tues. 26 Oct.

Middlesbrough: Arrived: Oct. 25: Abbey Holme, Rich: Imports, San Antonina (sic) 14,400 cwts. wheat.

Nov 13

Stockton: Sailings: Nov 11: Abbey Holme, Rich, London, light.

1886 The Standard (London) Mon. 15 Nov. p.6
Gravesend: Arrival: Nov 14: Abbey Holme, Stockton.   [Survey: London in December.]

1886-7 [15th voyage]

1887 The Dundee Courier and Argus Sat. 8 Jan.
Spoken: Abbey Holme, steering south, Jan 2 49 N., 28 W.

1887 The Mercury (Hobart, Tasmania) Tues. 5 Apr. p.2
Hobart: Arrived: Apr. 4: The stout wooden barque Abbey Holme made her second appearance in our waters at an early hour yesterday morning, and dropped anchor off Macquarie Point after an uneventful passage of 101 days from Gravesend, and 94 days from leaving her anchorage in the Downs. The voyage out has been fairly fine, only the average amount of bad weather being encountered. The vessel sailed from the London Docks at 10 a.m. on December 23. Arrived at Gravesend the same afternoon, and took on board a quantity of gunpowder for the Tasmanian Government. Left Gravesend at 7 a.m. on the 24th., and anchored in the Downs the same day, but owing to the prevailing westerly winds and bad weather, could not leave until the night of the 29th December. Start Point and the Lizard were abeam on the 31st, with easterly winds and fine, weather, crossing the Bay of Biscay the barque had principally north-westerly winds and fine weather which held until reaching the Madeiras on January 9th. That land of the vine was run out of sight next day and north to north easterly winds carried the ship to San Antonio, off Cape De Verde, which was made and passed on January 17th. Light and variable winds with fine weather but little rain succeeded to the Equator, which was crossed on January 29th in long. 24deg. W.; thence to 25deg. S. south-east breezes and moderately fine weather were met with. Moderate N.W. to S.W. winds accompanied the barque to Prince Edward Islands, which were passed on 5th ult. From this point to sighting the South-West Cape of Tasmania on the 1st inst., had N.W. to S.W. winds, increasing at times into a whole gale, with high and confused seas. Light variable winds with occasional foggy weather, accompanied often with heavy rains, succeeded until passing the South-West Cape, when a heavy gale, with terrific squalls, stopped further progress. On Sunday afternoon the wind lulled a little, and shifted a point or two to the southward. A pilot was taken on board at 6 p.m. the same evening, and she finally came to an anchor about 1 a.m. yesterday. The barque has on board a full cargo of merchandise for this port, including a quantity of gunpowder, which she discharged at the powder jetties in the Domain yesterday, and will berth at the Wharf this morning.
May 11 p.2
The crew of the barque Abbey Holme was engaged in bending sails yesterday. The barque will leave for Tolcahuano (sic) either to-day or to-morrow.
May 12 p.2
The barque Abbey Holme hauled into the stream yesterday afternoon. Capt. Rich expects to get away for Chili to-morrow.
May 16 p.2
Sailed: May 15th: Abbey Holme, barque, 516 tons, J. Rich, for Tolcahuano (sic), South America, in ballast.

1887 The Liverpool Mercury Mon. 12 Dec. p.3
Falmouth: Arrived: Dec 10: Abbey Holme, from Iquique.
Dec. 16 p.3
Falmouth: Sailed: Dec. 15: Abbey Holme, for London.

1887 The Daily News (London) Mon. 19 Dec. p.2

London, Victoria Dock: Arrivals: Dec. 17: Abbey Holm (sic), Iquique.
Dec. 20 p.6
Entered Inwards: London Custom House: Abbey Holme, Iquique, R.V.D. [Royal Victoria Dock], *Hine Bros. and Willis.* [Survey: London in January 1888.]

1888-9 [16th voyage]

1888 The Standard (London) Sat. 11 Feb. p.6
Gravesend: Sailing: Feb. 10: Abbey Holme, Nelson N.Z.

1888 The Evening Post (N.Z.) Wed. 4 Apr. p.2
The barque Abbey Holme, of Maryport (sic), Rich, bound from London to Nelson, N.Z., put into Dover on 15th February, having lost anchor and 15 fathoms chain, and broken hawspipe.

1888 At Nelson Port (N.Z.) the "The Nelson Evening Mail" reported several times.
Apr. 6 p.2
The barque Abbey Holme left London for this port on February 21, and may be looked at the end of May. She is a small vessel, and when she left the East India Dock was drawing 14ft 8in forward and 14ft 9in aft.
May 25 p.2
The Financial Statement, which on the present occasion is looked forward to with more than ordinary interest, is to be delivered on Tuesday n xt (sic). The Nelson consignees by the barque Abbey Holme, now 100 days out from London, are keeping an anxious eye on the signal staff, as her arrival before the delivery of the budget speech and the alterations in the tariff which are expected, will probably mean a saving of some hundreds of pounds to them.
May 31 p.2
There are as yet no signs of the barque Abbey Holme now 103 days out from London to this port. She is a small vessel of the 500 tons register, and therefore would not make the passage as quickly as a larger one moreover at this time of the year it is generally difficult for a sailing vessel to travel along the coast at any speed owing to the light and baffling winds which prevail, but if the Abbey Holme has had anything like moderate weather she cannot be far away, and therefore may be looked for any day.
June 8
This barque was in sight at at (sic) early hour this morning, but owing to light winds she did not make much progress during the day, and will not reach the outer anchorage before dusk. She has made rather a long passage of 110 days. The Abbey Holme, brings a general cargo, including 500 cases of dynamite for Messrs. Wilkins & Field, which will be placed in their magazine on the Boulder Bank. She will probably be towed into harbor to-morrow morning.

{http://freepages.genealogy.rootsweb.ancestry.com/~shipstonz/nelson2.html}
Abbey Holme from London 20-02-1888: Nelson 09-06-1888: 110 days: J.H. Rich: Voy. 3: No passengers.

1888 The Colonist Nelson (N.Z) Mon. 11 June p.3
The barque Abbey Holme, of Liverpool, Captain John H. Rich, was towed into harbor yesterday morning, and berthed alongside the Railway wharf. She left the East Indian decks, London, on the 10th February, but anchored in the Downs till the 12th, awaiting a favorable wind. Having weighed anchor she proceeded as far as Dungeness, when the weather became so threatening that she put back to the Downs, and it was blowing a heavy s.s.w. gale with terrific hail and sleet squalls when she again dropped anchor. By

the 14th the weather had sufficiently moderated to warrant another start, but it was found that her anchor had got foul of something, and with the heavy pitching of the ship the starboard chain carried away, and the hawse pipe got broken. On the 15th she proceeded to Dover harbor, where a new anchor and fifteen fathoms of chain and hawse pipe were obtained, and she again set sail on the 18th. The vessel passed the Lizards just before midnight on the 19th, a gale from the N.E. then blowing with heavy snow squalls, but she had fair winds and fine weather across the Bay of Biscay. S.E. gales and high seas were then encountered for four days, but with fine weather and fresh N.E. winds she passed San Antonio (Cape de Verd Islands) on the 8th March. The Equator was crossed on the 15th March, in longitude 27 west, 26 days from Dover, but the fresh trade winds being well southerly she made rather a bad course, being carried a long way to the westward. The S.E. trades were lost in latitude 30 S., and from there fresh winds from N.E. to N.W. carried the vessel past Inaccessible Island, which was sighted on the 7th April. For six days before reaching the meridian of the Cape heavy squalls with a mountainous sea were experienced, and the meridian of the Cape was passed on the 23rd April. Fresh westerly winds, with occasional gales and high seas, were then encountered until the South coast of Tasmania was passed on the 25th May, the vessel running her easting between 43 and 44 degrees South. Light to moderate winds with fine weather prevailed till in latitude 41 S. and longitude 170 E., when moderate westerly winds favored her course till land was made to the S.W. of Cape Farewell, when the wind increased and the sea rose. The Spit light was passed at 7 a.m. on June 7, when light and variable winds from the South, varied with occasional squalls, retarded her arrival. The Nelson Lighthouse was made at 5 p.m. on the 8th, and the pilot boarded the vessel next morning. No ice was seen during the voyage, and not a vessel of any kind was sighted from the Cape of Good Hope till the vessel had arrived in Tasman Bay.

1888 The Nelson Evening Mail (N.Z.) Mon. 18 June p.2
At the Police Court to-day a Russian with an unpronounceable name, a seaman on board the barque Abbey Holme, was charged with assaulting Constable Phair at the Port and a man who went to his assistance, and with misconducting (sic) himself generally. He was sentenced to a month's imprisonment with hard labor.
July 6
The Abbey Holme has finished ballasting, and will be towed to the outer anchorage by the Charles Edward to-night.
July 7
The Abbey Holme was towed to the outer anchorage by the Charles Edward last night. While in harbor advantage was taken of the fine weather to clean and paint her, with the result that she presented quite a different appearance to what she did on her arrival, when she was covered with barnacles and grass. Captain Rich will not therefore now require to dock his vessel at Lyttelton. The Abbey Holme will probably sail to-night.
July 13
Sailed: July 12, barque, Abbey Holme, 500, Rich, for Lyttelton, last night. She loads there with grain for London.

1888 The Star (N.Z.) Mon. 16 July p.2
Lyttelton: The barque Abbey Holme, which sailed from Nelson on July 5 for this port, was at anchor off Nelson harbour on July 11, the weather being then unfavourable for her to proceed on her voyage.
13 Aug.
The inclemency of the weather during the past week has greatly interrupted the working of perishable cargo. The barque Abbey Holme, would probably have been a full ship ere

this but for the rain. If the weather improves, to-morrow afternoon should see the Abbey Holme ready for sea.
18 Aug.
Lyttelton: Sailed 17— Abbey Holme, barque. 516 tons. Rich: [she] *was towed to sea yesterday morning with a cargo of produce on board loaded by the New Zealand Shipping Company. She is bound for London direct.*

1889 The Standard (London) Tues. 8 Jan. p.6
Gravesend: Arrivals: Jan.7: Abbey Holme, Lyttelton, N.Z.
Jan. 9 p.6
South West India Dock: Arrived: Abbey Holme, from Lyttelton, N.Z.
Jan. 21 p.6
South West India Dock: Left: Abbey Holme, for dry dock.

1889-90 [**Fl corr**. 17th voyage]

1889 The South Australian Register (Adelaide) Wed. 22 May p.4
Port Adelaide: Arrived: Tuesday, May 21: Abbey Holme, barque, 516 tons, John H. Rich, master, from London: General Cargo.
The Abbey Holme is one of a line of vessels which for a long course of years visited this port, and being a well-built craft usually commanded home freights. The vessel, which returned on Tuesday morning, is a fine barque, and has made a fair passage, and on reaching the Bell Buoy on Tuesday morning was taken in charge by Pilot Walsh, and at once made signal for steamtug, which towed her to the magazine ground, where some combustibles were to be discharged. The master is a good old specimen of a British shipmaster, who has had a long colonial experience, having been a frequent visitor to Sydney, Melbourne, and Pirie, but he was never here before. He reports leaving London on January 30, but through bad weather was compelled to come to in the Downs, when he slipped his cable and proceeded down channel with strong winds and coarse weather. After clearing the land had a fine passage over the Bay of Biscay, and such favourable weather on the southern route that on February 26 sighted the island of Saint Antonio and fell in with good north-east trades which lasted to 21½° north, when south and south-east winds set in. Crossed the Equator on March 8, in 28° 26', and carried fresh south-east winds to 17* south, when north and north-east winds prevailed to 27*, when south-east and southerly winds supervened to 36* south. Crossed the prime meridian on April 11, and the Cape of Good Hope in 43* S. on April 16. Then had strong breezes and heavy seas during the passage of the Indian Ocean, which, however, did no serious damage. After passing the meridan (sic) of Cape Leuwin on May 9 some very light winds and variables prevailed till the 15th, when strong westerly gales set in, and so continued till making Cape Borda.
June 13 p.4
Sailed, June 12: Abbey Holme, Barque, for Newcastle.

1889 The Sydney Morning Herald Thurs. 20 June, p.6
Newcastle: Arrival: June 19: Abbey Holme from Adelaide.
July 18 p.3
Port of Newcastle: Cargos despatched: July 6: Abbey Holme for Valparaiso with 736 tons coals.

1889 Maryport Advertiser Fri. 9 Aug. p.2
Sale by Private Treaty: Iron Barque "Abbey Holme" of Liverpool: Gross Tonnage, 534, Net, 515, Built in 1869: For Sale, by Private Treaty, by order of the Administors of the

late Robert Hine, of Umballa, Bengal, India, Esquire, deceased, 4-64th shares of the above vessel: Maryport, 30th July 1889.
Aug. 30 p.3
Valparaiso: At: Abbey Holme, barque, from Newcastle N.S.W.

[Fl corr. Newcastle (N.S.W.) July 6 – Aug 25 Valparaiso Sep 27 -- ??? Pisagua Oct 29 –]

1890 The Scotsman Mon. 3 Mar. p.4
Queenstown: Arrived: Mar. 1: Abbey Holme, from Pisagua (nitrate).

1890 The Standard (London) Tues. 4 Mar. p.6
Queenstown: Sailings: Mar. 3: Abbey Holme, Leith.

1890 The Scotsman Sat. 15 Mar. p.7
Leith: Arrived: Mar. 13: Abbey Holme, 516, Rich, from Pisagua, nitrate of soda.
Apr. 9 p.5
Leith: Sailed: Apr. 7: Abbeyholme (sic), 516, Rich, for Middlesborough, light.
[Survey (fifth survey) in Leith in April.]

1890 The North-Eastern Daily Gazette (Middlesbrough) Wed. 9 Apr. Second Edition
The Gale: Wreck off South Shields. A Schooner's Narrow Escape.
Shortly before the Abbey Holme struck on the South Pier yesterday afternoon a schooner which was making for the Tyne under sail was observed to be drifting into a dangerous position. The coastguardsmen and a few brigadesmen who happened to be on the pier, seeing the condition of affairs, took the precaution to run the rocket van, containing the life-saving apparatus, along towards the eastern extremity of the structure. A steamtug, however, got the vessel in tow, and took her safely into the harbour. The sea was running very high, and breaking with great force over the Tyne piers. At times the mammoth crane on the Tynemouth Pier was totally obscured from view by the white clouds of spray which went over it. The gale continued to prevail last evening, and vessels making for the Tyne were severely buffeted in entering the harbour.

1890 The Maryport Advertiser Fri. 11 Apr.
Wreck of a Maryport Barque: Gallant Rescue of the Crew.
The weather on the coast on Tuesday at South Shields was cold and stormy, and with strong gales from the north-east, a high sea prevailed. In the afternoon the alarm gun was fired, and thousands of people made their way to the seaside to ascertain the cause. It was seen that a large vessel had struck on the north side of the South Pier, and was bumping heavily upon the rock, the sea at the same time making a clear breach over her. The brigadesmen were soon upon the scene, and lifeboats were also dispatched from North and South Shields. The South Shields brigadesmen threw rocket lines from the pier, and by this means communication was established with the stranded vessel. The first person to be landed by the breeches buoy was the captain's wife, a stout elderly woman. She was in a very prostrate condition and was assisted along to the Watch House and there carefully attended to Dr. Crease, the honorary surgeon of the brigade, was already at the place, and under his direction the poor woman gradually recovered from the shock which she had sustained. In the meantime the rest of the hands on board, consisting of the captain, second mate, two apprentices, and five runners, were got safely ashore. The seas all the time had been driving along and over the pier with unabated fury, and it was almost a miracle that none of the men were washed into the seething waters. The whole of the rescued were soon comfortably located at the brigade house on the South Pier. They were supplied with dry clothing,

hot tea, and other refreshment. It was ascertained that the vessel was the iron barque Abbey Holme, of Liverpool, and that she was being towed from Leith to Middlesbrough in ballast. The captain, Mr. J.H. Rich, stated that he left Leith at half-past 3 o'clock on Tuesday morning, and, when off the Tyne, he determined on account of the stormy state of the weather, to put into Shields harbour for shelter. When just outside the piers the hawser broke, and the vessel drifted helplessly down upon the South Pier. She struck the east-end, and gradually forced her way towards the jetty of the Tyne General Ferry Company where she became fast. The following are the names of the rescued people:-- Captain John Hoare Rich and his wife; Richard Bidwell, mate; Arthur Lowdon and William Fitch, apprentices; Thomas Bain, John H. Bowersby, Alexander Dalgleish, Robert Adams, and John Anderson, runners. There was a muster of 34 brigadesmen, including several of the officers, to assist the local coastguardsmen in the rescue which was effected within an hour. The Abbey Holme is a vessel of 516 tons register, and was built at Sunderland in 1869. She is owned by Messrs. Hine Brothers, Customs House Buildings, Maryport. During the rescue of the crew two members of the South Shields Volunteer Life Brigade (Messrs. J.W. Swainston and B. Heron) went on board the vessel and assisted in getting the captain's wife on shore by means of the rocket cradle. In an interview with a reporter the mate stated that the barque, which was in ballast, left Leith that morning in tow of the tug William Fenwick, also of Leith. There was at the time of leaving, eight o'clock, a strong northerly wind, which increased as the vessel proceeded on her voyage. At the time she was under foresail, four under mainsails, mainsail, and four topsails. As she kept continually over-running the tug they had to furl all the sails, and brace the yards fore and aft. The gale increased, and with difficulty they reached the Tyne. Just on entering the hawser parted, and the vessel struck as above described. On Tuesday evening a great quantity of the deck fittings were washed ashore, and it was feared the barque, which still preserved an even keel, would become a total wreck.

The Abbey Holme has been surveyed and certified as a total wreck.

[**Fl corr**. April 9th 1890 "Abbey Holme" This vessel sailed from Leith on the 7th inst. In tow for Middlesbro on Tees, & we much regret to inform you that in entering the Tyne last night for shelter during a strong northerly gale, the tow-line parted, & the vessel drove on the Rocks at South Shields. Our superintendent being at the time at Sunderland we wired him to proceed to Shields immediately. He has called in two independent Surveyors today, who have examined the Ship, & report her to be a total wreck. She is insured at the rate of £5500. Chartered freight is also covered. Yours truly, Hine Bros.]

[**Fl corr**. Custom House Buildings Maryport 16th May 1890
Dear Sirs,
Barque "Abbey Holme" 17th voyage.
We beg to enclose statement of a/c, from which you will see the vessel has made a profit of £1298: 16/10 exclusive of insurance. From this we deduct £248: 10/2 cost of insurance and add to the balance £1: 19/2, brought forward from last a/c making £1052: 5/10 available for division.

We divide £960, £15 per shares, & carry the balance of £92: 5/10 forward. Herein please find our cheque for £30 being amount due you on your 2/64 shares, receipt of which you kindly acknowledge.

Referring to our letter of the 9th ulto. In which we informed you of the loss of this fine little ship; we are now engaged in collecting the amount of insurances, which were effected prior to her loss, to charge, along with Leith outward expenses; and these will appear in a supplementary a/c, when we are in a position to send out Total Loss a/c, is which the £92: 5/10 above referred to will be shewn.

    A meeting of Owners will be held at our Offices on Thursday next the 22nd inst. At 2.30 o'clock p.m.

    Yours faithfully Hine Bros.]

Abbey Holme, wreck at Sunderland April, 1890: John Mounsey

DENTON HOLME

Official No.	**47182**	Code letters	VMNJ
Built	1863 June	Belfast (Harland & Wolff)	
Deck	Two	Build	Clincher
Masts	Three	Gallery	None
Beams	Two tiers	Bulkheads	Three (cemented)
Rigging	**Barque**	Head	Demi-Woman
Stern	Round	Framework	Iron.
Tonnage	**998**	Length 213.2 feet; Breadth 31.1 feet; Depth 21.7 feet.	

After Abbey Holme was wrecked on 8 April 1890, Hine Bros. bought the last of their working sailing vessels.

[**MNL** 1880: Star of Denmark of Belfast: Owner: John Corry, Rosenheim, Croydon, Surrey.]

1890 Sydney Morning Herald Sat. 31 May p.8
The iron barque Star of Denmark, 996 tons registered, – has been sold for £6650.

1890 The Belfast News-Letter Sat. 3 May p.4
Change of Name of Vessel.
I Wilfrid Hine of Maryport, hereby give Notice in consequence of the Ships owned by my Firm of Hine Brothers having the distinctive name of "Holme", it is my intention to apply to the Board of Trade, under section 6 of the Merchant Shipping Act, 1871, in respect of my ship Star of Denmark, of Belfast, Official Number 47,182, of gross tonnage 998 tons, of register tonnage 998, heretofore owned by: James Porter Corry of Belfast; John Corry, younger, of Belfast; Robert William Corry of Belfast; William Corry of London; John Corry of London; For permission to change her name to 'Denton Holme' to be registered in the said new name at the Port of Maryport, as owned by Wilfrid Hine.
Dated at Maryport, this 1st day of May, 1890.   Wilfrid Hine.

1890 Maryport Advertiser Fri. 30 May
The Holme Fleet: Messrs Hine, Brothers, Maryport, have just added to their fleet of iron sailing ships a very fine iron vessel of the registered tonnage of 998, with a dead weight carrying capacity of 1,550 tons. She is 213 feet long, 32 feet beam, and 22 feet depth of hold, and is the highest class at Lloyds'. Until now she has been the property of Sir James Corry & Son, Belfast, and was built by the celebrated Belfast builders, Messrs Harland & Wolff. She is an extra strong vessel, her plates being of unusual thickness. Messrs Hine have received permission from the Broad of Trade to change her name, which hitherto has been Star of Denmark, of Belfast. She is now called Denton Holme, of Maryport. Captain J. H. Rich, of Maryport, for many years master of the Abbey Holme, has been appointed to the command. The vessel is now loading a general cargo in Glasgow for Western Australia, from whence she loads a return cargo for home, and has every prospect of a very successful voyage before her under her new flag.
June 27 p.
Denton Holme, barque, left Glasgow for Freemantle (sic) 25th.

1890 The West Australian (Perth) Fri. 26 Sept. p.3
Shipwreck at Rottnest. The Denton Holme Ashore.
The Vessel Abandoned. All Hands Saved.
The utmost excitement was manifested in Fremantle, yesterday morning, when the news was circulated that a large vessel had gone ashore at Rottnest. Despite the inclemency

of the weather many persons frequented the vicinity of the jetty in order to ascertain news of the disaster. The first information of the casualty was brought ashore early in the morning by Pilot Gilmore, who rowed a small dingy five miles in order to bring the tidings, and to secure the necessary help from the mainland. He was compelled to adopt this course owing to the calm at the time the vessel went ashore, and as the pilot boat could not be sailed with sufficient speed, when it had got some distance, he embarked in a small boat, and in the teeth of threatening weather brought the news to the harbour authorities.

The Denton Holme, formerly known as the Star of Denmark, and built about 27 years ago, is a barque of 998 tons, owned by Messrs. Hine Bros., and was bound from Glasgow laden with 1,275 tons of pipes for the Perth Water-works, and from 250 to 300 tons of general cargo. She sailed on June 23rd, so that she has been about 90 days on the voyage. At 11.55 on Wednesday evening the barque was sighted by those on duty at the Lighthouse on Rottnest, and in accordance with the usual custom the pilot boat in charge of Pilot Butcher, was manned, and put off to the vessel. The weather at this time was moderate, although there was every indication of a storm, the sea being comparatively calm. The crew of the pilot-boat watched the progress of the big vessel, and wondered that she did not stop. It seemed that she hugged the shore too closely and the result was soon discerned, for the barque suddenly struck between the Transits and the Kingston Spit on the one side, and nearly on the same spot where the s.s. Macedon and the schooner Janet were wrecked some years ago. Of course alacrity was the order of the night on board the barque, and the necessary signals of distress were shown. These were immediately observed by those at the Lighthouse and the crew of the fast approaching pilot boat, and the necessary return signals were made. The pilot boat got alongside, and Pilot Butcher soon boarded, while in the meantime, Pilot Gilmore had made all necessary arrangements for assistance. The weather was calm, but the atmospherical indications were anything but favourable, and it was deemed advisable to at once despatch news to the mainland. As already related Pilot Gilmore arrived safe and sound, and it was not long before the Chief Harbour Master, Captain Russell, was aroused and informed of what had taken place. With all possible speed Captain Russell and the harbour crew assembled at the jetty, and the s.s. Rescue, belonging to Captain Fothergill, having got steam up, a start was made for the scene of the wreck. In addition to the harbour crew, the members of the pilot crew were taken on board, they having by this time succeeded in gaining the port.

Information was left by Capt Russell that the s.s. Cleopatra was to be despatched before noon to act as a tender, but while she was getting up steam one of the boiler-tubes burst and she was rendered heure de combat.

The news of the wreck reached the port shortly after daylight, and about 8 o'clock the Rescue was ready. This was quick work, when it is considered that the crew had to be sought and steam got up, and other arrangements made.

On the arrival of the tug at the scene of the shipwreck it was found that Pilot Butcher had rendered assistance of the utmost value, in fact he almost lost his life in his efforts. Just at daybreak the glass began to fall rapidly, and a north-west gale swept over the coast, accompanied with drenching showers of rain. Pilot Butcher at once saw the advisability of making things secure, so he began to remove the ship's papers, the captain's chronometer, money, and other valuables. The sea was now rising rapidly, and while jumping from the ship to his boat he miscalculated the distance, and fell headlong into the ocean, a huge wave sweeping over him as he fell. Fortunately he was almost at once hauled on board again. Despite this accident Pilot Butcher continued at his post until after noon, manfully doing his duty, and materially assisting the captain in endeavouring to float the vessel owing to the increasing wind and rising sea, this was found to be a difficult task, and on the arrival of the tug it was deemed advisable to leave the vessel. About noon the arrangements for leaving the vessel were made, and the seventeen sailors and their effects were conveyed in the boats to the tug which had got under the shelter of the island. The ship was lying with her head south, and she went further on the reef, and at the time of the abandonment water was coming in at her fore compartment. A heavy sea was running breaking over the ship's stern, and it was dangerous for anyone to remain on board, as there was a possibility of her breaking up at any moment. The last to leave the vessel were the Captain and Pilot Butcher.

Mr. H. King's Statement.

Mr. Harry King, representative of the agents, who went off with the Rescue, stated that on arrival at the vessel it was found that she was in a precarious position. A boat in charge of Pilot Butcher came off, and gave the information that the captain and the crew were ready to leave, and that the ship's papers and other valuables had been removed to the island. Four boats' crews were then picked up, one boat being cut adrift. The ship was making a little water, but owing to the heavy sea no one from the tug went on board.

The Captain's Report.

Captain Rich, the commander, who was here six years ago in charge of the Abbey Holme, was interviewed by our representative last night and furnished the following report:- Left Glasgow on June 23rd, and experienced strong southerly winds in St. George's Channel and then had fair winds and fine weather until reaching Cape de Verd Islands. After that had variable winds to 12½ deg., then S.W. and S.S.W., strong occasionally, with heavy seas as far as 15 W. longitude. Continued to have similar weather with occasional squalls and met the south-east trades 5½ deg. N. Crossed the equator 35 days out and had fresh south-east trades to 25 deg. S. Then N.E. and northerly winds to the vicinity of Tristan d'Acuna, and had strong westerly winds to the Cape, after which fair winds prevailed. When in longitude 65 E. had a heavy gale from the north which shifted suddenly to the S.S.W. With the tremendous sea caused by the gale from the northward and also the one from the south the two seas met causing the vessel to roll and labour very heavily. When the vessel was heavily lurching the pipes could be heard shifting in the lower hold. This caused great anxiety on board, as the safety of the vessel was endangered. The next day it was found that several pipes had shifted in the lower hold, but it was impossible to get at them on account of them being stored between the deck beams. This occurred several times, owing to the heavy rolling of the ship, and we were compelled to keep her before the seas, so that it would ease her rolling. At one time I thought we should have to bear for the Mauritius, but after a consultation with the chief officer, it was determined to continue the voyage. Nothing of any moment occurred until we sighted Rottnest Light on Wednesday evening at 9 o'clock. We passed the light about 11 o'clock, and kept on a course along the island and at midnight showed two blue lights for the pilot. These were not answered and at 20 past 12 we fired two more lights, the vessel being kept in towards the land in order to pick up the pilot. A light was shown on the Island, and at that time I considered my vessel was close enough to the land and was in the act of wearing her round on the other tack to lay to for the pilot when I observed breakers on the starboard beam. I got the yards trimmed as quickly as possible, but immediately afterwards the vessel took the ground and remained fast. The pilot boat and Pilot Butcher got alongside about 2 o'clock ; we trimmed the yards and made every effort to get the ship under weigh, but without success. Pilot Butcher considered it was advisable to get a boat away to the shore so that assistance could be obtained from Fremantle, and this was accordingly done. On the return of the pilot we fired several sky rockets and burned blue lights to attract attention and obtain assistance, and at daylight the signals of distress, N.C., were hoisted. In the meantime we kept sounding the pumps and they were kept at work until the ship was left. There seemed no chance of the vessel floating, she was thumping and labouring heavily, and we thought it was best to get the boats out, and this was done. The pilot considered it best to clew the sails up to keep the vessel from forging ahead, which would have placed her in a more dangerous position. Between 10.30 and 11 o'clock the tug boat Rescue arrived from Fremantle, having on board the Chief Harbour Master, Capt. Russell, Capt. Fothergill, Mr. Harry King, representing the agents (Messrs. Dalgety & Co.), Pilot Gilmore and the harbour crew. The sea was mountainous, driving heavily over the ship, and there was no chance of the tug getting alongside. Pilot Butcher took five of the ship's crew in a boat and proceeded to the tug. They encountered some very heavy seas, and several times were in great danger of being capsized, but by skilful navigation they reached the tug in safety. A consultation was held with Capt. Russell, and the boat returned again to the ship, meeting with more difficulties on the way. It was reported to me that the Harbour Master intended to run the tug under the lee of the shoal of the reef, and that as soon as we saw him there the boats were to leave the vessel and the tug would pick them up. We were advised to leave the ship as our position was indeed precarious, and every moment it was expected that the heavy seas would break her up. About noon, orders were given to my chief officer to man the boats, and the men and himself soon got them ready to cast adrift. The men were got away first, and then Pilot Butcher, myself, and four men left in the last boat and proceeded to the tug, in which we were conveyed to Fremantle, the four boats being taken in tow by the steamer. One boat had to be cut adrift from the bow of the vessel to keep the others from fouling. I must give great praise to Pilot Butcher for the pluck and energy he displayed throughout a most trying period, while the members of my crew are also deserving of every praise for the cool manner in which they stuck to me under the serious difficulties in which we were placed. We arrived at Fremantle about 4.30, and I saw to the housing of the crew and officers, together with their effects. When we left the vessel was in a most dangerous position, and the storm was increasing in violence. The vessel was straining greatly, the masts at times almost coming entirely over, while the water was coming into the fore cabin.

Later Particulars. Fremantle, 10 o'clock.

The barque has gone ashore within 50 yards of the spot were the s.s. Macedon, and the schooner Janet were wrecked. The master of the Denton Holme suggests that it is only right that a pilot schooner should be stationed on the outside of Rottnest Island, to pick up vessels about to enter the Port.

The arrival of the Rescue with the crew and officers and the rescuing party was watched by a great crowd of the inhabitants, who assembled on the small jetty. This occurred shortly after 4 o'clock, but it was some time before all the men got ashore, as they had to load the small boats with the baggage saved from the wreck. On landing they were besieged by persons anxious to glean particulars, but as they had undergone sufficient privations and were cold and hungry, they made their way into town to seek lodgings and refreshment. Messrs. Dalgety & Co. made every effort to look after the men's comfort, and in an hour's time they were all safely housed.

The particulars of the casualty were telegraphed to Melbourne by Mr. E. Solomon, agent of the Underwriters' Association.

During last night the weather continued very stormy, the wind blew strong from the north west, and it is expected that the vessel will be a total wreck by morning, there being no prospect of a change.

It is understood .that the cargo is mostly insured in Australasian offices.

1890 The West Australian (Perth) Tues. 7 Oct. p.3
The official enquiry into the stranding of the Denton Holme barque, was held yesterday morning before Mr. L. W. Clifton, Collector of Customs, Mr. B. Fairbairn, R.M., and Capt. Owston and Captain Patterson of the Deveron, the two latter acting as nautical assessors. .

The following charges were preferred against the captain.

1. For that Capt. Rich, after signalling for a pilot at 11.30 p.m. on the 24th Sept., did neglect to heave to, and did stand in with all sail set on a NE, NNE course till 12 o'clock.

2. For that after signalling for a pilot the second time at midnight you did neglect to heave to, but continued the course towards the land of Rottnest Island.

3. For that after sighting Rottnest light to the time of the Denton Holme stranding, you did neglect to heave the lead, when the sailing directions state "that a vessel approaching the port of Fremantle from N. and W. should not come nearer than the 30 fathoms line."

4. That having an Admiralty Chart of the Port of Fremantle, you did neglect to consult it after midnight and take cross bearings when the Port light on Arthur's Head was in view till after the vessel struck on the Transit Reef.

Mr. Dymes appeared for the captain of the barque, and Capt. Russell for the Harbour authorities.

Capt. Rich, having heard the statements made at the preliminary enquiry read over, was then sworn and stated that the barque Denton Holme was laden with general cargo and pipes, and was bound from Glasgow to Fremantle. Everything went well until September 25th. The remainder of his evidence was similar to that given at the preliminary enquiry.

In Cross-examination the witness stated that he held the blue lights and they burned about three minutes. His side lights could be seen about five miles off. He received no signal from the Pilot station, the first thing being a flash light from the pilot boat just before boarding. There was a flash from the island, but he did not know what it meant.

By Mr. Dymes : He considered that if the pilot had come off sooner, the accident would not have occurred. He stood in to assist the pilot as he knew he had only a small boat.

John Johnson, a member of the pilot crew, said that on the night of the 24th September about 5 minutes to 12, he flared up and received an answer from the lighthouse. At that time he sighted a vessel burning blue lights. He immediately reported to Pilots Butcher and Gillmore, and got orders to call the crew and man the boat, and went off to the ship in twenty minutes from the time he saw the blue lights.

Wm. Samuel Smith, second mate, of the Denton Holme, gave similar evidence to that given at the preliminary enquiry.

Pilot Butcher, of Rottnest said that he was called at midnight on the 24th inst. As a rule it was the duty of the lighthouse keeper to sight a vessel first. After receiving the signal and rousing the crew he got under weigh within 20 minutes or half an hour. They were about an hour in making for the ship. They would have got there sooner, but he burned blue lights and tried all he could to attract the ship's attention away from danger as at that time he did not know she was on the reef. When no movement was made witness thought there was something wrong, and put off in the dingy, and found the ship was on the reef. The barque would have been safer if she had kept a little further off, and then they could have boarded her. He had been a good many years pilot, and had seen the Macedon wrecked just outside where the barque was. The steamer went ashore late in the afternoon, and the weather was fine and calm. He had seen the Janet on this reef, there being a moderate breeze from the S.W. and the weather squally. Both these vessels became total wrecks.

By Capt. Ouston : All on board were sober, when I got on board.

By Capt. Russell: I was on board the vessel a long time. I got one of the ship's boats and went ashore to heliograph. When I went ashore I met Mr. Timperley about half past two in the morning.

Capt. Russell referred to this statement, as it had been said that the pilot did not get aboard until after 2 o'clock, whereas he had been on board, taken soundings, got goods ashore, and landed again, at Rottnest by that time.

Cross-examination continued : I called Mr. Timperley before I went off, and when I saw the vessel I thought she was much closer than she should have been. She was too near the Duck Rock. I then made great haste to get off. My instructions are not to flash signals from the boat, when there is danger to the boat. I had to make a round about course to the vessel.

By Mr. Dymes : Under ordinary circumstances it took him about half an hour to get to a ship. The quickest time on record in which he had got to a ship was about half an hour, and at other times he had had to chase a ship as far as Fremantle before he got to her. One time he was twelve hours "boxing" after ship, because she would not wait for him.

By Captain Owston: We have nothing with which to warn vessels when they are in danger, except for the flare-up. I could not say when I first saw her if she was on the reef.

By Capt. Russell : If I had been captain of the ship I should have hove to with the ship's head off from the shore.

At this stage the enquiry was adjourned until half-past two o'clock. On resuming, Capt. Fothergill was called, and stated that he was master mariner, and well acquainted with the port. He had visited the Denton Holme. He noticed a white sandy mark coming away from the vessel, and going in a S.S.E. direction to Phillip Island, when it went on the south passage. He pointed out the position of the ship at present. There was a current running, from the wreck S.S.E. This current, as he observed, would tend to put the ship on the rocks. The average time from seeing the signals from the lighthouse and the pilot coming on board, would be an hour and a half. He thought it would add to the safety of ships coming to this port if there was a permanent red light fixed at the lookout station at Bathurst Point, such a light to be seen only when a ship was in danger.

Capt. Russell, the Chief Harbour Master, considered that the lighthouse was in a proper position at Rottnest, but the light was not sufficiently powerful and ought to be improved. There was a lookout station at Bathurst Point. The pilot quarters were at Thompson's Bay, about a quarter of a mile from the Point. There were no means of signalling by code by day and by lights at night. He thought Captain Fothergill's suggestion was a very good one. He thought that a ship coming in should keep the lead going, especially at night, and the captain of the Denton Holme should have done so. If he had, the casualty might have been avoided.

Mr. Dymes then addressed the Court on behalf of the captain, maintaining that the proper precautions were taken and that everything was in favour of the captain not easting the lead, owing to the prevailing fine weather.

The Court adjourned, and on returning into Court gave the following decision:-" We have carefully considered this case, and we take a most lenient view of it. The vessel has been lost through the captain's neglect, and we suspend his certificate for three months from the date that the vessel went ashore. In the meantime he can use his mate's certificate if he likes, and with regard to costs we make no order."

1890 The West Australian (Perth) Thurs. 9 Oct.p.3

To the Editor.

Sir,- I have sailed with Captain Rich of the Denton Holme for the last two years, and now the enquiry as to the cause of the wreck is over, I feel it is only just on my part to let the public know what sort of a commander he is. That he has committed an error in judgment none can deny, but that he was guilty of any negligence is far from the fact. He is, and always has been ever since I have sailed with him, a most cautious, particular and careful commander, who would run no risks and always kept his ship and crew in the most perfect order and discipline. He was most assiduous in all ways and spent far more time, day and night, on deck than is usual with captains and is in every way a competent experienced commander with whom any man might be proud to sail.

I am, etc.,　　　　Thomas Hole ; Chief Officer of the Denton Holme;

1918 The Advertiser (Adelaide) Sat. 5 Oct. p.11

Captain Thos. Soley Hole, of Port Adelaide, died on Thursday at Sister Wilson's Nursing Home, at Woodville. About three months ago he had a paralytic stroke, which deprived him of speech. He was born at Chudleigh, Devon, on October 27, 1838, and obtained his master's certificate under the British Board of Trade Teignmouth on January 31, 1867. He paid his first visit to Port Adelaide in the Torrens over 30 years ago, and ever since has made the Prince Alfred Sailors' Home his abode when at Port Adelaide. He sailed in Adelaide-owned vessels for about 30 years. He was on the barque Elizabeth about 30 years ago as mate, and was chief officer of the Denton Holme, Torrens, and the barque Wild Wave. His last trip was with the Wild Wave last year, and he broke his arm on the voyage. His widow resides in England, and she has been seriously ill. Captain Hole earned the high regard of all who knew him.

AIKSHAW

Maryport Maritime Museum (Allerdale Borough Council)

AIKSHAW

Official No.	**72922**	Code letters	WTFL
Built	1875 Sept.	In Sunderland (W. Doxford & Sons)	
Deck	One	Build	Clincher
Masts	Three	Gallery	None
Beams	Two tiers	Bulkhead	One (cemented)
Rigging	**Barque**	Head	¾ woman
Stern	Elliptic	Framework	Iron.
Tonnage	**573**	Length 171.0 feet; Breadth 28.9 feet; Depth 18.0 feet.	
		New ship	

This barque was commissioned by either Hine Brothers or E.W. Tyson or both. Hine Bros. were most probably at least part owners and/or managing owners. After Tyson died in 1881 the Aikshaw was fully a Hine Brothers vessel.

[**LR** 1875 Supplement: Captain Tyson: Owners, Hine Bros. / E.W. Tyson, Maryport.
[**LR** 1876 Captain Tyson: Owner, E.W. Tyson, Maryport.
[**LR** 1877 Captain Tyson: Owners Hine Bros., Maryport.
[**MNL** 1878: Owner: Edward William Tyson, Aikshaw, Cumberland.]

TRS 1/629
1875: Aikshaw: Sunderland sailed Nov. 29. [Survey: Sunderland in November.]
Owner: Edward William Tyson address, Aikshaw, Aspatria, Carlisle.
Captain: Edward William Tyson (33) Born Maryport (27756) from the Knight Templar.
Mate: G. Tate (24) Born Sunderland (97266).
Commenced 29-11-75 Sunderland.

1875 The Liverpool Mercury Mon. 20 Dec. p.3
Deal: passed: Dec. 18: Aikshaw, Valparaiso.

1875 Adair's Maryport Advertiser Fri. 24 Dec. p.8
Off the Isle of Wight: Aikshaw, Tyson, landed Pilot, all well.
1876 May 19 p.8
Valparaiso: Arrived: Mar. 16: Aikshaw, Tyson, after a passage of 96 days.

TRS 1/629
At Valparaiso Thomas Duffy (42) Edinburgh, A.B., and O.W. Briggs (31) Denmark, Cook, left behind both suffering from the effects of syphilis, they have received their effects and the balance Duffy £ 3.19/- at 42d $ 22.57 cts. And Briggs £ 4 16/- at 42d $ 33. 14.
1876 Aikshaw: Valparaiso sailed Mar. 21: Iquique arrived May 22 and sailed June 16.

1876 Lloyd's List Oct. 20 col. 7
Queenstown: Arrived: Oct. 19: Aikshaw, Tovison (sic), Iquique (nitrate).
Oct. 24 col. 8
Queenstown: Sailed: Oct. 23: Aikshaw, Newcastle.
Nov. 4. col. 4
The Lizard: Passed: Oct. 31: Aikshaw from Queenstown for Newcastle.
Nov. 14 col. 7
Shields: Arrived: Nov. 11: Aikshaw, Tyson from Iquique. [Survey: Newcastle in December]

[**MNL**: 1876 p.119: Owner: Edward William Tyson, Aikshaw, Cumberland.]

1877 The Newcastle Courant Fri. 23 Feb. p.2

Nisi Prius Court, Saturday.--Action to Recover Demurrage.

[The] plaintiff, Mr Tyson, part owner of the ship Aikshaw; the defendants, Messrs A. Gibbs and Co., shipbrokers, &c., London. .... On May 2, 1876, a charter party was made at Valparaiso between agents for the Lima Associated Banks, of the one part, and agents for the master and owners of the British barque Aikshaw," to take a cargo of nitrate of soda to England. The vessel took in a cargo of 891 tons of nitrate of soda at Iquique, and the charter party stipulated that 30 working days were to be allowed, for loading the cargo, and it was to be discharged "as fast as the custom of the port will allow," and demurrage was fixed at £10 per day. Owing to the nitrate of soda having to be carried in bags through the surf to lighters at Iquique and then taken to the ship, it was necessary to allow a long time for loading the ship. On November 11th the Aikshaw arrived at Newcastle-upon-Tyne, and the plaintiff gave notice to Messrs Scott Brothers, Newcastle, the consignees of the cargo, that the vessel would be ready for discharging on the 14th. A Stevedore was employed by the plaintiff, and undertook to discharge the cargo at the rate of 70 tons a day. The discharging of the cargo commenced, and on 30th November the plaintiff, considering the ample time had been allowed for discharging the cargo, gave notice to Messrs Scott that the lay days for discharging the cargo had expired, and that demurrage would be charged for every day from December 1st. The discharging of the cargo was not completed until December 23rd; and this action was brought to recover demurrage for 17 days, the other five days in December not being claimed for, owing to the plaintiff having been engaged on the five days in taking in coal to "stiffen" the ship.—The jury gave a verdict for the defendants.

1877 The Liverpool Mercury Sat. 27 Jan. p.7
Shields: Sailed: Jan 26: Aizshaw (sic), for Singapore.
Jan. 31 p.3
Deal: Passed: Jan 30: Arkshaw (sic), from Shields for Singapore.
Apr. 18 p.3
Spoken: Aikshaw (barque) bound S., March 18, 8 S. 28 W.

1877 The Straits Times (Singapore) Sat. 2 June p.23
Shipping in the Harbour: Aikshaw – Tyson – Brit. Bark – 575 – May 30 – Shields – Lying at the roads –Gilfallan, Wood & Co. – Discharging.

1877 Straits Times Overland Journal (Singapore) Sat. 9 June p.15
Singapore: Arrivals: Wednesday, 30th May: British barque Aikshaw 575 tons, Tyson, Shields 26th Jany.
July 7 p.13
Singapore: Departures: Tuesday 3rd. June (sic) [July?]: British barque, Aikshaw, Tyson, for London.
TRS 1/629 Singapore: David Horn (35) London A.B. put in prison 3-7-77

1877 The Daily News (London) Wed. 28 Nov. p.3
Gravesend: Arrivals: Nov. 25: Aikshaw from Singapore. [Survey: London in December]

TRS 1/629 Captain: Edward William Tyson, 33, Maryport, same ship. Mate: George Tate, 25, Sunderland, same ship, C/97266. William Mitchell, 48 Cornwall, ship British Duke, at Liverpool: Joined 1878, 14 Jan. 10 a.m.—Carpenter: Wages £5. 10 advanced on Entry per Calendar Month, £8. 5.
6/2/79 London Discharged Balance of wages on Discharge £52. 7. 5.
Mate £ 4.15 per month: Cook £5.00: A.B. £3.5: O.S. £2.5

1878 The Standard (London) Mon. 21 Jan. p.7

Deal: Sailings: Jan. 19: Aikshaw, Auckland, N.Z.

TRS 1/629 Captain: Tyson. Mate: Tate.
At Auckland: 3 deserters all A.Bs.

1878 Evening Star (Auckland) (N.Z.) Mon. 12 May [incorrect:: 13 May] p.2
Auckland: The fine iron barque Aikshaw, commanded by Captain Tyson, arrived in harbour this morning from London, after a lengthy passage of 98 days from land to land, and 108 days from London. She left London on January 17, and anchored in Gravesend next day. Left the Downs on the 19th and Start Point on the 29th, the weather then being very bad, the wind blowing in heavy squalls from the N.W., accompanied with hail. This weather continued, with little change, until February 6, when it moderated. On the 9th February Fred Campbell, an A.B., fell over a bucket and broke his thigh bone. Crossed the Equator on the 28th February, in lat. 8 miles (sic) north, and 27th 4? west. The weather was then good. On March 4th spoke the barque Annie Fish, bound to New York. Passed the meridian of the Cape of Good Hope on March 28, in lat. 43* 15' S., and long. 16* 47 east. The weather was very bad here, and the wind blew almost a hurricane. On the 29th the foretopmast-staysail blew away owing to the weight of the wind. On April 15th the weather was just about the same. That day the martingale-stay and jibboom carried away. The crew refused to obey the orders of the Captain, and one of their number was put in irons. This was sufficient to quell the mutiny. The main-top-gallant stay was blown away on Saturday, April 27th, and on May 2nd a terrific gale accompanied by rain and a heavy sea set in. The main topsail was blown clean away. The weather continued bad, until sighting the Three Kings, at midnight on Friday. Fine weather was experienced down the Coast. The Aikshaw brings no passengers, but a full general cargo of merchandise. She comes consigned to Messrs Shaw Saville and Co's agent. As there is no cargo on board, she was brought up the harbour and anchored on the wharf at noon. The Aikshaw is a fine new iron barque. She was built in 1875 and this is her second voyage.
Imports: 2 crates toilet-ware, 1 bale door mats, 2 do. carpets, 2 cases trimmings, 1 do. furniture, 1 do. Utrecht velvet, 7 do. iron bedsteads, 1 do. net curtains, 1 case cane-seats chairs, 4 cases furniture, 5 cases chimney and toilet glasses, 1 case bassinetts – T. & H. Cooke.
100 brls salt herrings, 100 brls. Red herrings, 29 pkgs, agricultural machines, 2 cases sawmill machinery. – John Reid and Co.
871 cases, 10 pieces and packages, 533 casks, 4766 packages, 32 bales, 22 packets, 200 kegs, 50½ hhds., 5 drums, 59?9 slates, 489 bars iron, and 102 iron plates, 1000 bags, 25 tons pig iron, and 10 cases for transhipment to Napier.
100 cases. – Henderson and Mac a lane. (sic). [Macfarlane?]
9 bales, 123 cases, 130 packages. – Owen and Graham.
[May 14 p.2] *10 cases ...... -- Wilson and Horton.*
2 crates toilet ware, 1 bale door mats, 2 bales carpets, 2 cases trimmings, 2 cases furniture, 1 case Utrecht velvet, 7 cases iron bedsteads, 1 case net curtains. – Winks and Hall.
1 tank figs, 30 cases Bell and Black's plaid vestas, 20 do. 250's, 15 bags Barcelona nuts, 115 boxes cleme raisins, 7 barrels tar, 3 bales seaming, and roping twine, 30 kegs Ewebank nails, 2 cases slate pencils, 6 do. school slates, 2 do. envelopes, 2 do. notepaper. – E. and H. Isaacs.
5,000 Countess slates, 50 cases Red Heart rum, 50 cases condensed milk, 6 cases assorted cigars. – Kummer and Co.
[May 17 p.2] *12 cases maccaroni (sic) and vermicelli. – T.H. Hall and Co.*

May 22 p.2
The barque Aikshaw, from London, is turning out her cargo in excellent condition.
June 10 p.2
The barque Aikshaw entered out at the Customs to-day for Guam, in ballast.
Police Court: This Day: (Before R.C. Barstow, Esq., R.M.): Desertion:
R.W. Benson **[TRS 1/629:** Benson (17) of London O.S. Cuthbertson (16) apprentice] *and John Cuthbertson, boys on board the barque Aikshaw, were brought up, under the Merchant Shipping Act, charged of desertion. The prisoners pleaded not guilty. Captain Tyson said that Cuthbertson was an indentured apprentice and Benson an A.B. on board the Aikshaw. They left on June 5th, taking their clothes with them. He gave them no permission to leave. By way of defence, Benson said he had shipped at 1s. a month, and as he didn't think he was receiving proper treatment he left. Cuthbertson could only say that he had deserted because he did not like the ship; in fact he was tired of it. They were sentenced to a month's imprisonment with hard labour, and ordered to pay the costs of the action.*
June 13 p.2
The barque Aikshaw cleared at the Customs to-day, for Guam, in ballast.
June 17 p.2
Auckland: Departures: Aikshaw, barque, for Guam, sailed this morning.

1878 The Argus (Melbourne) Fri. 21 June p.6
Spoken: March 4: Aikshaw from London to Auckland, 7 S. 40 W. [?]
July 16 p.4
Newcastle: Arrived: July 14: Aikshaw from Auckland. [Survey: Newcastle (N.S.W) on July.]

1878 The Sydney Morning Herald Wed. 17 July p.4
Newcastle: Shipping arrivals have been exceedingly slack during the week and consequently the harbour is becoming thinned of tonnage, the chief arrivals, foreign-going, being Aikshaw, barque, 573, from Auckland, destination uncertain.
July 31 p.4
Newcastle: July 29: The barque Aikshaw has cancelled her Hongkong Charter, and fixed for Lyttelton, term withheld.
TRS 1/629: 3 deserters in Newcastle, 1 O.S. 2 A.B.

1878 The Argus (Melbourne) Fri. 2 Aug. p.4
Newcastle: Sailed: July 31: Echshaw (sic), for Lyttelton.

1878 The Star (Canterbury) (N.Z.) Tues. Aug. 13 p.2
Lyttelton: Arrived: Aug. 12: Aikshaw, barque, 573 tons, Tyson from Newcastle, last night.

1878 The Press (Canterbury) (N.Z.) Wed. 14 Aug. p.2
Lyttelton: Aikshaw will be berthed at the No 3 Wharf .
Imports: Per Aikshaw—873 tons coal.
The barque Aikshaw, Captain Tyson, left Newcastle on July 31st, and had a fresh easterly gale for two days, after which experienced moderate westerly weather to passing the Kaikouras on the morning of the 11th inst.; thence light and variable winds to arrival in harbour on Monday night. Captain Tyson reports that the barque Queen of the West and the brig Raymond were ready for sea when he left, and they would in all probability have sailed about the 2nd of August.
Sept. 12 p.2
The Aikshaw cleared for Oamaru yesterday with part cargo of wheat for London aboard. She fills up at the Southern port, sailing thence to the United Kingdom with all possible despatch.

TRS 1/629: 3 deserters. All A.Bs.
Sept. 14 p.2
Lyttelton: Sailed: Sept. 14: Aikshaw, barque, 590 tons, Tyson, for Oamaru.

We shall let the "North Otago Times" take over:
Sept. 10 p.2
Let us earnestly hope that the Aikshaw and the Celestial Queen are but the fore-runners of an established line of vessels which shall have for their New Zealand destination the port of Oamaru.
Sept. 11 p.2
A large vessel, presumed to be the Aikshaw, now due, arrived last night, and anchored outside.
Sept. 16 p.2
It will be seen by a telegram in our shipping column that the barque Aikshaw sailed from Lyttelton for the port on Saturday [14th]. She comes here to load grain for London direct.
Sept. 18 p.2
A large ship, supposed to be the Aikshaw, lay in the offing the greater part of yesterday, but the wind falling light was unable to come in.
Sept. 19 p.2
The Aikshaw Captain Tyson came into the Bay yesterday morning and dropped anchor about noon at the outer anchorage. As we have already stated, she comes here to load grain for the Home Country. She is a fine iron vessel of 573 register and was build at Sunderland in 1875. She is on her first voyage to New Zealand having brought a cargo of coals to Lyttelton from Newcastle N.S.W. She left Lyttlelton on Saturday last and experienced a heavy southerly gale till the evening of that day afterwards calms and N.E. winds to arrive as above.
Sept. 24 p.2
The Aikshaw has recovered a remarkably quick dispatch in loading, considering the slow process of rowing off cargo boats, and the want of a steam winch for hoisting purposes.
Sept. 25 p.2
The barque, Aikshaw, has had a quick despatch, her loading, which was only commenced on Thursday last, having been completed at 8 o'clock yesterday morning. She cleared out for the Home Country yesterday, with a cargo consisting altogether of 900 tons wheat, 550 tons of which were shipped at this port and the balance at Lyttelton, Messrs. P. Cunningham and Co., being the consignors. The Aikshaw will probably sail this morning, and we heartily wish her a safe and prosperous voyage.
Sept. 26 p.2
The barque, Aikshaw, Capt. Tyson, set sail for the old country about 7 o'clock yesterday, with a fair wind. She was soon out of sight.

1879 The Liverpool Mercury Thurs. 16 Jan. p.3
Spoken: Aikshaw, from Oamaru for channel Nov. 7: 42 S. 38 W. [Off Argentina]

1879. January 16, she reached Schull, Cork (Ireland) for orders.

[A personal letter]
Barque Aikshaw
Schull, Near Queenstown, Ireland,
Jany 1879, Satury night
My Dear Wife
        I sent one letter away this afternoon because I know you must be anxious to hear some news from me. I thought we would have sail.d to day but the wind was Contrary we

Bargae Hickshaw
Jan ... Sculld
Satur 14/st New Buckinstown
Ireland

My Dear Wife
I sent one letter away
this afternoon because I
know you must be ...
anxious to hear some news
from me I thought we would
have sail'd to day but the
wind was Contrary we are
to leave the first chance
... few lines ...
... in your letter
Dear Wife ...
... as sure ... so far
God knows we have
had some trouble ...
have Thought on you
Dear Wife often

See overleaf a transcript of this letter by William Mitchell

wondering how you can
manage. God knows it
is not my fault I tried
My best Never mind we
are coming to London,
and when we get paid
he will find out several
things will come to light.
Little as he may think
of now. Dear Wife I,
hope you have enjoyed
good health. I am
very sorry to say my
Eyesight is failing
very fast Never mind
we will meet again
shortly please the Lord
give my respects to
thy. Middlttons. tell
them I hope soon
to see them

My Dear I hope next
Sunday be home if
I have one left I hope
Bill is a good boy
I have to call him a
Young man now I
wipe Dear Wife I have
never had such a bad
time as this Nothing but
Bad weather all the way
out and the Same home
12 Months hard Labour
starved half the time I
hope you have not lost
all the Home If you
have I cannot blame
you. you may think
because I am thousands
of Miles away from
You

are to leave the first chance. I sent a few lines for Mrs Sales in your letter Dear Wife I am very thankful we have come so far God Knows we have had some trouble I have thought on you Dear Wife often wondering how you can manage. God knows it is not my fault I tried my best Never mind we are coming to London and when we get paid he will find out several things will come to light Little as he may think of now. Dear Wife I hope you have enjoyed good health. I am very sorry to say my Eyesight is failing very fast. Never mind we will meet again shortly please the Lord give my respects to they Middeltons. tell them I hope soon to see them My Dear I hope next Sunday be home if I have one left I hope Bill is a good boy (Ill?) [I'll?] have to call him a young man now I expect. Dear Wife I have never had such a bad time as this Nothing but Bad weather all the way out and the same home 12 months hard Labour starved half the time I hope you have not lost all the Home If you have I cannot blame you. You may think because I am thousands of miles away from you that I forget you. The further away from you the more anxious thoughts this have been a sore trial for me this time among Ice and Snow and how we got clear of the Ice it was a miracle By Gods good will and power. never mind I hope this is my last voyage If I can get anything to do on Shore because I am not so young as I was I find age creeping on me fast. I have had a good trial (?) of the sea I would like to have been Like Billy, he had more sense then I had. [written across] I will say a few more words when we sail because the Pilot when (?) he leave the Ship will take the Last Letters on shore when we Sail it is uncertain any how we must trust to providence for all things I expect it will be a Sunday Sail very likely. [across another page] this is Saturday night. I hope you are all happier then I am. My respects to all Inquiring Freinds (sic). Good Night and God Bless you my Darling., I am your Afft Husband Wm Mitchell

Carpenter Barque Aikshaw.

TRS 1/629
Aikshaw: Voyage: London 4.4.78 to London 6.2.79
William Mitchell (aged 48) Cornwall (formerly on the "British Duke" Plymouth 1877), Carpenter, discharged in London on 6/2/1879. signed by William Mitchell.

{Marriage: 7-7-1863: Andrew William Mitchell—Elizabeth Lock—St Thomas, Stepney, Middlesex}

[[England and Wales Census 1881]]

Thomas Sale	Head	M.M.	52	M.E.O.T, Middlesex	
Mary Sale	Wife	M.F.	43	ditto	
Thomas Sale	Son	U.M	20	ditto	
Joseph Sale	Son	U.M	17	ditto	
Sarah Sale	Dau	U.F.	15	ditto	
William Sale	Son	U.M	14	ditto	
Mary Sale	Dau	U.F.	10	ditto	
Helena Sale	Dau	U.F.	9	ditto	
Elizabeth Mitchell	Lodger	M.F.	43	Holborn, Middlesex,	Sailors Wife

98 St. Ann's Rd., Mile End Old Town, Middlesex

[See Mitchell again on the Myrtle Holme (Vol. 2), date 1881 in Adelaide.]

1879 The Glasgow Herald Thurs. 6 Feb. p.6
Deal: Passed: Feb.5: Aikshaw, Oimara (sic), N.Z for London.

1879 The Standard (London) Fri. 7 Feb p.7
Gravesend: Arrivals: Feb. 6: Aikshaw, Oimaru (sic), N.Z. [Survey: London in March]

1879 The Times (London) Fri. 21 Feb. p.2
[Advert] *Roberts & Co's Java, China and Japan Lines: Batavia, Samarang & Sourabaya (Indonesia): Aikshaw: A1 100: S.W.I.D.* [South West India Dock, London]

Edward William Tyson of Staveley Kendal was buried 14 Feb. 1881 aged 37. He left a wife and three children, the youngest only five months old. [See Addenda of Captains and Family].

TRS 2/4
Aikshaw: Shares: 15 Feb. & 15 Nov. 1877 and 18 June 1879. Edward William Tyson 8; Jane Tyson 3; Edward Thomas Tyson 4; William Tyson 2. [no Hines]

TRS 1/629
1879: Captain G.T. Tate, 27, Sunderland. Owner Ed. W Tyson, Maryport.
Sailed from London Apr. 4.
1879: Aikshaw: Batavia arrived July 29, sailed Aug. 30: Samarang arrived Sept. 9, sailed Oct. 3. Sourabaya arrived Oct. 9, sailed Oct. 20.

1879 The Argus (Melbourne) Mon. 29 Sept. p.4
Port Batavia: Loading: Aikshaw, 573 tons: Aug. [Survey: Batavia in August.]
Oct. 6 p.4
Via Torres Straits and Sydney we have advices from Batavia to 6th September ....Vessels loading Aikshaw for Melbourne.

1879 The Maitland Mercury & Hunter River General Advertiser (NSW) Tues. 7 Oct. p.7
At Batavia on the 6th inst. Aikshaw loading raw sugars, for Melbourne.

1879 Bijvoegsel Tot De Nieuwe Amsterdamsche Couran Algemeen Handelsblad I. Zondag 12 October (No 15381)
Batavia: Vertrokken [Sailed]: *Sept. 2: Aikshaw, Tate, Samarang.*
Nov. 27 (No 154339)
Soerabaja, Binnengekomen [Arrived]: *Oct. 9: Aikshaw, Tate, id* [Samarang].
Dec. 9 No (15439)
Soerabaja: Vertrokken [Sailed]: *Oct. 19: Aikshaw, Tate, Probolingo.*

1880 The Argus (Melbourne) Wed. 7 Jan. p.4
Ships to Arrive (at Melbourne): Sailed: Aikshaw: Sourabaya: Nov. 18, tonnage 573.
Jan. 30 p.4
The Aikshaw; a barque from Sourabaya: was reported yesterday as passing Cape Otway at a quarter past 8 p.m.
Feb. 3 p.4
Melbourne: Arrived: Feb. 2: Aikshaw, barque, (573 tons, G. Tate, with 750 tons sugar) which arrived yesterday, is from Java, with a full cargo of sugar. She left Probolingo, her port of loading, on November 22, and cleared Balli Straights on November 27. In the S.E. trades latitudes the winds were light, and after parting with these the barque had light variable winds to Cape Otway, which was made on Thursday last. On Friday and Saturday afterwards she had to contend against strong gales from E.S.E. to E., and the Heads were not entered until Sunday last. There she was towed up the river to Yarraville refinery, the agents being the Victorian Sugar Company.

1880 The Williamstown Chronicle (Victoria) Sat. 14 Feb. p.3
Footscray Police Court: Thurs. Feb. 12. Before Messrs. Morris, W. Mitchell, & Campbell.

  Alleged Assault.--Charles Bailer, cook and steward on the ship Aikshaw proceeded against Thomas Taylor a seamen on the same vessel for an assault alleged to have been committed on the 4th inst. Defendant had been arrested on warrant, and kept in the lock-up two days before being bailed out.

Mr. Harcourt appeared for complainant, and Mr. A. Read for defendant.

Charles Bailer on oath said that on the day named, he was scrubbing out his cabin when defendant went and complained of his tea being black, and struck him on the side with his hand, and said said (sic) he would be the death of him (witness), if he went in the ship. The mate heard the disturbance, and separated them. Afterwards defendant got a stick and dodged him round the galley.

To Mr. Read: I obtained the warrant against defendant. Did not tell the magistrate I was struck by a billet of wood. He must have misunderstood me if he thought so. *Witness here prevericated a great deal and was cautioned by Mr. Read, who told him to leave the box.*

The case was dismissed with £1 1s. costs in default of distress, fourteen days imprisonment.

<u>*Wages*</u>.*--Captain Tait (sic), of the same vessel was summoned by a seaman named August Louis, for £22 wages said to be due.*

Mr. Harcourt appeared for complainant, and Mr. Read for defendant.

It was stated that complainant sued for the amount on account of the cruelty he had received on the voyage from London, and also for having been kept short of provisions.

The following evidence was taken August Louis deposed: I joined the vessel in London. Remember being in the port of Samarang, Java.

Mr. Read objected to the question.

Mr. Harcourt said he was going to complain of the captain wilfully leaving his men without food.

Witness continued: The bread was not fit to eat, and I complained to the captain, when he said "You can go aft; and leave when you like." We had also a quantity of bad fat given instead of lean meat.

Mr. Read again objected, stating that they were being sued for wages and not the condition of the food.

Mr. Harcourt: It is ill usage to deprive the men of their food.

Witness continued: At Samarang, the captain one night said I want to see the lighters empty before the men knock off. The captain was drunk at the time. I said I would not work any more. The captain then kicked me in the abdomen. His brother took him away. He afterwards struck me and gave me a black eye. The captain sent some flour on shore at Samarang which left us without sufficient food to proceed to Melbourne. We were short of bread. He said you will get as much as each other. We met a barque outside Cape Otway, and got a bag of flour from it. The reason I did not complain at Samarang was because the captain said he would give me my discharge at Melbourne. Was certain that some flour was sold at Samarang by the captain. I am afraid to go in the ship again as he might kick me again.

To Mr. Read: I did not ask the captain not to lag me. Could not swear how many days I was on full allowance of all provisions except bread. The first ship we met the captain obtained some bread from. I showed the crew where I was kicked. The captain told me one time he would kick my liver out.

The magistrates did not consider the case of ill-usage maintained, and though the provisions might have run short there was a remedy for that. They dismissed the summons for wages in this case and also in another of a similar nature, in which a seaman had sued for a similar amount.

Disobedience of Orders.--The complainant in the last case were then proceeded against by Captain Tait for continued wilful disobedience of orders.

The Captain stated that from the 4th to 7th of the present month he had frequently given defendant orders on the ship to go to work, and he positively refused to do so.

The first mate gave similiar evidence.

Sentenced to one hour's imprisonment.

Feb. 21 p.2

Captain Tate, of the Aikshaw, was summoned, in the City Court on Wednesday for illegally landing a pig. Mr.Gurner prosecuted, and Mr. Stewart appeared for the defence. The vessel came from Java, and discharged at the Sugar Works, where the pig was put ashore. That is contrary to law, as there are stringent regulations against landing pigs before inspection. A penalty not exceeding £100 is laid down, so that a very heavy fine is in the power of the bench. Mr.Stewart said his client pleaded guilty although the matter was wrongly brought here instead of at Footscray. The captain had to comglain (sic) of the customs officer's delay in informing him of the summons. In consequence of this he had incurred a penalty, on demurrage, for the detention of his vessel, to the amount of £45, or £15 a day for three days. He was ignorant of the law. The bench inflicted a fine of £1.

1880 The Argus (Melbourne) Mon.23 Feb. p.4

Port Phillip Heads: Sailed, Feb. 22: The Aikshaw, barque, for Port Pirie, S.A., was towed from the bay on Saturday [21st.] by the Hercules.

TRS 1/629 2 deserters in Melbourne.

[**LR** 1879: Captain Tyson amended Tait: Owners Hine Bros, Maryport.]
[**LR** 1880: Captain Tait amended G. Tate: Owners Hine Bros. Maryport.]
[**MNL** 1880: Owner: Edward William Tyson, Aikshaw, Cumberland.]
[**MNL** 1882 & 1883: 72977 Aikshaw, Maryport, 573, Mrs. Hannah B. Tyson, Maryport]

1880 The South Australian Register Sat. 3 Apr. p.2

Port Pirie: Sailed: March 26: Ackshow (sic), barque, 573 tons, Tait (sic), for the United Kingdom – 32,474 bshls wheat.

TRS 1/629 1 deserter 17-3-80

1880 The Dundee Courier and Argus Mon. 26 July p.

At St. Helena: (by telegraph, dated Madeira, July 22): Aikshaw.

1880 Nieuwe Amsterdamsche Courant. Algemeen Handelsblad Don. (Thurs.) 29 Juli p.6

St. Helena: Binnengekomen [Arrived]: 9 Juli: Aikshaw, Tate, Port Pirie n. het Kanaal [the Channel].

1880 The South Australian Register Mon. 1 Nov. p.5

Aikshaw, 4,059 qr., from Port Pirie, 44s 9d., for Newry.

1880 The Freeman's Journal (Dublin) Sat. 25 Sept. p.3

Newry: Arrived: Sept. 24: Aikshaw, of Maryport, Tate, master, from Australia, wheat.

Oct. 6 p.3

Newry: Sailed: Oct. 5: Aikshaw, of Maryport, Tate, master, for Glasgow, ballast.

1880 The Glasgow Herald Wed. 6 Oct. p.8

Glasgow: Arrived: Oct. 5: Aikshaw, 573, Tait (sic), from Newry, ballast.
Oct. 18 p.8
At Glasgow for Honolulu. HI—The magnificent Iron Clipper Barque "Aikshaw," 573 tons register, classed 100 A1 at Lloyd's. Has the greater portion of her Cargo engaged, and will meet with prompt despatch—For freight, &c. apply to Allan C. Gow & Co. 19 Waterloo Street; or to Geo. Gray MacFarlane & Co., 4 West Regent Street.
[Survey: Clyde (Glasgow) in November.]

TRS 1/629
Managing Owner: Edw. W. Tyson, Maryport. Master: G. Tate.

1880 The Glasgow Herald Mon. 15 Nov. p.8
Glasgow: Sailed: Nov. 13: Aikshaw, 573, Tait (sic), for Honolulu, general.
Nov. 17 p.6
The Tail of the Bank: Sailed: Nov. 16: Aikshaw, 573, Fate (sic), from Glasgow for Honolulu: general.
Nov. 18 p.6
Lamlash: Put in: Nov. 16: Aikshaw for Honolulu.
Nov. 19 p.6
Lamlash: Sailed: Nov. 18: Aikshaw, Honolulu.
1881 Feb. 11 p.6
Spoken: Aikshaw, from Glasgow for Honolulu, Dec. 26, in lat. 4 S., long. 27 W.

TRS 2/7 note in Index
Edward William Tyson of Maryport Mariner died at Maryport 11 March 1881 , having bequeathed all his property to his wife, Hannah Beeby Tyson for whom letters of administration was granted at Carlisle on 29 March 1881.

TRS 2/4
Aikshaw: Shares: Hannah Beeby Tyson 10, William Tyson 2. [no Hines] 30 March 1881.

1881 Saturday Press , Honolulu H.I., Sat. 23 Apr. p.2
Honolulu: Arrived: April 17: Brit bk Aikshaw, Tate, from Glasgow last Sunday, after a passage of 153 days. She brings a general cargo to Messrs. G.W. Macfarlane & Co, which she is discharging at the old Steamship dock. After discharging she will be laid on for San Francisco, to sail in about two weeks.
May 7 p.2
The British bark Aikshaw is at the old Steamship wharf, discharging her cargo very slowly, and loading sugar also, by degrees; if they hurry up she may get off for San Francisco about the middle of next week.
A Naval Court was held yesterday by H.B.M. Consul-General to investigate charges brought by several of the crew of the British bark Aikshaw against the first mate. The Court found the drunkenness not proved, but carelessness and leaving the deck when on watch was proved, and the mate censured accordingly. The master was also censured for the lax state of discipline in his ship, as revealed by the enquiry. The Court decided that the crew had no sufficient grounds for not carrying out the terms of their agreement.

TRS 1/629
George Forman 32 (Maine) A.B. May 13 1881 Imprisonment by the local court for breach of laws of the Hawaiian Kingdom.
May 14 p.2
Port of Honolulu: Sailed: May 13: Brit bk Aikshaw, Taita (sic), for San Francisco. Aikshaw got off for the Coast yesterday, with a large sugar cargo, 1,915,870 lbs, which

is the largest cargo that has ever left Honolulu, being 184,500 lbs more that the amount carried by the Willard Midget.

1881 The Saturday Press, Honolulu, H.I., Sat. 21 May p.2.
Exports: For San Francisco, per Aikshaw, May 13—1,915,870 lbs sugar, 81 buchs bananas Val Dom. $123, 324. 42; Val Foreign $720. 00.
For San Francisco, per Aikshaw, May 13th--Mr. Hundley [Hendley?]*, Mrs. Keys, Miss Keys, Master Keys.*

1881 Daily Alta California Mon. 6 June p.4
San Francisco: Arrived: Br bark Aikshaw, Tate, 23 days from Honolulu; mdse, to J D Spreckels & bros. Sailed May 13th, first part moderate N E trades, following by strong easterly winds, which continued to June 3 d. lat. 42 20 N; thence northerly and westerly winds to port.
Importations: Honolulu. Per Aikshaw 13,096 bags 1781 kegs sugar.
June 16 p.4
Wheat market British bark Aikshaw 596 tons Cork U.K. £3. 17s. 6d.
July 22 p.4
San Francisco: Sailed: July 22: Aikshaw, Taite (sic), Cork.
[Surveys: San Francisco in June & July.]
TRS 1/629 2 deserters.

1881 Advent Review & Sabbath Herald. Battle Creek, Mich. Tues. Aug. 16, p. 124, Vol 58. No. 8
Ship-Labor in California.
Bro. H. C. Palmer, ship missionary in California, in making his report for the quarter ending July 1, says that several of the officers and men on ships visited by himself this quarter, had previously heard of our papers in Europe, and had become greatly interested. There seems to be more of an eagerness to investigate the doctrines taught by our publications than ever before. He says that our denomination is the only one that visits the ships at that place (San Francisco), and that it is a matter of surprise and wonder to the sailors how we can afford to donate so largely for their benefit. This feeling Bro. P. turns to account by asking if they are not willing to use of their means for the benefit and gratification of their friends in worldly matters, and then drawing a contrast between things of a temporal and an eternal nature. The point thus made, he says, is always acknowledged in a kind and thoughtful manner. The Seaman's mission has recently been supplied with Bibles from the American Bible Society, which is a great help to his work. The islands around Alaska and the North Pacific have been well supplied with reading matter the last quarter. An interest has also been awakened on Pitcairn Island. Bro. Palmer says: "The result of the labor this quarter has been of greater significance than that, of last quarter. I ask the prayers of all God's people in behalf of this work, and that I may have a greater consecration to it. I feel that the Lord has blessed the efforts put forth; to his name be all the glory and praise."

No of ships visited during the quarter, 79

" "   *pages of tracts distributed, 37,508*
" "   *copies of Signs " 4,258*
" "   *Good Health " 86*
" "   *Tidende " 324*
" "   *Harolden " 335*
" "   *Stimme " 61*
" "   *Frenchpaper ' 24*

" "   other periodicals ' 66
" "   Annuals ' 179
Donations received, $2.50

Bro. P. appends the following interesting notes to his report:—
Ship Arcadia : Captain interested.
" La Escocesa : Captain very much interested.
" Glory of the Seas : Steward and wife much interested.
Promise to distribute reading matter, and to write on arriving at home.
" Polynesian : Captain and wife much interested.
" Pomona: Gave two Bibles to men in the forecastle. Several were much interested; distributed extra reading matter.
" Inglewood: Second mate, carpenter, and sailmaker much interested.
" Olympus : Captain gave $2.00 to the cause, and promised to see me on his return. Seemed much impressed with evidences of the second advent. Gave him Thoughts on Daniel and on Revelation.
" Hagarstown : Captain acquainted with our people in the Bast. Subscribed for Signs.
" Legal Tender (a whaler),: Captain and friend very much interested; have much hope in their cases.
" Oiluruum : Second mate and steward much interested. Asked for extra reading matter, and seemed deeply affected.
" Aikshaw : A great anxiety manifested to read by officers and crew.
" Alpheta : Officers and crew anxious to read. Gave extra reading matter. M. L. H.

1881 The Maryport Advertiser and Weekly News Fri. 30 Dec. p.5
Queenstown: Arrived: Dec. 28: Aikshaw, Tate, from San Francisco.
TRS 1/629
Queenstown: M. Turning (28) Kingstown A.B. left in prison 29-12-81.

1882 The Liverpool Mercury Wed. 4 Jan. p.3
Queenstown: Sailed: Jan 3: Aikshaw, for Barrow.

1882 The Maryport Advertiser and Weekly News Fri. Jan. 6 p.8
Barrow-in-Furness: Arrived: Jan. 3: Aikshaw, Tate, from San Francisco via Queenstown.

TRS 1/629
1882: Managing Owner: Edw. W. Tyson, Maryport. Master: Tate. Glasgow 11-11-80 to Barrow 4-1-82.
1882 Aikshaw: Master G. Tate, C/97266: Managing Owners Hine Bros. of Maryport.
Barrow: Sailed: Jan. 20. Liverpool: Arrived: Jan. 23.

[Long voyage] Liverpool--Maryport 2.3.82 – 10.7.84.
Aikshaw: Master G. Tate: Registered Managing Owners Hine Bros. Maryport.

1882 The South Australian Register (Adelaide) Fri. 16 June p.4
Port Adelaide: Arrived: Thursday, June 15: Aikshaw, barque, 573 tons, G. Tate, master, from Liverpool March 3. Harrold Brothers, agents.
The Aikshaw, barque, from Liverpool, made an ordinary passage, having the usual run of wind and weather. Prior to reaching the longitude of the Cape she sprung the maintopsailyard, which was the only casualty of any consequence which occurred. She reached the Bell Buoy on Thursday, and on the pilot boarding he let go an anchor for a very short time, when the tug was in attendance, and towed the vessel to the wharf.

Port Adelaide: Friday, June 30. [Before Mr. R. J. Turner. S.M].
Geo. Tate, master of the Aikshaw, was charged with using threatening language to Water-police Constable Baker. It appeared that a seaman of the ship had been fined at the Court, and a dispute arose on the subject between the captain and the constable. Ultimately the former said he would give the latter a hiding but for his uniform, and the constable said he had a right to be on board the other's ship. Fined 5s.

1882 The South Australian Advertiser (Adelaide) Fri. 1 July p.6
George Tate, master of the ship Aikshaw, was charged with using threatening language towards Constable Baker. There was some contradictory evidence offered, the police constable and another officer stating that the captain threatened to thrash the informant, and two or three other witnesses alleging that Constable Baker insulted the defendant and provoked him to threaten to give informant "a good hiding." The S.M. considered there was provocation, and fined defendant 5s. and costs 10s.
July 4 p.4
Sailed: July 2: Aikshaw, barque, for Newcastle.
TRS 1/629 1 deserter 1-7-82.

July 12 p.5
New South Wales. Sydney, July 11. The barque Aikshaw, from Adelaide, while being towed into Newcastle yesterday during a heavy swell, narrowly escaped an accident, owing to the parting of the tow line of Nobbys. The signal gun was fired, but the tug picked her up again without mishap.

1882 The Sydney Morning Herald Tues. 11 July p.4
Newcastle: Arrivals: July 10: Aikschan (sic), from Adelaide.
Aug. 22 p.4
Newcastle: Departures: Aug 21: Arkshaw (sic) for Valparaiso, with 1966 (sic)-- tons coal.
TRS 1/629
Newcastle: Samuel Dunne (21) Belfast A.B. and C. Kahlan (25) Hamburg A.B. in gaol.
1882: Aikshaw: Valparaiso arrived Oct. 10, sailed Oct 14: 1 deserter.
Iquique arrived Nov. 29, sailed Dec. 28: 1 deserter.

1883 Nieuwe Amsterdamsche Courant Algemeen Handelsblad. Woensdag 17 Januari (No 16545)
Iquique 31 Dec. Vertrokken [Sailed]: *Aikshaw, Tate, Hampton.*

1883 New York Herald Wed. 21 Mar. --triple sheet-- p.10
Spoken: Bark Aikshaw (Br) Tate, from Iquique for Hampton Roads, Jan 24, lat 35 S, lon 89 W.

1883 The New-York Times Thurs. 10 May p.5.
Norfolk, Va., May 9. – Last evening as the United States steamer Alliance was coming up Hampton Roads from outside the capes without a licensed pilot aboard, as is now the custom on naval vessels, she came into collision with the bark Aikshaw, from Iquique for New-York, which was lying at anchor about two miles from Thimble Light. The bark had her bowsprit and forward rigging carried away. The Alliance was not injured.

1883 New York Herald Sat. 12 May --with supplement-- p.10
New York: Arrivals: May 11: Bark Aikshaw (of Maryport, E.), Tate, Iquique, Dec. 31. via Hampton Roads, with nitrate of soda to Bowring & Archibald. Passed Cape Horn Feb 12, and crossed the Equator March 30, in lon 35; off Cape Horn had a strong N W gale, smashed a boat. [Survey: New York in May.]
May 16 --triple sheet-- p.10

Norfolk, Va, May 15.—The injury to the British bark Aikshaw which was recently in collision with the United States steamer Alliance at the mouth of the Chesapeake Bay, has been compromised, the United States authorities paying all damages.

1883 The New-York Times Wed. 13 June
New-York: Cleared: June 12 Aikshaw, (Br.,) Tate, Sydney, N.S.W.
June 17
New-York: Sailed: June 16: Bark, Aikshaw for Sydney.
TRS 1/629 5 deserters in New York.

1883 The Argus (Melbourne) Wed. 26 Sept. p.6
The barque Aikshaw 75 days from New York, for Sydney, was spoken by the General Picton on September 2.
Oct. 4 p.6
The barque Aikshaw from New York for Sydney passed Wilson's Promontory at 20 minutes to 6 p.m. yesterday. [which suggests Aikshaw sailed via the Cape of Good Hope.]

1883 The Sydney Morning Herald Wed. 10 Oct. p.6
Sydney: Arrivals: October. 9: Aikshaw, barque, 596 tons, from New York June 16, arrived yesterday evening from New York with a general cargo, and anchored in Watson's Bay for inspection by the health officer. She will most likely be granted pratique this morning, and be towed to Neutral Bay.

The internet has furnished some details of the crew and passengers in Sydney. {mariners.records.nsw.gov.au/1883/10/8310.htm} {from the Internet: Source Authority of New South Wales Shipping Master's Office}
Aikshaw of Maryport. George Tate – Master. 573 tons. From the Port of New York to Sydney (N.S.W.) Oct. 13 1883: George Tate, Master: William Frodson [Jackson?], 1st Mate, 26, Maryport: John Holme, 2nd Mate, 25, Maryport: Bernard Olsen, Carpenter, 34, Norway: Josep Nigun, A.B., 25, Finland: R.S. Hockly, Sailmaker - A.B., 26, London: O.W. Snarberg, A.B., 29, Sweden: Axel Berghils, A.B., 23, Finland: O. Nilsen, A.B., 24, Sweden: William Sweetman, A.B., 29, Halifax: Thomas Larkin, Cook & Steward, 43, Belfast: Nathaniel Bradley, A.B., 23, Glasgow: Ralph Colin McClean, Apprentice, 16, Maryport: John Gorley Crone, Apprentice, 17, Maryport: William Arthur Armstrong, Apprentice, 17, Maryport: George …. Evans, Boy, 21, Sydney (N.S.W.): Carl Johanssen, A.B., 27, Finland:
Passengers: Mrs. Tate, Adult; Master Tate, Child.
TRS 1/629 At Sydney: George ......Evans (21) Sydney in Hospital.

We shall have a break in Sydney. The nationalities and ages are interesting, as all officers and apprentices were from Maryport (except for the Captain). Briefly we delve into the {**FS:** 1881 Census}. We chase the apprentices. William Armstrong (most probably) lived at 73 King street, Maryport, (Crosscanonby) as a clogger, 15, born in Maryport living with his mother, Head, Mariner's Wife 50, born in Maryport. John G. Crone lived at 121 High street, Maryport (Crosscanonby) a scholar, 15, born in Carlisle. He lived with his mother, Head, Mariner's Wife, 42, born in Carlisle. Ralph McLean lived at 34 Bents Maryport (Ellenborough & Ewanrigg) with Robert Levison Head, 57, born in Whitehaven a Blacksmith Ironworks, his wife Eliza Levison, 62, born Scotland, Elizabeth Rothery Unmarried, 18, born in Maryport, General Servant (Domestic). Ralph was 14 years old, a nephew, born in Carmarthen Wales and was a scholar.

1883 The Sydney Morning Herald Wed. 24 Oct. p.8
Departures: Oct. 23: Aikshaw, barque, 573 tons, Captain George Tate, for Port Augusta, via Newcastle: Exports 100 tons coal: was towed to sea last evening:

Passengers: Mrs. Tate and Master Tate.
25 Oct. p.6
Newcastle: Arrivals: Oct. 24: Aikshaw from Sydney.
Nov. 15 p.8
Newcastle: Departures: Nov. 13: Aikshaw, for Port Augusta.
Nov. 24 p.8
Wilson's Promontory: Inward: Nov. 23: 6.45 a.m.: Aikshaw, barque.

1883 The South Australian Register (Adelaide) Fri. 7 Dec. p.4
Port Augusta: Arrived: Dec. 4: Aikshaw, barque, 573 tons, Tate, master, from Newcastle. Cargo 897 tons coal
1884 Jan. 4 p.7
Marine Board: Thursday, January 3.
Casualty Reports.—Reports were received from various sources as to damage to the grounding of the Aikshaw.
Jan. 30 p.4
Port Germein: Sailed: Jan. 29: Aikshaw, United Kingdom.
Feb. 9 p.4
Exports from Port Pirie: Jan. 26, Aikshaw, 32,502 bushels wheat, U.K.
TRS 1/629 5 deserters in Port Augusta.

1884 The Maryport and Workington Advertiser Fri. 22 Feb. p.8
Port Augusta: Sailed: Dec. 17: Aikshaw, for Channel.

1884 New York Herald Wed. 11 June Tripe Sheet p.10
Spoken: April 7th, lat 28 35 S, lon 10 57 E. bark Aikshaw (of Maryport), from Port Pirie for Cork, 69 days out. [via Cape of Good Hope]

1884 The Morning Post (London) Sat. 3 May p.6
St. Helena: Arrivals: (By tele. dated Madeira, May 2) Aikshaw

1884 The Liverpool Mercury Wed. 25 June p.3
Queenstown: Arrived: June 24: Aikshaw, from Adelaide.
July 9 p.3
Queenstown: Sailed: July 8: Aikshaw for Maryport.

1884 The Maryport and Workington Advertiser Fri. 11 July p.8
Maryport: Arrived: July 10: Aikshaw, Tate, from Port Pirie, via Queenstown.
Aug. 1 p.5
Liverpool: Arrived: July 31: Aikshaw, Tate, from Maryport.

1884 The Argus (Melbourne) Mon. 18 Aug. p.3
Wheat Market: the Aikshaw at 39s 6d for Maryport.

[**LR** 1883: Aikshaw, Bk, G. Tate, 573/55, Hine Bros, Maryport 100A1]

The voyage from Liverpool to Maryport was 861 days or 2 years 4 months 8 days

1885 Otago Daily Times (N.Z.) Mon. 12 Jan. p.2
Port Chalmers: Arrival of the Aikshaw. The barque Aikshaw, from Liverpool. Arrived at Port Chalmers on Friday afternoon. She was met in the Lower Harbour by the Customs steam launch, and all being well on board, was at once cleared in by Mr. R. T. Macdonnell, the tide-surveyor. The Aikshaw is a smart-looking iron barque of 573 tons register, and was built in 1875 under special survey, by Doxford and Sons, of Sunderland, her class at Lloyd's being 100 A1. She has a raised quarter-deck and

topgallant forecastle, and is altogether a well-found vessel. She brings 900 tons of general cargo and 14 tons of dynamite, which is stowed in a properly-constructed magazine. She is consigned to Messrs Neill and Co. (Limited), of this city, and will discharge at the Dunedin wharf. The Aikshaw left Liverpool on September 19, was towed down to the Skerries, and thence had light variable winds until she cleared the Channel, on September 22, when the winds flew into the N. W., and carried her into the Bay of Biscay; she experienced light airs and calms while crossing the Bay, and took up the N. E. trades off the Island of Madeira on October 11. The trades were light and unsteady, and gave out in latitude 10 N, longitude 27 W, on October 23; thence she had light adverse winds and calms until October 26, in latitude 4 N, when the S.E. trades were picked up; she crossed the equator on October 28, in longitude 81 W., had moderate S.E. trades, and lost them in latitude 30 S. on November 8; thence she experienced variable winds, and sighted the Island of Tristan d'Acunha on November 18; crossed the meridian of Greenwich November 21 in latitude 42 S., and rounded the Cape of Good Hope on November 29 in latitude 44 S.; she took the steady westerlies off the pitch of the Cape, and made her easting between the parallels of 46 and 48 S. latitude, carrying strong passage winds across the Southern Ocean, and meeting very heavy weather. The meridian of Cape Leuwin was crossed 20 days after she rounded the Cape of Good Hope; thence she met very unsteady winds and weather until January 4, when she encountered a very heavy N.E. gale, with high seas and rainy weather; the gale moderated on the evening of the same day, and on the 6th inst. she passed through Foveaux Strait; met a strong N.E. gale on the 7th inst., which was followed by a another from the N.W. on the 8th, on the evening of which day it backed to the S.W. and increased to a perfect hurricane; the gale moderated at 4 a.m. yesterday, and she made Cape Saunders at 10 a.m., was off the Heads at 2 30 p.m., crossed the bar in tow of the Plucky at 4 p.m. and anchored in the Powder-ground at 5.30 p.m. No ships bound for the Colonies were spoken, nor was any ice observed in the Southern Ocean. Captain Tate reports that on December 19, on latitude 47 S., longitude 104 E., she passed at 10 a.m., a spar, with canvas attached, apparently a mast and sail, also the side of a deckhouse painted white.
Jan. 30 p.2
Departures: Aikshaw, barque, 573 tons, Tate, was towed from Dunedin to sea yesterday, and sailed in ballast for Oamaru (sic), at which port she is to load for Home.

1885 The Timaru Herald (N.Z.) Fri. 30 Jan. p.2
Port of Timaru: Wool is now coming to hand freely, though the broken weather we have lately experienced has considerably retarded shearing. The wool is mainly merino clips. The barque Aikshaw left Port Chalmers for this port yesterday under charter to the N.Z.S. Company.
Feb. 5 p.2
Port of Timaru: Arrived: Feb. 4: Aikshaw, barque, 573 tons, Tate, from Port Chalmers: The barque Aikshaw arrived in port yesterday from Port Chalmers. She left on Monday afternoon, and had strong N.E. gales the same night, accompanied by heavy rain, which took off about four o'clock the next morning. The weather remained calm till 4 p.m. on Tuesday, when the wind came up from the S W. and brought with it heavy rain, lightning and thunder. Timaru was sighted at daybreak yesterday morning, and the vessel was towed to the buoys as above.
Feb. 6 p.2
The barque Aikshaw was discharging her ballast into the boats yesterday. The ballast is being thrown into the sea on the land side of the T wharf.

1885 The Star (N.Z.) Fri. 6 Feb. p.4

The Timaru Excursion.

[By our Special Reporter.] Another Success. Within the memory of men, and not very old men, either, a Christchurch resident used to look upon a journey to Timaru almost in the light of a journey to the end of the earth, wherever that may be. Those were the days when the Timaru surf was the terror of "all that travelled by water," while those who "travelled by land" stood in equal awe of the rivers, some half-dozen of which had to be crossed on the journey. Things are different now, verily. Yesterday, over 2000 of the inhabitants of Christchurch—a host equal in number to a third of the present population of Timaru—left the City of the Plains in the morning, had a "good time" in the Southern town, and were back in Christchurch before the night was very old.

Free Trips. The harbour works were, of course, the centre of attraction to the visitors. The Harbour Board had generously given the use of their tug Titan, which ran several free trips round the harbour, and had crowded decks on each occasion. There was only one vessel in the basin, the barque Aikshaw, which had arrived on the preceding day from Port Chalmers. The sea was rather rough, but the barque rode at her moorings in peace and security behind the sheltering mole. The operations of the large crane employed in placing the concrete for the monolith at the end of the breakwater, were watched with great interest by crowds of people, and the beach was dotted with groups enjoying the fresh sea breeze. Others filled up the five hours by a walk round the town, those who had known Timaru in former years noting the improvements which had taken place since their former visits. By half past 5 o'clock a move began to be very generally made in the direction of the railway station, and half an hour later the first train left for Christchurch, followed in about ten minutes' time by the second. A large crowd of the residents assembled to see the visitors off. One satisfactory feature of the day was the very orderly behaviour of all; a drunken man was a rarity, and the police had no more to do than on days which were not signalised by an excursion. The run home occupied about four hours and a half, the second train reaching town: at half-past 10 p.m.

1885 The Timaru Herald (N.Z.) Mon. 9 Feb. p.2

The Barque Aikshaw took in about 260 bales of wool from the wharf on Saturday. She was hauled off about three o'clock in the afternoon.

Feb. 13 p.2

The barque Aikshaw was hauled to the wharf yesterday morning but no cargo was put on board owing to the large number of excursionists on the wharf.

Feb. 17 p.2

Arrest: Two seamen belonging to the Aikshaw were arrested last evening by Detective Kirby for larceny. They will make their appearance at the Resident Magistrate's Court this morning.

Feb. 19 p.2

The barque Aikshaw was hauled to the wharf yesterday morning, and during the day took in about 220 bales of wool. Up to last night she had 2033 bales on board.

Feb. 20

Aikshaw only took a few bales of wool yesterday, owing to the large number of excursionists on board and on the wharf.

Feb. 21 p.2

Resident Magistrate's Court, Timaru: At this Court at 10 a m. on Thursday, the Resident Magistrate (J. S. Boswick, Esq.) heard the civil action James Williamson and James Murray (the Dunedin Iron and Woodware Company) v. George Tate (master of the barque Aikshaw), claim £13 16s 6d, for non-delivery of certain goods from London, viz., five bundles of iron, value £13 4s, and one coil of wire, 12s 6d. Mr. C.T.H. Perry appeared for plaintiffs, and Mr. Hamereloy for defendant. Captain Tate admitted receiving the goods on board, and his chief officer proved that they were delivered at Dunedin. After argument a nonsuit, with costs 21s, was given. Papers, &c, Received.

The barque Aikshaw finished loading wool for Home yesterday. The railway has only been engaged 32 hours loading her, during which time they have put on board 2454 bales of wool, besides a quantity of tallow and skins. She expected to sail about the beginning of next week.

A Tribute to the Port.
To The Editor of the Timaru Herald.
Sir, — Will you kindly give me space in your paper in order to express the pleasure I feel in stating my opinions concerning the future port of Timaru (of course we really cannot call it a completed port yet), and also to thank the Harbormaster (Captain Webster) and his assistants for the care and attention they have shown me during my stay here. We have now only been here sixteen days, and during this time have discharged 50 tons of ballast and loaded 2466 bales of wool, besides 24 casks of tallow, and I am pleased to state that during the whole of this time my vessel never had to leave the wharf through stress of weather. At the same time I found it very inconvenient to heave off to the buoys to give place to a small steamer. But of course this will change in time as the harbor increases. I am, &c, George Tate, Master Barque Aikshaw. Timaru, Feb: 20th.

Feb. 23 p.2
The cargo of the barque Aikshaw is valued at £48,520.

Feb. 27 p.2
Timaru: Sailed: Feb. 26: The Aikshaw 573 Tate, for London. She was towed to sea by the Triton yesterday forenoon, and picking up a rattling N.E. breeze, soon ran out sight.

1885 The Standard (London) Tues. 11 June p.6
London, West India Dock: Arrived: Arkshaw (sic) from Timaru.

TRS 2/5
Aikshaw: Shares: Hannah Beeby Tyson 8, Edward Thomas Tyson 3. [no Hines] 26 June 1885. [in Red: Wilfrid Hine is still Manager]

1885 The Times (London) Mon. 17 Aug. p.2.
[Advert] *Trinder Anderson & Co's Line: Fremantle and Champion Bay; Aikshaw -573- London – sailed.*

1885 The West Australian (Perth) Fri. 25 Sept. p.3
The London Shipping:
The following is the passenger list per Aikshaw, which cleared 5th August, 1885 Steerage: John Steenson, Martin Hession, Thomas Bryan, Thomas Molloy, Michael Halloran, Edward Grealy, Patrick Luiskey, Jane McGuire, Amy McGuire, Robert McGuire, Frederick Rudd, Emma Rudd, James Powell, Caroline Powell, James Powell, Mary Powell, Fred Powell, Margaret Grigsley, William Grigsley (sic), Thomas Grigsley (sic). 20 souls, equal to 17 statute adults.

Nov. 17 p.3
Fremantle: Arrivals: Nov. 14th: Aikshaw, barque, G. Tate, master, from London. Passengers: John Steenson, Martin Hession, Thos. Bryan, Thos. Molloy, Michael Halloran, Edward Grealy, Patrick Linskay [Luiskey?], Jane McGuire, Fred. Rudd, Margaret Grigsby, Wm. Grigsby, Thos. Grigsby, Emma Rudd, Amy Mc'Guire, James Powell, Caroline Powell, Mary Powell, James Powell, Fred. Powell.
[One missing. Namely Robert McGuire.]
Nov. 19 p.3

The barque Aikshaw, which arrived at Fremantle on Monday, brought to this Colony about twenty immigrants. She left London Docks on August 7, and arrived here after an average passage of 98 days. She made no calls on the way out. When in the tropics, she was becalmed for about a week, and when in the same latitude as the Cape of Good Hope, had the only day of bad weather she experienced. The crowning of Neptune was duly observed when passing the Equator, both among the crew and the passengers. In the tropics, she sighted the new ship, the Fairholme, whose captain accepted the courteous invitation of Captain Tate of the Aikshaw to dine, while at the same time the passengers of the latter vessel were given a trip to the Fairholme. An occurrence, which nearly had a fatal result, happened when the Aikshaw was becalmed. Two of the sailors went overboard to have a swim, when a shark made for them and they were rescued only just in time. On the whole, the Aikshaw had a good voyage, and the passengers, who were made comfortable, enjoyed the passage.

Maryport and Workington Advertiser Fri. 15 Jan. p.8 (1886)
A Remarkable Occurrence at Sea.
A letter has been received from Mr. John Crone, of Maryport, at present on board Messrs. Hine Brother's vessel, the Aikshaw, in which the following remarkable occurrence is related:-- A short time back, whilst an emigrant ship was proceeding on her passage to Freemantle (sic), (Western Australia), a young female emigrant dropped her child overboard, whether accidentally or purposely, cannot positively be asserted. The next day a shark was caught, and when the fish was opened, the body of the child was found in it.
[see John Crone apprentice in 1883]

1885 The West Australian (Perth) Tues. 29 Dec. p.3
At the Fremantle police court on Saturday W. Emanuel, a sailor belonging to the Aikshaw, was charged with being drunk and disorderly and resisting the police. He had a bottle of whiskey in his pocket at the time, and, succeeding in breaking away from the police, he rushed along the jetty, and falling across the rails bruised and cut his face severely and broke the bottle. The police said when the accused fell they thought, from the violence of the fall, that he had killed himself. He was fined 10s. or 14 days. The fine was paid.

1886 The Police Gazette Western Australia. Published by Authority – Wednesday Jan 6 p.2.
Adolph Janssen, middling stout, age about 32 years, 5 feet 10 inches high, brown hair, light whiskers, long visage, fair complexion, slightly bow legged, deserting the barque "Aikshaw." Dated Fremantle, 30th. December, 1885

1886 The West Australian (Perth) Tues 12 Jan. p.3
Fremantle: Departure: Jan 8 – Aikshaw, barque, Tate, master for Valparaiso.

1886 The Inquirer and Commercial News (Perth) Wed. 13 Jan p.2
A trip to Scarborough:
The sea view at Scarborough requires only to be seen to be appreciated — the islands of Rottnest, Carnac, Garden Island, and the Fremantle shipping, forming one of the most charming panoramas capable of being compassed by the human eye, and irrespective of the hundred and one other estimable features of the place, that of itself is well worth the ride out to see. For some hours during our stay the good ship Aikshaw, on her voyage to South America, was in sight, and with all sails bent to a light but fair breeze, the dot on the ocean was watched with an interest that spoke volumes of the bracing influences of the change of (.........) thus afforded to the little band of citizen travellers.

1886 Maryport and Workington Advertiser Fri. 7 May p.8
Talcahuano [south of Valpariaso]*: Sailed: Apr. 3: The Aikshaw for Matanzas.* [very near Valpariaso]

1886 The Liverpool Mercury Mon. 16 Aug. p.7
Lizard: Passed: Aug. 14: Aikshaw from Matanzas.
Aug. 23 p.7
Falmouth: Sailed: Aug. 22: Aikshaw for Goole.

1886 The Standard (London) Mon. 31 Aug. p.6
Hull: Arrivals: Aug. 29: Aikshaw, Matanzas.

1886 The York Herald Tues. 21 Sept. p.7
Goole: Sailed: Sept. 20: Aikshaw, Tate, London, ballast.

1886 The Standard (London) Sat. 25 Sept. p.6
London: East India Dock: Arrived: Aikshaw, to load for Gisbourne.

TRS 2/5

Aikshaw: Shares: Hannah Beeby Tyson 8, William Tyson 1, Jane Tyson 3, Wilfrid and Alfred Hine (Joint owners) 2. Remarks, Wilfrid Hine of Custom House Buildings, Maryport designated Managing owner per Form No 556/1885 under the hand of the said. Wilfrid Hine and Alfred Hine, jointly owners of two shares, and dated 12th Nov. 1886.

19 Nov. 1887 Hannah Beeby Tyson, Wilfrid and Arfred Hine 2. [in Red: M.O. [Manager Owner]]

TRS 1/629 Captain Geo. Tate, 1837, Sunderland, Aikshaw, C/01031: 1st Mate J Myers, 1837, Sunderland, Castle Holme in Maryport: 2nd Mate W. Cobb, 1866, Sunderland from Castle Holme in Maryport.

1887 The Argus (Melbourne) Thurs. 27 Jan. p.6
Spoken: Dec. 13: The barque Aikshaw, 52 days out of London, for Gisborne, New Zealand, by the Daphne in lat. 37½deg. S and lon. 20½deg, W; she reported all well.

1887 Poverty Bay Herald (N.Z.) Mon. Jan 3. p.2
At the Harbor Board meeting to-morrow tenders will be opened for lightering the Aikshaw with plant, also for timber and coal and block moulds.
Feb. 14 p.2
Gisborne: Arrival of the Aikshaw.
The barque Aikshaw, 573 tons, (Capt. G. Tate) left the London docks on October 21st, in tow of the steam tug. She anchored in the Downs during the night and got under way next day, being towed into the Channel. The tug left the ship off Dungeness. Experienced moderate weather to the Equator, which was crossed on Monday, Nov. 22. In consequence of the illness of the captain previous to this, a course was shaped for Funchal, Madiera, but on nearing that island the captain showed signs of improvement and directed the chief officer, Mr. Myers, to proceed on the voyage. She got in the S.E. trades when in about 5 North latitude. Passed the latitude of the Cape on Dec, 11th. On Jan, 1st, when in lat. 45.27 S. and long. 52.50 E., the captain died at 7.30 a.m., and was buried at sea. Fresh westerly winds were experienced to within a short distance of making the land, the easting being run down in about lat. 45 S. At noon on Feb. 3 sighted the Suares. On Feb. 6th a heavy gale was experienced which did some slight damage and split some sails. Light variable weather till reaching Table Cape on Saturday last, and anchored in the Bay at 3 p.m. the same day. Mr. Myers, chief officer, took command after Capt. Tate's death, and has brought the ship into port in the most

creditable manner. The Aikshaw brings plant and cement for the Harbor Board, consigned to Common, Shelton and Co. An enquiry will be held by the Collector of Customs to-morrow to verify the cause of the captain's death.
Feb. 16 p.2

Mr. John Bourke, Secretary for the Harbor Board, yesterday had occasion to wire to the Board's agents in London to inquire if the cargo of the ship Aikshaw was insured to the roadstead or the wharf. A reply was recived that the insurance was to the wharf. The message was sent from the office at 3.30 yesterday afternoon and the reply was received at 11.14 this morning.
Feb. 18 p.2

Last night two of the Aikshaw's crew made their escape from the ship in one of the boats. They were not missed until this morning. Captain Myers then came on shore to look for them and discovered the boat on the beach.
Mar. 4 p.2

The schooner Orpheus got slightly damaged lightering the Aikshaw this morning. She had her bulwarks aft smashed in through bumping against the barque.
Mar. 30 p.2

The contractor asks for extension of time:-- Aikshaw: There is now only about a hundred tons of cargo in the Aikshaw, principally cement. During the fortnight about 225 tons of cement was landed and stored, and 200 tons of plant, including all the heavy portion.
Apr. 4 p.2

Aikshaw (Capt. Myers) sailed at 5 a.m. to-day for Lyttelton in ballast. The Aikshaw has been lying in the Bay for over seven weeks discharging her cargo of plant and cement for the Harbor Board.
Apr. 13 p.2

With all their anxieties the members of the Harbor Board are still inclined to be witty at times. When the question of making provision in a case of distress was being discussed last night, one member generously suggested that they should each contribute a guinea, and the Chairman double. Someone suggested that the Chairman was entitled to a remission altogether, when another member was struck with the happy idea that it was the Engineer who should stand the two guineas. Later on the private generosity of members was appealed to on behalf of a proposed testimonial to the mate of the Aikshaw. Mr. Dickson thought the best form of a testimonial would be to get photographs of all the heavy machinery that had been delivered, accompanied with the thanks of the Board. A still more facetious member suggested that photos of the members themselves be presented!

1887 The Star (N.Z.) Tues. 12 Apr. p.2
Lyttelton: Arrived: April 11: Aikshaw, barque, 573 tons, Tate (sic), from Gisborne. Vessel at the Wharves: Brier Holme
TRS 1/629 Master: Henry Humphreys, 1834, Liverpool from Brier Holme joined at Lyttelton 16.4.87. Custom House Lyttelton 1877 22/4/87 certify that Henry Humphrey as Master. 2 deserters 18.2.87
Apr. 23 p.2
Lyttelton: Sailed: April 23: Aikshaw, barque, 573 tons, Humphreys, for Falmouth or Queenstown for orders.

1887 Poverty Bay Herald (N.Z.) Sat. 30 Apr. p.2
The barque Aikshaw left Lyttelton last week for London with 840 tons of wheat.

1887 The Freeman's Journal (Dublin) Fri. 5 Aug. p.3
Queenstown: Arrivals: Aug. 4: Arkshaw (sic), (Brit), 574, Humphrays (sic), Lyttleton, wheat.
TRS 1/629

Waterford: Arrived: Aug. 25: Aikshaw.

1887 Maryport Advertiser Fri. 16 Sept. p.5
Liverpool: Arrived: Sept. 11: Aikshaw, Humphreys, from Waterford. [Surveys: Liverpool: September & October.]
Oct. 28 p.5
Ship Shares for Sale:--On Friday, afternoon, at the Coffee Tavern, Maryport, Mr. T. Boyd offered for sale by auction, in two lots, seven 64th shares in the iron clipper barque Aikshaw. There was, however, only a small attendance, and no business was done.

1887 The Argus (Melbourne) Sat. 24 Sept. p.6
Coast cargo of New Zealand wheat per Aikshaw has changed hands at 29s. 9d.

TRS 1/629
Master, Humphreys, 1853, Liverpool, C/01031: William Cobb, 1866, Sunderland, "from Lance", 2nd Mate.

{www.archives.qld.gov.au/downloads/Indexes/immigration/*U-V.pdf*}
Index to Registers of Immigrant Ship' Arrivals 1848-1912. Series ID 13086.
Aikshaw: 26 Jan 1888: IMM/126 360 Z1967 M1706
Humphreys - (Captain): Blease Alwood H 31:

1888 The Brisbane Courier Tues. 24 Jan. p.4
In Moreton Bay: January 23: Aikshaw, barque, 573 tons, from Liverpool 15th. October, with a general cargo, arrived off Cape Moreton at 3.40 p.m. yesterday, after a passage of ninety-nine days.
Jan. 25 p.4.

Brisbane: The barque Aikshaw, from Liverpool, was towed up the river by the Boko on yesterday morning's tide, and berthed alongside Messrs. Parbury, Lamb, and Co's wharf, Eagle-street, where she will commence discharging on Friday, to-morrow being a public holiday. This vessel, which is consigned to the agency of Messrs. Quinlan, Gray, and Co., brings about 1100 tons of general merchandise, including a quantity of machinery for Messrs. R. R. Smellie and Co, and 300 steel rails for Cooktown. The Aikshaw, although a stranger in the port of Brisbane, has for some years past been engaged in the trade between Great Britain, the Australian colonies, and New Zealand, and has earned the reputation of being a fast sailer. She is an old vessel, having been launched from the yards of W. Doxford and Sons, of Sunderland, as far back as October of 1875. The hull is constructed of iron and measures 171ft in length by 28.9ft. beam and 18ft. depth of hold, which gives a tonnage of 573 tons net, 596 tons gross, and 553 under deck. She is divided into two compartments by an airtight bulkhead, and when leaving the builder's yards was classed 100 Al at Lloyd's. She is owned by Hine Bros. and belongs to Maryport. She has the appearance of being a strong serviceable vessel and carries 875 tons dead weight on a mean draft of 16ft. 4in. There is a very neat and comfortable-looking half-poop saloon wherein accommodation is provided four first-class passengers in addition to the captain and officers.

The Aikshaw, which is under the command of Captain Henry Humphreys, sailed from Liverpool on the 15th October, and at the outset encountered variable winds and weather. These lasted until the north-east trades were picked up. The island of Madeira was sighted on the sixteenth day out, and the first of the north-east trades was felt in lat. 29deg. 11min. N., long. 20deg. 29min. W. They proved moderate in force, and were lost in 8deg. N. lat., 24deg. 54min. W. long, on the 10th November. They were followed by southerly winds, which lasted for seven days. She crossed the equator on the l5th. of

November in long. 29deg. 19min. W., and picked up the south-east trades three days later in 5deg. 28min. S. lat, and 32deg. 39min. W. long. They were also moderate, and carried the vessel to 22deg. 28min. S. lat., which point was reached on the 25th November. She then experienced northerly and southerly winds for four or five days. Sighted Tristan da Cunha on the 3rd December, and crossed the meridian of Greenwich in 39deg. S. lat. 16 miles west of the 7th. The meridian of the Cape of Good Hope was crossed of the 12th December, and from that date she experienced from fresh gales to strong winds from north-west to south-west and west until reaching 139deg. E. long. On the 18th of December when in 46deg. 24min. S. lat. she passed an iceberg about 15ft. high and about 100ft. long. From the meridian of Greenwich to 139deg. E. long., a distance of 5800 miles, the vessel made the splendid average of 200 miles per day, but after that she had to steer a zig-zag course all the way to Cape Moreton, having met with nothing but northerly and baffling winds, the passage from there occupying sixteen days. The south end of Tasmania was rounded on the 9th of January, and she was off Point Danger at noon on Sunday, Point Lookout at 5 p.m., and Cape Moreton at 7.30 p m. She then made signals for a pilot, but getting no reply and the wind shifting to the eastwards, Captain Humphreys worked his vessel to seaward and did not again reach the Cape until Monday afternoon. She was towed across to the roadstead that evening.
Feb. 23 p.6
In regard to the vessels in harbour, the Aikshaw sails (in sand ballast) hence shortly for Port Pirie, where she will load grain for a port in the United Kingdom yet to be determined upon. She takes from here 400 tons of smelting coke for use in the silver mines in the Broken Hills district.
Feb. 29 p.3
Queensland: Aikshaw, barque, Port Pirie, cleared Moreton Bay during Wednesday night.

TRS 1/629 Brisbane 3 deserters: Port Pirie 2 deserters.

1888 The Mercury (Hobart) Sat. 24 Mar. p.2
Port Pirie: Arrived: Mar. 19: Aikshaw, from Brisbane.

1888 The Argus (Melbourne) Fri. 24 Aug. p.7
A Wheat ship damaged: London Aug 21.
The barque Aikshaw, which left South Australia on the April 16 with 32,584 bushels of wheat for the United Kingdom has arrived at Dublin. She encountered very severe weather on the voyage, and sustained considerable damage.

1888 The Daily News (London) Tues. 21 Aug. p.6
(From Lloyd's, August 20): Wrecks and Casualties: Aikshaw, barque, of Maryport arrived at Ringsend, Dublin, August 20, from Port Pirie with wheat. The master reports during heavy gales and high sea had two boats stove and deck-house and galley damaged.

1888 Maryport and Workington Advertiser Fri. 24 Aug. p.8
Queenstown: Arrived: Aug 20: Aikshaw, Humphreys, from Port Pirie (for orders).
Dublin: Arrived: Aug. 21: Aikshaw, Humphreys, from Port Pirie.

1888 The Freeman's Journal (Dublin) Mon. 27 Aug. p.3
Imported per Aikshaw from Port Perie (sic), 17,660 bags wheat.

TRS 1/629
Dublin: Sailed: Sept. 2. Liverpool for Dry Dock or Flushing Dock: arrived: Sept. 3.

1889 The South Australian Register (Adelaide) Sat. 26 Jan. p.4
Adelaide: Arrived: Friday, January 25: Aikshaw, barque, 573 tons, H. Humphreys, from Liverpool October 19: No passengers.

The Aikshaw, barque, from Liverpool, is one of the past schools of iron ships built of thick plating, and bearing in her appearance the evidence of lasting to an interminable time. She has the usual Liverpool cargo, which put her well down in the water. On leaving on October 19 she had very fine weather for several days, but after October 24 south-west gales and high seas were encountered until reaching the north east trades on November 14. The winds were light and variable, and it was December 1 before crossing the Equator, and the south-east trades were equally perplexing, but attended by heavy rain. On December 9 sighted Trinidad, and after passing 16* S. had moderate winds, mostly from the northward to 36* S, 22* W., when fresh breezes to heavy gales continued till crossing the meridian of the Cape on December 26, and boisterous weather prevailed to Cape Leuwin. The vessel was promptly attended by pilot and tug, and was at once towed into harbour.

Vessels Spoken.—By the Aikshaw—On October 29, the barque Albion, ten days out from Cardiff, bound to Santos. On November 18 the ship Stockbridge, from Liverpool to Melbourne, in lat. 13* 16' N., long 25* 36' W. On December 9, in lat. 20* S., long. 29* 37' W., the barque Annot Lysle, of Liverpool, bound north.

Feb 18 p.3
Departures: Feb. 11: Aikshaw, barque, 375, H. Humphreys, for Rangoon.

1889 Maryport Advertiser Fri. 1 Mar. p.3
Adelaide: Sailed: Feb. 26 (sic): Aikshaw, barque, Humphreys for Rangoon.
May 24 p.3
Rangoon: sailed: May 22: Aikshaw (barque), Humphreys, to River Plate.
Aug. 30 p.3
At Talcahuano:: Aikshaw barque from Rangoon.
1890 Jan. 3
Iquique: Sailed: Dec. 11 [1889]*: Aikshaw for Falmouth.*

1890 The Glasgow Herald Tues. 18 Feb. p.8
Vessels Spoken: Aikshaw (British barque), Iquique for the Channel, Feb. 1. 3 N., 30 W.
Mar.12 p.11
Vessels Spoken: Aikshaw, for the Channel, March 2, 48 N., 26 W.

1890 Western Mail (Cardiff) Wed. 9 Apr. p.4
Cardiff, Roath Docks: Arrivals: Apr. 7: Arkshaw (sic) 573, Ostend, ballast.
Apr. 29 p.4
Cardiff: Cleared: Apr. 28: Aikshaw, B, 854 rails for Buenos Ayres.
May 1 p.4
Cardiff, East Bute Dock: Sailed: Apr. 29: Arkshaw (sic) (Dawson), Buenos Ayres.

[**LR** 1889: Aikshaw, Bk, H. Humphreys/ Dawson, 573/558, Hine Bros, Maryport 100A1]

1890 The Glasgow Herald Mon. 21 July p.8
Rosario [Argentine]*: Arrived: July 16: Aikshaw, from Cardiff.*
1891 Feb. 28 p.11
Spoken: Dec. 27: Aikshaw, Iquique to Cork, 56 S. 65 W. [The Horn]

1891 The Standard (London) Mon. 23 Mar. p.6
Falmouth: Arrivals: Mar. 21: Aikshaw, Iquique.
Mar. 24 p.6
Falmouth: Sailings: Mar. 22: Aikshaw, Ostend.
Apr. 7 p.6

London: Surrey Commercial Dock: Arrived: Apr. 6: Aikshaw, from Ostend.
Apr. 9 p.1
[Advert] *Devitt and Moore's Australian Line: Hobart – Aikshaw: W. Cobb: W.I. May 25.*
May 8, p.6
Gravesend: Sailing: May 7, Arkshaw (sic), Hobart.

1891 The Mercury (Hobart) Tues. 16 June p.2.
Aikshaw was to have left London for Launceston and Hobart on May 7, with a large cargo including a quantity of railway iron for the Government.
July 10 p. 2.
Defence Stores.--Invoices have been received of the expected arrival from London for the Defence Department of the following military stores, ex Aikshaw:- For Hobart direct - Cartridges, S.A. ball, M.H. rifle; 250,000; cartridges, S.A. ball, M.H. carbine, 50,000; cartridges, S.A. blank, B L: rifle, 100,000; shells, empty, for 64-pr. R.M.L. 30; shells, empty, for 12 pr. B.L., 75; Sponges for R.M.L. 2.5 gun, 4; material and small stores, torpedo service, quantity annual demand. For Launceston direct, per Aikshaw -- Cartridges, S.A. ball, M.H. rifle, 250,000; shell, empty, for 12pr., B.L., 30.

1891 Examiner Launceston (Tasmania) Sat. 15 Aug. p.2
Tamar Heads: Arrived: August 14, 8.10 a.m., Aikshaw, bk, anchored outside Heads: 12.35 p.m., in tow of tug Wybia.
Launceston: The bark Aikshaw, which left London on May 30 (sic) for this port, arrived at the wharf about 7 p.m. yesterday after a passage of 75 (sic) days. Captain Cobb was too fatigued to give a report of the voyage last evening and we are consequently compelled to hold it over until our next issue. [Cannot find it].

1891 The Mercury (Hobart) 2 Sept. 2 p.2
Aikshaw cleared Low Head for Hobart at 2.55 p.m. yesterday
Sept. 5 p. 2.
Hobart: Aikshaw, barque, from London, via Launceston. Left London on May 7 and arrived at Launceston on August 13, 98 days out. She left Launceston on the 1st inst., and passed through Banks' Straits on the 2nd and had Eddystone abeam at 1 p.m. same day. Entered the river at daybreak yesterday, arriving here at 3 p.m., after a smart run round of three days. Dirty weather was experienced on entering Banks' Straits with strong north-easterly winds, when the wind veered round to the N.N.W., and afterwards north-east to Cape Pillar. ….She is owned by Messrs. Hine Bros., of Maryport, England, Captain Wm. Cobb being in command, assisted by Messrs. James Allen and Daniel Turney as first and second officer respectively. After discharging her cargo for this port, the Aikshaw will sail for Newcastle to load coals for the West Coast of South America.
Sept. 14 p.2
Aikshaw, barque, 573 tons, Wm. Cobb, for Valparaiso, via Newcastle. Left at 2.40 p.m. on Saturday.

1891 The Sydney Morning Herald Sat. 19 Sept. p.8
Newcastle: Arrivals: Sept. 18: Aikshaw, from Hobart.
Oct. 2 p.6
Newcastle: Departures: Oct. 1: Aikshaw, barque, for Valparaiso with 890 tons coal.
1892 Jan. 19 p.4
Valparaiso: Arrivals: Nov. 20: The barque Aikshaw from Newcastle.

1891 The Morning Post (London) Mon. 28 Dec. p.8
Lloyd's agent at Antofagasta telegraphs:--"The Ackshaw (sic) is totally lost; part of the crew were saved and landed here."

1892 Launceston Examiner Fri. 22 Apr. p.2

Sad news has just been received by a gentleman who has always taken a great interest in sailors and apprentices visiting this port. The intelligence is to the effect that the bark Aikshaw, which visited this port some months back, struck on the rocks at Valparaiso about last Christmas and sunk in seven minutes. Ten of the crew got into a boat, and that also struck on the rocks. The master, Captain Bulman (sic), the mate, and the youngest apprentice were dragged over the rocks in a naked condition. The only thing saved was a blanket, which they had to cut up for caps and shoes, on account of the heat of the sun. They had walked three miles without clothing, and would have had to walk 50, when fortunately they saw a tug boat and were rescued. On examination by a doctor they were found to be badly bruised, but no bones were broken.

Apr. 28 p.2.

We are glad to be able to report that from a letter received by the last mail from the second mate we learn that more lives were saved than at first reported. It appears that some order given by the captain was not distinctly heard and that the anchor was let down in 45 fathoms of water and that the ship sank after striking on the rocks; that 10 of the crew and officers got into a boat, which was wrecked against the rocks. The following were saved - Captain Cobb, first mate (Wm. Allen), second mate (Turney) carpenter, two apprentices (Smith and Bulmer), [see Myrtle Holme 1897] one A.B. seaman. Five were drowned, including one apprentice. Aikshaw was wrecked or foundered on Christmas Eve. The two apprentices went home on board the Castle Holme and the two mates went on board the Elder, having 200 (sic) passengers on board which was unfortunately wrecked on January 17, but all were saved. It appears it was only the boy that was hauled over the rocks. It is presumed that the mate in writing to Bulmer's friends confined himself to facts concerning the boy, to whom he was much attached, as according to Miss Bulmer's letter only two were saved. The Aikshaw left here for Hobart, thence to Newcastle, and afterwards to Valparaiso.

Wreck Report for Aikshaw, 1892:: Portcities Southhampton
(No. 4482) "Aikshaw."
Finding of a Naval Court of Inquiry held at Valparaiso on the 5th and 6th of January 1892. Present:
Mr. Adolph F. Howard, British Vice-Consul, Valparaiso, President.
Mr. Alexander McB. Elliott, Master Mariner and Surveyor to Lloyd's at Valparaiso, and Mr. William Kydd, Master of the "British Empire", of London, official No. 63,517, members.
Mr. Frederick J. T. Dawson, Clerk to the Court.

The Court, pursuant to an order from Her Britannic Majesty's Consul-General at Valparaiso, proceeded to investigate the cause and manner of the stranding and loss of the British barque "Aikshaw", of Maryport, official No 72,922, and having deliberately weighed and considered the evidence and observations preferred by the master, officers, and part of the crew of that vessel –

The Court finds—

That the "Aikshaw", an iron barque of 573 tons register, belonging to the port of Maryport, sailed from Antofagasta at 6.45 a.m. on the 24th December last, laden with a part cargo of coal, bound for Tocopilla, and at about 1 p.m. the same day was stranded on a sunken rock close inshore, between Jorges Point and Roca Blanca (lat. 23*32' S., long. 70*34' W.), and became a total loss.

That Alfred Vincent, William Wieg, Peter Nielsen, Hazlett Irvine Lewers, and William Tarbuck, were drowned owing to the smashing of the boat, and getting entangled in the wreck.

That from the evidence adduced, the Court is of opinion that the cause of the loss of the ship was due to the strong current and heavy swell setting towards the shore, and to the prevailing light winds, and there being no anchorage.

The Court is, however, of the opinion that had the vessel been tacked before she got so close in shore the casualty might have been avoided, and whilst recommending that Mr. William Cobb, the master, be supplied with a duplicate of his certificate, doth admonish him to be more cautious in the future.

Further, the Court doth recommend that duplicates of the certificates of Mr. James Allen, the mate, and Mr. Daniel L. Turney, the second mate, be issued to them.

The Court avails of this opportunity to express its high approbation of the humane conduct and energy displayed by Mr. Daniel L. Turney, the second mate, in saving the lives of Mr. James Allen, the mate, Julian R. Bulmer, apprentice, and Samuel Nimmo, the cook.

(Signed) William Kydd. Alex. McB. Elliot. A.F. Howard, President of the Naval Court. Fred. J.T. Dawson, Clerk to the Court.

1892 The Mercury (Hobart) Tues. 24 May p.2

The British Board of Trade have awarded their Silver Medal for gallantry in saving life at sea to Mr. Daniel Stalker Turney, late second mate of the barque Aikshaw of Maryport, in recognition of his services in rescuing life on the occasion of the wreck of the Aikshaw near Antofagasta South America on December 24, 1891. During the stay of the Aikshaw in this port Mr. Turney had made a few friends who will, no doubt, be glad to hear of his bravery and its reward.

****

{www.anmm.gov.au/webdata/resources/ Certificate Registers of Certificate of Competency Masters and Masters, Colonial Trade.}

Bulmer, Julian Ralph No.47: 17 Aug 1889: 1st Mate: Brisbane: Birth Kentish Town London: 1876.

{bmd} Julian Ralph Bulmer Marriage 1904 Sept. Holyhead (Anglesey) Vol. 11d Page 795.

DX/741/6

In the year 1930 I received a letter from Thos. Carey J.P. an octogenarian of Maryport, saying that as the only representative living of the late owners of the Barque Aikshaw" 795 (sic) tons, registered Messrs. Hine Bros. and Willis of Maryport and London, He had lately come into possession of that ship's brass bell which had recently been recovered from the scene of the wreck off Antofagasta, Chile, 40 years ago, the bell was little the worse for its long immersion in the sea.

Doxford & Sons (**added**: the builders Sunderland) 1875 was clearly visible upon its surface. Mr. Carey hearing that I was the youngest member of the crew when the wreck took place asked me if I could remember the names of the Captain and Officers and anything about the loss of the ship. Well I certainly could, as every detail of the voyage and shipwreck is as vivid in my mind to-day as when it occurred in the year 1891. Since then it has occurred to me that it might be of interest to listeners to hear an account of this tragedy which in the ocean going sailing ship was I am afraid not an infrequent ending of some fine ships although the public personally heard very little about the business except the bare fact that such and such a ship had been lost. As an introduction I may mention the fact I was born in London and educated at the Royal Mathematical School, Christs Hospital, Newgate Street, and had never seen the sea until just previous to my first voyage in the "Aikshaw" but I developed an intense desire to go to sea after reading such Authors as Marryat, Jules Verne, Clark Russell and Knigton (sic), and I would not be satisfied until I was placed in the Royal Mathematical School, founded expressly by King Charles II to train boys for his Majesty's Navy and Merchant Service and eventually when I left school at 15 years of age, taken by my Mother and handed over to the Mate (Mr Allen) of the Bark "Aikshaw" lying in the London dock fully loaded, bound for Tasmania.

The "Aikshaw" was destined never to return, she was loaded with every conceivable form of merchandise, including Locomotive Engines, and all manner of railway equipment. The voyage to Launceston passed without much incident worth recording, except we suffered the usual hardships and discomforts undergone by the crew of sailing vessels whilst the "Easting down" in the "roaring forties" that is to say wet decks and wet clothes for weeks at a time, rough seas would come roaring on board sweeping everyone off their feet and half drowning them, there was no means of drying one's clothes either. After about 120 days sailing we sighted the Island of Tasmania (sic) [report of 1891 The Mercury (Hobart) 5 Sept. p.2: Aikshaw: Left London on May 7 and arrived at Launceston on August 13, 98 days out.] I definitely remember on hearing the coast, scenting the delicious perfume coming from the direction of the land. We towed about 30 miles up the river Tamar, discharged half our cargo and sailed round to Hobart Town and discharged the remainder, took in ballast and sailed for Newcastle N.S.W. Loaded a cargo of coal, sailed for Valparaiso, Chile, through Cook's Straits en route, arrived at Valpariaso (sic), had orders to proceed to Antofagasta to discharge, when most of the cargo had been discharged we had orders to sail to Tocopilla, some distance up the coast to discharge the remainder and load Nitrate for the United Kingdom. We hove up anchor and sailed from Autofagesta (sic) at 4 a.m. on Christmas Eve 1891 and shortly after mid-day the ship was a total wreck and half the crew drowned. It happened like this, a few hours after we got under way, the wind shifted and we had to beat out of the Bay. About 8 bells (noon) after we had been alternately trimming and ballast in the hold, orders came "all hands dinner" we had no sooner taken our dinner (consisting of pea soup and salt pork) remember Autofagasta (sic) is almost in the tropics and rather hot down in the "hakf (sic) deck," the apprentices apartments, about 12x8x7 feet inside the deck [all scored out], than another order came "all hands 'bout ship', I suppose she had approached too near the land, and I immediately ran with the kid (tin basin, sailors carry their food in) of pea soup to the galley to be kept warm, that was the last I saw of any dinner or any other meal that day. We hauled the yards round in a vain endeavour to tack ship but the ship being in ballast and having a very light draft and consequently not steering well, would not answer her helm, and missed stays and ran right on to the rocks and heeled over.

The Captain gave orders to put out a boat, then I well remember, that thinking the ship could be saved if some assistance could be got, and in my wisdom and in-experience thought the Captain was acting too hastily in ordering us to leave the ship, I ran up to him and said "shall I run up a flag signal and ask for assistance Sir?"--we would be seen from the Port, but I received the abrupt order, no my lad get into that boat, so I had to obey, this was a most difficult job, but eventually the boat was lowered into the water full of men, but before we could haul it clear of the foundering ship, she heeled over, crushing violently [scored out], the boat between herself and the rocks, all hands in the boat except myself were either killed or drowned. I was thrown into the sea, with wreckage, spers (sic), swinging yards, sails, etc., all round a terrible turmoil but I struggled, swimming for dear life, clutching at anything I could get hold of, thrown up and down with every heave the ship gave, then almost on her beam ends, the sea doing its best to pound her to pieces which it eventually did in about an hours time, at last after struggling for which seemed an age, exhausted and almost done for, I came bobbing up close to the main top (a platform at the top of the lower rigging about 30-40 feet up the mast, I got hold of this and embraced it with both arms, then I saw the 2nd. Mate and an apprentice named Turney & Smith respectively who threw me a line from where they were safely standing on the rocks having got there by climbing along the mast when in a horizontal position, I caught this rope and secured it under my arm pits and let myself go, they they (sic) hauled me through the sea, wreckage and over the rocks to safety. These two on their arrival home were presented with a R.H.S. testimonial, I certainly own my life to them. Nine out of the total crew of 17 were drowned. The Captain jumped from the unturned bottom of the ship and swam round reaching safety.

We recovered nothing from the wreck except some blankets which we wrapped round our feet to protect them from the rocky road over the mountain over which we should have had to tramp about 15 miles to the Port but as luck would have it we had been seen from the Port, and a launch was sent to our assistance into which we managed to get after climbing along the rocky coast for some distance. I can assure you, the next day Christmas Day I was feeling very sore with a broken rib and sundry wounds on my body the scars of which are visible to-day. I felt in no mood to enjoy the festivities of the season. A collection of clothes was made from the ships in the harbour and the inhabitants on shore which resulted in my being presented with a uniform which fitted me like a glove (**added**: too much, the trousers split after a day or two), and was by no means comfortable considering the heat, but I was very glad of it under the circumstances. After I recovered we all sailed for Valpariaso in the "Catchapole" R.M.S. one of the coast mail boats which sail as far north as Lima and south as far as Conception. At Valpariaso (sic) a court of enquiry before the British Consul was held into the cause of the disaster, that over and Firnished (sic) with a new rig-out I was given orders to join the Bar (**added**: que Castle Holme), loading Nitrate for the United Kingdom (at Iquique) some hundreds of miles up the coast, we again embarked on the "Catchapole" and had a glorious time feasting on fruit all day long and calling at a great many ports en route, such as Taltal, Chanaral, Carrizal, Coqueinbo (sic) [Coquimbo?], Housca [Huasco?] etc., I finished my apprenticeship in the C. H. became 2nd Mate and Mate before I left her finally but not without going through more thrilling experiences.

A strange sequel happened, the remaining (sic) survivors of the wreck of the "Aikshaw" who embarked on the P.S.N.C. Commadore ship "John Elder" not many hours after leaving Valpariaso, for Liverpool, the ship ran aground in a fog off Conception, and I think became a total loss although no lives were lost. If I were asked whether, If I had my life over again I would chose (sic) the sea as a career, I think I would say Yes! but conditions for seafarers general to-day, have improved almost beyond belief, both with regard to the personal confort (sic) and freedom from risks, bearing in mind the wonderful discoveries scientists have made, such as wireless direction finders, (**added**: Radar) echo sounding machines, improved compasses, (**added**: Gyroscopic), and various other devices to eliminate the risks, that hitherto were always present while at sea, then again, gone are the magotty biscuits, salt-beef and non-vegetable monotonous diet of 50 years ago, and in their place thanks to the research chemists, and his food storage appliances, a varied diet, similar to the best thatcan (sic) be procured on shore is now enjoyed by the sailor. A youth who goes to sea to-day is in an infinitely better position regarding his personal comforts than he would have been 50 years ago, but I doubt very much whether all this comparative comfort and luxury will be likely to foster and encourage the finest qualities of character and endurance which the older and harder methods produced. *Signed* J. R. Bulmer MBE.

{www.plimsoll.org/resources/SCCLibraries/WreckReports/16249.asp}: "John Elder" (s.s.): Finding and Order of a Naval Court of Inquiry assembled at the British Consulate General at Valparaiso, on the 26th, 27th, 28th, 29th, and 30th days of January 1892, and the 1st and 2nd days of February 1892.
The Court, pursuant to an order from the Honorable Hedworth Lambton, Captain, Royal Navy, proceeded to investigate the circumstances attending the wreck of the British steamship "John Elder," of the port of Liverpool, official number 63,313, when on a voyage from Valparaiso to

Liverpool, and the cause of such wreck, and to inquire into the conduct of the master, officers, and crew of the said vessel, and having deliberately weighed and considered the evidence and observations preferred by the master, officers, passengers, and crew of that vessel --

The Court finds;--That the steamship "John Elder," 4,160.10 tons, belonging to the port of Liverpool, sailed from Valparaiso about 4 p.m. on Saturday, 16th January 1892, laden with a general cargo, as well as 139 passengers, bound for the port of Talcuhuano, and at about 6.20 a.m. on Sunday, January 17th, was stranded in foggy weather on Carranza Rocks, where she eventually became a total wreck on January 20th:. That the passengers were all safely landed about 11 a.m. on the day of stranding: That when the boats were ordered out it was done quietly; but, although there was no lack of personal exertion on the part of the officers, the boats were neither properly manned, provisioned, or found: That the chief officer should have been placed in command of the boats, containing as they did more than 120 passengers, including many women and children: That the boats were despatched to the northward without due thought or proper precautions, the second officer, who was in charge, not even having a compass in his boat: That after three or four hours' rowing about the passengers were all safely landed without much difficulty about half a mile from the scene of the wreck.

1902 The Western Mail (Perth) Sat. 29 Mar. p.27
The s.s. Workfield 2,678 tons berthed at Perth. The Chief officer is Mr. J. G. Crone, who has previously visited Fremantle with the immigrant barque Aikshaw 20 years ago. [Most probably the apprentice for Aikshaw in 1883.]

+++++++++++++
Let us follow (a few snippets) of some immigrants landed in Fremantle/Perth in 1885.

1932 The Western Mail (Perth) Thurs. 11 Feb. p.7
"Golden Days." A Voice from the Past.
The following letter to the Editor, written by Mr. Fred. W. Rudd, now of Stratton Strawless, Norwich, England, and formerly of the goldfields, Mundijong, Bellevue and Perth in this State, will no doubt prove of interest to readers of "The Western Mail." Mr. Rudd takes us back to Coolgardie, where he was camped three years before Arthur Bayley made his epoch-making find.
He writes:-- "A copy of 'The Western Mail' dated October 1, 1931, has just reached me. On page 5 you have an article 'Golden Days,' the reading of which thrilled me, and impelled me to write this. "The account of Tim Moon finding the plate nailed to a tree, stating that 'as far back as '86 Anstey and party had pegged out a claim not far from Coolgardie' literally made me jump. It was the hand that is writing this that painted that account on the plate and nailed it to the tree.
Here is a copy of the plate:
+ **Fred W. Rudd. + + Anstey Prospecting Coy., + + November. 1889. +**
(Not '86 as mentioned in your article).

"You can verify this my (sic) a diary that I handed to Cornthwaite Hector Rason on a visit to England in 1907 and which, is, for aught I know, still in the W.A. Agent-General's office in London. The diary gives a daily account of the trip which occupied severel (sic) months. I forget the number of my Miner's Right, but it was under 100. I called at the office of the Mines Department when on a visit to W.A. a few years ago, but their records don't go back so far, although they showed me a copy of another and later Miner's Right I held in 1900, I think, for the Serpentine area.

"It was not so much gold as water we were looking for at Coolgardie. Gold was a secondary consideration then. Sit for two and a half days on the back of a camel in the out-back of the West in November, without a drop of water, and you'll give all the gold ever discovered for a quart of dirty water--or all that ever will be discovered for a gallon from the Swan Brewery. I know!

"You will gather from the enclosed leaflets of lectures that many and strange things have happened to me since those stirring days -- all the lectures being my own experiences in the lands mentioned. For three seasons I lectured for the Empire Marketing Board; now for the Selbourne Society. London.

"I am putting my experiences into book form, and I guess they should be interesting as I am working a strange love triangle through it.

"In addition to the lands mentioned, I have traversed U.S.A. from west to east, and south to Los Angeles. I landed first in Western Australia from the barque Aikshaw, of Maryport, 657 tons, on November 14. 1885. Since then I have spent 26 years in the country (three trips). At that time there were only three main streets in Perth-Front, Middle, and Back streets (St. George's-terrace, Hay and Howick streets, and Murray-street). I was one of Foy and Gibson's first customers (ask Arthur or Charles Amies if they know me).

"How rapidly time flies. It seems but a few years since the foregoing events happened. They come crowding on my memory, which, fortunately, is remarkably good.

"I well recollect the building of the Midland Railway of W.A., on which I was afterwards an employee, and I could 'pitch' a few good yarns of that time -- also as checker on the old Fremantle jetty, when Customs and railway were under Clayton Mason.

"They were happy days. Whatever happened was all in the day's work. I never heard of any going hungry -- one was usually sure of a damper and a tin of dog, especially after Upton Sinclair's book 'The Jungle.'

"However, I must 'ring off.' It will be rather late for a Christmas greeting, but I wish you 'all the best' for the new year.

"Fred and John Mosey know me well. I doubt if Australia has a greater 'booster' than I."

Accompanying Mr. Rudd's informative letter were the leaflets he mentioned. His lectures are on "A Cruise Through the Islands of the Pacific," "Japan, the Land of Many Wonders," "Australia, the Land of Opportunity," "Canada, "South Africa," "Fifteen Years in the Australian Bush," and "Round the World in Sixty Minutes." Copies of eulogistic Press reports lead one to believe that these lectures, illustrated by lantern slides as they are, must be nearly as interesting to English people as his letter published here -- with will be to "old timers in this State -- and that is saying a lot!

1939 The Western Mail (Perth) Thurs. 26 Jan. p.11
First Claim on Coolgardie.

Dear "Non-Com.,"--A copy of "The Western Mail" of 1-12-38 has just reached me containing John Meiklejohn's letter about the "First Lease on Coolgardie."

Let me say right here that I am quite sure he has stated in all his Communications to the Dolly Pot (which I have read with more than passing interest) what he firmly believed to be true. What he didn't know was true also. I'm sure he--like myself--realises we are never too old to learn.

Re his request for further information on the subject: To give details of the formation of the Anstey Prospecting Co. and its operations would provide sufficient copy to crowd out every contributor to the Dolly Pot for many weeks. However, I am writing my autobiography which I hope someone will publish, and in it will give details not only of my trip to Coolgardie, but of my 26 years' residence in various parts of W.A. My last visit ended in 1924--my first began in 1885. In this way I hope your contributors to the Dolly Pot may get all the information I am able to give, as I will let you know when (if) I can find a publisher.

Now for a few details: The Anstey Co. consisted of eight contributing members. We had in our employ three paid men, Glass, Payne and Greaves. Our first prospecting began at Enuin on Geo. Lukin's station--and it was here that Payne (not Greaves as has been stated) struck the first piece of reef gold in the east. Anstey, who was a most excitable man, rushed into town and a rush followed.

This was late in 1888. On his return to Enuin I accompanied him. The find there was not a paying one, so we decided to return to town, where I built an assaying laboratory at the back of Leake and Harper's office in St. George's-terrace for his private use, as he thought then of assaying for the public, but as small finds were being discovered further east, the company decided to have another try.

Fully equipped with three camels and seven horses we started again for Enuin-- Anstey, Glass and myself. Arriving there we learnt that Fraser had just come in from what was afterwards Golden Valley. Southern Cross had not then been located.

It was here that Nature took her first toll before she gave up her treasures of The Golden West. Tim Shea and Harry Beadle started off one morning for the new find, but never arrived there. Their bodies were found by parties that went out to search for them.
I may say that all the requirements of the Mining Act were complied with. On our return from Coolgardie we showed our samples to Warden Troy (I am not quite sure whether it was Troy or Finnerty) and returned to Perth with them, where Anstey assayed them.

I am taking up too much space so can only answer J.M.'s question: "Why had such an important event remained so long unknown. "I left W.A. in 1907. The fact of my having pegged six claims on Coolgardie was known to many Perthites and old prospectors whether J.M. knew it or not. Since 1907 till 1917 I was knocking round the world--six years in the Far East and lost touch with W.A. until I returned in 1921.

In 1924 I called at the Mines Department in Perth and found to my surprise that they had no records of any mining transactions previous to 1890. If they had ever recorded any they were lost. How's that for W.A. in the 80's?
Fred W. Rudd,
Jarrahdale, Stratton Strawless, Norwich, England.

+++++++++++++
{**FS:** 1881 Census}

Robert McGuire	Head M M	40 Isle of Man	Mariner
Jane McGuire	Wife M F	30 Scotland	
Emmy McGuire	dau U F	4 Liverpool	

5 Boarders and a nurse
Rathbone Place 4, Liverpool

{**bmd**} Birth Amy Frances McGuire Sept. 1876 Liverpool 8b 136
Birth Robert Patrick McGuire Sept. 1884 Liverpool 8b 136

1895 The Western Mail (Perth) Mon. 9 Sept. p.6
Government Gazette: Appointments: Post and Telegraph department: Miss Amy McGuire to be telephone attendant, Fremantle.

1922 The Western Mail (Perth) Thurs. 28 Sept. p.18
Deaths.
McGuire.--On September 18 at 15 Malcolm-street, Fremantle, Jane, beloved wife of Mr. Robert McGuire, of Fremantle Harbour Trust, and loving mother of Mrs. Hunt, Mrs. Biggs, Dallas and Allan and of the late William, Eric and Leslie; aged 78 years.
A patient sufferer at rest.

1929 The Western Mail (Perth) Fri. 2 Aug. p.19
A Wharfside Identity. Old Watchman's Retirement.
After 48 years' continuous service on the waterfront at Fremantle Mr. Robert McGuire recently retired at the age of 89 years. From 1881 until a few weeks ago he served in various capacities among the shipping at Fremantle, where he was well-known to ship's companies and local

shipping men. Born on the Isle of Man in 1840 Mr. McGuire followed in the footsteps of his forefathers and went to sea at an early age. He sailed out of Liverpool in some of the crack windjammers of the seventies and eighties, in the Australian, wool and the China tea trade. In 1881 he was cast away on a timber ship that grounded in Hampton Harbour, on the North-West coast, and after making his way to Fremantle he found employment on the waterfront. He was given a position with the Harbour and Lights Department and was appointed as signalman at Fremantle during the period when that service was under the control of the Harbour and Lights Department. He retired from that service and became a watchman on the wharf. At his retirement he was watchman in charge of Robb's Jetty.

1932 The Western Mail (Perth) Tues. 2 Aug. p.1
Deaths.

McGuire: On August 1, 1932, at Fremantle, Robert McGuire of 15 Malcolm-street, Fremantle, husband of the late Jane McGuire, and loving father of Amy (Mrs E. Hunt, Fremantle), Eleanor (Mrs. C. Biggs, Belmont), Deallas (?), (Fremantle), and Allan (Wyndham): aged 92 years.
Aug. 3 p.12
Mr. Robert McGuire, who died at East Fremantle on Monday at the age of 92 years, was well known in Fremantle and in other parts of Western Australia. He spent about 50 years in this State, coming here from the Isle of Man, where he was born. For about 25 years he was in charge of a lighthouse which stood at Arthur's Head, Fremantle, and which was then the leading light for ships entering Fremantle. It was demolished in 1905. Later Mr. McGuire joined the Harbour Trust and had charge of the loading and discharging of cattle at Robb's Jetty for 25 years. He retired two years ago. Two of Mr. McGuire's sons were killed by aborigines in the North-West.

+++++++++++
1887 The Western Mail (Perth) Sat. 15 Jan. p.15
At the Perth Police Court on Tuesday: George Haynes, assistant machinist at the office of the West Australian was charged with absenting himself from his work without leave. His defence was that he had been dismissed by the machinist Steenson, but this was denied by Steenson, and Mr. Hackett, the manager, stated that Steenson had no power to dismiss the defendant.-- Fined £5 and costs.

1896 The Western Mail (Perth) Tues. 24 Mar. p.4
Valedictory.-- The employees in the composing and machine departments of the West Australian and the Western Mail office on Saturday evening, entertained Mr. J. Steenson at a farewell social in the Hotel Metropole. The foreman of the composing room, Mr. J. Gibbney, presided, and there was a large attendance, including several gentlemen who were present by special invitation. The chairman, in proposing the "Health and Success of Mr. Steenson," mentioned that for upwards of ten years Mr. Steenson had filled the position of machinist in the office. During that time he had faithfully discharged the duties entrusted to him. No greater proof of that could be afforded than the fact that the proprietors had asked him to express their thorough appreciation of Mr. Steenson's long and loyal services, and to state that though his association with the office was being severed, they would continue to take a practical interest in his welfare. (Applause.) As for Mr. Steenson's fellow-workers, they one and all had a high regard for him, regretted that they were about to lose his companionship, and cordially wished him every possible good fortune. (Hear, hear.) The toast was drunk with musical honours. Mr. Steenson suitably responded. He was, he said, highly gratified at what had been said concerning himself. The toasts of "The Proprietors," "The Visitors," "The Secretary (Mr. Green)," and "The Chairman" were heartily received. Many capital songs and several excellent recitations were given, the proceedings closing shortly before midnight.

1898 The Western Mail (Perth) Sat. 22 Oct. p.4
Funeral Notices: The Friends of the late Mrs. Sarah Thomson, formerly of South Australia, are respectfully invited to follow her remains to the place of interment, the Wesleyan Cemetery, Perth. The funeral is appointed to leave her son-in-law's (Mr J. Steenson's) residence, Tea Gardens, South Perth, at 3 o'clock, to morrow (Sunday) afternoon.

Donald J, Chipper, Undertaker, Hay-st, Perth.

1903 The Western Mail (Perth) Tues. 27 Jan. p.4
Freemasonry: The consecration ceremony…………..following officers: tyler, Bro. J. Steenson.

1907 The Western Mail (Perth) Sat. 5 Oct. p.9
At the Government Printing Office, a few days ago, Mr. John Steenson the Government Printing Office, a few days ago, Mr. John Steenson was presented with a token of esteem from his fellow-employees. Mr. Steenson has decided to sever his connection with the office, to start in business on his own account. The presentation took the form of a gold medal, suitably inscribed.

1909 The Western Mail (Perth) Fri. 13 Aug. p.3
Women's Christian Temperance Union. The Perth Union. The following officers elected: vice-president: Madam Steenson.

1929 The Western Mail (Perth) Mon. 17 June p.1
Funeral Notices: The Friends of Mr. John Steenson, Officer-in-Charge North Perth Fire Brigade Station, are respectfully invited to follow the remains of his late beloved wife, Annie, to the place of interment, the Methodist portion of the Karrakatta Cemetery.

1935 The Western Mail (Perth) Tues. 16 July p.1
Deaths: Steenson: The Friends of the late Mr. John Steenson, of 22 Gill-street, North Perth and late of the North Perth Fire Brigade Station.
The Brethren of the above Lodge.
M.U.O.F.S., Loyal City of Perth Lodge.
W.A. Fire Brigades Industrial Employer's Union.
Swan River Rowing Club.

1935 The Western Mail (Perth) Thurs. 18 July p.13
Funeral: The Late Mr. John Steenson.
On July 14 last Mr. John Steenson passed away at the St. John of God Hospital at the age of 78 years. He had been connected with fire brigade work for the last 48 years, and only retired from active duty a few months ago. The service at the graveside was conducted by the Rev. Arthur Lyons in the presence of a large gathering of firemen and other friends. The chief mourners were Mr. and Mrs. A. Jewell (daughter and son-in-law), A. and N. Fielding (cousins) and F. C. Jewell.

CONCLUSION

During nearly 45 years that Wilfrid Hine had been either manager or owner of sailing vessels, there had been revolutions in shipping. In 1862 sail ruled the waves. The most beautiful, fast and graceful ships were plying their trade especially between China and Europe. British shipping was supreme as the main rival, America, was torn apart by the Civil War 1861-1865. Yet within a few years several factors meant that sail would be superseded by steam. As the industrial age rolled on, steam propulsion became progressively efficient. The opening of the Suez Canal in 1869 was a mortal (though lingering) blow to sail, as suddenly shipping could avoid the long and dangerous routes via Cape of Good Hope or the Horn. (The draught of the big sailing ships could not use the Suez Canal.) The famous Cutty Sark built in 1869 was converted as a barque in 1877 and then plied mainly between Britain and Australia as a woolship. Up to the 19th century steamships and barques co-existed, but steam became increasingly dominant. However, one owner Gustaf Erickson had a last sailing empire in Mariehamn, Aland Islands Finland. The last commercial sailing ship went round Cape Horn with cargo with wheat from Port Victoria Australia to Falmouth in 1949. It was Erickson's Pamir, four masted, steel hulled barque, 3,020 tons burthen, a giant.

While the steam fleet expanded, the Hine Brothers' sailing fleet gradually decreased. Some vessels were sold and some were wrecked and not replaced. Since 1876 they did not acquire any sailing vessels except the Denton Holme bought in 1890; presumably a replacement for the Abbey Holme which sank the same year. It was a failure as that also was wrecked the same year.

There were still four ships or barques commissioned by the Hine Brothers in Sunderland between 1875 and 1876 which plied mainly between England and Australia and were the only four working sailing vessels which reached the 20th century. These we shall follow in Volume Two, namely: Brier Holme, Castle Holme, Eden Holme and Myrtle Holme.

ADDENDA OF VESSELS AND CAPTAINS

Abbey Holme   63204   JHPP   barque
1869 -1873   Wedgwood Robinson   *Mrs. Robinson 1871.*
1873 -1876   John Henry Randall
1876 -1882   William Bryce
1882 -1890   John Hoare Rich   *Mrs. Rich & son 1885, 90.* **wrecked**

Aikshaw   72922   WTFL   barque
1875 -1879   Edward William Tyson
1879 -1887   George T. Tate (Died at Sea). *Mrs. Tate & Master Tate 1883.*
1887 -1890   Henry Humphreys
1890 -1891   Dawson
1891 -1891   William Cobb   **wrecked**

Aline   58065   HPLB   barque
1872 -1880   John Graham Turney   **wrecked**

Brier Holme   76136   WTRF barque
1876 -1891   John Johnston
1891 -1904   John Hoare Rich   *Mrs. Rich, 1896-99, 1902* **wrecked**

Byron   4621   JDHB   brigantine
1867 -1868   Fearon
1868 -1871   Edward Ward   **sold**

Castle Holme   72923   WTCR ship/barque
1875 - 1877   Thomas Sawle
1877 - 1883   James Williamson   *Mrs. Williamson 1881, 82*
1883 - 1897   William Bryce
1897 - 1904   John N. Hurst: (Robert Dix)
1904 - 1908   George Holman   *Mrs. Holman 1905, 06* **sold**

Cereal   27518   barque
1871 -1872   James Hannah Ritchie   *Mrs. Ritchie 1872.* **abandoned burnt**

Clara   50799   brigantine
1874 -1876   George McLeod
1880 -1883   Hodgson / McCullough   **sold**

Clymene   89483   ketch
1893 -1908   **sold**

Denton Holme   47182   VMNJ barque
1890 -1890   John Hoare Rich   **wrecked**

Eden Holme   62035   NQMF barque
1875 -1876   John J. Robinson. (Died on s.s. Mersey when wrecked 1876 Aug 12.*)*
1876 -1896   John Henry Randall.   *Mrs. Randall: 1880, 86, 87, 90, 91, 92, 94.*
1896 -1904   John Wyrill
1904 -1907   George Harold Dulling   **wrecked**

Elizabeth   22859   snow/brig
1862 -1862   J. Wilkinson   **abandoned**

Glastry   60319   brig
1874 -1875   Shepherd
1875 -1876   John Saul   *Mrs. Saul 1875* **sold**

Glenfalloch   29821   QHGB   barque
1873 -1873   John Johnston
1874 -1874   Anderson
1874 -1876   John Johnston
1876 -1879   John Saul
1879 -1880   Nicholson
1880 -1883   John Saul,   *Mrs. Saul & child 1881.* **condemned & sold**

Hazel Holme   58782   JNFM   barque
1872 -1874   James Hannah Ritchie   *Mrs. Ritchie 1873*
1874 -1876   William Henry Clark
1876 -1877   Wilson Holmes
1877 -1878   Thomas Sawle   Died at Sea
1878 -1883   Joseph William Millican   *Mrs. Millican outward 1881,* & daughter *82*
1883 -1886   John Austin   **condemned & sold**

Hebe   42393   TLVM   brig
1863 -1868   Joseph Wilkinson
1868 -1869   John Smith   sold.

Hope   8093   brig
1870 -1871   John Fearon
1871 -1873   John Patterson   **vessel not heard since:** died at sea

Humberstone   46202   VHMC   barque
1865 -1869   Wedgwood Robinson   *Mrs. Robinson 1867,* 69
1869 -1869   William Clark
1869 -1870   John Smith   **wrecked** (died at sea)

James   70856   flat
1882 -1882   James Coleman   **wrecked**

Jane Harrison: 66308   barque
1872 -1873   J. Johnston   **abandoned**

John Norman   6044   JMDV   ship/barque
1872 -1873   Joseph H. Hurst
1874 -1876   William Bryce
1876 -1879   J. Tarney
1879 -1880   J. Turney
1880 -1882   Isaac Nicholson   **abandoned**

Maggie Gross   59256   JGPH   brigantine

| 1875 -1876 | Holmes | |
| 1876 -1877 | Thomas Wedgwood | **sold.** |

Myrtle Holme   72921   PCGN ship/barque
1875 -1882   James Ritchie   *Mrs. Ritchie (1 child or outward 2 children)*
1875, (with 3 children) 76, (with 3 children) 77, (& Miss Jessie Ritchie) 78, (& child) 80,
(& child) 81.
1882 -1883   John Austin
1883 -1892   Joseph William Millican   *Mrs.Lydia Millican (& children) 1883, (&*
child) 84, (& two children) 85.
1892 -1907   Wm. Cobb   *Mrs. Cobb* outward *1899, 1902, & son 06.*
                                                                        sold.

Robert Hine   60079   HDSN barque
1868 -1872   Joseph Wilkinson
1872 -1872   Edward Ward
1872 -1876   George Brown   *Mrs. Brown 1874*
1876 -1884   Edward Hall   **sold.**

Tom Roberts   18904   MDSF schooner
1873 -1876   Edward Hall
1876 -1876   Clark
1876 -1882   --------------?
1881 -1881   John Fearon
1882 -1882   Tully
1883 -1883   Kendall   **sold.**

Queen of the Fleet 38058   SHND barque
1872 -1875   Wilson Holmes
1875 -1875   James Tarney   **abandoned**

++++++++++++++++++++

Anderson: Glenfalloch 1874-74

Austin John: Myrtle Holme 1882-83: Hazel Holme 1883-86

Brown George: Robert Hine 1872-76

Bryce William: John Norman 1874-76: Abbey Holme 1876-82: Castle Holme 1883-97.

Clark William Henry: Humberstone 1869-69: Hazel Holme 1874-76

Cobb William: Aikshaw 1890-91: Myrtle Holme 1892-1907

Coleman James: James 1882-1882

Dix: Castle Holme 1903.

Dulling George Harold Eden Holme 1904-7

Fearon John: Hope 1870-71: Tom Roberts 1881-81
Fearon: Byron 1867-68

Hall Edward:	Tom Roberts 1873-76: Robert Hine 1876-84
Holman George:	Castle Holme 1904-8.
Holmes Wilson: **Holmes**:	Queen of the Fleet 1872-75: Hazel Holme 1876-77. Maggie Gross 1875-76
Humphreys Henry:	Aikshaw 1887-89.
Hurst Joseph N.:	John Norman 1873-74: [same person?] Castle Holme 1897-1904.
Johnston John:	Jane Harrison 1872-73: Glenfalloch 1873 & 74-76: Brier Holme 1876-91.
Lane John:	Glenfalloch ???
Millican Jos. William:	Hazel Holme 1878-83: Myrtle Holme 1883-92.
McLeod George:	Clara 1874-76
Nicholson Isaac:	Glenfalloch 1879-80: John Norman 1880-82
Patterson John Wood:	Hope 1870-73
Randall John Henry:	Abbey Holme 1873-76: Eden Holme 1876-95.
Rich John Hoare:	Abbey Holme 1883-90: Denton Holme 1890-90: Brier Holme 1891-1904
Ritchie Jas Hannah:	Cereal 1871-72: Hazel Holme 1872-74: Myrtle Holme 1875-82:
Robinson John J.:	Eden Holme 1875-76
Robinson Wedgwood:	Humberstone 1865-69: Abbey Holme 1869-73
Saul John:	Glastry 1875-76: Glenfalloch 1876-79 & 80-83
Sawle Thomas:	Castle Holme 1875-77: Hazel Holme 1877-79.
Smith John:	Hebe 1868-69 Humberstone 1869-70
Tate George:	Aikshaw 1879-87
Tarney James:	Queen of the Fleet 1875-75: John Norman 1876-79
Turney John Graham:	Aline 1875-79: John Norman 1879-80
Tyson Edw. William:	Aikshaw 1875-79
Ward Edward:	Byron 1868-71 Robert Hine 1872-72 (died abroad)
Wedgwood Thomas:	Maggie Gross 1876-1877
Wilkinson Joseph:	Elizabeth 1862-62 Hebe 1863-68 Robert Hine 1868-72
Williamson James:	Castle Holme 1877-83
Wyrill John:	Eden Holme 1896-1904

Austin John	b. Swansea 1838	C/22542 Liverpool 1866
Brown George	b. Maryport 1847	C/31031 Dublin 1867
Bryce William	b. Maryport 1842	C/32636 Liverpool 1869
Clark William Henry	b. Co. Kirkcudbright 1840	C/30750 Belfast 1864
Cobb William	b. Sunderland 1866	C/017472 - C/024982 South Shields
Dix Robert		C/015740
Dulling George Harald	b. Starcross 1878	C/036296 London 1904
Hall Edward John		C/16622
Holman G.		C/631810
Holmes Wilson		C/42494
Humphrey Henry		C/01031
Hurst Joseph H.		C/023190
Johnstone John	b. Carrickfergus 1838	C/26696 Dublin 1867
Lane John	b. Picton 1839	C/02308 Liverpool 1876 ??
Millican Joseph William	b. Maryport 1854	C/21977 ex C/029542 Liverpool 1878
McLeod George	b. Stornoway 1831	C/33008 Dundee 1870
Nicholson Isaac	b. Whitehaven, 1846	C/83246 Liverpool 1876
Randall John Henry		C/28286
Rich John Hoare		C/22773
Ritchie James Hannah		C/93623
Robinson John P.		
Robinson Wedgwood	b. Maryport 1847	C/49237
Saul John		
Sawle Thomas	b. Cornwall 1842	C/84419
Smith John		C/13207
Tarney James		C/94517
Tate George		C/97266
Turney John Graham		C/19279
Tyson Edward William	b. Staveley 1844	C/27756
Ward Edward		C/13207
Wilkinson Joseph		C/10151
Williamson James		
Wilson Samuel		C/91122
Wyrill John		C/17156

ADDENDA OF CAPTAINS AND FAMILY

Austin John
{bmd: Birth John Austin Sept. 1838 Swansea 26 418.}

{http://www.welshmariners.org.uk/search.php}
Austin John, Swansea, Born 1838 C/22542: [Liverpool, 1866]
2 mate Grace Piele 1860-1: mate John Richards 1861: mate Limena 1861-3: mate Acacia 1863-4: Slain Castle 1865-6: Captain Peri 1867-8: Capt. Flora 1868-9: Capt. Princess 1870: Capt. Clara 1871-4: Capt. Talca 1874-81: (address 3 Edward st. Swansea) Capt. Myrtle Holme 1882-6 (?) [only 1882-3 and Hazel Holme 1883-6]: Capt. Ordovic 1888 (died at sea 1892).

Brown George
[**Dir:** Bulmer's 1883 p.553] Brown George, master mariner, 18 Strand st.
Mrs. Brown known voyages: *Robert Hine, 1874.*

1879 Adair's Maryport Advertiser Fri. 5 Sept.
We are sorry to notice the death of Mrs. Brown, wife of Capt. G. Brown, of this town. She was on her voyage home from Genoa in the "West Cumberland" (ss), when she was attacked by dysentery. Owing to complete prostration she was left at Gibraltar under the best medical care. The disappearance of the dysentry left her in an excessively weak state, and she appears to have gradually sunk away. Her remains will be forwarded to Maryport. She had only reached her 32ⁿᵈ year. Her kind disposition had secured for her a large circle of friends, by whom her loss is deeply lamented.

1881 The Maryport Advertiser and Weekly News Fri. 3 June p.8
Marriages: Brown-Robinson: On the 1ˢᵗ inst., by licence at the Baptist Chapel, Maryport, by the Rev. H. C. Bailey Captain George Brown of the Steamer Thorn Holme, to Mrs. Barbara Robinson, both of Maryport.

Bryce William
{bmd: Birth William Bryce   1842 Cockermouth 25 96
          Marriage Wm Bryce June 1876 Cockermouth 10b 851 (Mary Steele)

[Maryport Cemetery] William Bryce Master Mariner of Maryport: Died August 5ᵗʰ 1913; 71 years: Mary wife died March 9ᵗʰ 1924; 77 years.
{Census 1881}

Charles Richard Steele	Head M M	60 Sunderland Durham Mining Engineer
Isabella Steele	Wife M F	60 Sunderland Durham
Thomas Steele	Son U M	27 Ellenborough Cumberland Mining Engineer
Mary Brice	dau M F	32 Sunderland Master Mariner's wife
John Chs. Brice	Gr. Son M	4 Brisbaine (sic) Australia

          (Ellenborough House, Ellenborough & Ewanrigg Cumberland)

{Qld Government Historical Birth Records}
1877/21656 John Charles Bryce – William and Mary Steele 13/02/1877

[**Dir:** Kelly's 1897 p.304] Private dwelling Bryce Wm, 21 North st. Maryport.
[**Dir:** Bulmer's 1901 p.757] Bryce Mr. Wm, 21 North st. Maryport.

Cobb William
{Guildhall Lloyd's Masters}
Cobb William b. Sunderland 1866.
{bmd: Birth Cobb William Sept. 1866 Sunderland 10a 495

1899 The South Australian Register Thurs. 14 Sept p.4

Cobb—Parker.—On the 3rd August, at St. Paul's Church, Port Adelaide, by the Rev. Canon Somwell, William youngest son of Joseph Cobb, of Sunderland to Laura Elizabeth, eldest daughter of Harry Parker, of Rosemead, Alberton.

Mrs. Cobb known voyages: Myrtle Holme: Mrs. Laura Cobb (married in Adelaide) return 1899, Mrs. Cobb 1902, Mrs. Cobb & son 06.

1901The Advertiser (Adelaide) Wed. 2 Oct. p.4

Mr. Henry Parker, of Port Adelaide died at his residence, Princes-street, Alberton, on Monday evening, after an illness extending over a week. The deceased gentleman was born at Port Adelaide, and was a son of Mr. T. H. Parker who, for several years, conducted a butcher's business at the seaport. Mr. H. Parker, who followed the same calling, represented West ward in the Port Adelaide Corporation from 1894 till the end of 1896, and again during 1898 and 1899. Mrs. Parker and two daughters, survive him. The eldest daughter married Captain Cobb, the master of the well-known barque Myrtle Holme.

1903 Dec. 3 p.4

Births: Cobb.-On the 18th October, at their residence, 53, Amberley-street, Sunderland, Durham, England, the wife of Captain Cobb, of the barque Myrtle Holme, of a son. Both doing well.

1907 Aug. 16 p.4

Fremantle, August 15. The R.M.S. Ormuz arrived at 7 a.m. to-day with the following passengers:-- For Adelaide—Captain and Mrs. Cobb and son.

Aug 20 p.6.

Adelaide: Arrived: August 19: Ormuz R.M.S. Passengers: Captain and Mrs. A (sic). Cobb and son.

Captain A. (sic) Cobb, for many years master of the barque Myrtle Holme, a well-known trader between London and Port Adelaide, was, with Mrs. Cobb and their infant son, a passenger to Adelaide by the R.M.S. Ormuz. Captain Cobb, who was for over 15 years connected with the Myrtle Holme, has retired from the sea in order to accept a position as manager of the Spencer Gulf Stevedoring Company at Port Perie.

Dulling George Harald

{Guildhall Masters}

Dulling George Harald b. Starcross 1878; C036296 London 1904 vol 76 1904-07

Dulling George (father) b. Dawlish Devon 1844 C96388 Plymouth 1874 vol 18 1874-79 vol 31 1880-83 1885-87 vol 46 1888-95 vol 61 1897-1901 1903 vol 1905

{bmd: Marriage George Dulling (father) – Sarah Foote Sept 1865 Newton A 5b 221

Birth George Harold Dulling Jun 1878 St. Thomas (Devon) 5b 82

{Census 1881}

Sarah Dulling	Wife (head)	M F 37 Kenton	Devon wife of Master mariner
Amy G. Dulling	dau	F 9 Dawlish	
Henry H. Dulling	son	M 7 Dawlish	
Ethel M. Dulling	dau	F 4 Dawlish	
George H. Dulling	son	M 2 Kenton	
Mary A. Dulling	Mother in Law	W F 60 Mamhead	Formerly Dom. Servant
(2 Strand, Kenton)			

{bmd} Death Sarah Dulling Dec 1902 (50) St. Thomas 5b 27

1934 The Mercury (Hobart) Wed. 3 Oct. p.11

At Launceston Show:

There was a good entry of fat pigs, and Captain G. H. Dulling, a St. Leonards breeder, won most of the awards. They were shapely animals, in the pink of condition, and of good length.   The judge favoured the bacon pen exhibited by Captain Dulling in preference to that shown by the Spring Hill Dairy, because they were of uniform length, though not nearly so heavy. The second pen was on the heavy side. The judge said that Captain Dulling attributed his success to cross-breeding between the Middle York and Gloucester Old Spot, using the latter preferably as the mother of the litter. Bacon curers were heard to remark that they were not enamoured of the large white, and still less of the Old Spots, unless crossed judiciously. Captain Dulling was the only exhibitor of Old Spots, and the aged boar was a mammoth pig.

1937 The Mercury (Hobart) Fri. 27 Aug. p.11
Obituary: Capt. G.H. Dulling: Former Master Mariner.
Capt. George Harold Dulling, died at his home, 110 Elphin Rd., Launceston, yesterday, aged 59 years, after an illness of about five weeks.
Born at Exeter, England, he was the second son, of the late Capt. George Dulling, who was associated with the famous Holme line of wool clippers, trading between Australia and England some years ago. Receiving his early training in the vessels of the line, Capt. Dulling's first visit to Tasmania was as second officer in the Myrtle Holme. In 1905, at the age of 24, he was appointed captain of the Edenholme (sic), a frequent visitor to Tasmania. He was perhaps the youngest master trading out of England. In 1907 he retired from the sea, and for several years was engaged in farming at St. Leonards, but because of ill-health took up his residence in Launceston. On several occasions he was nautical assessor of Courts of Marine Inquiry.
He took a keen interest in sport, especially bowls and cricket, and was a prominent member of the A.B.C. Bowling Club. This week he was re-elected a vice-president of the Northern Tasmanian Cricket Association. He married Miss Neille Quigley, and there is a family of two daughters--Mary and June--and three sons--Phillip, James, and Kenneth. A younger brother, Phillip Dulling, who was in his last year of apprenticeship, was lost in the wreck of the Brier Holme, off the South-West Cape, Tasmania, in 1904. The funeral is appointed to leave his late residence at 3 p.m. today for Carr Villa Cemetery.

Fearon John
[Dir: Bulmer's 1883 p.623] Netherton: Fearon John, master mariner, 17 Victoria terrace.

Hall Edward.
[bmd] Marriage Edward Hall   Margaret Jenkins. Sept. 1857 Aberystwyth 11b 85
{bmd} Death Edward Hall – June 1901 76, Aberystwyth 11b 47
{FS: 1881 Census

Margaret Hall, 49,	Wife Head,	M. F. 1832	Wales, Mariner's Wife
Sarah Anne Hall, 22,	Dau.	S. F. 1859,	Wales, Dressmaker
Harriet Hall, 18,	Dau.	S. F. 1863,	Wales, Dressmaker
Susannah Maude Clayton, 8,	Grand Niece,	S. F. 1873,	Wales, Scholar.

Address: 10 Penmaesglas Rd., Aberystwith, Cardiganshire, Wales.

[Newspaper cutting, unfortunately details unknown, supplied from the Aberystwyth Museum]
Death of Captain Hall. We regret to announce the death of Capt. Edward Hall, 5, Custom House Street, which took place at the residence on Tuesday morning at the age of 76 years. Deceased has attended Divine service at Tabernacle Chapel on Sunday morning, and was also present at Trefechan Sunday School in the afternoon. He complained of feeling unwell on Sunday evening and did not go to chapel. His condition became worse. Dr. Rowlands was called early on Monday, and he found Capt. Hall suffering from great weakness of the heart. He gradually sank and passed away in the early hours of Tuesday morning. He was born in London, and came when very young with his mother to Aberystwyth, where he made his home. He was for some

years in the Royal Navy, serving on board H.M. St. Howe. He was always proud to relate how he attended as senior page on Queen Adelaide on a voyage to Madeira, via Lisbon, and back in 1846-47. Leaving the Royal Navy, he bought a vessel of his own, the "Bee," which he subsequently sold and bought the "Exchange." With these he traded between the ports of Cardigan Bay. After sailing them for some years he entered the service of Messrs. Hive (sic) Bros. of Maryport, as captain, first of the "Tom Roberts," and afterwards for many years of the barque "Robert Hive (sic)." During these years he traded mostly to the coast of Chili and the Pacific. He made a voyage round the world on three occasions. He also served as captain of the steamship "Ivy Holme". He attributed all his success in life to the Sunday School and the fact that at the first formation of the Temperance Society he had enrolled himself a member. He was a member of the old Moderation Society, formed in 1835, and afterwards of the first Total Abstainer Society formed in 1836. He strictly adhered to his temperance convictions all his life in all climates and under all conditions. He was one of the most faithful members of Tabernacle chapel, and during the whole of his lifetime had been a member of Trefechan Sunday School, and a teacher for many years. He was a strict Sabbatarian, and on no account would he sail his boats on Sunday. For this past seven years he had retired from active work, after a severe illness constructed as the result of an accident while on a voyage from Waterford to Dublin. Erysipelas set in after the accident, and he lay for a long time at Dublin Hospital. He married Margaret Jenkins, daughter of the late David Jenkins [chain-anchor maker] blacksmith, South-road, who died about nineteen months ago. There were three children of the marriage, viz, Mrs. Sarah Ann Williams, who is married to the Rev. John Williams, B.A., Dolgelley, Mr. Edward Hall, borough surveyor, Carnarvon, and Miss Harriet Hall, who resided with his father. Captain Hall's death is deeply regretted by his numerous friends, and much sympathy is felt with the family in the bereavement. The funeral takes place on Friday at the cemetery.

Letter
[in pencil note: Tardcu [? Sent by] Captain Edward Hall to son-in-law John Williams husband of Sarah Ann Hall]
5 Customhouse street: Aberystwyth: Sept 17th 1896
My dear John & Family.

We were very Pleased to Learn by by (sic) yesterday s post that you continue to Improve dayly which is most encouraging how very fortunate Miss Williams s sPirit has Proved under the trying Circumstances we are also very glad to Learn that the dear Children are all right although the Weather of late if the same as with us here, has not been favourable for outdoor exercise we note you report William Evans and his Aunt's trip to Bournmouth (sic) and trust that they enjoyed themselfs we also would fain take a run over and see you all but that treat must be Postponed for the Present. and be thankfull for the good news that we are favoured with Dayly. we also sincerely trust that you are abl (sic) to Put off for the Present all anxiety re your Onerous dutys that have to be Laid aside for the Present for once you are able to resume duty you will soon get all into order again. even anxiety on that .... Important as it is would be most Injurious Just now. but rather may we all be enabled to review with Gratitude God s, Providential and Mercyfull care, in the midst of your Late Experience. we will not task your strength with a long Epistle today you have our Prayers and best wishes for a speedy recovery to your usual good health and usefullness.
We all write in kind Love and best wishes for you all hoping that when restored to Convalesceny that you will be very carefull to Pay Due attention to the Doctors instructions and not task yourself to (sic) much on getting into Harness.
Ever your affectionate Father.
Edward Hall.

Holman George Albert
{Louise May [Mary?] Holman (nee Titley): born at Wynward, Tasmania.}
1923 The Examiner (Tasmania) Mon. 24 Sept. p5

A well known figure in the nautical community, Capt. William Joseph Titley; passed out at 80 years of age at his residence, 44 Eardley-street, on Saturday. For many years he was connected with shipping along the North-West Coast, and was also harbourmaster of Stanley. He leaves a family scattered living in various parts of the world, including Mrs. E. J. Atkinson (Launceston), Mrs. George Holman (in England, the wife of the captain (sic) of the ill-fated Briar (sic) Holme and the Castle Holme), a married daughter in West Australia, and a son, Mr. James Titley (Tas.). The funeral leaves deceased's late residence at 3 p.m. to-day for Carr Villa.

Mrs. Louise Holman known voyages: Castle Holme, 1905, 06.

Holmes Wilson
[Holme Line] Agreement 1887 Earl of Carrick
Wilson Holmes 55 Harrington (Address:- I Curzon st. Maryport)
{bmd} Marriage Wilson Holmes – Betsy Benn, Jun 1848 Cockermouth 25 82
{FS: Census 1881}

Betsy Holmes	Wife Head	M F 58 Maryport	
Joseph Holmes	Son	U M 23 Maryport	Ship Broker
Anne Holmes	Dau	U F 20 Maryport	At Home

(6 Well Lane, Maryport)
[Dir: Blumer's 1883 p.574] Holmes Wilson, master mariner, 6 Well lane.
Master Mariner, Holmes Wilson, 79 High street.
[p.557]Holmes Capt. Wilson, 79 High street.
[Dir: Kelly 1894 p.199 & 1897 p.201] Holmes Wilson, master mariner, 77 High st.
{bmd} Death Wilson Holmes Mar 1900 (78) Cockermouth 10b 492
Death Betsy Holmes Jun 1902 (80) Cockermouth 10b 412

Johnston John
[Brier Holme: 1877: Agreement: Master: John Johnston (39) born Carrickfergus 1838]
[Dir: Bulmer's 1883 p.558] Johnston John, master mariner, High st.
Johnston John, master mariner, 33 Catherine st.
[Dir: Kelly's 1894 p.199] Johnstone John, master mariner, 23 North st.
[Dir: Bulmer's 1901 p.760] Johnstone John, master mariner, 23 North st.

1906 The Register (Adelaide) Fri. 29 June p.7
Many nautical men at Port Adelaide will remember Capt. Johnstone who for many years visited the Port as master of the Maryport barque, Brier Holme. In a recent issue of The Maryport News appears a notification of his retirement from active sea service, and an appreciative article concerning his long experience as an A.B. before the mast, mate, and master. Capt. Johnstone began his sea life in 1850, and after serving in coasting vessels joined the wooden vessel Gam Jam (sic) [Gamjam], and made two voyages in her to India, and arrived on the first occasion just in time to see Sir Colin Campbell leave for the relief of Lucknow to the stirring strains of "The Campbells are coming," played on the pipes of a Highland regiment. He also saw the arrival of H.M.S. Shannon, and the start up country of the Naval Brigade, under the command of Capt. Peel, a son of the great Sir Robert. On returning to Maryport Capt. Johnstone joined the schoner (sic) Martha Grace, taking the place of a friend who was ill. She was bound from Maryport to Dublin with coal, and was commanded by Capt. John Benn, father of Mr. Benn, who until recently was coxswain of the Maryport lifeboat. The others on board were Mr. John Wilson, Capt. Johnstone, and a dog. This was in October, 1859, a time well remembered by old seafaring men, because of the fearful gale of that month, which wrecked the Royal Charter, a big sailing ship with an auxiliary screw, on her homeward voyage from Australia to England. The Martha Grace was caught in the storm off the

Calf of Man, and the captain and Mr. Wilson were washed over board, while Capt. Johnstone, who was steering, only escaped through being lashed to the tiller. The vessel drifted at the mercy of the wind and sea for 36 hours and was eventually sighted by the William Carey which took off the man and dog. During the years that followed Capt. Johnstone served in the North American and East Indian trades, gained his master's certificate at Dublin in 1869, and in October, 1872, began that long and honourable connection with Messrs. Hine Brothers (owners of the Holme line) which lasted up to the day of his retirement. In 1876 he joined the Brier Holme, then just launched at Sunderland and for 15 years sailed that vessel, mainly in the Australian trade. In 1891 he exchanged for steam, being appointed master of the Forest Holme, and had some trying experiences. Once, in 1893 the vessel was struck by a tidal wave on the way across the Atlantic to Nova Scotia, and had her decks smashed in. Twelve months later the ship ran over some submerged danger, and lost her tail shaft and propeller, and three or four years afterwards she came into collision with an iceberg and had her bows stove in.

McLeod George

[Dir: Butcher's Swansea Commercial Directory 1881-82 p.283] Swansea: McLeod, master mariner, 11 New Fleet st.

{FS: Census 1881}

George Mcleod.	Head	53,	M. M. 1828, Scotland, Head. Master Mariner.
Barbara do	Wife	42 (sic)	W.M. 1829 (sic), Scotland.
Annie do	Dau.	22,	S. F. 1859, Scotland, No Occupation.
Jane do	Dau.	14,	S. F. 1867, Scotland, Scholar.
Roderick do	Son	11,	S. M. 1870 Scotland, do
John do	Son	9,	S. M. 1872 do do
George D. do	Son	6,	S. M. 1875 Wales do
Alexander M. do	Son	2,	S. M. 1879 do do

Address: 11 Fleet Street, Swansea (Town), Glamorganshire, Wales.

Millican Joseph William

{bmd} Birth Joseph William Millican   Mar. 1854 Cockermouth 10b 423

{bmd} Death Joseph William Millican (78) Mar. 1932 Birkenhead 8a 752

{bmd} Death Lydia C. Millican (83) Mar. 1941 Birkenhead 8a 1094

{   } Marriage: At Fremantle Millican Joseph William married Lydia Caroline Jones. Registration Number 5082 Registration 1881.

1877 Rockhampton Bulletin, Rockhampton, Thurs. 19 Apr. p.2

In the Infant School: -------promotions -------: Miss L. Jones to the position of assistant teacher, Class III: Miss Jones ----passed with great credit. [She was] *prepared for the examination by Miss Aird, head mistress of the Infant School.*

1881 The Capricornian, Rockhampton, Queensland Sat. 12 Mar. p.11

A pleasing recognition of a teacher's services was made at the William-street Public School on Monday afternoon, when Miss L. C. Jones, assistant in the Girls' School, was made the recipient of a handsome testimonial on the occasion of her resigning her position, which she had held for nine years. The presentation, which took the form of a piece of plate, was made by Miss Morrison, the head teacher, on behalf of the teachers and scholars. Miss Morrison expressed her regret at losing the assistance of Miss Jones, whom she said was greatly respected by both the teachers. Miss Jones had won the good will of all by her excellent qualifications and kindly manner. Miss Jones acknowledged the gift in suitable terms.

1881 The Capricornian, Rockhampton, Queensland Sat. 30 Apr. p.1

Marriage: Millican--Jones. On the 23 instant, at the Johnston Memorial Church, Freemantle (sic), West Australia by the Rev. Joseph Johnston, Joseph William Millican, captain of the barque Hazel Holme, and eldest son of the late Captain John Millican of Maryport, Cumberland, England, to Lydia Caroline (Lily) eldest daughter of Edward Jones, of Rockhampton and Townsville, and formerly of Knockvicar House, County Roscommon, Ireland.

{bmd}	Birth	Elsie Hazel Millican	Mar 1882	Cockermouth	10b 539
	Birth	Percy John do	Dec 1883	Cockermouth	10b 567
	Birth	Myrtle Gwendoline do	Sep 1885	Poplar	1c 632
	Birth	Douglas George do	Dec 1887	Cockermouth	10b 581
	Birth	Norman Shera do	Mar 1890	Cockermouth	10b 595
	Birth	Ivy do	Mar 1891	Ulverston	8c 810
	Birth	Victor Howard do	Dec 1894	Cockermouth	10b 603

1882 The Morning Bulletin, Rockhampton (Queensland) Mon. 17 Apr. p.1
Birth: Millican:--On the 18th February, at her residence, 32 High-street, Maryport, Cumberland, England, the wife of Captain J. W. Millican, of a daughter (Elsie Hazel).
1884 The Morning Bulletin, Rockhampton (Queensland) Mon. 4 Feb. p.1
Birth: Millican:--On December 4, 1883, at her residence, 32 High-street, Maryport, Cumberland, England, the wife of Captain J. W. Millican, of the "Myrtle Holme" of a son.

[Dir: Bulmer's 1883 p.561] Millican Joseph William, master mariner, 32 High street.
[Dir: Kelly's 1894 p.200] Millican Joseph William, master mariner, 33 North street.
[Dir: Bulmer's 1901 p.761] Millican J. W, master mariner, 33 North street.
[Dir: Kelly's 1906 p.205] Millican Joseph William, master mariner, 8 High st.

[Census 1901]
Lydia C. Millican	Wife	M. F.	43	Ireland	
Elsie H. do	Dau.	S. F.	19	Maryport	Music Teacher
Myrtle do	Dau.	S. F.	15	London	School Teacher
Dougas G do	Son	S. M.	13	Maryport	
Norman S. do	Son	S. M.	11	Maryport	
Ivy Lilian do	Dau.	S. F.	8	Maryport	
Victor H do	Son	S. M.	6	Maryport	
Agnes J. Walker		S. F.	19		General & Servant Domestic

{http://genforum.genealogy.com/hine/messages/359.html}
British War Graves.
Douglas Alfred Hine:-- Rank: Flight Lieutenant (Pilot):-- Location: Rheinberg War Cemetery - Kamp Lintfort:-- County: Nordrhein-Westfal:-- Country: Germany Other Details: 118483. 431 (R.C.A.F.) Sqdn. Royal Air Force Volunteer Reserve. 23rd June 1943. Age 31. Son of Ernest William Hine and of Myrtle Gwendoline Hine (nee Millican); nephew of E. Hazel Nelson of Oxton Birkenhead. 3. C. 4.

Mrs. Lydia Millican known voyages: Hazel Holme, (marriage in Adelaide) *outward 1881* (& daughter) 82*:* Myrtle Holme, (& children) *83,* (& child) *84,* (& two children) *85.*

1882 The Morning Bulletin (Rockhampton, Queensland) Wed, 13 Dec. p.2
Rockhampton: Departures: Dec. 12: Queensland s., 309 tons, Captain J.H. Meaburn for Brisbane via ports: Passengers: Mrs. Millican and child.

1882 The Brisbane Courier Sat. 16 Dec. p.4
Brisbane: Arrivals: Dec. 15. Queensland, A.S.N. Company's 309 Captain J.E. Meaburn from Rockhampton, via Bundaberg and Maryborough. Passengers: Mrs. J.W. Millican.

1886 The Morning Bulletin, Rockhampton (Queensland) Tues. 6 Apr. p.4

In Keppel Bay: Arrivals: Apr. 4: Barcoo, s.s., 1505 tons, Captain W. W. Hampton, from Sydney and Brisbane. Passengers: Mrs. J.W. Millican and child. From Sydney bound for Cooktown via ports, arrived at Keppel Bay on Sunday afternoon, and after transhipping mails and passengers, resumed her voyage.

1886 The Morning Bulletin, Rockhampton (Queensland) Wed. 17 Nov. p.4

An entertainment of a musical character was given at the Benevolent Asylum last evening by ladies and gentleman connected with the Wesleyan Mutual Improvement Class. It was devised for the amusement of the inmates of the Asylum, and those who attended doubtless enjoyed it. The programme was well arranged, and included several good numbers. Among the performers were the Misses Kavanagh, Miss Donaghey, Mrs. T. B. Holmes, Mrs. J. Flint, Miss Daglish, Mrs. Millican, Mrs. Carroll, Mrs. Martin, Miss Jones, Mr. G. B. Jones, Mr. W. Donaghey, Mr. J. Flint, Mr. T. M. Martin, Professor Toeplitz, and Mr. N. South. The Rev. T. B. Holmes opened the proceedings with a brief address; and, during an interval, Mr. H. Mills, Secretary of the Benevolent Society, thanked the Association on behalf of the Committee and the inmates of the Asylum. He remarked that the Wesleyan Association was the first that had entertained the residents in the Asylum, and hoped the concert was the first of a series. [??]

Nicholson Isaac

{www.plimsoll.org/}   Wreck of "Fanny" 47667: Board of Trade Wreck Report, at Sourabaya, 3rd March 1881: Present, Isaac Nicholson, Master of the English Ship "John Norman".

Patterson John Wood

[Maryport Cemetery] Erected in affection remembrance of John Wood Patterson, beloved husband of Phebe Patterson who was lost at sea during a storm, on the 1st. Feb. 1873. while in command of the Brig Hope, which left Maryport for Swansea, 29th. Jan. aged 34 years.

Randall John Henry

Mrs. Randall known voyages: Eden Holme, 1880, 86, 87, 90, 91, 92, 94.

Rich John Hoare

{bmd}	Birth	Charlotte Price	June 1841	Cockermouth 25 91

{FS: 1861 census}
Charlotte Price (1841) of Maryport: Location in 1861 Birkenhead, Tranmere.

{bmd}	Marriage	John H. Rich – Charlotte Price Sept. 1864		Birkenhead 8 a 625
{bmd}	Birth	Thomas A. Rich	Jun 1866	Cockermouth 10b 544
	Birth	John Hoare Rich	Dec 1870	Cockermouth 10b 523

{FS: 1871 census}
Rich Charlotte (1841) Location in 1871 Whitechapel Aldgate.

[Dir: Post Office 1873 p.985] Master Mariner: Rich John Hoare, 12 Camp st., Maryport.

{bmd}	Birth	Joseph Price Rich	Sept 1879	Cockermouth 10b 579

{1881 census}

Charlotte Rich	Head	Wife	M. F	40 Maryport	
Thomas A. Rich		son	U. M	14 Maryport	Engine Fitter at works
John H. Rich			U. M	10 Maryport	Scholar
Joseph P. Rich			U. M	1 Maryport	
Mary Price	Mother		W F	73 Maryport	
Mary A. Blacklock		Niece	U F	16 Maryport	

(6 North place Maryport).

[**Dir:** Post Office 1873 p.985] Master Mariner: Rich John Hoare, 12 Camp st. Maryport.
[**Dir:** Bulmer's 1883 p.563]   Rich John, master mariner, 6 North st.
[**Dir:** Kelly's 1894 p.200] Rich John Hoare, master mariner, 29 North st.
[**Dir:** Bulmer's 1901 p.760]   John Rich, master mariner, 6 North st.

[**MNL&MD** Annual Appendage 1864. p.144: No. Cert. 22773: Class Examined, Class Mate (1 M) 1863, Liverpool: Rich, John Hoare.]

[**LR** 1870: Queen of May, Bk, E. Deady/ J.H. Rich, 314, Hrrngt 1856, S. Martin, Workington, A1]
[**LR** 1872: Queen of May, Bk, J.H. Rich, 314, S. Martin, Workington, A1, **recked** (sic)]

1872 Adair's Maryport Advertiser Fri. 5 July
Wreck of the "Queen of May."—In the fearful hurricane which took place at East London, on the 20th of May, in which several vessels were wrecked and some lives lost, the "Queen of May," Capt. Rich, of Maryport, is named as one of the sufferers: but are glad to add all hands are saved except an apprentice boy.

1879 The Liverpool Mercury Fri. 18 July p.3
Births: Rich—July 15, at 6, North-street, Maryport, the wife of Captain J.H. Rich, of the barque Edward Barrow, of a son.

[**LR** 1883:(64834 LRVG), Edward Barrow, Rich, Bk, 932/880, Nova Scotia, P. Dodgson, Maryport]
[**RAFS** 1884: Edward Barrow , J.H. Rich, Bk, Br, Halifax, 958, 1871 Pearson Dodgson.]

{**bmd**} Death Charlotte Rich, 86 age, Plymouth Dec 1927 (??)

Mrs. Charlotte Rich known voyages: Abbey Holme, 1885 (& son), 1890 (wrecked): Brier Holme, 1896, 97, 98, 99, (4th voyage to Tasmania in a vessel under Capt. Rich's command) & 1902.

Ritchie, James Hannah
{New Zealand History online: {www.bdmhistoricalrecords.dia.govt.nz}
Port Chalmers Marriages: Jane Mathieson, 18y, James Ritchie, 24y, 6 June 1865.
Parish Code 19/16/02

1865 Otago Witness (N.Z.) 17 June p.10
Port Chalmers: Inwards: June 12: Brothers, 32 tons, Jack, master, from Hukitika, ballast.
July 29 p.10
Port Chalmers: Outwards: July 26: Brothers, 32 tons, Ritchie, master, Oamaru, sundries.
1866 Jan. 6 p.10
Port Chalmers: Outwards-Coastwise: Dec. 30: Brothers, 32 tons, Ritchie, master, for Oamaru, with stores.

1866 Otago Daily Times (N.Z.) Thurs. 15 Feb. p.4
Port Chalmers: Departures: Feb. 14: Brothers, 32 tons, Ritchie, Moeraki, in ballast.
Feb. 20 p.4
Port Chalmers: Inwards: Feb.19: Oamaru, 25 tons, Mayne, master from Oamaru, wool.
Mar. 3 p.4
Port Chalmers: Inwards: Mar. 2: Oamaru, 25 tons, J. Maine (sic), from Oamaru.
Mar. 9 p.4
Port Chalmers: Outwards: Mar. 8: Oamaru, 25 tons, Ritchie, Master, for Oamaru, cargo.
Mar. 12 p.4
The "Grey River Argus" of the 28th reports: "Much anxiety was, on Monday last, expressed in town in consequence of a signal flying from the Mary Ann Christina lying in the roadstead that the Captain urgently required the services of a medical practitioner. ………. Dr. Foppoly……… was conveyed to the Mary Ann Christina, where he found the Captain Beer had been confined to his bed for ten days previous to arrival in

consequence of a severe attack of rheumatic fever. Luckily the Doctor had taken out some medicines specially applicable and was thus enabled to render material service.
Mar. 19 p.4
Port Chalmers: Arrivals: Mar. 18: Oamaru, schooner, Ritchie, from Oamaru, with wool, stone, and produce. Master, agent.
Apr. 6 p.4
Port Chalmers: Arrivals: Apr. 3: Oamaru, schooner, Ritchie, from Oamaru, with wool. In port – Mary Ann Christina, schooner, Grey River.
Apr. 21 p.1
[Advert] *For Sale: The Well-known Clipper Schooner: Mary Ann Christina: 80 tons Burthen: Well found in stores, &c, For terms, &c., Apply to H. Houghton and Co., Agents. Stafford street.*
Apr. 23 p.4
Port Chalmers: Arrivals: Apr. 12: Oamaru, schooner, Ritchie, from Oamaru, with wool, stone, and produce. Master, agent.
Apr. 28 p.4
Port Chalmers: Outwards—Coastwise: Apr. 27: Mary Ann Christina, 41 tons, Ritchie, Master, for Oamaru. Master agent. Exports: 12 tons coal. A M'Kinnon.
May 4 p.4
Port Chalmers: Departures: May 3: Oamaru, schooner, Hamilton, for Oamaru with cargo.
May 9 p.4
Port Chalmers: Inwards: May 8: Oamaru, 25 tons, Hamilton, from Oamaru with cargo.

1866 The Timaru Herald (N.Z.) Fri. 18 May p.3
Oamaru (From our own Correspondent.) May 12. I have to corroborate previous accounts of progress here. Our motto is "onward." In addition to the two steamers and small coasters which call at this port, our Beach-master, Captain Sewell, has lately purchased a vessel named the "Mary Ann Christina" which is intended, as well as his other vessel, "the Oamaru" to ply steadily here, and is to be hoped, with the opening up of the stone trade and other traffic, all there may find freights.

{Birth David Ritchie: No. 1866/6336, registration.}

1866 Otago Daily Times (N.Z.) Thurs. 11 Oct. p.4
Birth: On the 9th October, at Port Chalmers, the wife of Captain J. Ritchie, of a son.

1866 Otago Witness (N.Z.) 15 Dec. p.10
Port Chalmers: Inwards: Dec. 8: Mary Ann Christina, 38 tons, Ritchie, master, from Oamaru, cargo.
Port Chalmers: Outwards: Dec. 12: Mary Ann Christina, 38 tons, James Ritchie, Oamaru, cargo.

1867 Otago Daily Times (N.Z.) 3 Apr. p.4
April 2—Mary Ann Christina, 38 tons, Ritchie, master, from Oamaru.

1867 The Daily Southern Cross (N.Z.) Tues. 28 May p.4
The Mary Ann Christina is the property of Captain Sewell, of Oamaru, and is insured in the New Zealand Insurance Office.

1867 The Oamaru Times and Waitaki Reporter (N.Z.) Fri. 31 May p.2
Port of Oamaru: It is rumoured that the New Zealand Insurance Company intend presenting Captain Ritchie, of the Mary Ann Christina, with a testimonial, as a mark of their appreciation of his conduct during the late gale, when his vessel was placed in such imminent danger.—Evening Mail (Dunedin).

1867 Otago Daily Times (N.Z.) Mon. 10 June p.4

Port Chalmers: The schooner Mary Ann Christina sailed yesterday for Invercargill, under the command of Captain Jones, her late chief officer. Her late master, Captain Ritchie, takes charge of the barque Eleanor, purchased by him for the intercolonial trade.

July 20 p.4

The barque Eleanor, which has lain in Port Chalmers since her arrival from St John's, New Brunswick, on February the 9th, 1865, was purchased by Capt., Ritchie of this port about three weeks ago. Since then she has received a thorough overhaul at the hands of the carpenters and riggers, and is now ready for sea. She is expected to sail for Newcastle N.S.W., to-day.

July 22 p.4

Port Chalmers: Departures: July 21: Eleanor, barque, 411 tons, Ritchie for Newcastle, in ballast. Master, agent.

Aug. 2 p.4

Died: On the 1st August, at Mount street, Port Chalmers, James Hannah, the infant son of Captain James Ritchie, aged 10 months.

Aug. 3 p.1

Funeral Notice: The friends of Captain Ritchie, of the barque Eleanor, are respectfully invited to attend the funeral of his late son, to the Port Chalmers Cemetery, on the 3rd inst., at 3 p.m. R, Bauchop, Undertaker. Port Chalmers, August 1st, 1867.

{Death Jas. Hannah Ritchie 1867/2050, registration.
Birth Robert Ritchie: No. 1868/7217, registration. [?]}

Nov. 1 p.4

Birth: On the 28th October, at her residence, Port Chalmers, the wife of Captain James Ritchie, of a son.

Port Chalmers: At the Heads: Aug. 30: Eleanor barque, 411 tons, Ritchie, from Newcastle, with coals. Keith Ramsay, agent.

Dec. p.2

Imports: Per Eleanor, from Newcastle; 570 tons coal. The barque Eleanor, from Newcastle, was towed up to a discharging berth on Saturday evening. She sailed from Newcastle on the 24th ult., and had light easterly winds for the first two days. On the 27th a gale sprang up from S.S.W., and backed round northerly to east, and blew heavy. The gale then made a circle by veering round southerly to S.W., and continued to blow for three days. Light winds and fine weather were then experienced to nearing the Solander, when a heavy N.N.W. gale was encountered, when she bore away for the south of Stewart's Island, which was passed on Wednesday last. On getting under lee of the island the wind died away, and light northerly and north-east winds prevailed from thence to arrival. We are indebted to Captain Ritchie and his chief officer for Sydney and Newcastle papers.

1868 Jan. 23 p.4

Outwards: Eleanor, 411 tons, James Ritchie, for Newcastle, N.S.W.

1869 Jan. 6 p.2

The barque Eleanor is rapidly discharging her cargo, and will sail for Newcastle about beginning of next week under the command of Captain Cordon M'Kinnon. Captain Ritchie, her former master, owing to domestic affliction, remains on shore for this trip.

Jan. 18 p.1

Funeral Notice: The Friends of Captain James Ritchie are respectfully invited to follow the remains of his late wife to the Port Chalmers Cemetery, at two o'clock on Tuesday.

page 2

The shipping in the Bay yesterday hoisted their colours half-mast, as a mark of respect to Captain James Ritchie, late of the Eleanor, whose wife died on Saturday, after a lingering and severe illness.

Mar. 1 p.2

Port Chalmers: Arrivals: Feb. 28: Eleanor, barque, 396 tons, M'Kinnon, from Newcastle. Imports 550 tons coal.

Mar. 16 p.1

[Advert] For British Columbia: The Clipper Barque Eleanor: will sail for the above colony on Monday the 22ⁿᵈ inst. Parties desiring to proceed to California, or other west coast ports of North America, should make early applications to Capt. Ritchie on board. or Keith Ramsay. Dunedin.

Mar. 20 p.2

The barque Eleanor, which was advertised for British Columbia, has been taken off the berth for the present, her destination being Newcastle, for which port was expected to sail last evening.

Mar. 23 p.2

Port Chalmers: Arrivals: Mar. 22: Maria, ship, 747 tons, Duncan, from Newcastle: Passenger: Mrs. Duncan.

The ship Maria, previously reported from Newcastle at the Heads, was towed up to a discharging berth by the tug Geelong yesterday forenoon.

The barque Eleanor, for Newcastle, made another attempt to get underway yesterday forenoon, but being close down in the lee bank, she took the ground, about high water, before she had sufficient steerage way. Signals were at once made for a tug, but the Geelong having blown off her steam after towing up the ship Maria, it would have taken her a considerable time to get upstream again, and the barque was left hard and fast throughout the ebb. An attempt was to be made at high water last night to tow the barque into deep water.

Mar. 27 p.2

Port Chalmers: Departures: Mar. 26: Eleanor, barque, 366 tons, Ritchie for Newcastle.

June 1 p.2

Port Chalmers: At the Heads: Maria, ship, 747 tons, Duncan, for Puget Sound. Mr. Joseph Asher accompanies her as supercargo.

Dec. 13 p.2

Port Chalmers: Arrivals: Dec. 12: Eleanor, barque, 396 tons, Ritchie, from Newcastle.

1869 The South Australian Advertiser, Adelaide Mon. 27 Dec. p.2

Adelaide: Arrived: Dec. 24: Maria, ship, 747 tons, Jno. Duncan, master from Vancouver's Island September 20, via Melbourne December 17 Passengers—Mr. Peterson (supercargo), Mrs. Duncan, and Mr. Asher, in the cabin.

1869 Otago Daily Times (N.Z.) 31 Dec. p.2

Port Chalmers: Customs Entries: Outward Foreign: Dec. 30: Eleanor, barque, 396 tons, Crone, for Newcastle.

1870 Jan. 1p.2

The Ship Maria, from Puget's Sound with timber, arrived at Port Phillip Heads on the 12ᵗʰ December, and received orders to proceed to Adelaide with her cargo, from thence she was to proceed to Newcastle and load coal for this Port.

Jan.3 p.2

Port Chalmers: Departures: Jan. 2: Eleanor, barque, 396 tons, Crone, for Newcastle.

1870 The South Australian Advertiser, Adelaide Sat. 15 Jan. p.2

Adelaide: Arrived: Jan. 14: Coorong, 304 tons, from Melbourne Jan. 12: Passenger in cabin, Captain Ritchie.

In Harbour: Maria, ship, 747 tons, J. Duncan, from Vancouver's Island.

Jan. 20 p.3

Police Court—Port Adelaide: John Duncan, master of the vessel Maria, on the information of James Ritchie, master mariner, for assault, was found guilty, and fined 1s. and costs.

1870 The South Australian Register, Adelaide Fri. 21 Jan. p.4

The Maria, which brought here a cargo of timber from Puget Sound, has changed owners, and also masters. Captain Duncan resigning charge to Ca tain (sic) Ritchie. The former returns by the St. Leonards to London en route for Glasgow, where there is a vessel of 1,200 tons building for him by the same Company in whose service several of the best years of his life has earned this appreciation.

Mar. 9 p.4

Adelaide: Cleared out: Mar. 8: Maria, ship, 747 tons, Ritchie, master, for Liverpool, via Yankalilla. No Passengers.

1870 The South Australian Advertiser, Adelaide, Mon. 28 Mar. p.2

Adelaide: Arrived: Mar. 26: Maria, 747 tons, James Ritchie, from Yankalilla, bark laden, for Liverpool. Passengers—Mr. Frewin in the cabin; and 4 stevedores in the steerage. Cargo—614 tons bark. 7 casks tallow, 3 tons gum, Bean Bros.; 37 cases jam, Elder, Smith, and Co.; 57 bales rags. The Maria, for Liverpool, has loaded cargo at the outports, and on Saturday returned to the roads to embark passengers, take on board sea stock, and prepare for departure. She appears to be in want of dead weight from behavior under canvas, but perhaps, when the cargo settles down she will stiffen. The master speaks favorably of the facilities offered at the outports for loading by means of sailing freighters, but is somewhat surprised at the space occupied by the bark. Passengers are notified by advertisement to be on board on Monday at noon.

1870 The South Australian Register, Adelaide Fri. 8 Apr. p.4

Marriages. Ritchie—Frewin—On the 6th April, at St. Margaret's Church, Woodville, by the Ven. Archdeacon Marryat, Captain James Ritchie, Port Chalmers, New Zealand, to Mary Hannah, third daughter of Thomas Frewin, Esq., H. M. Customs, Queenstown.

{Genes Reunited: Mary Hannah Frewin, S, 26, father—Thomas, married James Ritchie, 29, S, father David on 6 Apr. 1870 at St. Margaret Church, Woodville, SA b 83. p. 8.)

Apr. 15 p.2

Maria, 747 tons, J. Ritchie, for Liverpool. Passengers—W. Leaver, J. Skelton, R. Barnes, J. Evans, J. Dudson, Mrs. Dudson and three children, Miss Smith and Mrs. Ritchie.

Apr. 19

Adelaide: Sailed: Apr. 17: Maria, ship, for Liverpool.

1870 English Supplement to the Launceston Examiner sat. 12 Nov. p.4S

Ships Arrived at Liverpool: Maria, Ritchie, Adelaide, 5th Sept.

1871 The Bury and Norwich Post, and Suffolk Herald Tues. 24 Jan. p.8

Shipwreck on the Norfolk Coast—Bacton: Monday.—(By telegraph.)—Mr. William Cubitt reports that the ship Maria, of Dunedin, 749 tons has gone ashore at Bacton during a strong easterly wind and in a heavy sea. The crew of nineteen men have happily been saved by the lifeboat Recompense, belonging to the National Lifeboat Institution and stationed at this place.

1871 Otago Times Daily (N.Z.) Mon. 3 Apr. p.2

The Loss of the Maria: The English papers report the loss of the ship Maria, belonging to Messrs Guthrie and Asher, of Dunedin. The intelligence is confirmed by a letter from his captain, which states that she sailed from Porgrund, Norway, on January 4th, bound to Melbourne with a cargo of Baltic deals consigned to her owners. On the 6th encountered heavy gales of wind which drove the ship in sight of Sunderland under close reefed topsails. After the gale abated thick weather set in, and on the morning of the 22nd, at 2 o'clock, the ship went ashore at Bacton on the east coast of England. On the 23rd, the crew were taken off by the Bacton life boat. On the 26th, a survey was held on the vessel by Lloyd's Agent and Captain Francis, the result of which was the condemnation of the ship as a wreck, her back being broken, and most of her poop and bulwarks washed off. The whole of the ship's furniture, including spars, sails, ropes, anchors, and chains, with the whole cargo of timber, were expected to be saved, a great portion of both having been landed before Captain Ritchie closed his despatch. The hull of the vessel was then buried ten feet in the sand. Both the hull and cargo were covered by insurance.

1874 Otago Daily Times (N.Z.) Wed. 21 Jan. p.4
Shipping: Port Chalmers: Departures Otago, ship, 992 tons, Stewart, for London: Passengers: Saloon, Mrs. Ritchie and two children. [see Hazel Holme]

{bmd} Birth   Jessie Ritchie   Sept 1876   Stepney 1c 480
{www.access.prov.vic.gov.au/public/PROVguides/}
Index to Unassisted Inward Passenger Lists to Victoria 1852-1923
Jan. 1877: Myrtle Holme: Captain, Jas. Ritchie.
Mrs. Ritchie, adult: Robt. Ritchie, child: David Ritchie, child: Jessie Ritchie, child: Miss Ward, adult.

This database is a searchable list of passengers travelling on ships leaving Victoria.
Mar. 1877: Myrtle Holme: destination London.
Mr. Carme (sic), (age) 37: Mrs. Carme (sic), 32: William Collard, 25: R. Gilbraith, 28: Mr. Hunt, 36: Mrs. Hunt, 31: Miss Martin, 14: Caroline Perrins, 14: Jas. Robertson, 37: Mrs. Robertson, 35: Mrs. Ritchie, 30: Ritchie; 002 children with, child: Miss Ward, 26.

Index to Unassisted Inward Passenger Lists to Victoria 1852-1923
Dec. 1877: Myrtle Holme: Captain, Jas. Ritchie.
Mrs. Ritchie, adult: Robert Ritchie, 10: David Ritchie, 9: Jessie Ritchie, 1.

Index to Unassisted Inward Passenger Lists to Victoria 1852-1923
Apr. 1879: Myrtle Holme: Captain, James Ritchie.
Mary H. Ritchie, 36: Jessie Ritchie, 3: Ada Tylon (sic), 19.

This database is a searchable list of passengers travelling on ships leaving Victoria.
May 1879: Myrtle Holme: destination Newcastle.
Mrs. Johnson, adult: Ada Tuxtton, (Turton ?), Adult: Mrs. Ritchie, adult: Ritchie, child.}

{FS: 1881 census}

William Garberry	Head	M	M	32	Gilcrux Cumberland	Engine Driver Iron Works.
Jane Garberry	Wife	M	F	29	Sedburgh York	
Sarah Isabella Garberry	dau		F	6	Dearham	Scholar
Thomas Garberry	son		M	3	Maryport	Scholar
David Ritchie	Boarder		M	13	New Zealand	Scholar
Robert Ritchie	Boarder		M	12	New Zealand	Scholar

          (91 John St. Crosscanonby Maryport).

Mrs. Mary H. Ritchie known voyages: Cereal, 1872 (burnt): Hazel Holme, 1873, Myrtle Holme, (1 child or outward 2 children) 1875, (with 3 children) 76, (with 3 children) 77, (& Miss Jessie Ritchie) 78, (& child) 80, (& child) 81

[Dir: Kelly's 1894 p.200] Ritchie James, master mariner, 132 High st.
[Dir: Bulmer's 1901 p.762] Ritchie James, master mariner, 132 High st.

1900 The Gazette, Montreal Fri. 8 June p.10
Montreal: Captain James Ritchie, commodore of the Holme line fleet was in the city yesterday on a flying trip from Quebec, where his vessel the Isleholme (sic) is

discharging coal.   The Isleholme (sic) is the latest requisition of the Holme line and during the summer months will run between London and Quebec.
{bmd}   Death   James Hannah Ritchie (63) Sept. 1905 Cockermouth 10b 384.
           Death   Mary H. Ritchie (74) Mar. 1918 Cockermouth 10b 821.

1905 Otago Witness Illustrations (N.Z.) 6 Dec. p.48.

The Manchester Guardian of Friday, September 29, says: — "Captain James Hannah Ritchie, commodore-captain of the Holme line, of Maryport, died, yesterday at Maryport. He had had a varied and adventurous career. He tried his luck twice at the gold diggings, sailed his own ship in the New Zealand coastal trade, was wrecked in the s.s. Fern Holme, off Newfoundland, and had the barque Seiriol Wyn burned under him in mid-Atlantic. Unlike most seamen, he was a non-smoker and a strong tee-totaller, and would allow no alcohol on his ship. He was 63 years of age."

[This is beyond the scope of this book. However, our Captain James Ritchie was not involved with vessels such as the "Wakool (screw steamer) 1863 and the "Gundagai" (paddle steamer) 1863. Both were brought over by Capt. James Ritchie from Adelaide (originally from Goolwa on the Murray River) where he lived with his family. He worked in New Zealand for a couple of years and presumably captained the Prince Alfred and the Waipa (government vessels).

Three sailing vessels at that time were the "Emerald", "Emu" and "Prince Consort" but their captain was David Ritchie.]

John J. Robinson
Captain of Eden Holme: 1875-76

1876 Adair's Maryport Advertiser Fri. 18 Aug. p.8
Wreck of the Steamer Mersey belonging to Maryport.

On Sunday orning the melancholy tidings were received by telegram of the wreck of the Mersey, a fine steamer, which sailed from Barrow on Thursday last, with a cargo of pig iron for Antwerp. She was commanded by Capt. Robinson, an experienced seaman, and brother-in-law to the owners Messrs Hine Brothers, Maryport. Her crew consisted of seventeen, two only of whom were saved. The captain, mate, and some others belonging Maryport all perished. A second telegram received on Monday states that a schooner remained by the wreck for three hours, but could not discover nothing of other survivors. It appears the vessel had struck a sunken rock off Schooner Island, in St. Bryde's Bay, Pembrokeshire, in a dense fog at 1.30 on Friday. The crew being on what is called weekly pay there is no perfect list kept at the office. Captain Robinson leaves a widow and two children, and others in Maryport leave orphans and widows. .....
Those who perished belonging to Maryport are Capt. Robinson, Charles Robinson, his consin (sic), mate, Arthur Forster, second engineer, and Paul Radnor a seaman.

Robinson Wedgwood
{bmd} Marriage Wedgwood Robinson – Sarah Robertson Dec 1854 West Derby 8b 708.

{FS: Census 1881}
Wedgewood Robinson M. M 47 Maryport   Master Mariner
Sarah Robinson   M. F 50 Lamplugh
Jane Reid   U. F 22 Maryport   General Serv. Domestic
8 Lawson St.
[Dir: Bulmer's 1883 p.563] Robinson Wedgewood master mariner 8 Lawson st.

1889 The Maryport Advertiser and Weekly News Fri. 21 June p.3
Death of Captain Robinson, of Maryport: It is with the deepest regret that we have to announce the death of Captain Robinson, one of the best known and most popular of the inhabitants of Maryport. For a considerable number of years the late Captain Robinson was in the service of Messrs. Hine Brothers, ship owners and brokers, of Maryport, had for the past fifteen years the deceased captain had superintended the building off all sailing vessels for the firm. Only on Thursday last the captain was superintending the stowage of the s.s. Chittadong, which was been loaded with rails, and on Saturday he succumbed after only a few hours' illness. Captain Robinson made himself a favourite with all by his genial and cordial manners, and in him the poor of the town lose a staunch friend and benefactor. The funeral took place of Tuesday afternoon, and it was very largely attended by friends and others who were anxious to show their respect for the dead and their sympathy for the widow and relatives. The principals of the firm for which the late captain had worked as well and zealously were both present, and the office staff was also represented. Flags were flying at half mast high at Messrs. Hine's offices, Messrs. Ritson and Co's yard, the harbour-master's office, and also on several ships in the harbour, as a token of respect for the memory of the deceased.

Mrs. Sarah Robinson known voyages: Humberstone, 1867, 69. Abbey Holme, 1871.

Saul John
{bmd} Birth Martha Holmes Dec 1850   Cockermouth Vol 25 104
       Marriage John Saul – Martha Holmes Mar 1872 Cockermouth 10b 718

Marriage certificate 1872: Crosscanonby: March 6: John Saul, 22, Bachelor Mariner, Maryport, father Daniel Saul, carpenter:::Martha Holmes, 21, Spinster, -------,Maryport, father Wilson Holmes, mariner.

{FS: Census 1881}

Martha Saul	Wife (head)	M. F 30		Maryport
John Saul	son	U. M 1		Maryport

7 Well Lane Maryport

[Dir: Bulmer's 1883 p.563] John Saul, master mariner, 7 Well lane.

[Dir: Kelly's 1894 p.200] John Saul, master mariner, 79 High st.
Mrs. Saul (Private Resident) 79 High st.

[Dir: Kelly's 1897 p.200] Mrs. Saul (Private Resident) 79 High st. [No Master Mariner.]

[Dir: Bulmer's 1901] Mrs. Martha Saul, Maryport, 79 High st.

Mrs. Martha Saul known voyages: *Glastry 1875: Glenfalloch* (& child) *1881-83 (one voyage)*

Sawle Thomas

{bmd} Born Thomas Sawle Jun 1842 Truro 9 323 or 328
Marriage Thomas Sawle – Eliza J. Baird? Beard? [Bryant] Jun 1866 Truro 5c 269
Born Andrew Seymour B. Sawle Dec 1875 Truro 5c 269
Death Elizabeth Sawle Jun 1877 Truro 5c 105

{Guildhall Lloyd's Captains Registers} Volume 1869.
Thomas Sawle b 1842 Cornwall cert. no. C84,419

1876 Royal Cornwall Gazette Sat. 23 Dec. p.8
Deaths: Sawle: At the residence of her father, Mr. Bryant, Beacon Cottage, St. Agnes, Dec. 16, Susanna Seymour, the beloved wife of Capt. Thomas Sawle, of German, and of the ship "Castle Holme," of Sunderland, aged 33. Mrs. Sawle was a most affectionate wife and mother, and was greatly esteemed and respected by all who knew her. Australian and Sydney papers will please copy

1878 Royal Cornwall Gazette Fri. 10 May p.6
Deaths: Sawle: At sea (while on a voyage from Australia to London). March 1, Capt. Thomas Sawle, of the barque Hazel Home (sic) (late of Portscatha), aged 36.

.

{rootsweb.ancestry.com}
10 May 1878 Admin. (with the Will) of personal estate of Thomas Sawle, effects under £400, formerly of St. Agnes, late of German's, master mariner, widower, died 1 Mar 1878 at sea. Principal registry under usual limitations to Nicholas Bryant, grandfather and guardian of Andrew Seymour Bryant Sawle an infant, the son and only next of kin.

{FS: Census 1881} Beacon, St. Agnes.

Nicholas Bryant	Head	M M 62	St. Agnes	Cornwall	General Agent
Mary A. Bryant	Wife	M F 59	St. Agnes	Cornwall	Farming (35 acres)
A. T. (sic) Sawle	Gson	U M 5	St. Agnes	Cornwall	
Mary Menadue		M F 46	St. Just	Cornwall	Genl. Serv.

{bmd} Marriage Andrew Seymour B. Sawle – Susan Jenkins Dec. 1899 Truro 5c 260

Smith John

[Maryport Cemetery] John Smith who was lost in the China Seas. October 21st 1870 Aged 33 years. Widow Sarah Scott died 13 June 1913. Aged 73 years.

Tarney James

[Dir: Bulmer's 1883 p.565] Tarney James, master mariner, 12 Church st.

Tate T. George

{bmd} Birth George Tate Dec 1851 Sunderland Vol 24 Page 333.
[Agreement] on Aikshaw 1877 George Tate 25 Sunderland Mate (1852)
Died at Sea on Aikshaw Jan 1 1887
Mrs. Tate known voyage: *Aikshaw, 1883* (& Master Tate, child)

Turney John Graham
{bmd} Marriage John Graham Turney – Mary Stalker Sept 1866 Liverpool 8b 5

[**Dir:** Post Office 1873 p.985] Master Mariner: Turney Jhn. 7 Ellenborough pl. Maryport

{FS: 1881 census}

Mary Turney	(Wife) Head	F	39 Maryport	Master Mariner's Wife
Sarah F. Turney	dau	F	13 At sea	Scholar
Richard A. Turney	son	M	10 Maryport	Scholar
Daniel S. Turney	son	M	7 Maryport	Scholar
John G. Turney	son	M	5 Maryport	
Mary S. Turney	dau	M	1w. Maryport	

7 Ellenborough pl. Maryport

[**Dir**: Bulmer's 1883 p.566]
Turney John Graham Turney, master mariner, 7 Ellenborough pl., Maryport.
[**Dir**: Bulmer's 1901 p.763] Turney Capt. John Graham Turney, retired master mariner, 7 Ellenborough place, Maryport.
Turney Daniel Stalker, chief mate, 6 Ellenborough pl Maryport
{bmd} Marriage Daniel Stalker Turney -- ?? Sept 1896 Cockermouth 10b 923
      Marriage Julian Ralph Bulmer -- ?? Sept 1904 Holyhead (Anglesey) 11b 795
      (One of the apprentices saved by Daniel Turney when the Aikshaw was wrecked).

Captain J. Turney "Southella" Steam ship 1281 tons, featured in Lloyd's of 1882 only one year. {www.plimsoll.org/resources/SCCLibraries/.../15408.asp?view=text} Port Cities Southampton: Board of Trade Wreck Report for 'Esk Holme', 1892 Captain John Graham Turney.

{bmd} Death John Graham Turney Mar 1906 (67) Cockermouth 10b 413
      Death Mary Turney Jun 1913 (71) Cockermouth 10b 731

[Maryport Cemetery] In Loving Memory: Captain John Graham Turney of 7 Ropery Maryport, who died January 27 1906. Aged 67 Years: Also of Mary his wife who died on the 18 May 1913 of 7 Ropery Maryport. Aged 71 Years: Also of Esther Jane Turney, Daughter of the (Ropery) who died on the 12 Feb 1923, Aged 49 Years.

Tyson Edward William
{bmd} Edward William Tyson Birth Dec 1843 Cockermouth 25 89
      Edward William Tyson Death Mar 1881 Kendal 10b 425
{Cumberland roots} (Baptisms).
13-10-1875 (No. 135)   William son Edward William & Hannah Tyson of Maryport a Captain
14-01-1877 (No. 161)   Jane Robson dau. David (sic) William & Hannah Tyson of Cooper a Sea Captain
18-06-1880 (No. 215)   Annie Mary dau Edward William & Hannah Tyson of Westnewton a Sea Captain
      (Burial)
14-02-1881 (no. 38)   Edward William Tyson of Staveley, Kendal aged 37 yrs.

TRS 2/7 note in Index

Edward William Tyson of Maryport Mariner died at Maryport. [Will] 11 March 1881, having bequeathed all his property to his wife, Hannah Beeby Tyson for whom letters of administration was granted at Carlisle on 29 March 1881.

{FS: 1881 census}

Hannah B. Tyson	Visitor (Widow) Head	F	40	Aikshaw
William Tyson	son	M	5	Aikshaw
Jane R.	dau	F	4	Aikshaw
Annie M.	dau	F	7 m	Maryport
Mary Ferguson	Servant	F	26	Overby Servant Dom
(At Aspatria)				

[Dir: Bulmer's 1901: Hannah B. Tyson, 3 North st, Maryport]

Ward Edward
{bmd} Marriage Edward Turnbull Ward – Mary Sherwood Dec 1871 Cockermouth 10b 871

1872 Adair's Maryport Advertiser Fri. 13 Sept.
Death of Capt. Ward. –Yesterday morning brought the melancholy tidings of the death of Edward Ward, of the ship "Robert Hine." It appears the deceased had experienced indifferent health on the outward voyage, and when at Guayaguil (sic) his illness culminated in the breaking of a blood vessel on the 9th of August, and he was interred on the following day. Capt. Ward was in the prime of life, a young man who was greatly esteemed, and held a high character, and good prospects in his profession in the merchant service. –Shortly before sailing from this country, he married the eldest daughter of Mr. Sherwood, the photographer, and the tidings of this sudden calamity to his young widow and family is a severe shock.
Sept. 27 p.8
Birth: On the 24th, the wife of late Capt. Ward, of a daughter.

Wilkinson Joseph.
[Dir: Post Office 1873 p.892: Wilkinson Joseph, master mariner, 17 Corkickle, Whitehaven.]
{bmd: Marriage; June 1861: Joseph Wilkinson—Mary Braithwaite: Whitehaven 10b 790}

{FS: 1881 census}

Mary Wilkinson	Head	F M	51	Beckermont	Master Mariners Wife
Joseph Wilkinson	son	M S	14	Whitehaven	Scholar
Eleanor Wilkinson	dau	F S	14	Whitehaven	Scholar
Braithwaite Wilkinson	son	M S	7	Whitehaven	Scholar
Eleanor Wilkinson	mother-in-law	F W	76	Rottington Cumberland	
(17 Corkickle, Preston Quarter, Cumberland)					

[Dir: West Cumberland 1883 p.264: Wilkinson Joseph, master mariner, 17 Corkickle, Whitehaven.]

Maryport Advertiser and Weekly News, Fri. 2 Nov. p.4 1883.
Death of Captain Wilkinson. We regret to note the death, on Saturday last, at Cork……. Whitehaven, of Captain Joseph Wilkinson who has been many years acted as marine superintendent for Messrs. Hine Brothers' steamers. His connection with Mr. Wilfrid Hine, and subsequently with the firm of Messrs. Hine Brothers, extended over a period of 23 years. He was a faithful servant, and always enjoyed the full confidence and respect of his employers. All the new steamers that this firm have built were modelled and constructed under his supervision. Captain Wilkinson was born at Flimby in the year 1827, and leaves a widow and three children.

{Preston Quarter Cemetery, Whitehaven:
To the Memory of Joseph Wilkinson Whitehaven Master Mariner late Superintendent of the Steamship under the management of Messrs Hine Brothers Maryport. Born 15th August 1827. Died 3rd Nov. 1885. This Monument is erected by the Masters of the several Steam and Sailing Ships of the above firm as a token of esteem and respect for his character and high moral worth. Mary wife of the above born 25th January 1830. Died 20th December 1908. Eleanor Wilkinson daughter of Joseph and Mary Wilkinson born 18th August 1866. Died 9th December 1939.}

Williamson James
Mrs. Williamson known voyages: Castle Holme 1881, 82. (Born c 1831.)

Wyrill John
{bmd}

Marriage	John Wyrill -- Eliza Shaw Jun 1863		Scarbro' 9d 482
Birth	Arthur James Wyrill Mar 1865		Scarbro' 9d 299
Birth	Ada Wyrill Sept. 1866		Scarbro' 9d 299
Birth	Kate or Kate Hall Wyrill Sept. 1868		Scarbro' 9d 305
Birth	Elizabeth Wyrill Sept. 1872		Scarbro' 9d 329
Birth	Florence Wyrill Mar 1875		Scarbro' 9d 344
Death	Florence Wyrill Sept. 1875		Scarbro' 9d 268
Birth	Thomas Edward Wyrill Mar 1877		Scarbro' 9d 358

{FS: Census 1881}

Maria A. Shaw	Sister in Law (Head)	U. F 37 Scarborough	Mariner's Wife
Ada Wyrill	Dau	F 14 Scarborough	Scholar
Kate H. Wyrill	Dau	F 12 Scarborough	Scholar
Thomas E. Wyrill	Son	M 4 Scarborough	

3 Spring Hill Ter. Falsgrave (Scarborough). York

Somehow the Head must have been Captain John Wyrill, then Maria Shaw would have been his sister-in-law and Eliza would have been the mariner's wife.
(Where Mrs. Eliza Wyrill and daughter Elizabeth are not known. Arthur James most probably would have been at sea. He eventual become a captain of the Missionary ship, "John Williams" in Australia).
[**Dir**: Kelly's of N&E Riding of Yorkshire 1893 p.285] Wyrill John, master mariner, 161 Falsgrave rd. [p.267] Shaw Mrs. 159 Falsgrave rd.
{bmd} Marriage Maria Ann Shaw – William Needem Newlove or Henry Hepburn Forrester 1887 Scarbro' 9d 499.

Death Eliza Wyrill Sept 1905 (64) Scarborough 9d 243
Death John Wyrill Mar 1921 (84) Scarborough 9d 485

GLOSSARY

AB:	Able Rating or Seaman
Abeam:	At right angles to vessel
Aft:	At or towards the stern
Aloft:	Upper righing, overhead
Amidships:	The middle part of the vessel
Apprentice:	Also officer material
Barque or bark:	A vessel having three or more masts, with fore-and-aft rigged on the after mast and square-rigged on all other masts.
Bending the sails	To secure the sails to their spars.
Brig/Snow:	Two-masted square-rigged vessel, with an additional lower fore-and-aft sail on a gaff and a boom to the mainmast
Brigantine:	Two-masted vessel with a square-rigged foremast & fore-and-aft-rigged mainmast.
Broach:	Veer or cause (a ship) to veer and present a side to the wind and waves
Binnacle:	The housing of the ship's compass
Bosun (boatswain):	The crew's foreman, who is gives out the duties on board.
Bows:	The forward part of the vessel
Bowsprit:	The spar projecting forward from the vessel's stem.
Bulkhead:	Partition or walls (dividing sections)
Clipper:	Vessel of any size or rig designed for speed esp. one with raking bows
Doldrums:	Equatorial ocean-region of calms, sudden storms, & light unpredictable winds
Draught:	Depth of water needed to float a ship
Easting:	Sailing in an easterly direction in southern latitude where fair winds prevail
Fathom:	A depth of six feet of water
Fo'csle:	The forward deck, usually raised above the main deck. Below this was usually the crew's quarters
Half Deck:	From mainmast to quarter-deck. Area given as living quarters to the apprentices
Heave—hove—tr. Colloq:	To throw
Heave-to—hove-to:	To bring a vessel head to wind with some sails 'backed' or sheeted to the windward, i.e to bring to a standstill
Jib-boom:	An extension to the bowsprit that supports the flying-jib.
Jury-rig:	A substitute or a temporary rig used after a vessel has lost a mast or spars
Leeward:	The side which is away from the wind
List:	The tilt of the vessel from one side to the other, to port or to starboard
Log:	The log book of the vessel or the instrument to measure the vessel's speed
Ketch:	Two-masted fore-and-aft rigged sailing boat with a mizzen-mast stepped forward of the rudder and smaller than its foremast
Flat:	A boat with a flat bottom for transport in shallow water
Poop:	The stern of a ship
Pooped:	Ship received a wave break over the stern and could cause the vessel to sink
Mainmast:	The middle or mainmast on a fully-rigged or three-masted barque
OS:	Ordinary seaman
Port(side):	Left hand side of the vessel looking toward the bows
Quarterdeck:	The part of the deck which covers the quarters
Reefing:	Reducing the area of sail which is spread to the wind

Ship:	Fully-rigged sailing vessel, with three or more masts, square-rigged on all masts
Stern:	The rear part of the vessel
Stove in:	Broken by external force. Smashed in from the outside.
Smack:	A small but fully-decked vessel
Topgallant:	The mast holding the topmast holding upper and lower topgallants sail
Topmast:	The mast holding the upper and lower topsails
Topsail schooner:	A fore-and-aft rigged vessel of two or more masts having two square topsails, or a single square topsail on the foremast
Trim:	A vessel's trim, her position in the water in relation to the horizontal. If level, she is 'in trim.' If down by the head or stern she is 'out of trim'
Windward:	Towards the wind
Weep:	Leaking very slowly
Yard:	A spar suspended from the mast and spreading the head of a square sail
Yawl:	Vessel with 2 masts, main & mizzen, mizzen small stepped abaft the rudder post.

BIBLIOGRAPHY

1. Ian Hine *A Cumberland Endeavour* (2012)

2. John D. Wells *Solway Winds* Pitcairn Publishing (2004)

3. John D. Wells *Maryport. The Passing Years.* Printed by Titus Wilson & Son, Kendal ISBN 0-9549240-1-0 (2006).

4. John D. Wells *Maritime Maryport.* Printed by Titus Wilson & Son, Kendal ISBN 0-9549240-3-7 (2012).

5. Basil Lubbock *The Nitrate Clippers* Publisher Kessinger Publishing Co. (2005)

6. Basil Lubbock *The Colonial Clippers* Publishers Brown, Son & Ferguson (1966).

7. Sir Henry Brett *White Winds Fifty Years of Sail in the New Zealand Trade* Vol 1 (1925) Vol 2 (1928)

8. *Capt. Brown's Experience on Board the Barque "Robert Hine"* Jas. Starr Printer and Bookbinder, Wigan (1899)

9. Dallas Murphy *Rounding the Horn* Weidenfeld & Nicolson (2004)

10. John Nicholson *The Incomparable Captain Cadell* Allen & Unwin (1950)

11. John Harrison *Where the Earth Ends* John Murray (2000)

12. Joseph Conrad *The Mirror of the Sea*

13. Hugh Falkus *Master of Cape Horn. The Story of a Square-rigger Captain and his World. William Andrew Nelson 1839-1929* London Victor Gollancz Ltd. 1982.

Films

a. DVD (Sailing) Around Cape Horn (aboard a square rigger 1929)—Capt. Irving Johnson.

b. Video: NMM: Square Rigger of the 1930s: Including "The Cape Horn Road: Allan Villiers.

INDEX

Hine Sailing Ships & others (<u>bold</u>—illustrations)

Hine Captains and Wives

Captain		Mrs.
Anderson	270, 298-299	
Austin	193-195, 298-299, 301-302	
Brown	127-129, 132-135, 299, 301-302, 321	127-130, 299, 302
Bryce	159,166-168, 231, 233-38, 297-299, 301-302	231, 302
Clark	20, 104-105, 174, 178-179, 298-299, 301	
Cobb	281 (2nd mate), 283 (2nd mate), 286-87, 297, 299, 301-303	299, 303
Coleman	110, 298-299	
Dawson	285, 297	
Dix	297, 299, 301	
Dulling	297, 301, 303-304	303-304
Fearon	27-28, 65, 106, 297-299, 304	
Hall	103-104, **114**, **116**, 1334, 136-141, 299-301, 304-305	**116**, 304-305
Holman	297, 300-301, 305	297, 305-306
Holmes	41, 54-57, 86-87, 179-181, 298-301, 306, 318	55, 306
Humphreys	282-285, 297, 300	
Hurst	viii, 159, 166-167, 297-298, 300-301	
Johnston	39, 50, 206-209, 297-298, 300-301, 306-307	
Lane	213, 215, 300-301	
Millican	184-193, 298-301, 307-308	
McLeod	91-94, 297, 300-301, 307	307
Nicholson	159, 169-171, 211, 298, 300-301, 309	
Patterson	65-66, 298, 300, 309	309
Randall	221-222 (mate), 227-231, 297, 300-301, 309	297, 309
Rich	121, 238-243, 245-251, 253, 255, 257, 297, 300-301, 309-311	
Ritchie	38, 175-178, 297-301, 310-316	
Robinson John	297, 300-301, 317	317
Robinson Wedg	vii, 1, 13-15, 17-20, 121, 208, 218-225, 227, 234, 297-298, 300-301, 317	
Saul	76-78, 88, 210-216, 298, 300-301, 317-318	77, 214, 298, 317-318
Sawle	181-184, 297-298, 300-301, 318	318
Smith	9-10, 20-23, 75, 298, 300-301, 318	23, 318
Tate	261-263 (mate), 268-282, 297, 300-301, 318-319	275-276, 297, 319
Tarney	57, 159, 168-169, 298-301, 318	
Turney	147-154, 169, 297-298, 300-301, 319	319
Tyson	261-265, 268, 270, 297, 300-301, 319	268, 270-271, 319-320
Ward	vii, 1, 15 (mate), 28-30, 123, 127, 297, 299-301, 320	127, 320
Wedgwood	87-88, 299-300	
Wilkinson	vii, 1, 6-9, 121, 123-127, 298-301, 320-321	320-321
Williamson	126, 297, 300-301, 321	297, 321
Wyrill	127, 297, 300-301, 321	321

Mrs.

Mrs. Millican/ nee Caroline Jones	187-188, 190, 193, 298-299, 307-309
Mrs. Rich/ nee Charlotte Price	243, 250-251, 297, 309-310
Mrs. Ritchie/ nee Jane Mathieson (1st)	310-312
Mrs. Ritchie/ nee Mary Frewin (2nd)	38, 176-177, 297-299, 314-316
Mrs. W. Robinson/ nee Sarah Robertson	15, 18-20, 220, 297-298, 317

Ship-owners

Wilfrid Hine/Wilfred/W.	iii, vii-ix, **x**-xiv, 1-2, 6-8, 13-15, 20, 22-23, 27-28, 32, 37-38, 71, 94, 111, 121, 123, 126-127, 138, 134, 147, 151, 153, 159, 166-169, 174-176, 186, 206-207, 211, 215, 218, 236, 296, 320
Alfred Hine	v, viii, **x**-xiv, 1-2, 65, 71, 308
Hine Brothers/Bros.	i, iii, v-xv, 1, 55, 71, 76, 86, 91-92, 94, 103, 106, 110, 121, 127, 137, 140, 153, 159, 169, 174, 193, 195, 214, 216, 238, 241, 243, 247, 251, 253-254, 261, 270, 276, 283, 285-286, 296, 307, 317, 320-321
Richard Nicholson & Son(s) of Liverpool	vii, viii, 1, 6, 8, 14, 28, 121, 126, 159, 218